THE EFFECTIVENESS OF INTERNATIONAL ENVIRONMENTAL AGREEMENTS
A Survey of Existing Legal Instruments

D1522944

THE UNITED NATIONS CONFERENCE ON ENVIRONMENT AND DEVELOPMENT

THE EFFECTIVENESS OF INTERNATIONAL ENVIRONMENTAL AGREEMENTS

A Survey of Existing Legal Instruments

edited by
PETER H. SAND
Principal Programme Officer,
United Nations Conference on Environment and Development

CAMBRIDGE
GROTIUS PUBLICATIONS LIMITED
1992

SALES &
ADMINISTRATION   GROTIUS PUBLICATIONS LTD.
PO BOX 115, CAMBRIDGE CB3 9BP,
ENGLAND

FAX   0223 311032 (from abroad: 44 + 223 + 311032)

British Library Cataloguing in Publication Data

Effectiveness of International Environmental Agreements: Survey of Existing Legal Instruments
  I. Sand, Peter H.
  341.762

ISBN 1-85701-004-3 (PAPERBACK)
ISBN 1-85701-003-5 (HARDBACK)

Printed by The Burlington Press (Cambridge) Limited, Foxton, Cambridge

TABLE OF CONTENTS

PREFACE

The United Nations Conference on Environment and Development (UNCED, Rio de Janeiro, 3 - 14 June 1992) marked the opening for signature of two new global environmental treaties -- the United Nations Framework Convention on Climate Change, and the Convention on Biological Diversity -- as well as the adoption of the "Rio Declaration on Environment and Development" and of an agreed action programme leading up to the year 2000 and into the 21st century (Agenda 21). Together with a consensus on non-mandatory forest principles, and a recommendation to start negotiations on a further global convention on desertification, the Conference thus added substantially to the growing body of law on environment and sustainable development.

Yet the major significance of the Rio Conference for the evolution of international law in this field may well lie elsewhere. The adoption of Agenda 21 was preceded by an intensive debate on the adequacy and effectiveness of existing international legal mechanisms, in the course of which the UNCED Preparatory Committee undertook a survey of 124 multilateral environmental instruments, related bilateral agreements, and their interface with relevant trade and development regimes. The outcome of this debate is reflected in chapters 8(B) and 39 of Agenda 21, and to some extent in the institutional arrangements under chapter 38 -- i.e., the specific review functions of the new UN Commission on Sustainable Development with regard to the implementation of environmental agreements. It will be important, however, to keep in mind the background of these recommendations, which were based on an evaluation of the survey results compiled in the present volume, drawing on contributions from an international team of experts and edited in light of the final UNCED documents.

Research on the effectiveness of international environmental regimes has only just begun. The UNCED survey is but a start, a benchmark study that will need to be carried forward and refined by future re-assessments, especially through the Commission on Sustainable Development. The follow-up programmes outlined in Agenda 21 provide guidance for this purpose.

Many people contributed to this UNCED project. In addition to the work undertaken -- under severe time pressure -- by the co-authors of individual chapters, the co-operation of the secretariats and depositaries of the international agreements and instruments concerned is gratefully acknowledged. Special thanks are due to Andrea Petznek, for research assistance in compiling the background information; to Karen Esposito, for managing and processing the initial survey; and to Lila Sandoval, for finalizing the revised text.

Peter H. Sand
Geneva, July 1992

CONTRIBUTORS

Ambassador Richard E. Benedick, World Wildlife Fund, Washington/D.C. (USA)

Hon. Prafullachandra N. Bhagwati, former Chief Justice of the Supreme Court (India)

Ambassador Alexander Borg Olivier, LL.M., LL.D. (Malta)

Professor Alan E. Boyle, Faculty of Law, Queen Mary and Westfield College, University of London (United Kingdom)

James O'Grady Cameron, LL.M., (Australia), Centre for International Environmental Law, King's College, London

Professor Guillermo J. Cano, Fundación Ambiente y Recursos Naturales, Buenos Aires (Argentina)

Professor Günther Doeker, LL.M., Ph.D., Free University of Berlin (Germany)

Malcolm J. Forster, LL.M., Freshfields Environment Group, London (United Kingdom)

Professor David A.C. Freestone, Law School, University of Hull (United Kingdom)

Thomas Gehring, Dipl. Pol., research assistant, Free University of Berlin (Germany)

Parvez Hassan, LL.D., Lahore (Pakistan), Chairman of the Commission on Environmental Law, World Conservation Union

Wordsworth Filo Jones, LL.M. (Sierra Leone), environmental consultant

Professor Alexandre C. Kiss, Director of the Environmental Law Centre, University of Strasbourg (France)

Katharina Kummer, Lic. en droit (Switzerland), research assistant, University of London

Professor Barbara Kwiatkowska, Faculty of Law, University of Utrecht (Netherlands)

Professor Virginia A. Leary, Faculty of Law, State University of New York at Buffalo (USA)

Maria Rita Mazzanti, LL.B., Rome (Italy), formerly with the Legal Division of the International Atomic Energy Agency

Thobeka Mjolo-Thamage, LL.M. (South Africa), Centre for International Environmental Law, King's College, London

David M. Ong, LL.M. (Malaysia), research assistant, University of Hull

Ralph U. Osterwoldt, LL.B., M. Litt., formerly with the Department of the Environment, Ottawa (Canada)

Ricardo Pronove III, LL.M. (Philippines), United Nations Institute for Training and Research, Geneva

Jonathan C. Robinson, LL.M., Centre for International Environmental Law, King's College, London (United Kingdom)

Ambassador Alberto Székely (Mexico), member of the International Law Commission of the United Nations

Marceil D. Yeater, J.D. (USA), consultant to the UNEP International Register of Potentially Toxic Chemicals, Geneva

CRITERIA FOR EVALUATION

The UNCED Preparatory Committee, at its second session in March-April 1991, established an open-ended Working Group III to deal with legal, institutional and all related matters, and specifically entrusted it with the task, among others, to "prepare an annotated list of existing international agreements and international legal instruments in the environmental field, describing their purpose and scope, evaluating their effectiveness, and examining possible areas for the further development of international environmental law, in the light of the need to integrate environment and development, especially taking into account the special needs and concerns of the developing countries" (decision 2/3, A/46/48, Part I, annex I).

At its third session in August-September 1991, the Preparatory Committee formulated a set of proposed "criteria for evaluating the effectiveness of existing agreements and instruments", to serve as a basis for compiling the necessary background information for an agreed list of such agreements and instruments in cooperation with the international secretariats concerned, as applicable (decision 3/25, A/46/48, vol. II). The criteria, which thus provided the framework for the present survey, read as follows:

CRITERIA FOR EVALUATING THE EFFECTIVENESS OF EXISTING AGREEMENTS OR INSTRUMENTS

(Some of the criteria listed may not be applicable to all agreements or instruments to be evaluated.)

A.   Objectives and achievement

1.   What are the basic objectives formulated in the international agreements and instruments evaluated, and how do these objectives relate to the effective integration of environment and development?

2.   In the case of regional agreements and instruments, what is their actual and potential bearing on global environmental protection and sustainable development?

3.   Do these agreements or instruments take into account the special circumstances of developing countries?

4.   To what extent have the basic objectives (environmental/developmental) formulated in international agreements and instruments been met, and how is goal achievement measured?

B.   Participation

5.   Is membership limited or open-ended?

6.   Are reservations possible, and to what extent have they been used?

7. What is the current geographical distribution of membership in existing environmental agreements and instruments, especially as regards developing countries?

8. What is the record of actual participation by developing countries in the negotiation and drafting of these agreements and instruments, and in programme activities and meetings organized under these agreements and instruments?

9. Which incentives (e.g. financial, trade, technology benefits) are available to encourage participation and facilitate implementation by developing countries?

10. Which measures have been taken to promote and support the effective participation of developing countries in the negotiation and operation of international agreements or instruments, including technical and financial assistance and other available mechanisms for this purpose?

11. Which factors influenced the participation, especially of developing countries, in the agreement or instrument? for example:

   (a) Financial resources required and available for participation in the agreement or instrument;

   (b) Technical assistance required and available for participation in the agreement or instrument;

   (c) Scientific assistance required and available for participation in the agreement or instrument;

   (d) Information on the (operation of the) agreement or instrument to Governments, parliaments, press, non-governmental organizations, industries and the general public;

   (e) Role of parliaments, press, non-governmental organizations, industries and public opinion in general;

   (f) Availability of reservations.

C. Implementation

12. To what extent has the implementation of agreements or instruments been constrained or accelerated by provisions regarding their entry into force?

13. What are the commitments imposed on parties by these agreements and instruments, and how is compliance by parties with their commitments monitored and measured?

14.   How do parties report on their performance in implementing agreements and instruments, and to what extent have they complied with reporting duties?

15.   Which are the specific requirements (if any) of data supply and data disclosure, and to what extent have they been met by the parties?

16.   Which possibilities exist to promote compliance and to follow up on non-compliance, and to what extent have they been used?

17.   Which mechanisms are available to deal with disputes over implementation and to what extent have they been used?

18.   Which factors influenced the implementation? for example:

(a)   Financial resources required and available for implementation of the agreement or instrument;

(b)   Technical assistance required and available for implementation of the agreement or instrument;

(c)   Scientific assistance required and available for implementation of the agreement or instrument;

(d)   Information on the (operation of the) agreement or instrument to Governments, parliaments, press, non-governmental organizations, industries and the general public;

(e)   Role of parliaments, press, non-governmental organizations, industries and public opinion in general;

(f)   International supervisory or implementing bodies;

(g)   Obligations to report on compliance and/or to supply and disclose data;

(h)   Non-compliance procedures and procedures for settlement of disputes (including fact-finding procedures).

D.   Information

19.   In which form and in which languages are the texts of existing agreements and instruments published and disseminated?

20.   How is current information on the operation and implementation of international agreements and instruments made available to Governments, to the industries concerned and to the general public?

21. What additional materials are available to provide guidance for the implementation of international agreements and instruments at the national level?

22. To what extent is the above information used in international and national training and education programmes?

E. Operation, review and adjustment

23. Which are the institutional arrangements for international administration of existing agreements and instruments?

24. What are the annual (1990) costs of international administration (secretariat, meetings, programmes) of agreements and instruments, and how are they financed?

25. Which are the main benefits and the main cost elements of national participation in existing agreements and instruments, and which possibilities exist to reduce participation costs for developing countries?

26. Which mechanisms are available to ensure that scientific knowledge and advice is taken into account in policy-making decisions under these agreements and instruments?

27. How do these arrangements and mechanisms ensure the effective participation of (a) national authorities, especially from developing countries; and (b) non-governmental participants, including the industries concerned and the scientific community?

28. Which mechanisms are available to ensure periodic review and adjustment of international agreements and instruments in order to meet new requirements, and to what extent have they been used?

F. Codification programming

29. Which new drafts, or draft revisions of existing agreements and instruments, in the environmental field are currently under preparation or negotiation?

30. To what extent and through which mechanisms is drafting coordinated with related work regarding other agreements and instruments?

31. Which are the remaining gaps that need to be covered by legal provisions?

32. To what extent are mechanisms other than formal agreements or instruments contributing to the development of international law in the field of the environment?

SUMMARY REPORT ON THE SURVEY

The research papers assembled in the present volume are part of the preparatory work for the United Nations Conference on Environment and Development (UNCED), undertaken by the UNCED Secretariat in response to a request by Working Group III of the Preparatory Committee, at its third session in August-September 1991, to compile the necessary background information for a survey of existing international environmental agreements and instruments, in accordance with the evaluation criteria formulated by the Committee (A/46/48, vol. II, Annex I, decision 3/25).

From October 1991 to January 1992, thirteen research papers were prepared for this purpose by a team of legal experts, in consultation with the international secretariats and depositaries of the instruments concerned, whose cooperation is gratefully acknowledged. The results of this research, as summarized by the UNCED Secretariat in document A/CONF.151/PC/103 and Addendum 1, are as follows:

OBJECTIVES AND ACHIEVEMENT

The present survey covers existing international agreements and international legal instruments in the environmental field, mainly as recorded in the 1991 UNEP Register of International Treaties and Other Agreements in the Field of the Environment (UNEP/GC.16/INF.4) and listed in document A/CONF.151/PC/77, with the specific amendments made by the Preparatory Committee at its third session (decision 3/25, annex III (A/46/48), vol. II). By definition, therefore, the majority of the agreements and instruments selected are oriented towards environmental conservation and protection against pollution; 25 (mostly on marine living resources and transboundary freshwaters) may be described as oriented primarily towards rational utilization and management of resources; and 21 deal with both environment and development aspects. Even development-oriented agreements, however, give recognition to the long-term goal of environmental sustainability of resource use, as illustrated by the 1946 International Convention for the Regulation of Whaling (No. 57) and the 1983 International Tropical Timber Agreement (No. 25).

The basic objectives of most agreements and instruments surveyed here (usually stated in preambular or introductory provisions) are formulated in highly general and abstract terms, which makes it difficult to evaluate actual goal achievement. Measurable objectives --such as quantitative targets and technical criteria for compliance - are found in very few agreements, such as international environmental standards for motor vehicles, aircraft and ships (Nos. 28, 30 and 36), the biodegradability limits set by the 1968 European Agreement on the Restriction of the Use of Certain Detergents in Washing and Cleaning Products (No. 97), and the emission reductions laid down in protocols to the 1979 Convention on Long-range Transboundary Air Pollution (No. 31) and to the 1985 Vienna Convention for the Protection of the Ozone Layer (No. 33). In some instances, objectives were subsequently specified and elaborated by joint interpretative or programmatic declarations by the Parties to an agreement, at their regular meetings (as in the case of the 1978 Treaty for Amazonian Cooperation, No. 21; and the 1983 International Undertaking on Plant Genetic Resources, (No. 26)) or at separate ministerial-level conferences (as in the case of the marine environment conventions for the North Sea and the Baltic Sea (Nos. 43-45)). Following the 1987 Report of the World Commission on Environment and Development, the postulate of "sustainable development", and the consequential integration of environment and development objectives, has figured prominently as a common denominator in authoritative statements issued in the context of many different agreements and instruments.

More than half (73 out of 124) of the agreements and instruments covered by the present survey are regional or subregional in scope, including seven non-mandatory sets of recommendations (by the Organisation for Economic Cooperation and Development, (OECD) (Nos. 3 and 100)). Though geographically restricted, these agreements or instruments can nevertheless have a bearing on global environmental protection and sustainable development: (a) because of the overall ecological significance of the area concerned (such as the 1959 Antarctic Treaty (No. 14) or the 1978 Treaty for Amazonian Cooperation (No. 21)); (b) because of the proportionate contribution of certain regions (such as those covered by the Economic Commission for Europe (ECE) and OECD) to the overall volume of global pollution; (c) because of the acknowledged "demonstration effect" of regional regulatory models for countries outside the region (such as the ECE motor vehicle standards, (No. 28) or the European Free Trade Association pharmaceutical standards, (No. 98)); or (d) simply because, in the absence of applicable global controls, an aggregate of regional regimes may be the only option currently available to deal with a world-wide environmental problem (such as marine pollution from land-based sources (under Nos. 44-49), depletion of marine living resources, (under Nos. 58-69) or management of transboundary freshwaters (under Nos. 72-93)).

Some agreements or instruments generally address relations with developing countries (e.g., the 1989 Lomé IV Convention (under No. 9)) or seek to balance specific North-South interests regarding natural resource exports/imports (e.g., under Nos. 18 and 25), access to such resources (e.g., under Nos. 26 and 67) or regarding compensation for on-site conservation measures (under the 1972 World Heritage Convention, (No. 17)). By contrast, 19 agreements apply between developing countries only, 26 are exclusively between industrialized States, and a further 10 regional agreements include European developing countries only. To the extent that the remaining other agreements and instruments refer to the special circumstances of developing countries at all, they do so (a) by providing for technical assistance (e.g., the 1972 London Dumping Convention (No. 35) and most of the United Nations Environment Programme (UNEP)-sponsored regional seas conventions, (Nos. 46-55)); and (b) by permitting flexible derogations from uniform standards according to the special circumstances and abilities of countries (e.g., under the International Civil Aviation Organization (ICAO) standards for aircraft emissions (No. 30); or under the International Labour Organization (ILO) conventions on the working environment (Nos. 110-116)). The most detailed recent provisions in this respect are those of the 1987 Montreal Protocol on Substances That Deplete the Ozone Layer (under No. 33).

As pointed out in paragraph 5, the lack of precise objectives is a major difficulty in measuring achievement; membership statistics alone are not sufficient as indicators. Nevertheless, a number of attempts have been made to evaluate the overall effectiveness of international environmental agreements and instruments, either by the Parties, by the secretariats, or by independent observers. In the case of the 1972 London Dumping Convention (No. 35), a self-evaluation by the Parties was submitted to the Preparatory Committee in 1990 (A/CONF.151/PC/31); the UNEP secretariat submitted an evaluation of the 1985 Montreal Guidelines on Land-based Sources of Marine Pollution, based on questionnaire replies from the Parties (A/CONF.151/PC/71). Similar earlier evaluations had been undertaken by UNEP for its 1978 Principles on Shared Natural Resources (No. 6) and the 1982 Guidelines on Offshore Mining (No. 37); see progress reports A/37/396,

UNEP/GC.13/9/Add.1, UNEP/GC.14/25, and UNEP/GC.15/9/Add.2. While another UNEP report on the 1982 World Charter for Nature (under No. 1) considered regular monitoring of the implementation of the Charter "an essential requirement for its fulfillment", no further evaluations have been undertaken; the same is true for the 1980 UNEP/World Meteorological Organization (WMO) Provisions for Cooperation Between States on Weather Modification (No. 32). In 1986, the secretariat of the Food and Agriculture Organization of the United Nations (FAO) carried out an evaluation of its 1985 International Code of Conduct on the Distribution and Use of Pesticides (No. 101) (see FAO/AGP.GC/89/BP.1); another review is currently in preparation. Other external reviews of the Code's implementation were undertaken by non-governmental and industry organizations in 1987, 1988 and 1989.

Comparative analyses of environmental agreements and instruments have also been prepared by the World Bank (for its 1992 annual report), by UNEP (for its 1992 "State of the Environment" report), and by the Office for Ocean Affairs and the Law of the Sea of the Secretariat (A/CONF.151/PC/69, submitted to the Preparatory Committee in 1991, covering Nos. 43-55; and the study of an expert group on the conservation and management of the living resources of the high seas, convened in July 1991 and covering Nos. 57-69), as well as by individual member States and competent academic research institutions. In particular, in an investigation initiated in 1990, the United States International Trade Commission identified 170 bilateral and multilateral environmental agreements with a view to periodic evaluation (Report to United States Senate Committee on Finance, USITC: 235/1991); and the United States General Accounting Office in January 1992 completed an evaluation of eight major international environmental agreements (Nos. 18, 25, 31 (c), 33 (a), 35 36 (a), 57, 103). In June 1991, the Norwegian Fridtjof Nansen Institute issued preliminary findings of its evaluation of the effectiveness of five international environmental agreements (Nos. 14(b), 31, 43, 45, 57) (Report R:007-1991); and in December 1991, the Center for International Affairs of Harvard University presented an evaluation of the effectiveness of international environmental institutions, covering several of the agreements and instruments listed here (Nos. 31, 33, 36, 43-45, 57-69, 101-102). The present summary also draws on the results of those studies.

PARTICIPATION

Less than half of the 124 agreements and instruments surveyed are open to global membership, although several of the regionally restricted agreements allow other States to join upon approval by the original signatories. The geographical scope of some multilateral agreements actually is so narrow as to render them less significant than some bilateral agreements, which in certain regions (especially on the American continent) play a far greater role in practice and therefore should duly be taken into account in global comparison. In view of the total volume of existing transboundary agreements in this field, however (estimated at close to 2,000 for shared water resources and another 2000 for fishery resources alone, according to FAO Treaty records), the present survey had to be limited to an analysis of representative samples of bilateral agreements on environment and development.

A number of legally binding agreements make use of the possibility of reservations or other devices permitting national exceptions in order to facilitate wider participation. Under several nature conservation conventions, for example, reservations may be entered against the listing of particular species of wildlife (Nos. 18, 22, 23). In the field of aircraft engine emissions, the well-established system of notification of national differences under the

1944 Chicago Convention (No. 30) allows for a degree of technical differentiation compatible with basic requirements of uniformity; similarly, the recent Volatile Organic Compounds Protocol to the 1979 Convention on Long-Range Transboundary Air Pollution (No. 31/d) gives signatories a range of regulatory options and base years from which to select. Several of the ILO conventions on the working environment (No. 111, 115) permit temporary derogations under certain circumstances. In some cases, the reservations and exemptions may assist countries, during an initial phase, in adjusting their national regulations to full compliance. Concern has been expressed, however, that excessive use of reservations by Parties could undermine the global effectiveness of an environmental protection regime. Several agreements therefore expressly prohibit reservations, or make them subject to unanimous approval by all Parties (under the 1949 Agreement on the General Fisheries Council for the Mediterranean (No. 60) and the 1960 Convention on Third Party Liability in the Field of Nuclear Energy, No. 117); or limit them to specified procedural aspects such as dispute settlement (under the ECE motor vehicle regulations (No. 28) and the International Atomic Energy Agency (IAEA) conventions on nuclear accidents, No. 109).

The membership statistics provided in the annex to the present report at first glance seem to reflect an overall balance of industrialized and developing countries. Closer analysis on a country-by-country basis reveals, however, that the total figures per treaty are misleading. The vast majority of ratifications by developing countries concern general declaratory instruments not involving active participation for Member States; by contrast, developing countries are under represented in agreements dealing with operational aspects of environment and sustainable development, especially considering the full range of existing treaty law in this field. When comparing the membership of individual countries in the 38 legally binding global agreements listed, it appears that those countries which participate in more than 25 agreements are virtually all industrialized States; whereas those countries participating in less than 10 agreements are virtually all developing countries. At the same time, more than half of the regional agreements and instruments concern the European and North American region, mostly without any participation from developing countries. This "clustering" of membership is only partly explained by the fact that some of the older agreements originated in industrialized States and consequently might be expected to have reflected the priorities and interests of those States. Chronological comparison indicates, conversely, that more than two-thirds of the agreements now listed date from the post-1972 period, during which global treaty negotiations could at least numerically be expected to have been dominated by developing countries.

Further imbalances become apparent from data concerning the actual participation by developing countries in the governance of existing agreements and instruments, including programme activities, working groups and regular review meetings. For example, at the 1991 Geneva meeting of the Conference of the Parties to the Migratory Species Convention (No. 22), which then had a fairly balanced membership of 18 industrialized and 19 developing countries, there was an official participation of delegations from 14 industrialized and only 6 developing countries.

In response to these imbalances - which may be assumed to reflect structural problems of financial and staff resources for participation - several international agreements and instruments have developed special incentives to encourage participation and facilitate implementation by developing countries. A number of special funds have been set up for this purpose under different agreements, starting with the World Heritage Fund of the 1972 Convention Concerning the Protection of the World Cultural and Natural Heritage (No. 17); though primarily used to finance on-site projects implementing the Convention, the World

Heritage Committee recently decided to make an allocation from the fund in order to assist experts from the least developed countries to participate in the work of the Committee. Under the 1971 Ramsar Convention (No. 16), a Wetland Conservation Fund was launched in 1990 to assist developing countries in implementing the Convention; also, the regular budget includes a budget line to support the participation of developing countries in meetings. Under the 1979 Migratory Species Convention (No. 22), in addition to the existing trust fund for the participation of developing countries in expert meetings, the 1991 Conference agreed to earmark a sum equivalent to 10% of the regular budget for technical assistance. An International Fund for Plant Genetic Resources operates under the 1983 International Undertaking on Plant Genetic Resources (No. 26). Under the 1987 Montreal Protocol (No. 33(a)), an Interim Multilateral Ozone Fund became operational in 1991, in addition to the trust funds established to finance meeting attendance by developing countries.

Other incentives for wider participation for developing countries, as reported by the secretariats of international agreements and instruments, relate primarily to the availability of technical assistance and training directed at national capacity-building, to enable countries to comply with the technical requirements of agreements. While technology transfer is mentioned prominently in some agreements (including Part XIV of the 1982 Convention on the Law of the Sea, (No. 38); the ozone layer agreements (under No. 33); and the 1989 Basel Convention on Hazardous Wastes, No. 103), the main significance of these provisions appears to have been as a framework for multilateral and bilateral programmes of financial assistance. In the context of the 1979 Convention on Long-range Transboundary Air Pollution and its protocols (No. 31), a task force on technology exchange was established in 1988 (recently merged with a new Working Group on Technology) mainly to promote the transfer of environmental technologies to economies in transition.

On the whole, the participation of developing countries in existing environmental agreements and instruments may be said to have been influenced by a combination of factors, including the availability of financial resources, technical and scientific assistance, and pressure by parliamentarians, non-governmental organizations, industries, the press and the general public. Flexible treaty provisions, including the availability of temporary derogations and reservations, are also likely to have played a role in some cases.

IMPLEMENTATION AND INFORMATION

The entry into force of legally binding agreements depends on the agreed minimum number or threshold of ratifications. While high thresholds may be justified by a desire to ensure a high degree of instant uniformity and to avoid competitive disadvantages for early participants, the drawback is long delays in implementation, as illustrated by the 1982 Law of the Sea Convention (No. 38), (requiring 60 ratifications and still not in force) and several marine pollution conventions (delayed by the minimum tonnage requirements under agreements Nos. 36 and 121). The reverse tendency of other agreements therefore has been to accelerate entry into force by lowering the threshold, to only three ratifications (as in the 1986 IAEA conventions on nuclear accidents, No. 100) or to a minimum of two, as in the case of the ILO conventions on the working environment (Nos. 110-116), the Red Cross protocols (No. 5) or the ECE motor vehicle regulations (No. 28). Alternatively, international technical rules may be brought into effect without requiring ratification (in the form of annexes as under Nos. 18, 22, 31, 33 etc.) or even by "tacit consent" (e.g., under Nos. 30 and 36). Parties may also agree to waive consent requirements voluntarily (as under the

1967 Tlatelolco Treaty, No. 107) or to apply agreements on an interim basis (as under the 1991 Espoo Convention, No. 11).

Once an agreement has come into force, compliance by the Parties with their commitments may be controlled by a variety of techniques developed under different international regimes. Apart from joint scientific monitoring of national environmental parameters (e.g., the EMEP monitoring programme under No. 31 (a) and mutual recognition of inspections (e.g., under Nos. 50 and 98), the method most frequently used is periodic reporting by all Parties, followed by joint public review of the information submitted.

There are wide differences in the quality of national performance reports as a means to monitor compliance with international agreements and instruments. Some agreements (such as the 1978 Treaty for Amazonian Co-operation, No. 21) contain no reporting duties; in others (such as the 1968 African Convention on the Conservation of Nature and Natural Resources, (No. 15)) a general duty to report on implementation is stipulated but has never been applied, in the absence of appropriate mechanisms or procedures. In some instances (such as the 1982 World Charter for Nature, No. 1 (a), and other UNEP-sponsored guidelines), reports on implementation were initially not foreseen but were subsequently solicited from Governments and by ad hoc questionnaires from the secretariat, sometimes with disappointing results. In the case of agreements on marine living resources (e.g., Nos. 60 and 66) and the 1983 International Tropical Timber Agreement (No. 25), reporting concerns general fishery data and trade data rather than information on compliance. As a rule, reporting results are noticeably better where they are based on an internationally agreed format and according to agreed reporting schedules with recurrent deadlines.

One of the most elaborate reporting schemes is that of ILO. Pursuant to Article 22 of the ILO Constitution, States having ratified ILO conventions must report on their laws and practices applying the conventions, currently at four-year intervals. After preliminary review by the secretariat, the reports are examined by an independent Committee of Experts, which may direct questions and observations to the States concerned, and are then submitted to the intergovernmental Committee on Standards of the annual ILO Conference for public discussion. A special feature of the ILO review procedure is the active participation of non-governmental workers' and employers' organizations. Compliance of States with their reporting obligations has generally been good, and over the past five years, of the 178 national reports due for the ILO working environment conventions (Nos. 110-116 in the present survey), 158 were duly submitted; it is noteworthy, however, that 15 of the 20 missing reports concerned developing countries.

Other organizations have encountered more serious problems of reporting. Only about 60% of the Parties to the 1972 London Dumping Convention (No. 35) complied with their obligation to report on dumping activities; the percentage of Parties reporting under the 1973-1978 MARPOL Convention for the Prevention of Pollution from Ships (No. 36) is approximately 30%, with major gaps particularly in developing countries (of the 70 national reports received from 1986 to 1990, 58 were from industrialized States). While the 1983 International Tropical Timber Agreement (No. 25) had 46 Parties (21 importing/industrialized countries and 25 producing/developing countries) in 1990, only 15 (12 importing and 3 producing countries) submitted the required data on their harvesting and trading of timber. Under the 1973 Convention on International Trade in Endangered Species (CITES) (No. 18), only 38% of the industrialized States and only 19% of the developing countries Parties submitted their 1989 annual reports on trade movements, and reports were frequently late or incomplete. Of the 31 Parties to the 1979 Convention on Long-range Transboundary Air Pollution (No. 31), seven (one developing and six industrialized countries) failed to submit their 1990 major review reports. About 80% of the Parties to the 1987 Montreal Protocol on Substances That Deplete the Ozone Layer (No. 33 (a) responded to the requirement for reporting baseline consumption data; however, data from many countries were incomplete, which prompted the establishment in 1990 of an <u>ad hoc</u> Group of Experts on the Reporting of Data. The 1991 Meeting of the Parties urged developing countries to inform the secretariat of any difficulties they face in reporting data so that assistance can be provided to remedy the situation.

Once national data are received, they need to be processed and analyzed, frequently by specialized external experts, for example by the IUCN/UNEP/WWF Wildlife Conservation Monitoring Centre under the 1973 Endangered Species Convention (No. 18); by the international centres of the EMEP monitoring programme under the 1979 Long-range Transboundary Air Pollution Convention (No. 31), and on behalf of HELCOM under the 1974 Baltic Marine Environment Convention (No. 44); and by the International Council for the Exploration of the Sea (No. 63) under several agreements on marine living resources. The ultimate responsibility for evaluation of national reports remains, of course, with the intergovernmental Conferences of the Parties.

Under the 1973 Endangered Species Convention (No. 18), the secretariat takes up cases of non-compliance directly with the Parties concerned (more than 100 cases annually) and transmits the information received in response to the Conference of the Parties for action, which in serious cases may decide to suspend wildlife trade with a Party in non-compliance. Under the European Community (EC) Treaty, as amended by the 1986 Single European Act (No. 9), the EC Commission has in a large number of cases (242 until 1990) lodged proceedings against member States for non-compliance with environmental directives; more than half of these proceedings were based on complaints by individual citizens or groups. While complaint procedures are also foreseen in other agreements (e.g., complaints by Governments to the United Nations Security Council under the 1977 Environmental Modification Convention, (No. 4), or under the 1972 Biological Weapons Convention, (No. 25)), these have not been used in practice. Similarly, the mechanisms for complaints and inquiry available under Articles 24-26 of the ILO Constitution have so far been invoked only once in connection with an ILO convention on the working environment (No. 112: a 1987 complaint by a trade union was declared "not receivable" on procedural grounds). A new procedure to follow up on non-compliance was introduced in 1990 under the 1987 Montreal Protocol on Substances That Deplete the Ozone Layer (No. 33 (a)); the procedure is being elaborated further by an <u>ad hoc</u> legal expert group. A new complaints procedure was also introduced in the 1991 Volatile Organic Compounds Protocol to the Long-range Transboundary Air Pollution Convention (No. 31 (d)).

Even though many of the global and regional agreements surveyed contain provisions and detailed annexes for dispute resolution - including references to binding arbitration or judicial settlement, though usually on an optional rather than a compulsory basis - so far there are no known cases in which any of these provisions were invoked or used. While the 1974 Nordic Environment Protection Convention (No. 2) and the 1974-1977 OECD Principles Concerning Transfrontier Pollution (No. 3) may be said to have promoted equal rights of access and non-discrimination in national judicial and administrative proceedings, they have not directly been applied in disputes.

It may be concluded, therefore, that the implementation of agreements or instruments has mainly been influenced by such factors as financial resources, technical and scientific assistance, public information and national reporting duties. By contrast, international supervisory bodies, non-compliance procedures and dispute settlement procedures so far have not played a major role.

The annex to the present volume provides bibliographic source references to some major international collections in which the full texts of the 124 agreements and related instruments covered by the present survey are reproduced. In addition, several Governments (e.g., Canada and Hungary) have recently published complete national compilations of the environmental agreements and instruments to which they are Parties. The secretariats or depositaries identified in the annex frequently issue further information and guidance material to assist in the implementation of agreements; examples are the CITES Directory and Identification Manual (under No. 18), the Handbook of the Antarctic Treaty System (under No. 14), and the Handbook for the Montreal Protocol on Substances That Deplete the Ozone Layer (under No. 33 (a)).

Information on basic treaty data, entry into force and membership is annually updated in the UNEP "Register of International Treaties and Other Agreements in the Field of the Environment". Several international secretariats issue periodic newsletters for use by Governments, the industries concerned and the general public. A wide range of additional information is available from non-governmental organizations and institutions, such as the Environmental Law Centre of the International Union for Conservation of Nature and Natural Resources (IUCN), and in the context of specialized international training programmes as organized by the United Nations Institute for Training and Research (UNITAR), the International Maritime Law Institute of the International Maritime Organization (IMO), and the International Development Law Institute (IDLI).

OPERATION, REVIEW AND ADJUSTMENT

A directory of the secretariats or depositaries for 124 agreements and instruments is given in the annex to the present volume. There are major differences, depending on whether the attributes of a secretariat include specific monitoring or reporting functions, and/or the co-ordination or technical-financial administration of international programmes and projects. While most treaty secretariats are part of larger international organizations, making budgetary specification difficult, the following table compares the 1990 annual budgets of eight major international secretariats:

Agreement (No.)	Short title (and location)	Staff (Professional and General Service)	Annual budget (Millions of dollars)	Main funding source
18	CITES (Lausanne)	18	2.46	Parties
25	ITTO (Yokohama)	20	2.36	Parties
31	LRTAP (Geneva)	7	1.30	UN/ECE
33	Vienna/Montreal (Nairobi)	6	2.30	Parties & UNEP
35	LDC (London)	5	0.76	IMO
36	MARPOL (London)	20	3.03	IMO
57	IWC (Cambridge)	13	1.31	Parties
103	Basel (Geneva)	4	0.68	Parties & UNEP

Source: Revised from US General Accounting Office, GAO/RCED-92-43, 1992.

The budgets given above refer to international administration and meeting costs and do not include the participation costs of the Parties, such as travel to meetings under the agreement. Even with a minimum attendance at only two or three one-week meetings at the secretariat headquarters (actual meeting numbers in 1990 were much higher), travel alone would on average require at least US$ 10,000 per year/per Party. As indicated in paragraph 14 above, some travel funding is normally available to facilitate participation by experts from developing countries, either from one of the trust funds established for this purpose, or from secretariat funds.

A number of agreements and instruments provide for the establishment of scientific advisory bodies to contribute expertise for policy-making, especially in periodic reviews and assessments. As an alternative to in-house advice, an existing international institution may be designated for this purpose (as in the case of the International Council for the Exploration of the Sea (No. 63)).

Non-governmental organizations have traditionally played a major role in the negotiation and implementation of international environmental agreements. Under identical provisions of the 1973 Endangered Species Convention (No. 18) and the 1979 Migratory Species Convention (No. 22), the UNEP secretariat thus regularly draws on the services of "suitable intergovernmental or non-governmental international or national agencies and bodies technically qualified in protection, conservation and management" of wildlife. While in conventions on the working environment (Nos. 110-116) workers' and employers' organizations are formally recognized as part of the ILO tripartite system of decision-making, most other environmental agreements or instruments contain no express reference to the status of non-governmental organizations.

Procedures for periodic review and adjustment have been built into several of the most recent international environmental agreements, so as to provide a "feedback loop" for new scientific information:

(a)   Under the 1987 Montreal Protocol on Substances that Deplete the Ozone Layer (No. 33 (a)), four assessment panels co-ordinated by an "Open-ended Working Group" reported to the 1990 London meeting of the Parties and provided the basis for a series of far-reaching amendments. The next round of assessments is now underway.

(b)   Under the 1988 Nitrogen Oxides Protocol to the Long-range Transboundary Air Pollution Convention, (No. 31 (c)), regular reviews are undertaken by a new Working Group on Strategies; the group developed the "critical loads" approach, and submitted its first report in 1991.

(c)   Under the 1989 Basel Convention on Hazardous Wastes (No. 103), an evaluation of the treaty's effectiveness is to be undertaken three years after its entry into force and at least every six years thereafter.

CODIFICATION PROGRAMMING

A number of new draft conventions and protocols are currently in preparation, including the following: an ILO convention on prevention of industrial disasters (1993); an IAEA nuclear safety convention (1993); an ECE convention on transboundary impacts of industrial accidents (1992[1]); an ECE convention on protection and use of transboundary watercourses (1992[1]); a revision of the 1985 Sulphur Emissions Protocol under the Long-range Transboundary Air Pollution Convention (No. 31) (1993); a revision of the 1958 ECE Motor Vehicle Agreement (No. 28 (1992)); a Council of Europe convention on civil liability for damage resulting from activities dangerous to the environment (1992); a liability protocol under the 1989 Basel Convention on Hazardous Wastes (No. 103) (1992); a revision of the 1974 Baltic Marine Environment Convention (No. 44) (1992[1]); a possible merger of the 1972 Oslo and 1974 Paris conventions on marine pollution in the North Sea (Nos. 43 and 45) (1992); new protocols on offshore mining and on hazardous wastes under the 1976 Mediterranean Convention (No. 46) (1992), and on land-based marine pollution both under the 1981 West African Convention and under the 1983 Caribbean Convention (Nos. 48 and 52) (1992-1993).

An in-depth review of the law-making work of all international organizations in this field was last undertaken in 1980-81 (Environmental Law: UNEP Report No.2, 1981). Following the discontinuation of the earlier surveys of legislative activities in the UN system - which had at least provided mutual information to the various secretariats - there is currently no formal mechanism for co-ordinating this kind of drafting work; the retrospective summary of past activities in the United Nations Juridical Yearbook continues to suffer from a severe publication lag (the most recent volume published covers the year 1985). Yet the volume of current drafting suggests a need for timely co-ordination, which should also include liaison with related drafting work outside the United Nations system (as already initiated for airborne marine pollution under Nos. 31 and 44-45, or with regard to protection of the environment in times of armed conflict under Nos. 4-5).

Future codification projects in this field will have to take into account, in particular, the ongoing work of the International Law Commission on four topics: state responsibility; international liability for injurious consequences arising out of acts not prohibited by

---

[1]   Already completed prior to June 1992.

international law; crimes against the peace and security of mankind; and the law of non-navigational uses of international watercourses. Another area requiring close co-ordination with other United Nations bodies is the relationship between existing agreements or instruments in the environmental field and relevant international trade agreements or instruments, taking into account the 1990 Declaration on International Economic Cooperation, in particular the revitalization of economic Growth and Development of the Developing countries; the International Development Strategy for the Fourth United Nations Development Decade; and progress in the preparation of a Code of Conduct for Transnational Corporations, and the draft guidelines on sustainable development imperatives being prepared by the UN Centre on Transnational Corporations. In this context, the recent decision by Council of the General Agreement on Tariffs and Trade (GATT) to reactivate its Group on Environmental Measures and International Trade is significant, in view of the Group's agenda to consider:

(a)   trade provisions contained in existing multilateral environmental agreements (in particular Nos. 18, 33 (a) and 103) vis-à-vis GATT principles and provisions;

(b)   multilateral transparency of national environmental regulations likely to have trade effects;

(c)   trade effects of new packaging and labelling requirements aimed at protecting the environment.

It should also be kept in mind that the evolution of international law in the field of environment and sustainable development is influenced by mechanisms other than formal legal agreements or instruments:

(a)   In addition to the non-mandatory "soft law" instruments already listed (Nos. 1, 3, 6, 10, 26, 32, 37, 39, 71, 100-102, 105), there are a number of programmatic instruments which, because of their adoption at interministerial or other high-level intergovernmental meetings, serve as normative reference for further law-making. Examples are the action plans adopted in the context of the UNEP regional seas programme (reflected in Nos. 46-49, 51-52, 54-55) and the Zambezi River action plan (No. 90); the role of the International North Sea and Baltic Sea Conferences in shaping the revisions of the OSPARCOM and HELCOM conventions (Nos. 43-45); and the corresponding role of the 1991 Rovaniemi Conference and Declaration in the development of a new Arctic Environment Protection Strategy.

(b)   The relative weight of standards and guidelines adopted by competent international technical bodies, even without legally binding effect, in influencing State practice can be virtually equivalent to that of formally binding agreements or instruments in this field. Examples are the food quality standards of the joint FAO/World Health Organizations (WHO) Codex Alimentarius Commission, which only become binding upon unilateral governmental acceptance; and the entirely indicative WHO guidelines for drinking-water quality and ambient air quality. Where compliance with such reference norms is made a condition of technical assistance (as in the case of the IAEA basic nuclear safety standards) or of financial assistance (through the World Bank's internal "operational directives" for projects, e.g., on international waterways and on environmental assessment), these instruments acquire special significance for future international law-making.

FOLLOW-UP: AGENDA 21

In the context of its recommendations for future action ("Agenda 21"), the UNCED Preparatory Committee examined possible areas for the further development of international environmental law, in the light of the need to integrate environment and development, especially taking into account the special needs and concerns of the developing countries (Terms of Reference of Working Group III, decision 2/3, A/46/48, vol. I, annex I). In addition to the research papers subsequently compiled in the present volume and the summary report prepared by the UNCED Secretariat (A/CONF.151/PC/103 and Add.1), the Preparatory Committee had before it the expected outcomes formulated at the third session (decision 3/25, annex I, A/46/48, vol. II), as well as the conclusions of the 1990 Siena Forum on International Law of the Environment (A/45/666), the Beijing Symposium on Developing Countries and International Environmental Law (12-14 August 1991), the UNEP Meeting of Senior Government Officials Expert in Environmental Law for the Review of the Montevideo Programme (30 October-2 November 1991, UNEP/Env.Law/2/3), and relevant recent comments by Governments and international organizations in the context of the United Nations Decade of International Law (as summarized in the 1991 Report of the Secretary-General of the United Nations (A/46/372)).

The outcome of this comprehensive examination is reflected in chapter 39 (International legal instruments and mechanisms) of Agenda 21, as drafted at the fourth session of the Preparatory Committee (A/CONF.151/4, Part IV) and finalized at the Conference in Rio de Janeiro from 3 to 14 June 1992.

The UNCED Preparatory Committee also considered the need for providing an effective legal and regulatory framework at the national and local level, including national monitoring of legal follow-up to international instruments. The outcome of this analysis - which must be seen in conjunction with chapter 39 - is reflected in chapter 8 (programme area B) of Agenda 21 (Integrating environment and development in decision-making, A/CONF.151/4, Part I).

AGENDA 21 - CHAPTER 39:
INTERNATIONAL LEGAL INSTRUMENTS AND MECHANISMS

Basis for action

The following vital aspects of the universal, multilateral and bilateral treaty-making process should be taken into account:

(a)   The further development of international law on sustainable development, giving special attention to the delicate balance between environmental and developmental concerns;

(b)   The need to clarify and strengthen the relationship between existing international instruments or agreements in the field of environment and relevant social and economic agreements or instruments, taking into account the special needs of developing countries;

(c)   At the global level, the essential importance of the participation in and the contribution of all countries, including the developing countries, to treaty-making in the field of international law on sustainable development. Many of the existing international legal instruments and agreements in the field of environment have been developed without adequate participation and contribution of developing countries, and thus may require review in order to reflect the concerns and interests of developing countries and to ensure a balanced governance of such instruments and agreements;

(d)   Developing countries should also be provided with technical assistance in their attempts to enhance their national legislative capabilities in the field of sustainable development;

(e)   Future codification projects for the progressive development and codification of international law on sustainable development should take into account the ongoing work of the International Law Commission; and

(f)   Any negotiations for the progressive development and codification of international law concerning sustainable development should, in general, be conducted on a universal basis, taking into account special circumstances in the various regions.

Objectives

The overall objective of the review and development of international environmental law should be to evaluate and to promote the efficacy of that law and to promote the integration of environment and development policies through effective international agreements or instruments, taking into account both universal principles and the particular and differentiated needs and concerns of all countries.

Specific objectives are:

(a)   To identify and address difficulties which prevent some States, in particular developing countries, from participating in or duly implementing international agreements or instruments and, where appropriate, to review or revise them with the purposes of integrating environmental and developmental concerns and laying down a sound basis for the implementation of these agreements or instruments;

(b)   To set priorities for future international law-making on sustainable development at the global, regional or sub-regional level, with a view to enhancing

the efficacy of international law in this field through, in particular, the integration of environmental and developmental concerns;

(c)   To promote and support the effective participation of all countries concerned, in particular developing countries in the negotiation, implementation, review and governance of international agreements or instruments, including appropriate provision of technical and financial assistance and other available mechanisms for this purpose, as well as the use of differential obligations where appropriate;

(d)   To promote, through the gradual development of universally and multilaterally negotiated agreements or instruments, international standards for the protection of the environment that take into account the different situations and capabilities of countries.   States recognize that environmental policies should deal with the root causes of environmental degradation, thus preventing environmental measures from resulting in unnecessary restrictions to trade.   Trade policy measures for environmental purposes should not constitute a means of arbitrary or unjustifiable discrimination or a disguised restriction on international trade.   Unilateral actions to deal with environmental challenges outside the jurisdiction of the importing country should be avoided.   Environmental measures addressing international environmental problems should, as far as possible, be based on an international consensus.   Domestic measures targeted to achieve certain environmental objectives may need trade measures to render them effective.   Should trade policy measures be found necessary for the enforcement of environmental policies, certain principles and rules should apply.   These could include, inter alia, the principle of non-discrimination; the principle that the trade measure chosen should be the least trade-restrictive necessary to achieve the objectives; an obligation to ensure transparency in the use of trade measures related to the environment and to provide adequate notification of national regulations; and the need to give consideration to the special conditions and development requirements of developing countries as they move towards internationally agreed environmental objectives.

(e)   To ensure the effective, full and prompt implementation of legally binding instruments, and to facilitate timely review and adjustment of agreements or instruments by the parties concerned, taking into account the special needs and concerns of all countries, in particular developing countries;

(f)   To improve the effectiveness of institutions, mechanisms and procedures for the administration of agreements and instruments;

(g)   To identify and prevent actual or potential conflicts, particularly between environmental and social/economic agreements or instruments, with a view to ensuring that such agreements or instruments are consistent.   Where conflicts arise, they should be appropriately resolved;

(h)   To study and consider the broadening and strengthening of the capacity of mechanisms, inter alia in the United Nations system, to facilitate, where appropriate and agreed by the parties concerned, the identification, avoidance and settlement of international disputes in the field of sustainable development, duly taking into account existing bilateral and multilateral agreements for the settlement of such disputes.

<u>Activities</u>

Activities and means of implementation should be considered in the light of the above Basis for Action and Objectives without prejudice to the right of every State to put forward suggestions in this regard in the General Assembly of the United Nations. These suggestions could be reproduced in a separate compilation on sustainable development.

A.   Review, assessment and fields of action in
international law for sustainable development

While ensuring the effective participation of all countries concerned, Parties should at periodic intervals review and assess both the past performance and effectiveness of existing international agreements or instruments as well as the priorities for future law-making on sustainable development. This may include an examination of the feasibility of elaborating general rights and obligations of States, as appropriate, in the field of sustainable development, as provided by General Assembly resolution 44/228. In certain cases, attention should be given to the possibility of taking into account varying circumstances through differential obligations or gradual application. As an option for carrying out this task, earlier UNEP practice may be followed whereby legal experts designated by governments could meet at suitable intervals to be decided later with a broader environmental and developmental perspective.

(a)   Measures in accordance with international law should be considered to address, in times of armed conflict, large-scale destruction of the environment that cannot be justified under international law. The General Assembly and the Sixth Committee are the appropriate fora to deal with this subject. The specific

competence and role of the International Committee of the Red Cross should be taken into account.

(b)   In view of the vital necessity to ensure safe and environmentally sound nuclear power, and in order to strengthen international cooperation in this field, efforts should be made to conclude the ongoing negotiations for a nuclear safety convention in the framework of the International Atomic Energy Agency.

B. Implementation mechanisms

The parties to international agreements should consider procedures and mechanisms to promote and review their effective, full and prompt implementation. To that effect, States could, <u>inter alia</u>:

(a)   Establish efficient and practical reporting systems on the effective, full and prompt implementation of international legal instruments;

(b)   Consider appropriate ways in which relevant international bodies, such as UNEP, might contribute towards the further development of such mechanisms.

C. Effective participation in international law-making

In all these activities and others that may be pursued in the future, based on the above Basis for Action and Objectives, the effective participation of all countries, in particular developing countries, should be ensured through appropriate provision of technical assistance and/or financial assistance. Developing countries should be given "headstart" support not only in their national efforts to implement international agreements or instruments, but also to participate effectively in the negotiation of new or revised agreements or instruments and in the actual international operation of such agreements or instruments. Support should include assistance in building up expertise in international law particularly in relation to sustainable development, and in assuring access to the necessary reference information and scientific/technical expertise.

D. Disputes in the field of sustainable development

In the area of avoidance and settlement of disputes, States should further study and consider methods to broaden and make more effective the range of techniques available at present, taking into account, among others, relevant experience under existing international agreements, instruments or institutions and, where appropriate, their implementing mechanisms such as modalities for dispute avoidance and settlement. This may include mechanisms and procedures for the exchange of data and information, notification and consultation regarding situations that might lead to disputes with other States in the field of sustainable development and for effective peaceful means of dispute settlement in accordance with the Charter of the United Nations including, where appropriate, recourse to the International Court of Justice, and their inclusion in treaties relating to sustainable development.

AGENDA 21 - CHAPTER 8 (B):
PROVIDING AN EFFECTIVE LEGAL AND REGULATORY FRAMEWORK

Basis for action

Laws and regulations suited to country-specific conditions are among the most important instruments for transforming environment and development policies into action -- not only through "command and control" methods but also as a normative framework for economic planning and market instruments. Yet although the volume of legal texts in this field is steadily increasing, much of the law-making in many countries seems to be ad hoc and piecemeal, or has not been endowed with the necessary institutional machinery and authority for enforcement and timely adjustment.

While there is continuous need for law improvement in all countries, many developing countries have been affected by shortcomings of laws and regulations. To effectively integrate environment and development in the policies and practices of each country, it is essential to develop and implement integrated, enforceable, effective laws and regulations that are based upon sound social, ecological, economic and scientific principles. It is equally critical to develop workable programmes to review and enforce compliance with the laws, regulations, and standards that are adopted. Technical support may be needed for many countries to accomplish these goals. Technical cooperation requirements in this field include legal information, advisory services and specialized training and institutional capacity-building.

The enactment and enforcement of laws and regulations (at the regional, national, state/provincial or local/municipal level) is also essential for the implementation of most international agreements in the field of environment and development, as illustrated by the frequent treaty obligation to report on legislative measures. The survey of existing agreements undertaken in the context of conference preparations has indicated problems of compliance in this respect, and, where appropriate, the need for improved national implementation and, where appropriate, related technical assistance. In developing their national priorities, countries should take account of their international obligations.

Objectives

The overall objective is to promote, in light of country-specific conditions, the integration of environment and development policies through appropriate legal and regulatory policies, instruments and enforcement mechanisms at the national, state, provincial, and local level. Recognizing that countries will develop their own priorities in accordance with their needs and national, and where appropriate, regional plans, policies and programmes, the following objectives are proposed:

(a)   To disseminate information on effective legal and regulatory innovations in the field of environment and development, including appropriate instruments and compliance incentives, with a view to encouraging their wider use and adoption at the national, state, provincial, and local level;

(b)   To support countries which request it in their national efforts to modernize and strengthen the policy and legal framework of governance for sustainable development, having due regard for local social values and infrastructures;

(c)   To encourage the development and implementation of national, state, provincial and local programmes which assess and promote compliance and respond appropriately to non-compliance.

Activities

A. Make laws and regulations more effective

Governments, with the support of competent international organizations, where appropriate, should regularly assess the laws and regulations enacted and the related institutional/administrative machinery established at the national/state and local/municipal level in the field of environment and sustainable development, with a view to rendering them effective in practice. Programmes for this purpose could include the promotion of public awareness; preparation and distribution of guidance material; and specialized training, including workshops, seminars, education programs, and conferences, for public officials who design, implement, monitor and enforce laws and regulations.

B. Establish judicial and administrative procedures

Governments and legislators, with the support, where appropriate, of competent international organizations, should establish judicial and administrative procedures for legal redress and remedy of actions affecting environment and development that may be unlawful or infringe on rights under the law and should provide access to individuals, groups and organizations with a recognized legal interest.

C. Provide legal reference and support services

Competent intergovernmental and non-governmental organizations could cooperate to provide Governments and legislators, upon request, with an integrated programme of environment and development law (sustainable development law) services, carefully adapted to the specific requirements of the recipient legal and administrative systems. Such systems could usefully include assistance in the preparation of comprehensive inventories and reviews of national legal systems. Past experience has demonstrated the usefulness of combining specialized legal information services with legal expert advice. Within the United Nations system, closer cooperation between all agencies concerned would avoid duplication of databases and facilitate division of labour. These agencies could examine the possibility and merit of performing reviews of selected national legal systems.

D. Establish a cooperative training network for
sustainable development law

Competent international and academic institutions could - within agreed frameworks - cooperate to provide, especially for trainees from developing countries, postgraduate programmes and in-service training facilities in environment and development law. Such training should address both the effective application and the progressive improvement of applicable laws; the related skills of negotiating, drafting and mediation; and the training of trainers. Intergovernmental and non-governmental organizations already active in this field could cooperate with related university programmes to harmonize curriculum planning and to offer an optimal range of options to interested Governments and potential sponsors.

E. Develop effective national programmes for reviewing and enforcing
compliance with national, state, provincial and local
laws on environment and development

Each country should develop integrated strategies to maximize compliance with its laws and regulations relating to sustainable development, with assistance from international organizations and other countries as appropriate. The strategies could include:

(a)   Enforceable, effective laws, regulations and standards that are based on sound economic, social and environmental principles and appropriate risk assessment, incorporating sanctions designed to punish violations, obtain redress, and deter future violations;

(b)   Mechanisms for promoting compliance;

(c)   Institutional capacity for collecting compliance data, regularly reviewing compliance, detecting violations, establishing enforcement priorities, undertaking effective enforcement, and conducting periodic evaluations of the effectiveness of compliance and enforcement programmes; and

(d)   Mechanisms for appropriate involvement of individuals and groups in the development and enforcement of laws and regulations on environment and development.

F. National monitoring of legal follow-up to
international instruments

Contracting parties to international agreements, in consultation with the appropriate secretariats of relevant international conventions as appropriate, should improve practices and procedures for information on legal and regulatory measures taken. Contracting parties to international agreements could undertake sample surveys of domestic follow-up action subject to agreement by the sovereign States concerned.

Means of implementation

(a)   Financing and cost evaluation

        The Conference secretariat has estimated the average total annual cost (1993-2000) of implementing the activities of this programme to be about $6 million from the international community on grant or concessional terms. These are indicative and order of magnitude estimates only and have not been reviewed by Governments. Actual costs and financial terms, including any that are non-concessional, will depend upon, inter alia, the specific strategies and programmes Governments decide upon for implementation.

(b)   Scientific and technological means

        The programme relies essentially on a continuation of ongoing work for legal data collection, translation and assessment. Closer cooperation between existing databases may be expected to lead to better division of labour (e.g., in geographical coverage of national legislative gazettes and other reference sources) and to improved standardization and compatibility of data, as appropriate.

(c)   Human resources development

        Participation in training is expected to benefit practitioners from developing countries and to enhance training opportunities for women. Demand for this type of postgraduate and in-service training is known to be high. The seminars, workshops, and conferences on review and enforcement that have been held to date have been very successful and well attended. The purpose of these efforts is to develop resources (both human and institutional) to design and implement effective programmes to continuously review and enforce national and local laws, regulations, and standards on sustainable development.

(d)   Strengthening legal and institutional capacity

        A major part of the programme should be oriented towards improving the legal-institutional capacities of countries to cope with national problems of governance and effective law-making and law-applying in the field of environment and sustainable development. Regional centres of excellence could be designated and supported to build up specialized databases and training facilities for linguistic/cultural groups of legal systems.

CHAPTER I

GENERAL ENVIRONMENTAL CONCERNS

Alexandre C. Kiss and Parvez Hassan

This chapter covers the following 11 international legal instruments of general environmental concern, in chronological order:

(1)   the 1972 UN **Stockholm Declaration on the Human Environment**;

(2)   the 1974 **Nordic Convention on the Protection of the Environment**;

(3)   the 1974 OECD **Principles Concerning Transfrontier Pollution**, and related recommendations;

(4)   the 1977 UN **Environmental Modification Convention (ENMOD)**;

(5)   the 1977 Red Cross **Protocols (Relating to the Protection of Victims of Armed Conflicts)** Additional to the 1949 Geneva Conventions;

(6)   the 1978 UNEP **Shared Natural Resources Principles**;

(7)   the 1980 **European Outline Convention on Transfrontier Co-operation**;

(8)   the 1980 UN **Convention on Prohibited Conventional Weapons** and related protocols;

(9)   the 1986 **Single European Act** amending the 1957 Rome Treaties Establishing the European Communities, and related instruments;

(10)   the 1987 UNEP **Goals and Principles of Environmental Impact Assessment**; and

(11)   the 1991 ECE **Convention on Transboundary Environmental Impact Assessment**.

A list showing the status of ratifications as of 1 January 1992 is annexed (pages 54-58).

(1) Declaration on the United Nations Conference on the Human Environment
(Stockholm, 16 June 1972)

Objectives and achievement

According to the preamble of the Declaration, "the protection and improvement of the human environment is a major issue which affects the well-being of peoples and economic development throughout the world; it is the urgent desire of the peoples of the whole world and the duty of all Governments." Following the adoption of the Declaration by the Stockholm Conference, the UN General Assembly by Resolution 2994 (XXVII) of 15 December 1972 drew it to the attention of governments and of the newly established UNEP Governing Council.

The Stockholm Declaration proclaims in its Principle 8 that "economic and social development is essential for ensuring a favourable living and working environment for man and for creating conditions on earth that are necessary for the improvement of the quality of life". The principles which follow add that "environmental deficiencies generated by the conditions of underdevelopment and natural disasters pose grave problems and can best be remedied by accelerated development through the transfer of substantial quantities of financial and technolgical assistance as a supplement to the domestic effort of the developing countries and such timely assistance as may be required" (Principle 9). Principle 10 insists on the necessity of the stability of prices and adequate earnings for the developing countries. Principle 11 proclaims that the environmental policies of all States should enhance and not adversely affect the present or future development potential of developing countries, while Principle 12 insists on the duty to take into account the circumstances and particular requirements of developing countries and any costs which may emanate from their incorporating environmental safeguards in their development planning and the need for making available to them additional international technical and financial assistance for this purpose. Principles 13 to 17 advocate development planning policies and measures, including demographic policies, while Principle 23 recognizes that it is essential in all cases to consider the systems of values prevailing in each country, and the extent of the applicability of standards which are valid for the most advanced countries but which may be inappropriate and of unwarranted social cost for the developing countries.

The Stockholm Declaration is at the basis of the development of international environmental law during the decades which followed. The "Action Plan for the Human Environment" and also adopted by the Stockholm Conference may be considered as an explicitation of that Declaration and the progress made in its implementation is in part an application of the Stockholm Declaration. One may stress in particular the activities of UNEP in this regard (GEMS, INFOTERRA, the International Register of Potentially Toxic Chemicals), the United Nations conferences on water resources (Mar del Plata, 1977), on desertification (Nairobi, 1978), and the UNEP Regional Seas Programme which has achieved the conclusion of treaty systems for eight regions including more than 100 states, the great majority of which are developing countries, etc.

Participation

Even if some States did not attend the Stockholm Conference, mostly for political reasons which were independent of environmental considerations, virtually all States accept by now the principles proclaimed at Stockholm and often invoke them.

Most resolutions adopted by the UN General Assembly in environmental matters as well as many international multilateral agreements make reference to the Stockholm Declaration as a leading text in this field. Similarly, for scientists, non-governmental organizations and the general public, the Stockholm Declaration constituted and still constitutes authoritative guidance for action.

Implementation

In the field of international environmental law, Principle 21 of the Stockholm Declaration is particularly relevant. It reads as follows:

"States have, in accordance with the Charter of the U.N. and the principles of international law, the sovereign right to exploit their own resources pursuant to their own environmental policies, and the responsibility to ensure that activities within their jurisdiction or control do not cause damage to the environment of other states or of areas beyond the limits of national jurisdiction."

This principle, though part of a nonbinding text, is generally recognized today as having become a rule of customary international law. It has been reaffirmed a number of times in declarations adopted by the United Nations General Assembly (including the Charter of Economic Rights and Duties of States of 12 December 1974, General Assembly Resolution 3281/XXIX) and by other international organizations and conferences (Preliminary Declaration of a Programme of Action of the European Communities in respect of the Environment, Official Journal of the European Communities, 20 December 1973; Final Act, Helsinki Conference on Security and Cooperation in Europe, 1 August 1975). Its contents were inserted in the UN Law of the Sea Convention (No. 38 in the present survey), Article 194 (2), as well as in the ASEAN Convention on the Conservation of Nature and Natural Resources (No. 27, Art. 20). The preamble to the 1979 Geneva Convention on Long-Range Transboundary Air Pollution (No. 31) reproduced principle 21 as "expressing the common conviction of States" on this matter.

The Stockholm Declaration has been issued in the six official languages of the United Nations (e.g., in UNEP Environmental Law Guidelines and Principles, No. 1) and in many other languages of the world, and has been widely disseminated by the UN and by NGOs. It is reproduced in many publications relating to environmental law.

Operation, review and adjustment

The Nairobi Declaration adopted by the UNEP Governing Council at its session of a special character on 18 May 1982, and especially the **World Charter for Nature** adopted by UN General Assembly Resolution 37/7 on 28 October 1982, may be considered as updating and complementing the principles of the Stockholm Declaration.

In a 1984 progress report from the UNEP Executive Director to the Governing Council (UNEP/GC.12/INF/4), the regular monitoring of the implementation of the World Charter for Nature was described as "an essential requirement for its fulfillment". However, no further reviews of governmental compliance appear to have been undertaken.

(2) Nordic Convention on the Protection of the Environment
(Stockholm, 19 February 1974) and related agreements

Objectives and achievement

The main objectives of the 1974 Convention are to ensure non-discrimination and equal rights of access between Governments and citizens of the Nordic countries in cases involving transboundary environmental impacts. The Convention applies in all cases where an "examining authority" (judicial or administrative) decides on the permissibility of environmentally harmful activities, or where compensation is claimed for harm caused by such activities; it does not apply to cases that were already pending at the time of its entry into force, or to cases governed by other special agreements. The Nordic countries have indeed concluded a number of related agreements on specific environmental matters, such as the **Nordic Agreement on Co-operation Over National Territorial Boundaries with the Aim of Preventing or Limiting Damage to Man or Property or the Environment in the Event of Accidents** (Stockholm, 20 January 1989).

While the Convention is thus sub-regional in scope, it has served as a model for the development of more general rules of international law, e.g., in the OECD Principles Concerning Transfrontier Pollution (No. 3 below), and for bilateral agreements outside the Scandinavian sub-region.

According to an evaluation conducted in 1981 by the Nordic Council of Ministers, the basic principles of the Convention has proved to be effective, although some of its provisions (e.g., on-site inspections under Article 10, and advisory opinions by a joint commission under Article 12) had never been applied. Subsequent non-governmental evaluations carried out in 1985 and 1991 indicate that the Convention was invoked in a number of licensing and compensation claims proceedings, and that it has been effective mainly in encouraging notification and administrative co-operation with regard to transfrontier pollution risks, whereas in some cases its provisions were either not observed or declared to be inapplicable.

Participation

The Convention is restricted to Nordic countries (currently Denmark, Finland, Norway and Sweden), the legislation of which presents many similarities and which have a background of longstanding co-operation in various fields. It entered into force on 5 October 1976. No accession and no reservations are foreseen by the Convention; however, Iceland may accede to the 1989 Agreement.

Implementation and information

When environmentally harmful activities are foreseen or have taken place, the Contracting Parties must ensure equality of access in all administrative and judicial proceedings to nationals of other Contracting States (Convention, art. 3,5, 6). They appoint a special "supervisory authority" to be entrusted with the task of safeguarding general environmental interests insofar as regards nuisances arising out of environmentally harmful activities in another Contracting State (Convention, art.4). Each State defrays the cost of activities of the supervisory authority (Art. 8). The Convention also provides for consultations, upon requests regarding the permissibility of environmentally harmful activities which entail or may entail considerable nuisance in another State (Article 11).

According to the 1989 Agreement, each Contracting State undertakes to provide necessary assistance in the event of an accident or imminent threat of an accident in accordance with its possibilities to do so (Article 2). An authority in a Contracting State which in the event of an accident is responsible for taking measures to prevent or limit damage to man or property or the environment may request assistance directly from a competent authority in another Contracting State (Article 3). For the practical implementation of the Agreement, the competent authorities in each Contracting State are expected to be in direct contact with each other (Article 6 (2)). As far as possible, the parties will eliminate provisions in their national legislation to the extent that they prevent such cooperation (Article 1(2)). In principle, the assisting State has a right to reimbursement for costs incurred for the assistance rendered (Art. 4).

According to the Convention, where the permissibility of environmentally harmful activities which entail or may entail considerable nuisance in another Contracting State is being examined by the appropriate authority of the State where the activities are being carried out, the Government of each State may demand that an opinion is given by a commission. This commission consists, unless otherwise agreed, of a chairman from another Contracting State and three members from each of the States concerned. The case cannot be decided upon until the commission has given its opinion (Article 12 (1)).

Both instruments were drafted in Danish, Finnish, Norwegian and Swedish. Unofficial English and French translations are available for the Convention, and an unofficial English translation for the Agreement.

Competent "supervisory authorities" for the purposes of the Convention have been designated in all Contracting States. According to Article 6 (1) of the 1989 Agreement, the Contracting States inform each other about the organization and competent authorities in their States and any changes in legislation and other substantial changes which are of importance for the Agreement. The States also promote the development of direct co-operation in the field.

One criticism made in non-governmental evaluations is the lack of information abount the Convention among administrative authorities, which in some cases may have accounted for a failure to observe notification provisions.

Operation, review and adjustment

The Swedish Government is the depositary both of the 1974 Convention and the 1989 Agreement. According to Article 6 (3) of the Agreement, meetings shall be held when suitable. Co-ordination of follow-up activities is ensured by the Nordic Council of Ministers and its "Officials' Committee for Environmental Affairs", with a secretariat in Copenhagen (Denmark).

At the time of signature of the Convention, the Contracting Parties also adopted a **Protocol** interpreting certain provisions. To date there have been no amendments or proposals for amendment.

(3) OECD Principles Concerning Transfrontier Pollution
(Paris, 14 November 1974) and related recommendations

Objectives and achievement

The set of principles concerning transfrontier pollution was adopted by the Council of the Organisation for Economic Cooperation and Development (OECD) as an annex to its Recommendation C(74)224 of 14 November 1974. Its objective is to initiate action for preventing and controlling transfrontier pollution. During subsequent years, specific recommendations further elaborated the principles formulated by the 1974 instrument: on **Equal Right of Access in Relation to Transfrontier Pollution** (Recommendation C(76)55 Final, of 11 May 1976); on the **Implementation of a Regime of Equal Rights of Access and Non-discrimination in Relation to Transfrontier Pollution** (Recommendation C(77)28 Final, of 17 May 1977) and on **Strengthening International Co-operation on Environmental Protection in Frontier Regions** (Recommendation C(78)77 Final of 21 September 1978).

These texts represent a first formulation of concepts which have since been widely accepted as a basis of customary and codified international law. The very definition of pollution, first used by the 1974 Principles, has been adapted for use in many international conventions (No. 46 in the present survey: 1976 Barcelona Convention for the Protection of the Mediterranean Sea against Pollution, Article 2(a); No. 31: 1979 Geneva Convention on Long-Range Transboundary Air Pollution, Art. 1; No. 38: 1982 UN Convention on the Law of the Sea, Art. 1(1)(4), etc.). The 1978 UNEP Principles of Conduct in the Field of the Environment for the Guidance of States in the Conservation and Harmonious Utilization of Natural Resources Shared by Two or More States (No. 6 below) were partly inspired by the OECD Principles. Several specific principles of the OECD Recommendations have also been generally recognized:

- the duty to warn potentially affected countries of any situation which may cause any sudden increase in the level of pollution in areas outside the country of origin of pollution (Principle 9): UNEP Shared Resources Principles (No. 6) 9(1); UNCLOS (No. 38), Article 198; ASEAN Convention on the Conservation of Nature and Natural Resources (No.27), Art. 20(d); Vienna Convention on Early Notification in the Case of Nuclear Accident or Radiological Emergency (No. 85), Art. 2.

- assistance to other States in an environmental emergency (Principle 10): UNCLOS (No.38), Art. 199; Vienna Convention on Assistance in the Case of a Nuclear Accident or Radiological Emergency (No. 85), Art. 1; International Convention on Oil Pollution Preparedness, Response and Co-operation (No. 41), Art. 7; etc.

- prior information and consultation on works or undertakings which might create a significant risk of transfrontier pollution (Principles 6, 7 and 8): Kuwait Convention on the Protection of the Marine Environment from Pollution (No. 47), Art.11; ASEAN Agreement on the Conservation of Nature and Natural Resources (No. 27), Art. 20; UN Charter of Economic Rights and Duties of States, Art. 3; Espoo Convention on Environmental Impact Assessment in a Transboundary Context (No. 11 below), Art. 3-5, etc.

The principles of non-discrimination and equality of access (Articles 4 and 5 of the 1974 Recommendation) have mainly influenced national legislation and national judicial decisions.

Participation

The OECD instruments were adopted by the 24 member countries of that organization (19 Western European States, Australia, Canada, Japan, New Zealand, USA), none of which is a developing country. However, later evolution shows that some of the principles have been widely accepted by the international community as a basis for customary and codified rules.

Implementation and information

Since these instruments are mere recommendations, they have no binding character. However, the very fact that the States which adopted them are OECD members creates for these States pressures to observe them, as they reflect common views and intentions.

These recommendations should govern the general attitude of States members of OECD and do not exclusively concern the reciprocal relations between them. They may be considered as applicable by OECD members to non-members, which including developing countries. Also, one may recall that OECD has recently adopted a recommendation to ensure that member countries consider environmental aspects in the identification, planning, implementation and evaluation of development projects which are proposed for funding.

OECD documents are generally available in English and French.

Operation, review and adjustment

The costs of the international administration of these instruments are covered by the general budget of the OECD secretariat located in Paris (France). The costs of national implementation measures by the member of OECD (warning, information and consultation) are, as a rule, borne by the States which initiate them. For the cost of assistance in environmental emergencies specific rules are generally adopted in bilateral or multilateral agreements.

The principle of equal right of hearing includes that whenever a project, a new activity or a course of conduct may create a significant risk of transfrontier pollution and is investigated by public authorities, those who may be affected by such pollution should have the same rights of standing in judicial or administrative proceedings in the country where it originates as those of that country. On the other hand, whenever transfrontier pollution gives rise to damage in a country, those who are affected by such pollution should have the same rights of standing in judicial or administative proceedings in the country where such pollution originates as those of that country, and they should be extended procedural rights equivalent to the rights extended to those of that country. These provisions of Principle 5, further developed in subsequent recommendations, ensure the participation of individuals and non-governmental entities, without making any distinction as to the country of residence of the persons whom they concern.

The OECD Council ensures the progressive elaboration and adjustment of the 1974 Principles and related instruments.

(4) Convention on the Prohibition of Military or Any Other Hostile Use of Environmental Modification Techniques (ENMOD),
(Geneva, 18 May 1977)

Objectives and achievement

According to its preamble, the objective of the ENMOD Convention is to prohibit effectively military or any other hostile use of environmental modification techniques in order to eliminate the dangers to mankind from such use.

According to Article 3 of the Convention, this instrument shall not hinder the use of environmental modification techniques for peaceful purposes and shall be without prejudice to the generally recognized principles and applicable rules of international law concerning such use. It is also provided that the States Parties facilitate and have the right to participate in the fullest possible exchange of scientific and technological information on the use of environmental modification techniques for peaceful purposes.

The events of the Gulf War demonstrated the reality of the risks envisaged by the Convention, as well as the limitations of international treaty law to cope with these risks: Kuwait actually was the only country in the region to have become a Party to the Convention, albeit with a reservation to the effect that it was bound "only towards States Parties thereto".

Participation

Membership is open to all States. The Convention entered into force on 5 October 1978. As of 1 January 1992, there were 55 Parties to the Convention, including 29 developing countries. While only Kuwait entered the above-mentioned formal reservation, several other States made interpretive declarations at the time of ratification.

Negotiations on the ENMOD Convention were carried out by the U.N. Committee on Disarmament (predecessor of the Conference on Disarmament 1969-1978). The following developing countries were then members of that body: Argentina, Brazil, Burma, Egypt, Ethiopia, India, Iran, Mexico, Mongolia, Morocco, Nigeria, Pakistan, Peru, Romania, Yugoslavia and Zaire.

Implementation and information

Commitments imposed upon parties of the ENMOD Convention are:
- not to engage in military or any other hostile use of environmental modification techniques having wide-spread, long-lasting or severe effects as the means of destruction, damage or injury to any other State Party (Article 1(1));
- not to assist, encourage or induce any state, groups of States or international organization to engage in activities contrary to this general prohibition (Article 1 (2));
- to take any measures considered as necessary in accordance with national constitutional processes to prohibit and prevent any activity in violation of the provisions of the Convention anywhere under its jurisdiction or control (Article 4);
- to consult one another and to co-operate in solving any problems which may arise in relation to the objectives of, or in the application of the provisions of, the Convention (Article 5).

When there is a request from a State Party of consultation for solving a problem which may arise concerning the application of the convention, the Secretary-General of the United Nations, as depositary shall convene a Consultative Committee of Experts. Any state party may appoint an expert to this Committee. The Committee transmits to the Secretary General a summary of its findings of fact incorporating all views and information presented to it during its proceedings (Article 5 (1) (2)).

Any State Party which has reason to believe that any other State Party is acting in breach of obligations deriving from the provisions of the convention, may lodge a complaint with the UN Security Council. Such a complaint should include all relevant information as well as all possible evidence supporting its validity. Each State Party undertakes to co-operate in carrying out any investigation which the Security Council may initiate on the basis of the complaint. The Security Council shall inform the States Parties of the results of the investigation. Each Party to the convention undertakes to provide or support assistance to any State Party which so requests, if the Security Council decides that such Party has been harmed or is likely to be harmed as a result of violation of the Convention.

The ENMOD Convention has been adopted in Arabic, Chinese, English, French, Russian and Spanish. It has been published with other multilateral treaties, especially by UNEP and the UN Department of Disarmament Affairs.

Operation, review and adjustment

International administrative functions with regard to the Convention are carried out by the UN Department for Disarmament Affairs in New York, within the general United Nations budget.

According to Article 8, five years after the entry into force of the Convention, a conference of the States Parties was to be convened, in order to review the operation of the Convention and, if necessary, to eliminate the dangers of military or any other hostile use of environmental modification techniques. This conference met in 1984: the participating States expressed their conviction that the provisions of the Convention remained effective in preventing the dangers of military or any other hostile use of environmental modification techniques. Other conferences could be convened periodically on request of the majority of the Contracting States. Following consultations during the second half of 1991, a majority of States Parties have expressed their wish to convene a Second Review Conference in September of 1992 and requested the Secretary-General of the United Nations to provide the necessary services for the preparation and holding of the conference.

Any State Party to the Convention may propose amendments. Proposed amendments shall be submitted to the depositary who shall circulate them to all states parties. An amendment shall enter into force for all states parties which have accepted it, upon the deposit of instruments of acceptance by a majority of states (Article 6). No amendments have been made to date.

(5) Protocol I (Relating to the Protection of Victims of International Armed Conflicts) Additional to the 1949 Red Cross Conventions

(Geneva, 8 June 1977), and related Protocol II

Objectives and achievement

The purpose of the Protocol (and of the simultaneous **Protocol II Relating to the Protection of Victims of Non-International Armed Conflicts**) is humanitarian. Their preambles refer to the necessity to reaffirm and develop provisions protecting the victims of armed conflicts and to supplement measures intended to reinforce their application. The objectives require limiting the means and methods of warfare, including means which would cause widespread, long-term and severe damage to the environment and thereby prejudice the health or suvival of populations. No specific development issues are raised.

The Geneva Conventions and their Additional Protocols are global in scope. The environmental objectives are contained in two provisions of Protocol I (Articles 35(3) and 55) and in one section of Protocol II (Article 15). In both Protocols nuclear power stations are given special protection against attack (Protocol I, Art. 56; Protocol II, Article 15).

Articles 35(3) and 55 remind governments that protection of the environment is an issue also in times of armed conflict. Although the standards set by Protocol I are not particularly strict, the rules are proof of growing general awareness of the need to protect the environment.

Participation

Parties to the 1949 Geneva Conventions may become party to the Protocols. As acceptance of the 1949 Conventions is almost universal (166 States as of 1 January 1992) participation in the Protocols is de facto open-ended. Reservations are possible, but no reservations have been made to the provisions concerning the environment.

Among the 108 Parties to Protocol I, 76 are developing countries; so are 61 among the 98 Parties to Protocol II. Developing countries have also fully participated in the negotiation of the protocols by the 1974-1977 Diplomatic Conference, and in many respects played a leading role. The International Committee of the Red Cross (ICRC) has always shown special concern for the implementation of humanitarian law in the Third World, in particular through its network of delegations. ICRC delegates, for example, produce information and dissemination material and assist Governments in their efforts to prepare for implementation of international human rights law in times of armed conflict.

Implementation and information

Implementation of the Protocols was accelerated by the provision for entry into force six months after only two instruments of ratification or accession were deposited.

The commitments of the Parties are to respect and ensure respect for the Protocols during armed conflicts, including respect for civilian objects and civilian populations and limiting the means and methods of warfare. Precautionary measures must be taken by both sides to the conflict and all parties must give orders and instructions to ensure observance of the instruments. Article 85 requires that legal advisers be available to military commanders to advise them on the appropriate instruction to be given to the armed forces on application of the Conventions and Protocols.

A function of supervision is assigned to a Protecting Power - a neutral or other state not a party to the conflict - or to an impartial humanitarian organization such as the ICRC. Parties to a conflict are obliged to designate and accept Protecting Powers. In addition to the role of the Protecting Powers and the ICRC, Article 90 of Protocol I provides for the establishment of an International Fact-Finding Commission to be composed of fifteen members of high moral standing and acknowledged impartiality. States parties must separately agree to accept the competence of the Commission which has the power to examine the facts concerning alleged serious violations of the Conventions or of the Protocol and to use its good offices to restore respect for the law. During a conflict ICRC delegates are authorized to go to all places where there are protected persons; prisoners of war or civil internees and to carry out their humanitarian duties.

Article 91 provides for state responsibility and the possibility of compensation in the case of violations. Individual responsibility for grave breaches (war crimes) has not been extended to the provisions concerning environmental protection.

There is no compulsory reporting mechanism. However, the States Parties to Protocol I must communicate to each other official translations of the Protocol and the laws and regulations they adopt to ensure its application (Article 84).

Public opinion, NGOs and international supervisory bodies and procedures play a decisive role in the implementation of the Red Cross conventions and their protocols.

The official languages of the treaties are Arabic, Chinese, English, French, Russian and Spanish. Other language editions are produced by the authorities in the countries concerned. Article 83 of Protocol I requires dissemination of knowledge concerning humanitarian law and Article 19 of Protocol II declares that this instrument must be disseminated as widely as possible.

Current information on the operation and implementation of the Protocols is provided by the ICRC Annual Reports as well as by current information material published by ICRC. The ICRC, the League of Red Cross and Red Crescent Societies and national societies conduct education and training programmes.

Operation, review and adjustment

The implementation of rules on the protection of the environment in armed conflict is only one aspect of ICRC activities, covered by the regular ICRC budget. ICRC operations are covered by voluntary contributions from States. Developing countries are therefore free to determine the amount of their financial contributions to the ICRC.

Periodic review and adjustment of the Protocols is an informal process. The ICRC takes up new issues for study and informal discussion with Governments. This can result in a formal procedure: a meeting of the States Parties to Protocol I will be convened upon the request of any State and the approval of the majority of States Parties, to consider general problems concerning application of the Protocol. The Swiss Federal Council, as depositary of the Conventions and Protocols, acts with regard to amendments to both Protocols and revisions of Annex I to Protocol I.

(6) UNEP Principles of Conduct in the Field of the Environment for the Guidance of States in the Conservation and Harmonious Utilization of Natural Resources Shared by Two or More States
(Decision 6/14 of the Governing Council of the United Nations
Environment Programme, 19 May 1978)

Objectives and achievement

The principles aim at the rational use of shared natural resources in a manner which does not adversely affect the environment. They encourage States sharing a natural resource to co-operate in the field of the environment, hence promote the effective integration of environment and development.

In its subsequent Resolution 34/186 of 18 December 1979, the UN General Assembly requested all States "to use the principles as guidelines and recommendations in the formulation of bilateral or multilateral conventions regarding natural resources shared by two or more States, on the basis of the principles of good faith and in the spirit of good neighbourliness and in such a way as to enhance and not to affect adversely development and the interests of all countries and in particular of the developing countries". The latter part of this interpretive statement corresponds to Principle 15 of the guidelines.

Progress reports on the implementation of these principles were considered by the UN General Assembly in 1981, 1985 and 1987. The reports, partly based on the replies to questionnaires circulated by UNEP to all UN member States and international organizations, indicate growing acceptance of the principles as reference source in drafting national and international legal instruments.

Participation

The Principles are addressed to all member States of the United Nations. As from a legal point of view they constitute recommendations, States have accepted only the responsibility to implement them but no binding legal obligation. Developing countries took an important part in their elaboration, within the UNEP Working Group of Legal Experts which drafted the principles from 1976 to 1978, in the UNEP Governing Council which adopted them and, finally in the UN General Assembly which recommended their implementation to all States.

Implementation and information

The main factor promoting compliance with the Principles, beside their intrinsic value, has been the general development of international environmental law. Most of these Principles had already been formulated either in the 1972 Stockholm Declaration (No. 1 above, e.g., Principle 3(1) which reproduces verbatim Principle 21 of that declaration), or, sometimes in a different way, by the OCDE Principles Concerning Transfrontier Pollution (No. 3 above). Thus the main significance of the UNEP Principles is on the one hand to expand the international rules concerning transfrontier pollution to the use of shared natural resources, on the other hand, to contribute to the transformation of such rules into customary norms of international law. According to the replies to a 1984 UNEP survey, at least 24 States drew upon the Principles on Shared Resources when negotiating particular agreements with other states or, at least, contemplated the future use of the Principles (Afghanistan, Argentina, Benin, Bolivia, Botswana, Egypt, El Salvador, Finland, Germany, Greece, Guatemala, Guinea Bissau, Hungary, Jordan, Lesotho, Mozambique, Niger, Poland, Rwanda, Switzerland, Uganda, Vietnam, Zaire, Zimbabwe; see document UNEP/GC.13/9/Add.1).

The Principles have been published and disseminated in all official UN languages, together with other UNEP documents. As such, they may not have been given the wider public attention which they deserved beyond the Governments of countries which have effectively drawn upon them when drafting international treaties or adopting national legislation.

Operation, review and adjustment

The usual mechanisms of UNEP are available to ensure review and adjustment of the Principles. So far, no need has been felt for such revision or adjustment. To some extent, the more specific principles and guidelines subsequently developed and adopted within the framework of UNEP (e.g., Nos. 10,37, and 39 below, and specific agreements such as the 1987 Action Plan for the Environmentally Sound Management of the Common Zambezi River System) may be considered as a further elaboration of the Principles.

(7) European Outline Convention on Transfrontier Co-operation Between Territorial Communities or Authorities
(Madrid, 21 May 1980)

Objectives and achievement

According to the Preamble, the aim of this Convention is to ensure the participation of the territorial communities or authorities of Europe in the achievement of greater unity between the member States of the Council of Europe, by fostering co-operation between such communities or authorities at frontiers in various fields such as regional and economic development as well as environmental protection. Public facilities and services should be improved and mutual assistance granted in emergencies.

Contracting parties undertake to facilitate and foster transfrontier co-operation between territorial communities or authorities. Transfrontier co-operation should thus contribute to the economic and social progress of transfrontier regions. In an Appendix to the Convention, model agreements, statutes and contracts on transfrontier co-operation between territorial communities or authorities are proposed to the States Parties and provide texts for such co-operation, inter alia, in the field of nature conservation (places requiring protection, natural parks), water conservation (pollution control, treatment plants), protection of the atmosphere (air pollution, noise abatment, noise-free zones, etc.), energy (power stations, gas, electricity and water supplies), wastes (refuse disposal plant, sewerage).

Agreements have been concluded in application of the Convention, creating working communities between local and regional authorities (Jura, Alpine Regions, Pyrenees, etc.). Several bilateral and sub-regional treaties on transfrontier co-operation can also be mentioned (e.g., between Belgium, Germany, Luxembourg and the Netherlands). Informal co-operation is frequent and shows that the reality of co-operation is well advanced.

Participation

The Convention is open to member States of the Council of Europe. As of 1 January 1992, 16 of the 25 member States were Contracting Parties. European non-member States can be invited to participate by a unanimous vote of the Committee of Ministers of the Council of Europe (Articles 9 and 10). Reservations have been made by several Contracting Parties. Efforts are underway for the withdrawal of these reservations.

Technical and scientific co-operation between regions is particularly important for local and regional authorities (exchange of information, education, planning, etc.). The Parliamentary Assembly of the Council of Europe, composed of representatives of the national parliaments of the member States, and especially a Standing Conference for Local and Regional Authorities in Europe played a prominent role in the drafting and the promotion of the Convention.

Implementation and information

In application of Article 9 (2), the Convention entered into force three months after the deposit of the fourth instrument of ratification, on 22 December 1981. The low number required for entry into force accelerated the implementation of the Convention.

Contracting Parties have accepted the commitment to facilitate and foster transfrontier co-operation between territorial communities or authorities within their jurisdiction. They should endeavour to promote the conclusion of any agreements and arrangements that may prove necessary for this purpose with due regard to the different constitutional provisions of each State. They also should encourage any initiative by territorial communities and authorities inspired by the outline arrangements between territorial communities and authorities drawn up in the Council of Europe. In this perspective, they should consider the advisability of granting to territorial communities or authorities engaging in transfrontier co-operation in accordance with the provisions of the Convention the same facilities as if they were co-operating at national level (Article 5).

The implementation of the Convention is evaluated by the Parliamentary Assembly of the Council of Europe and in particular by the Standing Conference for Regional and Local Authorities in Europe as well as by the European Conference of Frontier Regions (which meets every three years). The Council of Europe proceeded to an evaluation of the impact of the Convention by sending out a questionnaire to the governments of the States Parties to the Convention. The answers were analysed by a restricted committee of governmental experts which also studies the problem of reinforcing the scope of the Convention by means of an additional protocol.

According to Article 8, the Contracting Parties forward to the Secretary General of the Council of Europe all relevant information concerning the agreements and arrangements provided for by the Convention. In addition, Article 6 foresees that each Contracting Party shall supply to the fullest extent any information requested by another Contracting Party in order to facilitate the performance by the latter of its obligations under the Convention.

Regional and local authorities, universities, but also interest groups, individual initiatives etc. contributed to creating different permanent structures and practices of transfrontier co-operation, often in an informal manner, but in the spirit of the Convention and often making reference to it.

The languages of the Convention are English and French. The publications of the Council of Europe regularly provide information on the Convention and its implementation, through periodical reports and studies. The Parliamentary Assembly of the Council of Europe adopted several recommendations concerning transfrontier co-operation. Seminars have also been organized on this issue.

Operation, review and adjustment

The Secretariat of the Council of Europe in Strasbourg (France) ensures the administration of the Convention, with costs covered by the general budget of the Council of Europe. No extra charge is imposed upon the States which are Parties to the Convention. A Committee of Governmental Experts reviews the legal and other problems of transfrontier co-operation, as national constitutional provisions often raise obstacles to full implementation and make it difficult for regional and local authorities to use the possibilities of the Convention. The Committee is currently evaluating the results of the Convention and proposals for the necessary adjustments. The elaboration of an additional **protocol** is being discussed.

(8) Convention on Prohibitions or Restrictions on the Use of Certain Conventional Weapons Which May be Deemed to be Excessively Injurious or to Have Indiscriminate Effects
(Geneva, 10 October 1980) and related protocols

Objectives and achievement

The Convention is a framework treaty allowing for a gradual expansion of categories of conventional weapons to be covered through additional Protocols. In its present three Protocols, adopted at the same time as the Convention, it provides new rules for the protection of civilians and civilian objects and, in some cases, military personnel as well.

A direct reference to environmental protection is contained in the preamble which recalls "that it is prohibited to employ methods or means of warfare which are intended, or may be expected, to cause widespread, long-term and severe damage to the environment". Furthermore, Protocol III on Prohibitions or Restrictions on the Use of Incendiary Weapons prohibits, in Article 2(4) to make forests or other kinds of plant cover the object of attack by incendiary weapons except when such natural elements are used to cover, conceal or camouflage combatants or other military objectives, or are themselves military objectives.

Participation

Membership is open to all States. The Convention was elaborated by a special UN Conference, held from 1979 to 1980 with the participation of 85 States. It entered into force on 2 December 1983 and, as of 1 January 1992, had 32 Parties, including 14 developing countries.

Upon accession, States Parties have to express consent to be bound by at least two of the Protocols (Art. 4 (2)). While the Convention does not make provision for reservations, a number of States made interpretive declarations at the time of signature or ratification.

Implementation and information

The parties to the Convention, upon their consent to be bound by protocols, undertake to eliminate or restrict the use of weapons such as non-detectable fragments, mines, booby traps and other devices as well as incendiary weapons.

Efforts to include in the Convention a mechanism for verification of compliance were unsuccessful.

The languages of the Convention are Arabic, Chinese, English, French, Russian and Spanish. The text of the Convention is disseminated together with other instruments of humanitarian law. It is also used in the same way in international and national training and education programmes. According to Article 6, the Parties undertake, in time of peace as in time of armed conflict, to disseminate the Convention and those of its annexed protocols by which they are bound as widely as possible in their respective countries and, in particular, to include the study thereof in their programmes of military instruction, so that those instruments may become known to their armed forces.

Operation, review and adjustment

The Secretary General of the United Nations, who is the Depositary of the Convention, ensures its administration, through the UN Department for Disarmament Affairs. At any time after the entry into force of the Convention any Contracting Party may, in addition to proposing new additional Protocols, also propose amendments. If a majority including at least 18 Parties so agree, the Secretary General of UN convenes all Contracting Parties to a conference. At the conference, additional Protocols and amendments are adopted and enter into force in the same manner as the Convention and its protocols. If, after a period of 10 years following the entry into force of the Convention no conference has been convened, any Contracting Party may request the depositary to convene all the Contracting Parties to a conference to review the scope and operation of the Convention and its Protocols. This Review Conference may also consider proposals for additional Protocols or for amendments.

(9) Treaties Establishing the European Communities
(Rome, 25 March 1957)
as amended by the **Single European Act**
(Luxembourg, 18 February 1986, and The Hague, 28 February 1986)

Objectives and achievement

Since a widespread concern for the environment did not yet exist at the time of signature of the treaties creating the European Communities (EC, i.e., the European Economic Community, the European Coal and Steel Community, and the European Atomic Engery Community), it is normal that those treaties did not contain any provision concerning environmental protection. After the 1972 Stockholm Conference (see No. 1 above), a political decision taken outside the statutory organs of the Communities, by a meeting of the heads of State or Government of the nine member countries resolved the problem. It proclaimed the necessity to improve the quality of life, and invited the Community institutions to establish an action programme setting forth a precise calendar. As a result, consecutive four-year programmes of action were elaborated and about 200 legal instruments (decisions, directives and regulations) were adopted. However, the legal basis of Community action in this field has really been clarified only by the Single European Act of February 1986, in force since 1 July 1987.

According to Article 130 R of the Single European Act, action by the Community relating to the environment has the following objectives:
(a) to preserve, protect and improve the quality of the environment;
(b) to contribute towards protecting human health;
(c) to ensure a prudent and rational utilization of natural resources.

The global bearing of EC action on environmental protection and sustainable development is due to the following facts:
(i) EC legislation and action concern 360 million persons living in the most industrialized part of the world. Ensuring environmental protection in this area means a considerable contribution to the protection of the global environment and to a rational management of natural resources.
(ii) Owing to its quasi-federal structures (including a Council, Commission, Parliament and a Court of Justice), the EC can adopt and enforce advanced environmental regulation which may constitute a model and an incentive for other parts of the world (e.g. EC legislation on the protection of the aquatic environment, or on wastes).
(iii) The EC participates as a Contracting Party in all the major international conventions related to environmental protection.

The EC and 69 African, Caribbean and Pacific States (ACP) signed on 15 December 1989 the **Fourth ACP-EC Convention** ("Lomé IV"). Applicable for a period of ten years, this treaty, which is entirely devoted to economic co-operation with, and assistance to developing countries, contains a chapter specifically related to protection of the environment and conservation of natural resources. In proposing an integrated approach both horizontal and preventive, the treaty seeks economic and social development based upon a sustainable balance between economic objectives, management of natural resources and the value of human resources. Special attention is given to development programmes and to international movement of toxic wastes. The EC has also entered into other specific agreements with developing countries in the Mediterranean, in Asia and in Latin America.

As a result of EC action, national environmental legislation was improved and developed in its member States.

Participation

Membership in the EC is geographically restricted. The admission of new member States is subject to a strict procedure. While there have been no reservations, interpretative declarations were made by signatory countries when the Single Act was adopted.

Twelve European states are currently EC members. Treaties of co-operation have been concluded with the ACP countries (Lomé IV) and with individual developing countries. Common institutions have been created for co-operation between the EC and the ACP countries (Council of Ministers, Committee of Ambassadors, Joint Assembly). The entire programme of the EC - ACP co-operation foresees ECU 10.8 billion as assistance to developing countries and 1.200 billion as loans (approximately US$ 12 billion and 1.4 billion). The Lomé Convention also includes technical assistance and large facilities for trade between developing countries and the EC.

Implementation and information

The EC has strong regulatory powers. Regulations that are obligatory and immediately applicable in the member states have been mainly adopted in matters concerning the external trade of the Community (e.g., Regulation 348/81 related to the importation of products derived from cetaceans). In all other questions related to environmental protection, mainly directives have been adopted so far. These texts bind every member State to achieve the stated result, but leave to national authorities the choice of means.

Certain directives impose upon member States the obligation to report to the Commission, one of the EC bodies. However, the EC also has the power to supervise, on its own, the implementation of the rules which it adopts. After adoption of a directive by the Council where the member States are represented as such, the Commission addresses an official letter to each member State, transmitting the directive and notifying the State of the time limits for incorporating it into domestic law. Close to three months before the limit fixed for this incorporation, the Commission reminds Governments who have not carried out their obligations that they must transform the directive into measures applicable in their internal law. Information on implementation is addressed by the States to the Commission, but the latter also may derive information from formal or informal contacts, written or oral, from the national authorities responsible for the application of directives. There also exists a complaint procedure open to individuals and non-governmental groups which may initiate action by the Commission. In case of breach, Article 169 of the Treaty of Rome permits the Commission to begin a procedure involving three phases: an official of notice letter addressed to the State, an opinion exposing in detail the infraction, and, finally, a referral to the Court of Justice of the European Communities. By 31 December 1989, in regard to the environment, the Commission had considered more than 400 cases of infraction. Of these, it had transmitted 240 letters of notice, issued 74 opinions and referred 28 cases to the Court.

The EC has an information service with offices in the member States. Its Official Journal publishes in all the languages of the Communities all acts adopted by them. EC law is taught in the universities of the member States, and special programmes of teaching and internships are organized. In addition to general information on action by the EC in the field of environmental protection, special activities - e.g. the European Year of the Environment - have also been undertaken and played an important role in raising public awareness.

Operation, review and adjustment

The institutions of the Communities and especially the Commission ensure the administration of EC legislation, financed from a common budget. The Lomé Convention with the ACP States includes an important chapter (Title III) on co-operation for the funding of development: while the ACP States have the responsibility of determining objectives and priorities and of selecting projects and programmes, the Community has the responsibility to decide on the funding of projects and programmes (Article 222).

According to the Single Act, in preparing its action relating to the environment, the Community shall take account of available scientific and technical data and of the environmental conditions in the various regions of the Community (Article 130 R (3). Decisions on environmental questions are taken after extensive scientific, economic and legal studies.

The European Parliament, composed of representatives directly elected by the peoples of the member states participates in the elaboration of the EC policy in different fields. It is also constantly informed of the implementation of such policies. The EC Commission maintains liason with non-governmental organizations.

(10) UNEP Goals and Principles of Environmental Impact Assessment
(Decision 14/25 of the Governing Council of the United Nations Environment Programme, Nairobi, 17 June 1987)

Objectives and achievement

As indicated in the preliminary note of the instrument, environmental impact assessment of planned activities has the purpose of "ensuring environmentally sound and sustainable development". Three objectives are designated:
- to establish that before decisions allow to undertake or to authorize activities that are likely to significantly affect the environment, the environmental effects should be taken into account;
- to promote implementation of appropriate national procedures in order to implement environmental impact assessment (EIA);
- to encourage countries to develop reciprocal procedures for notification, information exchange and consultation on activities that are likely to have significant transboundary environmental effects.

No specific mention is made of developing countries. However, the instrument lists among the activities which should be subject to EIA those which concern categories of resources (water, tropical rainforests), or environmental problems (such as increased soil erosion, desertification, deforestation) having a special importance for developing countries (footnote to Principle 2).

EIA procedures have been adopted in the national legislation of different countries. To a considerable extent, the first draft of the European Convention on Environmental Impact Assessment in a Transboundary Context (see No. 11 below) was based on the Goals and Principles developed under UNEP auspices.

Participation

The Principles were drafted by a UNEP Working Group of Experts on Environmental Law, in which developing countries had a large representation. They were approved by the Governing Council of UNEP as being addressed to all countries in the world.

Implementation and information

According to Principle 12, States should endeavour to conclude bilateral, regional or multilateral arrangements, as appropriate, so as to provide, on the basis of reciprocity, notification, exchange of information, and agreed-upon consultation on the potential environmental effects of activities under their control or jurisdiction which are likely to significantly affect other States or areas beyond national jurisdiction.

At its fifteenth session in 1989, the UNEP Governing Council by its decision 15/41, taking into consideration a report prepared by the Executive Director on the implementation of Goals and Principles, called on Governments to increase their use and authorized the Executive Director to continue to seek the views of Governments and relevant international organizations for further development in this field.

The Goals and Principles have been published in Arabic, Chinese, English, French, Russian and Spanish, in documents distributed by UNEP.

Operation, review and adjustment

The Goals and Principles are administered by UNEP, with the costs of work relating to their dissemination and review covered by the regular budget of the Programme Activity Center for Environmental Law and Institutions, Nairobi. Initiatives for review and, if necessary, for adjustment are to be taken within the UNEP Governing Council, whose system-wide medium-term environment programme (SWMTEP) envisages the preparation of a binding international **convention** on this subject.

(11) Convention on Environmental Impact Assessment in a Transboundary Context

(Espoo, Finland, 25 February 1991)

Objectives and achievement

This regional convention may be considered as one of the results of the Final Act of the Conference on Security and Co-operation in Europe (CSCE, Helsinki, 1975) and of subsequent CSCE meetings in Madrid and Vienna. It was prepared under the auspices of the UN Economic Commission for Europe (ECE).

The main objective of the Convention is to take all appropriate and effective measures to prevent, reduce and control significant adverse transboundary environmental impact from proposed activities, by the establishment of an environmental impact assessment procedure that permits public participation (Art. 2 (1)(2)). This means that a Contracting Party under whose jurisdiction a proposed activity which is likely to cause significant adverse transboundary impact is envisaged to take place, ensures that the affected Party is notified in advance (Articles 2, paragraphs 3 and 4, and 3). By applying environmental factors at an early stage in the decision-making process and such procedures contribute in a significant way to the effective integration of environment and development.

Participation

The Convention is open to ECE member States, regional economic integration organizations such as the European Community and European States not members of the United Nations which have consultative status with ECE. As of 1 January 1992, 27 European States, Canada, the USA and the European Community had signed it and one State (Albania) had ratified. While the Convention does not contain an article on reservations, several States made interpretive declarations upon signature.

Although no mention is made of developing countries, the bilateral and multilateral co-operation foreseen by Appendix VI of the Convention includes institutional, administrative and other arrangements which could be used for the transfer of technology and for other forms of assistance to such countries.

It should be stressed that the Espoo Convention derives to some extent from the UNEP Goals and Principles of Environmental Impact Assessment (No. 8 above), as well as the earlier Nordic Environmental Protection Convention (No. 2 above), and principles on environmental impact assessment elaborated under the auspices of the ECE can be considered as one of the first transformations of those principles into a binding instrument. The Espoo Convention may be useful as a model when principles of information and consultation in order to avoid transboundary environmental harm, stated in other regional arrangements, especially those adopted between developing countries, will be developed. (e.g., under the Kuwait Convention on the Protection of the Marine Environment from Pollution, No. 47, Art. 11; ASEAN Agreement on the Conservation of Nature and Natural Resources, No. 27, Art. 20)).

It may also be expected that through the Espoo Convention technical, financial and managerial assistance will be provided to countries with economies in transition and those developing from an economic point of view, to establish EIA systems and to promote the precautionary principle and sustainable development.

Implementation and information

While the Espoo Convention has not yet entered into force, the signatories decided by way of a resolution (ECE/ENVWA/19) to initiate interim measures of implementation, including a first meeting held in Geneva in December 1991. Article 11 stipulates that the Parties, who are to meet in principle once a year, shall keep under continuous review the implementation of this Convention and, with this purpose in mind, shall review the policies and methodological approaches to environmental impact assessment by the Parties with a view to further improving environmental impact assessment procedures. They also should exchange information regarding experience gained in concluding and implementing bilateral and multilateral agreements and seek, where appropriate the services of competent international bodies and scientific committees in methodological and technical aspects pertinent to the achievement of the purposes of the Convention.

The Parties concerned shall determine whether and to what extent it is necessary to undertake a post-project analysis related to the likely significant adverse transboundary impact of the activity for which an environmental impact assessment has been undertaken under the Convention. This includes the surveillance of the activity and the determination of any adverse transboundary effect (Article 7). When, as a result of post-project analysis, the state of origin or the affected state has reasonable grounds for concluding that there is a significant adverse transboundary impact or factors have been discovered which may result in such an impact, it shall immediately inform the other Party. The Parties concerned shall then consult on necessary measures to reduce or eliminate the impact.

Another original solution adopted by the Espoo Convention is the inquiry procedure provided for in Appendix IV. Environmental impact assessment procedures should be initiated with respect to proposed activities which are listed in Appendix I to the Convention. If there is a doubt whether such an activity is likely to have a significant adverse transboundary impact, the state which could be affected shall notify the Secretariat that it submits the question to an inquiry commission. The notification shall state the subject-matter of the inquiry and all States Parties to the Convention will immediately be informed of it by the Secretariat. The inquiry commission consists of three members: both the requesting party and the other party to the procedure appoint a scientific or technical expert and the two experts so appointed shall designate by common agreement the third expert who shall be the president of the commission. The parties to the inquiry procedure must facilitate the work of that commission by providing it with all relevant documents, facilities and information and by enabling it to call witnesses or experts and receive their evidence. If one of the parties to the inquiry procedure does not appear before the commission or fails to present its case, the other party may request the commission to continue the proceedings and to complete its work. The final opinion of the commission must be based on accepted scientific principles and reflect the view of the majority of its members, although it also may include any dissenting view. It shall be presented to the parties and to the secretariat within two months. The final opinion of the inquiry commission is to advise the concerned Parties in the likelihood of significant adverse transboundary impact.

Article 15 concerns the settlement of disputes about the interpretation or application of the Convention. The parties must seek a solution by negotiation or by any other method of dispute settlement. A Party to the Convention may declare at any time that for a dispute not resolved by such means it accepts as compulsory in relation to any Party accepting the same obligation, the jurisdiction of the International Court of Justice or arbitration in accordance with the procedure set out in Appendix VII to the Convention. The Appendix reproduces rules generally followed in this matter, but some of its provisions may be stressed. The tribunal may take all appropriate measures in order to establish the facts but has to protect the confidentiality of any information it receives in confidence. It may, at the request of one of the parties, recommend interim measures of protection. It may hear or determine counter-claims. Finally, its award shall be accompanied by a statement of reasons.

The languages of the Convention are English, French and Russian. The Secretariat transmits to the Parties reports and other information such as proposed amendments (Article 14) or the submission of a matter to an inquiry commission (Appendix IV(1)). Other communications concerning the participation in the Convention are transmitted to the Parties by the Secretary-General of the United Nations who is the depositary of the convention.

The effective participation of national authorities and industries concerned is ensured by the fact that States Parties must impose national environmental assessment procedures on determined activities. Thus, national authorities collect the information which the authors of determined proposed activities must submit to them. Such activities are listed in Appendix I, the information to be transmitted is determined in Appendix II, while Appendix III lists the general criteria to assist in the determination of the environmental significance of activities not listed in Appendix I. The procedure may also imply the participation of scientific experts.

According to Article 2 (6), the State of origin of a proposed activity which may cause transboundary environmental impact must provide an opportunity to the public in the areas likely to be affected to participate in relevant environmental impact assessment procedures regarding such activities, and shall ensure that the opportunity provided to the public of the affected State is equivalent to that provided to the public of the State of origin.

Operation, review and adjustment

The main body set up by the Convention is the meeting of the Parties, to be held as far as possible in connection with the annual sessions of the Senior Advisers to ECE Governments on Environmental and Water Problems (Art.11). The Executive Secretary of the UN Economic Commission for Europe carries out the secretariat functions, through the ECE Environment and Human Settlements Division in Geneva.

The Meeting of Parties considers and, where necessary, adopts proposals for amendments to the Convention (Article 11(2)(e). Any Contracting Party may propose amendments by submitting them in writing to the secretariat. The proposed amendments shall be discussed at the next meeting of the parties. Agreement on the proposed amendment should be reached by consensus, but if no agreement is reached, the amendment shall as a last resort be adopted by a three-fourth majority vote of the Parties present and voting at the meeting. The amendments adopted shall be submitted by the Secretary General of the United Nations to all Parties for ratification, approval or acceptance. They shall enter into force for parties having ratified, approved or accepted them on the ninetieth day after the receipt by the depositary of notification of such acts by at least three fourth of these Parties.

Codification programming

Under the auspices of the Senior Advisers to ECE Governments on Environmental and Water Problems, two further legal instruments have been prepared for adoption and signature at a CSCE conference in Helsinki on 18 March 1992:
- a **Convention on the Protection and Use of Transboundary Watercourses and International Lakes**; and
- a **Convention on Transboundary Impacts of Industrial Accidents**.

STATUS OF RATIFICATIONS AS OF 1 JANUARY 1992

GLOBAL INSTRUMENTS (Treaty numbers see page 28)

Parties	4	5	8
Afghanistan	x		
Albania			
Algeria	x	x	
Angola		x	
Antigua & Barbuda	x	x	
Argentina	x	x	
Australia	x	x	x
Austria	x	x	x
Bahamas		x	
Bahrain		x	
Bangladesh	x	x	
Barbados		x	
Belarus*	x	x	x
Belgium	x	x	
Belize		x	
Benin	x	x	x
Bhutan			
Bolivia		x	
Botswana		x	
Brazil	x		
Brunei Darussalam		x	
Bulgaria	x	x	x
Burkina Faso		x	
Burundi			
Cambodia			
Cameroon		x	
Canada	x	x	
Cape Verde	x		
Central African Republic		x	
Chad			
Chile		x	
China		x	x
Colombia			
Cook Islands			
Comoros		x	
Congo		x	
Costa Rica		x	
Cote d'Ivoire		x	
Cuba	x	x	x
Cyprus	x	x	x
Czech & Slovak Fed. Rep.	x	x	x
Democ. People's Rep. of Korea	x	x	
Denmark	x	x	x
Djibouti		x	

Parties	4	5	8
Dominica			
Dominican Republic			
Ecuador		x	x
Egypt	x		
El Salvador		x	
Equatorial Guinea		x	
Estonia*			
Ethiopia			
Fiji			
Finland	x	x	x
France			x
Gabon		x	
Gambia		x	
Germany	x	x	
Ghana	x	x	
Greece	x	x	
Grenada			
Guatemala	x	x	x
Guinea		x	
Guinea-Bissau		x	
Guyana		x	
Haiti			
Holy See		x	
Honduras			
Hungary	x	x	x
Iceland		x	
India	x		x
Indonesia			
Iran (Islamic Republic of)			
Iraq			
Ireland	x		
Israel			
Italy	x	x	
Jamaica		x	
Japan	x		x
Jordan		x	
Kenya			
Kiribati			
Kuwait	x	x	
Lao People's Democratic Rep.	x	x	x
Latvia*			
Lebanon			
Lesotho			
Liberia		x	
Libyan Arab Jamahiriya		x	
Liechtenstein		x	x

Parties	4	5	8
Lithuania*			
Luxembourg		x	
Madagascar			
Malawi	x	x	
Malaysia			
Maldives		x	
Mali		x	
Malta		x	
Marshall Islands			
Mauritania		x	
Mauritius			
Mexico		x	x
Micronesia			
Monaco			
Mongolia	x		x
Morocco			
Mozambique		x	
Myanmar			
Namibia		x	
Nauru			
Nepal			
Netherlands	x	x	x
New Zealand	x	x	
Nicaragua			
Niger		x	
Nigeria		x	
Niue			
Norway	x	x	x
Oman		x	
Pakistan	x		x
Palau			
Panama			
Papua New Guinea	x		
Paraguay		x	
Peru		x	
Philippines			
Poland	x	x	x
Portugal			
Qatar		x	
Republic of Korea	x	x	
Republic of Yemen	x	x	
Romania	x	x	
Rwanda		x	
St. Kitts & Nevis		x	
St. Lucia		x	
St. Vincent & the Grenadines		x	

Parties	4	5	8
Samoa		x	
San Marino			
Sao Tome & Principe	x		
Saudi Arabia		x	
Senegal		x	
Seychelles		x	
Sierra Leone		x	
Singapore			
Solomon Islands	x	x	
Somalia			
South Africa			
Spain	x	x	
Sri Lanka	x		
Sudan			
Suriname		x	
Swaziland			
Sweden	x	x	x
Switzerland	x	x	x
Syrian Arab Republic		x	
Thailand			
Togo		x	
Tonga			
Trinidad & Tobago			
Tunisia	x	x	x
Turkey			
Tuvalu			
Uganda		x	
Ukraine*	x	x	x
Union of Soviet Socialist Rep.*	x	x	x
United Arab Emirates		x	
United Kingdom	x		
United Republic of Tanzania		x	
United States of America	x		
Uruguay		x	
Vanuatu		x	
Venezuela			
Viet Nam	x	x	
Yugoslavia*		x	x
Zaire		x	
Zambia			
Zimbabwe			

* Membership status subject to further clarification.

REGIONAL INSTRUMENTS

(2) <u>Nordic Convention on the Protection of the Environment</u> (Stockholm 1974)

Denmark
Finland
Norway
Sweden

(3) <u>OECD Principles Concerning Transfrontier Pollution</u> (Paris 1974)

Australia	Japan
Austria	Luxembourg
Belgium	Netherlands
Canada	New Zealand
Denmark	Norway
Finland	Portugal
France	Spain
Germany	Sweden
Greece	Switzerland
Iceland	Turkey
Ireland	United Kingdom
Italy	United States of America

(7) <u>European Outline Convention on Transfrontier Co-operation Between Territorial Communities or Authorities</u> (Madrid 1980)

Austria	Liechtenstein
Belgium	Luxembourg
Denmark	Netherlands
Finland	Norway
France	Portugal
Germany	Spain
Ireland	Sweden
Italy	Switzerland

(9) <u>Single European Act</u> (Luxembourg and The Hague 1986)

Belgium	Italy
Denmark	Luxembourg
France	Netherlands
Germany	Portugal
Greece	Spain
Ireland	United Kingdom

(11) <u>Convention on Environmental Assessment in a Transboundary Context</u> (Espoo 1991)

Albania

CHAPTER II

NATURE CONSERVATION AND TERRESTRIAL LIVING RESOURCES

Malcolm J. Forster and Ralph U. Osterwoldt

This chapter covers the following 16 international legal instruments on nature conservation and terrestrial living resources, in chronological order:

(12) the 1949 Washington **Convention on Nature Protection and Wildlife Preservation in the Western Hemisphere,**

(13) the 1950 **International Convention for the Protection of Birds**, and related instruments;

(14) the 1959 **Antarctic Treaty**, and related instruments;

(15) the 1968 **African Convention on the Conservation of Nature and Natural Resources;**

(16) the 1971 Ramsar **Convention on Wetlands of International Importance Especially as Waterfowl Habitat**, as amended;

(17) the 1972 **Convention Concerning the Protection of the World Cultural and Natural Heritage;**

(18) the 1973 Washington **Convention on International Trade in Endangered Species of Wild Fauna and Flora**, as amended;

(19) the 1973 Oslo **Agreement on Conservation of Polar Bears;**

(20) the 1976 Apia **Convention on Conservation of Nature in the South Pacific;**

(21) the 1978 Brasilia **Treaty for Amazonian Co-operation;**

(22) the 1979 Bonn **Convention on the Conservation of Migratory Species of Wild Animals;**

(23) the 1979 Berne **Convention on the Conservation of European Wildlife and Natural Habitats;**

(24) the 1979 Lima **Convention for the Conservation and Management of the Vicuña;**

(25) the 1983 **International Tropical Timber Agreement;**

(26) the 1983 FAO **International Undertaking on Plant Genetic Resources;**

(27) the 1985 ASEAN **Agreement on the Conservation of Nature and Natural Resources**.

A list showing the status of ratifications as of 1 January 1992 is annexed (pages 117-122).

(12) Convention on Nature Protection and Wildlife Preservation in the Western Hemisphere
(Washington, 12 October 1990)

Objectives and achievement

Two objectives are expressed in the preamble of the Convention: to protect all species in their natural habitat to prevent extinction and to preserve extraordinary scenery and natural areas. Conserving habitats to protect species was a visionary approach in its time. The Convention's primary focus is to establish national parks and wilderness reserves (defined in Article I). Parties also agree to adopt laws and regulations to protect nature outside of especially protected parks and reserves (Art.V); to protect migratory species and species listed in an Annex (Art. VIII); and to control the import/export and transit of protected fauna and flora (Art. IX). As a framework for cooperation, the Convention provides specifically for scientific collaboration in Article VI.

The combined territories of the Parties to the Convention contain approximately 25 percent of all species on Earth and the largest intact tropical forests. As the Convention focusses on the need to conserve habitats, the Parties will need to squarely address the challenge of linking environmental protection and sustainable development.

Of the 21 Parties, 20 are developing countries. The Convention predates and does not reflect the current distinctions drawn between groups of countries on the basis of their degree of development. Their special circumstances are taken account of within the framework of the Organization of American States and informally between the Parties engaged in co-operation on particular matters.

The Convention has been cited by officials as one of the factors in inspiring and providing uniform criteria for the establishment of national parks, wilderness reserves and environmental protection laws by the Parties. Yet numerous national laws appear to have been drafted without reference to the Convention's requirements. Some Latin American countries are recently calling for revitalization of the Convention to incorporate concepts of biodiversity and sustainable development. Following the 1976 OAS General Assembly resolution (AG/RES. 218 (VI-0/76) to evaluate progress in meeting the terms of the Western Hemisphere Convention, studies indicated that the effectiveness of the Convention has been seriously limited by lack of an intergovernmental mechanism, technical commission or supporting administrative unit, lack of periodic specialized conferences, and lack of updating to add measures required by present conservation needs and sustainable development.

Five technical meetings recommended adopting legal measures to assure ecological stability and diversity, biological productivity, sustained yield of renewable resources, soil, watershed, and maritime ecosystem conservation, integrated rural development, environmental monitoring, education, and research, Since 1988, the OAS General Secretariat, complying with OAS General Assembly resolution AG/RES.948 (XVIII-0/88), has studied the creation of an "Inter-American System for Nature Conservation," as recommended by the Inter-American Juridical Committee.

Participation

Membership is restricted to "the American Governments" by Article XI, i.e., members of the Organization of American States (OAS). Of 19 Parties to the Convention, all but the United States are developing countries. Bolivia, Colombia, and Cuba, have signed but not ratified the convention. There is no article providing for reservations.

The 21 Parties and Signatories cover all of the Western Hemisphere except for 4 regions, namely, the islands of the Caribbean Sea and Gulf of Mexico where only Cuba, Hispaniola, and Trinidad and Tobago are represented; Northeastern South America with the absence of Guyana, and French Guyana; the Central American countries of Honduras and Belize; and Canada, which has only recently (1990) joined the Organization of American States and thus become eligible for membership to the Convention.

The developing countries of Latin America were instrumental in negotiating and drafting the Convention between December 1938 and October 1940. Since the late 1970's, the Organization of American States has renewed efforts to realize the potential of the Convention and five groups of technical experts have convened meetings to discuss training needs in resource conservation, marine mammals, conserving the Western Hemisphere ecosystems, migratory animals and their ecosystems and, finally, legal aspects of the Convention.

While the Convention itself is silent on incentives and measures to encourage participation, financial, technical and scientific assistance is provided by some Parties to implement activities under the Convention. The United States Fish and Wildlife Services has secured matching funds from interested organizations such as the World Wildlife Fund to carry out work in Latin America, particularly: local training for wildlife biologists and managers, research on endangered species, technology transfer, technical workshops, national fauna and flora inventories, identifying key habitat, and developing conservation management funds. Political focus is on activities to develop local capabilities within developing countries.

Information on the Western Hemisphere Convention is limited to that produced by the Organization of American States' Secretariat and the Parties and is not generally available to the press, interested organizations or the public. The lack of awareness about the Convention is due to the lack of a coordinating body or administrative structure to implement review and promote its terms by such measures as regular meetings of and reports by the Parties.

Implementation

The Convention on Nature Protection and Wildlife Preservation in the Western Hemisphere entered into force on 30 April 1942, after five ratifications in accordance with Article XI.3, and less than 2 years after it was opened for signature by the American Governments on 12 October 1940. The relatively low threshold number of ratifications accelerated the Convention's entry into force.

By the Convention, the Parties agree to establish parks and reserves, to adopt suitable laws and regulations, and to cooperate. The Convention provides that Parties "shall" take measures to protect migratory birds (Article VII) and to control the import and export of protected species (Article IX). By the hortatory Article III, the protection of species in the Annex to the Convention is declared to be of special urgency and importance. This is of limited value because the Annex (i) is not a single comprehensive list of species agreed by the Parties, but rather a compilation of national lists, (ii) reflects the status quo rather than stimulating additional protection, (iii) is mostly outdated (no revisions have been submitted since 1967), (iv) has no provisions for amendment, nor common criteria for listing, nor obligations for concerted action. The flexibility in the terms of Article VIII as in other provisions, leaves much action to the discretion of the Parties.

No commitments to monitor or to report are specifically provided for by the Convention. The scientific knowledge resulting from collaboration under Article VI is to be made available to all the Parties through publication. Submission by national authorities of lists of species to be added to the Annex to the Convention implies no requirement for any specific data on the conservation status of those species, because their listing in the Annex is not subject to any criteria agreed by the Parties.

Operation, review and adjustment

The Secretariat of the Organization of American States (OAS) in Washington serves as depositary and convention secretariat. The OAS has convened several regional meetings on environmental protection.

Following a 1988 report by the Inter-American Juridical Committee and a 1989 secretariat study on creation of an "Inter-American System of Nature Conservation", an OAS Working Group report has recommended the establishment of a comprehensive environmental programme of action for the region, including further measures to implement the 1940 Convention.

Rather than adopting a new Convention to establish such a "System," one alternative to be considered by the OAS Permanent Council is to establish a technical office to implement the existing Western Hemisphere Convention. A permanent office of the Convention would function to collect and disseminate information, including lists of protected species, stimulate financial cooperation, and act as an administrative secretariat for regular technical committee meetings. The OAS Secretariat study (CP/doc.2036/89, at p. 18) noted that establishing an office and implementation of the WHC would not alone adequately address current conservation needs, thus the call for a programme of action and an inter-American "System".

(13) International Convention for the Protection of Birds
(Paris, 18 October 1950), and related instruments

Objectives and Achievement

The principal objective of the Convention is expressed to be the conservation of birds in the wild state. The Convention obliges Parties to confer protection on all birds (at least during the breeding season) and to migrant species during their return flight to their breeding grounds. Furthermore, endangered species are to be accorded year-round protection. The Convention also requires the prohibition of the import, export, transport, sale, offer for sale or possession of live or dead specimens of birds killed or taken in contravention of the requirements of the Convention, although there are a number of exceptions to this general principle. Prominent among these exceptions is the killing or taking of birds in defence of crops or other harvested commodities and for scientific or educational purposes, as well as the raising of gamebirds and species used in falconry. Similar prohibitions (and exceptions) apply to the removal or destruction of nests, eggs, young, etc. Particular reference is made to the control of dangers presented to birds by oil-spills, lighthouses, power-lines, pesticides, etc.

There are also prohibitions on certain methods of taking birds (where this is permissible under the terms of the Convention). These include bird-lime, lights, automatic weapons, the use of vehicles or motor-boats, etc. Each party must compile a list of the species which can lawfully be taken or kept in captivity within its jurisdiction, together with the conditions applicable. Parties must also take steps to discourage trade in wild birds.

Though global in scope, the Convention only has European Parties. It does not in terms address the special situation of developed countries. Indeed, of its Parties, only Turkey and Yugoslavia may be considered as falling into that category. Reference is made (in Article 6) to the special economic importance of some species in some of the Scandinavian countries, but this is a specific, not a general, reference.

Like its predecessor, the 1902 **Convention for the Protection of Birds Useful to Agriculture**, the Convention is, in practice, entirely moribund. The functions which the Convention was originally intended to have performed are now overlain by those of the Berne Convention on the Conservation of European Wildlife and Habitats and the Bonn Convention on the Conservation of Migratory Species of Wild Animals (Nos. 22-23 below), both of which by their inclusion of developing countries that are also range States of the species protected by the Conventions have assumed much of the role foreseen for this Convention in the developing world.

Participation

Access to the Convention is open to all States. The Convention makes no provision for reservations. Membership of the Convention is entirely made up of European states. There are no parties from Africa, Asia, Australasia or the Americas.

Implementation and information

In addition to the obligations referred to in part A above, Parties are also required to provide and (if necessary) create reserves for breeding, feeding and resting on migration.

They are also obliged to conduct programmed of environmental education as to the need to preserve and protect birds. There is no systematic monitoring of compliance by States Parties, implementation being regarded as a matter entirely for the individual States. There is no procedure for reporting.

The Convention contains no provisions for regular meetings of the Parties at which the operation of the Convention may be reviewed and reports received from States Parties. Nor does it contain provisions as to the settlement of disputes.

The text of the Convention is available in English and French.

Operation, review and adjustment

Depositary functions for the Convention are discharged by the French Foreign Ministry. There are no other institutional arrangements, and no financial provisions.

The Conventions contains no express requirement that activities in pursuance of its requirements be based upon scientific advice. The Convention does not expressly provided for the setting up of any scientific committee, or similar institution. Nor is there any provision for reference to any scientific bodies existing independently of the Convention. In practice, non-governmental organizations such as the International Council for Bird Preservation (ICBP) have served as centres for the distribution of information on the Convention.

Codification programming

Aside from bilateral agreements for the protection of migratory birds (addressed separately in Research Paper No. 35) and subregional arrangements such as the 1970 **Benelux Convention on the Hunting and Protection of Birds**, the most active legal instrument in this field continues to be the 1979 **Directive on the Conservation of Wild Birds** adopted by the Coucil of European Community (EC), repeatedly amended and supplemented, and enforced by the EC Commission, through compliance and reporting requirements ultimately sanctioned by the European Court of Justice.

(14) The Antarctic Treaty
(Washington, 1 December 1959), and related agreements and protocols

Objectives and Achievement

The Antarctic Treaty provides the umbrella for an inter-linked system of international agreements of importance for the environment. These include:-
-       The Antarctic Treaty
-       over 200 agreed measures adopted under the Treaty
-       The Convention on the Conservation of Antarctic Seals (1972)
-       The Convention on the Conservation of Antarctic and Marine Living Resources, 1980
-       The Convention on the Regulation of Antarctic Mineral Resource Activities, 1988
-       The Protocol on Environmental Protection to the Antarctic Treaty, 1991.

The Antarctic Treaty reserves Antarctica exclusively for peaceful purposes, banning all activities of a military character, as well as nuclear explosions and disposal of radioactive wastes there. It guarantees freedom of scientific research in Antarctica and establishes the basis for international co-operation therein. The Treaty's juridicial provisions, which permit the Parties to agree to disagree over the existence of territorial sovereignty in Antarctica, provide the basis for regulating human activities in Antarctica. On that basis, extensive action has been taken in the field of environmental protection. The Convention on the Conservation of Antarctic Marine Living Resources applies an innovative ecosystem management to fishing activities in Antarctic Waters. Most recently, the Parties concluded the **Protocol on Environmental Protection to the Antarctic Treaty** (Madrid, October 1990). In it, the Parties commit themselves to the comprehensive protection of the Antarctic environment and dependent and associated ecosystems and designate Antarctica as a natural reserve, devoted to peace and science. Building on the existing body of measures adopted under the Antarctic Treaty, the Protocol elaborates detailed, mandatory rules to ensure that activities in Antarctica do not result in adverse environmental effects.

Though defined in regional terms, all the elements of the Antarctic System acknowledge the importance of the Antarctic environment on the global scale. Initially, this was usually expressed in terms of the value of the region as a resource for scientific activity. Recent elements of the System, however, reflect the potential contribution of the Antarctic ecosystems to the health of the global environment. For example, among the matters which are to be taken into account under the Protocol in conducting activities in Antarctica is the significance of research carried on there to the understanding of the global environment. While the elements of the Treaty system routinely stress that the management of the Antarctic region is undertaken by the Parties to the Treaty for the benefit of humanity in general, there is no express treatment of the special position of developing countries.

The consensus of opinion is that the Antarctic Treaty system has resulted in the effective preservation of the Antarctic environment. The system has demonstrated an anticipatory approach to environmental issues. Concern over the impacts of fishing activities led to conclusion of the Convention on the Conservation of Antarctic Marine Living Resources in 1980 (CCAMLR). At the tenth annual meeting of the Commission established under CCAMLR in November 1991, a precautionary catch limit for Antarctic krill was agreed. Concern over the possibility of mineral resource activities in Antarctica led to the conclusion of the Convention on the Regulation of Antarctic Mineral Resource Activities in 1988. That Convention, however, has been overtaken by the Madrid Protocol's indefinite ban on Antarctic mineral resource activities, which for the next 50 years can only be set aside by consensus and subsequent ratification of all Antartic Treaty Consultative Parties. Concern for the possible impacts of other human activities have resulted in the extension and codification of detailed mandatory rules for environmental protection are incorporated in the system of annexes that form an integral part of the Madrid Protocol. Specific annexes have been adopted setting forth strict requirements relating to procedures for environmental impact assemssment; conservation of Antarctica fauna and flora; waste disposal and waste management; the prevention of marine pollution and area protection and management, respectively. Further annexes may be added following entry into force of the Protocol.

Participation

The Antarctic Treaty is open for accession by all members of the United Nations and by any other State that may be invited to accede, with the agreement of all Antarctic Treaty Consultative Parties. The Consultative Parties - those entitled to full participation in the regular consultative meetings held under the Treaty - comprise the 12 original signatories, as well as such other acceding Parties that demonstrate their interest in Antarctica by the conduct of significant scientific research there. There are now 26 Antarctic Treaty Consultative Parties, and 14 Contracting Parties that are not Consultative Parties. The latter participate as observers in consultative meetings. Three States that were non-members of the United Nations have been invited to accede to the Treaty following expression of interest therein: the Republic of Korea, the Democratic People's Republic of Korea, and Switzerland. The Antarctic Treaty makes no provision for reservations and the Protocol expressly prohibits their use.

At present, the 26 Consultative Parties comprise 12 from Europe, 1 African state, 4 states from the Asian region, 2 from the Pacific region, 1 North American state and 6 states from Latin America and the Caribbean. In addition, there are 14 other Parties, 8 from Europe, 1 from Asia, 1 from the Pacific, 1 from North America and 3 from Latin America and the Caribbean. There is no evidence that the ratification provisions have materially affected the implementation of the Treaty, although the scientific research activity criterion for becoming a Consultive Party may have inhibited accession.

Those developing countries which are numbered among the original Consultative Parties have participated throughout the period of operation of the Treaty system. Consultative Meetings have, on the whole, been well-attended by developing countries, whether Consultative Parties or not. Some Consultative Parties have assisted developing countries in their aspirations to establish themselves as Consultative Parties, e.g. by providing logistic or other support for expeditions.

Parties have been motivated by a range of factors. Many of the original Parties were concerned to promote scientific research activities in the region, while not compromising their territorial claims. Later adherents have also wished to promote scientific research, but some Parties have also been anxious to broaden the base of representation in the Treaty system, particularly of developing countries. In recent years, public attention (especially that focused by NGO and media activity) has played a supporting role in stimulating governmental activity in respect of Antarctic affairs generally. Discussion of Antarctica has also taken place in the UN General Assembly.

Implementation and information

The Antarctic Treaty and Antarctic Treaty system impose a wide range of obligations on Parties. These include prohibitions on all military activities, nuclear explosions and disposal of radioactive waste in Antarctica, as well as requirements to exchange and make freely available data and observation resulting from scientific research activities. There is an extensive set of binding conservation measures relating to marine living resources, including obligations to collect and effort statistics. All human activities are subject to detailed rules relating to environmental impact assessment; conservation of native fauna and flora, including prohibitions on introduction of alien species; waste disposal and waste management; prevention of marine pollution and an extensive system of protected areas. Related provisions call for environmental monitoring. The Antarctic Treaty accords to Parties rights of on-site inspection to promote compliance. Both the Convention on the Conservation of Antarctic Marine Living Resources and the Madrid Protocol build on and extend these provisions.

The various elements of the Treaty system make provision for the reporting of the activity of Parties in the Antarctic region. The most recent of these, in the Protocol, provide that Parties must inform all other Parties of their own compliance measures and those which they have taken in order to ensure that others comply with the terms of the Protocol. In addition, each Party is under an obligation to inform all the others of any such activity . There are also provisions for mutual inspection by Parties of each other's installations and activities in the Antarctic area. The Protocol also calls for annual reporting by each Party on what steps have been taken to implement the Protocol. There are also specific requirements under the individual components of the Treaty System, such as catch data and exploitation effort (see, e.g. CCAMLR). Reports on the operation of the various components of the Treaty System are made to the Consultative Meetings of the Parties, at which serious allegations of non-compliance are discussed. In some cases, e.g. CCAMLR, the Meeting of the Parties to the individual component will address allegations of non-compliance, sometimes in response to reports by the Secretariat.

Both the Antarctic Treaty and the Convention on the Conservation of Antarctic Marine Living Resources provide for disputes among Parties to be resolved by peaceful means, including referral of such disputes by mutual agreement to third party procedures for settlement. The Madrid Protocol adds compulsory procedures (at the request of any party to a dispute) for its mandatory provisions, based on a choice of forum approach (either the International Court of Justice or the special arbitral tribunal provided for in a schedule to the Protocol).

Materials relating to the Treaty System are available in English, Spanish, French and Russian. Extensive documentation relating to the elements of the Treaty System are published and disseminated by the Consultative Meetings and by the Secretariats of the various constituent elements of the System. In addition, the Scientific Committee on Antarctic Research (SCAR) produces scientific reports relating to Antarctic research. The materials referred to are generally available for educational and training use.

Operation, Review and adjustment

The Meeting of the Consultative Parties is the principal organ of the Treaty System. There is a permanent Secretariat for CCAMLR. The Protocol establishes a Committee for Environmental Protection composed of representatives of Consultative Parties. Parties themselves bear the costs of participation in the affairs of the Treaty System. There are no mechanisms for alleviating the cost burden on developing countries.

The Treaty and its various component instruments contain requirements that activities in the Antarctic region be scientifically sound. The work of SCAR forms an integral part of the input to decisions taken by the Consultative Meetings. The new Protocol also requires that environmental policies drawn up and adopted by the Consultative Meeting shall draw upon "the best scientific and technical advice available". National governmental authorities of Parties have access to the Consultative Meetings, whether as Consultative Parties or as non-consultative parties. Meetings are also attended by observers from SCAR and the CCAMLR Commission, as well as from other intergovernmental organizations (e.g., IOC, ICAO, IMO, WHO, WMO, WTO, UNEP), the World Conservation Union (IUCN) and the non-governmental umbrella organization dealing with Antarctic Affairs (Antarctic and Southern Ocean Coalition - ASOC).

The Antarctic Treaty contains a provision that, as from the expiry of 30 years from its coming into force (i.e. as from 23 June 1991) any Consultative party may request the convening of a conference of all Parties to review the operation of the Treaty.

Codification Programming

In recent years, the Treaty System has developed by means of the negotiation of additional component instruments (CCAMLR, the Minerals Convention, the Protocol, etc.) rather than by fundamental revision of the Treaty itself. Part of this process has involved the consideration of the application of other conventions to the operation of the Treaty System - see, e.g., the provisions relating to the applicability of MARPOL (No. 36 in the present survey) in the annex to the Protocol relating to control of marine pollution in the Treaty area.

(15) African Convention on the Conservation of Nature and Natural Resources

(Algiers, 15 September 1968)

Objectives and achievements

The principal objective of the Convention is to promote the taking of the necessary measures to ensure the conservation, utilization and development of soil, water, flora and faunal resources of the continent, in accordance with scientific principles and having due regard to the best interests of the people. The Convention therefore proceeds on the assumption that nature and natural resource conservation must be closely linked to and integrated with development. A striking feature of the Convention (which is quite elderly by the standards of major multilateral conservation treaties) is the inclusion of an article which require States Parties to ensure that, when development plans are being drawn up, full consideration should be accorded to ecological as well as to economic and social factors and the conservation and management of natural resources are to be regarded as "an integral part" of national and/or regional development plans. Indeed, it is the view of the Secretariat of the Organization of African Unity (OAU) that the primary purpose of the Convention is developmental.

This nexus is carried through into those articles of the Convention which impose specific obligations relating to the conservation of each class of resources. The articles on soil conservation call for the improvement of soil quality and protection from erosion, taking care to underline the connection between these matters and the adoption of sound agricultural practices, the potential effect on soil quality of agrarian reform, the constructive role of planned land-use (especially in connection with activities which might otherwise accelerate soil deterioration (e.g. by removing vegetation cover). The provisions governing water resources, as well as calling for the prevention and reduction of water pollution, also oblige states parties to endeavour to guarantee sufficient and continuous supplies of "suitable" water for their populations, e.g. by co-ordination and careful planning of water resources development projets. Provisions relating to the conservation of flora seek to promote the utilisation and development of those resources, seeking the adoption of scientifically-based management plans for forests and rangelands which have particular regard for social and economic needs, soil productivity, etc. Those provisions also address some of the negative aspects of grazing and other practices, e.g. the firing of bush to promote grass-growth, over-grazing, insensitive bush-clearance, etc. Similarly, faunal resources are to be conserved, wisely used and developed "within the framework of land-use planning and of economic and social development", in accordance with scientifically-based management plans. In addition to the provision of protected areas, States Parties are called upon to manage wildlife resources in the wider countryside on the basis of optimum sustainable yield compatible with other land-uses.

The Convention contains provisions relating to the control of hunting; the establishing and management of protected areas and species; the control over the traffic in specimens and trophies; conservation education; etc. It also contains a short article which rather baldly obliges States parties to "reconcile" customary rights with the terms of the Convention. The Convention is indeed careful throughout to integrate environmental obligations with the demands of economic and social development (see, e.g. Articles II,IV,V,VI,VII,IX,XIII).

The Convention, though regional in scope, is of potential significance to global environmental protection and sustainable development, in that it has been accepted by the vast majority of African states, is of wide import, seeks (albeit in somewhat general terms) to address environmental management within the framework of development and is structurally integrated into a prominent continental international political institution. The Convention thus provides a foundation and a mandate for national and supranational environment activities in Africa. It pays particular attention to the establishing of protected areas to conserve representative samples of ecosystems and particularly those which are in any respect peculiar to the territories of the States parties. Furthermore, the Convention calls for special measures of protection for a large number of endangered species of animals, fishes and plants which were seen by the Parties as being of particular significance. Because of their global impacts, therefore, the Bamako Convention (No. 80 in the present survey) which seeks to regulate the transboundary movements of hazardous wastes and their disposal, and the African Convention on Nature and Natural Resources which basically addresses the issues of biodiversity, necessarily have a bearing on global environmental and sustainable development

Participation

Membership in the Convention is restricted to member States of the OAU.

The Convention makes provision for reservations, but not in respect of the substantive articles relating to the management of the various categories of resources. The right to enter a reservation, therefore, is confined to "implementation" questions such as research, environmental education, the integration of environmental concerns into development plans, inter-state co-operation, etc. In fact, the right to enter a reservation is rarely used, as the practice of the OAU is, so far as possible, to seek consensus on issues such as those addressed by the Convention.

The level of activity in respect of the Convention is very low. The last meeting of the Parties took place in 1985. At that meeting, a proposed revision of the Convention was considered and States Parties were asked to submit their comments on the draft revisions. Very few have done so.

The OAU Secretariat takes the view that participation in the Convention was influenced by financial, technical and scientific factors and by the role of parliaments, press, etc. The Secretariat is of the opinion that States perceive it to be in their own interests to accede to the Convention and that they feel under a sense of obligation as members of the OAU to support it in this field.

Implementation and information

The entry into force provisions only required four ratifications from a relatively large number of potential Parties. The threshold of ratifications required did not seriously handicap the effectiveness of the Convention.

There is no systematic monitoring of compliance by States Parties, implementation being regarded as a matter entirely for the individual States. The Convention provides for States Parties to submit reports to the OAU on the implementation of the Convention (and for the submission to the OAU of other, more detailed information, such as the texts of legal instruments intended to give effect to the principles contained in the Convention). There is, however, in practice no mechanism for these reports to be made or received. The Secretariat is not given power of its own motion to report on the compliance of States Parties with the terms of the Convention. The practical result is that there is no reporting system in operation.

The Convention contains no provisions for regular meetings of the Parties at which the operation of the Convention may be reviewed and reports received from States parties. The OAU Secretariat is of the opinion that financial constraints have severely hampered the effectiveness of the Convention, in that many member States are unable to participate because the costs of travelling are beyond their means.

The Convention contains a short article (Article XVIII) on the settlement of disputes, which sees negotiation as the normal method of resolution, but which provides also for unresolved matters to be submitted to the Commission of Mediation, Conciliation and Arbitration of the OAU. The Convention is silent as to whether the determination of the Commission is binding. The procedure has never been used.

The text of the Convention is available in Arabic, English, French and Portuguese, the working languages of the OAU. In so far as this material is made available, distribution functions are the responsibility of the OAU (which includes the Convention on its mailing list of official publications). To a certain extent, the Convention is publicized by the activities of organizations (including NGOs) with which the OAU co-operates.

Operation, review and adjustment

Bureau functions for the Convention are discharged by the OAU Secretariat. There are no other institutional arrangements. Such costs as are incurred are carried on the general budget of the OAU itself and have not been determined as an individual cost item. The Convention itself does not address the cost burdens nor any financial matters.

The Convention requires in general terms that certain plans and programmes must be based upon scientific advice (Articles II,IV(a),V(1)(a),VI(1)(a)VII(1)(a), etc.), but does not expressly provide for the setting up of any scientific committee, or similar institution. Nor is there any provision for reference to any scientific bodies existing independently of the Convention.

The Convention provides that, after the expiry of five years after the date of entry into force of the Convention, any party may request a revision of the whole or any part of the Convention (Article XXIV(1)).

Codification programming

In 1985, a meeting of an expert group of lawyers was convened by the OAU to consider proposed amendments to the Convention, drawn up by the International Union for Conservation of Nature and Natural Resources (IUCN) in consultation with a number of African legal experts. The proposed amendments were then further revised by IUCN and resubmitted to the OAU for further consideration, which is still in train. The draft amendments (as modified in the light of the expert meeting) reflect developments since 1968 in modern international conservation instruments.

There may be some value in redefining some of the obligations in the Convention so as to recognise the need to maintain essential ecological processes and to conserve biological diversity. Specific provisions relating to endemic species; sustainable use of harvested resources; vegetation and forest cover, impact assessment, etc. Many of these matters are addressed in the proposed revision of the Convention. Reporting and financial provisions should also be included, together with (perhaps) provision for a permanent secretariat with a systematic network of focal points in national ministries. It would clearly be of value to provide for regular meetings of the parties to the Convention with a view to reviewing its progress and implementation (perhaps as a permanent item of business on the agenda of OAU ministerial meetings). The Convention Secretariat is clearly a suitable subject for donor assistance, as little amelioration in the Convention's position can otherwise be expected.

(16) Ramsar Convention on Wetlands of International Importance Especially as Waterfowl Habitat
(2 February 1971), as amended

Objectives and achievements

The basic objective of the Convention is to provide the intergovernmental framework for international cooperation for the conservation and wise use of wetland habitat and species. The integration of environment and development is explicitly provided for, especially in regard to the "wise use" provisions of the Convention.

The Ramsar Convention is global in scope.

The special circumstances of developing countries are taken into account in numerous resolutions adopted by the Conference of the Contracting Parties on development assistance requirements (e.g. Rec.C.3.4, C.3.5 and C.4.13).

Convention membership is expanding (64 Contracting Parties) along with a rapid expansion designated for the Convention's list of wetlands of international importance (currently 521). National wetland policies are under elaboration in several States. The Contracting Parties appear to be satisfied that basic objectives are being met, as reflected in their national reports submitted regularly to the Bureau.

Participation

Membership is open to all States.

Reservations are not envisaged for substantive provisions of the Convention. Some states have, however, made declarations at the time of accession as to the geographic scope of their membership.

Most industrialized countries are now members of the Convention, with membership by developing countries growing rapidly (38 of 64).

While only a few developing countries were involved in the drafting of the Convention and its adoption in 1971 in Iran, they have been fully involved in the development of the 1982 Paris protocol and the 1987 Regina amendments to the Convention. The current programme of the Convention stresses greatly activities in developing countries.

Co-operative arrangements have been promoted under the Convention including programmes between the Netherlands, Switzerland and France with African States and Canada and the USA with Latin American States. Current efforts are under development between Japan and Asian member States. Most notably, the "Wetland Conservation Fund" was launched by the Convention in 1990 to assist developing countries in the implementation of the Convention. First project allocations are planned for late 1991.

In addition, there is a separate budget line to support the participation of developing country delegates to Convention meetings.

Factors influencing participation include financial, technical, scientific and information assistance.

Implementation and information

The need to amend the Convention resulted in delays in reaching its present state of effectiveness. A decision by the Contracting Parties in 1987 to treat the amendments as if they were in force until such time as they entered into force has greatly facilitated matters since then.

There are four basic commitments:
- Designate at least one site onto the List of Wetlands of International Importance;
- Organize planning to promote the wise use of wetlands;
- Establish reserves for wetlands, whether or not included on the List;
- Cooperate for the management of shared wetlands and shared wetland species.

More specific obligations have been formulated by the Conference in the "Framework for the Implementation of the Ramsar Convention" (Doc. C. 4.12).

Parties report to each Conference of the Contracting Parties according to an agreed format. Reports are also required when the ecological character of a listed site is changing or is likely to change so that international consultations might be held on the problem. Compliance has been good for the formal triennial reports, but could be improved in the case of specific sites. Often the Bureau first hears of these problem areas from non-governmental sources.

A Ramsar data base has been elaborated with an agreed classification and data system for all wetland sites. The Contracting Parties have been very rigorous in assisting in the data supply and have reviewed entries prior to publication of Ramsar Directories.

A Monitoring Procedure was instituted in 1988 to assist countries in addressing management problems in Ramsar sites, used selectively due to funding restrictions (about 7 cases per year). In 1991 these have included Austria, Egypt, Mexico, Venezuela, USSR (Khazakstan).

The Convention contains no provision on dispute settlement. Disputes are resolved by discussions at the Conference of the Contracting Parties, followed by Conference recommendations.

The Convention is considered to have been successful because it is based on cooperation, not coercion or perceived penalties.

The text is available in all UN languages plus German. Dissemination is promoted by Unesco as Convention Depositary.

A "Ramsar Newsletter" is published three times a year in English, French and Spanish versions, with a German version planned as from 1992. An information brochure and information package are available in the same language versions; video and slide show is also available in these language versions. All are available to Contracting Parties, other governments and the general public free of charge (a project is now under elaboration to expand provision of such materials to developing countries, and to assist in the translation and printing of materials into local languages).

Special studies on experience in certain countries have been published (e.g., Implementation of Ramsar in Denmark) as well as publications on certain programme areas, including a series of case studies on Wise Use.

Ramsar publications and video have been used for training purposes recently, e.g., in Greece, Kenya, Sri Lanka and Japan.

Operation, review and adjustment ·

Secretariat functions are performed by a Bureau, hosted by the World Conservation Union (IUCN) in Gland, Switzerland, responsible to a Standing Committee of the Contracting Parties.

The latest core budget for 1991-1993 is Sfr. 3.3 million, covered by contributions from the Contracting Parties according to the UN scale of assessments. Projects are also undertaken outside the core budget, of at least a similar magnitude, funded mainly by France, the Netherlands, Switzerland, USA and as from 1992 by Japan.

In the case of most developing countries, costs of membership are low (e.g., Sfr. 119 per year under current budget). The Wetland Conservation Fund can provide tangible financial benefits as well as expert services.

Ramsar Conferences are expert conferences. In addition, expert groups such as the Wise Use Working Group have been established to guide policy decisions by the Conference of the Contracting Parties.

National authorities, especially from developing countries comprise the membership of Ramsar Committees. Participation by non-governmental observers is encouraged both in meetings of the Contracting Parties and in expert committees.

The Convention is reviewed at triennial meetings, the next one to be held at Kushiro in Japan in June 1993.

Codification programming

The Ramsar Bureau meets regularly with the secretariats of other international nature conservation conventions to exchange information and to coordinate action.

(17) Convention Concerning the Protection of the World Cultural and Natural Heritage
(Paris, 12 November 1972)

Objectives and achievement

The Convention is a legal instrument through which States voluntarily commit themselves to protect cultural monuments and natural sites within their territory that are recognized to be of such outstanding universal value that safeguarding them concerns humanity as a whole.

By regarding the heritage as both cultural and natural, the Convention reminds humanity of the fundamental need to preserve the balance between man and the environment, and of the interaction between man and nature. The relationship between environment and development is therefore essential to the Convention, although admittedly rather abstract. In concrete terms, however, World Heritage sites are the most attractive sites for visitors and tourist of the whole world. Hence, World Heritage sites have a dual function in providing income, particularly in developing countries, to held with the development process, as well as acting as centres for heightening awareness of all classes of society to the need to protect natural sites and cultural monuments that are part of the world heritage of mankind.

The Convention is global in scope.

Countries that are the most richly endowed with cultural and natural "treasures" are not always the most prosperous and may have difficulty in providing adequate protection. Through the World Heritage Fund established under the Convention, any individual, nation or institution may contribute to the protection of the heritage in countries where national resources are insufficient.

337 sites have been inscribed on the World Heritage List (245 cultural, 78 natural and 14 with both cultural and natural attributes). An evaluation is currently underway to assess the effectiveness of the Convention and the completeness of the List, especially in terms of coverage of cultural and biogeographical regions with respect to the criteria for cultural and natural heritage (see paras 24 and 36 of the Operational Guidelines).

Participation

The Convention is open to all UNESCO States and those non-member States which are invited to accede to the Convention by the General Conference of UNESCO.

The Convention makes no provision for reservations.

The current membership of 123 States Parties to the Convention includes 95 developing countries.

The Convention was negotiated under the auspices of UNESCO, IUCN and ICOMOS, in each of which organisations developing countries are well-represented. The meetings of the World Heritage Committee and the Bureau have been relatively well-attended by developing countries, but when meetings are held outside UNESCO Headquarters developing country attendance has fallen because of the costs of sending experts to such meetings. Nonetheless, many heritage sites have been nominated by developing countries.

The World Heritage Fund is designed to help the implementation of the Convention by developing countries, including preparatory assistance for nominations, technical co-operation for listed sites, training and emergency assistance. The World Heritage Committee has recently decided to make an allocation from the Fund in order to assist experts from the least developed countries to participate in the work of the Committee.

The World Heritage Committee makes the executive decisions as to the implementation of the Convention, including the allocation of funds. The membership of the Committee is equitably divided between the regions of the world and special measure have been taken to increase participation from least developed countries.

No formal investigation has been undertaken as to the factors which have attracted states to participate in the Convention. In all probability, many are attracted by the international prestige which attaches to designation as a World Heritage Site. Many states clearly see membership of the Convention as a method of obtaining assistance, whether technical or financial or both, for conservation projects. The Fund, for example, will make small direct grants for technical assistance, but it is more usual for the designation or assistance to be seen as a catalyst or as pump-priming, serving as a focus for attracting funds from UNDP, the World Bank or from bilateral aid agreements.

Implementation and information

Each State Party recognises that it has a duty to identify, protect, conserve and hand on to future generations the cultural and natural heritage which lies within its territory. Each State accepts an obligation to do its utmost to ensure the achievement of this goal, whether by expending its own resources or by mans of international collaboration and assistance. Monitoring and assessment is carried out through programmes of assessment at the Heritage Sites, by IUCN in the case of natural sites. IUCN prepares regular reports on the condition of these sites for the World Heritage Committee. The monitoring procedure is currently under review.

Each Party reports to the UNESCO General Conference. The Convention Secretariat itself does not require reports. The World Heritage Committee's own resources do not stretch to following up all the parties, even if they did present regular reports.

The only specific requirements for data disclosure are those surrounding the application for inclusion on the World Heritage List or on applications for financial assistance from the Fund. There is no established Secretariat procedure for obtaining further information about a particular site. The usual procedure would be to ask the Chairman of the appropriate Committee to put the question of the state of the site on the agenda for discussion. This kind of action is often triggered by a complaint from an interested member of the public.

The Convention contains no express provisions on dispute-settlement.

A review of the twenty years of operation of the Convention is currently underway. Implementation of the Convention would be facilitated by a rationalisation of the mechanisms within each State Party to deal with cultural and natural heritage in a co-ordinated manner; increased promotion of the aims of the Convention at the highest level; an expanded World Heritage Fund; and a strengthening of the Secretariat within UNESCO, which would enable more resources to be deployed on dealing with requests for assistance, meeting preparation, and external fund-raising.

The official text of the Convention is available in English, French, Spanish, Russian and Arabic.

The reports of the Committee and the Bureau, together with an updated World Heritage List and list of Parties, are sent to all States Parties regularly. The Convention is also the subject of an imaginative and energetic public information exercise. The Secretariat produces a range of promotional material, including posters, magazines, books, films, exhibitions, etc. Further promotion is carried out by the States Parties themselves.

The "Operational Guidelines for the Implementation of the World Heritage Convention" contain specific information for the use of member States.

This material is frequently used as basic resource material for international and national specialist training seminars organized under the World Heritage Fund.

Operation, review and adjustment

The Division of Ecological Sciences within the UNESCO Secretariat is responsible for administrative functions concerning natural sites under the Convention, with the World Conservation Union (IUCN) providing technical advisory services.

Approximately $30,000 is allocated under the UNESCO regular programme each year to cover the costs of meetings, adminstration, communications, etc. UNESCO also provides four professional and four general service staff under its regular programme and budget.

Contributions to the Fund are obligatory or voluntary. Obligatory contributions are assessed from time to time by the General Assembly of States Parties. It has traditionally been set at 1% of the State's annual UNESCO contribution. Thus, developing countries pay a relatively small sum, which they can frequently recoup in the form of technical assistance grants. Voluntary contributions are expected at least to equal the amount which would have been paid had the State opted for compulsory assessment.

The current level of annual funding generated is $2.3 million, which is about evenly divided between natural and cultural sites.

IUCN gives technical and scientific advice for natural heritage aspects.

Member governments participate as of right in Convention meetings. Non-governmental participation is ensured through IUCN and advisory services.

The Convention envisages an amendment procedure (Article 37), but no such amendment has taken place.

Codification programming

There are no current drafts or amendments to the Convention planned.

(18) Convention on International Trade in Endangered Species of Wild Fauna and Flora
(Washington, 3 March 1973)

Objectives and achievement

Although not explicitly stated in the text of the Convention on International Trade in Endangered Species (CITES), the objective of CITES, which is self-evident from the text, is to ensure, through international co-operation, that the international trade in specimens of species of wild fauna and flora does not threaten the conservation status of the species concerned.

The Convention does this by applying trade controls in party states in three main ways. First, it in effect prohibits (with limited exemptions) the commercial international trade in wild-caught specimens of species threatened with extinction (Appendix-I species). Secondly, it gives the responsibility to exporting states to limit, through a permit system, the trade in specimens of species which could become threatened with extinction if there were no such restriction (Appendix-II species). And finally, it requires parties to control trade in specimens of species which have been protected in certain states and listed by those states in Appendix III.

The provisions relating to trade in species in Appendix II are of particular relevance to the question of "environment and development". These measures are aimed at ensuring that the population of each species is

"maintained throughout its range at a level consistent with its role in the ecosystem in which it occurs and well above the level at which that species might become eligible for inclusion in Appendix I..." (Article IV.3)

When properly implemented, this provision ensures that any international trade in specimens of CITES Appendix II species is sustainable.

The potential benefits of well managed programmes for the sustainable use of wildlife, both to species and to local communities of people, have been amply elaborated elsewhere. While there is considerable use of wildlife at a local level, this Convention deals with use of living natural resources outside the countries of origin of those resources. This form of use allows direct financial benefits to be gained by the people and countries concerned. Moreover, in well developed systems such as wildlife ranching operations, by linking commercial use of species with the supply of specimens from managed wild populations, an incentive is provided to maintain wild habitat and populations in good condition.

The Convention is global in scope.

The bulk of international wildlife trade consists of movements of specimens originating in developing countries, for consumption in developed countries. However, developing countries often lack the resources they require to ensure that the trade controls imposed by the Convention are adequately enforced. For this reason, the provision of CITES are designed so that the responsibility for control of international trade is shared between the importing and exporting countries. The importing countries, which generally have better resources for the control of international trade, are obliged not to accept imports of specimens of species listed in the appendices unless the trade has been authorized by the exporting or re-exporting countries. Thus, as a generalization, the developed wild-life consuming countries are assisting the developing wildlife-producing countries to implement their management of wild fauna and flora.

Since the principal aim of CITES is to prevent international trade from threatening the survival of species, a very rough measure of its success can be formulated by examining the transfer of species from Appendix II to Appendix I.

The limitations of this yardstick must, however, be recognized. International trade is not the only threat to the survival of species. Populations of animals and plants may also be reduced by destruction or alteration of habitat, by natural disasters, by introduced species of competitors or predators, and so forth. Species whose populations have been reduced in size by these factors may be candidates for inclusion in Appendix I, as may those with naturally small or very geographically restricted population. It must equally be recognized that the meetings of the Conference of the Parties sometimes waive the normal criteria for inclusion of species in Appendix I (or Appendix II). Finally, the transfer of some species reflects improved knowledge of their status, which is in some cases a result of the monitoring instituted because of the Convention.

With these considerations in mind, the following are the results:

Fauna -   82 species (including subspecies or species populations) transferred from Appendix II to I;
  -           34 species transferred from Appendix I to II;
  -           18 species deleted from Appendix I;

Flora   -   50 species transferred from Appendix II to I;
  -           1 species transferred from Appendix I to II;
  -           8 species deleted from Appendix I.

Participation

Membership is open to all States.

General reservations are not possible under the Convention. However, specific reservations may be made:
  i)   at the time of the deposit of the instrument of ratification, acceptance, approval or accession with regard to:
         a)   any species included in Appendix I, II or III; or
         b)   any parts or derivatives specified in relation to a species included in Appendix III;
  ii)   with regard to amendments to Appendices I and II, within a period of 90 days following the adoption of such amendment; and
  iii)   with regard to species listed in Appendix III and any parts and derivatives of such species, at any time.
At present the following reservations are in effect;
         Reservations by 17 countries with regard to 34 taxa in Appendix I;
         Reservations by 4 countries with regard to 23 taxa in Appendix II;
         Reservations by 11 countries with regard to 12 taxa in Appendix III.
The Plenipotentiary Conference to Conclude an International Convention on Trade in Certain Species of Wildlife, which concluded the Convention International Trade in Endangered Species of Wild Fauna and Flora (February/March 1973), was attended by 91 countries, including 60 developing countries. As of January 1992, 84 of 112 Parties to the

Convention are developing countries.

In the meetings of the conference of the Parties, there is generally good representation from developing countries. In recent years their participation has been supported by a project to try to ensure the attendance of two representatives from each developing country.

Moreover, the establishment of the principal committees of CITES, which carry on the work of the Conference between the meetings of the conference of the Parties, the Standing Committee, Animals Committee and Plants Committee, are also established with regional representatives, so that the representation of developing country interests is assured.

With external funding, the Secretariat has organized a number of training seminars, both general and specific in scope. For example, general training seminars have been held for the Latin American countries, for the African countries and for the Asian and Oceanian countries. More specific seminars have been held on Enforcement, on Trade in Live Animals, on Trade in Plants, and on Trade in Reptile Products. The developing country Parties have been active and keen participants in these meetings.

The Convention does not specify incentives to encourage membership thereof nor to facilitate implementation. However, the Parties have adopted a number of Resolutions which create trade disadvantages for non-party states. From this point of view there is an incentive to become a party to CITES.

With regard to implementation, however, considerable efforts have been made by the Secretariat to facilitate the tasks of the Parties. In particular:

- training seminars have been organized (see paragraph 8 above);
- the Secretariat has provided a service of permit verification to the Parties, to check the authenticity and validity of export permits before they are accepted by importing states;
- technical assistance has been provided by the regular missions of staff of the Secretariat to the Parties to discuss problems in implementation and to try to find solutions;
- scientific assistance has been provided by the establishment, through the Secretariat, of a large number of studies of the status of and trade in species in Appendix II, to determine the permissible levels of trade;
- legal assistance has been provided by the use of the services of the IUCN Environmental Law Centre; and
- financial assistance has been provided through the Secretariat, for example in paying for the attendance of developing country representatives at meetings and seminars and paying for the printing of permits of some countries on security paper.

A major factor influencing the decision of many countries to become Party to CITES is the pressure that stems from adverse publicity about illegal or harmful wildlife trade and about the mortality of animals in the large-scale pet trade.

Probably the most significant influences are information on the convention to governments, parliaments, press, NGOs, industries and the general public; and the role of parliaments, press, NGOs, industries and public opinion in general.

However, this might give the false impression that all the pressure is negative. In reality, a large number of Parties were influenced by conservation motives. This is true both for countries which are primarily exporting wildlife, and concerned about their own living resources, and about countries which are primarily importing wildlife, and thus concerned about their effect on global biodiversity.

Implementation and information

The implementation of CITES has not been directly constrained or accelerated by specific provisions regarding its entry into force. Initial entry into force required a minimum of 10 ratifications, which took about two years (1 July 1975). The convention enters into force in a state 90 days after the date of the formal deposit of its instrument of ratification, acceptance, approval or accession with the Depositary Government (Articles XXI and XXII). On amendments, see paragraph 28 below.

The main constraint on the implementation of CITES in each Party has been the need to create national legislation. Although this is an obligation under the Convention, several countries have not complied even after being a Party for many years. Others have only incomplete legislation, lacking for instance means for sanctions against offenders.

Each Party has an obligation to control all trade in species of flora and fauna listed in the appendices to the Convention in accordance with the provisions laid down in the text, and to report on that trade. Furthermore, during the meetings of the Conference of the Parties, a number of Resolutions on implementation have been adopted, either to provide clarification or interpretation, where the text of the Convention is not sufficiently explicit, or to establish rules to deal with problems not foreseen in the Convention text. Although these Resolutions are not binding, Parties are nonetheless expected to adhere to the recommendations they contain.

Although there is no systematic monitoring of the compliance with these commitments, the Secretariat does keep details of infractions of the convention, many of which reflect poor implementation practices. It presents a summary of some of the most important cases at the meetings of the conference of the Parties.

The Parties have an obligation under Article VIII, paragraphs 7 and 8, to provide an annual report on trade and to provide a biennial report on legislative, regulatory and administrative measures taken. Unfortunately, not all Parties meet the reporting requirements and even those which do submit annual reports often submit them long after the agreed deadline (31 October of the year following the year to which a report applies). In addition, many of the reports submitted are incomplete; for example, statistics on the trade in flora or in Appendix III species may be deficient or missing.

The importance of the annual statistics reports has repeatedly been emphasized by the Secretariat and by the Conference of the Parties. They are vital as a way of monitoring the implementation of the Convention. The data are computerized by CITES Secretariat consultants, enabling analyses of the data to be conducted in many ways. A comparison of the reports of each Party with those of the other Parties often reveals information on trade of which it was unaware and can help to identify possible violations and frauds.

The specific requirements for reporting on their annual trade in CITES specimens are laid down in Article VIII of the Convention. Each party is required to maintain records of trade in specimens of species included in the appendices, covering: the names and addresses of exporters and importers; the number and type of permits and certificates granted; the states with which trade occurred; the numbers of quantities and types of specimens and names of species traded (including the size and sex of the specimens where applicable).

Additional guidance on the submission of annual reports has been given in Resolution Conf 2.16 and guidelines for the preparation of the CITES annual reports were provided by the Secretariat in 1982.

In spite of the above-mentioned Resolution (and others dealing with specific details of reporting) and the guidelines, the annual reports are continuous source of concern. As mentioned under paragraph 14 above, many Parties do not submit annual reports at all, others far too late and most reports that are finally submitted are incomplete. A detailed study undertaken for the years 1980-1985 showed that the percentage of Parties submitting their reports varied from 61% to 52% during that period.

The Secretariat is active throughout the year in helping the Parties to ensure compliance with the Convention, offering advice and assistance and verifying the validity and authenticity of permits and certificates.

When the Secretariat considers that the provisions of the Convention are not being correctly implemented, it is obliged to inform the Party concerned which should reply with the necessary information within one month (Resolution Conf 7,5). The information provided must then be reviewed by the Conference of the Parties which may make any appropriate recommendation. As indicated above, the Secretariat maintains a file of cases of non-compliance and provides a summary report to the meetings of the conference of the Parties.

Although the convention does not include any provisions to penalize Parties for non-compliance, the Parties prefer to avoid being cited in the alleged infractions report. Moreover, in the most serious cases of non-compliance, where there was no short-term option available, the conference of the Parties and/or the Standing Committee, advised by the Secretariat have gone so far as to recommend a cessation of trade with a particular country, pending the correction of the implementation problems that have been identified. This has invariably had beneficial results by providing an incentive to the Party concerned to that the necessary measures.

The resolution of disputes over interpretation and application of the provision of the CITES is dealt with in Article XVIII. It foresees negotiation between the Parties involved and, should this fail, reference to the Permanent Court of Arbitration at the Hague. So far such disputes are not known to have arisen.

(a) Financial resources for implementation are often inadequate at the national level, this limits not only the number of staff involved in the implementation of CITES (in some countries only one or two persons are involved in the implementation), but also the availability of communication equipment (fax/telex) and of properly printed CITES documents.

(b) Technical assistance is provided to parties by the Secretariat in the form of:
- training seminars (*);
- printing of permits (*);
- visits to the countries concerned to assist the Management Authority on specific problems;
- providing answers to any queries from any party.

(c) Scientific assistance for the CITES Management Authority of each Party is in principle provided by the Scientific Authority nominated by that Party in accordance with Article IX. In many countries, however, the scientists do not have easy access to the scientific data they need to make the determinations specified in the Convention. The sort of information required can often only be provided by special studies. Those are provided for by:
- certain countries;
- IUCN/SSC specialist groups (*);
- projects by CITES-Secretariat (*).

(d) Information about unsuccessful and successful implementation of CITES by individual countries is provided by the CITES Secretariat directly to the

Management Authorities of the countries concerned, as the Secretariat is obliged to do. In case of serious infractions, the CITES Secretariat may inform the Standing Committee of CITES, NGOs also provide information to the Secretariat, and often contact the governments of the countries concerned. They are, however, often inclined to involve the press as well.

(e)   The role of the parliaments, press, NGOs and public opinion is generally directed to the national implementation of the Convention, leading in some cases to more strict measures being taken by individual Parties. During these meetings, the presentations by NGOs (who have a right to be present if recognized by their governments or if being an international organization) frequently influence the decisions taken.

(f)   There are no international supervisory implementing bodies, other than the Secretariat of the Convention. The role of the CITES Secretariat is mainly an advisory one (Article XII, Article XV and Article XVI) its focus being on serving the Parties and assisting them in ensuring adequate implementation of the Convention. A special report on the infractions of the Convention is presented by the Secretariat to the meeting of the Conference of the Parties.

(g)   The reporting requirements have helped to identify illicit trade, leading to improvements in implementation in specific cases.

(h)   There are no non-compliance procedures contained in the text of the Convention. However, the Standing Committee of CITES has the possibility to recommend Parties to take certain measures against any Party (e.g., a ban on trade) which seriously and repeatedly infringes the rules of the Convention. Such recommendations have been made on a few occasions.
The procedures for settlement of disputes between Parties to the Convention are contained in Article XVIII.

The original text of the Convention was in Chinese, English, French, Russian and Spanish. Translations are also available in Danish, Dutch, German, Greek, Hungarian, Indonesian, Japanese, Polish and Portuguese, amongst other languages.

The working languages of the Convention are English, French and Spanish and all official texts (Conference proceedings, Conference documents, Resolutions, Notifications to the Parties, etc.) are in these three languages. Some special publications for information are only available in English but it is intended to produce French and Spanish versions where possible (e.g., Identification manuals).

Owing to restrictions on resources for interpretation, some Committee meetings are conducted only in one of the official languages, generally English.

The most up-to-date information on the operation of CITES is provided by the Secretariat in Notifications to the parties. These are sent to the Management Authorities of all Parties and are available by subscription to non-governmental organizations. The Secretariat also has direct contact with a number of conservation and trade organizations to whom information is made available on recent events and decision.

In addition, the Secretariat has many contacts with the press and, as a result, a large number of articles are published each year about the Convention. About five to ten press releases are issued each year by the Secretariat and a press kit is available for journalists.

The Parties, of course, have responsibility for ensuring that the citizens of their states are aware of any changes in the law, for example resulting from amendments to the appendices of the Convention.

Two publications in particular have been produced to aid implementation of the Convention, they are especially targeted at the Parties but are available to the public. These are the CITES Identification Manual and a book entitled 'The Evolution of CITES'. A video on wildlife trade and CITES has also been produced and distributed all over the world. A customs training package is in preparation.

The information provided by the Secretariat is know to be used in the training programmed of Customs services and Management Authorities, as well as in international conservation organizations, universities and schools.

Operation, review and implementation

The Secretariat of CITES is provided by UNEP, in accordance with Article XII of the Convention. An outposted UNEP unit in Lausanne (Switzerland) administers the Convention.

The primary source of funds for the CITES Secretariat are the contributions from outside (i.e., counterpart contributions).

Trust Fund

The Secretariat activities closely related to the terms of reference of the Convention (i.e., the operational costs) are entirely funded by the assessed contributions designated for each Party in accordance with the UN scale. The fixed level of assessment contributions to the Trust Fund agreed upon by the Conference of the Parties for 1990 amounted to SFR 3,859,950. As the individual level of contributions for each country and budget covering the CITES Secretariat operational costs were established in Swiss Francs (SFR), amount in US dollars are approximate:

Contributions received to
CITES Trust Fund in 1990   USD 2,750,000

Total of expenditures related
to the Trust Fund in 1990   USD 2,472,000

Counterpart Contributions

These contributions are intended to cover specific projects not necessarily covered by the budget approved by the Parties. Generally, these projects are for surveys of species or for improving enforcement of the Convention. The level of expenditures is equal to the amount of contributions received in the present or prior years and pledges. Unlike contributions to the Trust Fund, contributions for the projects can come from private industry, non-governmental organizations, Parties and any individual who wishes to donate funds.

Counterpart activities
expenditures in 1990   USD 534,864

The main cost of active participation in the Convention is the cost of administration and enforcement. The primary administrative requirement is that of keeping up-to-date on laws, regulations and recommendations concerning trade; reviewing applications for permits and certificates; and issuing the documents. There should also preferably be an internal inspection system (for example, for verifying claims that specimens are captive-bred or artificially propagated). In addition, there need to be sufficient checks on shipments at the ports of entry and exit, this role is generally delegated to Customs officers but some states have enforcement officers specifically designated to help ensure effectiveness of the controls.

The cost of reviewing permit applications must take into account the expenditure required for using or maintaining a Scientific Authority. The costs of issuing permits are in some cases augmented by the expense of establishing a computerized system which can be extremely high.

The costs of attending CITES meetings and committees can be significant for some countries but assistance is provided as far as possible, often through special projects established by the Secretariat.

Each Party is required to designate a Scientific Authority to advise its Management Authority on matters related to the issuance of export permits. The Scientific Authorities are generally also involved in or responsible for the preparation of proposals to amend the appendices. The delegation of the Parties frequently include representatives of the Scientific Authorities.

For the purpose of making scientific decisions related to the operation of the Convention, for example with respect to amending the appendices, the Conference of the Parties has established certain criteria which should be followed in making decisions. It has also established an Animals Committee, a Plants Committee and a Nomenclature Committee, all of which have responsibility for the consideration of scientific issues.

Projects exist to help ensure the active participation in meetings of representatives of developing countries party to CITES. In addition, the Convention makes specific allowance for the participation of non-governmental organizations qualified in protection, conservation or management of wild fauna and flora.

The Conference of the Parties meets every two to three years to review implementation of the Convention and to revise the appendices as appropriate. Amendments to appendices enter into force automatically in accordance with an accelerated procedure not requiring ratification. The review of implementation frequently results in resolutions to improve the national application by the parties.

In addition, there have been two Extraordinary Meetings which have agreed on amendments to the text of the Convention. Such amendments only enter into force for the Parties which have accepted them, sixty days after two-thirds of the states party to the Convention at the time of the agreement of the amendment have deposited their instruments of acceptance.

One of the amendments so far agreed is related to financial provisions and the other to accession to the Convention by regional economic integration organizations. The first has entered into force. The second has not yet been accepted by the required number of Parties.

Codification programming

The 8th Conference of the Parties to CITES, to be held in Kyoto, Japan in March 1992, will consider a large number of proposals for amendment of the appendices to the Convention.

Drafting is co-ordinated through the Secretariat, with other relevant conventions on wildlife conservation, including Nos. 12,13,15,16,17,19,21,22,23,24 and 57 in the present survey.

(19) Agreement on the Conservation of Polar Bears
(Oslo, 1973)

Objectives and achievement

The Agreement aims to protect polar bears by co-ordinating research, restricting killing and capture, and protecting the ecosystems, of which polar bears are a part.

A regional agreement between the five circumpolar States, its measures to protect the Arctic ecosystem where polar bears occur serve also to protect an important component of the global environment.

The countries within whose jurisdictions polar bears occur are all "developed countries".

The conservation status of polar bears is better now than when the agreement was signed in 1973. The five Parties co-operate on scientific research and management, and monitor the health of their own polar bear populations.

Participation

The membership and geographical distribution is limited to the circumpolar countries whose fauna include polar bears: Canada, Denmark (Greenland), Norway, U.S.A. and U.S.S.R.

No reservations are provided for.

No developing countries participate in the Agreement.

Political will, strengthened by scientific evidence and public concern about declining populations of polar bears was the main factor influencing the participation of the Parties.

Implementation and information

Entry into force occurred on 26 May 1976, in accordance with Article X(4) requiring ratification by three signatories, a majority of the five possible and eventual Parties. Signed in Oslo on 15 November 1973, it was not until 25 January 1978 that all five circumpolar States had ratified.

Commitments under the Agreement are clearly listed in Articles I to IX. In brief, each Party "shall" prohibit the taking (hunting, killing, capturing) of polar bears except for scientific purposes or traditional/aboriginal uses (Art. I); protect and manage polar bears populations and their habitats (Art. II); ban illegal traffic (Art.V); pass and enforce laws (Art. VI); and conduct national research. Co-operative measures oblige Parties to consult, exchange information and promote compliance by non-nationals.

Although there is no formal provision in the Agreement for regular reports or conferences, the Parties formally exchange all data gathered by each on research and management of polar bears within their jurisdiction at a "Consultative Meeting of the Contracting Parties" every four years. The 'Proceedings' of the meeting are published under the auspices of the International Union for the Conservation of Nature and Natural Resources (IUCN), most recently in April 1991. In addition, there are frequent informal communications on research and management results between two or more Parties. No penalties for non-compliance are provided, but progress to date indicates a mutual will by all Parties to comply.

No formal dispute settlement mechanisms are provided, but the Parties may raise differences at the meetings of the IUCN Polar Bear Specialist Group. No major disputes over implementation have been reported. Factors influencing implementation include the following:

(a)   Funds for its own research programme is provided by each Party.

(b)   Information on research technology, such as satellite telemetry is routinely exchanged among the Parties.

(c)   Scientific assistance has been available when required, for example in 1990, U.S. polar bear scientists trained U.S.S.R. personnel in certain research techniques.

(d)   Information is made available through meeting proceedings, scientific journals and ad hoc popular publications.

(e)   Public interest in the welfare of the polar bears is high and helps assure the compliance of the Parties to the Agreement.

The Agreement of ten articles is in the English and Russian languages, each text being equally authentic. It is disseminated through the IUCN and the wildlife agencies of the Parties. Information is made available to governments and interested parties through conference proceedings, scientific journals, and popular publications.

The modes of research and management done under the Polar Bear Agreement have served as models of international co-operation in conservation, such that they are cited and copied for application under other wildlife agreements (according to Canadian Wildlife Service).

Operation, review and adjustment

No administrative body such as a secretariat or commission has been provided for, nor established, to promote implementation of the Agreement. There has only been one consultative meeting of the Parties (in January 1981), to ensure continuation of the Agreement after the initial 5-year agreement.

Each Party is separately responsible for its scientific input into policy-making and for the participation of all interested groups. In Canada, for example, a 'polar bear technical committee' meets annually and advises those wildlife agencies with management responsibilities for polar bears. The Committee also serves as a conduit for information on the status of polar bears throughout the polar region.

Codification programming

At the meetings in the IUCN Polar Bears Specialist Group held to date, Parties agreed that the original terms of the Agreement served their purposes well, and thus no revision of that text has been undertaken.

The Agreement, while in the form and reflecting the substance of a Convention, does demonstrate that a regional group of countries with a limited conservation goal in common, can agree to co-operate within a streamlined framework, without formal obligations to meet and report regularly, and without the supervision of an international body. This model is however limited in its application to situations where a small number of countries, with adequate and similar domestic scientific and management capacity, agree to co-operate for the conservation of a small number of wildlife species.

(20) The Convention on Conservation of Nature in the South Pacific
(Apia, 12 June 1976)

Objectives and achievement

The principal objective of the Convention is to conserve the capacity of the South Pacific to produce renewable natural resources. The dependence of the peoples of the South Pacific region on these resources is recognized and their value from a nutritional and cultural point of view is accorded equal prominence with the more usual acknowledgement of their importance as scientific, educational, etc. resources.

The Convention pays particular attention to the establishing of protected areas to conserve representative samples of ecosystems, "superlative scenery", "striking geological formations", etc., many of which may be of more the regional importance. States parties are also required to have especial regard to the conservation of indigenous wildlife (particularly those species threatened with extinction)and migratory species.

The Convention makes some attempt to address the particular problems of South Pacific States, but the rather traditional "protected areas" approach is of limited value to many of these, which are fairly small island States. Some recognition appears in the Convention of the important role of custom in these States.

The relatively limited activities carried on under the auspices of the Convention tend towards the conclusion that States may perceive that its objectives can better be carried out within the framework of the South Pacific Regional Environmental Programme (SPREP, No.55 in the present survey) regional convention or the SPREP action programme.

Participation

The Convention is restricted to States which are members of the South Pacific Commission (or are eligible to become so). The Convention makes no provision for reservations.

The Convention merely makes provision for States Parties to enter into collaborative arrangements as to research, training, etc.

Implementation and information

Even though the entry into force provisions only required four ratifications from a relatively large number of potential Parties. The Convention only entered into force on 28 June 1990.

Parties are obliged to take steps to establish protected areas, in which taking of wildlife is restricted or prohibited and within which commercial activities are strictly controlled. Parties are also obliged to prepare inventories of indigenous species which are threatened with extinction. There are also obligations as to co-operation, research, training of conservation personnel, environmental education, etc

The Convention provides for notification of protected areas and of endangered indigenous species to the South Pacific Commission, which performs secretariat functions. It also calls for the conduct of consultations between the parties. The Commission is not given power of its own motion to report on the compliance of States Parties with the terms of the Convention. The Convention contains no provisions for regular meetings of the Parties at which the operation of the Convention may be reviewed and reports received from States Parties. It contains no provisions for settlement of disputes.

The text of the Convention is available in French and English. No additional information material is available.

Operation, review and adjustment

Bureau functions for the Convention are discharged by the South Pacific Regional Environment Programme, under separate budget revisions.

The Convention envisages that the Parties shall conduct research, including scientific research, "relating to the conservation of nature" and that the results of such research shall be disseminated and exchanged between the Parties. it does not, however, expressly require that decisions taken or programmes established under the Convention should be conditional on any particular scientific basis. The Convention does not expressly provide for the setting up of any scientific committee, or similar institution. Nor is there any provision for reference to any scientific bodies existing independently of the Convention.

The Convention contains no provisions for amendment or review of its terms. Indeed, it does not even make provision for a meeting of the Parties.

Codification programming

There are no proposals for amendments to the Convention, although a recent meeting of States which are Parties to the Convention (held under the auspices of the SPREP) concluded that the objectives of the Convention might be better addressed under the terms of other Conventions and programmes operative in the region, especially the Convention for the Protection of the Natural Resources and Environment of the South Pacific and related protocols (SPREP Convention) and the SPREP Action Plan for Managing the Environment of the South Pacific.

(21) Treaty for Amazonian Co-operation
(Brasilia, 3 July 1978)

Objectives and achievement

The objectives of the Treaty, as formulated in the Preamble, are to promote the harmonious development of the Amazon region, maintaining a balance between economic growth and conservation of the environment.

All Contracting Parties are developing countries. While the scope of the Treaty is limited to the Amazonian territories of the Contracting Parties, its wider significance for regional co-operation in Latin American and for the global environment has repeatedly been acknowledged.

Progress in achievement of the Treaty's objectives is reviewed by the Contracting Parties in regular ministerial and technical meetings, starting with the 1980 Belem Conference which entrusted the Amazonian Co-operation Council with a broad mandate for development and environment tasks.

Participation

Membership is restricted to the original Contracting Parties; no adherence is possible (Article XXVII). No reservations are permitted (Article XXVI).

The main factor influencing actual participation in the Treaty remains sub-regional political solidarity among the Amazonian basin countries, which is reflected in the series of declarations adopted at the annual ministerial conferences.

Implementation and information

The Treaty entered into force after ratification by all signatories, which was completed within two years after signature on 2 August 1980.

The Contracting Parties are committed to undertake joint action and efforts to promote the harmonious development of their respective Amazonian territories in such a way that these joint actions produce equitable and mutually beneficial results and also achieve the preservation of the environment, and the conservation and rational utilization of the natural resources of these territories. More specific commitments include co-operation in the fields of scientific research, health services, trade, tourism, natural and cultural heritage.

There are no obligations for reporting, monitoring or data supply. Compliance with the Treaty shall be ensured by permanent national Commissions to be established in each Contracting Party (Article XXII).

While there are no provisions on dispute settlement, the Contracting Parties "may, whenever necessary, set up special Commission to study specific problems or matters related to the aims of the Treaty" (Article XXIV).

Authentic treaty texts are available in Dutch, English, Portuguese and Spanish; texts have been reproduced in a number of international legal collections.

Operation, review and adjustment

The pro tempore secretariat of the Treaty rotates among member States (currently Ecuador, as host country of the next meeting of the Amazonian Co-operation Council). General support is also provided by the secretariat of the Organization of American States (OAS).

Codification programming

The treaty has provided the framework for a plurinational project on Amazonian co-operation carried out by the Organization of American States, which includes co-operation in the field of natural resources development and environmental management, and binational projects for transborder co-operation.

(22) Bonn Convention on the Conservation of Migratory Species of Wild Animals
(Bonn, 23 June 1979)

Objectives and achievement

The Convention, and its subsidiary "Agreements" between Range States through which listed species migrate, aim to conserve migratory species by Parties restricting harvests, conserving habitat and controlling other adverse factors. Sustainable utilization is an implicit goal.

With respect to endangered migratory species on Appendix I, Parties shall prohibit taking of animals with few extraordinary exceptions (Art. III.5) and shall endeavor to conserve habitat, remove obstacles, and control endangering factors (Art. III.5). "Agreements" to benefit species listed in Appendix II are generally regional, sometimes on a North-South gradient, but taken together should have a global effect. The Convention is silent on sustainable development.

Numerous migratory species range over both developed and developing countries, and future agreements will need to take into account of the special circumstances of developing countries. While the Bonn Convention text does not distinguish between Parties, the Conference of the Parties at its 1991 meeting resolved that a study be commissioned on the most effective means to ensure and fund the participation of developing countries in and implementation of the Convention (CMS/Res. 3.6 on Financial Matters, para. 6).

It is difficult and early to determine the extent to which the Convention has resulted in practical local implementation of conservation measures to control harvesting and protect habitat of listed migratory species. Goal achievement could be measured by the regional and species-specific Agreements drafted to date. Agreements have been completed on the conservation of:

(i)   seals in the Wadden Sea (entered into force 1 October 1991);
(ii)   bats in Europe (opened for signature, 25 November 1991);
(iii)   small cetaceans in the Baltic and North Seas (expected to be opened for signature, 31 March 1992)

Agreements are currently being drafted on conservation of:

(iv)   white storks in Europe and Africa;
(v)   waterfowl in the Western Palearctic region;
(vi)   Houbara bustard in the Gulf inter alia;
(vii)   waterfowl in Asia;
(viii) small cateceans in the Black and Mediterranean Seas.

Participation

Membership to the Convention is open to all States. Membership to "Agreements" under the Convention is limited to Range States (and the relevant "regional economic integration organizations") for the species covered, except for cetaceans, where any State may join.

(a)   The Convention provides for reservations on joining and on amendment of the Appendices with regard to species listed on the Appendices. To date, few have been entered. France, on joining the Convention in 1990, entered a reservation against one turtle species on Appendix I. The U.K. entered reservation against the addition of six turtles species to Appendix I in 1985 but withdrew the reservations in 1988. Norway entered reservations against the addition of two small cetaceans species to Appendix II in 1988 and has expressed its intent to enter reservations against a further three small cetaceans species added to Appendix II in 1991.

(b)   Agreements concluded or being negotiated under the Convention have varying provisions relating to reservations. For example, the Agreement on the Conservation of Seals in the Wadden Sea allows no reservations, whereas the Agreements on (i) Bats in Europe and (ii) Small Cetaceans in the Baltic and North Seas allow for reservations on species covered.

(a)   The Convention currently has 37 Parties (12 in Africa, 3 in America and the Caribbean, 5 in Asia, 16 in Europe and 1 in Oceania), of which more than half are developing countries.

(b)   To date, Agreements concluded under the Convention have focussed on Europe, although those currently being drafted for the White Stork and Western Palearctic waterfowl also cover African Range States and those for Asian waterfowl and the Houbara bustard are exclusively Asian in focus.

Of the 63 Governments which participated in concluding the Convention, 38 were developing countries. Draft agreements on species for which developing countries are Range States include those on (i) the White Stork and (ii) Western Palearctic waterfowl, whose sponsoring Party (the EC) has consulted European and some African Range States including those which attended the third meeting of the Conference of the Parties. Saudi Arabia is taking the lead to involve other developing country Range States of the Houbara bustard in an Agreement. The Secretariat will establish a working group including Asian participants to formulate the Asian Waterfowl Agreement.

Attendance at meetings of Conferences of the Parties by developing countries participation has been variable. For meetings where governments have been expected to fund their delegates' attendance, developing country participation has been low.

A trust fund assists developing country participants to attend meetings of experts and of the Standing Committee. Further, for attendance at meetings of the Conference of the Parties and of the Scientific Council, some funding support for representatives of developing country Parties has been made available by a few European governments. As a result, participation at meetings has been higher, but developing countries have not taken up all funding offers or opportunities. (Report of Secretariat, doc. CMS/Conf. 3.11). The 1991 third meeting of the Conference of the Parties agreed to the inclusion of a sum of about 10% of the total budget to assist developing countries, and the Standing Committee will determine how these funds should be spent (e.g., on travel or other activities).

To understand why some developing countries have not participated even when funds and other assistance are made available, Parties have resolved to commission a study "to ensure and fund developing country participation in and implementation of the Convention" (CMS/Res. 3.6).

Implementation and information

The Convention was concluded on 23 June 1979, signed by 28 States, and entered into force pursuant to Article XVIII(1) on 1 November 1983 after the relatively low threshold of 15 ratifications had been received by the Depositary (Germany).

Only with respect the endangered migratory species on Appendix I, are Parties under a strict legal obligation under Art. III(5) to prohibit their "taking", with few exceptions. Most other provisions are hortatory, encouraging Parties to conserve habitat, to control endangering factors and to conclude "Agreements" to benefit species. Regional "Agreements" can stipulate more precise and mandatory obligations and set up more localized and effective implementing mechanisms than the global and general framework of the Convention can. Guidelines for "Agreements" are set out in Article V, but it is too early to evaluate Parties' compliance, which will involve inter alia enforcing domestic regulations and cooperating in research, management and protective measures, to be monitored by interested Parties, scientists and organizations. One measure of compliance is the demonstrated successful conservation of an endangered migratory species.

Parties to the Convention should inform the Conference of the Parties of measures they are taking to implement the Convention for species listed on the Appendices; initially response was very poor, but has improved gradually so that at the 1991 meeting, nearly half the Parties submitted reports of variable comprehensibility. Parties also must inform the Secretariat of exceptions made to the prohibition on taking of Appendix I species, but although the Secretariat is aware informally of some cases of such taking, it has never been informed by Parties officially. Reporting requirements under Agreements varies, and since one Agreement has only just entered into force, no comment can be made on their effectiveness. Further reports should be make to the Conference of the Parties on the effectiveness of each Agreement pursuant to Article IV(3), but this must await their coming into force. There is no such requirement for Article IV(4) agreements.

Parties are required to inform the Secretariat of those species in the Appendices of which they are Range States. The Secretariat circulates Range State lists to Parties and experts for comments.

No provision explicitly promotes compliance or penalizes non-compliance.

Article XIII provides dispute settlement procedures (bilateral negotiation, followed by referral to the Permanent Court of Arbitration), which have not yet been used. Agreements may provide for disputes which cannot be resolved by the Parties to be referred to the Conference of the Parties (e.g., draft Western Palearctic Waterfowl Agreement, 1991).

Implementation of the Bonn Convention is influenced mainly by political will as well as all of the factors listed, including lack of or imbalance of financial, technical, and scientific resources, and the need for more information, publicity, and public interest. Reservations do not seem to have been an important factor.

The Convention, with 20 articles and 2 appendices, was adopted in English, French, German, Russian and Spanish versions, and its working languages are English, French and Spanish. Dissemination is mainly by the Secretariat. To date, authoritative texts exist only in English and German. Correction to the French and Spanish texts were agreed by the 1991 meeting of the Conference of Parties. The Convention will soon be registered by the Depositary with the UN Secretary-General, and published through United Nations channels.

The languages of the Agreements vary with the Range States: for example, English, German, Dutch and Danish for Wadden Sea seals; English, French and German for European bats; English, French, German and Russian for Baltic and North Sea small cetaceans.

Information on the Convention is provided (i) in papers for the Conference of the Parties, (ii) on request to the Secretariat, and (iii) at various international meetings. Information on Agreements should be provided by the secretariats of those agreements when they come into force, but could also be provided by the Bonn Secretariat. "Information Sheets" started in 1985 by the Secretariat streamlined responses to numerous similar requests, and after being discontinued for financial reasons, these will be re-instituted.

A Range State list for each Party has been prepared and will be up-dated based on comments from Parties. Draft instruments of accession and ratification in English, French, and Spanish have been prepared, and guidelines for Party reports to the Conference are being used on a trial basis.

No training and education programs have been formally requested information from the Secretariat.

Operation, review and adjustment

UNEP provides the Secretariat and administers the trust fund for the Convention. At present, institutional arrangements for Agreements vary, being undertaken by various international organizations or governments. Some Parties would prefer these centralized at the Bonn Convention Secretariat when resources permit. The Convention is financed entirely by the Parties, on the basis of the UN scale, with a maximum of 25% by any one Party. The agreements are also to be financed by the Parties to them, but the basis varies; none in force yet covers developing countries. The 1990 budget for the Convention adopted by the second Conference of the Parties was US $367,374 but in fact only US $292,234 were received in contributions from Parties during 1990 towards that year's budget.

The main benefits of participation in the Convention relate to the international support it provides for national conservation programmes, access to international scientific information and expertise as well as potential funding for specific projects in developing countries. The main costs of participation relate to expenses for meeting attendance and travel costs of national experts/delegates.

The Convention established a Scientific Council which provides scientific advice to the Conference, to the Secretariat and, when instructed, to the Parties. Agreements may provide for advisory bodies, (e.g., Baltic and North Sea small cetaceans) or advice from the Convention's Scientific Council (e.g., White Stork)). The scientific mechanisms do not ensure participation of national authorities; non-governmental expert participants may be selected for appointment to the Scientific Council by the Conference, or to working groups by the Scientific Council.

The Convention and all Agreements to date provide for regular (usually triennial) meeting of Parties, which can amend the instruments and actions under them. Meetings of the Conference of the Parties have been held in October 1985, October 1988 and September 1991.

Codification programming

Instruments for the White Stork, Houbara bustard and Western Palearctic waterfowl are currently under negotiation; agreements for Asian waterfowl and Mediterranean and Black Sea small cetaceans are being prepared.

The third meeting of the Conference of the Parties in 1991 requested its Standing Committee to look at harmonization between future instruments under the Convention. Agreements between Range States should take account of related instruments such as the 1971 Ramsar Convention on Wetlands (No. 16), the 1985 North American Waterfowl Management Plan, and the Convention on Biodiversity expected to be signed at UNCED in 1992.

A major informal instrument implementing the Convention is the UNEP/FAO Global Plan of Action for the Conservation, Management and Utilization of Marine Mammals (UNEP Regional Seas Reports and Studies No. 55), which has provided support for a number of projects concerning migratory species listed in the CMS appendices.

(23) Convention on the Conservation of European Wildlife and Their Natural Habitats
(Berne, 19 September 1979)

Objectives and achievement

The dual objectives of the Convention are the protection of species of wild flora and fauna and the conservation of their natural habitats. Particular emphasis is placed on the need to take steps to protect European species which are seriously endangered by extinction. Specific provisions protect the habitats of threatened species and those important for migratory species, that is wintering, feeding, breeding or moulting sites situated on migration routes.

The Convention arises out of the recognition that wild flora and fauna constitute a natural heritage of cultural, scientific and economic worth. This must be preserved for the benefit of current and future generations. These wild species are essential in maintaining biological balances. However, they are being seriously depleted, some being in danger of extinction. The main reason for the decline in these species is the alteration or destruction of their habitats. The natural environment has been damaged by human activity in a number of ways. Agricultural and industrial activity have created pollution and waste. Deforestation and land development has reduced the area in which wildlife can flourish. Tourism has led to further development, and certain leisure pursuits have contributed to erosion of the landscape (for example, skiing and heavy use of land by ramblers and mountain bikers). The Convention stipulates measures to ensure the special protection of specified species of wild plants from picking and collecting. It also seeks action to stop the depletion of endangered species wild animals by over-hunting or collecting.

The Convention recognizes that such protection of European wildlife requires Contracting States to take into account the conservation of protected habitats in their planning and development policies. In addition Contracting States must take the legislative and administrative measures necessary protection of the species listed in the appendices to the Convention. The Convention recognizes the need for co-operation between the contracting states in order to best achieve the Convention's goals. International co-operation is particularly stressed in relation to the protection of migratory species.

The Convention was established under the auspices of the Council of Europe in 1979, aimed at conserving European wildlife and natural habitats. Initially the signatories were member States of the Council of Europe (25 States in 1991). Consequently species listed in the appendices are those found in Western Europe. Similarly environmental guidelines issued by the Convention's Standing Committee are intended to protect categories of landscape (for example, forests, coastlines, mountains and flood-plains) in the form that they are found in continental Europe.

It has, however, always been recognized that the geographical scope of the Convention could logically, and perhaps even should necessarily, be extended to North Africa. There are two distinct grounds for such an extension. Firstly, the geographical and climatic conditions in countries along the North coast of Africa mean that these African countries contain habitats similar to the European landscapes which are the subject of the

Convention, and as a result many of the species listed in the Convention's appendices are to be found in North Africa. Species of birds protected by the Convention which migrate to North Africa for the winter constitute the second link.

The Berne Standing Committee commissioned a study addressing the question of extension to North Africa (de Klemm Report, 5 September 1991), which was discussed at the 11th meeting of the Standing Committee in December 1991. The de Klemm Report endorses the relevance of The Berne objectives to Africa North of the Sahara Desert. However, de Klemm questions whether full membership of the Bern Convention of North African states is practical and suggests that the Standing Committee might instead form an associative relationship with the North African states, aimed at promoting similar conservation measures in North Africa. Although Mauritania is characterized by a Saharan rather than a North African landscape, nonetheless the de Klemm report recommends that it should be treated as a country relevant to the Berne objectives. This is because a substantial number of the species of migratory birds listed under the Berne Convention migrate to Moritania for winter.

The attitude of the Convention decision-makers (ultimately the Council of Ministers, guided by the Standing Committee) on geographical extension of the Convention has changed in the light of the recent political change in Eastern Europe. Now the priority is to incorporate Eastern European countries as new participants in the Berne framework. In the past, the Committee of Ministers of The Council of Europe had invited some developing countries to join the Convention. However, only two - Senegal and Burkina Faso - accepted and ratified the Convention. It is likely that efforts to extend membership will now be re-directed towards Eastern European countries.

Developing countries would probably participate more in the work of the Convention if an effective and well-founded programme of cooperating between North and South was established. Although such a fund has been opened, Contacting States have failed to contribute.

Implementation of the Convention is mainly the responsibility of the individual Contracting States. However, the Standing Committee issues recommendations. For example, it has recommended Contracting States to designate areas of special conservation interest within their territory, where an area fits certain criteria laid down by the Standing Committee relating to important habitats or the protection of particular species. The same recommendation also envisaged the establishment of staffed agencies and the drafting of management plans by Contracting States to ensure the practical implementation of the Conventions' objectives.

Working groups have been established to produce reports on the population status of special species, for example small cetaceans. The reports of working groups' meetings represent the method of monitoring the practical steps which have been taken or should be taken to meet threats to wild life identified as endangered under the Convention. These reports give details of inter-State co-operation. Standing Committee recommendations on the protection of individual species, for example the wolf, also recommend specific steps which should be taken by individual countries. Nonetheless, these recommendations are of a broad nature, leaving the practical details of implementation to the discretion of the Contracting States. For example, Greece was advised to "draw up a national plan for the species, and therefore establish adequate wolf protection measures".

Participation

The Convention is restricted to member States of the Council of Europe and any other State which the Committee of Ministers of the Council of Europe may invite to sign, after having consulted the existing Contracting Parties. The Convention allows signatory States to make reservations. However, Recommendation No. 4 (1986) of the Standing Committee expresses concern at the large number of reservations which had been made by Contracting States, and discouraged such reservations.

See paragraph 3. So far membership has been concentrated on Western Europe and Scandinavia. Hungary and Bulgaria have recently adhered. The only participating States among developing countries are Turkey, Cyprus, Senegal and Burkina Faso.

No developing countries (except Turkey and Cyprus) were involved in the negotiation and drafting of the Convention. All signatories, including the small number of developing countries, are entitled to participate in the drafting of Standing Committee recommendations and other instruments made under the Convention. Each Contracting State is entitled to one vote on Standing Committee resolutions. Nonetheless, as explained under paragraph 3 above, the cost of sending delegations to participate in meetings organised under the Convention has limited participation by the developing countries. Non-contracting States may be invited to attend as observers by the unanimous decision of the Standing Committee.

The fund to promote North-South co-operation in the achievement of Convention objectives has been of little use due to lack of contributions from Contracting States. Adequate funding will be necessary to achieve worthwhile participation among poorer States. The de Klemm Report is clear that financial aid is a pre-requisite for the extension to Africa of the Convention objectives. No trade and technology benefits stem directly from participation in the Convention.

Implementation and information

The Convention is in full force as between the signatory States.

Reports on the performance of the contracting States in implementing the Convention appear to be adequate. They are largely provided by environmental and scientific bodies working within the various countries. These agencies also constitute the channels of co-operation between their contracting parties. Biannual Reports on implementation are presented to the annual Standing Committee meetings and the Standing Committee also commissions specialist reports by expert agencies (for example, the technical report on small cetaceans by Greenpeace).

There are no specific requirements of data supply and data disclosure either under the Convention or under Standing Committee Recommendations, though of course disclosure of relevant data would be covered by the general obligations under the Convention. No legal sanctions against non-compliance exist. Non-compliance can only be discouraged by political pressure (at the national, Council of Europe and non-governmental level).

Article 18 of the Convention governs the settlement of disputes. It expresses the desirability of settlement between the parties concerned, and places a duty on the Standing Committee to use its best endeavours to promote settlement. Failing agreement by negotiation, Article 18 sets out provisions for arbitration. In a dispute between two contracting States one of which is a European Economic Community member, the Community has a right to be made party to the dispute.

(e)   NGOs play a decisive role in implementing and encouraging compliance with their convention, both nationally and internationally.   Examples of NGOs which regularly attend are the International Union for Conservation of Nature and Natural Resources (IUCN) and Worldwide Fund for Nature, Greenpeace, the European Herpetological Society and the Royal Society for the Protection of Birds.   Acting as watchdogs, they report non-compliance to the Secretariat.   They also give expert technical assistance, propose new measures and subjects for research, and play a major role in presenting issues.   For example, the Swiss Nature Conservation League appealed to the Federal Court to overturn the permission granted by the Cantonal Authorities for an extended hydro-electrical power station.

(f)   The Standing Committee and the Council of Europe are the main supervisory bodies.

The text of the Convention is available in French and English.   All working documents appear in these two languages.

Current information and material appears to readily available from the Covention Secretariat in Strasbourg on request by interested parties.   After each meeting, the Standing Committee is under a duty to forward a report to the Committee of Ministers on its work and on the function of the Convention.   Governments of all contracting states would be supplied with Standing Committee instructions and material through their representatives on the Committee.   Above all, NGOs perform an important role in disseminating materials to influential parties and the general public.

It is not apparent that materials relating to the Convention are used in International or national educational programmes.

Operation, review and adjustment

Administration is carried out by the Secretariat.   The Secretariat comes under the auspices of the Council of Europe, which provides approximately £50,000 per year to finance its activities.   The Secretariat consists of two full-time workers, one administrator and one secretary.

One of the principal functions of the Convention is to promote scientific research leading to the conservation of wildlife and natural habitats.   It is therefore implicit in the Convention that any existing scientific advise should be fully taken into account by the Standing Committee in formulating policies.   However, the Convention does not specifically require the Committee to obtain scientific advise before taking policy decisions.

Any amendment to the text of the Convention proposed by a Contracting State or by the Committee of Ministers is subject to approval by the Committee of Ministers and unanimous acceptance by the Contracting States.   The Standing Committee may amend the appendices.   Consideration of periodic review of the Convention and instruments to adapt it to new requirements would be a matter for the meetings of the Standing Committees.   Since the final draft of the Convention in 1989, no amendments have been introduced (the Appendices have been modified twice).   However, more detailed guidelines have been drawn up within the broad framework terms of the Convention, in the form of one Resolution (No 1 of 1989, on conservation of habitats) and 18 Recommendations.   Subjects of the Recommendations include protection of the Valle Furlana in Italy, turtle nesting beaches in Greece and Turkey, prosecution of illegal hunting or trading in protected birds, and protection of the wolf, the bear, the lynx, molluscs, crayfish, etc.

Codification programming

It appears that drafting of instruments of the Convention, or any future amendment to the Convention, would take account of other environmental agreements and instruments. Thus, for example, the de Klemm Report (on possible extension of the Convention to Africa) addresses the issue of possible duplication of the African, Ramsar, Regional Seas and Bonn Conventions.

The Convention appears to have been reasonably successful in achieving co-operation between contracting states in formulating environmental policy. However, there is a vital need to set up the means of legal enforcement in contracting states of implementing measures [This might be possible, on the European Economic Community model, through action against the Governments of Contracting States for failing to implement measures in the form of national law, since such practical implementation is left to the discretion of contracting states as in the case with EC Directives]. As has been stressed above, any effective extension of the Convention to developing countries, and more immediately, to the economically disadvantaged countries of Eastern Europe, necessitates financial assistance for implementation measures in these countries. On a practical level, the Secretariat is at present under-staffed and under-funded. Geographic extension of the Convention and more vigorous implementation would require an extension of the central Secretariat, more funding and possibly provision of affiliated national secretariats.

(24) Convention for the Conservation and Management of the Vicuña
(Lima, 20 December 1979)

Objectives and achievement

The principal objective of the Agreement is the conservation and management of the vicuña. This objective is expressly related to the economic well-being of the peoples of the Andean region. Indeed, the Convention includes a commitment to the sustainable utilisation (under State control) of the vicuña with a view to providing a further source of income and resources for the population.

The Convention is of global significance in that it governs the conservation, management and exploitation of the entire world population of the vicuña. The Parties to the Convention are all developing countries.

The Convention is considered to have met its basic objectives, the population of vicuña in the member States having increased from an estimated 59,000 in 1978 to 160,000 in 1990.

Participation

The Convention is only open to States which are range states of the vicuña. There is an express provision prohibiting the accession of other States (Article 13), except as regards Argentina (as Party to the earlier 1969 Convention), which participated as observer until 1989 but has since become a Party. The Convention makes no provision for reservations.

The Convention was negotiated by all the concerned states. As to subsequent activity, all Andean States participate. The Convention was largely prompted by a common desire among the range states of the vicuña to collaborate to conserve the populations of that species and to manage them on a scientific basis for the benefit of the people of the region.

Implementation and information

The Convention provided for provisional application from the date of signature. This proved an effective method of avoiding delays in implementation, including meetings of the Technical-Administrative Commission from 1980 onwards.

The parties undertake to prohibit the hunting and trade of vicuña and its products. They also undertake to prohibit the export of fertile reproductive material and to set up national parks and other reserves for the benefit of the vicuña. There are also obligations to participate in training and technical assistance programmes, as well as public information tasks. There is also a commitment to regulate trade, should the stock levels rise to a point where such trade can be carried on.

The Convention established a Technical-Administrative Commission to oversee the working of the Convention. The parties also exchange information through the Multinational Documentation Centre established in Bolivia.

The Convention contains no express provisions on dispute-settlement, although the Technical-Administrative Commission is empowered to deal with problems of implementation, by way of decisions or recommendations.

Economic factors hampered the finding and execution of programmes for research, capacity building and monitoring.

The official text of the Convention is only available in Spanish, but unofficial translations in English and other languages are available.

The Convention provides for the dissemination and exchange of information about the conservation of the vicuña to be undertaken by each of the Parties as part of the discharge of its responsibilities under the Convention. Four issues of documents were published by the Documentation Centre in Bolivia, but further issues could not be produced for lack of funds.

Operation, review and adjustment

Each Party bears the costs of its participation and its share of meeting costs for the Technical-Administrative Committee.

Although the Convention does not envisage a regular review of its terms, the Technical-Administrative Committee takes decisions adjusting and supplementing the Convention as required.

Codification programming

There are no current proposals for amendments to the Convention. The establishment of a common fund to finance programmes for research, capacity-building and monitoring has been identified as a high priority for future action.

(25) The International Tropical Timber Agreement
(Geneva, 18 November 1983)

Objectives and achievement

The objectives of the ITTA are to promote the management of tropical forests on a sustainable basis and to provide a framework for co-operation between producing and consuming member states in the tropical timber industry. The expansion of tropical timber production by producing member states will promote the economic development of producing countries through increased export earnings. The ITTA aims to encourage the planning of tropical timber reforestation and the establishment of forest management in order to achieve a sustainable utilisation and conservation of tropical forests, both as an economic resource and an important factor in maintaining ecological balance in the regions concerned. Although the ITTA was first drafted as a commodity agreement, the final version adopted in 1983 was a comprehensive agreement to govern development the tropical timber industry in the context of environmental implications and the impact on the economies of producing regions. The Agreement entered into force on 1 April 1985. The operational activities under the ITTA began in November 1987, after the establishment of the Secretariat in Yokohama, Japan.

The membership of the International Tropical Timber Organisation ("ITTO") set up by the ITTA is categorized into producers and consumers of tropical timber. Almost all producers are developing countries, situated in the tropical belts of Africa, Asia and Latin America. The consuming countries are mainly developed countries in Europe, North America and the Far East.

Since almost all tropical timber producing countries are Parties, the potential importance of the ITTA and related instruments on the ecological balance is on a global level. The establishment of methods to manage tropical timber resources as renewable economic resources is essential to sustained economic improvement for much of the world's population, as well as to halting the environmental damage caused by rapid deforestation.

About half of the Parties involved in drafting the ITTA were developing countries. The ITTA recognises that financial and technical assistance to developing producer countries is a prerequisite of long term planning and forestry management. Studies, projects and guidelines under the ITTA are therefore undertaken conscious of the needs of developing countries, and in particular the necessity to integrate policies of economic development into measures to improve forestry management. The ITTA provisions on projects incorporate the needs of producer countries for technological transfer, training and investment. Thus the ITTA projects represent a conduit of external financial aid and know-how.

There are a few developing countries, such as China, Nepal and Egypt, amongst tropical timber consumer members of ITTO. Hence the ITTA makes provision for developing importing members whose interests are adversely affected by measures taken under the ITTA to apply for appropriate differential and remedial measures. On the other hand, all Contracting States must make an assessed contribution to the annual budget to cover the administrative costs of administering and supervising the implementation and operations of the ITTA; and must bear the expenses of their own delegations to the Sessions of the International Tropical Timber Council (ITTC) and its Permanent Committees, working parties, etc.

The ITTA states that the Council should review the world tropical timber situation annually with regard to trade economic, ecological and environmental aspects. Each year the Council must publish an annual report on its activities. In addition, reports on tropical timber issues are produced as part of ITTA project activity.

An Action Plan has been published as a result of the 9th Session of the Council in November 1990. This summarises activities envisages under the ITTA so far and identifies priority areas for programme development and project work. According to the Action Plan, the central objectives of the ITTA are yet to be achieved on any significant scale. The Action Plan underscores the consensus for the continuing depletion of the tropical forest base. Long-term management and forest policies are not being implemented. The key aim of the ITTA - a sustainable management of the resource base for the supply of wood raw material and other non-wood forest services and goods -is not being achieved because of socio-economic factors leading to deforestation and forest degradation. A prime objective of ITTO is the expansion of of forest estates to produce timber for processing within the producer countries, as opposed to exporting timber as unprocessed raw material. However, export of logs by producer countries still dominates. The Action Plan identifies the obstacles to economic development concurrent with environmental preservation as lack of investment in the timber processing industries in producer countries; lack of skill in operating harvesting equipment; and technical constraints due to the expense of forestry research and a breakdown in R&D co-operation.

On the other hand, the ITTO appears to have set up reasonably effective methods of monitoring the tropical timber position. The ITTO also seems to have been quite successful as an inter-governmental organisation responsible for co-ordinating research and project activity by international organisations and NGOs. Furthermore, the ITTO has succeeded in achieving almost comprehensive membership among producing and consuming countries. This has contributed significantly to enhancing the forum for consultation and co-operation between governments, conservations NGOs and timber trade associations. Nonetheless, the Action Plan concludes that the opportunities to conserve and utilise the world's tropical forest will remain illusive if the level of human and financial resources committed to it remains insufficient.

Participation

Membership is open to any state which produces or consumes tropical timber. Current membership is 48, including 22 producers and 26 consumers. Article 43 prohibits reservations.

Beyond contributions to the administrative budget and to ITTO secretariat, producer Governments' visibility and participation in the substantive work of ITTO could be further enhanced.

The ITTA places heavy emphasis on the means needed in order to achieve its ends (ie conservation alongside economic utilisation of the world's tropical forests). The ITTA recognises that such goals can only be achieved by planned development in the producing regions. This requires technical, educational and financial assistance to these regions as well as the promotion of trade and R&D in tropical timber. The incentive for participation by developing countries lies in the opportunity to benefit from financial, trade, investment and technological assistance and co-operation. However, while it is clear that the ITTA intends to facilitate implementation by developing countries, the human and financial resources devoted to this assistance are totally insufficient for the scale of the problems. The ITTA does provide in general terms for collaboration in technological transfer, training, research and market intelligence.

It seems that the very high level of membership among developing countries is due to the opportunity to benefit from financial, technical and scientific assistance, while it is likely that participation among developed countries, representing most of the consumers of tropical timber, has been influence by pressure from media, public opinion, Parliaments and NGO's in the current international atmosphere of concern for the role of tropical forests in the global environmental and development crisis.

Implementation and information

The provisions of Article 37 requiring a minimum package of ratifications, economically balanced between producer and consumer countries, delayed entry into force beyond the planned date of 1 October 1984 to 1 April 1985. However, several Governments opted for earlier provisional application (Article 36).

The ITTA itself only imposes obligations of a broad nature. The three ITTA duties for member countries are to pay the contributions to the Administrative Account, and (in the case of developed consumer members particularly) to the special account for projects; to provide data on tropical timber requested by the Council; and to use their best endeavours to co-operate to promote the attainment of the ITTA objectives. Members are obliged to accept decisions taken by the Council.

In December 1990 the Council adopted the "ITTO Guidelines for the Sustainable Management of Natural Tropical Forests" as an international reference standard, in the form of principles, to guide the development of more detailed national guidelines. Thus the legal implementation and enforcement of practical measures are left to member countries themselves, and are therefore subject to the economic and political pressures on law-makers in member states (principally producer countries). A competitive market price for timber (tending towards the marginal cost of production omitting costs of replacement) generally means that renewal of forest resources is not economically feasible.

The assessment of compliance by Parties with ITTA principles is the responsibility of the Council and permanent Committees. Emphasis is placed on monitoring and review of ITTO projects and the programme set up by the Action Plan. An expert Committee has been established for the technical assessment of project proposals. On the other hand, the Committee on Market Intelligence appears to have been fairly effective in obtaining information on the tropical timber market. It is also mandated to assist member countries to improve their own statistical services.

An example of assessment of implementation by ITTO itself rather than by national governments is the ITTO mission to Sarawak, Malaysia in 1989.

The ITTO has not succeeded in enforcing the obligation on members to contribute to its resources. Producer states have paid less than two-thirds of their assessed contributions to the administrative budget, and consumers have also fallen short. The development and environmental aspects of ITTO's remit (which are inextricably inter-dependent) do not appear yet to have achieved any measurable progress. Timber-dependent producer economies have felt no significant improvements yet. On the other hand, ITTA has been effective as a trade agreement in providing improved market information.

Detailed assessments of project proposals are carried out by the appropriate permanent Committee in pre-project studies. These are outlined in the ITTO Project Cycle. Parties are expected to report data on timber imports and exports, as a basis for teh ITTO annual assessment of the world tropical timber situation. For 1990, data were received from 24 consuming countries and 15 producing countries.

The ITTA provides that any complaint that a member has failed to fulfil its obligations under the ITTA, or any dispute on the application of the ITTA shall be referred to the Council for decision. It appears that ITTO is unlikely to pursue non-compliance in member states (primarily meaning producer countries) because of the political impossibility of ensuring compliance by Governments concerned.

The main cause of failure to achieve the ITTA's objectives for development and environmental protection is the failure to provide adequate financial resources to make sustained timber exploitation economically viable. In addition, even otherwise achievable levels of efficiency in timber use (for example, stemming from modern harvesting techniques), are being missed through inadequate technology or scientific know-how.

Public awareness of the danger to tropical timber forests, and the linked economic problems of the producing nations, has been raised by publicity from media and Non-governmental Organizations. This has raised pressure on the Governments of democratic developed countries to act to improve the situation. However, NGOs seem to have concluded that public opinion in developed economies is a better target for mobilization and near-term change than the long-term institution-building in which ITT now is engaged.

The ITTA was originally published in Arabic, English, French, Russian, Spanish and Chinese. Current information is available from the ITTO headquarters in Yokohama.

Under the terms of the ITTO Guidelines, national Governments should draw up and implement their own more detailed national Guidelines. However, such national Guidelines appear to be either non-existent or inadequately implemented.

Operation, review and adjustment

The ITTA established the International Tropical Timber Organisation, which functions through the International Tropical Timber Council and three permanent Committees. The Committees are:

(a)   Committee on Economic Information and Market Intelligence;

(b)   Committee on Reforestation and Forest Management;

(c)   Committee on Forest Industry.

The operational activities of the Council and the permanent Committees fall into two basic categories. The first category consists of the formulation and implementation of projects in research and development, market intelligence, processing, reforestation. The second category consists of monitoring commercial activity in tropical timber; reviewing the future need of the trade and assistance provided for production; and encouraging transfer of know-how and technology.

In 1989 the ITTO administrative budget was $2.54. million. In 1990, this rose to $2.8 million and in 1991 was $3.1 million. This is financed by contributions from all member States in proportion to their votes on the International Tropical Timber Council (ITTC). Administration is undertaken by the Secretariat, which performs support services to the Council and the Permanent Committees and the Organization as a whole. The Council is the governing body of the Organization. Its work consist in formulation of overall policies, approving the programme of work for the Organization, allocating funds for its implementation and undertaking an annual review and assessment of the tropical timber market and economy. Funding of project activities is from the Common Fund for Commodities; relevant regional and international financial institutions; and voluntary contributions from members and interested organizations. Generally target contributions from donor members are made at the bi-annual sessions of the Council. However, direct funding of ITTO's projects from the multilateral Common Fund has been delayed due to the late start-up of the operations of the Fund. Projects are proposed by member States, often with the technical advice of the Secretariat. Almost three quarters of the total US$ 44 million so far of project and pre-project funding has been provided by Japan. The idea is to persuade consumer States and their importing industries to contribute to ITTO as a gesture of commitment and political goodwill towards achieving sustainable use and conservation of tropical forests. However, this has not yet been achieved on a significant scale, except in the case of Japan.

Producer States are the intended beneficiaries of the three main ITTA programmes (ie market intelligence; reforestation and forest management; and further processing by developing countries), although market information may be of use to all parties in the timber trade. There is no provision in the ITTA to assist developing countries in bearing the expense of sending delegates to meetings and working parties, in order to play a more pro-active role in directing ITTO policies. Consumer States play an important role as donors supporting ITTO projects.

The ITTA envisages that policy should be based on scientific advice, and all projects must be expertly assessed before approval. For this purpose, the ITTA provides that the ITTO should, as far as possible, utilize facilities and expertise provided by existing national and international agencies and NGOs, and should collaborate with such organisations in research and data collection. It also allows the ITTO to use funds offered to it from these organisations. Any such organizations may request formally to be invited to meetings of the Council as observers. ITTO thus accepts earmarked funds to advance bilateral agendas whilst still pursuing its own multilateral theme.

The ITTA is subject to periodic extension or renewal by the Parties. A mechanism for amending the ITTA, involving the approval of at least two thirds of producing members and two thirds of consuming members is provided in Article 38. The intent of the drafters of the ITTA was to leave the Parties free to decide on any changes at any time it so decides. Further extension of the ITTA has been decided twice in 1989 and 1991, for two consecutive periods of extension 1990-1992 and 1992-1994

Codification programming

At the initiative of FAO, the Secretary-General of the UNCED convened an ad hoc meeting of heads of UN agencies and the ITTO in March 1991 to explore possibilities of instituting periodic consultations among the relevant Secretariats in order to co-ordinate current negotiations on legal instruments for climate change and biodiversity and a possible consensus on forests. ITTO participated together with FAO, UNESCO, WMO, UNEP, UN/DIEC and the Intergovernmental Negotiating Committees concerned.

(26) International Undertaking on Plant Genetic Resources
(Rome, 23 November 1983) as supplemented

Objectives and achievement

The objective of the Undertaking is to ensure that plant genetic resources are preserved and are made available as widely as possible for the purposes of plant breeding. This objective is expressly to be achieved for the benefit of present and future generations. The essence of the Undertaking is to conserve genetic resources specifically for the purposes of human development. The Undertaking is focused on plant genetic resources of economice and/or social interest, particularly for agriculture. Particular emphasis is given to cultivated varieties of plants, plants or varieties which have been in cultivation in the past, primitive versions of cultivated plants, wild relatives of such plants and certain special genetic stocks. The Undertaking is, therefore, largely concerned with plant genetic diversity which is, has been or may become of importance for agricultural use (especially food crops). The Undertaking also has regard to the destructive impact of development activities, as it calls for special efforts to be made in order to conserve plant varieties which are threatened with extinction as a result of deforestation (especially in tropical areas) or changes in agricultural practices. The Undertaking also envisages the setting up and development of an international network of centres at which plant genetic material would be held for the benefit of the international community.

The Undertaking forms an important element in FAO's Global System on Plant Genetic Resources as a co-ordinated attempt on the global level to accumulate an important resource for plant genetic material. The Undertaking covers <u>ex situ</u> as well as <u>in situ</u> conservation (see articles 3 and 4).

The Undertaking explicitly recognizes the difficulties faced by developing countries in plant genetic resource conservation. In the Resolution adopting the Undertaking, the General Conference of FAO recognized that, while a huge amount of plant genetic material was to be found in developing countries, there was a need to support and expand training and facilities for plant breeding in those countries. The Undertaking stipulates that access to the materials which have been collected or conserved in pursuance of its terms and the export of such material for scientific or plant-breeding purposes is to take place free of charge or on the basis of mutual exchange or, at the very least, on the most favourable terms having regard (among other things) to the characteristics of the person or entity making the request for transfer. The Undertaking also provides for special consideration to be given to the need to provide urgent funding in cases where there is reason to apprehend that the effective conservation of material held in a collection centre might be prejudiced.

Participation

The Undertaking is open to all FAO member States and to States which are not members of FAO but are members of the United Nations. As of January 1992, there were 104 States that are commited to the Undertaking. Of these, 32 are African States, 12 States from the Asian region, 26 European States, 23 States from the Latin American and Caribbean region, and 11 States from the Near East.

States may enter reservations to the Undertaking and many of them have taken advantage of the right to do so. Reservations have usually been entered because of possible conflicts between the terms of the Undertaking and national laws. Since the adoption of an agreed interpretation of the effect of the Undertaking, with the simultaneous recognition of Farmers' Rights and Plant Breeders in 1989, most reservations have been withdrawn.

The Undertaking provides a framework for financial and technical assistance to developing countries in identifying and conserving plant genetic resources and in plant-breeding operations. The Parties to the Undertaking endeavour to co-operate in order to strengthen the capabilities of developing countries in the identification and surveying of existing plant resources and in respect of plant breeding and seed multiplication and distribution. A financial mechanism, the International Fund for Plant Genetic Resources, has been set up to ensure the conservation and utilisation of plant genetic resources on the international plane. The Fund provides a channel for countries (and for intergovernmental and non-governmental organisations as well as commercial enterprises and individuals) to play a role in conserving the world's plant genetic diversity.

Implementation and information

Parties to the Undertaking agree to mount exploration missions to identify plant genetic resources which are potentially valuable and in danger of extinction and particularly those which are endangered by deforestation or development activities. They agree to put in place legislation to protect plants and their habitats and to take steps to collect genetic material (including collection into genebanks and living plant collections, such as botanic gardens, etc.). Parties accept that they must provide access to such plant genetic resources as they control and to allow the export of those resources to other States for the purposes of scientific research or plant-breeding. Furthermore, they accept that such access and export shall be granted free of charge, or on the basis of mutual exchange or on the most favourable basis (having regard to the identity of the transferee). Parties also pledge themselves to building up institutional and technical capabilities in developing countries, intensifying plant-breeding and germ plasm maintenance activities on the international plane, establishing international genebanks, building up an internationally co-ordinated network of collections, putting in place an international data system and providing an early warning system to alert the international community to threats to the continued security of any centre at which plant genetic material is collected. They also agree to do what they can to place plant genetic resource activities on a firm financial footing and, especially, to fund rescue work in cases where collections are at risk. There are also information and monitoring duties.

The Undertaking is regarded by the Parties and by FAO as not imposing an legally binding obligations on the Parties. Thus, the effect of the provisions outlined above is said to be merely to urge Parties to conduct their affairs in accordance with the principles set out therein.

Monitoring of the operation of the Undertaking is carried out by FAO through the medium of the Commission on Plant Genetic Resources, which is an intergovernmental forum having 128 state members with a wide and even geographical distribution. The Commission has established an intergovernmental Working Group with regional representation to deal with issues relating to plant genetic resources during the intervals between the meetings of the Commission.

States are required to provide the Director-General of FAO with annual reports of the steps which have been taken by them in pursuance of the terms of the Undertaking. There are no other specific data supply requirements set out in the Undertaking. The operation of the Undertaking is reviewed at regular meetings of the Commission (and the Working Group) on Plant Genetic Resources.

The Undertaking makes no reference to dispute settlement. Matters of controversy between the parties are usually resolved by negotiation and the agreed result endorsed, in appropriate cases, by the Commission or the FAO General Conference.

Material relating to the Undertaking is published in English, French, Spanish, Arabic and Chinese. Materials relating to the implementation of the Undertaking and to other aspects of the Global System are published both by FAO and by the International Board for Plant Genetic Resources. These include regular newsletters about recent developments, technical guidelines, scientific papers and research reports, identification manuals, directories of plant genetic resource collections, etc. Seminars are held to focus public attention on plant genetic resource issues and major public information campaigns are mounted.

The Secretariat is developing a Global Information and Early Warning System, which will publish a "State of the World's Plant Genetic Resources" and monitor the new developments in biotechnology related to the International Undertaking. A wide range of training activities are undertaken under the auspices of the Global System. These range from short, specialist courses on closely-defined topics and training programmes tailor-made for particular individuals or groups to funding postgraduate studies for sponsored students in university programmes.

Operation, review and adjustment

The implementation of the Undertaking is overseen by the Commission on Plant Genetic Resources and the Working Party. International administration costs are covered by the regular budget of FAO.

The main benefits accruing to developing countries from adherence to the Undertaking are the provision of scientific, technical and financial assistance in the identification, collection, conservation and management of plant genetic resources, together with access on favourable terms to such resources held by other states adhering to the Undertaking.

The Undertaking requires that activities embarked upon by Parties be in accordance with recognized scientific standards and that collecting and conservation of the material and the management of the centres where it is held be conducted in a scientifically-approved manner. These matters are also overseen by the Commission and the Working Party. National authorities are represented on the Commission and the Working Party. Non-governmental organisations also participate as observers in the meetings of the Commission.

Codification programming

The working of the Undertaking is reviewed on a continuing basis by the Commission and the Working Group. There are no proposals at present for any major review of the Undertaking.

(27) ASEAN Agreement on the Conservation of Nature and Natural Resources

(Kuala Lumpur, 9 July 1985)

Objectives and achievement

The principal objective of the Agreement is the maintenance of essential ecological processes and life-support systems, the preservation of genetic diversity and ensuring the sustainable utilisation of harvested natural resources with a view to attaining sustainable development. The Agreement seeks to integrate environmental matters as an integral part of development planning at all stages and at all levels. The Agreement incorporates a number of significant difference from other regional conservation agreements. Species protection provisions, for example, are cast in terms of the preservation of genetic diversity, with increased stress on habitat conservation; harvesting controls include consideration of dependent and related populations, etc. Extensive treatment is given to the conservation of vegetation cover and forest resource. Soil protection provisions consider downstream siltation problems, etc. The Agreement also addresses cross-sectoral environmental problems, such as the misuse of agro-chemicals, ill-considered development schemes giving rise to wetland drainage or deforestation, etc. The Agreement also calls for integrated pollution control and monitoring programmes and contains sophisticated provisions relating to land-use planning controls and environmental impact assessment.

The Agreement seeks to address environmental problems in the context of economic development. Sustainable development is a avowed objective and the importance of making development decisions in an environmentally literate manner is underscored, both in the recital of general principles in the Agreement and in individual articles (such as that which draws attention to the use of economic and fiscal devices to assist in pollution control - see Article 10(c)).

The Agreement is of general significance as representing a detailed set of environmental obligations which take account of modern conservation thinking. Examples are the stress laid upon the need to adopt a cross-sectoral approach to pollution control, the concentration on genetic diversity, the importance attached to reforestation, water catchment and watershed protection, the consideration of shared natural resources and transfrontier environmental impacts. The Agreement also displays a number of procedural features of interest, providing for regular meetings of the Parties, a designated secretariat, national focal points, provision for the amendment of the Agreement and the negotiation of protocols, etc.

The Agreement is regional in scope; all signatories are developing countries.

There has been little formal activity by the signatories subsequent to the signing of the Agreement in 1985. The Agreement requires a study on the existing legal position with respect of the environmental laws, regulations and administrative practices in each of the signatories. Except for the Philippines, these studies have not yet been completed. On the other hand, the Ministers of the Environment of the ASEAN countries meet regularly (most recently in January 1992) to discuss international environmental issues. A group of ASEAN Senior Officials on the Environment has also been formed and meets regularly over the last decade. ASEAN has established six working groups on environmental matters; these deal with nature conservation, marine environment, transboundary pollution, environmental management, environmental economics and education, information and public awareness.

Participation

The Agreement is restricted to States members of ASEAN, all of which are developing countries. The Agreement makes no provision for reservations.

Implementation and information

The entry-into-force provisions require ratifications from all six ASEAN States. This insistence on consensus is explicable in the context of a small, tightly-knit regional organisation. Six years after signature, however, the Agreement has still not received the necessary ratifications to enter into force.

The Parties undertake extensive commitments to adjust their domestic laws and practices to accommodate to principles referred to in 1 above. The Agreement is cast in mandatory language throughout (see, e.g. Articles 3(2),5, 6(1), 14), although the effect is qualified in places by requirements that States Parties need only "endeavour" to achieve the objectives described (see, e.g. Articles 6(2), 8(2), etc.). The Agreement provides, in principle, for the identification of adequate administrative machinery for the implementation of the principles contained in the Agreement (together with provision for co-ordination, where necessary) - see Articles 17 and 23. Hitherto, however, it would appear that there is no machinery established at an international level which is charged with monitoring compliance.

The Agreement contains provisions relating to the dissemination of the results of scientific research and specifically requires monitoring data and other information (including "reports and publications of a scientific, administrative or legal nature") and especially information about measures taken in pursuance of the Agreement to be communicated to the Secretariat. At present, however, there being no Secretariat appointed under the Agreement, such flow of information as occurs does so in the context of the other meetings and institutions referred to in 1 above. The Agreement confers wide but unspecified powers on the Secretariat, so (when it is appointed) it may have power of its own motion to report on the compliance of States Parties with the terms of the Agreement.

Article 28 specifically requires the preparation by States Parties of reports on the steps they have taken to put into effect the terms of the Agreement. The Agreement envisages the submission of reports to the Meeting of the Parties on the implementation and working of the Agreement and the posing of questions and enquiries by States Parties into these matters, and the Secretariat is required to assist in the discharge of these functions. The Meeting of the Parties is required to keep implementation under review.

The Agreement simply provides that disputes shall be settled amicably by consultation or negotiation.

The text of the Agreement is available in English and the national languages of the ASEAN countries. There are no special arrangements made at a governmental level for the dissemination of information, material, or for use in training programmes.

Operation, review and adjustment

The Agreement makes provision for a Secretariat to be designated on the coming into force of the Agreement. The provision sets out the functions of the Secretariat with some precision. As the Agreement is yet to enter into force, there is currently no Secretariat, and no financial costs. The Agreement only refers to financial matters in the context of the additional action which the Meeting of the Parties may wish to consider - Article 21(2)(d).

The Agreement refers, in the annunciation of its "fundamental principle", that scientific principles are to illuminate activities under the Agreement. It also envisages that the Parties shall conduct scientific research and that the results of such research shall be disseminated and exchanged between the Parties. It does not, however, expressly provide for the setting up of any scientific committee, or similar institution. Nor is there any provision for reference to any scientific bodies existing independently of the Agreement.

The Agreement provides that any Party may propose amendments, but does not envisage a regular review of its terms. The Meeting of the Parties, however, includes amongst its functions the need to review the Agreement.

Codification programming

There are no current proposals for amendments to the Agreement.

STATUS OF RATIFICATIONS AS OF 1 JANUARY 1992

GLOBAL INSTRUMENTS   (Treaty numbers see page 59)

Parties	13	16	17	18	22	25	26
Afghanistan			x	x			
Albania			x				
Algeria		x	x	x			
Angola			x				
Antigua & Barbuda			x				x
Argentina			x	x	x		x
Australia		x	x	x	x	x	
Austria		x		x		x	x
Bahamas				x			
Bahrain			x				x
Bangladesh			x	x			x
Barbados							x
Belarus*			x				
Belgium	x	x		x	x	x	x
Belize			x	x			x
Benin			x	x	x		x
Bhutan							
Bolivia		x	x	x		x	x
Botswana				x			
Brazil			x	x		x	
Brunei Darussalam				x			
Bulgaria		x	x	x			x
Burkina Faso		x	x	x	x		x
Burundi			x	x			
Cambodia			x				
Cameroon			x	x	x	x	x
Canada		x	x	x		x	
Cape Verde			x				x
Central African Republic			x	x			x
Chad		x		x			x
Chile		x	x	x	x		x
China			x	x		x	
Colombia			x	x		x	x
Cook Islands							
Comoros							
Congo			x	x		x	x
Costa Rica			x	x			x
Cote d'Ivoire			x			x	x
Cuba			x	x			x
Cyprus			x	x			x
Czech & Slovak Fed. Rep.		x	x				

Parties	13	16	17	18	22	25	26
Democr. People's Rep. of Korea							x
Denmark		x	x	x	x	x	x
Djibouti							
Dominica			x				x
Dominican Republic				x			x
Ecuador		x	x	x		x	x
Egypt		x	x	x	x	x	x
El Salvador			x	x			x
Equatorial Guinea							x
Estonia*							
Ethiopia			x	x			x
Fiji			x				x
Finland		x	x	x	x	x	x
France		x	x	x	x	x	x
Gabon		x	x	x		x	x
Gambia			x	x			
Germany		x	x	x	x	x	x
Ghana		x	x	x	x	x	x
Greece		x	x			x	x
Grenada							x
Guatemala		x	x	x			
Guinea			x	x			x
Guinea-Bissau		x		x			
Guyana			x	x			
Haiti			x				x
Holy See			x				
Honduras			x	x		x	x
Hungary		x	x	x	x		x
Iceland	x	x					x
India		x	x	x	x	x	x
Indonesia			x	x		x	
Iran (Islamic Republic of)		x	x	x			x
Iraq			x				x
Ireland		x	x		x	x	x
Israel				x	x		x
Italy	x	x	x	x	x	x	x
Jamaica			x				x
Japan		x		x		x	
Jordan		x	x	x			
Kenya		x	x	x			x
Kiribati				x			
Kuwait							x
Lao People's Democratic Rep.			x				
Latvia*							

Parties	13	16	17	18	22	25	26
Lebanon			x				x
Lesotho							
Liberia				x		x	x
Libyan Arab Jamahiriya			x				x
Liechtenstein		x		x			x
Lithuania*							
Luxembourg	x		x	x	x	x	
Madagascar			x	x			x
Malawi			x	x			x
Malaysia			x	x		x	
Maldives			x				
Mali		x	x		x		x
Malta		x	x	x			
Marshall Islands							
Mauritania		x	x				x
Mauritius				x			x
Mexico		x	x	x			x
Micronesia							
Monaco			x	x			
Mongolia			x				
Morocco		x	x	x			x
Mozambique			x	x			x
Myanmar							
Namibia				x			
Nauru							
Nepal		x	x	x		x	x
Netherlands	x	x		x	x	x	x
New Zealand		x	x	x			x
Nicaragua			x	x			x
Niger		x	x	x	x		x
Nigeria			x	x	x		
Niue							
Norway		x	x	x	x	x	x
Oman			x				x
Pakistan		x	x	x	x		
Palau							
Panama		x	x	x	x	x	x
Papua New Guinea				x		x	
Paraguay			x	x			x
Peru			x	x		x	x
Philippines			x	x		x	x
Poland		x	x	x			x
Portugal		x	x	x	x	x	x
Qatar			x				

Parties	13	16	17	18	22	25	26
Republic of Korea			x			x	x
Republic of Yemen			x				x
Romania		x	x				
Rwanda				x			x
St. Kitts & Nevis			x				
St. Lucia			x	x			
St. Vincent & the Grenadines				x			
Samoa							x
San Marino			x				
Sao Tome & Principe							
Saudi Arabia			x		x		
Senegal		x	x	x	x		x
Seychelles			x	x			
Sierra Leone							x
Singapore				x			
Solomon Islands							x
Somalia				x	x		
South Africa		x		x	x		x
Spain	x	x	x	x	x	x	x
Sri Lanka		x	x	x	x		x
Sudan			x	x			x
Suriname		x		x			
Swaziland							
Sweden	x	x	x	x	x	x	x
Switzerland	x	x	x	x		x	x
Syrian Arab Republic			x				x
Thailand			x	x		x	
Togo				x		x	x
Tonga							x
Trinidad & Tobago				x		x	x
Tunisia		x	x	x	x		x
Turkey	x		x				x
Tuvalu							
Uganda		x	x	x			
Ukraine*			x				
Union of Soviet Socialist Rep.*		x	x	x		x	x
United Arab Emirates				x			
United Kingdom		x	x	x	x	x	x
United Republic of Tanzania			x	x			x
United States of America		x	x	x		x	
Uruguay		x	x	x	x		
Vanuatu				x			
Venezuela		x	x	x			
Viet Nam		x	x				

Parties	13	16	17	18	22	25	26
Yugoslavia*	x	x	x				x
Zaire			x	x	x		
Zambia		x	x	x			x
Zimbabwe			x	x			x
European Economic Community					x	x	

REGIONAL INSTRUMENTS

(12) <u>Convention on Nature Protection and Wildlife Preservation in the Western Hemisphere</u> (Washington 1940)

Argentina	Mexico
Brazil	Nicaragua
Chile	Panama
Costa Rica	Peru
Dominican Republic	Trinidad and Tobago
Ecuador	United States of America
El Salvador	Uruguay
Guatemala	Venezuela
Haiti	

(14) <u>Antarctic Treaty</u> (Washington 1959)

Argentina	Hungary
Australia	India
Austria	Italy
Belgium	Japan
Brazil	Netherlands
Bulgaria	New Zealand
Canada	Norway
Chile	Papua New Guinea
China	Peru
Colombia	Poland
Cuba	Republic of Korea
Czech & Slovak Fed. Rep.	Romania
Democr. People's Rep. of Korea	South Africa
Denmark	Spain
Ecuador ·	Sweden
Finland	Switzerland
France	United Kingdom
Germany	USSR*
Greece	United States of America
Guatemala	Uruguay

(15) <u>African Convention on the Conservation of Nature and Natural Resources</u> (Algiers 1968)

Algeria	Morocco
Burkina Faso	Mozambique
Cameroon	Niger
Central African Republic	Nigeria
Congo	Rwanda
Cote d'Ivoire	Senegal
Djibouti	Seychelles
Egypt	Sudan
Gabon	Swaziland
Ghana	Togo
Kenya	Tunisia

Liberia
Madagascar
Malawi
Mali

Uganda
United Republic of Tanzania
Zaire
Zambia

(19) <u>Agreement on Conservation of Polar Bears</u> (Oslo 1973)

Canada
Denmark
Germany

Norway
USSR*
United States of America

(20) <u>Convention on Conservation of Nature in the South Pacific</u> (Apia 1976)

Australia
Cook Islands
Fiji
France
Samoa

(21) <u>Treaty for Amazonian Co-operation</u> (Brasilia 1978)

Bolivia
Brazil
Colombia
Ecuador

Guyana
Peru
Suriname
Venezuela

(23) <u>Convention on the Conservation of European Wildlife and Natural Habitats</u> (Berne 1979)

Austria
Belgium
Burkina Faso
Bulgaria
Cyprus
Denmark
Finland
France
Germany
Greece
Hungary
Ireland
Italy

Liechtenstein
Luxembourg
Netherlands
Norway
Portugal
Senegal
Spain
Sweden
Switzerland
Turkey
United Kingdom
European Economic Community

(24) <u>Convention for the Conservation and Management of the Vicuna</u> (Lima 1979)

Bolivia
Chile
Ecuador
Peru

* Membership status subject to further clarification.

CHAPTER III

ATMOSPHERE AND OUTER SPACE

Richard E. Benedick and Ricardo Pronove III

This chapter covers the following agreements and instruments on the environmental aspects of atmosphere and outer space, in chronological order;

(28)   The ECE Regulations Concerning Gaseous Pollutant Emissions from Motor Vehicles, pursuant to the 1958 **Agreement Concerning the Adoption of Uniform Conditions of Approval and Reciprocal Recognition of Approval of Motor Vehicle Equipment and Parts**, as amended and supplemented;

(29)   the 1967 **Outer Space Treaty**, and related instruments;

(30)   Annex 16 on Environmental Protection to the 1944 Chicago **Convention on International Civil Aviation**;

(31)   the 1979 Geneva **Convention on Long-range Transboundary Air Pollution**;

(32)   the 1980 UNEP **Provisions for Co-operation Between States on Weather Modification**; and

(33)   the 1985 Vienna **Convention for the Protection of the Ozone Layer**, with its 1987 Montreal **Protocol on Substances That Deplete the Ozone Layer**.

A list showing the status of ratifications as of 1 January 1992 is annexed (pages 144 - 148).

(28) ECE Regulations Concerning Gaseous Pollutant Emissions from Motor Vehicles, pursuant to the Agreement Concerning the Adoption of Uniform Conditions of Approval and Reciprocal Recognition of Approval for Motor Vehicle Equipment and Parts
(Geneva, 20 March 1958), as amended and supplemented

Objectives and achievement

The basic objectives of these technical regulations - which since 1970 have included rules on permissible exhaust emissions for petrol and diesel engines - are to define uniform conditions for licensing of motor vehicles and parts in the European region. While most of the over 90 regulations adopted focus on safety, they also standardize a growing range of environmental specifications for vehicle construction.

Though regional in origin, some of the Regulations are followed on a voluntary basis by a number of States outside Europe (e.g., Australia and New Zealand), including developing countries such as Singapore. Car manufacturers comply with the Regulations in order to obtain type approval for imports in all States following these standards.

The regulations have achieved a high degree of standardization of environmental requirements for motor vehicle construction and trade. Voluntary acceptance by non-member States may also be considered a success indicator.

Participation

Membership is currently restricted to member States of the United Nations Economic Commission for Europe (ECE) and States having consultative status with ECE. No reservations are permitted, except on the dispute settlement clause of Article 10, on which several countries have actually made reservations.

The current membership of 21 States includes 2 developing countries in Europe. Several developing countries apply the ECE Regulations on a voluntary basis.

The principal factor influencing participation has been the administrative and commercial advantage of uniform licensing regulations for trade in motor vehicles and parts. Environmental factors have, however, begun to influence participation, as several States have withdrawn from regulations which they do no consider sufficiently strict for pollution control purposes.

Implementation and information

Only two ratifications are required to bring new regulations into force, which has facilitated rapid implementation.

The Agreement requires mutual recognition of foreign documentation for motor vehicle licensing and the adjustment of national administrative procedures and controls for this purpose. Technical verification of compliance is left entirely to national authorities, and no international monitoring is foreseen. Parties only report information on their designated national agencies authorized to issue licensing documents in accordance with the Agreement.

Article 10 provides for dispute settlement, including recourse to international arbitration; however, Article 11 allows reservations on this clause (see section B above).

Implementation of the Agreement is influenced mainly by the effectiveness of national administrative institutions for motor vehicle licensing in member States.

The texts of the Agreement and its Regulations, as well as explanatory materials published by the ECE secretariat are available in English, French and Russian (e.g., "Transport Information 1990") and are distributed to Governments, the automobile industry and the general public.

Operation, review and adjustment

Regulations pursuant to the 1958 Agreement are adopted and revised by the ECE Inland Transport Committee, upon recommendation by its Working Party on the Construction of Vehicles (WP. 29). The preparation of environment-related Regulations is carried out through regular expert meetings in a sub-group on Pollution and Energy. Secretariat functions are performed by the ECE Transport Division. The costs of meetings, documentation and secretariat services for the Agreement and its Regulations are covered by the regular ECE budget (currently 2 professionals, 2 secretaries, and about 20 meetings annually).

The main benefits to member States relate to standardization of administrative procedures and removal of trade barriers for motor vehicles and parts, and the regular adjustment of national standards in accordance with international developments in vehicle safety and environmental protection. The main costs relate to the participation of national representatives in ECE meetings. No possibilities are available to reduce participation costs for developing countries.

The Agreement and its Regulations are regularly reviewed and revised at the meetings of the ECE Inland Transport Committee and its subsidiary expert groups. Representatives of national licensing authorities participate as members of delegations, and representatives of the automobile industry and other non-governmental organizations participate as observers.

Amendment of the Agreement is facilitated by the "tacit consent" procedure stipulated in Article 13, which brings amendments into force automatically in the absence of formal objections within a specified time period.

Codification programming

The two basic Regulations on pollutant emissions (No. 49 for diesel engines and No. 83 for gasoline engines) were revised at the 44th session of the ECE Inland Transport Committee in order to harmonize them with the recently amended "Clean Car" Directive of the European Community; both amendments are expected to enter into force on 1 January 1993. The Committee also recommended amendments to the 1958 Agreement, mainly with a view to taking into account recent environmental and safety developments in addition to the Agreement's traditional trade orientation. It has been proposed, furthermore, to broaden participation in the Agreement to include the European Community and member States of other UN regional commissions which will require changes in governance arrangements.

There is close co-ordination with related drafting work on directives for motor vehicles in the European Community, and with technical standards in the International Organization for Standardization.

(29) Treaty on Principles Governing the Activities of States in the Exploration and Use of Outer Space, including the Moon and other Celestial Bodies

(London, Moscow, Washington, 27 January 1967), and related agreements

Objectives and Achievement

Through the U.N. Committee on the Peaceful Uses of Outer Space (COPUOS), five treaties have been codified and three sets of principles have been endorsed. Although the treaties focus particularly on the peaceful exploration and utilization of space and celestial bodies, they contain provisions relating to States' responsibility in ensuring that their space activities do not harm the environment. The treaties that contain specific provision on environmental protection are, in addition to the 1967 Outer Space Treaty: the 1968 **Agreement on the Rescue of Astronauts, the Return of Astronauts and the Return of Objects Launched into Outer Space** (the Rescue Agreement); the 1972 **Convention on International Liability for Damage Caused by Space Objects** (the Liability Convention) and the 1979 **Agreement Governing the Activities of States on the Moon and Other Celestial Bodies** (the Moon Treaty). A fundamental premise of these treaties is that States should conduct their space activities with due regard to the peaceful co-existence of humanity and to the preservation of the space and Earth environment. In addition, States are urged to make available the benefits of the space technology to all countries, particularly the developing countries.

The specific provisions in the respective space treaties that relate to the environment and development are as follows:

<u>The Outer Space Treaty</u>

Article I calls for the exploration and use of outer space for the benefit of all countries, implying that space activities should promote the improvement of all humankind, including economic development.

Article IV obliges States to avoid nuclear contamination by not placing nuclear weapons around the Earth.

Article VI makes States internationally responsible for their national space activities, whether such activities are carried on by governmental agencies or non-governmental agencies. This responsibility would extend to any resulting environmental harm.

Article VII extends liability to States which have space objects that cause harm to another State, to its persons or on Earth.

Article IX, which is considered the primary article dealing with the environment, obliges States to conduct space exploration without interfering with rights of other States to engage in space activities and without introducing extraterrestrial matter that caused harmful contamination and adverse changes on the Earth.

The Rescue Agreement

Article 5 specifies that a State can take immediate action to eliminate possible harm of a space object that has landed in its territory if it is "hazardous" or "deleterious".

The Liability Convention

Generally, the Liability Convention seeks to enforce environmental protection by making States liable for space activities.
Article II provides that States will be absolutely liable for damage caused by its space objects on Earth.
Article VIII provides for a compensation scheme that an injured State may present to the liable State, Articles IX through XII describe how the claim for compensation should be pursued. By including a compensation claim provision, the Convention seeks to enforce the liability for harm that a space object can cause, including environmental harm.

The Registration Convention

Article 2 calls for U.N. registration of a space object that is launched into Earth orbit or beyond and Article 4 describes the type of information that should be provided. One of the purposes of this Convention is to allow for the gathering of information for proof of harm that could result on the Earth from a space activity.

The Moon Treaty

Article 7 obliges States to take measures to avoid harmfully affecting the environment of the Earth through the introduction of extraterrestrial matter or otherwise, implying that no forms of contamination should cause harm to the environment. Pursuant to Article 7, States must inform the U.N. Secretary General of any measures that are being adopted that may affect the Earth environment.

In addition to the space treaties, COPUOS agreed to a set of **Principles Relating to Remote Sensing of the Earth from Space**, adopted by U.N. General Assembly Resolution 41/65 of 3 December 1986. These Principles deal specifically with the effect and benefit of the application of space technology for the environment and development. Generally, the Principles recognize the utility of environmental data for resource management and development and call for the promotion of international cooperation regarding the disclosure of remote sensing data. According to Principle 1, the term remote sensing is the survey of the Earth's surface from space for the purpose of "improving natural resources management, land use and protection of the environment".

All of the above-mentioned instruments are global in scope. The 1967 Outer Space Treaty, as well as other space treaties and principles recognized that space exploration and use must benefit all countries, regardless of their level of development because space is the province of all humankind.

Through the process of codifying the space treaties which encourage the promotion of space exploration for all countries and the preservation of the environment, and by the drafting of new space law, COPUOS and the Secretariat can measure the achievements and progress of the space law instruments. During the COPUOS sessions and its two Subcommittees, the Scientific and Technical and Legal Subcommittees, the 53 Member States report on their respective space activities and progress they have achieved. This information is provided in the context of space treaties and principles already endorsed, e.g., in promotion of the remote sensing principles. In addition, the Secretariat provides documentation on programmes, seminars and workshops it sponsors through the Space Applications Programme of the U.N. Outer Space Affairs Division which promote the principles of the space law treaties.

Annually, the Inter-Agency Co-ordination Committee comprised of directors and experts in the United Nations system report on the progress of their space applications programmes that seek to monitor the environment, manage resources and promote economic development.

The space law treaties call for States to inform the Secretary-General of their space activities. Through the provisions of the Registration Convention, specifically Article IV, the international community is put on notice about the types of objects that are in space which could possibly cause harm to the environment or which are used to monitor the environment.

Participation

Membership in the above-mentioned instruments is open to all States. The space treaties contain no provisions on reservations. Dispute resolution is generally referred to consultations (Article IX of the Outer Space Treaty, Article XV of the Moon Treaty), to a Claims Commission (under the Liability Convention), or generally to "established procedures for peaceful settlement" (Remote Sensing Principles).

The developing countries have participated in the negotiation and drafting of the space law instruments. Nearly sixty percent of the membership of COPUOS is represented by developing countries. During the COPUOS sessions and its subcommittees, a special working group of the Group of 77 convene informally and submit working papers and statements concerning the application and promotion of space technology for their development. The participation and interests of the developing countries is demonstrated with the introduction of the newest item for the development of a set of draft principles for the dissemination of space technology to the developing countries.

One of the main purposes for establishing COPUOS was to study practical and feasible means to encourage international programmes in space activities. In accordance with the recommendations of the Second United Nations Conference on the Exploration and Peaceful Uses of Outer Space (UNISPACE) held in 1982, which focused on improving the effectiveness of institutional means of providing the benefits of space technology, the United Nations has conducted studies on space activities and their implication, and has sponsored workshops and seminary through its Programme on Space Applications to provide education and training in the fields of remote sensing, satellite communications, meteorology and basic space science in developing countries. The Inter-Agency Co-ordination Committee (described above) reviews the status and plans for fellowships, training, education and availability of expert services by the United Nations system for developing countries.

Codification programming

COPUOS is currently finalizing a set of **Draft Principles Relevant to the Use of Nuclear Power Sources in Outer Space**. These Draft Principles will represent international legal recommendations ensuring that nuclear power space missions are used as safely as possible to avoid any potential radiation contamination of the Earth.

Also, COPUOS has as a new agenda item "Legal Aspects Related to the Application of the Principle that the Exploration and Utilization of Outer Space should be carried out for the Benefit and in the Interests of All States, taking into Particular Account the Needs of Developing Countries". Through this draft Principle, COPUOS will seek to promote the principles of space law including the preservation of the Earth environment and the dissemination of space technology to developing countries.

In addition to the Earth environment, the issue of the problem of space debris and space pollution has received increasing attention. This problem could present an obstacle to future space development, particularly for the developing countries which have just started their space programmes or are planning the implementation of a space programme. During the 46th session, the U.N. General Assembly therefore called attention to the problem of space debris and considered that it could be an appropriate topic for in-depth discussion by the Committee on the Peaceful Uses of Outer Space.

(30) Annex 16 on Environmental Protection, to the 1944 Chicago Convention on International Civil Aviation
(Montreal, vol. I: Aircraft Noise, 1971; vol. II:
Aircraft Engine Emissions, 1981), as amended

Objectives and achievement

The objectives of these international standards and recommended practices, which were adopted by the Council of the International Civil Aviation Organization (ICAO) pursuant to Articles 37 and 54 of the Convention, are to standardize the required emissions limits for aircraft noise and gaseous pollutants, by way of uniform certification procedures. These provisions aim at reconciling the economic requirements of air transport development with environmental requirements, especially in the vicinity of airports.

The ICAO standards are global in scope. The possibility of national departures from global standards, provided under Article 38 of the Convention, was designed to allow a measure of flexibility especially for the benefit of developing countries.

The objectives are considered to have been met in that all newly designed aircraft engines meet the requirements of Annex 16, although a number of countries have filed notifications under Article 38 regarding different national standards.

Participation

Membership is open to all States. The current ICAO membership of 164 States includes 132 developing countries. Instead of reservations, national differences in standards are notified through the procedure under Article 38 of the Convention.

Annex 16 was originally drafted by a 14-member committee of experts nominated by States plus observers from international organization. Participation by developing countries has been very low, despite efforts to attract further nominations. There are no special incentives to encourage participation.

Implementation and information

Entry into force of ICAO Annexes is facilitated by a "tacit consent" procedure, enabling dissenting countries to notify their differences within a specified time limit, after which the Annexes become generally applicable. Notifications of national differences in standards are recorded and regularly communicated to all members, by way of supplements to Annexes. With regard to Annex 16, vol. II (aircraft engine emissions) as of January 1992, 11 member States had notified national differences, while 22 had reported conformity. The remaining 131 members are presumed to be tacitly conforming.

Provisions for dispute settlement and non-compliance are contained in Articles 84-88 of the Convention. Disputes are normally considered by the ICAO Council, with possible recourse to international arbitration or adjudication.

Potential factors affecting compliance include technical difficulties in meeting the requirements, disagreement with the need for specific aspects of the requirement and the cost of compliance testing. A problem of major concern to developing countries (as expressed in ICAO Assembly Resolution A28-3) are unilateral or regional operating restrictions on older aircraft not conforming to Annex 16.

Annex 16 is available in Arabic, English, French, Russian and Spanish. The ICAO secretariat publishes a wide range of information materials for Governments and public distribution. No technical guidance materials on Annex 16 have been issued.

Operation, review and adjustment

Annexes are adopted and revised by the ICAO Council upon recommendation by an expert committee. Administrative functions under the Chicago Convention are performed by the ICAO secretariat in Montreal (Canada). Several ad hoc meetings of expert committees on Annex 16 have been held since 1978. Costs of meetings, documentation and secretariat services are covered by the regular ICAO budget.

The main benefits of national participation in Annex 16 relate to environmental improvements through reduced engine emissions in the vicinity of airports. The main costs relate to the need for more sophisticated engine technology which is reflected in increased cost of aircraft.

Continuous review of Annex 16 by the expert committee and the ICAO Council takes into account inputs from manufacturers, operators, airport management, etc. The flexible ICAO procedure for amendment of technical annexes allows timely adjustment. An amendment to Annex 16, vol. II adopted on 4 March 1988 thus became nationally applicable on 17 November 1988.

Codification programming

The second meeting of the ICAO Committee on Aviation Environmental Protection, held in Montreal from 2 to 13 December 1991, recommended to the ICAO Council to tighten the standards for emissions of nitrogen oxides under Annex 16 (II) by 20%. The Committee also recommended changes to its work programme which will focus attention on the effects and control of aircraft engine emissions at high altitude.

There is currently no co-ordination with drafting work regarding other international agreements or instruments.

(31) Convention on Long-Range Transboundary Air Pollution
(Geneva, 13 November 1979), and related protocols

Objectives and achievement

The basic objectives of the Convention, concluded within the regional framework of the UN Economic Commission for Europe (ECE), are "to limit and, as far as possible, gradually reduce and prevent air pollution including long-range transboundary pollution" (Article 2). For this purpose, the Parties undertake "to develop the best policies and strategies including air quality management systems, and, as part of them, control measures compatible with balanced development, in particular by using the best available technology which is economically feasible and low- and non-waste technology" (Article 6).

The ECE region, comprising Europe and North America, accounts for about three quarters of global air pollution and is the heaviest consumer of natural resources and energy. The Convention which deals with problems of air pollution of the ECE region has therefore an important bearing on global environmental protection as well as potential impact on promoting sustainable development.

The Convention is the outcome of protracted East-West negotiation in the wake of the 1975 Helsinki Conference on Security and Co-operation in Europe. There is no reference to the special circumstances of developing countries.

After the entry into force of the Convention in 1983, the following supplementary protocols were concluded:

- the 1984 Geneva **Protocol on Long-term Financing of the Co-operative Programme for Monitoring and Evaluation of the Long-range Transmission of Air Pollutants in Europe** (EMEP), originally established in 1977 and consisting of a sampling network of 96 stations in 24 countries, co-ordinated by centres in Norway and the USSR;

- the 1985 Helsinki **Protocol on the Reduction of Sulphur Emissions or Their Transboundary Fluxes by at least 30 per cent** (by the year 1993, using 1980 levels as a basis), ratified by 20 States;

- the 1988 Sofia **Protocol concerning the Control of Emissions of Nitrogen Oxides or Their Transboundary Fluxes** (providing for a freeze of national emissions at 1987 levels by 1994, together with a package of abatement measures), ratified by 18 States, with a technical annex amended in 1991; and

- the 1991 Geneva **Protocol concerning the Control of Emissions of Volatile Organic Compounds or Their Transboundary Fluxes** (providing for a range of options for emission abatement, with four technical annexes), not yet in force.

A recent review showed that at least 24 Parties to the Convention had achieved a net reduction of sulphur emissions as compared to 1980; 12 countries had already reduced their emissions by 30% or more. Overall sulphur emissions in Europe dropped by 22% between 1980 and 1990. Ten countries have announced long-term national reductions of about 50% or more, four of these by even more than 65%.

Participation

Membership is restricted to ECE member States and regional economic integration organizations (the EC) and States having consultative status with ECE. Reservations are not foreseen and have not been entered.

Of the 33 Parties to the Convention, 4 are European developing countries; 2 other developing countries in Europe have not yet joined. Special efforts are made in the context of an ECE/UNDP project and through bilateral programmes, to assist these countries so as to enable them to implement or join the Convention. Among the factors influencing participation in the Convention and its protocols, the availability and public dissemination of scientific data obtained through the EMEP monitoring programme and other co-operative programmes on air pollution effects probably played a significant role.

Implementation and information

The Convention took more than three years to enter into force, as it required a minimum of 24 ratifications. However, the signatories had by special resolution agreed to implement the Convention on an interim basis, with an Interim Executive Body taking up its functions soon after signature and converting itself into a permanent institution (representing all Parties) in 1983.

Compliance with the commitments specified in Articles 2-9 of the Convention (including the obligation to submit annual reports and other information) is reviewed by the Executive Body at its annual meetings and in special four-year reviews undertaken on the basis of detailed questionnaires. At the same time, monitoring data on actual depositions of air pollution are collected and analyzed under the EMEP programme and submitted to the Executive Body. For the 1990 major review, 24 of the 32 Parties submitted their national reports, though several incomplete.

The national emissions data and other information required from Parties under Article 4 of the Helsinki Protocol and Article 8 of the Sofia Protocol are further specified in work plans for implementation of the Convention, adopted annually by the Executive Body. Annual data reporting to the EMEP international centres is generally satisfactory; major problems in the past concerned members recording "transboundary fluxes" rather than emissions of pollutants. Periodic public review of national reports and the data collected through EMEP and other co-operative programmes under the Convention has served as an effective mechanism to induce compliance. The publicity caused by NGO participation in the annual review meetings may be considered a contributing factor.

The dispute settlement clause of Article 13, which generally refers to negotiation or any other method acceptable to the parties, has not been invoked so far.

Factors influencing the implementation of the Convention include the availability of financial resources, and in the case of some Parties, technical and scientific assistance.

The Convention and its protocols were issued and distributed as ECE documents in English, French and Russian; they have been reproduced in numerous collections of international legal texts. Translations into other languages were published in the Official Journal of the European Communities, and in national legislative series. Current information on the operation and implementation of the Convention and its protocols is disseminated through documents for ECE meetings, the ECE "Air Pollution Studies" series, the unofficial "MonitAir" newsletter of the EMEP programme, public information brochures, etc.

In the context of EMEP and other monitoring programmes under the Convention, special manuals have been issued for the guidance of participating national institutions. Guidelines have also been developed and distributed for emission inventories and for uniform calculation of pollution control costs. Information documents and reports are provided upon request to schools and universities for use in both undergraduate and postgraduate programmes.

Operation, review and adjustment

Secretariat functions pursuant to Article 11 of the Convention are carried out by the UN Economic Commission for Europe, through the Air Pollution Section of the ECE Environment and Human Settlements Division in Geneva. Costs of meetings, documentation and secretariat services are covered from the regular ECE budget. International co-ordination costs for the EMEP programme are financed by assessed contributions from the Parties to a UN-administered trust fund (approximately $1 million for 1990); for other co-operative programmes and task forces, by voluntary contributions of "lead countries" and participating Parties.

The benefits of national participation in the co-operative programmes established under the Convention include access to specialized information, international scientific co-operation and expertise as a basis for national decision-making. The main cost elements are travel and participation expenses for national experts. While there are no formal procedures to reduce participation costs for developing countries, informal arrangements are frequently made to enable experts from economies in transition to participate in projects and meetings.

Following its re-structuring in November 1991, the Executive Body for the Convention has established several standing subsidiary bodies to provide the necessary scientific expert advice for policy-making decisions:

(a) the Working Group on (Air Pollution) Effects;

(b) the Working Group on Strategies with task forces on assessment modelling, emission projections and economic aspects;

(c) the EMEP Steering Body; and

(d) the Working Group on Technology.

The co-operative programmes established under the Convention operate by direct contact between the national environmental authorities and scientific institutions concerned. Non-governmental organizations and industry representatives participate regularly as observers in the meetings of the Executive Body and its subsidiary bodies.

Article 5 of the Sofia Protocol provides for systematic review of the protocol one year after its entry into force, taking into account the best available scientific substantiation and technological development; and for negotiations, starting no later than six months after entry into force, on further steps towards emission reductions. The Working Group on (Abatement) Strategies was established with a mandate, inter alia, to serve as a forum for this process. In a series of semi-annual meetings and in co-operation with other subsidiary bodies, it developed the "critical loads" approach as a basis for further regulatory action.

Codification programming

A revision of the 1985 Protocol on sulphur emissions is under preparation. Controls for transboundary air pollution by persistent organic compounds and by emissions of heavy metals have been identified as future priorities, and preparatory work on these topics was initiated in 1990.

Drafting work is co-ordinated, through the ECE secretariat, with other competent bodies, especially as regards airborne pollution of adjacent regional sea areas (e.g., the Baltic Sea, through the Helsinki Commission, see No. 44; and the North Sea, through the Oslo/Paris Commission, see Nos. 43/45).

(32) UNEP Provisions for Co-operation Between States in Weather Modification
(Decision 8/7/A of the Governing Council of UNEP, 29 April 1980)

These non-mandatory provisions were prepared by an informal UNEP/WMO working group of legal and scientific experts in 1975 and 1978, followed by governmental comments (WMO/UNEP/WG.26/5), and a further 1979 meeting of governmentally designated experts on the legal aspects of weather modification (WMO/UNEP/WG.26/8). After endorsement by the UNEP Governing Council, they were circulated to all States in July 1980 for "consideration in the formulation and implementation of programmes and activities relating to the field of weather modification", together with a set of Draft Guidelines for National Legislation concerning Weather Modification (WMO/UNEP/WG.26/6). They were issued in Arabic Chinese, English, French, Russian and Spanish as UNEP Environmental Law Guidelines and Principles No.3.

The provisions define weather modification activities as "any action performed with the intention of producing artificial changes in the properties of the atmosphere for purposes such as increasing, decreasing or redistributing precipitation or cloud coverage, moderating severe storms and tropical cyclones, decreasing or suppressing hail or lightning or dissipating fog". Because of the potential implications for agricultural development in particular, these issues have been of concern to a number of developing countries.

The main objectives of the provisions are to ensure that weather modification activities are conducted in a manner designed not to cause damage to the environment of other States or of areas beyond the limits of national jurisdiction, and that timely notifications and consultations are undertaken for this purpose.

Although the Governing Council in its decision requested follow-up reporting from WMO and the UNEP Executive Directory on a periodic basis, no such reports appear to have been submitted.

(33) Vienna Convention for the Protection of the Ozone Layer
(Vienna, 22 March 1985) and
Montreal Protocol on Substances That Deplete the Ozone Layer
(Montreal, 16 September 1987)

Objectives and achievement

The basic objectives of the Vienna Convention are "to protect human health and the environment against adverse effects resulting or likely to result from human activities which modify or are likely to modify the ozone layer" by adopting agreed measures to control human activities found to have adverse effects (art.2), by cooperating in scientific research and systematic observations (art.3), and by exchanging information in the legal, scientific, and technical fields (art.4). The Vienna Convention is the basic international instrument for "harmonizing the policies and strategies on research" (UNEP/OzL.Conv.2/3,p.4). The World Meteorological Organization (WMO), together with UNEP, plays a central role in this scientific effort.

The basic objectives of the Montreal Protocol are "to protect the ozone layer by taking precautionary measures to control equitably total global emissions of substances that deplete it, with the ultimate objective of their elimination on the basis of developments in scientific knowledge, taking into account technical and economic considerations and bearing in mind the developmental needs of developing countries" (preamble). The protocol is the basic international instrument for "achieving the harmonization of policies, strategies and measures for minimizing the release of substances causing or likely to cause modifications of the ozone layer" (UNEP/OzL.Conv.2/3,p.4).

These objectives relate importantly to effective integration of environment and development. Depletion of the ozone layer could adversely affect development prospects by aggravating health problems (skin cancer, cataracts, damage to the human immune system), reducing agricultural productivity, and affecting animal life, including the marine food chain. In addition, some of the controlled ozone-depleting substances are also major greenhouse gases; therefore, their limitation would help to mitigate adverse impacts of climate change on development, including changes in rainfall patterns, effects on agriculture, and rising sea level. Finally, the treaties' objectives involve, as detailed below, measures to assist developing countries to obtain advanced technologies for replacing or avoiding use of the controlled substances.

The Convention and its protocol are global in scope. The Vienna Convention commits parties to cooperate in research and development and transfer of technology and knowledge "taking into account in particular the needs of the developing countries" (art.4). The Montreal Protocol provides for a grace period for the implementation of control measures by developing countries (art.5), for a special financial mechanism to assist developing countries (art.10), and for transfer of technology to developing countries "under fair and most favourable conditions" (art.10A).

Achievement of objectives, as described below, has been considered and documented at the 1989, 1990, and 1991 annual Meetings of Parties to the Montreal Protocol and the 1989 and 1991 biennial Conferences of Parties to the Vienna Convention. Based on these reports, there has been considerable progress in achieving the objectives of the agreements. There has been intensive expanded international cooperation in research, monitoring, and exchange of information, including the formation of industrial consortia for cooperation in development and testing of alternatives to controlled substances. Production and consumption of controlled substances has declined substantially since the Montreal Protocol was signed, with most countries being well ahead of the treaty timetables. New technologies and substitute products have been, or are being, developed, and information and technology are being transferred to developing countries. Finally, more and more governments have accepted the commitments of the Montreal Protocol since the original 24 countries signed the treaty on 16 September 1987.

Participation

Membership is open. As of 1 January 1992, the Vienna Convention had 81 States Parties (plus the EEC), of which 49 were developing countries from every geographical region. The Montreal Protocol as of the same date had 75 States Parties (plus the EEC), of which 43 were developing countries with a similarly broad geographic distribution.

No reservations are admissible (Vienna Convention and Montreal Protocol, art.18).

Developing countries have had an active and expanding role in the negotiating and drafting of both agreements as well as in programme activities and working parties. For example, at the September 1987 negotiating session for the Montreal Protocol, over 60 nations participated, of which more than half were developing countries. Two and one-half years later, at the critical second Meeting of Parties in London in June 1990, during which the protocol was significantly strengthened and amended, 95 governments were represented, the great majority being from developing countries. Significantly, both parties and governments that were not yet parties (mainly developing countries) participated on an equal basis in the process of revising the original Montreal Protocol. This quality of participation has also characterized intersessional meetings.

The original Montreal Protocol signed in 1987 established a ten-year grace period before developing countries were obligated to follow the agreed reduction schedule for controlled substances (art.5). At the second Meeting of Parties in 1990, an Interim Multilateral Ozone Fund was established, with an initial three-year budget of up to US$ 240 million, to meet agreed incremental costs to developing countries of implementing the control measures (art.10). (When the protocol amendment enters into force in 1992, the "interim" fund will formally become the Multilateral Ozone Fund.) In addition, the revised protocol now contains a commitment "to ensure that the best available, environmentally safe substitutes and related technologies are expeditiously transferred [to developing countries]...under fair and most favourable conditions" (art.10A). Finally, the Montreal Protocol explicitly recognizes that "developing the capacity to fulfil the obligations [of developing countries]...to comply with the control measures...and their implementation by those same Parties will depend upon the effective implementation of the financial co-operation as provided by Article 10 and transfer of technology as provided by Article 10A" (art.5).

In accordance with article 4 of the Vienna Convention and article 10 of the Montreal Protocol, technical and financial assistance have been provided to developing countries to promote their participation in the process, including attendance at working party and intersessional meetings. According to information from the UNEP secretariat, the cost of participation of representatives from developing countries in meetings convened under the Vienna Convention and the Montreal Protocol in 1991 is estimated at US$ 820,000, which was met from the following sources: Vienna Convention Trust Fund, Montreal Protocol

Trust Fund, Finnish Ozone Trust Fund, and counterpart contributions. The 1992-1993 budget approved by the third Meeting of Parties to the Montreal Protocol includes estimated costs to support participation of representatives of developing countries of US$ 480,000 for 1992 and US$ 576,000 for 1993. It was noted at that meeting that there were substantial arrearages in agreed contributions by parties to the Vienna Convention and Montreal Protocol Trust Funds, and that the continued participation of representatives of developing countries was critically dependent on timely payment of outstanding pledges. Moreover, the UNEP Executive Director observed that "the Montreal Protocol and Vienna Convention Trust Funds are inadequate to assure the full participation of representatives from developing countries in the coming years" (UNEP/OzL.Pro.3/9, p.3).

The participation of countries -- developing as well as industrialized -- in the treaties was primarily motivated by a genuine and shared concern over the long-term risks to the environment, human health, and the development process itself if the ozone layer were allowed to deteriorate. Certainly the provision of financial assistance and technology were crucial factors, but it is interesting to note that even before these articles were explicitly agreed at the second Meeting of Parties in 1990, 28 developing country Governments (and 30 industrialized countries) had already ratified the protocol. Another favorable factor influencing the participation of developing countries was the adoption by the second Meeting of Parties in 1990 of balanced voting procedures for major revisions and decisions under the protocol, requiring a two-thirds majority of parties, comprising separate simple majorities among industrialized and developing countries.

Implementation and information

The Montreal Protocol entered in force as scheduled on 1 January 1989 when 29 governments, representing an estimated 83 percent of 1986 global consumption of controlled substances, had ratified the protocol; the treaty actually required only 11 nations representing at least two-thirds of global consumption (art.16). The amendment agreed to at the 1990 second Meeting of Parties -- which, among other features, added new chemicals to the list of controlled substances and established the financial mechanism -- was to enter into force on 1 January 1992, provided that at least 20 Parties had ratified the amendment (annex 2, art.2). This condition has not been met so far. In addition, other major adjustments and decisions agreed to at the 1990 Meeting of Parties -- including substantial strengthening of the reduction schedules for the original controlled substances, and the establishment of an Interim Multilateral Ozone Fund -- entered into force automatically in March 1991.

These are relatively expeditious provisions for entry into force. Significantly, most parties -- developing and industrialized countries alike -- have not waited for formal entry into force before implementing fundamental elements of the treaty, including reductions in production and consumption of controlled substances and development and transfer of technology. The primary motivation for this has been a universal recognition of the planetary dangers as the science continued to evolve.

Under the Vienna Convention, Parties report to the secretariat a summary of measures undertaken in the various categories of scientific research and cooperation, and these are reviewed and discussed at the biennial Conference of Parties. Under the Montreal Protocol, Parties are committed to: control measures to reduce production and consumption of specific substances (art.2); control of trade with non-parties (art.4); regularly scheduled assessment and review of control measures (art.6); reporting of data (art.7); co-operation in research, development, public awareness, and exchange of information (art.9); and establishment of a financial mechanism and transfer of technology (art.10 and 10A).

The heart of the Montreal Protocol obligations are the article 2 control measures relating to substances that deplete the ozone layer. As amended by the 1990 second Meeting of Parties, these commitments involve the phaseout of a specified list of chlorofluorocarbons and halons, and of carbon tetrachloride, by the year 2000, and the phaseout of methyl chloroform by 2005, with scheduled interim reductions for each of the above classes of chemicals.

Compliance with articles 2 and 4 is monitored and measured through the specific reporting requirements of article 7. Compliance with obligations in general is monitored through consultations among the parties and with the secretariat, through the Executive Committee of the Multilateral Ozone Fund (which comprises seven representatives each from industrialized and developing nations), and through deliberations of the annual Meeting of Parties.

Parties to the Montreal Protocol provide to the secretariat annual statistical data on production, imports, and exports of controlled substances, including imports and exports to Parties and non-Parties (art.7). There have been some problems regarding the completeness of data provided, both by industrialized and by developing countries (UNEP/OzL.Pro.3/L.4/Add.1). It has been recognized by the Parties that failure to report the required data could result in a situation of non-compliance.

At the third Meeting of Parties to the Montreal Protocol in June 1991, the Implementation Committee noted that reporting was not satisfactory: of 71 Parties (at that time), only 31 had reported complete data for 1986, which is the base year used to calculate required phasedowns of the original list of controlled substances. Of the remainder, 19 Parties had reported incomplete data, 6 had reported no data available and/or requested assistance, 2 had reported that their data were included in those of another party, and 13 Parties, including 4 EEC countries, had not reported data. Of 48 Parties required to report data for 1989, the base year for substances added to the controlled list at the 1990 Meeting of Parties, only 23 Parties had complied by May 1991, and only 20 had submitted complete data.

It was further noted that some developing countries were experiencing serious reporting problems owing to lack of technical and economic resources. The 1991 Meeting of Parties in a formal decision (III/7) recommended that developing countries should inform the secretariat of any difficulties they face in reporting data so that assistance can be provided to remedy the situation. Further, the secretariat will undertake the task of estimating 1986 per capita consumption of controlled substances for developing countries that have not reported data, with a view toward identifying countries that had a 1986 per capita consumption level of below 0.3 kg, and that consequently were eligible for the grace period and financial assistance provided for under articles 5 and 10 of the Montreal Protocol.

At the 1990 Meeting of Parties, an Implementation Committee was created consisting of five Parties (increased to 12 Parties, equally balanced between developing and industrialized nations, at the 1991 Meeting of Parties). The Implementation Committee was charged with considering and reporting to the Meeting of Parties any reported cases of non-compliance coming to its attention (Montreal Protocol Handbook, p.94). The Meeting of Parties itself, however, is ultimately responsible for deciding upon and calling for steps to bring about full compliance with the protocol, including measures to assist a Party's compliance.

At the 1989 Meeting of Parties, the Parties established an Ad Hoc Working Group of Legal Experts on Non-Compliance which has met in July 1989, April 1991, and

November 1991. In Decision III/2 of the 1991 Meeting of Parties, the Working Group was charged with "elaborating further the procedures on non-compliance," including specifically: identifying possible situations of non-compliance; developing an indicative list of advisory and conciliatory measures to encourage full compliance; reflecting on the role of the Implementation Committee in providing recommendations to the Meeting of Parties on specific steps in cases of reported non-compliance; considering the possible need for legal interpretation of protocol provisions; and drawing up "an indicative list of measures that might be taken by the Meeting of Parties in respect of Parties that are not in compliance with the Protocol, bearing in mind the need to provide all assistance possible to countries, particularly developing countries, to enable them to comply with the Protocol" (decision III/2). Up until now, these measures have not been used.

Article 11 of the Vienna Convention provides that disputes between parties should be resolved by negotiation or, if this proves unfeasible, through the good offices or mediation of a third party. The article further provides that a Party, at the time of its ratification or accession, may declare in writing that, for a dispute not resolved in accordance with the abovementioned procedures, it would accept one or both of the following means of dispute settlement as compulsory: arbitration in accordance with procedures adopted by the Conference of Parties, or submission of the dispute to the International Court of Justice. If parties have not accepted this procedure, the dispute shall be submitted to a conciliation commission created by the parties to the dispute, the recommendations of which "the parties shall consider in good faith."

While the provisions of this article also apply to the Montreal Protocol, the 1990 Meeting of Parties established the separate specific mechanisms outlined in 16, above, to apply to reported cases of non-compliance with the protocol. In addition, the amended article 5 provides that, if a developing country believes itself unable to comply with control measures because of inadequate financial or technological assistance provided under the protocol, it could notify the secretariat and the Parties would consider appropriate action at the next formal Meeting of Parties. In the interim, there would be no non-compliance procedures invoked against the notifying party. Decisions by the Meeting of Parties would be governed by a balanced voting procedure: a two-thirds majority of Parties, comprising separate simple majorities among developing and industrialized nations. Up until now, these mechanisms have not been used.

The texts have been published in all official United Nations languages. By decision II/7 of the second Meeting of Parties, UNEP was requested to prepare a <u>Montreal Protocol Handbook</u>, to include all texts, revisions, decisions by Parties, and other material relevant to the protocol's operation, and to update the <u>Handbook</u>, as necessary, following each meeting of Parties.

Working papers and reports of all meetings of parties, including intersessional and <u>ad hoc</u> working groups and assessment panels are available in all UN languages from the UNEP secretariat. This material is used by individual countries as well as UNEP for training and educational purposes. As an example, regional workshops were held by UNEP during 1990 in Malaysia and Mexico, and one for Africa is under preparation.

Operation, review and adjustment

The basic institutional mechanisms for administering these agreements are the biennial Conference of Parties to the Vienna Convention, the annual Meeting of Parties to the Montreal Protocol, and, for both treaties, the UNEP secretariat. The administration of the agreements by the secretariat and the parties has been characterized by a marked degree of flexibility in designing and establishing various subsidiary groups to deal with particular aspects of the agreements. Such mechanisms have included, for example, the Bureau of the Conference of the Parties to the Vienna Convention; the Meeting of Ozone Research Managers under the Vienna Convention; the Open-Ended Working Group of the Parties to the Montreal Protocol and the Bureau of the Montreal Protocol, which meet intersessionally to develop and negotiate recommendations for the Meeting of Parties on protocol revisions and implementation issues; the Executive Committee of the Multilateral Ozone Fund (with a small professional secretariat located in Montreal); the Implementation Committee and the Ad Hoc Working Group of Legal Experts on the Non-Compliance Procedure described in 16, above; the Open-Ended Working Group on Trade; the Ad Hoc Group of Experts on Data Reporting; the Ad Hoc Technical Advisory Committee on Destruction Technologies; and the three Assessment Panels described in 26, below: the Scientific Assessment Panel, the Technology and Economics Assessment Panel, and the Environmental Effects Assessment Panel.

The 1990 administrative budget for the Montreal Protocol was US$ 3.4 million. Budgets are approved on a rolling biennial basis; for 1991, the budget is US$ 2.4 million; for 1992, US$ 2.3 million; and for 1993, US$ 2.4 million. Budgets are financed by a Trust Fund, administered by the UNEP secretariat, to which parties contribute according to an agreed assessment schedule (Montreal Protocol Handbook, pp. 112-114). Administrative costs of the Vienna Convention are also funded through a Trust Fund administered by the UNEP secretariat. The 1990-1991 biennium budget amounted to US$ 0.8 million.

More broadly, the costs of implementing the provisions of the Montreal Protocol include such elements as costs of conversion of existing equipment and production facilities, costs of premature retirement of capital equipment, costs of imported products and materials, costs of patents and royalties, research and development into alternative products and technologies, retraining of labor, and similar items. The Multilateral Ozone Fund is designed to meet incremental costs to developing countries of meeting the obligations of the protocol; an indicative list of categories of such incremental costs is found in the Montreal Protocol Handbook, pp. 96-97. Specific country studies, undertaken by experts from the country concerned together with experts from such organizations as UNDP, serve to estimate the needs of individual developing countries.

The main benefits of participation in the Vienna Convention and the Montreal Protocol for all parties, developing and industrialized alike, are the avoidance of adverse health and environmental impacts. For developing countries, there is an additional element in the commitment by industrialized countries to transfer new and environmentally benign technologies as they are developed.

Scientific input into the policy-making process is a fundamental element of both the Vienna Convention and the Montreal Protocol. The Conference of Parties to the Vienna Convention established a biennial Meeting of Ozone Research Managers, composed of government experts on atmospheric research and on research related to health and environmental effects of ozone layer modification. This group, working closely with WMO, reviews on-going national and international research and monitoring programmes to ensure proper coordination of these programmes and to identify gaps that need to be addressed. The group produces a report to the Conference of Parties with recommendations for future research and expanded co-operation between researchers in developed and developing countries.

The Montreal Protocol established a Scientific Assessment Panel charged with "undertaking the review of scientific knowledge in a timely manner as dictated by the needs of the Parties" (Montreal Protocol Handbook, p.82). In addition, a Technology and Economics Assessment Panel, which included many industry and non-governmental representatives, analyzes and evaluates technical options for limiting use of ozone-depleting substances, estimates the quantity of controlled substances required by developing countries for their basic domestic needs and the likely availability of such supplies, and assesses the costs of technical solutions, the benefits of reduced use of controlled substances, and issues of technology transfer. An Environmental Effects Assessment Panel surveys the state of knowledge of impacts on health and environment of altered ozone levels and the resultant increased ultraviolet radiation reaching the Earth's surface. The panels, which involve experts from numerous developed and developing countries, produced their first comprehensive reports in 1989, providing the basis for the significant revisions of the protocol undertaken by the 1990 Meeting of Parties. A second major report, taking account of the evolving scientific and technological situation, is being produced in 1991 for consideration by the fourth Meeting of Parties in 1992.

The Parties to the Vienna Convention are committed to "enhancement of the capability of developing countries to contribute to ozone science research" (decision 5, first Conference of Parties). Parties in developing countries have been invited to identify, in a report to the secretariat, scientific institutes that could cooperate with those in developed countries, indicating present activities and future plans. Parties in developed countries were also asked to identify institutes that might assist developing country institutes in enhancing their contribution to ozone science research. The secretariat covered costs of participation of ten research managers from developing countries in the Meeting of Ozone Research Managers.

The 1991 Meeting of Parties to the Montreal Protocol decided "to encourage the participation of representatives of developing countries" in all meetings convened under the Montreal Protocol "and to provide, as far as possible, financial assistance for such participation" (decision III/6). An estimated $US 250,000 is required for participation of developing country experts in the second (1991) assessment process (UNEP/OzL.Pro.3/3, p.21), out of a total cost of US$ 820,000 for participation of developing country representatives in all meetings convened under the Vienna Convention and the Montreal Protocol.

It should be noted that deliberations of the Conference of Parties to the Vienna Convention, the Meeting of Parties to the Montreal Protocol, and the Open-Ended Working Group of Parties to the Montreal Protocol are open to all governments, whether or not they are Parties to the treaties, as well as to observers from international agencies, industry and non-governmental organizations. The assessment panels also include experts from the non-governmental sector.

Codification programming

The Open-Ended Working Group of the Parties to the Montreal Protocol is considering, on the basis of the Assessment Panel reports prepared during 1991, further revisions to the treaty to be presented to the fourth Meeting of Parties in 1992. Remaining issues under the Montreal Protocol that may require further legal interpretation include non-compliance procedures and consistency of the trade provisions with GATT.

Coordination occurs through the UNEP secretariat and through the currently ongoing UNCED process.

STATUS OF RATIFICATIONS AS OF 1 JANUARY 1992

GLOBAL INSTRUMENTS   (Treaty numbers see page 123)

Parties	29	30	33
Afghanistan	x	x	
Albania		x	
Algeria		x	
Angola		x	
Antigua & Barbuda	x	x	
Argentina	x	x	x
Australia	x	x	x
Austria	x	x	x
Bahamas	x	x	
Bahrain		x	x
Bangladesh	x	x	x
Barbados	x	x	
Belarus*	x		x
Belgium	x	x	x
Belize		x	
Benin	x	x	
Bhutan		x	
Bolivia		x	
Botswana		x	x
Brazil	x	x	x
Brunei Darussalam		x	x
Bulgaria	x	x	
Burkina Faso	x	x	x
Burundi		x	
Cambodia		x	
Cameroon		x	x
Canada	x	x	x
Cape Verde		x	
Central African Republic		x	
Chad		x	x
Chile	x	x	x
China	x	x	x
Colombia		x	x
Cook Islands		x	
Comoros		x	
Congo		x	
Costa Rica		x	x
Cote d'Ivoire		x	
Cuba	x	x	
Cyprus	x	x	
Czech & Slovak Fed. Rep.	x	x	
Democr. People's Rep. of Korea		x	

Parties	29	30	33
Denmark	x	x	x
Djibouti		x	
Dominica			
Dominican Republic	x	x	
Ecuador	x	x	x
Egypt	x	x	x
El Salvador	x	x	
Equatorial Guinea	x	x	x
Estonia*			
Ethiopia		x	
Fiji	x	x	x
Finland	x	x	x
France	x	x	x
Gabon		x	
Gambia		x	x
Germany	x	x	x
Ghana		x	x
Greece	x	x	x
Grenada		x	
Guatemala		x	x
Guinea		x	
Guinea-Bissau	x	x	
Guyana		x	
Haiti		x	
Holy See			
Honduras		x	
Hungary	x	x	x
Iceland	x	x	x
India	x	x	x
Indonesia		x	
Iran (Islamic Republic of)		x	
Iraq	x	x	
Ireland	x	x	x
Israel	x	x	
Italy	x	x	x
Jamaica	x	x	
Japan	x	x	x
Jordan		x	x
Kenya	x	x	x
Kiribati		x	
Kuwait	x	x	
Lao People's Democratic Rep.	x	x	
Latvia*			
Lebanon	x	x	

Parties	29	30	33
Lesotho		x	
Liberia		x	
Libyan Arab Jamahiriya	x	x	x
Liechtenstein			x
Lithuania*			
Luxembourg		x	x
Madagascar	x	x	
Malawi		x	x
Malaysia		x	x
Maldives		x	x
Mali	x	x	
Malta		x	x
Marshall Islands		x	
Mauritania		x	
Mauritius	x	x	
Mexico	x	x	x
Micronesia		x	
Monaco		x	
Mongolia	x	x	
Morocco	x	x	
Mozambique		x	
Myanmar	x	x	
Namibia		x	
Nauru		x	
Nepal	x	x	
Netherlands	x	x	x
New Zealand	x	x	x
Nicaragua		x	
Niger	x	x	
Nigeria	x	x	x
Niue			
Norway	x	x	x
Oman		x	
Pakistan	x	x	
Palau			
Panama		x	x
Papua New Guinea	x	x	
Paraguay		x	
Peru	x	x	x
Philippines		x	x
Poland	x	x	x
Portugal		x	x
Qatar		x	
Republic of Korea	x	x	

Parties	29	30	33
Republic of Yemen	x	x	
Romania	x	x	x
Rwanda		x	
St. Kitts & Nevis			
St. Lucia		x	
St. Vincent & the Grenadines		x	
Samoa			
San Marino	x	x	
Sao Tome & Principe		x	
Saudi Arabia	x	x	
Senegal		x	
Seychelles	x	x	
Sierra Leone	x	x	
Singapore	x	x	x
Solomon Islands		x	
Somalia		x	
South Africa	x	x	x
Spain	x	x	x
Sri Lanka	x	x	x
Sudan		x	
Suriname		x	
Swaziland		x	
Sweden	x	x	x
Switzerland	x	x	x
Syrian Arab Republic	x	x	x
Thailand	x	x	x
Togo	x	x	x
Tonga	x	x	
Trinidad & Tobago		x	x
Tunisia	x	x	x
Turkey	x	x	x
Tuvalu			
Uganda	x	x	x
Ukraine*	x		x
Union of Soviet Socialist Rep.*	x	x	x
United Arab Emirates		x	x
United Kingdom	x	x	x
United Republic of Tanzania		x	
United States of America	x	x	x
Uruguay	x	x	x
Vanuatu		x	
Venezuela	x	x	x
Viet Nam	x	x	
Yugoslavia*		x	x

Parties	29	30	33
Zaire		x	
Zambia	x	x	x
Zimbabwe		x	
European Economic Community			x

REGIONAL INSTRUMENTS

(28) <u>Regulations concerning gaseous pollutants emissions from motor vehicles, pursuant to the Agreement Concerning the Adoption of Uniform Conditions of Approval and Reciprocal Recognition of Approval for Motor Vehicle Equipment and Parts</u> (Geneva 1958)

Austria
Belgium
Czech & Slovak Fed. Rep.
Denmark
Finland
France
Germany
Hungary
Italy
Luxembourg
Netherlands

Norway
Poland
Portugal
Romania
Spain
Sweden
Switzerland
USSR*
United Kingdom
Yugoslavia*

(31) <u>Convention on Long-range Transboundary Air Pollution</u> (Geneva 1979)

Austria
Belgium
Bulgaria
Belarus*
Canada
Cyprus
Czech & Slovak Fed. Rep.
Denmark
Finland
France
Germany
Greece
Hungary
Iceland
Ireland
Italy
Liechtenstein

Luxembourg
Netherlands
Norway
Poland
Portugal
Romania
Spain
Sweden
Switzerland
Turkey
Ukraine*
USSR*
United Kingdom
United States of America
Yugoslavia*
European Economic Community

* Membership status subject to further clarification.

CHAPTER IV

MARINE ENVIRONMENT AND MARINE POLLUTION

Alan E. Boyle, David A.C. Freestone, K. Kummer and David M. Ong

This chapter covers the following 23 global and regional agreements and instruments on the marine environment and marine pollution:

I. GLOBAL MARINE ENVIRONMENT

(34) the 1969 Brussels **Convention Relating to Intervention on the High Seas in Case of Oil Pollution Casualties,** and its 1973 Protocol;

(35) the 1972 London **Convention on the Prevention of Marine Pollution by Dumping from Ships and Aircraft,** as amended;

(36) the 1973/78 MARPOL **Convention for the Prevention of Pollution from Ships;**

(37) the 1982 UNEP **Guidelines Concerning the Environment Related to Offshore Mining and Drilling Within the Limits of National Jurisdiction;**

(38) the 1982 **United Nations Convention on the Law of the Sea;**

(39) the 1985 UNEP Montreal **Guidelines for the Protection of the Marine Environment Against Pollution from Land-based Sources;**

(40) the 1989 **International Convention on Salvage;**

(41) the 1990 **International Convention on Oil Pollution Preparedness, Response and Co-operation;**

II. REGIONAL MARINE ENVIRONMENT

(42) the 1971 Nordic **Agreement Concerning Co-operation in Measures to Deal with Pollution of the Sea by Oil;**

(43) the 1972 Oslo **Convention for the Prevention of Marine Pollution by Dumping from Ships and Aircraft,** as amended;

(44) the 1974 Helsinki **Convention on the Protection of the Marine Environment of the Baltic Sea Area,** as amended;

(45) the 1974 Paris **Convention on the Prevention of Marine Pollution from Land-based Sources,** as amended;

(46) the 1976 Barcelona **Convention for the Protection of the Mediterranean Sea Against Pollution,** and its protocols;

(47) the 1978 Kuwait **Regional Convention for Co-operation on the Protection of the Marine Environment from Pollution,** and its protocols;

(48) the 1981 Abidjan **Convention and Protocol for the Protection and Development of the Marine and Coastal Environment of the West and Central African Region;**

(49) the 1981 Lima **Convention for the Protection of the Marine Environment and Coastal Area of the South-East Pacific,** and its protocols;

(50) the 1982 **Memorandum of Understanding on Port State Control** in Implementing Agreements on Maritime Safety and Protection of the Environment;

(51) the 1982 Jeddah **Convention and Protocol for the Conservation of the Red Sea and Gulf of Aden Environment;**

(52) the 1983 Cartagena **Convention for the Protection and Development of the Marine Environment of the Wider Caribbean Region**, and its protocols;

(53) the 1983 Bonn **Agreement for Co-operation in Dealing with Pollution of the North Sea by Oil and Other Harmful Substances;**

(54) the 1985 Nairobi **Convention and Protocols for the Protection, Management and Development of the Marine and Coastal Environment of the Eastern African Region;**

(55) the 1986 Noumea **Convention for the Protection of the Natural Resources and Environment of the South Pacific Region**, and its protocols; and

(56) the 1990 Lisbon **Agreement on Co-operation for Combating Pollution in the Northeast Atlantic.**

Other environment-related agreements and instruments primarily dealing with marine living resources will be covered in chapter V. Agreements dealing with liability for marine pollution damage will be addressed separately in chapter X.

A list showing the status of ratifications as of 1 January 1992 is annexed (pages 249 - 255).

I. GLOBAL MARINE ENVIRONMENT

(34) International Convention relating to Intervention on the High Seas in Case of Oil Pollution Casualties
(Brussels, 19 November 1969), and related 1973 protocol

Objectives and achievement

To confer power on the coastal State to intervene in the event of a pollution casualty on the high seas, threatening to damage or damaging its coastline or related interests. Parties to the Convention may take such measures on the high seas as may be necessary to prevent, mitigate or eliminate grave and imminent danger to their coastline or related interests from pollution or threat of pollution of the sea by oil, following upon a maritime casualty or acts related to such a casualty, which may reasonably be expected to result in major harmful consequences (Article 1).

The convention only relates to the extension of rights of the coastal State; it does not address special circumstances of developing countries.

One indicator of the extent to which this agreement has met its basic objectives is that no dispute is known to have arisen among any of the Parties concerning measures taken to deal with pollution casualties, nor is any Party known to have been obliged to pay compensation. The dispute settlement machinery has not been invoked (Art. 8).

Evidence of a negative lesson learned from the Convention is the subsequent reformulation of the basic principle of intervention in Article 221 of the 1982 UN Convention on the Law of the Sea (No. 38). The declared reason for this rewording was the 1969 Convention's failure to permit intervention by coastal States at a sufficiently early stage in a pending marine accident. A third measure is that the annual quantity of oil entering the sea due to tanker accidents has declined since 1974, but other factors, including lower volumes of oil transported during the early 1980s, and the impact of other international measures are probably the major cause of this limited decline (see the data given below under No. 36, for of annual accidental discharges).

Participation

Membership is open to States members of the United Nations or any specialized agency, or the IAEA, or parties to the Statute of the ICJ. Reservations are not prohibited (Art. 10). Geographical distribution of membership is as follows (as of 1 January 1992):

	(a) 1969 Convention (57 Parties)	(b) 1973 Protocol (26 Parties)
Europe:	20	15
Africa:	13	3
Asia:	4	1
Latin America:	5	1
Caribbean:	4	2
North America:	1	1
Australasia and Pacific Islands:	3	1
Middle East:	7	2

Total developing country participation: 33

48 countries participated in the drafting and negotiation of the Convention. Of these, 21 were developing States and 27 were developed States. 4 developing and 1 developed States attended as observers.

Implementation and information

The Convention provides for entry into force after fifteen States have become parties (Art. 11). It entered into force five and a half years after opening for signature.

The following commitments are imposed on Parties:

(a)   To consult with other States affected before taking measures (Art. 3(a));

(b)   To notify proposed measures to any person or company known to have interests which can reasonably be expected to be affected by those measures (Art. 3(b));

(c)   To use best endeavours to avoid risk to human life and to afford assistance to persons in need (Art. 3(e));

(d)   To notify without delay States and persons or companies concerned and the Secretary General of the International Maritime Organization (IMO) (Art. 3(f));

(e)   To set up and maintain a list of experts (Art. 4);

(f)   To ensure that measures taken are proportionate to the damage actual or threatened, and necessary to protect the interests of the coastal State (Art. 5);

(g)   To pay compensation for damage arising as a result of measures taken in contravention to the Convention, i.e., when such measures exceed those reasonably necessary to prevent, mitigate or eliminate grave and imminent pollution damage to the coastline or related interest;

(h)   Compliance is not monitored or measured, save that in case of dispute, Article 8 provides for unilateral resort to conciliation, or if unsuccessful, to arbitration.

The Parties are required to report on measures taken under the Convention to IMO and to other States affected. There are no requirements of data supply.

Unilateral resort to conciliation or arbitration is provided for by Article 8. There has been no known use of this Article.

The authentic text of the Convention is in English and French; it has been officially translated into Russian and Spanish. Texts were published by IMO, which also publishes treaty information periodically in its IMO News, and promotes the use of treaty materials in international training at the World Maritime University and the IMO Maritime Law Institute.

Operation, review and adjustment

The IMO secretariat in London acts as reporting facility, and depositary, and maintains a list of independent experts. International administrative costs for individual conventions are not specified within the IMO budget.

The convention has been adjusted by an ad hoc protocol in 1973. Art. 14 provides for a conference to revise or amend the Convention to be convened by IMO on the request of not less than one third of the parties.

Codification programming

No revisions are currently under consideration.

154

(35) Convention on the Prevention of Marine Pollution by Dumping of Wastes and Other Matter
(London, 29 December 1972), as amended

Objectives and achievement

The Convention's basic objectives are to take all practical steps to prevent the pollution of the sea by dumping of waste and other matter that is liable to create hazards to human health, to harm living resources and marine life, to damage amenities or to interfere with other legitimate uses of the sea (Article I).

Article 2 makes some allowance for the special circumstances of developing countries by requiring contracting parties to take effective measures individually "according to their scientific, technical and economic capabilities". Article 9 makes provision for the Parties to promote support for other Parties who require training of personnel, supply of equipment and facilities for research and monitoring and disposal and treatment of waste.

The extent to which basic objectives have been met can be measured as follows:
(a)   International action to prevent pollution by dumping. The Convention has enabled the implementation of the first control mechanism of a global kind based on the complete prohibition of dumping as sea of particular harmful substances and the establishment of licensing systems for the dumping at sea of all other substances. Since the entry into force of the Convention, increasing efforts have been made to reduce the amounts of hazardous wastes dumped and incinerated at sea by changing industrial processes and through the use of recycling methods and waste treatment techniques. As a result disposal of industrial waste by dumping shows a decrease from 17 million tons in 1979 to 6 million tons in 1987. In spite of these waste management efforts, disposal at sea of certain waste types, in particular dredged material and sewage sludge is continued to be considered a practicable and environmentally acceptable option. Nevertheless the amount of sewage sludge dumped has declined from 17 million tons in 1980 to 14 million tons in 1985 with a continuous decrease thereafter.
(b)   Reduction, control and phasing out of certain types of dumping by collective action of the Contracting Parties. As a result of the Consultative Meetings of Contracting Parties several resolution have been adopted concerning certain forms of dumping:

-      a suspension of all dumping at sea of radioactive wastes and other radioactive matter pending completion of additional scientific and technical studies and assessments, as well as additional studies on the wider political, legal, economic and social aspects of radioactive waste dumping.
-      the regulation and re-evaluation of incineration at sea of wastes and other matter, with a view to proceeding towards the termination of the incineration of noxious liquid wastes at sea by 1994.
-      the phasing out of sea disposal of industrial waste by 1995.

(c)   The adoption of supplementary regional agreements and actions plans for environment protection purposes covering the following sea areas:

- Mediterranean
- The Gulf Region
- The Wider Caribbean
- West and Central Africa
- East Asian Seas
- Red Sea and Gulf of Aden
- South West Pacific
- South East Pacific
- South Asia
- North Sea
- Baltic Sea.

(d)   Trends in the disposal of industrial waste disposed of by dumping or incineration at sea. These show a decrease from 17 million tons in 1979 to 6 million tons in 1987. IMO reports that this reduction has been achieved through the efforts of contracting parties to find alternative disposal methods, to reduce wastes and to use cleaner technologies. The amount of sewage sludge dumped had declined from 17 million tons in 1980 to 14 million tons in 1985, with a continuing decrease thereafter. A 1991 report on the Convention prepared by IMO (A/CONF.151/PC/31) concludes that it has provided an effective instrument for the protection of the marine environment.

Participation

The Convention is open for accession by "any State" (Art. 18). While reservations are not prohibited, no reservations have been entered.

The Convention has 67 Parties (as of 1 January 1992):

Europe:	26
Africa:	12
Asia:	4
Latin America:	9
North America:	2
Australasia and Pacific Islands:	5
Caribbean:	6
Middle East:	3

Total developing countries: 38

Only between 30 to 45 Parties attend Consultative Meetings, and only 15 to 20 participate in meetings of its subsidiary bodies. 43 States Parties sent delegations to the 1990 Consultative Meeting, of whom 19 were developing States. In addition 6 non-Parties, all developing States, sent observers. The Association of Pacific Island legislatures has also participated.

Article IX provides for the collaboration of Contracting Parties for the promotion of scientific, technical and other assistance to States which request it. This includes the supply of necessary equipment and facilities for research and monitoring, and support for the disposal and treatment of waste and other measures to prevent or mitigate pollution caused by dumping.

IMO in its role as the Secretariat for the London Dumping Convention, has been active in sponsoring international symposia and organising seminars for the exchange for scientific and technical information related to the implementation of the Convention. International development agencies and national development agencies of developed countries provide technical assistance. Several countries with experience of waste disposal at sea have offered on-the-job training for scientific/administrative staff from developing countries.

Several developing countries have become party to the Convention in view of the powers conferred by this treaty to States Party to regulate the dumping of wastes by national and foreign ships in the jurisdictional waters of States Party. Another factor of encouragement for developing countries to become party is that the implementation of the convention does not involve any substantive economic or financial burden.

On the other hand, in spite of the efforts to promote the goals of the convention undertaken at an international and regional level, the need to regulate the dumping of wastes at sea is still a low priority in the policy making activities of many developing countries. Further more, no provision has been made by the Contracting Parties concerning the financing of participation of developing countries at the Consultative Meetings.

Implementation and information

The Convention entered into force on the thirtieth day following deposit of the fifteenth instrument of accession or ratification. This occurred two years and eight months after opening for signature.

The following commitments are imposed:

(a)   Individually and collectively to promote effective control of all sources of pollution of the marine environment and taking all practicable steps to prevent pollution of the sea by dumping of waste and other matter (Art. 1).

(b)   To take effective measures individually and collectively to prevent marine pollution caused by dumping and harmonise their policies (Art. 2).

(c)   To prohibit dumping of waste or other matter except as specified (Art. 4).

(d)   To designate an appropriate authority to issue permits, keep records of dumping, monitor the condition of the seas, and report on these matters to IMO (Art. 6).

(e)   To apply measures required to implement the Convention for all vessels and aircraft registered in its territory of flying its flag; loading in its territory or territorial sea matter to be dumped; or believed to be engaged in dumping under its jurisdiction (Art. 7(1)).

(f)   To take measures to prevent and punish contravention of the Convention; develop procedures for effective application on the high seas (Art. 7(2)).

(g)   Compliance is monitored and measured by consultative meetings of the contracting parties, but no formal non-compliance machinery has been established.

The Parties are required to notify IMO directly or through regional secretariats of the nature, quantity, location, time and method of all matter permitted to be dumped, and of their monitoring of the condition of the sea, and of the criteria, measures and requirements adopted in issuing permits (Art. 6). Notification procedures adopted by the Consultative Meeting also call for the Parties to report compliance monitoring and environmental impact assessments. A report on the Convention prepared by IMO (A/CONF.151/PC/31) indicates that reporting is sufficient to enable some calculations of total dumping trends to be made. However, concern has been expressed with regard to notification by the parties. Only 60 per cent of contracting parties have fulfilled their obligations under the Convention in this respect, and the Consultative Meeting has sought more effective implementation. It should be borne in mind, however, that some parties, particularly developing States, do not carry out dumping at sea and may have nothing to report. The countries with the most consistent record of regular reporting are all developed industrialized nations.

The Consultative Meeting is able to exercise some control over compliance through notification of dumping activities and monitoring reports. There is no formal non-compliance procedure, no prior notification procedure and no multilateral consultation procedure. Some Parties have called for stronger compliance machinery. The Consultative Meeting has recognized the need for improved control of dumping in waters of non-contracting States by ships of Contracting Parties.

The Consultative Meeting adopted a provision for settlement of disputes, in 1978, which requires disputes concerning interpretation or application of the Convention to be settled by negotiation, or other agreed means; if settlement by these methods is not possible, the dispute shall be submitted by agreement of the parties to the dispute to the ICJ, or at the request of one of them to arbitration. There is no known use of the procedure.

The authentic text of the Convention is in English, French, Russian and Spanish. The secretariat and IMO make information available concerning the Convention's operation and implementation, including a comprehensive 1991 publication, The London Dumping Convention: The First Decade and Beyond.

Guidelines, recommendations and control and notification procedures have been adopted to assist effective implementation. These include:
(a)   Guidance for the application of annex III,
(b)   Procedures and criteria for determining emergency situations,
(c)   Criteria for the allocation of substances to annexes,
(d)   Reporting of sea disposal and monitoring,
(e)   Regulations and technical guidelines on incineration at sea,
(f)   Adoption of a hierarchical system of waste management.

Operation, review and adjustment

At the first Consultative Meeting, IMO was designated as the competent organization to be responsible for secretariat duties. Its duties include convening consultative meetings, preparing and assisting in the development of procedures for determining exceptional and emergency procedures, and communicating information and notifications received from contracting parties (Art. 14).
Consultative or special meetings of the parties have responsibility for keeping under review the implementation of the Convention, adopting amendments, inviting scientific studies, receiving and considering reports, promoting regional co-operation, developing emergency procedures and considering additional action (Art. 14)

The estimated annual cost of IMO international administrative work related to the London Dumping Convention for the most recent financial year is £452,000. The costs of national participation are limited to attendance at Consultative meetings and measures necessary to implement the Convention.

The Consultative Meeting requests advice on issues needing multi-disciplinary expertise from the Group of Experts on Scientific Aspects of Marine Pollution. It has also established ad hoc groups to provide advice on specific issues such as incineration at sea. An Inter-Governmental Panel of Experts on Radioactive Waste Disposal at Sea was established by the 10th Meeting in 1986. To assist in implementing the Convention the Consultative Meeting has established a Scientific Group on Dumping as its standing advisory body, responsible for responding to scientific requests, reviewing the provisions of the Annexes and making recommendations, reviewing scientific and technological developments, preparing lists of hazardous substances, developing guidelines on monitoring programmes, recommending the calling of scientific conferences, and generally maintaining awareness of the impacts on the marine environment of inputs from all waste sources. It is the task of this group to draw to the attention of the Consultative Meeting any emerging or worsening problems.

National authorities do not appear to participate effectively in the work of the Convention. The Consultative Meeting has only recently requested the secretariat to complete a list of national authorities responsible for implementing the Convention, to allow direct contact between them and the secretariat.

Non-Governmental Organizations do participate in meetings as observers and some have been active in lobbying the Consultative Meeting and in providing expert advice for delegations of some States parties at Consultative Meetings. Those listed as attending the Thirteenth Consultative Meeting in 1990 are:

International Association of Ports and Harbours
European Council of Chemical Manufacturers' Federations
Friends of the Earth International
Greenpeace International
International Union for the Conservation of Nature
Permanent International Association of Navigation Congresses
Association of Maritime Incinerators
Oil Industry International Exploration and Production Forum
Advisory Committee on Pollution of the Sea
Association of Pacific Island Legislature

The participation of the scientific community is indicated in section 26 above.

The regular Consultative Meetings are responsible for periodic reviews and adjustments. Article 15 of the Convention provides for amendment of the Convention and Annexes. Annex amendments take effect for all parties except those who express their non-acceptance within 100 days. These procedures have been used to amend the Convention in 1978 and to amend the annexes on several occasions. Regulations governing incineration at sea were adopted by amending Annex 1 in 1978; Annexes I and II were amended in 1980, and Annex III containing criteria for the issue of permits, in 1989.

Codification programming

Ongoing and future revision work includes:
(a)   Development of procedures for the assessment of liability;
(b)   Developing measures to improve control of dumping activities from ships flying the flag of a contracting party in waters of non-contracting parties;
(c)   Establishing amendments to the Convention with a view to clarifying the responsibilities and rights of coastal States to apply the Convention in a zone adjacent to their coasts.
(d)   Development of a long-term strategy for the Convention. Proposals under consideration include development of a comprehensive, global, multi-sectoral environmental protection and waste management framework; establishing a new convention covering land-based sources of pollution as well as dumping, on the basis of the "precautionary principle";

establishment of a global supervisory mechanism for all matters related to the marine environment; promotion of waste reduction and recycling technologies; improved enforcement mechanisms.

The Consultative Meeting and Secretariat are involved in co-ordinating work with a number of other instruments:

(a) Review of the preparatory process for establishment of the International Seabed Authority and environmental guidelines for seabed mining (under UNCLOS, No. 38;

(b) Consideration by an ad hoc Group of Legal Experts of the elaboration of standards compatible with the 1989 Basel Convention for the Control of Transboundary Movement of Hazardous Waste (No. 79);

(c) Consideration of improved liaison with regional organizations.

(36) International Convention for the Prevention of Pollution from Ships
(London, 2 November 1973), as amended

Objectives and achievement

The basic objectives of the Convention are to prevent the pollution of the marine environment by the operational discharge of oil and other harmful substances and the minimisation of accidental discharge of such substances.

The Convention is global in scope. Interests of developing countries are not specifically mentioned.

The 1990 GESAMP report estimates that 46% of total input of oil to the sea originates from shipping, including accidental spills. It reports a decline in oil spillages to 1986, due in part to a reduction in the volume of transported oil in the first half of the 1980s. It concludes that entry-into-force of Annex I of MARPOL has constituted to a major reduction in operational pollution from all types of vessels. Operational discharges have not been eliminated however. A report prepared by the U.S. National Academy of Sciences in 1990 for IMO found that a total of 568,800 tons of oil had entered the sea from ships in 1989, compared with 1.47 million tons in 1981. It too found that MARPOL had had a "substantial positive impact". Of this 1989 total however, only some 114,000 tons entered the sea accidentally; most of the remainder was intentionally discharged by tankers during the course of ballasting and tank cleaning and by other ships in the form of waste oil.

Participation

Membership is open to all States. Reservations are not prohibited, but no reservations have been entered.

Current membership (as of 1 January, 1992):

(a)   1973 Convention, 1978 Protocol, Annex I and Annex II. Total Parties: 70

Europe:	28
Africa:	12
Asia:	8
Latin America:	8
Caribbean:	4
North America:	1
Middle East:	5
Australasia and Pacific Islands:	4
Total Developing States:	41

(b)   Annex III
       47 Parties, not in force

(c)   Annex IV
       39 Parties, not in force

(d)   Annex V
       52 Parties, in force 18 February 1991.

41 developing and 30 developed States participated in the negotiation and drafting of the Original Convention in 1973. 7 developing States also attended as observers. Subsequent meetings of the Marine Environment Protection Committee are the main forum for further meetings and activities relating to the Convention. In 1990, 32 developing States and 19 developed States participated in these meetings.

Article 17 of the Convention states that the parties shall promote, in consultation with IMO and other international bodies, with assistance and co-ordination by the Executive Director of the United Nations Environment Programme (UNEP), support for those Parties requesting assistance for:

(a)   the training of scientific and technical personnel;

(b)   the supply of necessary equipment and facilities for reception and monitoring;

(c)   the facilitation of other measures and arrangements to prevent or mitigate pollution of the marine environment from ships; and

(d)   the encouragement of research.

Ratification and participation by developing States has been constrained by the financial costs of participation. On the other hand, the availability of technical assistance and the interests of developing nations with maritime interests are positive influences on national participation.

Implementation and information

The Convention provides for entry-into-force 12 months after at least fifteen States representing not less than 50% of gross merchant tonnage of world fleet have become parties. In practice, the Convention had attracted participation by States representing over 85% of gross merchant tonnage. Entry-into-force provisions do not, therefore, appear to have constrained the Convention's effectiveness. However, in the case of optional annexes which enter into force on the same terms, this does appear to have constrained entry-into-force for these parts of the Convention.

The Parties are committed:

(a)   To give effect to the provisions of the Convention and annexes in order to prevent pollution of the marine environment (Art. 1).

(b)   To prohibit violations, establish sanctions therefore under the law of the administration of the ship concerned, and take proceedings if informed of a violation and satisfied that sufficient evidence is available (Art. 4(1)).

(c)   To prohibit violations, and establish sanctions for violations within the jurisdiction of any party and either to cause proceedings to take place or furnish information to the administration of the ship (Art. 4(2)).

(d)   To apply the provisions of the Convention as may be necessary to ensure that no more favourable treatment is given to ships of non-parties (Art. 4(4)).

(e)   To co-operate in the detection of violations and enforcement of the Convention (Art. 6(1)).

(f)   To furnish evidence to the Administration that a ship has discharged harmful substances or effluents in violation of the regulations (Art. 6(3)).

(g)   The administration is required to investigate such reports, and, if sufficient evidence is available, to bring proceedings.

(h)   To arrange for the receipt and processing of all reports of incidents reported in accordance with Protocol I; notify IMO of such arrangements; relay without delay, any report to the administration of the ship and any other State affected (Art. 8).

(i)   To communicate to IMO various matters referred to in Article 11.

(j)   To conduct an investigation of any casualty producing major deleterious effects on the marine environment (Art. 12).

Compliance with these commitments is primarily monitored and measured by circulation to the parties of reports made to IMO under Article 11. Reports made by port States following inspections also enable compliance by flag States with their obligations to be monitored to some extent.

Under the mandatory reporting system of MARPOL, Annex I, annual reports are submitted to the Convention secretariat. These reports are then considered by the MEPC at its annual session. The following matters must be reported:

(a)   Annual enforcement report
-        reports by port/coastal States of violations referred to the responsible flag State;
-        reports by the flag State of violations on which it has taken in response to port/coastal State reports;
-        reports by flag States of cases of inadequacy of reception facilities referred by it to responsible port States;
-        reports by the port State on actions taken regarding the inadequacy of reception facilities, based on reports received by other States.

(b)   Annual summary report by the State's administration of incidents involving spillages of oil of more than 100 tons.

(c)   Annual assessment report
-        statistical report by the port State on the effectiveness of port State control (number of inspections and compliance rate);
-        reports by the port State on MARPOL violations by ships resulting in detention or denial of entry-into-port;
-        reports on penalties imposed by the port State for violations of MARPOL.

A survey of all types of reports for the period 1985-1989 discloses the following record of compliance with reporting requirements:

1990: 15 States (10 industrialized)
1988: 15 States (14 industrialized)
1987: 18 States (15 industrialized)
1986: 22 States (19 industrialized)

In a few cases, reporting States are not Parties to MARPOL but are reporting under the earlier 1954 OILPOL Convention. The percentage of Parties reporting is approximately 30%. The majority of States reporting are industrialized, and their reports are the most comprehensive and detailed. The quality of information supplied is often inadequate and insufficient to enable useful conclusions to be drawn.

Data supply requirements include the texts of laws and other legal instruments, a list of nominated surveyors, a number of specimen certificates issued under the regulations, a list of reception facilities, official reports showing the application of the Convention, an annual report of the penalties imposed (Art. 11).

There is no formal provision for a meeting of the Parties or for a non-compliance procedure. Non-compliance is an important issue in the deliberations of the Maritime Safety and Marine Environment Protection Committees of IMO, however. The report of the last sessions of MSC and MEPC are considered outstanding examples of the efforts undertaken by these bodies to press flag State compliance with the Conventions and, at the same time, extending port State control as a way of checking such compliance; through inspection of vessels and reporting of violations by port States. These procedures have been widely used, particularly in Europe, North American and Japan. Flag States are also required to comment on and explain deficiency reports submitted to IMO, and to respond to requests for information on the results of investigations into serious casualties, although it is recognized by IMO that the effective exercise of flag State jurisdiction remains inadequate.

There is no provision for dispute settlement, although resort to IMO is a possibility.

The Marine Safety Committee and the Marine Environment Protection Committee of IMO have reported a variety of causes which might contribute to the lack of effective implementation by flag States. These include:

(a)   Lack of trained and experienced technical personnel within the flag State administration;

(b)   The inability to retain skilled personnel;

(c)   Inappropriate delegation of inspection authority or the use of insufficiently qualified and experienced surveyors (Blanco-Bazan, 1991).

(d)   In addition, the record of port States in supplying reception facilities has been poor in some areas because of financial constraints. The provision of finance and technical assistance are important factors enabling some developing States to implement the Convention.

The English, French, Russian and Spanish texts are authentic. Official translations into Arabic, German, Italian and Japanese are called for. The treaty and annexes are published in updated form by IMO. Current information on the operation of the treaty is made available through IMO News, and through reports of the Marine Environment Protection Committee and Maritime Safety Committee of IMO.

IMO has adopted unified interpretations of Annexes I and II and a variety of resolutions of the Marine Environment Protection Committee and the IMO Assembly provide guidance to Parties on implementation of aspects of the Convention. These include guidelines for surveys under Annexes I and II; guidelines for implementation of Annex V; resolutions concerning reports of incidents; resolutions of the procedures for controlling ships and discharges under Annexes I and II; resolutions and specifications for equipment and technical aspects of pollution control. A manual on oil pollution provides practical information on preventing pollution in accordance with the Convention and is particularly aimed at developing countries. The International Codes for the Construction and Equipment of Ships Carrying Dangerous Chemicals in Bulk (the IBC and BCH Codes), and the International Maritime Dangerous Goods Code govern construction requirements under Annex II and packaging, marking and storage requirements under Annex III respectively.

The above-mentioned information is used in specialized international training programmes organized by IMO at the World Maritime University in Sweden and at the International Maritime Law Institute in Malta.

Operation, review and adjustment

The IMO secretariat receives reports, acts as depositary, and considers amendments to the Conventions and its Annexes. According to an unofficial estimate reported by the US General Accounting Office, IMO expenditure for MARPOL administration in 1990 amounted to US$ 3.03 million.

The main benefits of participation are the reduction in pollution for those States most likely to be affected, and the standardization of rules and procedures, facilitating the maintenance of freedom of navigation. The main costs are, for flag States, the costs of administering the system of certification and enforcement, and for port States, the cost of administering a system of inspection and enforcement. Participation costs for developing

States are most likely to be reduced by collaboration and co-operation with other States, whether through IMO or otherwise. The extraneous economic costs of participation are likely to be higher when only a few States in an individual region participate, since this may affect traffic patterns, to the detriment of parties implementing the Convention.

Scientific knowledge is available through IMO, which is responsible for issuing guidelines and amending the Convention. The Group of Experts on Scientific Aspects of Marine Pollution has made periodic reports on the state of the oceans and on the impact of pollution from ships. Non-governmental organizations participate with observer status at IMO meetings.

Article 16 of the Convention provides for amendments to the Convention, its appendices, annexes and protocols either by a Conference of the Parties, or through IMO. In practice, Appendices, Annexes and Protocols have been amended by IMO through the Marine Environment Protection Committee. The Convention and its Annexes were amended by Protocol in 1978 before entry into force, and further amended in 1984. Amendments have also been made to Annex I (1987, 1990); Annex II (1985, 1989, 1990); Annex V (1989 1990).

Codification programming

Proposals have been made for further amendments to the annexes to develop uniform standards for the construction of double hull ships and other designs intended to reduce the risk of pollution. The MEPC is also considering measures to reduce air pollution from ships.

The Marine Environment Protection Committee is responsible for co-ordinating work with other IMO conventions, and with relevant UNEP conventions such as the 1989 Basel Convention for the Control of Transboundary Movements of Hazardous Waste. Co-ordination with the 1982 UN Convention on the Law of the Sea (No. 38) is required with respect to:

(a)   enforcement by port States in cases of discharges outside the internal waters, territorial sea or exclusive economic zone of that State (Art. 218);

(b)   enforcement by coastal states within their exclusive economic zone (Art 220).

(37) UNEP Guidelines Concerning the Environment Related to Offshore Mining and Drilling Within the Limits of National Jurisdiction
(Nairobi, 31 May 1982)

Objectives and achievement

The objective of the Guidelines, produced as a result of a study by a UNEP expert group of the legal aspects of the issue, is to lay down basic standards for incorporation in national and regional rules, regulations, practices and procedures which will ensure that environmental considerations are effectively protected in national and international systems of authorization, environmental assessment, environmental monitoring, consideration of transfrontier impacts, safety measures, contingency planning, liability and compensation.

The Guidelines are global in scope. They relate directly to the need to protect the environment in an important sector of national economic development, i.e., in offshore mining and drilling. The Guidelines acknowledge the significance of the offshore industry to both developed and developing countries. They aim to assist Governments to develop national, regional and global regimes based on the best practice.

Two progress reports in 1985 and 1987 to the UNEP Governing Council indicated that very few governments had made use of the Guidelines (UNEP/GC.13/9/Add.1 and UNEP/GC.14/25). In 1989, seven Governments noted the compatibility of their own legislation with the Guidelines; seven intergovernmental organizations noted the significance of the Guidelines for their work (UNEP/GC.15/9/Add.2).

Participation

Experts from developing countries participated in the UNEP Working Group of Experts on Environmental Law which drew up the Guidelines. The Guidelines were endorsed by the UNEP Governing Council (GC) under Decision 10/14/VI and by the UN General Assembly (UNGA).

Implementation and information

The Guidelines impose no commitments; they constitute non-mandatory "soft law". The UNGA has recommended them to Governments (Resolution 37/217 of 20 December 1982). Following endorsement of the Guidelines by the UNEP Governing Council and UNGA, the UNGA asked the UNEP GC to submit periodic progress reports on the use made of these Guidelines. This was done in the UNGA fortieth and forty-second sessions.

There are no requirements for data supply.

Following discussion in UNEP GC and UNGA, Governments and international organizations were asked by letter from UNEP's Executive Director to report on the use made of the Guidelines in national law. Only two positive reports were received in 1984/5; reports from 4 governments and 4 UN bodies in 1987; and 7 governmental and 7 intergovernmental reports in 1988/9. The UNEP progress reports do not specify reasons for the low level of implementation by Governments. No dispute settlement mechanisms are included in the guidelines.

The Guidelines have been issued in Arabic, Chinese, English, French, Russian and Spanish. (UNEP Environmental Law Guidelines and Principles, No. 4)

Information on implementation is periodically provided to governments through reports to UNEP GC by the Executive Director. Consideration of the Guidelines is included in a number of national university courses.

Operation, review and adjustment

UNEP co-ordinates information on the use of the Guidelines. International administrative costs of dissemination and review are included in the regular budget of the UNEP.

IMO has suggested that the Guidelines be reviewed in the light of new IMO recommendations. This could be done through the UNEP Governing Council, based on further study by the UNEP Working Group of Experts on Environmental Law.

Codification programming

The Guidelines are designed to be taken into account in negotiation of regional and global conventions. This has been done in the negotiation of regional protocols in the Regional Seas Programme on off-shore operations in the Persian/Arabian Gulf (see the 1989 Kuwait Protocol on marine pollution resulting from exploration and exploitation of the continental shelf, under No. 42) and in the Mediterranean (see No. 41). They are also being taken into account in other regions.

The Guidelines require further transformation into intergovernmental agreements as well as national legislation. The Guidelines themselves, as a non-formal instrument, have contributed to the development of international law.

(38) United Nations Convention on the Law of the Sea
(Montego Bay, 10 December 1982)

Objectives and Achievement

The basic objective of the Convention is to establish "a legal order for the seas and oceans which will facilitate international communication, and will promote the peaceful uses of the seas and oceans, the equitable and efficient utilization of their resources, the conservation of their living resources, and the study, protection and preservation of the marine environment." (Preamble, para. 4). On the basis of recognition that "the problems of ocean space are closely interrelated and need to be considered as a whole" (Preamble, para. 3), the Convention lays down a series of interrelated legal regimes, integrating all elements, especially the rational exploitation and sound conservation of the living and non-living resources of the sea and the protection and preservation of the marine environment. The Convention also lays down the fundamental rule linking development to environmental protection:

"States have the sovereign right to exploit their natural resources pursuant to their environmental policies and in accordance with their duty to protect and preserve the marine environment" (art. 193).

This rule is set forth in the first provision of Part XII of the Convention devoted to the protection and preservation of the marine environment.

The Convention is global in scope. The special circumstances of developing countries are stressed throughout the Convention. Its provisions consistently recognize the special interests and needs of developing countries and especially in such contexts as the conservation and utilization of the living resources, technical assistance with respect to marine pollution, marine scientific research, and various aspects of the deep seabed regime. Moreover, an entire part - Part XIV - is devoted to the development and transfer of technology for promoting capacity building, particularly, of developing countries.

More specifically on the protection and preservation of the marine environment, the interests of developing countries are catered for by:

(a)   permitting States to use the best practicable means at their disposal and in accordance with their capabilities (Art. 194(1)).

(b)   Provision for scientific and technical assistance to developing States (Art 202).

(c)   According preferential treatment for developing States in the allocation by international organizations of appropriate funds and technical assistance and the utilization of their specialized services (Art 203).

(d)   Allowing for characteristic regional features, the economic capacity of developing States and their need for economic development to be taken into account in the development of global and regional rules, standards and recommended practices and procedures for the prevention, reduction and control of pollution from land-based sources (Art. 207(4)).

Since the Convention contains the global framework of general rules, realization of its objectives depends on the whole fabric of international and domestic law. Although the Convention has not entered into force yet, its basic objectives in the areas of environment and development have been incorporated in many global and regional instruments and national laws. Several international and regional organizations have also taken measures to adjust their mandate and activities to the provisions of the Convention. On the other hand, the Convention's basic objectives and provisions have not yet been met to a satisfactory degree in some important fields, such as the prevention, reduction and control of several sources of marine pollution, conservation and optimal utilization of the living resources, the capacity building of developing States in science and technology, and the rights of land-locked and geographically disadvantaged States. Goal achievement must be measured considering all these elements.

As regards protection of the marine environment, the Convention represents the culmination of important legal developments initiated by the Stockholm Declaration. The various multilateral treaties concluded during the Third UN Conference on the Law of the Sea and subsequent to the adoption of the Convention, e.g., regional agreements under the UNEP Regional Seas Programme, have contributed to the codification of international law relating to the environment. Thus its basic provisions regarding pollution from ships and dumping have been put into practice to a considerable degree by the 1973/1978 MARPOL Convention, the 1972 London and Oslo Dumping Conventions, the 1969 Convention Relating to Intervention on the High Seas, and regional protocols regulating dumping. The 1989 International Salvage Convention and the 1990 Convention on Oil Pollution Preparedness, Response and Co-operation are also intended to promote the objectives of co-operation and contingency planning to deal with marine pollution. Some aspects of the Convention not covered by these agreements, such as the extension of coastal State jurisdiction over pollution in the exclusive economic zone, have influenced the legislation of a small number of States, but the Convention's jurisdictional provisions, particularly Article 218 relating to port State jurisdiction over extra-territorial offenses, have not been widely implemented. As regards pollution from continental shelf operations or from land-based and atmospheric sources, some progress has been made at regional level in negotiating treaties for these purposes, in harmonizing national practices, and in securing implementation in national law. Regional agreements include the 1974 Paris Convention on The Prevention of Marine Pollution from Land-based Sources, the 1974 Convention on the Pollution of the Baltic Sea Area, the 1980 Athens Protocol on the Protection of the Mediterranean Sea Against Pollution from Land-based Sources, the 1983 Protocol for the Protection of the South East Pacific Against Pollution from Land-based Sources, the 1989 Kuwait Protocol on Marine Pollution from Exploration and Exploitation of the Continental Shelf and the 1990 Kuwait Protocol for the Protection of the Marine Environment against Pollution from Land-Based Sources. UN Doc, A/CONF.151/PC/71 lists action taken by States to implement or respond to the Montreal Guidelines for the Protection of the Marine Environment Against Pollution from Land-based Sources (QV). Not all States have participated in such regional arrangements, however, or adopted legislation to implement the Convention's purposes in these respects. The Convention has thus achieved some of its purposes by codification, and in some cases by stimulating the development of new rules of customary law and State practice.

Participation

Membership is open to all States; all self-governing associated States which have competence over matters governed by the Convention, including competence to enter into treaties in this respect; all territories enjoying full internal self-government recognized as such by the UN and which have competence over matters governed by the Convention; international organizations as defined (Art. 305).

Reservations are prohibited (Art. 309 and Annex IX).

As of 1 January 1992, 51 States have ratified or acceded to the Convention, consisting of:

3   from Europe
10   from Asia and Pacific
26   from Africa
12   from Latin America and the Caribbean

Except one State, all of these are developing countries.

During the Third United Nations Conference on the Law of the Sea, developing countries were fully represented and actively participated in the negotiation and drafting of the Convention. Indeed, the Conference would not have been held without the initiative of developing countries. Some of the most important concepts in the Convention derive from developing countries. Especially, the concept of the exclusive economic zone (EEZ) is based on the proposals vigorously advanced particularly by Latin American and African countries with a view to extending their exclusive jurisdiction over their natural resources from traditional 3 - 12 miles to 200 miles. A number of delegates from developing countries played important roles in the Conference, both formal and informal, including personal initiatives. Developing countries are very well represented also in the Preparatory Commission for the International Seabed Authority and for the International Tribunal for the Law of the Sea, which has been preparing for the two institutions to be set up under the Convention.

A number of incentives are available in the Convention to encourage participation by developing countries. These are, e.g., as follows:

(a)   The regime of the EEZ has radically expanded the resource base for many coastal States and particularly small island countries. Coastal States in general are also given certain leeway in the management of fisheries in their EEZ in that disputes relating to their sovereign rights over fisheries are exempt from compulsory binding dispute-settlement procedure.

(b)   The Convention establishes the regime to be applied to the deep seabed beyond the limits of national jurisdiction (the "Area"). It declares that the Area and its resources are the common heritage of mankind, and that activities in the Area shall "take into particular consideration the interests and needs of developing States ..." (arts. 136 and 140). In order to ensure these principles, the Convention specifically provides that the "effective participation of developed States in activities in the Area shall be promoted as provided for in [Part XI], having due regard to their special interests and needs ..." (art. 148).

(c)   The Convention has added a new dimension to the traditional regime of the continental shelf by requiring those States having a shelf broader than 200 miles to make financial or other contribution to the international community in respect of their mineral exploitation beyond 200 miles. Such contributions are exempted for developing States which are net importers of the mineral resources concerned. Further, such contributions are to be distributed to the Convention Parties "on the basis of equitable sharing criteria, taking into account the interests and needs of developing States ..." (art. 82).

(d)   The Convention establishes the concept and the regime of archipelagic States, with considerable benefits to qualifying countries. Like the EEZ, the concept of archipelagic State derives also from proposals by developing States. Fourteen countries - all of them developing - have declared themselves to be archipelagic States on the basis of the Convention.

(e)   Part XIV of the Convention is devoted to the development and transfer of marine technology, calling for co-operation in promoting the development and transfer of technology, particularly to developing States, with respect to the exploration and exploitation of marine resources, the protection of the marine environment, marine scientific research and other activities, " with a view to accelerating the social and economic development of the developing States" (art.266). The co-operative mechanisms in Part XIII on marine scientific research also contain a variety of benefits for developing countries. It should also be noted that the Third UN Conference on the Law of the Sea adopted a resolution on the development of national marine science, technology and ocean service infrastructures, urging the industrialized countries to assist the developing countries in those areas (Annex VI of the Final Act).

(f)   In the field of prevention and control of the marine environment, developing States are to be granted preference by international organization in the allocation of funds and technical assistance, as well as in the utilization of their specialized services (art. 203). Also, States are required to promote programmes of scientific, educational, technical and other assistance to developing countries for preventing and combating marine pollution. With regard to incentives to facilitate implementation, certain obligations of States are mitigated for developing countries. In particular, with respect to the duty to prevent, reduce and control marine pollution, States are required to take all necessary measures using "the best practicable means at their disposal and in accordance with their capabilities" (art. 194). Moreover, some of the provisions regarding transfer of technology and technical assistance referred to above would also indirectly facilitate the implementation of the Convention by developing countries.

No special measure was taken during the Third UN Conference to promote and support the effective participation of developing countries. This is also the case of the Preparatory Commission. The Office for Ocean Affairs and the Law of the Sea convenes, from time to time, groups of experts in order to consult on certain technical aspects of the implementation of the Convention as part of its activities for the consistent and uniform application of the Convention. The United Nations provides financial assistance to those experts who come from developing countries, out of voluntary as well as regular funds.

Implementation and information

There are numerous and substantial commitments imposed on parties throughout the Convention. In the field of the protection and preservation of the marine environment, States are obliged to take all measures necessary to prevent, reduce and control marine pollution from any source. Six sources are identified, with detailed obligations of States stipulated concerning each of them. They are also required to adopt laws and regulations, to co-operate in elaborating international rules, standards and recommended practices and procedures, and to enforce them.

Because of the nature of the provisions as framework rules, compliance with obligations are often monitored through the competent international organization like the International Maritime Organization.

There is no general performance reporting system in the Convention, except for Part XI relating to the deep seabed area. There is, however, a system of dissemination of information on such matters as charts and co-ordinates pertinent to jurisdictional limits. The coastal States must deposit a copy of such charts or list of co-ordinates with Secretary-General of the United Nations. Parties have also specific duties to give notice or notification to other parties concerned or to the international community at large on certain specific measures taken in compliance with specific provisions, such as construction and removal of artificial islands, enforcement measures taken for pollution control, and sea lanes and traffic separation schemes.

The Convention does provide for the Secretary-General of the United Nations to report to States and international organizations on issues of a general nature that have arisen with respect to the Convention (Art. 319 (1) (a)). The current annual report to the General Assembly under the item "Law of the Sea" may be viewed as an early implementation of that provision. States also often report on the measures they have taken at the General Assembly in connection with the annual debate on the same item.

Apart from the Convention provisions, States now as a matter of practice publicize new legislation and agreements through the Law of the Sea Bulletin (see (20) (c) below).

The Convention requires States to contribute and exchange, on a regular basis through competent international organization, "available scientific information, catch and fishing effort statistics, and other relevant data relevant to the conservation of fish stocks" (arts. 61 and 119). This applies to both the EEZ and the high seas.

With respect to marine scientific research, States and international organization are required to publish and disseminate information on proposed major research programmes and their results. For this purpose, States are obliged to "actively promote the flow of scientific data and information and the transfer of knowledge" resulting from such research, especially to developing countries (art. 244). With respect to the research conducted in the EEZ and the continental shelf, researching States and organizations must provide the coastal State with the reports on the research and, if requested, access to all data and samples obtained (art. 249).

The annual debate at the General Assembly on the law of the sea and its resolution provide opportunities for promoting compliance and following up on non-compliance in general terms. Mention should also be made of the practice among States to send formal protest notes against measures taken by other States which they consider contrary to, or not in conformity with, the Convention. Such protests are often published in the Law of the Sea Bulletin at the request of the States concerned. Once in force, the Convention's dispute settlement mechanisms discussed under (17) below will greatly enhance the ability to deal with non-compliance.

The Convention established an International Tribunal for the Law of the Sea as a means for the settlement of disputes concerning the interpretation or application of the Convention. The Convention also established a special arbitral procedure, to which disputes concerning the interpretation or application of its articles relating to the fisheries, protection and preservation of the marine environment, marine research, and navigation may be submitted.

The Convention provides for compulsory binding dispute-settlement procedures for those disputes which arise when a coastal State contravenes international rules and standards for the protection and preservation of the marine environment which have been established by the Convention or through a competent international organization or diplomatic conference (art. 197(1)). Disputes concerning the interpretation or application of the provisions with regard to fisheries are also to be settled through compulsory procedures, except where they relate to the sovereign rights of coastal State in its EEZ (art. 297(3)).

None of these procedures have been used because the Convention has not entered into force.

It should be noted that Resolution II of the Third UN Conference on the Law of the Sea establishes an interim regime governing preparatory investments in the activities in the deep seabed area before the entry into force of the Convention. In implementing resolution II, the Preparatory Commission has served as a mechanism to ensure that there were not disputes among the pioneer investors to be registered subsequently regarding overlapping of their deep seabed mining sites.

The Convention is done in six official languages of the United Nations. The text was published and disseminated in all languages in the form of an Official UN document. It is also contained in the Official Records of the Third UN Conference on the Law of the Sea. For wider distribution and use, the Convention text is made available, in all UN languages, as a separate UN publication together with the Final Act of the Conference and an index.

Current information on the developments relating to the Convention is made available to Governments, academic institutions, scholars and the industries concerned through the following publications, all prepared by the Office for Ocean Affairs and the Law of the Sea:

(a)   Report of the Secretary-General submitted annually to the General Assembly under the item, "the Law of the Sea", containing overview of trends and developments relevant to the Convention. The report is widely disseminated and used.

(b)   Annual Review of Ocean Affairs: Law and Policy, containing texts and selected extracts of documents emanating from global and regional organizations.

(c)   The Law of the Sea Bulletin, containing the texts of relevant national legislation and treaties as well as other latest information on the law of the sea, as soon as they are made available. This is published periodically, three or four times a year, and disseminated widely.

(d)   Annual Select Bibliography on the law of the sea.

The Office for Ocean Affairs and the Law of the Sea has been publishing three additional series of materials to provide guidance for the implementation of the Convention. These are:

(a)   Compilations of legislative materials on subject basis, such as the EEZ, the continental shelf, protection of the marine environment, marine scientific research, and maritime boundary agreements.

(b)   Legislative histories with respect to key provisions of the Convention, e.g., pollution by dumping, regime of islands, archipelagic States, and navigation on the high seas.

(c)   Publications providing guidance to the implementation of certain provisions, such as those relating to baselines and marine scientific research. Another publication, on the high seas fisheries is being prepared.

The Office has also published a compilation of declarations and objections thereto made by States with respect to the Convention.

These materials have been used in international and regional training and education programmes. The extent of their use in national programmes has not been monitored.

Operation, review and adjustment

The Secretary-General of the United Nations is designated as the depositary of the Convention. The Office for Ocean Affairs and the Law of the Sea, now part of the UN Office of Legal Affairs, is engaged in the day-to-day administration pertaining to the Convention - including its interim regime before entry into force, and the servicing of the Preparatory Commission for the International Seabed Authority and for the International Tribunal for the Law of the Sea.

The annual cost of the Office for 1990 was approximately US $4,500,000 excluding common services. Except for approximately $110,000 which was from the extrabudgetary sources, all were appropriated from the regular budget of the Organization.

The main benefits for States to be expected from the Convention are, inter alia, various additional uses of the sea, supplementary food resources and export earnings from living and non-living resources in the vastly expanded areas of their EEZs, new marine technologies, more efficient management of the ocean sector, as well as improved marine and coastal environment. These benefits of participation cannot be summarized in any general manner; they will vary according to the interests and perceptions of individual States. The Convention itself is a package deal based on consensus so it reflects a number of fundamental compromises among different groups of States, including maritime and coastal States, coastal and distant water fishing States, developed and developing States, land-locked and coastal States. In certain areas, where the Convention has already determined the development of international law, such as the extension of coastal State fisheries jurisdiction, it is questionable whether participation in the Convention is required to assure these gains. The main participation cost is the contribution to the running of the International Seabed Authority, the International Tribunal for the Law of the Sea and its Seabed Disputes Chamber. These costs fall mainly on developed nations and are offset in the case of developing nations by the arrangements for equitable sharing of deep seabed revenues. Participation costs for developing countries will be high, however, if the Convention is in force, if no deep seabed mining takes place, and if developed States do not become parties, and are therefore not contributors to the institutional costs.

States are also required to contribute funds or provide guarantees for the costs of the first operation of the Enterprise, the deep seabed mining arm of the Authority. This could be burdensome, but the present trend in the Preparatory Commission is to find ways of avoiding such costs, e.g. through a joint-venture.

Several provisions of the Convention require that States use scientific information or data for taking measures in such fields as the conservation of the living resources, and the elaboration of rules, standards and recommended practices and procedures for the protection and preservation of the marine environment (see also 15 above).

For establishing the outer limit of the continental shelf where it extends beyond 200 miles from the baseline, the Convention established a commission of scientific experts to which a coastal State must submit relevant information for recommendation on the establishment of such limits (art. 76).

The Convention establishes two subsidiary organs for the Council of the International Seabed Authority. The two organs, the Economic Planning Commission and the Legal and Technical Commission, give technical and scientific advice to the Council for its decision-making (arts. 164 and 165).

In the fields of the conservation of living resources and the protection and preservation of the marine environment, no provision is made for the participation of specific scientific experts from governments or other bodies in the decision-making process.

In the case of the commission on the limits of the continental shelf, however, it is to be comprised of experts in the relevant disciplines, serving in their personal capacities, selected with "due regard to the need to ensure equitable geographical representation" (Annex II). The Economic Planning Commission and the Legal and Technical Commission of the Authority's Council are also to be comprised of members with appropriate technical and scientific qualifications (arts. 164 and 165). However, with respect to the settlement of disputes relating to fisheries, protection of the marine environment and marine scientific research, the Convention provides for the creation of a special arbitral tribunal to be composed of experts in the respective fields (Annex VIII).

Codification programming

As part of its mandate, the Preparatory Commission is drafting regulations for the protection and preservation of the marine environment from activities in the deep seabed areas LOS/PCN/SCN.3/WP.6/Add.5 (1990).

There is no mechanism to ensure co-ordination in drafting clearly related instruments. Given what is stated in para. 30 (a) of page 24, co-operation is needed to ensure the compatibility between the regulations regarding pollution from deep seabed mining, ocean dumping and pollution from other maritime activities.

Decisions of international courts and arbitral tribunals as well as practice of States may be considered to be making important contributions to the development of international law relevant to the law of the sea. Already international tribunals are relying on the norms established in the Convention and determining proper implementation of the Convention. A number of guidelines, recommended practices and procedures have been prepared by competent international organizations in accordance with the Convention. These non-binding instruments have also contributed to the development of international law.

(39) UNEP Montreal Guidelines for the Protection of the Marine Environment Against Pollution from Land-based Sources
(Montreal, 19 April 1985)

Objectives and Achievement

The basic objective of the guidelines is to assist governments in the process of developing appropriate bilateral, regional and multilateral agreements and national legislation for the protection of the marine environment against pollution from land-based sources. They are of a recommendatory nature only, and serve as a checklist of basic provisions rather than as a model agreement.

The guidelines are global in scope.

The special circumstances of developing countries are taken into account by recognizing that States should act in accordance with their capabilities, and that internationally agreed rules and standards should take account of the economic capacity of States and their need for sustainable development (Arts. 4 and 5). The guidelines also recognize the desirability of promoting programmes of assistance to developing countries for the purpose of improving their capacity to prevent, reduce and control pollution from land-based sources, to assess its effects on the marine environment, and to enable them to establish infrastructure for the effective implementation of internationally agreed rules, criteria, standards and recommended practices and procedures related to protection of the marine environment (Art. 9)

Since 1985, when the guidelines were adopted, the following regional and bilateral agreements have been negotiated:

(a)   Kuwait Protocol on the Protection of the Marine Environment against Pollution from Land Based Sources, 1990 (No. 47).

(b)   US-Canada Agreement on the Conservation of the Marine Environment of the Gulf of Maine, 1989.

In addition, a draft protocol on the prevention of marine pollution from land-based sources has been prepared as part of a draft regional Convention on the Protection of the Black Sea Against Pollution, and new protocols on land-based pollution sources are currently in preparation under the 1983 Cartagena Convention for the Caribbean (No. 52) and the 1981 Abidjan Convention for West and Central Africa (No. 48). The International North Sea Conferences, held in 1987 and 1990, the Conference on Security and Co-operation in Europe, meeting in 1990, and the Baltic Sea States have all supported the adoption of stronger measures to control land-based pollution.

UNEP has reported on action taken to implement the guideline, based on replies from 34 governments and 38 international organizations (UN Doc. A/CONF.151/PC/71, 1991). These show that some States have taken action with the specific intention of implementing the guidelines, while in other cases action taken independently is nevertheless in conformity with them. The nature of the measures reported by individual States varies widely, however, and in some cases amounts to nothing of substance.

Participation

Funds have been made available by the World Bank, the EEC and the European Investment Bank to support national programmes in the Mediterranean. These have been of assistance to some developing countries in the region. The guidelines also call for technical assistance to be made available to developing countries, as indicated above. The only region in which such assistance has been reported on a significant scale is the Mediterranean.

Implementation and information

No commitments are imposed on States. Implementation has been reviewed by UNEP on an ad hoc basis.

Article 18 of the Guidelines calls for States to report as appropriate to the other States concerned on measures taken, results received and difficulties encountered in the implementation of applicable internationally agreed rules, criteria, standards and recommended practices and procedures. 34 States reported in 1990 to UNEP on their implementation measures under the guidelines. In most cases, however, reports will be submitted to regional institutions established under applicable regional agreements, such as the 1974 Paris Convention (No. 45 below).

The guidelines call for States to collect data on natural conditions in the region concerned, on the input of substances, and levels of pollution; they also call for timely notification of releases of land-based pollution likely to affect the marine environment. Implementation of these objectives will take place under applicable regional conventions and arrangements.

It is likely that the financial, scientific and technical resources required are the major factors influencing implementation of the guidelines in developing countries. In many cases these States have economic priorities which do not accord sufficient weight to the control of land-based pollution. The absence of non-compliance procedures or dispute settlement machinery under applicable regional instruments is also a relevant factor.

The guidelines are available in Arabic, Chinese, English, French, Russian and Spanish as published by UNEP.

Operation, review and adjustment

The guidelines call for institutional arrangements to be established, as they have been under most of the applicable regional agreements. The guidelines themselves are administered by UNEP. Work relating to dissemination and review of the guidelines is budgeted as part of the regular programme of the UNEP Environmental Law and Institutions Unit, Nairobi. Reviews of the guidelines are undertaken by UNEP as required.

GESAMP reports on the state of the marine environment, and scientific reports commissioned by regional institutions are available to policy-makers, but no mechanism for the dissemination of such knowledge is established under the guidelines.

Codification Programming

Proposals have been made for a global instrument to provide a framework for the control of land-based marine pollution. Some states favour a legally binding convention; others prefer a non-binding instrument consisting of a statement of principles and an "action plan". Alternatively, a combined instrument linking a global agreement and an action plan have also been proposed. The Intergovernmental Meeting of Experts (Halifax, May 1991) considered the merits of these proposals, but did not complete its work. It did conclude that substantial improvements were needed in existing legal and institutional frameworks at global and regional levels. A UNEP report (reproduced in UN Doc. A/CONF.151/PC/71, 1991) proposes the possible options of a global convention, a non-treaty instrument, and a global convention supplemented by an Action Plan.

There are no "gaps" as such waiting to be filled, save perhaps for the questions of liability for pollution damage (addressed in chapter X) and of mandatory consultation and notification in case of potential transboundary pollution. Rather, the issue is whether there should be a new global treaty to strengthen the present regime of regional and national action.

The Montreal Guidelines themselves have had some influence on State practice, and on subsequent drafting of regional agreements.

(40) International Convention on Salvage
(London, 28 April 1989)

Objectives and achievement

The objective of the convention is the establishment of uniform international rules on salvage operations in order to improve the safety of vessels, protect the marine environment, and provide incentives for persons carrying out salvage operations.

The convention is global in scope.

No special provisions are made for the situation of developing countries.

The convention is not yet in force.

Participation

The convention is open to all States.

States may reserve the right not to apply the convention to certain situations where their national interests alone are concerned, or where the property involved is maritime cultural property situated on the sea-bed. Reservations made at the time of signature are subject to confirmation upon ratification.

The convention was drafted by the Legal Committee of the International Maritime Organization (IMO). The final drafting was done by the International Conference on Salvage, which adopted the convention. Of the 66 States participating in the conference, 39 were developing countries.

The convention provides no special incentives for developing country participation. On the proposal of a group of Latin American States, the salvage conference adopted a resolution calling for assistance to Governments, upon their request, in the drafting of the legislation necessary for implementation of the convention.

Implementation and information

The convention establishes a régime for salvage operations, laying down the mutual rights and obligations of persons involved in such operations, and the contents of contracts on salvage. It does not impose obligations on States directly.

A resolution adopted by the salvage conference, calls on member states to transmit to IMO texts of national legislation relevant to the scope and objectives of the convention.

No dispute settlement mechanism is provided.

The convention was adopted in the official UN languages (Arabic, Chinese, English, French, Russian and Spanish). It is available in all these languages from IMO.

A resolution adopted by the salvage conference recommends that IMO promote public awareness of the convention by holding seminars, courses or symposia. It proposes that the study of the convention be included in the curriculum of existing IMO training institutions.

Operation, review and adjustment

Beyond assigning limited functions to IMO, the convention does not provide for institutional arrangements.

For the purpose of revising or amending the convention, a special conference may be convened by IMO.

(41) International Convention on Oil Pollution Preparedness, Response and Co-operation
(London, 30 November 1990)

Objectives and achievement

The first objective of the convention is the prevention of marine pollution by oil, in accordance with the precautionary principle. Secondly, the convention aims for the advance adoption of adequate response measures in the event that oil pollution does occur. To achieve these aims, mutual assistance and co-operation between party states is envisaged. The objectives of the convention have no direct implications for development issues.

The convention is global in scope.

No direct reference is made to the situation and needs of developing countries. The convention does, however, call for technical assistance to those parties which request such support (Art. 9).

Participation

Membership of the treaty is open to all States (Art. 15). Of the 90 States participating in the international conference which drafted the final text and adopted the convention, 68 were developing countries.

The convention does not include a provision on reservations.

The convention is not yet in force.

Beyond a very generally worded provision on technical co-operation (Art. 9), no incentive for developing country participation is provided. Resolution 6, adopted at the same time as the treaty, explicitly calls for provision of technical assistance to developing countries.

Implementation and information

Parties to the convention must require ships, offshore installations and sea ports under their jurisdiction to have oil pollution emergency plans (Art. 3). The convention establishes a reporting procedure on oil pollution incidents. Under this procedure, all persons concerned shall be required to report such incidents to the competent national authority, which must assess the incident and inform other states and/or IMO (Art. 4 + 5). Parties shall establish national and, as far as possible, regional systems for preparedness and response (Art. 6). They shall co-operate in pollution response (Art. 7), research (Art. 8), and technical matters (Art. 9).

Information on some aspects of implementation must be provided to IMO (Art. 6(3)).

Beyond the general obligations to co-operate in research and technical assistance (Art. 8 and 9), no provision for disclosure of data is made.

IMO shall act as clearing-house for such information as parties are required to provide to it (Art. 12). Parties shall evaluate the effectiveness of the convention together with IMO; no evaluation criteria or time scales are given (Art. 13).

The convention was established in the six official UN languages (Arabic, Chinese,

English, French, Russian, and Spanish). The text is available from IMO in all these languages.

Prior to the adoption of the convention, IMO elaborated a Guide to International Assistance in Maritime Pollution Emergencies, which was distributed at the diplomatic conference.

An Annex to the convention sets out the modalities of allocating the costs incurred by states in responding to oil pollution incidents. At the time of the adoption of the convention, the diplomatic conference adopted 10 resolutions, all which of are designed to provide more detailed guidance on various aspects of the implementation of the convention.

Following the adoption of the convention, IMO and industry representatives jointly established a steering group for education and training for oil spill preparedness and response.

Operation, review and adjustment

IMO was designated by the convention to act as clearing-house for information submitted to it by parties, and to facilitate co-operation among parties in technical and educational matters (Art. 12). These functions will be carried out after entry into force of the convention; no provision for an interim arrangement has been made. The convention also does not establish a meeting of the parties or similar institution.

Parties are required to evaluate the effectiveness of the convention together with IMO (Art. 13).

II. REGIONAL MARINE ENVIRONMENT

(42) Nordic Agreement Concerning Co-operation in Measures to Deal with Pollution of the Sea by Oil
(Copenhagen, 16 September 1971)

Objectives and achievement

The main objective of the Copenhagen Agreement is to ensure co-operation in dealing with any significant pollution of the sea by oil which threatens the coasts and related interests of one of the Contracting States. Another objective is to co-operate in furthering supervision of compliance with the 1969 Bonn Agreement for Co-operation in Dealing with Pollution of the North Sea by Oil. (This Agreement was replaced by the 1983 Bonn Agreement for Co-operation in Dealing with Pollution of the North Sea by Oil and Other Harmful Substances (No. 53 in the present survey).

Like the 1969 Bonn Agreement (later supplemented/replaced by the 1983 Bonn Agreement) the Contracting States of the 1971 Copenhagen Agreement undertake to share information about the sighting of oil slicks and the readiness of their respective equipment to deal with such slicks.

The Copenhagen Agreement goes further by providing more powers to Contracting States in the investigation of alleged offenses, including the power to take oil samples, under Art.7.

This Agreement therefore represents an early attempt at increasing environmental awareness and co-ordinating national regulatory efforts against oil pollution from ships.

Since this Agreement involves only the Nordic states, all of which are classified as developed countries, it does not need to take into account any special circumstances of developing countries.

The annual meetings of the Parties and the establishment of technical working groups which have prepared operational guidelines for the implementation of this Agreement indicate that its objectives have been achieved.

Participation

The Copenhagen Agreement was concluded between Norway, Denmark, Finland, and Sweden. It is a restricted agreement in that it was only open for signature by these four countries and came into force one month after their respective signatures. (Art.12) There is no provision in this agreement for the accession of other States; however, the Agreement is currently being expanded to include Iceland.

Reservations are not prohibited.

The current geographical distribution of membership is confined to what are commonly known as the Nordic countries, consisting of Norway, Denmark, Finland and Sweden. There are no developing countries in this group.

Public opinion had a positive influence on participation.

Implementation and information

Since the agreement was due to come into force one month after it had been signed by all four participating states (Art.12), and duly came into force in October,1971 after being opened for signature from 16 September 1971, implementation was indeed accelerated by the provisions regarding its entry into force.

The Parties undertake to inform each other of the sighting of any significant oil slick which may drift towards another party's territory. (Art.1)

Furthermore, any Contracting State threatened by significant oil pollution which may also affect another Contracting State is required to investigate the situation and communicate the results of this investigation without delay to the other state. (Art.2)

Should a Contracting State require assistance to deal with oil which is threatening its coast or related interests, it may request help from the other Contracting States. Any Contracting State which has been asked for assistance is required to do what is possible to render such assistance. (Art.3)

In furtherance of the main objective of co-operation, the Contracting States shall exchange information concerning (a)facilities for the reception of oily residues from ships; (b)national regulations which are relevant to the avoidance of oil pollution; and (c)the relevant authorities in the respective Contracting States dealing with oil pollution of the sea. (Art.8)

Art.9 requires the competent authorities to co-operate directly in the planning for the implementation of this Agreement.

Art.4 places a duty on Parties to provide and maintain stocks of slick-fighting equipment.

The Contracting State shall also inform the other Contracting States of the equipment it has for dealing with oil pollution. (Art.4(c))

Art.7 provides that the Contracting States shall render assistance to each other in the investigation of offenses against the regulations concerning pollution by oil.

The implementation of this commitment under Art.7 includes inspection of the oil record book, the ship's official log-book, and the engine room log, as well as the taking of oil samples.

The power to take oil samples (though presumably limited to ships registered in the Contracting State) provided an important element that had previously been lacking in the enforcement of preventive standards.

The Contracting Parties have been meeting regularly, and established technical working groups. In this way, their respective performances can be scrutinized.

These working groups have developed command structures, communications schemes, alarm procedures and exercise programmes as well as an exchange of information on equipment and national combating organizations, all of which are contained in a manual on co-operation which is updated periodically based on actual experience and exercises.

In addition to the requirements for sharing information set down in Articles 1, 2, and 8, which were explained earlier in answer to paragraph 1, Art.4(c) provides that a Contracting State shall inform the other Contracting States of the equipment it has for dealing with oil pollution.

Art.4(d) further obliges the Contracting States to inform each other of their experiences in the materials and methods of dealing with oil pollution.

Art.5 requires that the other Contracting States shall be informed of any action taken against an oil-slick, including the measures taken and their result.

A specific requirement of data disclosure is also to be found in Art.6. This provides that the competent authority of a Contracting State should be informed in any case where a vessel registered in that State has been observed committing an offence within the territorial or adjacent waters of the Contracting States against oil pollution regulations.

Aside from the provisions in this Agreement that deal with the exchange of information, and the exhortation contained in Art.9 to the effect that the competent authorities shall co-operate in planning and the other measures required of them; few possibilities exist within the framework of this Agreement to promote compliance and follow-up on non-compliance.

Thus, compliance is ensured through multilateral co-operation in enforcing both international and national regulations relating to the prevention of marine pollution from ships.

Since all the Contracting Parties to the Copenhagen Agreement are Contracting Parties to the Bonn Agreement or the Helsinki Agreement, or both, there has also been a good deal of experience of harmonization, in particular with respect to pollution reporting systems.

There are no mechanisms available within the framework of this Agreement to deal with disputes over its implementation.

A number of factors influenced implementation but public opinion and committed government policies probably have had the biggest influence.

The Copenhagen Agreement was done in a single copy in the Danish, Finnish, Norwegian and Swedish languages, all four texts being equally authentic. A manual on co-operation is updated periodically and the various reports have been in fulfilment of the exchange of information requirements. The above information is used in training exercises for oil spill response operations.

Operation, review and adjustment

There are no provisions for institutional arrangements in this agreement. But the Contracting Parties have met annually and have established technical working groups which provide some form of institutional structure.

The main benefit that is derived from national participation in this regional agreement is greater co-operation in the sighting and clearing-up of oil-slicks in the Nordic region. By co-operating with each other, the participating states will also be helping to ensure that a far larger area is covered than that which is within their own individual capacities to control. The participating states will benefit too from the exchange of information on new types of technology and new methods used for the cleaning-up of oil-slicks.

The main costs of national participation will go towards fulfilling the commitments imposed on the Contracting States by this agreement. This is especially true in respect of Art.4 which places a duty on Parties to provide and maintain stocks of slick-fighting equipment.

The technical workgroups and the manual for co-operation which is updated periodically help to ensure that scientific advice is taken into account.

The national authorities are already heavily involved in the implementation of this agreement through the information exchange and reporting requirements.

The annual meetings of the Contracting Parties would be the most appropriate forum for such a review. Although the Agreement is currently being expanded to include Iceland, the revised text is not yet available.

Codification programming

As mentioned above, the treaty is currently being expanded to include Iceland, but the revised text is not yet available.

As all the Parties to the present Agreement are also Parties to the Bonn Agreement (No.53) the Helsinki Convention (No.44), there is continuous co-ordination between them.

As its title indicates, the Nordic Agreement is solely concerned with co-operation in measures to deal with the pollution of the sea by oil, especially in the form of oil-slicks. This agreement leaves some gaps that need to be covered by further legal provision in terms of other different types of marine pollution. For example, although this Agreement was clearly inspired by the 1969 Bonn Agreement, it has not expanded its scope of application to include other harmful substances as the 1983 Bonn Agreement has done.

The ministerial-level International North Sea Conferences, the most recent of which was held in The Hague, on 8 March 1990 are useful mechanisms other than formal agreements which have contributed to the development of international law in this area. In the latest Conference, the Governments of Denmark, Norway and Sweden actually participated, while the Finnish Government sent an observer.

(43) Convention for the Prevention of Marine Pollution by Dumping from Ships and Aircraft
(Oslo, 15 February 1972) as amended

Objectives and achievement

The basic objectives of the Oslo Convention are set down in Art.1 where the Contracting Parties pledge themselves to take all possible steps to prevent the pollution of the sea by substances that are liable to create hazards to human health, to harm living resources and marine life, to damage amenities or to interfere with other legitimate users of the sea.

The Parties recognize that action on marine dumping must be taken at a regional as well as a global level. In line with the main objectives set down in Art.1, Art.4 states that the Contracting Parties shall harmonize their policies and introduce , individually and in common, measures to prevent the pollution of the sea by dumping from ships and aircraft.

The Oslo Convention was one of the earliest regional agreements for the protection of the marine environment. It represents an initial attempt at international regulation of marine pollution by dumping. This Convention has an actual bearing on global marine environmental protection because it actually set down a number of ground rules which did not exist before. For example, the notion that polluting substances can be classified into 'black' and 'grey' lists which are now to be found in practically all international treaties on marine pollution was initially derived from the Annexes to the Oslo Convention.

There are no developing countries in the area of application of this Convention.

The basic objective of preventing pollution of the sea area covered by the Convention has been met by a general prohibition of dumping without permits or approvals (subject to certain exceptions) and the institution of a strict system of legal controls over authorised dumping activities.

The addition of amending Protocols to the Convention, as well as the Decisions and Recommendations of the Oslo Commission have also been instrumental in setting-up a rigorous regime of controls which aims to be environmentally progressive.

Measuring goal achievement in terms of the total amount of industrial waste dumped over the years, a slight decrease has been noted. In 1976 the total amount of industrial waste dumped by the parties was approximately 7.2 million tonnes and in 1986 approximately 5.8 million tonnes.

Participation

The Oslo Convention on Dumping is a regional instrument in two respects: First, membership is limited to those states which were invited to the 1971 Oslo Conference on Marine Pollution. These states: Belgium, Denmark, Finland, France, the (then) Federal Republic of Germany, Iceland, the Netherlands, Norway, Portugal, Spain, Sweden, and the United Kingdom (all of which have signed the treaty) as well as the USSR, Poland, and Ireland which did not attend. Ireland has since become a party to the Convention on 25 January,1982 but the USSR and Poland, though invited to the Conference, have not yet joined the Convention.

Second, Art.22 provides that the Contracting Parties may unanimously invite other states to accede to the Convention. The participation of other states, ie. states outside the region, was not to ensure wider local application of the Convention but in order to have more effective protection of the marine environment from dumping in the area specified in Art.2. The net effect of Art.22 however is that although membership and participation in the Convention is limited to those countries which were invited to the Oslo Conference, there is scope for more widespread participation in the Convention.

Reservations are not prohibited. None have been made.

The current geographical distribution of membership is confined to those countries within the North East Atlantic region defined by Art.2, that were invited to the Oslo Conference (all of which are developed countries).

The fact that the Contracting Parties, being developed countries, have the financial, technical, and scientific resources available certainly has a positive influence on their participation. In the case of the Oslo Convention, the 'Stella Maris' incident caused immense public alarm and this too influenced participation in the Convention.

Implementation and information

Under Art.23(1) Convention requires ratification by seven parties to come into force.

Since the Convention entered into force on 7 April 1974, only slightly more than two years after it was concluded, the implementation of this Agreement was not constrained by these provisions.

On the other hand, however, the 1983 Protocol to the Oslo Convention Concerning Incineration at Sea which was done at Oslo, on 2 March 1983 took almost six years to come into force in 1989, and the 1989 Internal Waters Protocol done at Oslo on 5 December 1989 has not come into force yet.

The implementation of these Protocols has been constrained by the provisions regarding their entry into force which in both cases require all State Parties to the Convention to have deposited their instruments of ratification or accession.(Art.8 of the 1983 Protocol, and Art.9 of the 1989 Protocol)

The system of legal control established by the Oslo Convention is composed of principal rules (prohibiting or regulating dumping) coupled with certain exceptions. There is a separate set of provisions on the enforcement of the Convention. These are contained in Art.15 of the Convention.

The principal rules of the Convention are included in Art.s 5, 6, and 7 of the Convention. Under this system three categories of substances are subject to differing legal control. Under Art.5, dumping of substances listed in Annex 1 is prohibited entirely (with only certain exceptions to this rule under Art.s 8 and 9 of the Convention).

Art.6 provides that no substances listed in Annex 2 shall be dumped without a specific permit in each case from the appropriate national authority or authorities.

All other substances or materials fall under the third category and are subject to Art.7 of the Convention which states that no substances or materials shall be dumped without the approval of the appropriate national authority or authorities.

All dumping operations must therefore require the approval of the appropriate national authority, whatever the substance, the sole exception being cases of 'force majeure' covered by Art.8.

It is important to note here that the issue of permits (under Art.6) or approvals (under Art.7) remains the responsibility of the Contracting Party concerned in the case of ships or aircraft registered in its territory, or loading on its territory, or carrying out dumping operations within the limits of its territorial waters (and internal waters under the 1989 Internal Waters Protocol). It follows that one and the same consignment of waste may be the subject of more than one specific permit or approval, each being issued by one of the Contracting Parties concerned.

Art.15 sets out the enforcement provisions of the Convention. Most enforcement powers recognized to the Contracting Parties under Art.15 are existing rights of theirs under customary international law. These rights, however, are raised by the Convention to contractual obligations. By virtue of Art.15 the Contracting Parties are obliged to exercise their existing enforcement powers for the protection of the marine environment from dumping. Thus the enforcement powers of the Contracting Parties constitute both rights and obligations.

Under Art.15(1), each Contracting Party undertakes to ensure compliance with the provisions of this Convention, (a) by ships and aircraft registered in its territory; (b) by ships and aircraft loading in its territory the substances and materials which are to be dumped; and (c) by ships and aircraft believed to be engaged in dumping within its territorial sea. (Note: Art.2 of the Internal Waters Protocol which amends Art.15(1)(c) to include dumping within internal waters has not come into force yet.)

In respect of dumping on the high seas, each Contracting Party undertakes to issue instructions to its maritime inspection vessels and aircraft to report to its authorities any incidents which give rise to suspicions that unauthorized dumping has occurred or is about to occur.(Art.15(2))

Within its own territory, each Contracting Party shall take appropriate measures to prevent and punish conduct in contravention of the provisions of this Convention.(Art.15(3))

The Contracting Parties also undertake to assist one another as appropriate in dealing with pollution incidents involving dumping at sea (Art.15(4)), and to work together in the development of co-operative procedures for the application of the Convention, particularly on the high seas.(Art.15(5))

Art.16 establishes a Commission , made up of representatives of each of the Contracting Parties, that meets at regular intervals. The foremost duty of this Commission is to exercise overall supervision over the implementation of this Convention.(Art.17(a))

The Contracting Parties are further required to transmit their records of dumping permits and approvals issued, and of the dates, places, and methods of dumping which has taken place, to the Commission for its consideration.(Art.11) Such submissions shall follow the standard procedure, as defined by the Commission, for this purpose.(Art.17(b))

These reporting requirements appear to be complied with.

Art.11 requires each Contracting Party to submit records of the nature and quantities of the substances and materials dumped under permits or approvals issued by that Contracting Party.

Under Art.12, the Contracting Parties agreed to establish complementary or joint research programmes and more importantly, to transmit to each other the information obtained by such research.

Under Art.13, the Contracting Parties agreed to institute appropriate international organizations and agencies for monitoring the distribution and effects of pollutants in the area to which this Convention applies.

This requirement is fulfilled by the Joint Monitoring Group (JMG) which monitors the quality and quantity of pollutants introduced into the zone covered by the Convention through the reports on the quantities dumped.

Art.15(2) obliges each Contracting Party to report any unauthorized dumping incidents, if it considers it appropriate, to other Contracting Parties.

Under Art.15(4), the parties also undertake to exchange information on methods of dealing with such incidents.

These data supply and disclosure requirements were made more stringent at the First Meeting of the Oslo Commission in 1974 when it established a Prior Consultation Procedure (PCP) whereby Contracting Parties proposing to issue a permit for the dumping of wastes containing Annex 1 substances, must first inform the other members of the Commission.

The PCP now also requires Contracting Parties to give documented information as to alternative disposal methods to dumping that have been considered and rejected by the appropriate authorities.

The First Meeting of the Commission approved the use of a specimen form for the uniform entry of essential information in permits and approval documents. The frequency of the notification of these permits to the Commission was also agreed, ie. on a quarterly basis. In the case of specific permits issued under Art.6, these must be notified immediately. In this way compliance is promoted as all dumping is kept under constant supervision.

There is no provision in the treaty for settlement of disputes.

The text of this Convention was done in English and French, both of which are equally authentic. Certified copies of the text were sent to the Contracting Parties, and to the states referred to in Art.20, which were invited to the Conference on Marine Pollution at Oslo in October, 1971.(Art.27)

Current information on operation and implementation is disseminated through the Oslo Commission's Annual Reports of which there have been thirteen to date.

The Commission has produced a number of explanatory documents, including a Manual of Procedures and Decision.

Operation, review and adjustment

The main executive body of the Oslo Convention is the Oslo Commission where the parties meet annually. The Commission is assisted by a 'Standing Advisory Committee for Scientific Advice'(SACSA) and ad-hoc working groups, the 'Joint Monitoring Group'(JMG) and a permanent Secretariat in London, which operates jointly with the secretariat of the 1974 Paris Convention (No.45).

The annual costs of the administration of this Convention are not available.
Originally, the states agreed to contribute to a joint budget of GBP 122,000 to be equally distributed between both the Oslo and Paris Commissions.

Under the Financial Rules of Procedure adopted by the Oslo Commission at its First Meeting in Oslo, 1974 (later amended), Rule 3.2 provides that each Contracting Party contributes 2.5% towards the Commission's annual expenditure. The balance of the Commission's expenditure shall be divided among Contracting Parties in proportion to their Gross National Product in accordance with the scale of assessment adopted regularly by the United Nations General Assembly.

The Oslo and Paris Commissions have each set up their own standing scientific group. In the case of the Oslo Commission, this is the Standing Advisory Committee for Scientific Advice (SACSA) formed at the First Meeting of the Commission. On the recommendation of the standing scientific/technical group the Oslo Commission may decide to establish working groups to study specific issues or problems. In this way, scientific advice is taken into account in policy-making decisions.

In addition to this there is also a standing scientific group common to both Commissions called the Joint Monitoring Group (JMG) which provides scientific expertise on all monitoring issues. The JMG fulfils the requirements of Art.13.(See Q.15 on Monitoring). The overall system allows the Oslo and Paris Commissions to assess the consequences of decisions taken in implementation of the respective Conventions.

National Government representatives participate in OSPARCOM Meetings, although the degree to which each national delegation represents the views of national NGOs and the general scientific community varies.
The establishment of the North Sea Task Force provides an avenue for a wider representation of scientific views.

It is the duty of the Commission to review the efficacy of the control measures being adopted, and the need for any additional or different measures.(Art.17(c))

The Commission is also under a duty to keep under review the contents of the Annexes to this Convention, and to recommend such amendments, additions or deletions as may be agreed.(Art.17(d))

Codification programming

Discussions are in progress on the possible merger between the Oslo Dumping Convention and the 1974 Paris Convention for the Prevention of Marine Pollution from Land-Based Sources (No.45).

The Joint Monitoring Group (JMG) acts as the co-ordinating mechanism between these two conventions. The JMG's main function has been to establish the principles and procedures for a Joint Monitoring Programme which allows the respective Commissions to fulfil the requirements of Art.13 of the Oslo Convention and Art.11 of the Paris Convention. The JMG reports to the annual Joint Meeting of the Commissions on matters of joint interest.

The Oslo Convention only covers prevention of pollution from dumping in the sea. To be completely successful in its objectives other sources of pollution also need to be prevented from entering the sea. The proposed merger between the Oslo and Paris Conventions is therefore a step in the right direction.

The Declarations of the three ministerial-level North Sea Conferences which have been held in Bremen (1984), London (1987) and The Hague (1990) respectively, have laid down principles and targets for the reduction of marine pollution in the North Sea, including dumping. These have been implemented by the parties to the Oslo Convention.

(44) Convention on the Protection of the Marine Environment of the Baltic Sea Area

(Helsinki, 22 March 1974) as amended

Objectives and achievement

The basic objectives are set down in Art.3. The Contracting Parties undertake, individually and jointly, to take all appropriate legislative, administrative or other relevant measures in order to prevent and abate pollution and to protect and enhance the marine environment of the Baltic Sea Area.((Art.3(1))

The second undertaking of the Contracting Parties to ensure that the implementation of the present Convention does not increase pollution of the sea areas outside the Baltic Sea Area (Art.3(2)) has been subject to revision in order to make it more stringent.

It is now proposed that any measures taken to prevent pollution in the Baltic Sea Area shall not lead to unacceptable environmental strains on the air quality and the atmosphere or on waters, soil and underground sources, to unacceptable harmful or increasing waste disposal, or increased risk to the human health.

It is significant to note that the Contracting Parties were conscious not only of the economic, social, and cultural values of the marine environment of the Baltic Sea, but also the fact that the increasing pollution of the Baltic Sea Area originated from many sources.

In this respect, the present regional Convention recognises the link between all types of pollution from different sources and their threat to the overall socio-economic development of the countries of that region. It therefore has much actual and potential bearing on global environmental protection and sustainable development.

No developing countries are coastal states in the Baltic Sea Area. However, some central and east European countries could be considered economically developing countries.

Based on decisions by the Prime Ministers at the Baltic Sea Conference in Ronneby, Sweden in September 1990, an ad hoc HELCOM (Helsinki Commission) high-level Task Force with special emphasis on the less economically developed countries (economies in transition) in the region was established. The work started in late 1990 and is expected to be completed for ministerial consideration in spring 1992. The key elements of the programme should be under preparation by 1993.

The aim of the work is ambitious, to provide a concrete and action-oriented joint comprehensive programme to restore the Baltic to a sound ecological balance. The joint action plan will contain a list of priority actions needed to reverse the eutrophication of the Baltic Sea, to identify the problem areas, 'hot spots', and to suggest the procedure to finance the most urgent measures to reduce pollution.

The Baltic Marine Environment Protection Commission (established under Art.12(1)) makes recommendations on measures relating to the purposes of the present Convention.

The follow-up on the national implementation of the recommendations is based on the national implementation reports. Goal achievement is measured through pollution load compilations, periodic assessments as well as through ministerial meetings and conferences.

Participation

The present Convention was restricted to the Baltic Sea states which participated in the 1974 Helsinki Conference.(Art.26(1)) These states include Denmark, Finland, the (former) German Democratic Republic, the Federal Republic of Germany, Poland, Sweden, and the USSR all of which have become parties to the Convention.

The Convention is also open for accession to any other state, provided it is invited by all the Contracting Parties.(Art.26(1))

Reservations are not permitted under this Convention. (Art.25(1))

However, a Contracting Party is not prevented from suspending for a period not exceeding one year the application of an Annex, or part thereof, or amendments thereto, provided it informs the other Contracting Parties. (Art.25(2) and (3))

The Helsinki Convention covers the Baltic Sea proper with the Gulf of Bothnia, the Gulf of Finland, and the entrance to the Baltic Sea. There are no developing countries in this area. However, as stated earlier, a HELCOM Task Force has been established which will place special emphasis on the economies in transition in the Baltic Sea region.

Implementation and information

The present Convention entered into force two months after the deposit of the seventh instrument of ratification or approval.(Art.27) Since the Convention was signed on 22 March 1974 but only entered into force on 3 May 1980, more than six years later, the ratification process has been rather long.

The Contracting Parties have undertaken to prevent and control pollution from various sources including pollution from land-based sources (Art.6), disposal of wastes at sea by ships (Art.7) or through dumping (Art.9), and pollution from sea-bed activities (Art.10).

In addition to these obligations, the Contracting Parties have also undertaken to counteract the introduction into the Baltic Sea Area of hazardous substances as specified by Annex 1 (Art.5), and to take measures and co-operate according to Annex 6 in order to eliminate or minimize pollution of the Baltic Sea Area by oil or other harmful substances (Art.11).

The commitments imposed on the Contracting Parties are normally discharge limit values and operational requirements. The compliance by the Contracting Parties with their commitments is controlled by means of obligatory reporting according to a unified procedure, as well as by regular pollution load compilation projects and emission inventories.

Following the adopted reporting procedure, the Contracting Parties report on their performance in implementing HELCOM Recommendations every three years according to unified reporting formats. All the Contracting Parties comply with reporting duties satisfactorily.

The appropriate national authorities are obliged to inform the Commission of the quantity, quality and way of discharge of substances listed in Annex 2, in respect of land-based pollution.(Art.6(4))

Only dumping of dredged spoils is permitted and such dumping activities as well as emergency dumping are also reported to the Commission.(Art.9(6)) .

The Contracting Parties are required to develop and apply a system for receiving, channelling and dispatching reports on significant spillages of oil or other harmful substances.(Regulation 5 of Annex 6 on Co-operation in Combatting Marine Pollution)

The Parties must also provide information to the other Parties about their national organizations and regulations on combating pollution at sea by oil.(Regulation 9 of Annex 6)

The Contracting Parties have also agreed upon several monitoring programmes by which data on airborne pollution, radioactive substances and several determinants of the marine environment are collected. The collection of data is performed according to agreed guidelines. The collected data is stored on data bases which work on a consultancy basis for the Commission.

In addition to the monitoring data, data is also collected on emissions, releases, discharges from urban areas, industries and from rivers. Data collection on the monitoring programmes is well organized and the Contracting Parties fulfil their obligations well. However, the Contracting Parties have some problems in providing other monitoring data than the above-mentioned types of data.

The work of the Helsinki Commission (HELCOM) and its subsidiary bodies is focused on implementing the relevant provisions of the Convention, as well as on promoting the compliance of the obligations of the Contracting Parties under the Convention's regime. The decisions by the Commission are taken unanimously and decisions on measures are most often given in the form of Recommendations. The implementation of these Recommendations is under permanent review by the Commission, and the Contracting Parties report to every meeting of the Commission on progress and measures in their respective countries to ensure compliance with obligations arising from these decisions.

Art.18 deals with the procedure for the settlement of disputes and provides the Parties with a possibility to negotiate or request the mediation by a third Party in case of a dispute over the interpretation or application of the present Convention.

If an agreement cannot be achieved the Parties concerned can submit the case to a permanent arbitration tribunal, or to the International Court of Justice. These mechanisms have never been used.

The Helsinki Convention was drawn up in a single copy in the English language. Official translations into the Danish, Finnish, German, Polish, Russian, and Swedish languages were prepared and deposited with the signed original in Helsinki.(Art.29)

Information on the operation and implementation of the decisions by the Helsinki Commission is made available to governments through the annual activities reports as well as the reports from the annual Helsinki Commission meetings.

The Helsinki Commission has its own publication series called the 'Baltic Sea Environment Proceedings' in which periodic assessments, guidelines, seminars/symposia proceedings etc. can be published. Two hundred (200) copies of these are distributed to each of the governments for further dissemination among national authorities, industry and other interested parties. The BSEP are distributed to a large number of libraries, laboratories and institutions inside as well as outside the region.

In addition, bibliographic data (relevant reports, journal articles, books, conference documents, dissertations etc.) is compiled and made publicly accessible, either on-line (in Sweden and Germany) or on microfiche (until 1990) or printed in the Baltic Sea Environment Proceedings (BSEP, starting 1991). When compiling the bibliographic data, the original language is used (Danish, English, Finnish, German, Polish, Russian, and Swedish), but the English translation of the title and an abstract are included whenever possible.

In order to provide guidance for the implementation of the HELCOM decisions at the national level, the Committees of the Commission elaborate and adopt problem-oriented guidelines and manuals as well as arrange seminars/workshops on specific scientific and technological topics.

Seminars, symposia and workshops hosted by a Contracting Party are organized once or twice a year (sometimes in co-operation with other international organizations) to consider actual problems related to HELCOM goals (e.g. monitoring programmes, waste water purifications, reception facilities, etc.) Furthermore, co-operation with a special UNESCO school children project was established in 1991.

Operation, review and adjustment

The Baltic Marine Environment Protection Commission, also known as the Helsinki Commission or HELCOM was established under Art.12 of the present Convention. The Commission has established four permanent Committees and several ad hoc Working Groups as subsidiary bodies to the Commission itself or to the Committees. Pursuant to the administrative provisions for the Commission contained in Art.14, a Secretariat has been established in Helsinki to provide secretariat assistance to the Commission and its Committees and other subsidiary bodies. For the time being the staff comprises five persons in the professional category and seven persons in the general staff category.

The budget for the financial year 1990/91 amounted to circa. FIM 4.4 million and the income to the budget originates from equal contributions from the six(6) Contracting Parties as well as an extra contribution by Finland as the host country.

The budget for the HELCOM ad hoc high level Task Force, from 1 December 1990 to 30 November 1991, amounts to circa. FIM 2.7 million and the income consists of equal contributions from all six(6) Contracting Parties.

The main benefit would be better prevention of marine pollution in the Baltic Sea Area. This is achieved through regulation of pollution from various sources and greater geographical coverage of such regulation by this regional Convention. The main costs lie in setting-up the appropriate national institutional and organizational structures or expanding them in order to implement both the Convention obligations and the Recommendations of the Commission at the national level.

Inter-governmental organizations are invited to participate in relevant Committees and working groups either as observers or participants. Inter-governmental organizations participating in the work of HELCOM are UNEP, ECE, IMO, WHO/EURO, OSCOM/PARCOM, IBSFC, ICES, IAEA, WMO, IOC and CEC. The non-governmental organizations World Wide Fund for Nature (WWF), Greenpeace and Coalition Clean Baltic (CCB) have observer status to the Commission.

All the meetings are open to participants nominated by national authorities of the Contracting Parties.

Certain non-governmental participants who are experts working within bodies like the WWF are also invited or given the opportunity to comment on a topic or a specific document. The Baltic Marine Biologists (BMB) and Conferences of Baltic Oceanographers (CBO) are also invited to the work of the Commission.

The Convention provides for its own revision either at the request of the Commission or with the consent of the Parties.(Art.22)

Each of the Contracting Parties may propose amendments to the Articles (Art.23) or Annexes (Art.24).

The Annexes, which contain detailed operational obligations, are amended in a simplified manner according to which such an amendment shall be deemed to have been accepted at the end of a period determined by the Commission, unless within that period any one of the Contracting Parties has objected to the amendment.

Codification programming

The Helsinki Commission at its eleventh (11th) meeting decided to establish an ad hoc Working Group for the general revision of the Convention. The work of the Group is to be finalised by the end of 1991, and the revised instrument is supposed to be adopted at a conference to be held in April 1992.

The revision work is co-ordinated with the ongoing work on the revision of the Oslo/Paris Conventions (Nos.43 and 45) as well as aimed at ensuring the conformity of the Helsinki Convention with other international instruments, such as MARPOL73/78 (No.36) and the International Convention on Oil Pollution Preparedness, Response and Co-operation (OPRC, No.41).

The revision work is mainly concentrated on the following problems :

-Enlargement of the Convention Area by the inclusion of the internal waters of the Contracting States;

-Introduction of definitions such as the 'precautionary principle', 'best available technology', and 'best environmental practices', in the Convention text;

-Fundamental principles and obligations of the Contracting Parties in the Convention Area;

-Scope of application of the Convention;

-Harmful substances to be banned or limited in connection with discharges from land-based sources;

-Principles and obligations concerning land-based pollution;

-Introduction of new provisions on mutual information and consultation, public information; and environmental impact assessment in order to improve the implementation of the relevant instruments adopted by the Commission, as well as on nature conservation and bio-diversity.

Other mechanisms contributing to the development of international law in this area are, inter alia :

-Political declarations by the responsible ministers of the Contracting Parties. For example, the Ministerial Declaration of 1988, and the Baltic Sea Declaration 1990;

-Co-operation of the Baltic Sea States in the International Maritime Organization (IMO) as well as the exchange of information between the Helsinki Commission and other international organizations;

-International seminars, for example, the International Seminar on Protection of Special Areas, and the Seminar on Nature Conservation and Bio-diversity;

-Bilateral and multilateral sub-regional co-operation among the Contracting Parties, e.g., co-operation in combatting pollution, nature conservation, protection of the Gulf of Finland and the Gulf of Bothnia;

-Research and development programmes/projects carried out by the respective authorities of the Contracting Parties.

(45) Convention on the Prevention of Marine Pollution from Land-based Sources

(Paris, 4 June 1974), as amended

Objectives and achievement

The main objective of the Paris Convention is set down in Art.1 whereby the Contracting Parties pledge themselves to take all possible steps to prevent pollution of the sea by adopting individual and joint measures as well as harmonising their policies to combat marine pollution from land-based sources. The 1986 Paris Protocol has amended this Convention to include the prevention of pollution through the atmosphere by emissions into the atmosphere from land or from man-made structures. (This Protocol has not come into force yet.)

The objectives of this Convention do not expressly include the effective integration of environment and development.

The Paris Convention being one of the first international agreements aimed at the prevention of pollution from land-based sources, has much potential bearing on global environmental protection. The approach it adopted has been used as a model in other regional agreements (e.g., protocols listed under Nos. 41, 42, 44) as well as in the UNEP guidelines under No. 51.

All the states parties to this agreement are classified as developed countries by the United Nations.

Since the main objective of this convention is the reduction of 'pollution' from land-based sources, assessment of such a reduction is difficult to prove. But if an assessment of the trend in emissions is assumed to give some indication of the corresponding trend for pollution then it is possible to say, referring to the Quality Status Report (QSR) produced in connection with the 1987 North Sea Conference, that with few exceptions, contamination has been reduced or at least not increased over the last decade.

Participation

Membership of this Convention is limited to the States invited to the Diplomatic Conference on the Convention for the Prevention of Marine Pollution from Land-Based Sources held at Paris, and by the European Economic Community.(Art.22) These States were Austria, Belgium, Denmark, France, Federal Republic of Germany, Iceland, Luxembourg, The Netherlands, Norway, Portugal, Spain, Sweden, Switzerland and the United Kingdom. Finland and Italy were observers.

13 States have become Parties to this Convention. They are Belgium, Denmark, The EEC, France, Federal Republic of Germany, Iceland, Ireland, The Netherlands, Norway, Portugal, Spain, Sweden and United Kingdom.

As in the Oslo Convention, there is a provision which states that the Contracting Parties may, by unanimous vote, invite other states to accede to the Paris Convention.(Art.24(4))

Reservations are not prohibited. None have been made.

The current geographical distribution of membership is confined to the developed countries in the North East Atlantic area, specifically delimited by Art.2 of this Convention. It does not include any developing countries.

The availability of financial , technical, and scientific resources in these developed countries has certainly had a positive influence in respect of participation in this Convention.

Media attention and public opinion were also of much influence. The earlier negotiations and signing of the Oslo Convention on Dumping (No.36) paved the way for the Paris Conference which in turn led to the present Convention.

Implementation and information

The Paris Convention was concluded on 4 June 1974 and entered into force on 6 May 1978, on the thirtieth day following the date of deposit of the seventh instrument of ratification or accession.(Art.25(1))

Although the Convention entered into force in 1978, its activities commenced immediately following the signature of the Convention in 1974. Therefore the provisions regarding its entry into force have not constrained the implementation of this agreement.

The main commitments are contained in Art.4, which requires the Contracting Parties to implement, jointly or individually as appropriate, programmes and measures for the elimination as a matter of urgency, of pollution by the substances listed in Part 1 of Annex A and for the reduction or, as appropriate, elimination of pollution by substances listed in Part 2 of Annex A.

An important distinction which must be made is that what is required by this Convention is the elimination of **'pollution'** by the blacklisted substances (in Part 1 of Annex A); unlike the Oslo Convention which positively prohibits the dumping of blacklisted substances.

The Contracting Parties also undertake to adopt measures to forestall and, as appropriate, eliminate pollution by radio-active substances referred to in Part 3 of Annex A.(Art.5(1))

Under Art.6, the Contracting Parties shall further endeavour (a) to reduce existing pollution from land-based sources; and (b) to forestall any new pollution from land-based, including that from new substances.

Finally, each Contracting Party undertakes to ensure compliance with the provisions of this Convention and to take in its territory appropriate measures to prevent and punish conduct in contravention of the provisions of the present Convention.(Art.12(1))

In addition to this, the programmes and measures adopted by the Paris Commission (established by Art.15), by way of a unanimous vote, also have legal effect. Such programmes and measures shall commence for and be applied by all Contracting Parties two hundred (200) days after their adoption.(Art.18(3))

These commitments are measured by the permanent monitoring group set-up under Art.11.

The Commission has a duty to exercise overall supervision over the implementation of the present Convention.(Art.16)

The Contracting Parties are required to inform the Commission of the legislative and administrative measures they have taken to ensure compliance with the provisions of this Convention.(Art.12(2))

The Contracting Parties, in accordance with a standard procedure, are also required to transmit to the Commission: (a) the results of monitoring pursuant to Art.11, and (b) the most detailed information available on the substances listed in the Annexes to the present Convention.(Art.17)

In furtherance of the above reporting duty, the Contracting Parties are also required to improve progressively their techniques for gathering such information.(Art.17)

Under Art.10, the Contracting Parties have agreed to establish complementary or joint programmes of scientific and technical research, and to transmit to each other the information so obtained.

The permanent monitoring system set-up under Art.11 also requires extensive data to be supplied by the Parties.

The Contracting Parties are also required to exchange information in order to assist one another as appropriate to prevent incidents which may result in pollution from land-based sources.(Art.13)

A further requirement of disclosure of information to other Contracting Parties, through the Commission, occurs when special co-operative agreements are signed between Contracting Parties under the terms of Art.9.

It is the duty of the Commission to promote compliance by reviewing the general condition of the seas, the effectiveness of the control measures adopted and the need for any additional or different measures.(Art.16(b))

The Commission can also make recommendations when following-up on non-compliance.(Art.16(e) and (g))

When pollution from land-based sources of one Contracting Party prejudices the interests of one or more of the other Parties, the Contracting Parties concerned have undertaken to enter into consultation, with a view to negotiating a co-operation agreement. (Art.9(1))

In the event of a dispute, at the request of any Contracting Party, the Commission shall consider the question and may make recommendations with a view to reaching a satisfactory solution.(Art.9(2))

Any dispute between Contracting Parties relating to the interpretation or application of the present Convention, which cannot be settled otherwise by the Parties concerned, shall at the request of any of those Parties be submitted to arbitration under the conditions laid down in Annex B to the Convention.(Art.21) Annex B lays down the procedural rules for the constitution of an arbitral tribunal whose award shall be final and binding upon the Parties to the dispute.(Art.7(1) of Annex B)

These mechanisms have never been used.

The availability of financial, technical and scientific resources exerts a positive influence on implementation. But in the case of the Paris Convention, it was the weight of public opinion and media attention leading to government involvement at the ministerial-level North Sea Conferences that accelerated the implementation of the Paris Commission's decisions and recommendations. This is especially true in respect of PARCOM measures taken after the 1987 North Sea Conference.

The original text of the Paris Convention is in the French and English languages, both of which are equally authentic. Certified copies have been sent to each of the Contracting Parties and the States referred to in Art.22 which were invited to the Paris Conference.

Current information on operation and implementation is available through the publication of the Annual Reports of the Paris Commission, of which there are now ten.

There are numerous PARCOM Recommendations, Decisions, Guidelines, Reviews and Reports that have been published by the Paris Commission over the years to provide guidance for implementation.

Since this information is published regularly and distributed upon request, for e.g., in the Paris Commission's Procedures and Decisions Manual, it is widely used in government and industrial training as well as university education programmes, at least in the Contracting Party States.

Operation, review and adjustment

The Paris Commission (PARCOM) is the executive institution of this Convention. PARCOM shares a Joint Secretariat with the Oslo Commission (OSCOM) for the 1972 Oslo Convention (No.43) in London. The tasks of the Secretariat are mainly to organise and prepare the meetings of the Commissions, to distribute and translate documentation into English and French (which are the two official languages of the Convention), and to prepare matters for the Commissions and to issue reports (e.g. from the annual meetings of the Commissions).

There are no readily available figures for the annual costs. Originally, the states agreed to contribute to a joint budget for the Paris and Oslo Commissions of GBP(Great Britain Pounds) 122,000 equally distributed between the two Commissions.

The main benefits have been in the mutual undertakings by the Parties to reduce emission levels and to introduce co-ordinated environmental reporting and assessment. The Paris Convention has provided an important conduit for policy decisions taken at the INSCs.

The main cost elements would be in setting up the relevant institutions and technical expertise for the above mentioned assessments.

Art.4(3) requires Contracting Parties to take the latest technical developments into account when defining the programmes and measures to be adopted. This may be interpreted as ensuring that scientific knowledge is taken into account in policy-making decisions. But the formulation of emission limits and water quality standards in the first years of the Paris Commission were primarily influenced by economic/technical criteria and to a much lesser extent by 'ecological considerations'.

Only during the 1980s, as more general scientific knowledge improved and accumulated, has there been an improved balance between what is ecologically desirable and the regulatory decisions made.

A significant advance in this respect is PARCOM Recommendation 89/2 of 22 June 1989 On The Use Of Best Available Technology. The Contracting Parties agreed that the best available technology should be applied in the programmes and measures adopted under Articles 4 and 5 of the Convention in order to prevent pollution in Convention waters.

PARCOM ensures the effective participation of the national authorities through its standard reporting procedures and forms, (available in its Manual).

The establishment of the North Sea Task Force provides and important conduit for the views of the scientific community.

The Paris Commission, which is composed of representatives of the Contracting Parties themselves, can revise or amend this Convention and its Annexes.

The Commission may adopt recommendations for amendments to Annex A to the present Convention by a three-quarters majority vote of its members.(Art.18(4))

At the request of the Commission on a decision taken by a two-thirds majority of its members, the depository government (the Government of the French Republic) shall call a Conference for the purpose of revising or amending the present Convention.(Art.27(1))

Codification programming

Discussions are in progress with the intention of merging the Paris Convention with the 1972 Oslo Convention (No.43) whose own Commission shares its headquarters with the Paris Commission in London.

The Paris Commission (PARCOM) co-operates closely with the Oslo Commission at the operational level through annual joint meetings, the Joint Monitoring Group (JMG), the joint Secretariat and the Joint Group of Chairmen and Vice-Chairmen (CVC). The Joint Monitoring Group acts as a co-ordinating implementation mechanism between the present Convention and the 1972 Oslo Dumping Convention.

Working relationships have also been established with the Helsinki Convention on the Protection of the Marine Environment of the Baltic Sea Area (No. 44) and the Bonn Agreement for Co-operation in Dealing with Pollution of the North Sea by Oil and Other Harmful Substances (No.53). For example, in the OSPARCOM (Oslo and Paris Commissions) Secretariat in London, there is an administrative secretary who fills the secretarial functions of the Bonn Agreement.

The Paris Commission (PARCOM) also co-operates with bodies like the International Marine Organization (IMO) and the International Council for the Exploration of the Seas (ICES, No.63) in the monitoring of waste into water and to the surrounding environment.

The 1986 Paris Protocol amending the 1974 Convention (in force since September 1989) attempts to cover a gap by extending the scope of the Convention to include the prevention of pollution through the atmosphere by emissions into the atmosphere from land or from man-made structures.(Art.1 of the 1986 Paris Protocol)

The ministerial-level North Sea Conferences have made a significant contribution to the implementation of the Paris Convention, especially in respect to the setting of specific reduction targets for emissions.

The fact that the European Community (EC) is a party to the Convention, has had both positive and negative effects on the implementation of PARCOM. Positive effects since in a number of cases PARCOM was able to benefit from preparatory work done by the EC. Negative effects, since the EC Commission blocked several possible binding decisions due to lack of approval from its Council of Ministers.

(46) Convention for the Protection of the Mediterranean Sea Against Pollution
(Barcelona, 16 February 1976), and related protocols

- The 1975 Mediterranean Action Plan served as the basis for the development of a comprehensive, environmental programme in the region involving the Mediterranean coastal States and the numerous specialized bodies of the United Nations System: MAP.
Note: the relevant legal instruments are referred to in the following paragraphs as follows:
- Convention for the Protection of the Mediterranean Sea Against Pollution: **CONVENTION**
- 1976 Protocol for the Prevention of Pollution of the Mediterranean Sea by Dumping from Ships and Aircraft: **PROTOCOL I**
- 1976 Protocol concerning Co-operation in Combating Pollution of the Mediterranean Sea by Oil and other Harmful Substances in Cases of Emergency: **PROTOCOL II**
- 1980 Protocol for the Protection of the Mediterranean Sea against Pollution from Land-Based Sources: **PROTOCOL III**
- 1982 Protocol concerning Mediterranean Specially Protected Areas: **PROTOCOL IV**

Objectives and achievement

The convention, together with its protocols, constitutes the legal component of the Mediterranean Action Plan (MAP), which was adopted under the UNEP Regional Seas Programme.
Convention: As an umbrella treaty, its objective is the control of pollution of the Mediterranean Sea from all sources, and the promotion of co-operation among the riparian states to this end.
Protocol I: The objective is the protection of the marine environment of the Mediterranean against pollution by deliberate dumping of wastes and other harmful substances, through co-ordinated efforts of the riparian states.
Protocol II: The objective is the adoption of co-ordinated measures in case of grave and imminent danger to marine or coastal areas, resulting from spillage of oil and other harmful substances, and the promotion of preparedness for emergencies.
Protocol III: The objective is to implement Articles 4(2), 8 and 15 of the Barcelona Convention by co-operating in taking measures to protect the Mediterranean Sea against pollution from land-based sources. The protocol seeks to integrate environment and development by recognizing differences in the level of development between coastal states, and taking account of the economic and social imperatives of developing countries.
Protocol IV: The objectives are (1) the designation of areas which, in view of their vulnerability and their importance for the safeguard of natural resources and natural sites, and cultural heritage, need special protection; and (2) the adoption of measures for the protection of these areas.

The Barcelona Convention and its protocols are part of a global network of treaties regulating the protection of different regions of the earth against marine pollution. The widespread participation of states in these treaties gives them a standard-setting function on a world-wide scale. Regional regulation of marine pollution is in line with the 1982 UNCLOS (No.48), which refers to regional rules in various contexts.
The Barcelona Convention and its protocols, being the first of the UNEP Regional Seas Conventions, also had an influence on the elaboration of similar instruments for other

regions. The latest example of this is the ongoing elaboration of a treaty system to protect the Black Sea against pollution. This treaty system, which is being drafted by Bulgaria, Romania, Turkey, and the Soviet Union, is modelled on the Barcelona Convention and its protocols.

Protocol I: The objectives and provisions of this protocol are in line with those of the global 1972 Convention on the Prevention of Marine Pollution by Dumping of Wastes and Other Matter (London Dumping Convention, No.35). Article 1 of that treaty provides that states shall individually and collectively adopt measures to prevent dumping. The scope of Protocol I is broader in that it includes dumping from aircraft as well as ships. Together with other regional agreements restricting ocean dumping, it may contribute to a world-wide restriction of this practice. The protocol does not have a particular bearing on development issues.

Protocol II: This protocol is one of a series of legal instruments on the global and regional levels which provide for emergency preparedness in the context of marine pollution by oil and other harmful substances. Like other similar instruments, it provides evidence of an emerging "precautionary" approach to pollution; in this it may have an impact on the global approach to the issue. No significance for development issues is evident.

Protocol III: The actual and potential bearing of this protocol on global environmental protection and sustainable development is found in the extent to which it succeeds in reconciling the protection of human health and the natural productivity of the Mediterranean Sea with the economic development of surrounding nations. Present levels of pollution of the Mediterranean are unlikely to be indefinitely sustainable; to that extent the effective control of land-based pollution is likely to be essential for the attainment of sustainable development.

Protocol IV: Incorporating the concept of affording special protection to vulnerable or important ecosystems, this protocol takes special account of the characteristics of the Mediterranean as a semi-enclosed sea. Similar measures were adopted, on a global level, by the 1973 MARPOL Convention (No.36). No particular importance for development issues is evident.

The special needs of developing countries in the Mediterranean region are given priority, under article II(3) of the Convention, as regards technical and other possible assistance in fields relating to marine pollution.

Protocol III: The special circumstances of developing countries are taken into account particularly in Article 7, which allows for common guidelines, standards or criteria dealing with the control of land-based pollution to take into account local ecological, geographical and physical characteristics, the economic capacity of the parties and their need for development, the level of existing pollution and the real absorptive capacity of the marine environment. Article 10 also provides for the parties to co-operate in formulating and implementing programmes of assistance to developing countries in science, education, technology, training and the acquisition, use or production of appropriate equipment.

Protocol IV: Article 9 allows for parties to take into account the "traditional activities of their local populations" when promulgating protective measures. This provision is presumably aimed mainly at protecting traditional agricultural and fisheries activities in developing countries. Article 15 provides for the formation and implementation of programmes of mutual assistance and of assistance to those developing countries which express a need for it in the selection, establishment and management of protected areas.

Convention: One indication of the achievement of the basic aims of the Barcelona Convention is the adoption, between 1976 and 1982, of four protocols to regulate specific issues outlined broadly in the convention. Two more protocols to the convention are currently under preparation.

Protocol III: One measure of achievement is that the parties have reached agreement on the adoption of common measures setting environmental quality standards for bathing water and shellfish waters, and controlling pollution from a variety of substances listed in Annex I. They have not yet adopted common measures for other Annex I substances. It is clear from the meetings of the parties, and from the Conference on Security and Co-operation in Europe meeting on the Mediterranean in 1990, that control of sewage discharges, agricultural inputs and industrial waste generation remains inadequate, and that further measures are needed to implement the agreement effectively.

Mediterranean Action Plan (MAP): An indication of the satisfactory implementation of the MAP as such is the establishment, under the aegis of its Co-ordinating Unit, of four Regional Activity Centres which are responsible for carrying out specific activities under the MAP. These include activities in connection with the achievement of the MAP's priority targets, and the implementation of the protocols. In 1985, the parties reviewed their previous performance and agreed on 10 priority targets for the second decade of the MAP incorporated in what is known as the Genoa Declaration on the Second Mediterranean Decade.

In addition, numerous other projects are being carried out under the MAP. In 1990, for example, a total of over 100 scientific pollution research projects were carried out. Six studies were undertaken on the effects of global warming on deltas and other vulnerable areas; six more studies on the same subject are planned.

After the recent ratification of the Barcelona Convention and protocols by Albania, all riparian states of the Mediterranean are now participating in the MAP. This guarantees a widespread co-ordination in the protection of the marine environment of the region.

On the other hand, some party states have in the past failed to meet their financial and reporting obligations under the MAP.

Participation

Membership of the convention is restricted to the States invited to the Conference of Plenipotentiaries of the Coastal States of the Mediterranean Region held in Barcelona in 1976; to any state entitled to sign any of the protocols; and to the EC and other regional economic organization provided at least one of its members is a coastal state of the Mediterranean Sea Area. Other States may accede to the Convention and to any Protocol subject to prior approval by three-fourths of the Parties. Bulgaria, Romania and the Russian Federation recently indicated their intention to join the Convention and Protocols I and II.

Reservations to the convention or its protocols are not prohibited. Reservations have been made as follows: Convention: 2 States, Protocols I, II, III: 1 State, Protocol IV: 4 States.

Convention and Protocols I+II: Current membership extends to all coastal states of the Mediterranean. There are 19 parties, including the EC. Geographical distribution is as follows: - Europe: 11, - North Africa and Middle East: 8, total developing country participation: 12

Protocol III: 17 parties, including EC; geographical distribution as follows: - Europe: 11, - North Africa and Middle East: 6, developing countries: 10.

Protocol IV: 17 parties, including EC; geographical distribution as follows:
- Europe: 11, - North Africa and Middle East: 6, developing countries: 10.

Participation of developing countries in the MAP is high. Of the 4 Regional Activity Centres established under the MAP, 3 are located in developing countries.

As with every Action Plan under the UNEP Regional Seas Programme, financial support was initially provided by UNEP and other UN organizations to set up the MAP. In addition to contributions from party states, and from the EC and UNEP, the MAP continues to be supported financially by international funding bodies, e.g. the World Bank and the European Investment Bank. Such financial contributions are available to help parties implement the agreement and the programme of priorities established in 1985 by the Genoa Declaration on the Second Mediterranean Decade. Developing country representatives are sponsored by the MAP's support programme to participate in meetings and other activities. Under Article II(3) of the Convention, and Article 10 of Protocol III, assistance is available as an incentive to participation by developing states.

A recent initiative to integrate environment protection and development aims is reflected in the newly established Coastal Areas Management Programme (CAMP). The objective of this programme is to refocus MAP activities on the development of environmentally sound integrated management of the Mediterranean coastal through, among others, the process of integrated planning. This new orientation of MAP implies a harmonized involvement of all MAP components as well as relevant international bodies, for a better utilization of the limited resources of the Mediterranean region in the interest of the countries of the region and of their development, while being in accordance with sound long-term environmental management rules. Four coastal areas management programmes have been started in four Mediterranean coastal States (Kastela Bay, Yugoslavia; Izmir Bay, Turkey; Island of Rhodes, Greece and the Coastal Region of Syria). Five other projects are under preparation (Fuka, Egypt, Sfax, Tunisia and in Albania, Algeria and Morocco).

Implementation and information

The convention and its protocols all entered into force between two and four years after adoption.

Convention: The convention obligates parties to co-operate in taking appropriate measures for the protection of the marine environment of the Mediterranean region against pollution from all sources, and to co-operate in emergency response. To this end, protocols to the convention are to be adopted (Art. 3-9). Parties shall also establish joint programmes for pollution monitoring (Art. 10); exchange technical and scientific information, and establish procedures for liability and compensation (Art. 12).

Protocol I: The protocol prohibits the dumping of substances listed in Annex I. Dumping of Annex II substances requires a prior special permit, and dumping of all other substances requires a prior general permit (Art. 4-6). Permits shall be issued by the national authorities designated by party states only after careful consideration of the relevant factors, which are set forth in Annex III. Each party shall apply the protocol to activities under its jurisdiction.

Protocol II: Under this protocol, parties are required to maintain contingency plans and equipment for combating oil pollution. They shall monitor the state of the Mediterranean. In the event of spills of oil or other substances, they shall co-operate in salvage operations. In addition, parties shall exchange information and set up reporting requirements for shipmasters and pilots. They shall co-ordinate their activities through the regional centre.

Protocol III: The parties are committed to take all measures to prevent, abate, combat and control pollution caused by discharges from land-based sources; to eliminate pollution from Annex I substances; to limit strictly pollution from Annex II substances; to formulate progressively common guidelines, standards or criteria; to assess levels of pollution along their coasts and evaluate the effects of measures taken under the protocol; to co-operate in research and the provision of assistance; to inform each other of measures taken, results achieved and difficulties encountered.

Protocol IV: Parties shall establish protected areas based on their biological and ecological value as well as on their scientific, aesthetic, historical, archaeological, cultural or educational interest. These shall be safeguarded, or restored, to the extent possible. Measures to be adopted for the protection of these areas may include, among other things, prohibition of dumping, regulation of the passage of ships, regulation of fishing and hunting, and prohibition of destruction of plant and animal life. Parties shall give appropriate publicity to the establishment of protected areas. They shall establish a co-operation programme for the joint establishment of protected areas, and exchange scientific and technical information. The parties are committed to take all measures to implement the three action plans approved by the Contracting Parties concerning the protection of the Mediterranean Monk Seals, the Mediterranean Marine Turtles and the protection of Cetaceans in the Mediterranean.

Parties to the convention and the protocols report to each other through MEDU-UNEP, which was designated as the central clearing-house institution under the convention.

Article 11 of the convention, and the relevant provisions of protocols II, III and IV, require parties to exchange scientific and technical information and to co-ordinate their research.

MEDU-UNEP, which carries out the secretariat functions, may assist parties in implementing the provisions of the convention and its protocols. Performance evaluation is undertaken by the meeting of the contracting parties, which also has the function of making recommendations. Article 21 of the convention requires parties to co-operate in the development of procedures for compliance control. No such procedure has yet been established.

Article 22 of the convention calls on parties to settle disputes through negotiation or other peaceful means. If this cannot be achieved, parties may agree on dispute settlement through the arbitration procedure laid down in Annex A. This applies also to protocols I, II, and IV. Article 12 of protocol III provides for parties concerned in any dispute regarding land-based pollution to enter into consultations with a view to seeking a satisfactory solution. The matter may then be placed on the agenda of the next meeting of the parties, which may make recommendations for a solution. None of these procedures have been invoked by parties so far.

The official languages of the convention and the protocols are Arabic, English, French and Spanish. The texts are published by UNEP in a series which includes all UNEP-sponsored Regional Seas Conventions. Current information on operation and implementation is made available by the Co-ordinating Unit for the Mediterranean Action Plan (MEDU-UNEP) in Athens. MEDU-UNEP is responsible for two serial publications ("Mediterranean Action Plan Technical Reports" and "Medwaves"), and for publication of the reports of the meetings. UNEP has also published a directory of organizations involved in the implementation of the Action Plans of the Regional Seas Programme (Nairobi 1991), and a directory of the status of all agreements negotiated under the Regional Seas Programme (Nairobi 1990).

Various materials are provided under the MAP and its sub-programmes in particular during the annual celebration of the Mediterranean Environment Week. Measures referred to in paragraph 4 provide guidance on the implementation of the treaties.

Under the MAP, training courses and workshops are organized on subjects such as pollution prevention, control and response, and operation and maintenance of waste treatment plants and on GIS application, EIA application, oil and chemical pollution preparedness and response, and on response to accidental pollution. No information is available on the use of materials in these courses.

Operation, review and adjustment

UNEP is responsible under the Barcelona Convention for carrying out secretariat functions for the convention and the protocols (Art. 13). This is done by the Co-ordinating Unit for the Mediterranean Action Plan (MEDU-UNEP) in Athens. UNEP's Oceans and Coastal Areas Programme Activity Centre (UNEP-OCA/PAC) in Nairobi is responsible for overall co-ordination of the Regional Seas Programme. Article 14 of the convention provides for an ordinary meeting of the parties to keep implementation under review, adopt additional measures, and discharge other functions. Meetings of the parties to the protocols are held in conjunction with those of the parties to the convention. Their functions are essentially the same.
The following additional institutions have been established under the MAP:
- Regional Activity Centre for the Blue Plan (BP/RAC), located in Sophia Antipolis, France;
- Regional Activity Centre for the Priority Action Programme (RAP/PAC), in Split, Yugoslavia;
- Regional Activity Centre for Specially Protected Areas (SPA/PAC), in Tunis, Tunisia;
- Regional Marine Pollution Emergency Response Centre for the Mediterranean Sea (REMPEC IMO/UNEP), on the Manoel Island, Malta.
Up to the end of 1978, the Action Plan was mainly financed by UNEP, with governments of the region and collaborating UN Agencies contributing in kind. Since 1979, the Plan has been increasingly financed by Mediterranean Coastal States themselves, through the establishment of the Mediterranean Trust Fund (MTF). The main sources of finance of the Action Plan at present are cash contributions from Mediterranean governments on a scale agreed between them at meetings of the Contracting Parties. Other contributions, also from Mediterranean Coastal States, in cash and/or in kind, for specific aspects of the Plan, contributions in cash and kind by UNEP, and contributions in cash and/or in kind from the World Bank and the various collaborating UN Specialized Agencies.
During their 1991 meeting, the Contracting Parties approved a budget of approximately US $ 13 million for the 1992-1993 biennium. As agreed by the Contracting Parties in 1979, the Executive Director of UNEP was entrusted with the administration of the Mediterranean Trust Fund.
The main long-term benefit of participation in the MAP, and the convention and protocols adopted within its framework, is the reduction of the pollution of the Mediterranean. More specifically, participation in special programmes such as the recently established Coastal Area Management Programme (CAMP) benefits developing countries in particular, as it helps them implement the convention and the protocols on the national level. The main costs are the national measures needed for the implementation of the convention and the protocols. As financial and technical assistance are available from various sources under the MAP, these costs, especially for developing countries, are not very high.
The MAP, as other Regional Seas Programmes, is to a large extent implemented through designated national institutions. These are provided with the necessary assistance and training. To this end, existing global or regional co-ordinating mechanisms may be used.
One of the functions of the meetings of the contracting parties is to ensure periodic review and adjustment of the convention and its protocols.

Codification programming

The following new protocols to the Barcelona Convention are currently under preparation:

(1) Protocol on the Protection of the Mediterranean Sea against Pollution Resulting from Exploration and Exploitation of the Continental Shelf and the Sea Bed and its Sub-soil. This protocol is designed to respond to the obligation contained in Article 7 of the Barcelona Convention.

(2) Protocol on Transboundary Movements of Hazardous Wastes and their Disposal, designed primarily to prevent uncontrolled hazardous waste traffic from developed to developing countries in the Mediterranean Region.

In addition, amendments to some of the existing protocols were approved by the Seventh Ordinary Meeting of the Contracting Parties (1991). A new text of Annex IV to the IBS Protocol concerning airborne pollution in the Mediterranean was approved. The meeting authorized its Bureau to explore the feasibility to broaden the subject of the plenipotentiaries meeting on offshore protocol with amendments to the dumping protocol in order to include banning of incineration at sea and banning of dumping of industrial wastes in the Mediterranean.

Assessments and common measures relative to organophosphorus compounds, persistent synthetic materials, radioactive substances and pathogenic micro-organisms in the Mediterranean were also approved by the meeting.

These were in addition to the following previously approved measures:

- Interim Environmental Quality Criteria concerning Mercury Content of Seafood (Sept. 1985);
- Interim Environmental Quality Criteria concerning Microbial Concentrations of Bathing Waters (Sept. 1985);
- Maximum Concentration of Mercury in Effluent Discharges (Sept. 1987);
- Environmental Quality Criteria concerning Microbial Concentrations of Shellfish Waters (Sept. 1987);
- Control of Pollution by used Lubricating Oils (Oct. 1989);
- Control of Pollution by Cadmium and Cadmium Compounds (Oct. 1989);
- Control of Pollution by Organotin Compounds (Oct. 1989);
- Control of Pollution by Organohalogen Compounds (Oct. 1989).

A draft action plan to protect cetaceans in the Mediterranean was approved by the 1991 meeting of the Contracting Parties.

With a view to assist the Mediterranean States, in particular the developing states, in providing them with simple and yet adequate procedures and guidelines for their preparation of Environmental Impact Assessment (EIA) which could be used in the context of regional agreements on the protection of the marine environment, UNEP/MAP have developed and appropriate EIA approach which has been tested on the concrete case studies in Cyprus and Egypt and will be further tested and modified on the basis of experience gained through the preparation of additional case studies.

The drafting of legal instruments under the MAP is to a certain extent co-ordinated, through UNEP-OCA/PAC, with similar work done under the other Action Plans of the Regional Seas Programme. The scope of all Regional Seas Conventions and their protocols follow more or less the same format.

Remaining gaps include (general):

(1) Liability for damage: Article 12 of the Barcelona Convention obligates parties to adopt relevant measures. This remains to be done.

(2) Compliance monitoring: A formal procedure to monitor compliance and take measures

against offenders remains to be developed. Article 21 of the Barcelona Convention calls for the elaboration of such a procedure.

<u>Protocol III:</u> Common measures to control remaining Annex I substances and all Annex II substances.

<u>Protocol I:</u> Non-binding decisions of the parties to the London Dumping Convention and other dumping agreements contribute to an emerging international practice of phasing out ocean dumping of wastes.

<u>Protocol III:</u> UNEP's Montreal Guidelines on Marine Pollution from Land-Based Sources are contributing to the development of international law in this field, as are the declarations of parties to regional conventions, such as the endorsement of the "precautionary" approach to pollution control.

Several intergovernmental and non-governmental conferences on matters related to environmental protection and development in the Mediterranean (including the Conference on Security and Co-operation in Europe and the Charter on Euro-Mediterranean Co-operation concerning the Environment in the Mediterranean Basin - Nicosia Charter) have also addressed problems covered by the Barcelona Convention and its protocols, and have given support to their implementation.

208

(47) Kuwait Regional Convention for Co-operation on the Protection of the Marine Environment from Pollution
(Kuwait, 24 April 1978), and related protocols

Note: the relevant legal instruments are referred to in the following paragraphs as follows:
- Regional Convention for Co-operation on the Protection of the Marine Environment against Pollution: **CONVENTION**
- 1978 Protocol Concerning Regional Co-operation in Combating Pollution by Oil and Other Harmful Substances: **PROTOCOL I**
- 1989 Protocol Concerning Marine Pollution Resulting from Exploration and Exploitation of the Continental Shelf: **PROTOCOL II**
- 1990 Protocol for the Protection of the Environment against Pollution from Land-Based Sources: **PROTOCOL III**

Objectives and achievement

The convention, together with its protocols, constitutes the legal component of the Kuwait Action Plan (KAP), which was adopted under the UNEP Regional Seas Programme.
Convention: As an umbrella treaty, its objective is the protection of the Gulf against pollution from all sources, and the promotion of co-operation among the riparian states to this end. The convention takes account of the interrelated issues of environment and development by asserting the need for urban and industrial development to be carried out in such a way as to preserve, as far as possible, marine resources and coastal amenities.
Protocol I: The objective is co-operation between parties in the adoption of measures to combat marine pollution caused by accidental spillage of oil or other harmful substances.
Protocol II: The objective is the prevention and control of marine pollution resulting from offshore operations on the continental shelf.
Protocol III: The protocol aims at protection of the marine environment and coastal waters against pollution due to the release of untreated, insufficiently treated or inadequately disposed domestic and industrial discharges. The protocol was adopted in implementation of Articles 3(b) and 6 of the Convention.
The Kuwait Regional Convention and its protocols are part of a global network of treaties regulating the protection of different regions of the earth against marine pollution. The wide-spread participation of states in these treaties gives them a standard-setting function on a world-wide scale. Regional regulation of marine pollution is in line with the 1982 UNCLOS (No.38), which refers to regional rules in various contexts.
Protocol III in particular aims at reconciling environment protection and development priorities by making certain allowances for the different economic capacity of parties, and the need for sustainable development.
Convention: Article 12 calls for co-operation between parties in the provision of technical and other assistance related to marine pollution. No specific reference to the situation of developing countries is made, however.
Protocol I: Provision of assistance to developing countries may have played a role in the establishment of the Marine Emergency Mutual Aid Centre (MEMAC-ROPME), since the functions of that unit are very broad, including substantive assistance to contracting parties. There is no explicit reference to the needs of developing countries.
Protocol II: No provisions for the situation of developing countries.

<u>Protocol III</u>: Article 5 provides for the adoption of industrial planning programmes to ensure that the development of new industries is not inhibited by measures taken under the protocol. Guidelines and other regulations adopted in accordance with the protocol may take into account the different economic capacities of states, and the need for sustainable development. In addition, the protocol provides for scientific, technical and other assistance to parties that require it.

One indication of the achievement of the basic aims of the Kuwait Regional Convention is the adoption, between 1978 and 1990, of three protocols to regulate specific issues outlined broadly in the convention. The establishment of the Marine Emergency and Mutual Aid Centre (MEMAC-ROPME) in Bahrain in 1982, in accordance with the provisions of protocol I, is also an achievement indicator.

All coastal states of the Gulf are parties to the convention and protocol I, providing the basis for wide-spread co-ordination in the protection of the marine environment of the region. However, unilateral action during the Iran-Iraq war and the recent Gulf war caused major environmental damage and setbacks for the implementation of these agreements.

Participation

Membership of the convention and the protocols is limited to states which were invited to the Kuwait Regional Conference of Plenipotentiaries on the Protection and Development of the Marine Environment and the Coastal Areas in 1978 (namely the coastal states of the Gulf).

Reservations are not prohibited. No reservations have been made.

Current membership of the convention and protocol I includes 8 parties in the Middle East region, all of which are developing countries.

All party states participated in the drafting of the convention and protocols.

<u>General</u>: For the purpose of fact-finding missions and technical meetings, financial support was initially provided by UNEP and other UN organizations. However, the Kuwait Action Plan was set up with the financial support of contributions by the Contracting Parties to the Kuwait Regional Convention. A KAP Trust Fund was established for this purpose at UNEP, Nairobi to which substantial contributions were made by ROPME Member States.

<u>Convention</u>: The provisions on scientific information and technical and other assistance provide incentives for the participation of developing countries.

<u>Protocol I</u>: The establishment of the Marine Emergency Mutual Aid Centre (MEMAC) in accordance with Article 3 provides incentives for developing country participation. The functions of this centre are very broad, including substantive assistance to parties in implementing the convention. In addition, there is a requirement for information exchange.

<u>Protocol III:</u> The allowances made for development requirements, and the provision on scientific and technological co-operation provide further incentives.

Article 21 of the Convention facilitates amendments of technical annexes in response to scientific/technological changes.

Implementation and information

The convention and protocol I entered into force in the second year after adoption. Protocol II entered into force within the first year after adoption. Protocol III is not yet in force.

<u>Convention</u>: In order to prevent, abate and combat marine pollution, parties are required to adopt the necessary protocols, establish national standards, and co-operate with competent international organizations. They shall also promote technical and scientific co-

operation amongst each other. In their planning acuities, they shall endeavour to include environmental impact assessment.

Protocol I: Parties must provide the MEMAC and each other with information relevant to emergency response measures. They are required to take the necessary measures if pollution has occurred; for this they may request assistance from the MEMAC or directly from other parties. Parties to whom such a request is made must respond to the best of their abilities.

Protocol II: Parties are required to take all necessary measures, within their area of jurisdiction, to minimize environmental damage caused by offshore operations. To this end, they must establish a licensing system, and require prior environmental impact assessment for such operations. They shall ensure that such operations do not interfere with navigation, fishing or other activities. Operators of offshore installations must be required to be properly equipped, and to submit contingency plans for approval to the competent national authority. Discharges and disposal of waste in connection with offshore operations shall be controlled by national measures. Each operator of offshore installations shall be required to submit a "Chemical Use Plan" for approval by the national authority, and to comply with other regulations to be adopted under national law.

Protocol III: Contracting parties shall control sources of land-based pollution and adopt action programmes to this end. They shall develop guidelines and regulations for various sources of marine pollution, and for the quality of sea-water. Discharge shall be subject to a permit which specifies the modalities. The protocol also sets out requirements for monitoring, environmental impact assessment for projects in coastal areas, and scientific and technological co-operation.

Under Articles 9 and 23 of the convention, Contracting Parties are required to submit reports on measures adopted by them to the Council of the Regional Organization for the Protection of the Marine Environment (ROPME). Under protocol I, information shall also be submitted to the MEMAC. No information is available on the extent of compliance.

In the context of scientific co-operation, parties are required under Article 10 of the convention to exchange data. Protocol I merely provides a requirement for information exchange, without specific reference to data. Extent of compliance not known.

Protocol III requires parties to exchange data in specific fields, such as the results of environment monitoring, and the quantities of pollutants discharged from their territories. As the protocol is not yet in force, compliance cannot be assessed.

The institutions established under the KAP, namely ROPME and MEMAC, may assist countries in the fulfilment of their obligations under the Kuwait treaty system. Performance evaluation is undertaken by the Council of ROPME, in which all parties are represented. Article 24 of the convention requires parties to co-operate in the development of procedures for compliance control. No such procedure has yet been established.

Article 25 of the convention calls on parties to settle disputes through negotiation or other peaceful means. If this cannot be achieved, the dispute shall be submitted to the Judicial Commission for the Settlement of Disputes, operating with the framework of ROPME. This applies also to disputes concerning the protocols. There is no information on the extent to which these procedures have been invoked by parties.

Factors which influenced the implementation of the Convention and its Protocols are mainly the conflict in the Region even before the establishment of the ROPME Secretariat in January 1982, and partly the lack of financial resources, scientific expertise and technical capabilities.

The official languages of the convention and its protocols are Arabic, English and Persian. Current information on operation and implementation is made available by ROPME, which also publishes reports of surveys, studies, workshops, seminars and technical meetings. In addition, ROPME publishes a Quarterly Newsletter in Arabic and Persian.

The Regional Convention and the Protocols were developed and adopted by the States of the Region based on provisions of the international conventions and treaties. As regards conventions and treaties, individual Member States of ROPME have their own mechanisms for implementation. However, ROPME would provide them advisory assistance if requested.

Information received from international agencies are utilized by ROPME to a large extent in training programmes and programme implementation.

Operation, review and adjustment

ROPME is responsible for the technical co-ordination of the KAP. In accordance with the Kuwait Regional Convention, it consists of (1) the Council, which reviews the implementation of the convention and its protocols and carries out some other functions; (2) the Secretariat, which administers the convention and protocols; and (3) the Judicial Commission for the Settlement of Disputes. The MEMAC, established under protocol I, is in charge of development and technical co-ordination of response capabilities of party states.

Approximately US $3.5 million for operational expenses; programme implementation; training courses; workshops and seminars; legal/technical meetings; etc. Financing of ROPME activities are by contribution from ROPME Member States.

The main long-term benefit of participation in the KAP, and the convention and protocols adopted within its framework, is the reduction of the pollution of the marine environment of the Gulf. More specific benefits may be derived from the assistance provided to parties by the MEMAC. The main costs are the national measures and institutions needed for the implementation of the convention and the protocols. There is no information as regards the extent of these costs, and measures taken to reduce costs for developing countries.

Scientific data and other information received by ROPME from Member States and other sources are passed on to the National Focal Point designated by each Member State for their review and possible use in developing national environmental laws and regulations for protection and conservation of the environment.

The KAP, as other Regional Seas Programmes, is to a large extent implemented through designated national institutions. National authorities have important functions in the implementation of the protocols. Accordingly, they are provided with the necessary assistance and training. To this end, existing global or regional co-ordinating mechanisms may be used.

Review and adjustment of the Convention and its protocols is one of the main functions of the Council of ROPME, in which all states are represented.

Codification programming

Protocol III has not entered into force. A new draft Protocol for the Control of Transboundary Movement of Hazardous Wastes in the Sea Area is under development. One legal/technical meeting was held in December 1989 to review the draft Protocol. Two more meetings are planned to finalize the Protocol.

The drafting of legal instruments under the KAP is carried out by ROPME in consultation with Member States and in co-operation with UNEP.

Remaining gaps include:

(1) Liability for damage: Article 13 of the Kuwait Regional Convention obligates parties to adopt relevant measures. This remains to be done.

(2) Compliance monitoring: A formal procedure to monitor compliance and take measures against offenders remains to be developed. Article 24 of the convention calls for the elaboration of such a procedure.

(3) Protocol on accidental discharges from ships (cf. Article 4 of the convention).

(4) Protocol on dumping (cf. Article 5 of the convention).

<u>Protocol III</u>: UNEP's Montreal Guidelines on Marine Pollution from Land-Based Sources (No.39) are contributing to the development of international law in this field, as are the declarations of parties to regional conventions, such as the endorsement of the "precautionary" approach to pollution control.

(48) Convention for Co-operation in the Protection and Development of the Marine and Coastal Environment of the West and Central African Region,
(Abidjan, 23 March 1981), and related protocol.

Objectives and achievement

The basic objective of the Abidjan Convention, as a UNEP Regional Seas Convention, is the conservation of the environment of the West and Central African Region by the promotion, on a regional basis, of co-operation in the environmental protection and natural resources management in the marine and coastal areas of the region.

The importance of both environmental protection and development is expressly recognized both by the title and in the Preamble to the Convention in which the parties recognize the economic, social and health value of the marine environment and coastal areas of the region and the need for co-operation to ensure sustainable, environmentally-sound development through a co-ordinated and comprehensive approach. While conscious of the inter-generational responsibility of protecting this natural heritage for future as well as present generations, the parties recognize the threat to the marine environment, its ecological equilibrium, resources and legitimate uses which is posed by pollution and by the absence of an integration of an "environmental dimension" into the development process. The parties also note that existing conventions do not cover all aspects and sources of marine pollution and do not entirely meet the special requirements of the region.

One Protocol concerning co-operation in combating pollution in cases of emergency has been concluded under the Convention at the 1981 Abidjan Plenipotentiary Conference. The objective of the protocol is to establish a framework for co-operation to protect the marine and coastal environment from the threat and the effects of pollution deriving from the presence of oil or other harmful substances in the marine environment as a result of actual or potential marine emergencies (art. 3 and 4).

The concept of sound environmental management, the obligations to prevent, reduce and control marine pollution from its various sources in the region are in accordance with the approaches adopted by global conventions and with the concept of sustainable development, as is the development of EIA measures.

The regional nature of the agreement, based as it is on regional co-operation between predominantly developing countries recognizes their special requirements. Notable are the provisions of the Convention relating to technical and scientific assistance in fields relating to pollution and sound environmental management, and also the general obligations of co-operation, notably in emergencies but also in the exchange of data and scientific information.

Goal achievement can be measured on the basis of the degree of acceptance of the legal instruments, i.e., status of its signatures and ratifications; efficient participation in the programmes; level of contributions to the UNEP Trust Fund for the Protection and Development of the Marine Environment and Coastal Areas of the West and Central African Region (WACAF/TF); changes in national legislation; and allocations of funds in the national budget; production of reliable environmental data.

Participation

Membership is restricted. Initial signature and subsequent ratification, acceptance or approval of the Convention and its Protocol was limited to coastal and island states from Mauritania to Namibia inclusive. (Art.s 26-7).

Marine Environment and Marine Pollution

Subsequent accession is open to any African state (Art. 28(2)) or to any other State, subject to the prior approval of three quarters of the states entitled to initial membership which have become contracting parties (Art. 28(3)).

Reservations are not prohibited. None have been made.

Current Membership is confined to 10 coastal states of West Africa.

All the participating states are developing countries.

The primary incentive for participation and implementation is mutual and common benefit from a co-operative regional programme.

The Regional Seas programme is predicated on mutual assistance within the region. UNEP provides some "seed money" from its Environment Fund for initial programme development, but the primary financial responsibility for programme implementation, including participation at meetings lies with the regional Trust Fund.

To promote and support participation, UNEP has provided training, equipment, reference methods and financial support to undertake activities on marine pollution control, coastal erosion control, and assessment of critical habitats under the West and Central African Action Plan. UNEP (with IMO assistance) has supported projects on the Institution and Co-ordination of National Contingency Plans in the West and Central African Region. A number of national plans were developed and in 1985 a regional workshop on contingency planning was held. More recently, existing contingency plans are in the process to be updated.

Participation in the convention is critically dependent on the availability of financial, technical and scientific assistance.

Implementation and information

The Convention and Protocol required ratification by six states. They entered into force on 5 August 1984, some three and a half years after signature.

The Abidjan Convention is a framework Convention, consequently a number of its obligations are to co-operate. The principal obligations are:

Art. 4(1) obliges Contracting Parties, individually or jointly to take all appropriate measures ... to prevent, reduce and combat pollution of the Convention area and to ensure sound environmental management of natural resources, using best practicable means. To this end the parties undertake

- to co-operate in the formulation and adoption of protocols and other measures to facilitate the effective implementation of the Convention (Art. 4(2));

- to take all appropriate measures for the effective discharge of the obligations prescribed in the Convention and protocols and to harmonize their national policies in this regard (Art. 4(3)); and

- to co-operate in the competent international, regional and subregional organizations for the effective implementation of this Convention and its protocols, and to assist each other in fulfilling their obligations (Art. 4(4));

- to ensure that the implementation of those measures does not cause transfer of hazards or transform of one type or form of pollution to another. (Art. 4(5)).

The more specific objectives of the Convention require the Parties to take appropriate measures:

a) to prevent, reduce and combat pollution of the Convention area caused by pollution from ships (Art. 5);

b) to prevent, reduce and combat pollution of the Convention area caused by pollution from Dumping (Art. 6);

c) to prevent, reduce and combat pollution of the Convention area caused by discharges from land-based Sources (Art. 7);

d) to prevent, reduce and combat pollution of the Convention area caused by Sea-bed Activities (Art. 8);

e) to prevent, reduce and combat pollution of the Convention area resulting from discharges into the atmosphere from activities under their jurisdiction (Art. 9);

f) to prevent, reduce, combat and control coastal erosion in the Convention area resulting from human activities (Art. 10);

g)   to take all appropriate measures to protect and preserve rare and fragile ecosystems, as well as rare and depleted, threatened or endangered species of wild flora and fauna and their habitat in the Convention area (Art. 11);

h) to co-operate in responding to pollution emergencies in the Convention Area (Art. 12);

i) to develop, adopt and implement Environmental Impact Assessment guidelines and to disseminate information concerning them. (Art. 13);

j) to co-operate,   directly and through appropriate international and regional organizations, in scientific research, monitoring and exchange of relevant data and other scientific information; and to co-operate in the development of a regional network of national research centres to ensure compatible results (Art. 14).

k) to co-operate in the formulation and adoption of appropriate rules and procedures regarding liability and compensation for pollution damage (Art. 15).

Protocol concerning co-operation in combating marine pollution in cases of emergency.

This protocol implements Art. 12 of the Convention. It is distinctive in extending the definition of such emergency to include pollution caused by the failure of industrial installations. It requires parties:

a) to co-operate in taking necessary preventive and remedial measures (Art. 4);

b) to exchange relevant information (Art.s 5 and 6);

c) to establish reporting requirements for marine pollution incidents (Art. 7);

d) to render mutual assistance in the event of such an incident (Art. 8);

e) to develop and maintain marine emergency contingency plans and co-operate in the development of reporting procedures (Art. 9);

f) to comply with designated procedures when responding to marine emergencies (Art. 10).

Pursuant to Article 17(2)(vi) of the Convention, the Contracting Parties also take decisions regarding financial matters, including commitments for assessed contributions to the Trust Fund.

The Convention requires meetings of the Parties every two years (Art. 17) to review national reports on the implementation of the Convention and its protocol submitted in accordance with Art. 22. The Parties agree by Art. 23 to co-operate in the development of procedures to control the application of the Convention and its protocol.

Parties are obliged to submit reports for consideration by the Meetings of the Parties on the measures adopted in implementation of the Convention and its protocol in such form as such Meetings of the Contracting Parties shall determine (Art. 22).

The Convention requires Parties to   disseminate information concerning Environmental Impact Assessment guidelines they develop (Art. 13); and to co-operate, directly and through appropriate international and regional organizations, in scientific research, monitoring and exchange of relevant data and other scientific information; and to co-operate in the development of a regional network of national research centres to ensure compatible results (Art. 14).

The Protocol concerning co-operation in combating marine pollution in cases of emergency contains requirements for exchange of information regarding implementation of the protocol, including identity of national authorities, national laws and operational procedures (Art. 5); information on relevant research and development programmes, as well as on experiences in combating pollution by oil and other harmful substances (Art. 6); reports of marine pollution incidents and of presence, characteristics and extent of spillages of oil or other harmful substances observed at sea which are likely to present a serious and imminent threat to the marine and coastal environment of the region (Art. 7); principles to follow by each Contracting Party in the conduct of marine emergency responses (Art. 10).

Pending the establishment of a regional co-ordinating unit it appears these obligations have not been fulfilled.

The Convention contains provisions for settlement of disputes arising from interpretation or application of the Convention or its protocol (Art. 24). There is no report of them having been used.

Implementation has been influenced by the availability of financial, technical and scientific assistance; through pressure from parliaments, the press, NGOs and public opinion; and as a result of the reporting obligations mentioned in paragraph 14.

The Convention and protocol and the Action Plan are published in English and French. Each of the language texts is equally authentic. The texts are published in UNEP series.

Operation, review and adjustment

The depositary of the Convention and its protocol is the Government of the Côte d'Ivoire.

The Convention designates UNEP as the secretariat of the Convention.

Assessed contributions to the UNEP Trust Fund for the West and Central African Region for 1990 were $1,000,100. However, the Executive Director's report to the Governing Council indicates considerable arrears in the actual collection of contributions, which also prevented the establishment of the institutional infrastructure foreseen in the Convention.

Technical and scientific assistance (through IMO) has been made available through UNEP projects on contingency planning and for national capacity building. Participation in the Action Plan involves financial commitments. Financial difficulties have been a limiting factor in the implementation of the Convention and the participation of certain governments.

Expert meetings formulate recommendations to the biennial meetings of the Contracting Parties, including proposals for new protocols under the Convention.

The Convention envisages biennial Meetings of the Parties to review the annexes and protocols, and to consider new protocols and amendments to the Convention (Art. 17(2)); the first meeting was held in Abidjan in April 1985, and the second meeting in Dakar in January 1989. So far, no amendments to the Convention and Protocol have been proposed.

Codification programming

An additional protocol on land-based sources of marine pollution has been drafted by UNEP and it will be reviewed at the next meeting of the WACAF Steering Committee. Co-ordination is ensured through the UNEP secretariat (Programme Activity Centre for Oceans and Coastal Areas).

An additional protocol on specially protected areas is needed; also, problems of liability and hazardous waste management will have to be addressed in the future.

The UNEP West and Central African Action Plan is the major instrument contributing to implementation of the Convention and its protocol.

(49) Convention for the Protection of the Marine Environment and Coastal Areas of the South-East Pacific
(Lima, 12 November 1981), and related protocols.

Objectives and achievement

The basic objective of the Lima Convention, as a UNEP Regional Seas Convention, is the protection of the marine environment and coastal areas of the South-East Pacific Region from pollution by the promotion, on a regional basis, of co-operation in the areas of environmental protection and natural resources management in the marine and coastal areas of the region.

The importance of protecting the marine environment and coastal area of the region is expressly recognized in both the title and the Preamble to the Convention, and the need to reconcile such protection with the requirements of development is recognized inter alia in the provisions relating to Environmental Impact Assessment. In the Preamble the parties recognize the economic, social and cultural value of the South-East Pacific as a means of linking the countries of the region, and note that existing conventions do not cover all aspects and sources of marine pollution and do not entirely meet the special requirements of the region.

The Convention is supplemented by an Agreement and four protocols. The Agreement on regional co-operation in combating pollution of the South-East Pacific by hydrocarbons or other harmful substances in cases of emergency (Lima, 1981), together with a supplementary protocol (Quito, 1983) and a protocol for the protection of the South-East Pacific against pollution from land-based sources (Quito, 1983). Two further Protocols were completed in 1989, a protocol for the protection of the South East Pacific against radioactive pollution and a protocol for the conservation and management of protected marine and coastal areas of the South Pacific.

The objective of the 1981 Lima Agreement is to establish a framework for co-operation to protect the marine and coastal environment from the threat of pollution resulting from the presence of oil or other harmful substances. The 1983 Quito Supplementary Protocol provides detailed co-operative mechanisms to be used in the case of such an emergency. The 1983 Protocol on land-based sources of pollution aims to establish common standards and a co-operative regime to prevent, control and reduce pollution from such sources. The 1989 protocol for the protection of the South East Pacific against radioactive pollution establishes a regional regime for this purpose and the protocol for the conservation and management of protected marine and coastal areas of the South Pacific provides mechanisms for a regional protected areas system.

The concept of sound environmental management, the obligations to prevent, reduce and control marine pollution from its various sources in the region are in accordance with the approaches adopted by global conventions and with the concept of sustainable development, as is the development of EIA measures and regional action on land based sources of pollution.

The regional nature of the agreement, based as it is on regional co-operation between developing countries recognises their special requirements. Notable are the provisions of the Convention relating to technical and scientific assistance in fields relating to pollution and sound environmental management, and also the general obligations of co-operation, notably in emergencies but also in the exchange of data and scientific information.

The Convention has established the largest number of protocols of any of the Regional Seas Areas. The programme appears to be progressing well.

Participation

Membership of the Convention, Agreement and protocols is restricted to any State bordering the South East Pacific.

Reservations are not prohibited. None have been made.

Current Membership is 5: Chile, Colombia, Ecuador, Panama, Peru. All the participating States are developing countries. The primary incentive for participation and implementation is mutual and common benefit from a co-operative regional programme.

The Regional Seas programme is predicated on mutual assistance within the region. UNEP provides some "seed money" from its Environment Fund for initial programme development, but the primary financial responsibility for programme implementation, including participation at meetings lies with the regional Trust fund.

Technical and scientific assistance is designed to be available through the programme.

A training course and legal and technical expert workshop on the Contingency Plan for the combating of oil pollution in the South East Pacific in cases of emergency was convened in March 1985 by IMO/CPPS/UNEP (in co-operation with the Government of Panama). This reviewed the Regional Contingency Plan.

Implementation and information

The 1981 Convention required ratification by three states. It entered into force on 19 May 1986, some five years after signature.

The 1981 Agreement entered into force 14 July 1986. The 1983 Quito Supplementary Protocol entered into force 20 May 1987 and the 1983 Quito Protocol on Land-based Sources 23 September 1986.

The 1989 protocol for the protection of the South East Pacific against radioactive pollution and the 1989 protocol for the conservation and management of protected marine and coastal areas of the South Pacific are not in force having not yet received any ratifications.

The Lima Convention is a framework Convention, consequently a number of its obligations are to co-operate. The principal obligations are:

Art. 3(1) obliges Contracting Parties, individually or jointly to take all appropriate measures ... to prevent, reduce and control pollution of the Convention area from any source and to ensure sound environmental management of natural resources, using best practicable means. To this end the parties undertake

- to establish laws and regulations (no less effective than existing international rules, standards and recommended practices and procedures) for the effective discharge of the obligations prescribed in the Convention and protocols (Art. 3(3)).

- to co-operate on a regional basis in the formulation and adoption of effective rules, standards, practices and procedures to attain the objectives of the Convention (Art. 3(4));

- to take all necessary measures to ensure that activities under their jurisdiction do not result in damage by pollution and that such activities do not cause pollution outside their jurisdiction (Art. 3(5));

The more specific objectives of the Convention require the Parties to take appropriate measures:

a) to prevent, reduce and control pollution of the marine environment from land based sources, atmospheric sources, dumping, from vessels and other installations and devices. (Art. 4);

b) to prevent, reduce and control coastal erosion resulting from human activities (Art. 5);

c) to co-operate in cases of pollution resulting from emergency situations (Art. 6);

d) to collaborate in the establishment of pollution monitoring programmes (Art. 7);

e) to develop, adopt and implement Environmental Impact Assessment guidelines and to disseminate information concerning them (Art. 8);

f) to exchange relevant information among themselves (Art. 9)

g) to co-operate, directly and through appropriate international and regional organizations, in scientific research, monitoring and exchange of relevant data and other scientific information; and to co-operate in the development of national research programmes (Art. 10);

h) to co-operate in the formulation and adoption of appropriate rules and procedures regarding liability and compensation for pollution damage (Art. 11).

Agreement on regional co-operation in combating pollution of the South-East Pacific by hydrocarbons or other harmful substances in cases of emergency (Lima, 1981),

This protocol implements the general obligation of Art. 6 of the Convention. Its principal obligations require parties:

a) to co-operate in taking necessary measures to counteract harmful effects of marine pollution emergency situations (Art. I);

b) to endeavour to promote and establish contingency plans and programmes (Art. IV);

c) to carry out individual or collaborative monitoring activities (Art. V);

d) to exchange relevant information (Art. VII);

e) to co-ordinate communications for emergency use (Art. VIII);

f) to establish reporting procedures (Art. IX);

g) to establish common response and co-operative measures (Art. X and XI).

The supplementary protocol (Quito, 1983)

This protocol establishes detailed co-operation mechanisms in the event of an oil spill (Art. I) and details requirements for national contingency plans (Art. II)

The protocol for the protection of the South-East Pacific against pollution from land-based sources (Quito, 1983)

This protocol implements the general obligation of Art. 4(a)(i)of the Convention to endeavour to adopt appropriate measures to prevent reduce and control pollution from land based sources. Its principal obligations require parties:

a) to endeavour to prevent, reduce and eliminate pollution from land based sources by substances listed in Annex I (Art. IV);

b) to endeavour progressively to reduce pollution from land based sources by substances listed in Annex II(Art. V);

c) to endeavour to adopt rules and standards relating to land based sources of pollution (Art. VI) ;

d) to co-operate in combating land based pollution (Art. VII);

e) to establish monitoring programmes (Art. VIII);

f) to exchange relevant information among themselves and transmit it to the Secretariat (Art. IX);

g) to co-operate in the fields of science and technology (Art. X);

h) to refrain from causing damage by pollution to other parties (Art. XI); and to consult in cases where such damage is likely (Art. XII);

protocol for the protection of the South East Pacific against radioactive pollution

protocol for the conservation and management of protected marine and coastal areas of the South Pacific.

Financial commitments arising from the Action Plan are not based on the Convention.

The Convention requires meetings of the Parties every two years at the same•time as the meetings of the Permanent Commission of the South Pacific (Art. 12) to examine the extent to which the Convention is being implemented.

Similar provisions apply to the protocols.

Parties are obliged to submit reports to the Secretariat on the measures adopted in implementation of the Convention and its protocols in such form and at such intervals as such Meetings of the Parties shall determine (Art. 14).

The Convention requires parties to disseminate information on Environmental Impact Assessment through the Secretariat Organization (Art. 8) and to exchange information concerning national administration, programme development and research relating to marine pollution (Art. 9).

Agreement on regional co-operation in combating pollution of the South-East Pacific by hydrocarbons or other harmful substances in cases of emergency contains requirements for similar exchange of information (Art. VII) and for reporting procedures (Art. IX).

The protocol for the protection of the South-East Pacific against pollution from land-based sources contains requirements for reporting information on monitoring programmes (Art. VIII); exchange of information regarding implementation of the protocol, including identity of national authorities, national laws and operational procedures (Art. IX), and for the exchange of data and scientific information (Art. X).

There is no provision in the Convention relating to settlement of disputes arising from interpretation or application of the Convention or its protocols.

The Convention and protocols and the Action Plan are published in English and Spanish. The Spanish text is authentic. The texts are published in UNEP series.

Operation, review and adjustment

The depositary of the Convention and its protocols is the General Secretariat of the Permanent Commission of the South Pacific.

The Convention designates the Permanent Commission of the South Pacific (CPPS) as the Executive Secretariat under the Convention (Art. 13).

Mutual co-operation. Technical and Scientific assistance has been made available through IMO/CPPS/UNEP projects on contingency planning (see above). Participation in the Action Plan involves financial commitments. It seems likely that financial and other resource factors have inhibited the further development of the Action Plan and the Convention regime.

Communication directly with other parties and through the CPPS as Executive Secretariat, together with collaborative exercises, as required by the Convention and its protocols.

The Convention envisages biennial Meetings of the Parties to review the need for amendment or revision of the Convention and the protocols, and to consider the adoption of new protocols (Art. 12).

Two protocols were negotiated at a Meeting in Quito in 1983, and two further protocols in 1989.

Codification programming

The Permanent Commission of the South Pacific (CPPS), the depositary and Executive Secretariat, co-ordinates similar regional agreements and instruments.

The 1981 Action Plan for the Protection of the Marine Environment and Coastal Area of the South East Pacific is the major vehicle for practical implementation of the Convention and its protocols.

(50) Memorandum of Understanding on Port State Control in Implementing Agreements on Maritime Safety and Protection of the Marine Environment
(Paris, 26 January 1982)

Objectives and achievement

To improve and harmonize the system of port State control and strengthen co-operation and the exchange of information for the purpose of ensuring that effective action is taken by port States to prevent the operation of substandard ships and to avoid distorting competition between ports.

The actual bearing of the memorandum on global environment protection and sustainable development is that port State control has proved to be an effective means of policing marine pollution from ships and ensuring the enforcement of global conventions such as MARPOL. Its potential significance is that it may be possible to extend the scope of the scheme to include other states.

The special circumstances of developing countries are not taken into account.

The objectives of the memorandum have been met to the extent that over 70% of ships sailing to Western European ports are inspected annually, and that a high degree of compliance, averaging around 95% has been found. The parties have not however met their stated objective of achieving an annual total of inspections "corresponding to 25% of the estimated number of foreign merchant ships" entering the ports of each party over a 12 month period, but have achieved a figure of 18 to 20 per cent.

Statistical data provided by the MOU secretariat do not produce any clear evidence of improved quality of vessels visiting European ports, but officials in a number of ports were satisfied that there had been an improvement in the condition of vessels.

Participation

Membership may be expanded with the consent of those authorities presently participating in the memorandum.

Reservations are not provided for.

The geographical distribution of the memorandum is confined to Western Europe and contains no developing countries. No incentives are provided for participation by developing countries.

Implementation and information

The memorandum is not a treaty and entered into force on the date specified.

The parties undertake to give effect to the memorandum and annexes thereto, to maintain an effective system of port State control, to achieve an annual total of inspections corresponding to 25% of the number of foreign merchant ships entering the port during a 12 month period, to consult, co-operate and exchange information, to ensure that no more favourable treatment is given to ships entitled to fly the flag of non-party States, to avoid inspections within six months of a previous inspection, to ensure that hazardous deficiencies are removed before the ship proceeds, to report on inspections under the Memorandum. Compliance with the memorandum can be monitored by the Committee established under Section 6 of the memorandum.

Each authority is required to report on its inspections under the Memorandum and on their results. Information available from the secretariat does not enable the performance of individual States to be assessed.

Parties are required to exchange information with other authorities, to notify the flag State of action taken, to notify the next port of call where deficiencies cannot be remedied in the port of inspection, and to report as required in paragraph 14.

No provision is made for non-compliance.

No mechanisms of dispute settlement are provided.

None of the criteria listed appears to have influenced implementation.

The text is available in English and French.

Current information is made available through the secretariat's annual report.

Operation, review and adjustment

The Memorandum is administered by a Committee comprised of national authorities and the EEC. A secretariat is provided by the Netherlands Ministry of Transport and Public Works.

No budgetary information is available.

The main benefits are in the standard of ships using the ports of participating States, and the minimization of disruption to freedom of maritime navigation. The main costs are the provision of a system of periodic inspection. Developing countries can participate only with the agreement of present parties.

The Committee established by the Memorandum can take account of scientific knowledge.

The parties to the Memorandum are the relevant national authorities of the States concerned. No provision is made for NGO participation.

The Memorandum can be amended by 2/3 majority. Annexes may also be amended. The Committee established by the Memorandum is also required to keep the effectiveness of the Memorandum under review.

Codification programming

No revisions are currently under negotiation.

Initial drafting was co-ordinated with the 1973 MARPOL Convention.

The scheme is confined to Western Europe; it could be expanded.

The Memorandum itself may be considered as an informal mechanism contributing to the development of international law in this area.

(51) Regional Convention for the Conservation of the Red Sea and Gulf Of Aden Environment
(Jeddah, 14 February 1982), and related protocol

Objectives and achievement

The basic objective of the Jeddah Convention and its one Protocol on regional co-operation in combating pollution by oil and other harmful substances, as a UNEP Regional Seas Convention, is the conservation of the environment of the Red Sea and Gulf of Aden by the promotion, on a regional basis, of environmental protection and natural resources management in the marine and coastal areas of the region.

The importance of both environmental protection and development is expressly recognized in the Preamble to the Convention (the fifth of the UNEP regional seas conventions) in which the parties recognize the need to develop an integrated management approach to the use of the marine environment and the coastal areas which will allow the achievement of environmental and developmental goals in a harmonious manner. They recognize that pollution of the marine environment of the region by oil and other harmful or noxious materials from human activities on land and at sea, especially through indiscriminate and uncontrolled discharges presents a growing threat to marine life, fisheries, human health, recreational uses of beaches and other amenities, and mindful of the special characteristics of the region, particularly the vulnerability of its coral reefs recognize the need to ensure that urban and rural development and resultant land use should so far as possible preserve marine resources and coastal amenities so that such development does not lead to deterioration of the marine environment.

One Protocol has been negotiated under the Convention concerning co-operation in combating spills of oil and other harmful substances in cases of emergency. The Protocol was concluded at the Jeddah Conference in 1982.

The objective of the Spills protocol is to establish a framework for co-operation to protect the marine and coastal environment from the threat of pollution resulting from the presence of oil or other harmful substances in the marine environment as a result of marine emergencies.

The concept of sound environmental management, the obligations to prevent, reduce and control marine pollution from its various sources and the development of EIA measures are all in accordance with the approaches adopted by global conventions and with the concept of sustainable development.

The regional nature of the agreement, based as it is on regional co-operation between predominantly developing countries recognizes their special requirements. Notable are the provisions of the Convention relating to technical and scientific assistance in fields relating to pollution and sound environmental management, and also the general obligations of co-operation, notably in emergencies but also in the exchange of data and scientific information.

Information to be added.

Participation

Membership is restricted. Initial signature and subsequent ratification, acceptance or approval of the Convention and its Protocols was limited to states and regional economic integration organizations with relevant competencies which were invited to participate in the 1982 Jeddah Regional Conference of Plenipotentiaries. (Art. XXV)

Subsequent accession is limited to any State member of the Arab League (Art XXVI.2).

Reservations are not prohibited. None have been made.

All the participating states are developing countries.

The primary incentive for participation and implementation is mutual and common benefit from a co-operative regional programme.

The Regional Seas programme is predicated on mutual assistance within the region. UNEP provides some "seed money" from its Environment Fund for initial programme development, but the primary financial responsibility for programme implementation, including participation at meetings lies with the regional Trust fund.

Technical and scientific assistance is available through the programme.

Implementation and information

The Convention and the Protocol required ratifications by only four states to come into force - a small number for a regional Convention but only seven governments signed the Convention at the 1982 Jeddah Conference. They came into force 20 August 1985.

After the adoption of the regional Action Plan and the Convention and protocol, the Arab League Educational, Cultural and Scientific Organisation (ALESCO) was designated as responsible for such interim arrangements as may be necessary to achieve the objectives of the Action Plan until the establishment of the Regional Organisation for the Conservation of the Red Sea and Gulf of Aden Environment.

The Jeddah Convention is a framework Convention, consequently a number of its obligations are to co-operate. The principal obligations are:

Article 4(1) obliges Contracting Parties, individually or jointly to take all appropriate measures ... for the conservation of the Red Sea and Gulf of Aden Environment including the prevention, abatement and combating of marine pollution (Art III). To this end the parties undertake

- to co-operate in the formulation and adoption of protocols and other measures to facilitate the effective implementation of the Convention (Art. III(2));

- to establish national standards for the effective discharge of the obligations prescribed in the Convention and protocols and to harmonize their policies for this (Art. III(3)); and

- to co-operate in the competent international, regional and subregional organizations for the effective implementation of this Convention and its protocols, and to assist each other in fulfilling their obligations. (Art III(4));

- to ensure that the implementation of those measures does not cause transformation of one type or form of pollution to another which would be more detrimental. (Art III(5));

The more specific objectives of the Convention require the Parties to take appropriate measures:

a) to prevent, abate and combat pollution of the Sea Area of the Convention area caused by pollution from ships (Art. IV);

b) to prevent, abate and combat pollution of the Sea Area caused by pollution from Dumping (Art. V);

c) to prevent, abate and combat pollution of the Sea Area caused by discharges from Land-based Sources (Art. VI);

d) to prevent, abate and combat pollution of the Sea Area caused by Sea-bed Activities (Art. VII);

e) to prevent, abate and combat pollution of the Sea Area resulting from other human activities (Art. VIII);

f) to co-operate in responding to pollution emergencies in the Sea Area (Art. IX);

g) to co-operate, directly and through appropriate international and regional organizations, in scientific research, monitoring and exchange of relevant data and other scientific information; each party to designate a responsible National Authority for such co-operation (Art. X);

h) to give due consideration to marine environmental effects when planning or executing national projects and to develop standards in this regard (Art. XI);

i) to co-operate in the development of relevant programmes of scientific and technical assistance (Art. XII);

j) to co-operate in the formulation and adoption of appropriate rule and procedures regarding liability for pollution damage and for violation of the obligations of the Convention and its protocols (Art. XIII).

Because the Regional Organisation has yet to be established, monitoring of compliance with these obligations is undertaken by the Interim Council formed by ALESCO.

Financial commitments arising from the Action Plan are monitored through the Interim Council formed by ALESCO.

There is as yet no institutionalized system of reporting implementation of Convention obligations. Parties report on their performance in implementing the Convention through meetings of the Interim Council and directly through correspondence with the Executive Director of the Red Sea and Gulf of Aden Environmental Programme (PERSGA).

There are no direct obligations of data supply in the Convention.

The Protocol on regional co-operation in combating pollution by oil and other harmful substances in cases of emergency contains requirements (Art. VIII) for supply of information regarding national laws and contingency plans (Art. V), scientific and technical information (Art. VI), and reports of marine emergencies (Art. VII(2)) to a Marine Emergency Mutual Aid Centre.

Procedures to promote compliance and follow up non-compliance are envisaged through the Regional Organisation, which has not yet been established.

The Convention contains provisions for settlement of disputes arising from interpretation or application of the Convention (Art. XXIV). There are no reports that these procedures have ever been used.

Information to be added. Some financial assistance is provided through ALESCO for national research projects under the Action Plan.

The Convention and protocol and the Action Plan are published in Arabic and English. The texts are published in UNEP series.

Operation, review and adjustment

The depositary of the Convention and its protocols is the Government of the Kingdom of Saudi Arabia.

The Convention envisages the establishment of a Regional Organisation consisting of a Council and General Secretariat to be located in Jeddah.

In the interim the Arab League Educational, Cultural and Scientific Organisation (ALESCO) has responsibility for the implementation of the Action Plan. An office of the Red Sea and Gulf of Aden Environment Programme (PERSGA) has been set up in Jeddah.

As ALESCO is responsible for the interim arrangements pending the establishment of the Regional Organization, ALESCO allocates a lump-sum fund of about US $ 500.000 to cover the Biannual Budget of PERSGA.

Technical and Scientific assistance is available through PERSGA.

Until the envisaged General Secretariat of the Regional Organisation is established, the only mechanisms available are through the PERSGA office.

The Convention envisages regular Meetings of the Parties through the Council of the Regional Organisation to consider (inter alia) amendments to the Convention and the negotiation of further protocols (Art. XXI). No meeting of the Council has yet taken place.

(52) Convention for the Protection and Development of the Marine Environment of the Wider Caribbean Region
(Cartagena de Indias, 24 March 1983) and related protocols

Objectives and achievement

The basic objective of the Cartagena Convention, as a UNEP Regional Seas Convention, is formulated in its title which juxtaposes the two basic elements of this evaluation, namely the protection and development of the marine environment.

The importance of both these elements is expressly recognized in the Preamble to the Convention (which follows, but also adds to, the wording used by previous regional seas conventions) in which the parties declare that the protection of the ecosystems of the marine environment is one of their "principal objectives". While conscious of the inter-generational responsibility of protecting this environment for future as well as present generations, the parties also recognize the economic and social value of the marine environment to the region, and recognize the threat to the marine environment, its ecological equilibrium, resources and legitimate uses which is posed by pollution and by the absence of sufficient integration of an "environmental dimension" into the development process. The parties also expressly recognize the need to co-operate between themselves as well as with the competent international organizations in order to ensure "co-ordinated and comprehensive development without environmental damage." While the global nature of environmental problems is recognized by the need to secure the wider acceptance of international marine pollution agreements, the parties also note that these wider agreements do not cover all aspects of environmental deterioration and do not entirely meet the special requirements of the region.

Two Protocols have been negotiated under the Convention. A protocol concerning co-operation in combating oil spills in the wider Caribbean region, concluded at the 1983 Cartagena Meeting, provides for co-operation at both preventive and remedial levels to protect the marine and coastal environment (particularly of islands) from oil spill incidents. It has been provisionally extended by an annex to other hazardous substances.

The second protocol on Specially Protected Areas and Wildlife concluded in Kingston in 1990 (with annexes agreed in 1991) sets up a co-operative and common system for the establishment of protected areas and for the protection of wild flora and fauna and their habitat.

The concept of sound environmental management, the obligations to prevent, reduce and control marine pollution from its various sources and the development of EIA measures are all in accordance with the approaches adopted by global conventions and with the concept of sustainable development. The special needs of the smaller island developing countries [and territories] in the region are recognized expressly by the provisions of the Convention relating to technical and scientific assistance in fields relating to pollution and sound environmental management, but also by the general obligations of co-operation, notably in emergencies but also in the exchange of data and scientific information.

The regional nature of the agreement, based as it is on regional co-operation between predominantly developing countries recognizes their special requirements. Notable are the provisions of the Convention relating to technical and scientific assistance in fields relating to pollution and sound environmental management, and also the general obligations of co-operation, notably in emergencies but also in the exchange of data and scientific information.

The Convention and the first protocol have been in force since 1986. There is an extensive regional programme in operation (Caribbean Environment Programme, CEP), in which 28 States (23 developing countries) 7 territories and the European Community participate.

Participation

Membership is limited. Initial signature and subsequent ratification, acceptance or approval of the Convention and its Protocols was initially limited to states and regional economic integration organizations with relevant competencies which were invited to participate in the 1983 Conference of Plenipotentiaries in Cartagena de Indias in March 1983. (Arts 25 and 26).

Subsequent accession is limited to such states and organizations or to other states or relevant organizations which have received the prior approval of three fourths of the parties to the Convention or relevant protocol. In the case of regional economic organizations such approval may not be given unless it exercises competence in the fields covered by the Convention or relevant protocol and has at least one member state, belonging to the wider Caribbean region that is a party to the Convention and the relevant protocol.

Reservations are possible under the annexes to the 1990 Protocol. None have been made, so far.

Nineteen states are parties to the Convention and the first protocol, 15 of which are developing countries. Ten of the 14 signatories to the 1990 Protocol are developing countries.

Records of meetings indicated that the majority of the developed countries who are Contracting Parties have always participated in the negotiations and drafting process related to these agreement and instruments. Additionally, all developed countries of the Wider Caribbean Region participate in programme activities.

The majority of the countries in the region depend heavily on the marine environment for crucial economic activities such as fisheries and tourism. The five areas agreed by the parties for priority action under the CEP reflect these concerns, and the project designs include training workshops, funded pilot projects and technical and financial assistance with implementation in the five key areas:

Assessment and Control of Marine Pollution (CEPPOL), being jointly implemented with the Intergovernmental Oceanographic Commission (IOC/UNESCO)

Specially Protected Areas and Wildlife, programmes are in place for implementation, scientific training and assistance and project development;

Information Systems for the Management of Marine and Coastal Resources;

Integrated Planning and Institutional Development for the Management of Marine and Coastal Resources (IPID);

Education, Training and Public Awareness for the Management of Marine and Coastal Resources (ETA).

The Regional Seas programme is predicated on mutual assistance within the region. UNEP provides some "seed money" from central funds for initial programme development, but the primary financial responsibility for programme implementation, including participation at meetings lies with the Caribbean Trust Fund (CTF) (which is contributed by pledges from the participating States and Territories) and counterpart contributions from donor institutions.

Five meetings of the States and Territories participating in the Action Plan and Two Meetings of the Parties to the Convention have taken place (Guadeloupe, 1987; Kingston, 1990) together with Nine Meetings of the Monitoring Committee and the Bureau of the Parties. Decision No. 6 of the Ninth Meeting of the Monitoring Committee and Special Meeting of the Bureau of Contracting Parties, 12-14 June 1991 approved the funding of at least one representative from each contributing Government to attend the intergovernmental meetings of the Programme. Additionally, the Caribbean Trust Fund is used as a seed contribution to attract major financing from bilateral and multilateral sources. Several times fund raising to support participation by representatives of all the countries of the region, has been carried out successfully.

Workshops and other meetings organized for CEP through the RCU are wherever possible funded on the basis that at least one delegate will be supported from each participating State and Territory.

The financial undertaking to contribute to the CTF derives from participation in the Action Plan, rather than the Convention. Participation by one delegate at meetings will normally be funded by CTF (see above). Although a number of states are in arrears in honouring their pledges to the CTF, to date participation has been funded without discrimination between contributors and non-contributors. This may be about to change.

There is no evidence that lack of technical assistance is a deterrent to participation, although the number of meetings and workshops organized at regional and sub-regional level requiring attendance by senior technical officers does put a considerable strain on the operational efficiency of crucial departments, particularly in the small island states.

It is a key aim of the CEP programmes that they provide training and access to expertise in the designated areas. There is a general recognition that this is an incentive to participate.

The CEP is widely publicized in the region but competes with a number of other programmes for government and public attention. There is some evidence that NGO activity in some countries of the region has been considerably strengthened by the existence of the CEP. Regional NGOs attend and contribute to CEP meetings and provide important conduits of resources to governments, thus encouraging their participation in meetings etc.

CEP meetings operate by consensus. No reservations have been lodged to the Convention or its protocol. The availability of reservations was stressed in the SPAW Protocol negotiations to encourage wide participation. These powers have not [yet] been used.

Implementation and information

The Convention required nine ratifications to come into force - not a very high number for a large region. There is no doubt that a larger number would have slowed down entry into force, because of the often slow constitutional procedures in the participating states. The Convention took three years to come into force, in the ensuing five years the number of Parties has doubled.

The 1990 Protocol requires the same number of Parties.

The Cartagena Convention is a framework Convention, consequently a number of its obligations are to co-operate. The principal obligations are as follows:

Article 4(1) obliges Contracting Parties, individually or jointly to take all appropriate measures in conformity with international law and in accordance with the Convention and those of its protocols in force to which they are parties to prevent, reduce and control pollution and ensure sound environmental management, using for this purpose the best practicable means at their disposal and in accordance with their capabilities.

To this end the Parties undertake
- to ensure that the implementation of those measures does not cause pollution to the marine environment outside the Convention Area (Art 4(2));
- to co-operate in the formulation and adoption of protocols and other agreements to facilitate the effective implementation of the Convention (Art. 4(3));

- to co-operate in the competent international, regional and subregional organizations for the effective implementation of this Convention and its protocols, and to assist each other in fulfilling their obligations.

The more specific objectives of the Convention require the Parties to take appropriate measures:

a) to prevent, reduce and control pollution of the Convention area caused by pollution from ships (Article 5);

b) to prevent, reduce and control pollution of the Convention area caused by pollution from Dumping (Article 6);

c) to prevent, reduce and control pollution of the Convention area caused by discharges from Land-based Sources (Article 7);

d) to prevent, reduce and control pollution of the Convention area caused by Sea-bed Activities (Article 8);

e) to protect and preserve rare and fragile ecosystems as well as the habitat of depleted, threatened or endangered species (Article 10);

f) to co-operate in responding to pollution emergencies in the Convention Area (Article 11);

g) to develop, adopt and implement Environmental Impact Assessment measures and to disseminate information concerning them. (Article 12);

h) to co-operate, directly and through appropriate international and regional organizations, in scientific research, monitoring and exchange of relevant data and other scientific information; in particular the parties agree to assist each other with technical and scientific assistance relating to pollution and sound environmental management, taking into account the special needs of the smaller island developing countries and territories (Article 13).

<u>Protocol Concerning Co-operation in Combating Oil Spills in the Wider Caribbean region</u>
This protocol implements Art. 11 of the Convention. It requires parties:

a) to co-operate in taking necessary preventive and remedial measures (Art. 3);

b) to exchange relevant information (Arts 4 and 5);

c) to establish reporting requirements for marine pollution incidents (Art. 5);

d) to render mutual assistance in the event of such an incident (Art. 6);

e) to follow common response strategies (Art. 7).

<u>Protocol on Specially Protected Areas and Wildlife</u>

This implements the general obligation of Art. 10. It requires parties to take necessary measures to protect and preserve and manage in a sustainable way areas that require protection and threatened or endangered species of flora and fauna (Art. 3). In furtherance of this parties shall:

a) establish protected areas (Art 4);

b) take measures to protect such areas (Art. 5);

c) establish management plans for such areas (Art. 6);

d) co-operate in the listing and protection of designated areas (Art. 7-9);

e) take national measures to protect wild flora and fauna (Art. 10);

f) adopt co-operative measures for the protection of threatened and endangered species (Art 11);

g) publicize national protection measures and develop relevant educational programmes (Art 16);

h) encourage, develop and co-operate in relevant scientific, technical and management research (Art. 17);

Financial commitments arising from the Action Plan are not based on the Convention

The Convention requires meetings of the Parties every two years (Art. 16). Such meetings have as one of their functions the consideration of national reports on the implementation of the Convention and its protocols submitted in accordance with Art. 22.

No such reports have yet been required of parties.

Under Art 19 of the 1990 Protocol, each party is obliged to report periodically through its focal point to the Regional Co-ordinating Unit on a range of issues relating to protection of areas and species under its jurisdiction.

These Country reports are to be made available by the RCU to the Scientific and Technical Committee (STAC) to discharge its obligation to advise the parties on a range of issues (Art 20) including implementation.

The Meetings of the Parties to the Protocol are also mandated to "keep under review and direct" the implementation of the Protocol in the light of country reports and the advice of the STAC.

The Convention requires Parties to submit reports on implementation in such form and at such intervals as may be determined by the meeting of the parties (Art. 22; see also Article 4 of the Oil Spills Protocol, and Article 19 of the 1990 Protocol). Reporting is done on a survey basis.

The Convention requires parties to disseminate information concerning Environmental Impact Assessment guidelines they develop (Art. 12); and to co-operate, directly and through appropriate international and regional organizations, in scientific research, monitoring and exchange of relevant data and other scientific information; and to co-operate in the development of a regional network of national research centres to ensure compatible results (Art. 13).

Such information is to be exchanged under the research and information programmes developed by the RCU, see 9 above.

The Protocol concerning co-operation in combating oil spills in the wider Caribbean region contains requirements for exchange of information regarding implementation of the protocol, including identity of national authorities, national laws and operational procedures (Art. 4), reports of marine pollution incidents (Art. 5).

This is done through an IMO regional officer in Puerto Rico.

The Convention contains provisions for settlement of disputes arising from interpretation or application of the Convention or its protocols, and an Annex on Arbitration (Art. 23). These procedures have not been used, to date.

Implementation has been perceived as an integral part of the work programmes of the CEP. There are not yet a sufficient body of specific obligations on parties to assess successful implementation. The establishment of the UNEP Regional Co-ordinating Unit (RCU) in 1987 has positively influenced the implementation of the Convention.

Regional evidence generally suggests that this may become a problem through shortage of available and suitably qualified legal, scientific and technical personnel in the smaller states as well as available resources.

The Convention and protocols (as all the official documentation emanating from the Programme) is in three languages: English, French and Spanish. The texts are published in UNEP series and also by the Regional Co-ordinating Unit.

Current information on the operation and implementation of the Convention and its Protocols is made available to the Governments through specially prepared reports prior to Intergovernmental Meetings ("Report of the Executive Director" or "Note of the Secretariat") and through information packages being disseminated from the RCU regularly (average of 5 times per year). Industries and a wide variety of institutions and experts (about 5,000) are informed though technical reports and through the newsletter of the Caribbean Environment Programme, CEPNEWS, which is widely circulated within the region and outside.

Reports of workshops and meetings relating to issues of implementation are circulated as above. Practice is as yet limited on this.

Assistance from the Caribbean Trust Fund has been programmed for the development of national legislation.

The RCU also publishes a series of technical and training reports - CEP Technical Reports available to participating governments and the public. Approximately 10 reports have appeared to date.

The work plan for the forthcoming biennium includes regional and subregional workshops in the five designated priority areas, see paragraph 9 above. These workshops draw on regional and international expertise, constitute in themselves training and education, and also generate material for national implementation, training and education. The information as stated above is being used for training opportunities on numerous occasions. Recently, the Caribbean Environment Programme organized and executed an international course (8 weeks) on ocean policy and marine management in conjunction with the international Ocean Institute (Malta and Canada) and the University of the West Indies (Jamaica).

Operation, review and adjustment

The depositary of the Convention and its protocols is the government of Colombia.

The Convention designates UNEP as the Secretariat and to perform the functions set out in Article 16(1). To this end UNEP has established a Regional Co-ordinating Unit (RCU) in Kingston, Jamaica.

The parties designate appropriate channels of communication with the RCU - so called Focal Points - which are regularly published and updated.

The legal instruments form an integral part of the Caribbean Environment Programme. The 1990 cost for implementation of the Convention and its Protocols was approximately US $1.6 million being provided by the Caribbean Trust Fund (approximately 45%, contributions by participating States and Territories), the Environment Fund of UNEP (approx. 10%), and Counterpart Contributions (approx. 45%).

Participants in the Caribbean Action Plan pledge annual contributions to the CTF. These are de facto calculated by the RCU.

National participation is not formally dependent on contributions to the CTF as all projects and activities of CEP are of a regional nature, therefore the entire region benefits regardless of which countries have contributed to the Caribbean Trust Fund. Most of the specific activities such as information exchange and technical assistance will also continue to be available for all countries. The status of pledges is published, however, in the documentation of the Intergovernmental Meetings. As of 1991, support for the participation of Governments in the Intergovernmental Meetings of the Caribbean Environment Programme will be given only to Governments "contributing to CTF". Counterpart contributions from participating developed countries and from donor agencies contribute an increasingly large portion of funding of new programme initiatives.

The RCU provides the main conduit for this. It has an expert advisory group on the CEP and through its various sector Programmes is developing expert group consultations and information systems for both regional and national use (eg CEPNET). Regional expert bodies from the public and private sector participate in these programmes. Regional Activity Networks (RANs) have been established and Regional Activity Centres (RACs) are planned for development of regional expertise in aspects of the CEP.

Under the 1990 Protocol a Scientific and Technical Committee will develop similar systems. Until the Protocol enters into force an Interim S&T Committee (ISTAC) will perform this function. The SPAW programme eg envisages SPAW management training, promotion of regional standards and evaluation of protected areas.

(a) National experts are nominated by focal points in all participating states to take part in CEP activities wherever possible on a funded basis.

(b) NGOs are invited to meetings as observers on a non-funded basis. Regional NGO scientific experts participate in the CEP Experts Group and play a role in providing human and other resources for workshops etc. There is no record of industry participation in the programme.

Meetings of the Contracting Parties are convened every two years, since the Convention entered into force (October 1987, January 1990, November 1992). Special Meetings of the Bureau of Contracting Parties are being convened annually since the First Meeting of Contracting Parties in October 1987 (September 1988, January 1990, June 1991). These meetings agree on the convening of Ad Hoc Meetings of Experts to develop new legal instruments or adjust existing ones. Such meetings were convened in October 1988, June 1989 and November 1990 on the SPAW Protocol and expert meetings for the development of a protocol on land-based sources of pollution will be convened during 1992.

Codification programming

The technical annexes to the 1990 Protocol on Specially Protected Areas and Wildlife, on which negotiations began in October 1988, were completed in June 1991.

The Oil Spills Protocol of 1983, temporarily extended to other spills of all hazardous substances by the 1983 Cartagena Conference is being renegotiated to extend formally to all such substances. A draft was discussed at the Second Meeting of the Parties in January 1990 and a redraft will be available for discussion at the Third Meeting in November 1992.

A Protocol on the control of transboundary movement of hazardous waste was proposed at the Second Meeting of the Parties and a Resolution approved to that effect. Initial papers have been prepared.

A Meeting of Experts for the development of a Protocol on Land Based Sources of Pollution is planned for 1991.

Expert Groups and Plenipotentiary Conferences have available as information documents relevant global and regional treaties. The RCU is a part of the UNEP and is therefore able to advise on similar agreements and negotiations elsewhere.

Attendance of representatives of international and regional organizations provides some information of other relevant developments. This is also provided by national delegations which participate in subregional and other regional groupings.

There are still a number of issues to be covered at the regional level. One such issue being discussed is the transboundary movement of wastes.

A number of projects and activities are currently being implemented by the UNEP Caribbean Environment Programme such as the development of regional standards, guidelines, etc. These projects and activities contribute to the development of the legal framework. Among the projects and activities mentioned above are those which address coastal water quality and effluent standards (domestic, agricultural and industrial waste; pesticides; marine debris); promotion of regional standards for protected areas and wildlife management evaluation and assessment of parks and protected areas; standards for environmental impact assessment; guidelines for environmental management of contaminated bays and coastal areas; educational standards for natural resource management training. Additionally, the Programme provides support to the development of national legislation for protected areas and wildlife.

234

(53) Agreement for Co-operation in Dealing with Pollution of the North Sea by Oil and Other Harmful Substances
(Bonn, 13 September 1983), as amended

Objectives and achievement

The main objective of this Agreement is to provide a framework of obligations for co-operation between the Contracting Parties whenever the presence of oil or other harmful substances polluting the North Sea area presents a grave and imminent danger to the coast or related interests of one or more of the Contracting Parties.(Art.1) By including 'other harmful substances' this Agreement extends its coverage further than the 1969 Bonn Agreement which it effectively supersedes.

In a Decision Concerning Amendments of the 1983 Bonn Agreement (taken in Bonn, 22 September 1989), the Contracting Parties agreed to further extend the scope of the Agreement to include surveillance conducted as an aid to detecting and combating such pollution and to preventing violations of anti-pollution regulations.(Art.1(2)) This amendment has yet to come into force.

This Agreement does not make any express link between the environment and development.

This Agreement only applies when pollution from oil or other harmful substances presents a grave and imminent danger within the North Sea area (defined in Art.2).

The new amendment including surveillance within the scope of this Agreement, represents a preventive approach which is more in line with current environment treaty practice.

This Agreement may provide a useful guide to other coastal states which border semi-enclosed seas.

There are no developing countries in the North Sea area within which this Agreement applies.

The present Agreement entered into force on 1 September 1989. But since 1977 the Contracting Parties have met annually within the framework of the earlier 1969 Bonn Agreement.

A working group on operational, technical and scientific issues has been established and a Bonn Agreement Counter Pollution Manual has been developed which describes, inter alia, the operational arrangements for joint spill response. This is kept up to date at regular intervals. The goals of this Agreement have therefore been achieved.

Participation

Membership is limited to States invited to the Bonn Conference of the same name in 1983 (Art.18(1)) and the EEC (Art.18(2)). Other coastal states of the North East Atlantic area may be unanimously invited to accede to this Agreement.(Art.20) To date eight States and the EEC have become parties.

Reservations are not prohibited and have not been used.

The current geographical distribution is confined to the North Sea area (as defined by Art.2) and the North East Atlantic area (under Art.20). It does not include any developing countries.

The perceived need by Governments in the North Sea area for co-operation and co-ordination of measures taken against pollution by oil and other harmful substances is a significant factor influencing participation in this Agreement.

Media attention on incidents like the grounding of the 'Torrey Canyon' and subsequent public opinion expressing fears of pollution also positively influenced participation in this Agreement.

Implementation and information

The text of the Agreement provides that it shall enter into force on the first day of the second month following the date on which all the States invited to the Conference and the EEC have signed.(Art.19) Since the Agreement only came into force on 1 September 1989, nearly six years after it was signed, the provision for its entry would seem to have constrained its entry into force.

The Contracting Parties undertake to inform the other Contracting Parties of, inter alia, (a) their national organization for dealing with pollution from oil or other harmful substances, (b) the competent authority responsible for receiving and dispatching reports of such pollution, and (c) their national means for avoiding or dealing with such pollution (Art.4).

Each Party also undertakes to inform any other Contracting Party whenever it becomes aware of a casualty or the presence of oil slicks to which this Agreement applies.

The Parties are also under a duty to request masters of their flag ships and registered aircraft to report to them all casualties causing or likely to cause marine oil or other pollution.(Art.5(2))

The North Sea area of application under the Bonn Agreement is divided into zones in which a particular Contracting Party is obliged to take initial response action.(Art.6(2)) The Contracting Party is also obliged to immediately inform the other Parties of any action which it has taken.(Art.6(3))

In addition to the above, the Parties are also required to jointly develop and establish guidelines for the practical, operational, and technical aspects of joint action (Art.3(2)), and co-ordinated surveillance (under the amended Art.3(2) in Art.3 of the 1989 Decision which is not yet in force).

The Contracting Parties report on their performance to the Meetings of the Parties (required under Art.12(1)), which have been held annually since 1977. It is the duty of these meetings to, inter alia, (a) exercise overall supervision over the implementation, and (b) review the effectiveness of the measures taken under this Agreement.(Art.14)

As mentioned earlier, the Parties have undertaken to inform other Parties of their national organizations for dealing with pollution, and their authorities for receiving and despatching pollution reports, as well as their national means of dealing with such pollution and new ways in which such pollution may be avoided.(Art.4)

The Parties are required to, and have developed a standard pollution reporting form called POLREP for communication among Parties in the event of a pollution incident.(Art.5(2))

If such an incident does occur, the Parties are required to immediately inform all other Parties of its assessments and of any action which it has taken.(Art.6(3))

The Bonn Agreement Counter Pollution Manual which describes the operational arrangements for joint spill response is also kept up to date.

Aside from the annual meetings of the Contracting Parties which supervise the implementation of this Agreement (Art.14(a)), the Parties have developed the following mechanisms for promoting compliance :

(a) An agreed command structure for joint combating operations;

(b) An agreed procedure for radio communications in joint combating operations;

(c) Procedures for alarm exercises to test the readiness of Contracting Parties to respond in pollution incidents; and

(d) Guidelines for exchange of information on pollution incidents and the effectiveness of response.

There are no mechanisms for dealing with disputes.

Media attention to oil spill incidents, combined with increasing public disapproval, especially after the 'Torrey Canyon' incident, has been a main influencing factor in the implementation of this agreement.

The Bonn Agreement was done in English, French, and German, all texts being equally authentic.

Through the Bonn Agreement Counter Pollution Manual which is kept up to date at regular intervals and takes into account experience gained from combating operations as well as joint exercises and technological developments.

The Counter Pollution Manual provides such guidance and it is supplemented by the information provided by the Parties themselves, in fulfilment of their obligation to inform the other Parties under Art.4.

The joint guidelines developed under Art.3(2) for the practical, operational, and technical aspects of joint action may provide additional guidance.

The information above is available at both the international and national levels and can therefore be used in training and education programmes.

Operation, review and adjustment

There are no provisions for institutional arrangements in this Agreement. But, as mentioned earlier, the Parties have met annually since 1977 (as provided for by Art.12) and established a working group on operational, technical and scientific questions.

There is also an administrative secretary who fills the secretarial functions of the Bonn Agreement, as provided for by Art.15(1). This person is attached to the Oslo/Paris Commission Secretariat in London.

Each Contracting Party contributes 2.5% towards the annual expenditure of the Agreement. The balance is divided among the Parties in proportion to their gross national product in accordance with the scale of assessment adopted regularly by the United Nations General Assembly. In no case does the contribution of a Party to this balance exceed 20% of the balance.(Art.15(2))

The main benefit derived from participation in this Agreement is greater co-operation in the sighting and clearing-up of oil-slicks in the designated North Sea area. By co-operating with each other, the participating states will also be helping to ensure that a far larger area is covered than that which is within their own individual capacities to control. The participating states will benefit too from the exchange of information and new methods used for the cleaning-up of oil slicks.

The main costs will go towards fulfilling the commitments imposed on the participating states.

The undertaking by the Parties in Art.4 to inform the other Parties of new ways of avoiding pollution, and new methods of dealing with it will help to ensure that the latest scientific knowledge is taken into account.

The arrangements for co-operation laid down by this Agreement involve the full participation of the national authorities. (Art.s 3,4,5,6, and 9)

One of the duties of the annual meetings of the Parties is to review the effectiveness of measures taken. (Art.14(b)) This has been used recently to make the Decision Concerning Amendments of the 1983 Bonn Agreement (Bonn,22 September 1989) which are not in force yet.

Codification programming

As mentioned above, there have been some amendments to the Agreement which have not come into force yet.

There has been some co-ordination between this Agreement and the work of the Paris and Oslo Commissions (43 and 45).

The Bonn Agreement basically facilitates co-operation between its Parties. It is by no means a complete marine pollution agreement covering all aspects of pollution, such as the different types and sources of pollution.

The ministerial-level North Sea Conferences have contributed greatly to the development of this Agreement, culminating in the 1989 Decision to amend the Bonn Agreement which was prompted by paragraph 16, sub-paragraphs 46 to 50 of the Ministerial Declaration of the Second International Conference on the Protection of the North Sea, held in London from 24-25 November 1987.

(54) Convention for the Protection, Management and Development of the Marine and Coastal Environment of the Eastern African Region
(Nairobi, 21 June 1985)

Objectives and achievement

The basic objective of the Nairobi Convention, as a UNEP Regional Seas Convention, is formulated in its title which concerns the protection, management and development of the marine environment of the region.

The importance of both environmental protection and development is expressly recognized in the Preamble to the Convention in which the parties recognize the economic and social value of the marine and coastal environment of the region and the need for co-operation to ensure a co-ordinated and comprehensive development of the natural resources of the region. While conscious of the inter-generational responsibility of protecting this environment for future as well as present generations, the parties recognize the threat to the marine environment, its ecological equilibrium, resources and legitimate uses which is posed by pollution and by the insufficient integration of an "environmental dimension" into the development process. The global nature of environmental problems is recognized by the need to secure the wider acceptance of international marine pollution agreements, but the parties also note that these wider agreements do not cover all aspects of environmental deterioration and do not entirely meet the special requirements of the region.

Two Protocols have been concluded under the Convention, both at the 1982 Nairobi Plenipotentiary Conference: the first concerning protected areas and wild fauna and flora in the region, the second concerning co-operation in combating marine pollution in cases of emergency in the region.

The objective of the first protocol is to establish close co-operation to protect and improve the state of wild fauna and flora and natural habitats in the region by the establishment of specially protected areas in the marine and coastal environment.

The second protocol is to establish a framework for co-operation to protect the marine and coastal environment from the threat of pollution resulting from the presence of oil or other harmful substances in the marine environment as a result of marine emergencies.

The concept of sound environmental management, the obligations to prevent, reduce and combat marine pollution from its various sources and the development of EIA measures are all in accordance with the approaches adopted by global conventions and with the concept of sustainable development. Regional agreements are, however, considered more effective in solving regionally shared problems, taking into account the special needs and characteristics of the region and the common interests of the countries concerned.

The regional nature of the agreement, based as it is on regional co-operation between predominantly developing countries recognizes their special requirements. Notable are the provisions of the Convention relating to technical and scientific assistance in fields relating to pollution and sound environmental management, and also the general obligations of co-operation, notably in emergencies but also in the exchange of data and scientific information.

The Convention has not yet entered into force.

Participation

Membership is restricted. Initial signature and subsequent ratification, acceptance or approval of the Convention and its Protocols is limited to states and regional economic integration organizations with relevant competencies (having at least one Member State in the region) which were invited to participate in the Conference of Plenipotentiaries in Nairobi in June 1982. (Art. 26).

Subsequent accession is limited to such states and organizations or to other states or relevant organizations which have received the prior approval of three fourths of the parties to the Convention or relevant protocol (Art. 28).6.

Reservations are not prohibited. None are recorded.

The Convention is not yet in force (requiring 6 ratifications/accessions) but has 5 signatories and has been ratified by 3 States. All the States in the region which qualify to participate are developing states.

The developing States of the region negotiated and signed the Convention and protocols. There have been no meetings of the parties as the Convention has yet to enter into force; however, in the interim period a meeting of the Bureau of the Contracting Parties is held annually, in which 5 out of 9 States in the region participate.

The Regional Seas programme is predicated on mutual assistance within the region. UNEP provides some "seed money" from central funds for initial programme development, but the primary financial responsibility for implementation of the regional Action Plan including attendance at meetings lies with the parties through the regional Trust Fund. The Chairman of Bureau has been requested by the signatory governments to undertake missions to the countries of the region to urge early ratification of the Convention and its Protocols.

Participation is considered to depend on the availability of financial, technical and scientific assistance.

Implementation and information

The Convention and its Protocols require ratifications by only six states. They have not yet entered into force, having received only 3 ratifications.

The Nairobi Convention is a framework Convention, consequently a number of its obligations are to co-operate. The principal obligations are:

Art. 4(1) obliges Contracting Parties, individually or jointly to take all appropriate measures ... to prevent, reduce and combat pollution of the Convention area and to ensure sound environmental practices, using best practicable means. To this end the parties undertake

- to co-operate in the formulation and adoption of protocols and other measures to facilitate the effective implementation of the Convention (Art. 4(2));

- to take all appropriate measures for the effective discharge of the obligations prescribed in the Convention and protocols and to harmonize their national policies in this regard (Art. 4(3)); and

- to co-operate in the competent international, regional and subregional organizations for the effective implementation of this Convention and its protocols, and to assist each other in fulfilling their obligations (Art. 4(4)).

- to ensure that the implementation of those measures does not cause transformation of one type or form of pollution to another which would be more detrimental. (Art. 4(5));

The more specific objectives of the Convention require the Parties to take appropriate measures:

a) to prevent, reduce and combat pollution of the Convention area caused by pollution from ships (Art. 5);

b) to prevent, reduce and combat pollution of the Convention area caused by pollution from Dumping (Art. 6);

c) to prevent, reduce and combat pollution of the Convention area caused by discharges from Land-based Sources (Art. 7);

d) to prevent, reduce and combat pollution of the Convention area caused by Sea-bed Activities (Art. 8);

e) to prevent, reduce and combat pollution of the Convention area resulting from discharges into the atmosphere from activities under their jurisdiction (Art. 9);

f) to take all appropriate measures to protect and preserve rare and fragile ecosystems, as well as rare and depleted, threatened or endangered species of wild flora and fauna and their habitat in the Convention area (Art. 10);

g) to co-operate in responding to pollution emergencies in the Sea Area (Art. 11);

h) to take all appropriate measures to prevent, reduce and combat environmental damage caused by engineering activities in the Convention area (Art. 12);

i) to develop, adopt and implement Environmental Impact Assessment guidelines and to disseminate information concerning them. (Art. 13);

j) to co-operate, directly and through appropriate international and regional organizations, in scientific research, monitoring and exchange of relevant data and other scientific information; and to co-operate in the development of a regional network of national research centres to ensure compatible results (Art. 14).

k) to co-operate in the formulation and adoption of appropriate rule and procedures regarding liability and compensation for pollution damage (Art. 15).

Protocol on protected areas and wildlife

This protocol implements the general obligation of Art. 10 of the Convention. Its principal obligations require parties:

a) to take all appropriate measures to maintain essential ecological processes and life support systems; to preserve genetic diversity and to ensure sustainable utilization of harvested natural resources; also to endeavour to protect and preserve rare and fragile ecosystems and rare, depleted, threatened or endangered species of wild flora and fauna in the region and their habitats (Art. 2);

b) to take all appropriate measures to ensure the strictest protection of endangered wild fauna (Art. 4);

c) to take all appropriate measures to ensure protection of depleted or threatened wild fauna (Art. 5);

d) to co-ordinate their protection efforts for the protection of migratory species (Art. 6);

e) to take all appropriate measures to prohibit introduction of alien or new species (Art. 7);

f) to establish protected areas in areas under their jurisdiction and collaborate in their promulgation and enforcement (Art.s 8-16);

g) to develop and co-ordinate relevant scientific and technical research; exchange relevant information and develop technical and other co-operation (Art.s 17-19)

Protocol concerning co-operation in combating marine pollution in cases of emergency.

This protocol implements Art. 11 of the Convention. It requires parties:

a) to co-operate in taking necessary preventive and remedial measures (Art. 3);

b) to exchange relevant information (Art. 4);

c) to communicate information concerning, and reporting of, marine pollution incidents (Art. 5);

d) to render mutual assistance in the event of such an incident (Art. 6); and

e) to take all necessary measures in the event of such an incident (Art. 7).

Because the Convention and its protocols are not yet in force these obligations are not yet binding.

According to Article 17(1)(f), of the Convention, the Contracting Parties may also take decisions on financial commitments to the Trust Fund for the Implementation of the Action Plan for the Eastern African Region.

These obligations are not yet operative. However, co-operative activities corresponding to them are already being undertaken on a voluntary basis under the UNEP Action Plan for the Eastern African Region.

The Convention requires parties to disseminate information concerning Environmental Impact Assessment guidelines they develop (Art. 13); and to co-operate, directly and through appropriate international and regional organizations, in scientific research, monitoring and exchange of relevant data and other scientific information; and to co-operate in the development of a regional network of national research centres to ensure compatible results (Art. 14).

The Protocol on protected areas and wildlife requires parties to exchange information on relevant scientific and technical research. (Art. 18)

The Protocol on regional co-operation in combating pollution by oil and other harmful substances in cases of emergency contains requirements for exchange of information regarding implementation of the protocol, including identity of national authorities, national laws and operational procedures (Art. 4), reports of marine pollution incidents (Art. 3).

Obligations for compliance are not yet operative.

The Convention contains provisions for settlement of disputes arising from interpretation or application of the Convention (Art. 24) and an Annex on Arbitration of such disputes. These obligations are not yet operative.

Pending the entry into force of the Convention and its protocols, implementation remains voluntary.

The Convention and protocols and the Action Plan are published in English and French. The texts are published in UNEP series.
Information is disseminated through international meetings, the UNEP Governing Council, as well as scientific and popular publications.

Operation, review and adjustment

The depositary of the Convention and its protocols is the Government of the Republic of Kenya.

The Convention designates UNEP as the Secretariat and to perform the functions set out in Art. 16(1). These are currently carried out by the UNEP Programme Activity Centre for Oceans and Coastal Areas, in Nairobi.

Pending the entry into force of the Convention, a Bureau composed of 5 out of the 9 coastal States meets annually on a rotating basis. Administrative costs of interim implementation are covered in part by the UNEP secretariat budget, and in part by the Trust Fund for the Implementation of the Action Plan for the Eastern African Region (pledged contributions for 1990: $250,000).

The Convention envisages regular Meetings of the Parties (Art. 17) as well as the negotiation of further protocols (Art. 18).

Codification programming

Once the Convention enters into force a priority for drafting of an additional protocol will be control of pollution from land-based sources and related internal waters; also, problems of liability and hazardous waste management will have to be addressed in the future.

The UNEP Action Plan for the Eastern African Region is the major instrument that will contribute to implementation of the Convention and its protocols once they become operative.

242

(55) Convention for the Protection of the Natural Resources and Environment of the South Pacific Region
(Noumea, 24 November 1986), and related protocols

Objectives and achievement

The basic objective of the Noumea Convention, as a UNEP Regional Seas Convention, is the protection of the natural resources and environment of the South Pacific Region by the promotion, on a regional basis, of co-operation in the areas of environmental protection and natural resources management in the marine and coastal areas of the region.

The importance of both environmental protection and development is expressly recognized in the Preamble to the Convention in which the parties recognize the economic and social value of the natural resources of the region and the need for co-operation to ensure a co-ordinated and comprehensive development of the natural resources of the region. While conscious of the inter-generational responsibility of protecting this natural heritage for future as well as present generations, the parties recognize the threat to the marine environment, its ecological equilibrium, resources and legitimate uses which is posed by pollution and by the insufficient integration of an "environmental dimension" into the development process. The parties also note that existing conventions do not cover all aspects and sources of marine pollution and do not entirely meet the special requirements of the region.

Two protocols have been concluded, both at the 1986 Noumea Conference of Plenipotentiaries. The first concerns the prevention of pollution of the South Pacific region by dumping. The objective of this protocol is to take a co-ordinated regional approach to the issue of dumping consistent with the 1972 Convention on the Prevention of Marine Pollution by Dumping of Wastes and other Matter, 1972 (No.35).

The second Protocol concerning co-operation in combating pollution in cases of emergency, have been concluded under the Convention, The objective of the protocol is to establish a framework for co-operation to protect the marine and coastal environment from the threat of pollution resulting from the presence of oil or other harmful substances in the marine environment as a result of marine emergencies.

The concept of sound environmental management, the obligations to prevent, reduce and control marine pollution from its various sources in the region are in accordance with the approaches adopted by global conventions and with the concept of sustainable development, as is the development of EIA measures. Regional action on dumping consistent with the London Convention is particularly relevant.

The regional nature of the agreement, based as it is on regional co-operation between predominantly developing countries recognizes their special requirements. Notable are the provisions of the Convention relating to technical and scientific assistance in fields relating to pollution and sound environmental management, and also the general obligations of co-operation, notably in emergencies but also in the exchange of data and scientific information.

The Convention only entered into force in 1990.

Participation

Membership is restricted. Initial signature and subsequent ratification, acceptance or approval of the Convention and its Protocols was limited to those states invited to participate in the Noumea Plenipotentiary Meeting, 24-25 November 1986 (Art.s 28-9).

Subsequent accession is open to any state referred to above, or, subject to the prior approval of three quarters of the parties to any other state (Art. 28).

Reservations are not prohibited. None have been made.

Current membership is 10 States/territories: Australia, Cook Islands, Fiji, France, Marshall Islands, Micronesia, New Zealand, Papua New Guinea, Solomon Islands and Western Samoa.

With the exception of Australia, France and New Zealand, all the participating states are developing countries.

The majority of participating States are developing countries. The Convention came into force in 1990.

The primary incentive for participation and implementation is mutual and common benefit from a co-operative regional programme.

The Regional Seas programme is predicated on mutual assistance within the region. UNEP provides some "seed money" from its Environment Fund for initial programme development, but the primary financial responsibility for programme implementation, including participation at meetings lies with the regional Trust fund.

Technical and scientific assistance is designed to be available through the programme.

A number of expert meetings were held prior to the 1986 Noumea Conference to assist the negotiations.

A workshop on Marine Pollution Prevention, Control and Response was convened in November 1984 by SPC, SPEC, IMO and UNEP (with US Coast Guard assistance) with 26 participants from 17 countries in the region.

Implementation and information

The Convention required ratification by ten States. It entered into force on 23 August 1990, some four years after signature.

The Protocols require the same number of Parties.

The Noumea Convention is a framework Convention, consequently a number of its obligations are to co-operate. The principal obligations are:

Art. 5(1) obliges Contracting Parties, individually or jointly to take all appropriate measures ... to prevent, reduce and control pollution of the Convention area from any source and to ensure sound environmental management of natural resources, using best practicable means. To this end the parties undertake

- to use their best efforts to ensure that the implementation of those measures does not result in an increase in marine pollution outside the Convention area (Art. 5(2));

- to co-operate in the formulation and adoption of protocols and other measures to attain the objectives of the Convention (Art. 5(3));

- to co-operate taking into account the competent international, regional and subregional organizations to attain the objectives of this Convention and its protocols, and to assist each other in fulfilling their obligations (Art. 5(4)).

- to establish laws and regulations (no less effective than existing international rules, standards and recommended practices and procedures) for the effective discharge of the obligations prescribed in the Convention and protocols (Art. 5(5)).

The more specific objectives of the Convention require the Parties to take appropriate measures:

a) to prevent, reduce and control pollution in the Convention area caused by discharges from ships (Art. 6);

b) to prevent, reduce and control pollution in the Convention area caused by discharges from land-based Sources (Art. 7);

c) to prevent, reduce and control pollution in the Convention area resulting from Sea-bed Activities (Art. 8);

d) to prevent, reduce and control pollution in the Convention area resulting from discharges into the atmosphere from activities under their jurisdiction (Art. 9);

e) to prevent, reduce and control pollution in the Convention area caused by dumping (Art. 10);

f) to prevent, reduce and control pollution in the Convention area resulting from storage of toxic and hazardous wastes (Art. 11).

g) to prevent, reduce and control pollution in the Convention area which might result form the testing of nuclear devices (Art. 12).

g) to prevent, reduce and control environmental damage, particularly coastal erosion, in the Convention area caused by coastal engineering projects (Art. 13).

h) to protect and preserve rare and fragile ecosystems, as well as rare and depleted, threatened or endangered species of wild flora and fauna and their habitat in the Convention area (Art. 14);

i) to co-operate in responding to pollution emergencies in the Convention Area (Art. 15);

j) to develop, adopt and implement Environmental Impact Assessment guidelines and to disseminate information concerning them. (Art. 16);

k) to co-operate, directly and through appropriate international and regional organizations, in scientific research, monitoring and exchange of relevant data and other scientific information; and to co-operate in the development of a regional network of national research centres to ensure compatible results (Art. 17);

l) to co-operate, directly and through appropriate international and regional organizations, in the provision of technical and other assistance in the fields of pollution and environmental management (Art. 18);

m) to transmit to the Organisation information on the measures adopted in implementation of the Convention and its protocols (Art. 19);

n) to co-operate in the formulation and adoption of appropriate rules and procedures regarding liability and compensation for pollution damage (Art. 20).

Protocol for the prevention of pollution of the South Pacific region by dumping:

This protocol implements the general obligation of Art. 10 of the Convention. Its principal obligations require parties:

a) to take all appropriate measures to prevent reduce and control pollution of the Protocol Area by Dumping (Art. 3);

b) to prohibit the dumping of substances listed in Annex I of the Protocol, except as provided in the Protocol (Art. 4);

c) to prohibit the dumping of substances listed in Annex II of the Protocol, except with a prior special permit (Art. 5);

d) to prohibit the dumping of substances not listed in Annexes I or II of the Protocol, except with a prior general permit (Art. 6);

e) to designate appropriate authority(ies) to issue permits, keeps record and monitor the condition of the Area in accordance with the Protocol (Art. 11);

f) to apply the implementing measures to its flag vessels and aircraft, to vessels and aircraft loading in its territory and to vessels, aircraft or platforms believed to be dumping in areas under its jurisdiction; to prevent conduct in contravention of the Protocol; and to co-operate in the effective application of the Protocol on the high seas (Art. 12);

g) to report dumping incidents (Art. 14).

<u>Protocol concerning co-operation in combating marine pollution emergencies in the South Pacific region:</u>

This protocol implements Art. 12 of the Convention. It is distinctive in extending the definition of such emergency to include pollution caused by the failure of industrial installations. It requires parties:

a) to co-operate in taking necessary preventive and remedial measures (Art. 4);

b) to exchange relevant information (Art.s 5 and 6);

c) to establish reporting requirements for marine pollution incidents (Art. 7);

d) to render mutual assistance in the event of such an incident (Art. 8);

e) to develop and maintain marine emergency contingency plans and co-operate in the development of reporting procedures (Art. 9);

f) to comply with designated procedures when responding to marine emergencies (Art. 10).

Financial commitments arising from the Action Plan are not based on the Convention.

The Convention requires meetings of the Parties every two years (Art. 22) to assess periodically the state of the environment in the Convention Area and to consider information on national measures adopted by each party in implementation of the Convention (as required by Art. 19).

Parties are obliged to submit information for consideration by the Meetings of the Parties on the measures adopted in implementation of the Convention and its protocol in such form and at such intervals as such Meetings of the Parties shall determine (Art. 19).

The Convention requires parties to exchange information concerning the administration and management of protected areas (Art. 14), communicate information on Environmental Impact Assessment to the Organisation (Art. 16), to co-operate, directly and through appropriate international and regional organizations, in scientific research, monitoring and exchange of relevant data and other scientific information (Art. 17), and to transmit to the Organisation information on the measures taken to implement the Convention and its protocols, as required (Art. 19).

The Protocol for the prevention of pollution of the South Pacific region by dumping contains the requirement that parties report, if appropriate, dumping incidents to the Organisation and any other party concerned (Art. 14).

The Protocol concerning co-operation in combating marine pollution emergencies in the South Pacific region contains requirements for exchange of information regarding implementation of the protocol, including identity of national authorities, national laws and operational procedures (Art. 4), communication of information concerning, and reporting of, pollution incidents (Art. 5).

The Convention contains provisions for settlement of disputes arising from interpretation or application of the Convention or its protocol (Art. 26) together with an Annex on Arbitration. They have not yet been used.

The Convention and protocols and the Action Plan are published in English and French. Each of the two language texts is equally authentic. The texts are published in UNEP series.

Operation, review and adjustment

The depositary of the Convention and its protocols is the Director of the South Pacific Bureau for Economic Co-operation (now the South Pacific Forum Secretariat, see No. 67).

The Convention designates the South Pacific Commission as "the Organisation" but this role has been delegated to the South Pacific Environmental Programme (SPREP).

Technical and scientific assistance has been made available through

SPC/SPEC/IMO/UNEP projects on contingency planning (see above). Participation in the Action Plan involves financial commitments. It seems likely that financial and other resource factors have inhibited the implementation of the Convention and the participation of certain governments.

Communication directly with other parties and through the organisation, together with collaborative exercises, as required by the Convention and its protocols.

The Convention envisages biennial Meetings of the Parties to review the review the annexes and protocols, and to consider new protocols and amendments to the Convention (Art. 22). The first meeting was held in July 1991

Codification programming

The South Pacific Commission, the depositary and Secretariat, is in a position to co-ordinate similar regional agreements and instruments.

The 1982 UNEP Action Plan for Managing the Natural Resources and Environment of the South Pacific Region is the major instrument for practical implementation of the Convention and its protocols. The Plan was revised by an intergovernmental meeting in 1991.

(56) Agreement on Co-operation for Combating Pollution in the Northeast Atlantic
(Lisbon, 17 October 1990)

Objectives and achievement

The objective of the agreement is the protection of the coastal regions of the Northeast Atlantic against pollution by hydrocarbons and other noxious substances. In particular, the agreement aims for the provision of rapid response measures in case of accidents to ships and platforms resulting in such pollution.

The agreement complements the network of existing regional conventions for the protection of the marine environment, covering a geographical area for which no regional regulation of accidental pollution from ships exists as yet. The regulation of this issue on a regional basis is also in line with the global rules of the 1982 UNCLOS (No. 46), which leave room for regional rules on various aspects of protection of the marine environment.

Participation

Membership is restricted to the signatories of the agreement (Spain, France, Morocco, Portugal, and the EC). By unanimous decision, the Parties can invite other States to accede to the agreement.

The agreement does not prohibit reservations.

Of the signatory states, 3 are European and one is North African. In addition, the EC is also signatory to the agreement.

Implementation and information

Party States must have immediately available equipment to deal with spills of oil or other noxious substances. They shall also set up a national system for the prevention of pollution and the mitigation of its effects; monitor shipping activities; and set up personnel training programmes in the relevant fields (Art. 4,12). Parties shall co-operate in these activities and assist each other as necessary (Art. 5,10). They shall obligate persons under their jurisdiction to report to the national authority any incident leading to pollution (Art. 7). The area covered by the agreement is divided into zones, which each party being responsible for activities in one zone (Art. 8,9, Annex 1).

The agreement obligates Parties to inform each other of relevant activities, and on incidents of pollution (Art. 4+5). In view of the very small number of parties, there is no institutionalized reporting system.

No requirement for data supply exists.

The meeting of the parties has a general supervisory function with respect to the implementation of the agreement (Art. 17).

No dispute settlement mechanisms are provided.

The official languages of the agreement are Arabic, Spanish, French and Portuguese, with the French text considered the authentic one in case of divergences.

Operation, review and adjustment

The agreement establishes a meeting of the parties to carry out overall supervision and review the treaty's effectiveness (Art. 15-18). An International Centre is also established to assist parties in the implementation of the convention (Art. 18,19, Annex 2).

The meeting of the parties shall regularly review the effectiveness of measures adopted in accordance with the agreement (Art. 17).

STATUS OF RATIFICATIONS AS OF 1 JANUARY 1992

GLOBAL INSTRUMENTS   (Treaty numbers see page 149)

Parties	34	35	36	38	40	41
Afghanistan		x				
Albania						
Algeria			x			
Angola				x		
Antigua & Barbuda		x	x	x		
Argentina	x	x				
Australia	x	x	x			
Austria			x			
Bahamas	x		x	x		
Bahrain				x		
Bangladesh	x					
Barbados						
Belarus*		x				
Belgium	x	x	x			
Belize				x		
Benin	x					
Bhutan						
Bolivia						
Botswana				x		
Brazil		x	x	x		
Brunei Darussalam				x		
Bulgaria	x		x			
Burkina Faso						
Burundi						
Cambodia						
Cameroon	x			x		
Canada		x				
Cape Verde		x		x		
Central African Republic						
Chad						
Chile		x				
China	x	x	x			
Colombia			x			
Cook Islands						
Comoros						
Congo						
Costa Rica		x				
Côte d'Ivoire	x	x	x	x		
Cuba	x	x		x		
Cyprus		x	x	x		
Czech & Slovak Fed. Rep.			x			

Parties	34	35	36	38	40	41
Democr. People's Rep. of Korea			x			
Denmark	x	x	x			
Djibouti	x		x	x		
Dominica				x		
Dominican Republic	x	x				
Ecuador	x		x			
Egypt	x		x	x	x	
El Salvador						
Equatorial Guinea						
Estonia*			x			
Ethiopia						
Fiji	x			x		
Finland	x	x	x			
France	x	x	x			
Gabon	x	x	x			
Gambia			x	x		
Germany	x	x	x			
Ghana	x		x	x		
Greece		x	x			
Grenada				x		
Guatemala		x				
Guinea				x		
Guinea-Bissau				x		
Guyana						
Haiti		x				
Holy See						
Honduras		x				
Hungary		x	x			
Iceland	x	x	x	x		
India			x			
Indonesia			x	x		
Iran (Islamic Republic of)						
Iraq				x		
Ireland	x	x				
Israel			x			
Italy	x	x	x			
Jamaica	x	x	x	x		
Japan	x	x	x			
Jordan		x				
Kenya		x		x		
Kiribati		x				
Kuwait	x			x		
Lao People's Democratic Rep.						
Latvia*						

Parties	34	35	36	38	40	41
Lebanon	x		x			
Lesotho						
Liberia	x		x			
Libyan Arab Jamahiriya		x				
Liechtenstein						
Lithuania*			x			
Luxembourg		x	x			
Madagascar						
Malawi						
Malaysia						
Maldives						
Mali				x		
Malta		x	x			
Marshall Islands			x	x		
Mauritania						
Mauritius						
Mexico	x	x		x	x	
Micronesia				x		
Monaco	x	x				
Mongolia						
Morocco	x	x				
Mozambique						
Myanmar			x			
Namibia				x		
Nauru		x				
Nepal						
Netherlands	x	x	x			
New Zealand	x	x				
Nicaragua						
Niger						
Nigeria		x		x	x	
Niue						
Norway	x	x	x			
Oman	x	x	x	x	x	
Pakistan						
Palau						
Panama	x	x	x			
Papua New Guinea	x	x				
Paraguay				x		
Peru			x			
Philippines		x		x		
Poland	x	x	x			
Portugal	x	x	x			
Qatar	x					

Parties	34	35	36	38	40	41
Republic of Korea			x			
Republic of Yemen	x			x		
Romania						
Rwanda						
St. Kitts & Nevis						
St. Lucia		x		x		
St. Vincent & the Grenadines			x			
Samoa						
San Marino						
Sao Tome & Principe				x		
Saudi Arabia					x	
Senegal	x			x		
Seychelles		x	x	x		
Sierra Leone						
Singapore			x			
Solomon Islands		x				
Somalia				x		
South Africa	x	x	x			
Spain	x	x	x			
Sri Lanka	x					
Sudan				x		
Suriname	x	x	x			
Swaziland						
Sweden	x	x	x			
Switzerland	x	x	x			
Syrian Arab Republic	x			x		
Thailand						
Togo			x	x		
Tonga						
Trinidad & Tobago				x		
Tunisia	x	x	x	x		
Turkey			x			
Tuvalu			x			
Uganda				x		
Ukraine*		x				
Union of Soviet Socialist Rep.*	x	x	x			
United Arab Emirates	x	x				
United Kingdom	x	x	x			
United Republic of Tanzania				x		
United States of America	x	x	x			
Uruguay			x			
Vanuatu			x			
Venezuela						
Viet Nam			x			

Parties	34	35	36	38	40	41
Yugoslavia*	x	x	x	x		
Zaire		x		x		
Zambia				x		
Zimbabwe						

REGIONAL INSTRUMENTS

(42) <u>Nordic Agreement concerning Co-operation in Measures to Deal with Pollution of the Sea by Oil</u> (Copenhagen 1971)

Denmark
Finland
Norway
Sweden

(43) <u>Convention for the Prevention of Marine Pollution by Dumping from Ships and Aircraft</u> (Oslo 1972)

Belgium
Denmark
Finland
France
Germany
Iceland
Ireland

Netherlands
Norway
Portugal
Spain
Sweden
United Kingdom

(44) <u>Convention on the Protection of the Marine Environment of the Baltic Sea Area</u> (Helsinki 1974)

Denmark
Finland
Germany

Poland
Sweden
USSR*

(45) <u>Convention on the Prevention of Marine Pollution from Land-Based Sources</u> (Paris 1974)

Belgium
Denmark
France
Germany
Iceland
Ireland
Netherlands

Norway
Portugal
Spain
Sweden
United Kingdom
EEC

(46) <u>Convention for the Protection of the Mediterranean Sea against Pollution</u> (Barcelona 1976)

Albania
Algeria
Cyprus
Egypt
France
Greece

Malta
Monaco
Morocco
Spain
Syria
Tunisia

Israel   Turkey
Italy   Yugoslavia*
Lebanon   EEC
Lybia

(47) <u>Kuwait Regional Convention for Co-operation on the Protection of the Marine Environment from Pollution</u> (Kuwait 1978)

Bahrain   Oman
Iran (Islamic Republic of)   Qatar
Iraq   Saudi Arabia
Kuwait   United Arab Emirates

(48) <u>Convention for Co-operation in the Protection and Development of the Marine and Coastal Environment of the West and Central African Region</u> (Abidjan 1981)

Cameroon   Ghana
Congo   Guinea
Cote d'Ivoire   Nigeria
Gabon   Senegal
Gambia   Togo

(49) <u>Convention for the Protection of the Marine Environment and Coastal Area of the South-East Pacific</u> (Lima 1981)

Chile   Panama
Colombia   Peru
Ecuador

(50) <u>Memorandum of Understanding on Port State Control in Implementing Agreements on Maritime Safety and Protection of the Marine Environment</u> (Paris 1982)

Belgium   Netherlands
Denmark   Norway
Finland   Poland
France   Portugal
Germany   Spain
Greece   Sweden
Ireland   United Kingdom
Italy

(51) <u>Regional Convention for the Conservation of the Red Sea and Gulf of Aden Environment</u> (Jeddah 1982)

Egypt   Somalia
Jordan   Sudan
Palestine, represented by the   Yemen
  Palestine Liberation Organization
Saudi Arabia

(52) <u>Convention for the Protection and Development of the Marine Environment of the Wider Caribbean Region</u> (Cartagena 1983)

Antigua & Barbuda
Barbados
Colombia
Costa Rica
Cuba
Dominica
France
Grenada
Guatemala
Jamaica

Mexico
Netherlands
Panama
St. Lucia
St. Vincent & the Grenadines
Trinidad & Tobago
United Kingdom
United States of America
Venezuela

(53) <u>Agreement for Co-operation in Dealing with Pollution of the North Sea by Oil and Other Harmful Substances</u> (Bonn 1983)

Belgium
Denmark
France
Germany
Netherlands

Norway
Sweden
United Kingdom
EEC

(54) <u>Convention for the Protection, Management and Development of the Marine and Coastal Environment of the Eastern African Region</u> (Nairobi 1985)

France
Kenya
Seychelles

(55) <u>Convention for the Protection of the Natural Resources and Environment of the South Pacific Region</u> (Noumea 1986)

Australia
Cook Islands
Fiji
Marshall Islands
Micronesia
Papua New Guinea
Samoa

* Membership status subject to further clarification.

CHAPTER V

MARINE LIVING RESOURCES

Alberto Székely and Barbara Kwiatkowska

This section of the survey covers the following 14 international agreements on marine living resources, in chronological order:

(57) the 1946 Washington **Convention for the Regulation of Whaling**, as amended;

(58) the 1948 Baguio **Agreement for the Establishment of the Indo-Pacific Fishery Commission**, as amended;

(59) the 1949 Washington **Convention for the Establishment of an Inter-American Tropical Tuna Commission**, and related agreements;

(60) the 1949 Rome **Agreement for the Establishment of the General Fisheries Council for the Mediterranean**, as amended;

(61) the 1952 Tokyo **Convention for the High Seas Fisheries of the North Pacific Ocean**, as amended;

(62) the 1952 Santiago **Convention on the Organization of the Permanent Commission on the Exploitation and Conservation of the Marine Resources of the South Pacific**, and related agreements;

(63) The 1964 Copenhagen **Convention for the International Council for the Exploration of the Sea**, as amended;

(64) the 1966 Rio de Janeiro **Convention for the Conservation of Atlantic Tunas**, as amended;

(65) the 1973 Gdansk **Convention on Fishing and Conservation of the Living Resources in the Baltic Sea and Belts**, as amended;

(66) the 1978 Ottawa **Convention on Future Multilateral Co-operation in the Northwest Atlantic Fisheries**;

(67) the 1979 Honiara **South Pacific Forum Fisheries Convention** and related agreements, including the 1989 **Convention on the Prohibition of Driftnet Fishing in the South Pacific** and its protocols;

(68) the 1980 London **Convention on Future Multilateral Co-operation in the North-East Atlantic Fisheries**;

(69) the 1982 Reykjavik **Convention for the Conservation of Salmon in the North Atlantic Ocean**; and

(70) the 1988 Bangkok **Agreement on the Network of Aquaculture Centres in Asia and the Pacific**.

Agreements and instruments generally regarding the marine environment and marine pollution have been covered separately in chapter IV; the 1980 Canberra Convention on the Conservation of Antarctic Marine Living Resources is addressed, together with other instruments on Antarctica, in chapter II; sample bilateral agreements on fisheries are discussed in chapter XII, also with reference to the regional 1991 Dakar Convention on Fisheries Co-operation among West African States.

A list showing the status of ratifications as of 1 January 1992 is annexed (pages 298 - 301).

Existing international fisheries commissions have generally been established in response to specific management needs, upon the initiatives of particular States or groups of States. The constitution of the Food and Agriculture Organization of the United Nations (FAO) provides for the creation of regional and subregional fisheries commissions, and several such commissions have been created in this context. Moreover, the FAO Committee on Fisheries (COFI) provides a forum for the discussion of fisheries issues world-wide, including the activities of the fisheries commissions. To this end, in 1984 FAO sponsored the World Fisheries Conference, and it has promoted the creation of regional and sub-regional fisheries bodies and provided some oversight of its own. However, fisheries management and conservation issues has also been dealth with in other fora, including the UN General Assembly.

An evaluation of existing agreements regarding high seas fisheries was conducted by a group of experts on the legal regime for high seas fisheries convened by the UN Office for Ocean Affairs and the Law of the Sea (now part of the Office of Legal Affairs) in July 1991. The Office is expected to prepare general guidelines for effective implementation of the regime of the UN Convention on the Law of the Sea (No. 38) in this respect.

There is only one global body concerned with the conservation and management of a high seas fishery resource, namely, the International Whaling Commission (IWC) (No. 57). Other fisheries commissions are regional in scope, being concerned with fisheries generally or with a specific species, within a particular area. These areas are generally very broad, comprising large expanses of the Atlantic and Pacific oceans or the Indian ocean. Some of these commissions are only concerned with high seas and straddling stocks; others have the function of seeking to harmonize the management activities of member States within their Exclusive Economic Zones or with straddling stocks between economic zones. Some, such as the South Pacific Forum Fisheries Agency (No. 67) or the Inter-American Tropical Tuna Commission (No. 59), are also concerned with highly migratory species.

Two broad functions are performed by fisheries commissions, depending on their constitution, one scientific and the other management. The first involves collection, exchange and assessment of scientific information and data. The other involves the formulation of appropriate standards and guidelines for States and promoting their implementation. Some commissions have their own scientists for obtaining and assessing information, but most of them rely on member States to provide both with the commissions serving only as a forum for discussion. In other cases, member States exercise within the framework of the commission the responsibilities of management, including standard-setting, determining allowable catches, establishing management measures which include allocation og quotas and effort limitations, monitoring and surveillance.

Useful reference sources are the FAO reviews of "Activities of International Organizations Concerned with Fisheries" (FAO Fisheries Circular No. 807, 1987), and of "FAO Regional Fishery Bodies and their Role in TCDC and ECDC" (FAO Doc. COFI/89/3, 1989). Further updated information will be found in FAO Fisheries Circular No. 835 entitled "Summary Information on the Role of International Fishery Bodies with Regard to the Conservation and Management of Living Resources of thie High Seas" (1991), which is currently being revised.

(57) International Convention for the Regulation of Whaling
(Washington, 2 December 1946), as amended

Objectives and achievement

The objective of the Convention is to adopt regulations for purposes of conservation and utilization of whale resources, and to serve as an agency for the collection, analysis and publication of scientific information related to whaling. The preamble to the Convention recognizes "the interest of the nations of the world in safeguarding for future generations the great natural resources represented by the whale stocks" and the need "to provide for the proper conservation of whale stocks and thus make possible the orderly development of the whaling industry".

The Schedule to the Convention, adopted and revised annually since 1949 at meetings of the International Whaling Commission (IWC), is an integral part of the Convention. Its purpose is to lay down the specific conservation regulations applicable.

Initially, there was no agreement on the adequacy or accuracy of scientific information about stocks, and the IWC did not have authority to adopt measures that might have been effective in controlling or limiting whaling, such as restrictions on the entry of vessels. As a result, quotas were never sensitive to the particular stocks, nor were they set at levels that would ensure sustainability, and wasteful competition and depletion was not avoided. From 1964, the IWC started taking significant management decisions, subsequently influenced by the 1972 Stockholm Conference (see No. 1) resolution calling for a 10 year moratorium on all commercial whaling, which led to the adoption of a new management procedure in 1975. It required that only those stocks which were determined to be greater than the given stock level (protection level) could be harvested, and catches were to be allowed only within the annual increments (sustainable yield) of the population. As this scheme still did not satisfy some of the member States, the IWC agreed in 1982 to set a zero quota from the 1985/86 pelagic season for all stocks commercially exploited, a moratorium which is still in force, and initiated a comprehensive assessment of whale stocks in this context.

Today, aboriginal subsistence whaling and catches for scientific purposes are the only whaling activities authorized by the IWC. With all commercial whaling banned, other issues have arisen, such as the interrelationship of whales with other species and their environment, the prevention of disturbance from whale watching, and other non-consumptive uses.

Participation

The IWC is the only existing global body concerned with the conservation of a high seas fishery resource, since it has a mandate that applies to all waters around the world in which whaling is carried out. As will be seen, especially as compared with the other regional experiences evaluated here, the IWC is concerned with ocean harvesting. Still, two thirds of the coastal States of the world are absent from it.

The 37 Parties to the Convention include 18 developing countries. There is no restriction as to the States that may become Parties to the Convention. While the Convention does not provide for reservations, Parties may "opt out" of amendments to the schedule by way of objection within specified time limits.

Implementation and information

Commitments relate to the substainable utilization of whale stocks, including restrictions on whaling activities, and the provision of data. Compliance with the whaling regulations is monitored by national inspectors and international observers, and their reports and the data submitted are reviewed by the IWC Infractions and Scientific Committees as appropriate.

Implementation is through internal legislation, copies of which are forwarded to the IWC Secretariat. Data requirements are laid down in paragraphs 24-31 and Appendix A of the Schedule. Response has been generally adequate, with some problems in the past.

The International Observer Scheme encourages full and accurate reporting of catches. The Convention stipulates penalties for infractions (Article IX) and reports on these are reviewed by the Infractions Sub-committee each year. In addition, the Aboriginal Subsistence and Scientific Committees monitor and report on relevant matters. Following the 1986 ban on commercial whaling, only "subsistence" and "scientific" whaling data are required from 6 members, all of which have provided their reports. At least one member nation unilaterally induces the less willing to conform to IWC decisions by the threat or imposition of trade sanctions or sanctions relating to fishing rights in exclusive economic zone.

The Convention is published by the Commission and has also been printed by some member Governments. English is the official and working language of the Commission (Rule of Procedure N.1).

The Commission publishes (Convention Article IV, paragraph 2) the Annual Report of its activities for each financial year (1 September - 31 August) and the Chairman's Report of each Annual Meeting, as the authoritative record (Rule of Procedure F.2(e)). It also maintains and publishes catch and related data on whaling operations. Furthermore, Rule of Procedure H.2(e) defines one duty of the Secretary to the Commission as to receive, tabulate and publish notifications and other information required by the Convention in such form and manner as may be presented by the Commission.

Operation, review and adjustment

The IWC secretariat is located in Cambridge, United Kingdom. The annual budget for 1990 was UK£812,000, financed mainly by contributions from Contracting Governments, with some small income from sales of publication, etc.

The IWC allots part of its budget towards a research fund for projects related to whales. The Commission collects and analyzes statistical information concerning whale stocks. The most important project has been the Comprehensive Assessment of Whale Stocks. The IWC Scientific Committee reviews scientific information related to whales and whaling, the scientific programmes of the Parties, the scientific permits and the scientific programmes for which the Parties plan to issue such permits.

The main benefit of participation for Governments is having a direct part in the conservation of whale stocks and regulation of the whaling industry through an appropriate international organization. The main cost element is the financial contribution required towards funding the Commission's work. There are no special provisions relating to the economic circumstances of Governments, the formula for contributions being based largely on the degree of involvement.

Convention Article V, paragraph 2(b) requires that amendments to the provisions of the Schedule with respect to the conservation and utilization of whale resources be based on scientific findings.   Article III, paragraph 1 describes how the IWC is composed of one member from each Contracting Government, who may be accompanied by one or more experts and advisers. These delegates may include industry and other non-governmental representatives as well as scientific advisers. Non-member Governments, intergovernmental organizations and international non-governmental organizations may also attend meetings by invitation in an observer capacity (Rule of Procedure C.1). There are no special arrangements for developing countries.

The Commission has from time to time established Committees or Working Groups to look at the operation and possible revision of the Convention. In general though, most Contracting Governments take the view that the Schedule to the Convention has proved to be a sufficiently flexible instrument to meet the changing circumstances.

Codification programming

A Working Group on the Revision of the Schedule and the Operation of the Convention will meet in June 1992. No drafts or texts are available so far.

Some Governments take the view that the International Convention for the Regulation of Whaling covers all cetaceans both large and small, while others believe that each nation generally has competence to regulate small cetaceans. In the absence of agreement, there is no global treaty dealing with direct and incidental catches of the latter, or their conservation, although a number of regional fishery agreements function for the conservation of small cetaceans.   The IWC - along with other organizations concerned - contributed to the elaboration of the 1984 UNEP/FAO Global Plan of Action for the Conservation, Management and Utilization of Marine Mammals.   The UNEP System-Wide Medium-Term Environment Programme for 1990-1995 provides for giving high priority to implementation of this Global Plan of Action, for which the IWC, along with FAO, UNESCO/IOC, UNEP and IUCN, carries major responsibilities.

Amongst several complementary regional initiatives is the 1991 Agreement on the Conservation of Small Cetaceans of the Baltic and North Seas, adopted within the framework of the 1979 Bonn Convention on the Conservation of Migratory Species of Wild Animals (No. 22 above); is a follow-up to the Ministerial Declaration of the Third International Conference on the Protection of the North Sea, The Hague, 8 March 1990.   Another important initiative is the UNEP Draft Action Plan for the Conservation of Cetaceans in the Mediterranean Sea, which was considered by the 7th Meeting of the UNEP Mediterranean Action Plan, Cairo, 8-11 October 1991, and which envisages appealing to the IWC to designate the Mediterranean Sea Area as a whale sanctuary as well as undertaking other conservation measures (doc. UNEP(OCA)/MED IG.2/3/Add.2).

(58) Agreement for the Establishment of the Indo-Pacific Fishery Commission
(Baguio, 26 February 1948), as amended

Objectives and Achievement

The purpose of the Indo-Pacific Fishery Commission (IPFC) is to promote the full and proper utilization of living aquatic resources by the development and management of fishing and culture operations and by the development of related processing and marketing activities.

The scope of the Agreement includes all species of marine and fresh water resources between India and Sri Lanka to the west and Hawaii to the east, but none of the South Pacific island States has joined the organization. In December 1990, an IPFC Ad Hoc Committee on structure, functions and responsibilities of the Commission agreed that its area of competence did not need to be precisely defined, on the understanding that in practice it would give priority to marine fishery resources in the new FAO Statistical Area 71. In addition, it felt that it was necessary to abandon the reference to the "Indo-Pacific region", and to refer to the "Asia and Pacific region". The Commission will consider these suggestions at its next meeting.

The Agreement has a bearing on environment protection and sustainable development of fisheries in the region adjacent to the IPFC region since some species covered by the 1948 agreement are migrating both in the IPFC region and in adjacent areas.

The Commission is empowered to encourage, recommend and, as appropriate, undertake training and extension activities. This has been mainly done for the benefit of developing countries. Some of the subsidiary bodies of the Commission (such as its South China Committee) have supervised field development projects funded by UNDP for the benefit of developing countries.

A detailed evaluation of the Commission's activities has been undertaken by a Committee ("Review of the structure, functions and responsibilities of the IPFC and its subsidiaries", IPFC/90/8, 1990), which will be considered by the Commission at its next session.

Participation

The Agreement is open to acceptance by all FAO member nations. The Commission may by a two-thirds majority of its membership admit to membership other States that are members of UN, any of its specialized agencies or the International Atomic Energy Agency. Acceptance of the agreement may be made subject to reservations, this possibility was not used so far.

The Agreement entered into force on 9 November 1948 (less than one year after signature), and was amended in 1952, 1955, 1958, 1961 and 1977. The current 19 member countries include 13 developing countries.

Lack of financial resources required is very likely the main constraint on participation by developing countries in meetings of IPFC.   The expenses of experts invited with the concurrence of the Director-General to attend meetings of the Commission, Committees or Working Parties in their individual capacity are borne by the budget of the FAO.   In exceptional cases, the Secretariat may financially assist participants from developing countries to attend meetings.

Implementation and information

Parties to the IPFC agreement are expected to attend the meeting of the Commission and its subsidiary bodies; to provide fishery statistics on a timely basis; and to comply with the recommendations formulated by the Commission. The Secretariat is following up the performance of members of the Commission in implementing the recommendations formulated by the Commission and its subsidiary bodies.

The data to be supplied are mainly fishery statistics. The matter is dealt with by a subsidiary body of the Commission, the Standing Committee on Resources Research and Development, which under its terms of reference is to encourage the improvement of national statistics in the region. Progress has been slow in collecting adequate statistical data, and assessing the impact of the fisheries on the stocks of fish. No recommendations for management have been made so far by the Commission.

During the 1970s, stock assessment studies were made by a special ad hoc group of experts serving the Commission. Concerned over the conditions of certain fisheries, in both the Western Pacific and Indian Oceans, the group strongly recommended that the Commission be given authority and the funding necessary to collect basic data on harvesting activities and the habits of the major species.

The Commission is entrusted with promoting and conducting scientific research, publishing and disseminating information. coordinating research, and recommending member action on cooperative research. The Parties are to share information to the maximum possible extent. At the 1988 meeting of the Standing Committee for the Indian Ocean Marine Affairs Cooperation Conference (IOMAC), it was reconfirmed that the lack of reliable estimates of fishery resources in 200-mile zones was a major problem. Lack of data management capabilities in marine affairs is another problem in the Indian Ocean, depriving States in the region of access to increased amounts of data from remote sensing and other activities.

Disputes regarding the interpretation or application of the IPFC agreement can be referred to a committee composed of one member appointed by each of the Parties of the dispute and in addition an independent chairman chosen by the members of the Committee. The recommendations of such a committee, while not binding in character, should become the basis for renewed consideration by the parties concerned of the matter out of which the disagreement arose. If as a result of this procedure the dispute is not settled, it can be referred to the International Court of Justice in accordance with the Statute of the Court, unless the parties to the dispute agree to another method of settlement.

Financial and technical assistance are considered the most important factors influencing implementation.

The text of the IPFC agreement is available in both French and English and is published and disseminated in the FAO Basic Texts. Information concerning the operating and implementation of the IPFC agreement is made available to Governments by reports of the meetings of the Commission and its subsidiary bodies. For the general public, an information brochure was published several years ago at the twenty-fifth anniversary of the Commission. A revised version of this booklet is to be published in 1992 .

Operation, review and adjustment

The Secretariat of IPFC is provided by FAO. The Secretary is appointed by the Directory-General of FAO. The Headquarters of the Commission is at the headquarters of the FAO Regional Office for Asia and the Pacific in Bangkok, Thailand. The Secretary may rely on specialists of the FAO Fisheries Department in various disciplines. The annual cost of running IPFC is about US $200,000 and is financed by the regular programme of FAO. Activities of the Commission are from time to time supported through regional projects funded by external donors.

Countries participating in the activities of IPFC benefit from the research and studies made by the Commission. The main cost involved for them is their participation in meetings.

Under Rule III of the Rule and Procedure, the agenda of each regulatory session of the Commission should include an item dealing with proposals for amendment, if any, to the agreement.

Codification programming

At its twenty-third Session, held in Colombo in May 1990, the Commission established an <u>Ad hoc</u> Committee comprising representatives of six member countries:
- (i)   to review the objectives, role and functions of IPFC;
- (ii)   to identify the factors which may have limited the efficiency of IPFC; and
- (iii)   to make recommendations to Member States for rationalizing the activities of IPFC.

The <u>Ad hoc</u> Committee met in Bangkok in December 1990 and its recommendations for rationalizing the activities of the Commission will be considered by the IPFC at its next session.

(59) Convention for the Establishment of the Inter-American Tropical Tuna Commission
(Washington, 31 May 1949), and related agreements

The original objective of the Convention was to have the Inter-American Tropical Tuna Commission (IATTC), under its Director of Investigation, serve as a scientific organization, to collect data and undertake studies on yellowfin and skipjack tuna in the Eastern Pacific Ocean. The Director was put in charge of gathering information on the biology of tunas, and recommending appropriate conservation measures, when necessary, for the populations of fishes covered by the Convention.

The Parties to the Convention are Costa Rica, France, Japan, Nicaragua, Panama, the United States and Vanuatu. Canada, Ecuador and Mexico became Parties to the Convention but later withdrew. The IATTC is headquartered in La Jolla, California.

Tunas, as highly migratory marine species are, transboundary resources par excellence and therefore typically require the effective enforcement of special international legal rules, designed to regulate the behaviour of fishing fleets so as to provide for their sustainable utilization.

For more than a quarter of a century, the Commission was able to develop an international conservation regime which was to become a model of success for other migratory species and marine regions of the world. As soon as 200 mile zones were widely established, however, and because of the impressive volumes of tuna species in the Eastern Pacific Ocean, mostly yellowfin and skipjack, that region soon became a significant laboratory to put the said rules to a test.

During the early 1960s the IATTC staff's investigations revealed that yellowfin were in danger of being overfished, and the Commisssion's Yellowfin Regulatory Area (CYRA), covering an area of more than 5 million square nautical miles with, in some parts, a breadth of more than 1,000 miles from shore, was established in 1962. The CYRA was drawn from San Francisco to Valparaiso, although historical evidence has shown no evidence of significant concentrations of the resource either in the United States or in Chile.

An annual maximum permissible global catch quota in the CYRA was first recommended for yellowfin tuna in 1962 at an IATTC meeting held in 1961. Quotas were also recommended for 1963, 1964 and 1965 but none were implemented until 1966. Procedurally, the Director of the IATTC secretariat recommends an overall quota for yellowfin tuna at the IATTC meeting. Then the IATTC meeting is adjourned and an intergovernmental meeting is convened. At this meeting representatives of the governments discuss such things as special quotas. Then, if they agree on these, the IATTC meeting is reconvened and the special quotas are incorporated into the IATTC resolution for regulations.

Under the quota system, the catch was undertaken in a competitive manner, on a first-come, first-served basis, which meant that each State was free to catch as many tons of the fish as its individual fleet's capacity allowed, and as long as the catch of all fleets combined did not exceed the global quota. When the information available led the Director to conclude that the agreed quota was about to be reached, he would recommend both the closure of the open fishing season, as well as the allowance for a so-called last fishing trip. During the last trip, each boat was authorized to cover the maximum of its carrying capacity.

Since 1969, small special quotas were authorized during the closed seasopn for small and newly constructed boats from developing coastal member States. This regime, while subject to difficult annual renegotiations, operated successfully, and the recommended total quota for 1977 was more than twice that for 1966. Maintenance of the stock of yellowfin at about its optimum level is partly responsible for this, although at least two other factors contributed: First, the fishery expanded further offshore, encompassing a greater portion of the CYRA. Second, the average size of the fish caught increased to nearer the optimum size than had been the case during the 1960s. However, when at the Third United Nations Conference on the Law of the Sea a consensus started emerging on the right of coastal States to establish a 200 mile Exclusive Economic Zone, the regime needed to adapt. Following a proposal put forward by Mexico in 1975, endorsed by Costa Rica, negotiations were begun on a sustainable regime for yellowfin tuna in the Eastern Pacific Ocean, which have not yet been concluded. At the core of the controversy was the initial resistance on the part of the United States against its exclusion from tuna fishing in the newly created 200-mile zones, which it had previously dominated through the largest fleet in the region. The United States did not recognize coastal State sovereign rights over tuna in these zones until almost 15 years later. In addition, tuna embargoes were imposed, on the basis of domestic legislation, on tuna-fishing countries which did not abide by the restrictions placed by that legislation on incidental dolphin mortality.

In the course of these developments, both the coastal States of the Eastern Tropical Pacific and the distant-fishing States remained divided, seeking alliances where they could find them. In 1983, the United States negotiated with Costa Rica, Guatemala, Honduras and Panama an **Interim Agreement**, which was signed in San José and has not yet come into force, to establish an access regime for United States vessels through the issuing of license permits, and pending the establishment of a new regional conservation regime. On the other hand, on 21 July 1989 Ecuador, El Salvador, Mexico, Nicaragua and Peru signed the Lima **Convention Establishing the Eastern Pacific Tuna Organization**, which is not yet in force either, and which contemplates a conservation regime where foreign fleets would only participate in the harvesting of surpluses left by coastal State fishing. Both instruments are open to adherence by other States.

Another significant development in this context was the adoption of a resolution by the OLDEPESCA Conference of Ministers (including Bolivia, Ecuador, El Salvador, Guatemala, Guyana, Mexico, Nicaragua, Panama, Peru and Venezuela) in November 1990, approving an international programme for the reduction of capture and incidental mortality of marine mammals in commercial fishing operations. This programme is of importance to the high seas tuna fisheries in the Eastern Pacific.

(60) Agreement for the Establishment of the General Fisheries Council for the Mediterranean,

(Rome, 24 September 1949) as amended in 1963 and 1976

Objectives and achievement

The purpose of the Agreement is to promote the development, conservation, rational management and best utilization of living marine resources. The General Fisheries Council for the Mediterranean (GFCM) is one of the regional bodies of the Food and Agriculture Organization of the United Nations (FAO) created under Article 14 of the FAO Constitution. Along with the IPFC created in 1948 (No. 58 above), it is one of the oldest of the nine FAO regional fishery bodies. The GFCM provides a forum for member States of the United Nations having a mutual interest in the development and proper utilization of all living marine resources in - as was specified by the 1976 amendments - "the Mediterranean and the Black Sea and connecting waters". This area coincides with FAO Statistical Area 37, which also falls wholly within the competence of the International Commission for the Conservation of Atlantic Tunas (ICCAT, No. 64 below).

The Agreement has a bearing on environmental protection and sustainable development of fisheries resources outside the region since some species covered by the agreement are migrating in both the Mediterranean and the Atlantic Ocean. The GFCM evolved from being primarily a fisheries research organization into an organization competent - as a result of the 1976 amendments - in all matters pertaining to conservation and rational management of fisheries. As is the case with many other fishery organizations, the detailed recommendations and other activities of GFCM contribute to the implementation of broad policy objectives laid down in the GFCM Agreement.

Both the Mediterranean and the Black Seas are semi-enclosed and are thus characterized by very slow water exchange and cumulative effects of pollution. The Mediterranean is connected to the Atlantic through the narrow Gibraltar Strait, and to the Red Sea by an artificial waterway, the Suez Canal, while the Black Sea is in turn connected to the Mediterranean through the Bosphorus and Dardanelles Straits. Both the Mediterranean and the Black Seas are shelf-locked, while the Black Sea is also zone-locked by 200 mile exclusive economic zones established by the four bordering states. The Mediterranean remains one of but a few regions worldwide not covered by overlapping 200 mile zones. Although four GFCM members are member States of the European Communities (EC), the EC Common Fisheries Policy established in the context of 200 mile zone extensions does not apply to the Mediterranean.

The Council is empowered to encourage, recommend, co-ordinate, and, as appropriate, undertake research and development activities including co-operative projects. These projects are normally taking into account the special needs of developing countries.

Since the establishment of the GFCM, total fish catches in the region almost tripled. It is difficult, however, to ascertain the influence of the Council's work on this figure.

Participation

The GFCM Agreement is limited to members and associate members of FAO. Membership in GFCM of other (non-FAO) members of the United Nations and of its specialized agencies or the IAEA requires a two-thirds majority decision of the GFCM and is contingent upon the assumption of such proportional shares in the expenses of the Secretariat as may be determined in the light of the FAO Financial Regulations. The 1963 Amendments specified that the provisions concerning membership did not affect the membership status in the GFCM of States non-members of the United Nations which had become Parties to the GFCM Agreement prior to the date of these Amendments. The GFCM members, when accepting the Agreement, state explicitly to which territories their participation extends; in the absence of such declaration, participation is deemed to apply to all territories for the international relations of which the member is responsible.

The GFCM Agreement permits reservations which, however, shall become effective only upon unanimous approval by the GFCM members. No reservations have been made so far.

Entry into force required five ratifications and took more than two years after signature (20 February 1952). Current membership includes all States bordering the Mediterranean and the Black Sea except the USSR; it thus includes all developing countries in the area. In practice, developing countries do not attend meetings of the Council as regularly as the developed countries. Some developing countries, however, have a very good record of attendance. In exceptional cases, the Secretariat may financially assist experts from developing countries to attend meetings. Lack of financial resources required is very likely the main constraint on participation by developing countries in meetings of GFCM.

Implementation and information

Parties to the GFCM Agreement are expected to attend the meeting of the Council and of its subsidiary bodies; to provide fisheries statistics on a timely basis; and to comply with recommendations formulated by the Council.

The Secretariat is following up the performance of Contracting Parties in implementing the recommendations formulated by the Council. This is done by sending reminders to Contracting Parties and by asking them to report verbally during sessions of specialized subsidiary bodies. A recommendation periodically followed up concerns the mesh size for trawl nets. Fifteen years after the formulation of this recommendation by GFCM, it appears that although several countries did change their legislation to this effect, the recommendation is still not fully complied with by fishermen.

The data to be supplied are mainly fisheries statistics. The timeliness and quality of the statistics supplied to the Council needs to be improved. This matter is dealt with by a Working Party on Fisheries Economics and Statistics, the terms of reference are as follows:

    (i)   determine the most relevant catch, effort, social and economic data on fisheries needed for bio-economic analyses, review the quality of data being collected, and recommend cost-effective methods for obtaining such data;

    (ii)   promote bio-economic and socio-economic research on fisheries and strengthen the exchange of economic expertise among member of GFCM;

(iii)   study the economic and socio-economic effects of fishery management measures;

(iv)   develop analytical tools, such as computerized bio-economic models to facilitate fishery economics research.

Lack of data can be a major drawback for conservation and utilization measures. For instance, in small-scale fisheries, countries encounter problems in recording data partly because fishermen do not understand the reporting forms and, as information is voluntary, there is a reluctance to give details on private business matters. Some countries use the marketing system to check reported catch data under which some information on the small-scale sector inevitably escapes recording. By 1989 no country had yet responded to the FAO enquiry concerning catch and effort statistics (initiated in 1988 for 1987 data) and only two-thirds of the Mediterranean states had replied to an aquaculture questionnaire (introduced in 1984). As data collected by FAO on fleet size and structure is on a global and national basis, such data does not distinguish between fleets operating in different areas for distant-water fishing or coastal states of the Mediterranean. Nevertheless, the GFCM Secretariat agreed in 1989 to produce a document summarizing data on Mediterranean fleets to facilitate the availability of data in this field.

Disputes regarding the interpretation or application of the GFCM agreement can be referred to a committee comprised of one member appointed by each of the parties to the dispute and an independent chairman chosen by the members of the committee. The recommendations of the committee, while not binding in character, must be considered by the parties concerned. If the dispute is not settled as a result of this procedure, it can be referred to the International Court of Justice in accordance with the Statute of the Court, unless the parties to the dispute agree to another method of settlement.

Factors constraining implementation include financial and technical assistance needs, as well as reporting obligation.

The text of the GFCM agreement is available in both French and English and is published and disseminated in the FAO Basic Texts, and in the United Nations Treaty Series (UNTS). 1963 Amendments were adopted in English, French and Spanish. The Reports of GFCM sessions, GFCM Statistical Bulletin, and the GFCM Circular are published by the FAO. The GFCM considers the need to improve statistical reporting and to review data included in the Statistical Bulletin to be essential, both for catch reporting and in assembling an improved data base on fleet size and fishing effort.

Information concerning the operating and implementation of the GFCM agreement is made available to Governments by reports of the meetings of the Council and its subsidiary bodies. For the general public, an information brochure published in 1989 ("40 Years of GFCM") is available.

Operation, review and adjustment

The GFCM consists of the Council comprising all members, each delegate having one vote, and meeting at least every two years; the Executive Committee meeting before and after Commission sessions; and the Secretariat. Other committees - such as the existing Committee on Fisheries Management - and working parties may be established only subject to the availability of the necessary funds in the approved FAO budget. The same relates to the recruitment or appointment of specialists at the expense of FAO, for consideration of specific problems. The GFCM Technical Consultations depend on the availability of funds. Before taking any decision involving expenditures in connection with the establishment of committees and working parties and the recruitment or appointment of specialists, the GFCM must have before it a report from the FAO Director-General on the administrative and financial implications thereof. The GFCM sessions and other meetings are attended by observers from non-participating States and several international organizations, such as UNESCO and its IOC, EEC, ICCAT, and ICES.

The annual cost for operating the GFCM is about US$ 300,000, which is financed by the regular programme of FAO. One GFCM member country which is not a member of FAO contributes in cash to GFCM activities.

Countries participating in the activities of GFCM benefit from research and studies made by the Council. The main cost involved for them is participation in meetings. While in some cases, the GFCM Secretariat was able to obtain assistance to facilitate participation by developing countries, the expenses of delegates and their alternates, experts and advisers to GFCM sessions, to committees and working parties are normally covered by their respective Governments. The same applies to the expenses of research and development projects undertaken by individual members, whether independently or upon GFCM recommendation. In addition, the members cover expenses of cooperative research projects in mutually agreed form and proportion. Cooperative projects must be submitted to the GFCM prior to implementation, and contributions to such projects must be paid into a trust fund administered by FAO according to its Financial Regulations.

Under Rule IV of the Rules of Procedure, the agenda of each regular session of the Council includes an item dealing with proposals for amendment to the Agreement. Amendments were adopted, and entered into force, in 1963 and 1976.

Codification programming

Under Article V of the GFCM Agreement, the members of the Council undertake to give effect to management measures recommended by the Council unless an objection is lodged within a given period of time. While a number of recommendations of the Council are not formulated under the binding procedure of Article V, they have an influence on the national fishery regulations of member countries.

As a regional body of FAO, the GFCM is guided in its activities by the 1984 FAO Strategy for Fisheries Management and Development, which formulated guidelines to be taken into account by coastal states in order to achieve rational management and optimum use of the living resources. The progress achieved by the Strategy and the associated five Programmes of Action is reviewed every four years, the first such evaluation having taken place in 1987. The new FAO Strategy on Fisheries Research Needs of Developing Countries will also be of essential importance for the future functioning of the GFCM.

(61) International Convention for the High Seas Fisheries
of the North Pacific Ocean
(Tokyo, 9 May 1952) as amended

Objectives and achievement

The Parties to this convention seek to ensure the maximum sustained productivity of the fishery resources in the region and, on a free and equal footing, to encourage their conservation and to advance the scientific studies and measures needed to achieve that conservation.

The Parties may undertake jointly or individually the protection of a stock. In the latter case, their main obligations are:

(i)   Whenever a Party undertakes to protect a stock of fish, to prohibit its own national and vessels from taking, loading, processing, having on board, or shipping such fish;

(ii)   When it has adopted conservation measures as to a stock of fish, to ensure that its own nationals and vessels abide thereby; and

(iii)   To adopt and enforce necessary laws and regulations with penalties to achieve that end.

The North Pacific as a whole, in terms of tonnage produced, is the most important fishing region in the world, although most of the fish are caught in the Northwest Pacific. In 1984, 31.9% of the world's total catch came from the North Pacific, of which almost 90% were caught in the Northwest Pacific.

Ten years before, when 200 mile zones had not been claimed in the region, China and the Democratic People's Republic of Korea derived about 100% of their catches there, Japan 91.2%, the Republic of Korea 89.9%, the Soviet Union 33.3%, the United States 12.5% and Canada 13%. At that time, and despite various bilateral and multilateral agreements applicable in the region, most of the stocks fished were, in fact, unregulated. The impact of extended national marine jurisdictions, starting in 1976, has been that, mostly as a result of the 1978 Protocol to the Convention, all stocks are now regulated.

One of the most acute problems of high seas fishing in the Northeast Pacific Ocean is the one related with straddling stocks, that is, stocks that straddle the high seas and the outer limit of the Exclusive Economic Zones of coastal States. Thus, this problem has emerged directly as a by-product of the extension of national marine jurisdiction up to 200 nautical miles. This problem also arises in other parts of the world, and remains to be resolved.

Participation

The Convention applies to the North Pacific and adjacent waters outside the Territorial Seas.

There are three Parties to this Convention: Canada, Japan and the United States. The International North Pacific Fisheries Commission (INPFC) established by the Convention is headquartered in Vancouver, Canada.

Implementation and information

The Convention's Commission, which works through its three national interest sections, studies anadromous stocks and makes recommendations for their conservation. It disseminates its own study results, and any other data and reports. The Commission also fosters scientific cooperation with regard to non-anadromous species found both in high seas areas and in the EEZs, such as marine mammals, shrimps, squid, groudfishes and king and tanner crabs. Contributions from the Parties to the INPFC budget amounted in 1988 to US$ 289,580, in 1989 to US$ 344,500.

The INPFC regularly publishes Annual Reports and a Bulletin in English and Japanese, as well as a Statistical Yearbook in English; the 1988 Statistical Yearbook was published in 1991. It also issued the INPFC Handbook of the basic texts, which was revised in 1990 with a view to including the 1986 Annex and new Memoranda of Understanding between the Parties.

Codification Programming

Article IV of the Convention states that the Parties shall work towards the establishment of an international organization with broader membership, dealing with species of the Convention area other than anadromous species. When such an international organization comes into existence, the functions of the Commission shall be transferred to the new body.

In October 1990, Canada hosted in Ottawa discussions with the United States, the USSR and Japan, which focused on the principal elements to be addressed in a new convention for anadromous species in the North Pacific. In September 1991, negotiations on the proposed new convention were concluded with an ad referendum text of a Convention on Anadromous Stocks in the North Pacific Ocean in September 1991. All functions of the Commission are expected to be transferred to this new Convention and possibly to other organizations such as the North Pacific Marine Science Organization established under the 1990 Pacific International Convention for the Exploration of the Sea (PICES, see No. 63), subject to agreement by the Contracting Parties.

(62) Convention Establishing the Permanent Commission **on the** Exploitation and Conservation of the Marine Resources of the South Pacific
(Santiago, 18 August 1952)

The Convention is designed to implement the Santiago Declaration on the Maritime Zone, adopted by Chile, Ecuador and Peru on the same date. Colombia joined later. These four States are the Parties to the Convention. The Permanent Commission of the South Pacific (CPPS) which it establishes rotates its headquarters among the Members States' capital cities.

Although the Convention does not precisely define its area of application, with the adherence to the CPPS of Colombia, the South Pacific system of agreements applies to a vast expanse of marine areas lying between coastal area of Central America and that of Antarctica. Since Panama has joined the CPPS Parties through the 1981 Lima Convention for the Protection of the Marine Environment and Coastal Area of the South-East Pacific (No. 40) and its 1983 Quito Protocols, this could open the way for an eventual Central American participation in CPPS, as there is no other sub-regional organization available in the hemisphere concerned with all fisheries aspects of the Eastern South Pacific.

The Santiago Declaration constituted one of the earliest precedents of the so-called 200-mile movement, and was adopted to obtain the greatest benefits from the conservation, protection and regulation of the utilization of the natural resources off their coasts and up to the limit claimed. Also on the basis of the Declaration, the three original Parties have concluded several other agreements, including the 1952 Santiago Regulations Concerning Whaling in the Waters of the South Pacific, as well as the Agreement supplementary to the Santiago Declaration, the Convention on the Legal Personality of the CPPS, the Agreement Relating to Penalties, the Agreement Relating to Measures of Supervision and Control in the Maritime Zone of the Signatory States, the Agreement Relating to the Issue of Permits for the Exploitation of the Marine Resources of the South Pacific, the Agreement Relating to the Regular Annual Meeting of the Permanent Commission, and the Agreement Relating to a Special Maritime Frontier Zone, all of them adopted in Lima in 1954.

The Foreign Ministers of the Parties adopted in 1981 the Declaration of Cali, expressing the intention to conduct studies to ensure the conservation and optimum utilization of tuna, and in 1984 the Viña del Mar Declaration, setting as policy objectives, among others, co-operation with other States of the South Pacific Basin, the adoption of common policies among Latin American States, reaffirming that each State is entitled to fix the total allowable catch for its own waters and its own harvesting capacity, reaffirming the responsibility for the conservation and protection of living resources of their maritime jurisdiction areas and adjacent high seas areas, continuing efforts to negotiate an agreement on the preservation and optimum utilization of tuna in the Eastern Pacific.

Thus, the South Pacific system of agreements gives the Permanent Commission special responsibility not only for all living marine resources, but also for the marine environment and mineral marine resources within the 200 mile national zones of the Parties, and to seek the co-operation of third States to regulate the exploitation of living resources beyond those zones. The CPPS is cooperating with FAO in the collection of fisheries statistics in the entire FAO Statistical Area 87, which includes a substantial area of the high seas.

Through its three main Commissions, the Legal Commission, the Commission for Scientific Research and the Commission on Coordination and Administrative Affairs, the CPPS unifies the measures of the member States related to marine hunting and fishing of species common to their national jurisdiction zones, with the objective of achieving their conservation. With that in mind, the CPPS establishes conservation measures such as protected species, open and closed seasons, time and methods of fishing and prohibited methods, and it promotes studies and the collection of statistical and other information, harmonizes national conservation and utilization measures, and prevents over-exploitation. CPPS is also exploring the possibility of designating the marine region as a cetacean sanctuary, in order to provide for their protection, especially from incidental fishing. Furthermore, under its auspices the 1981 Lima Convention for the Protection of the Marine Environment and Coastal Areas of the South-East Pacific was concluded, as well as its 1983 Quito Protocols (No. 49).

The General Secretariat of the CPPS and the National Sections for each of the Parties which it coordinates, implement the South Pacific system of agreements. The CPPS's Coordinating Committee for Scientific Research includes Assistant Secretaries for Scientific Affairs, technical directors of fisheries research institutes, directors of fisheries, directors of technical bodies for oceanography research in the navy, directors of national institutes for scientific and technological research, directors of natural resource and environmental assessment, and national representatives of universities and institutes conducting research in the field of ocean sciences. The achievements of CPPS were recognized in 1991, when it was selected to serve as secretariat for the Consultative Transpacific Fisheries Committee, which is the first result of tri-regional cooperation in the Pacific Basin.

(63) Convention for the International Council for the Exploration of the Sea
(Copenhagen, 12 September 1964), as amended

Objectives and achievement

The objective of the treaty is to provide a new constitution for the International Council for the Exploration of the Sea (ICES), which was originally established in 1902. The function of this body is to promote research into fields relevant to the sea, in particular living resources.

The work of ICES concentrates on basic research, with the focus on the Atlantic Ocean, and it has made significant contributions to monitoring of the state of the marine environment and marine living resources. While ICES itself is not a regulatory body, its Advisory Committees on Fishery Management (AFCM) and on Marine Pollution (ACMP) provide scientific information and advice, including recommendations for management measures, to several other international agreements and bodies in their fields (e.g., Nos. 66, 68, 69 below).

Participation

Membership is open to States participating in the work of the Council (Art. 16 (1)). The geographical distribution of present membership covers the European and North American regions; no developing countries participate.

The treaty does not include a provision on reservations.

Implementation and information

Entry into force was facilitated by a special clause reducing the number of ratifications required (Article 16, paragraph 3), which brought the treaty into force on 22 July 1968.

Although member States are not legally required to report on their performance in implementing agreements, there is a system of reporting research activities through the respective twelve Subject/Area Committees. Also, there is an essential obligation to report commercial fishery and aquaculture statistics for the Northeast Atlantic. There are other occasional requests for reporting or submitting other scientific information or data. Since the secretariat serves as a data centre for oceanographic, marine pollution, and fishery data, the member States are generally obliged to provide relevant data to the respective data bases.

The membership rights of a State which has not paid its financial contribution to the Council for two consecutive years may be suspended until it has met its obligations (Art. 14 (6)). The treaty establishes no specific dispute settlement procedure. The Council itself and the Consultative Committee may excercise authority in the settlement of disputes.

The offical texts of the treaty are in English and French, also published in the UNEP series of Selected Multilateral Treaties in the Field of the Environment.

Operation, review and adjustment

The treaty specifies the functions of the International Council for the Exploration of the Sea, as well as a number of subsidiary bodies, including a Consultative Committe and a Finance Committee (Art. 12), serviced by a secretariat in Copenhagen (Denmark). The institutional mechanisms are financed through counterpart contributions from Contracting Parties (Art. 14). Pursuan to an amendment protocol adopted in 1970, the annual budgets are approved by majority vote.

A major activity is the provision of scientific advice to member countries and several international commissions for marine fisheries and marine pollution control. In this context, the ICES secretariat serves as a centre for various international databases. The scientific work is performed by national scientists in member country research institutes.

Codification programming

A new regional **Convention Establishing the North Pacific Marine Science Organization** (PICES), signed on 12 December 1990, will enter into force 60 days upon deposition of the third instrument of ratification. Signatories include Canada, China, Japan, the USSR and the United States. While PICES is not officially related to ICES, its creation, structure, and purpose stem from the fact that people familiar with or in some cases intimately involved in ICES were instrumental in stimulating the establishment of PICES. "PICES" was chosen to denote Pacific ICES because the tasks of the new organization are very similar to those of ICES. The objective of PICES is to coordinate basic and applied marine research in the North Pacific region on fisheries and marine pollution issues.

276

(64) International Convention for the Conservation of Atlantic Tunas
(Rio de Janeiro, 14 May 1966), as amended

The objectives of the Convention are to maintain tuna populations at levels which will permit the maximum sustainable catch for food and other purposes. Studies shall include research on fish abundance, biometry and ecology; the oceanography of their environment; and the effects of natural and human factors upon their abundance.

The Convention applies to the Atlantic Ocean and adjacent seas (including the Mediterranean Sea). The International Commission for the Conservation of Atlantic Tunas (ICCAT) shall be responsible for the study of the populations of tuna and tuna-like fishes (the Scombriformes, with the exception of the families Trichiuridae and Gempylidae and the genus *Scomber*) and such other species of fishes exploited in tuna fishing in the Convention area as are not under investigation by another international fishery organization. The longitude of 20 degrees East has been used, for scientific purposes, as the border between the Atlantic and the Indian Ocean.

Based on the Convention, ICCAT was established and started its activities in 1969. The Commission's secretariat is located in Madrid. The Commission is presently comprised of 22 countries, including 14 developing countries. A Protocol enabling the European Community to become a Party to the Convention was adopted in Paris in 1984, but has not yet come into force.

The Commission established a Standing Committee on Research and Statistics, a Standing Committee on Finance and Administration, and an Infractions Committee. Four panels have also been established by the Convention to consider and, if necessary, initiate regulatory measures on species covered by the Convention.

ICCAT implements the Convention by co-ordinating scientific research, collecting and disseminating statistics and other information on the biology and ecology of tunas, and oceanographic conditions, and analyzing all this information regarding the stock status of fish. If, based on scientific findings, the Commission considers it necessary, it recommends to the Contracting Parties regulatory measures to ensure the maximum utilization of the populations of fish. Such regulatory measures may include a minimum and/or maximum size of fish which may be caught, restrictions on the amount of catch and/or effort, etc. The Commission has also adopted a resolution in support of 1989 UN General Assembly Resolution 44/225, regarding large-scale pelagic driftnet fishing.

Although scientific studies are conducted by the national institutes of the Contracting Parties, under the auspices of the Commission, there have been special programmes organized by the Commission and partly funded by it. Such programmes include the "International Cooperative Tagging Programme" (1970-present), the "International Skipjack Year Programme" (1979-1983), the "International Yellowfin Year Programme (1985-1988), the "International Albacore Research Programme" (1987-present), and the "Enhanced Billfish Research Programme" (1987-present). The billfish programme is funded wholly by donations from private sources.

The regulations which have been adopted and recommended by the Commission to the Contracting Parties include minimum size regulation for tropical tuna, bluefin tuna and swordfish; limits on fishing mortality for bluefin tuna and swordfish; and catch limitations for West Atlantic bluefin tuna.

(65) Convention on Fishing and Conservation of the Living Resources in the Baltic Sea and the Belts
(Gdansk, 13 September 1973), as amended

Objectives and achievement

The Gdansk Convention, in view of the importance of "maximum and stable productivity of living resources" to the Baltic Sea States and the joint responsibility of these States for the conservation and rational exploitation of such resources, provides a co-operative framework enabling the Baltic Sea States to preserve and obtain the optimum yield of all fish species and other living marine resources, and to put into effect projects for the conservation and growth of these resources. The International Baltic Sea Fishery Commission (IBSFC) is entrusted by the Convention with furthering these objectives.

A 1982 Protocol amended the Gdansk Convention with a view to adapting it to the extension of fishery limits in the Baltic Sea beyond the traditional 12 miles and to allow for participation by the European Community (EC).

The Gdansk Convention covers all waters of the semi-enclosed (zone/shelf-locked) Baltic Sea and the Belts that consist wholly of territorial seas and exclusive fishery and economic zones, but the Convention area excludes internal waters of the coastal States. The western boundary of the Convention area coincides with the eastern limit of the area covered by the NEAFC Convention (No. 68 below).

The Gdansk Convention does not specify the relationship between its objectives and the effective integration of environment and development, but the basic importance of this relationship follows from the Baltic Sea Declaration adopted by 5 Contracting Parties to the Gdansk Convention plus Denmark and Germany as well as Czechoslovakia and Norway at the Conference on the Environment of the Baltic Sea Area, held in Ronneby, Sweden, 2-3 September 1990. The Ronneby Declaration, considering that the exploitation of natural resources (including living resources) in the Baltic Sea should be consistent with sustainable development, envisages closer co-operation between the IBSFC and the Baltic Marine Environment Protection Commission (Helsinki Commission) as well as undertaking "to integrate environmental considerations into the procedures for planning future development in all economic and social processes."

While The Gdansk Convention has no direct bearing on global environmental protection and sustainable development, its implementation may impact upon integrated ocean management of neighbouring seas, especially the North Sea, to which the Baltic is connected through the narrow Danish Straits (the Little and Great Belts and the Sound), permitting only a very low rate of water exchange. The importance of the Baltic Sea to "adjacent sea areas" is emphasized in the 1990 Ronneby Declaration in recognition of the particular sensitivity of the Baltic marine environment and the need to take urgent action to protect and preserve this environment for present and future generations.

An assessment of the Gdansk IBSFC Convention must take into account a wide range of constraints on co-operative efforts of the Baltic Sea States, in particular: limited fishery resources; the Baltic's zone/shelf-locked character; difficult climatic and other geographical conditions; severe pollution of the Baltic environment; pronounced political and economic differences between the Baltic Sea States; problems posed by accession of the EC to the Gdansk Convention; as well as diminished competence of the IBSFC as a result of coastal State rights within the new fishery and economic zones. Against this background, the

Gdansk Convention - in spite of continuing difficulties to establish total allowable catches (TACs), quota allocation, and enforcement of IBSFC recommendations - appears to have achieved a substantial measure of success in the rational conservation and optimum utilization of the Baltic Sea fisheries.

Participation

As a result of the 1982 amendments, the Gdansk Convention is open to accession not only by States interested in the preservation and rational exploitation of the living resources of the Baltic Sea and Belts (as was already the case before the amendments), but also to any "intergovernmental economic integration organization" to which competence in matters regulated by the Gdansk Convention has been transferred by its member States, which in practice means the European Community; there are no developing countries among the six coastal States concerned.

The Gdansk Convention does not provide for reservations. The Convention's amendments procedure has been applied for the purpose of the 1982 Protocol.

Implementation and information

The Baltic Sea stands out as a region where all except two (including Polish/Danish boundary that involves Bornholm) maritime boundaries have already been delimited. This testifies to the Baltic Sea States' willingness to avoid boundary conflicts and may be a facilitating factor in any fishery dispute resolution. In the absence of a dispute settlement clause in the Convetion, bilateral fishery agreements provide for settling disputes by consultations and, where such consultations fail, as in the case of the EC/Sweden Agreement, by arbitration.

The IBSFC decisions and recommendations acquire - under the Gdansk Convention - binding force upon their adoption by a two-thirds majority (thus requiring four affirmative votes of presently five Parties), but the IBSFC position is weakened by a clause providing for entry into force of any recommendation related to the area within the fisheries jurisdiction of a given Party only on condition of its affirmative vote. The entry into force of an IBSFC recommendation is subject to an opting-out procedure preventing a Party from being bound by any recommendation to which it objects. To reduce the danger of certain measures being applied only by some of the IBSFC members, a recommendation ceases to have any effect if more than three parties object. Parties may withdraw from a recommendation at any time after it has entered into force (withdrawals becoming effective one year after the IBSFC has been notified to this effect). These procedural rules are modelled on the 1980 NEAFC Convention (No. 68 below).

The IBSFC reviews compliance with its recommendations but has no authority to recommend any enforcement measures.

The Gdansk Convention was concluded in seven equally authentic languages: Danish, Finnish, German, Polish, Russian, Swedish, and English. The working language of the IBSFC is English. The IBSFC regularly publishes proceedings of its sessions, fisheries rules (recent edition issued in 1984) and occasional publications.

All IBSFC recommendations binding on its members are published as legislative acts (decrees, ordinances, etc., and EC Council Regulations) in national official gazettes and the <u>Official Journal of the European Communities</u> [OJEC]; the IBSFC conservation measures having been implemented by the EC two years after EC accession by Council Regulation No. 1866/86, as amended by Regulations No. 2178/88 and No. 887/89.

Operation, review and adjustment

The IBSFC consists of all members - each having one vote - and a Secretariat (located in Warsaw, Poland). The Commission adopts its own rules of procedure, financial rules and biennial budget. Each Party to the Gdansk Convention pays the expenses of its own participation in IBSFC meetings. In spite of major differences in the level of economic development, contributions to the budget are shared in equal parts between the Parties. The total IBSFC budget for 1991 amounted to US$ 123,400.

The IBSFC sessions, originally scheduled biennially, take place (since 1977) annually, and may be attended by observers (without the right to vote), including ICES (No. 63), NEAFC (No. 68 below) and the Helsinki Commission (No. 44). Representatives of the IBSFC participate in turn as observers in meetings of these organizations as well as the FAO Committee on Fisheries (COFI). The IBSFC and the NEAFC, jointly with the ICES providing scientific advice to both of them, have since 1985 held Dialogue Meetings, to promote discussion and understanding between fishery managers and scientists and to strengthen the relationships between the three organizations.

(66) Convention on Future Multilateral Cooperation in the Northwest Atlantic Fisheries
(Ottawa, 24 October 1978)

Objectives and achievement

The 1978 Ottawa Convention establishing the Northwest Atlantic Fisheries Organization (NAFO) replaced the 1949 International Convention for the Northwest Atlantic Fisheries and the International Commission for Northwest Atlantic Fisheries (ICNAF). The 1978 NAFO Convention was the first of four treaties introducing a new system which permitted participation by the European Community (EC) as a Contracting Party and which adapted fisheries management to Coastal State rights within the 200 mile exclusive economic and fishery zones.

NAFO's overall function is "to contribute through consultation and cooperation to the optimum utilization, rational management and conservation of the fishery resources of the Convention area", i.e., all waters - within or outside the 200 mile zones - of the Northwest Atlantic. This area coincides exactly with FAO Statistical Area 21. The species covered by NAFO are all fishery resources, except salmon, tuna and marlin, cetacean stocks managed by the International Whaling Commission (IWC, No. 57), and sedentary species. The anadromous stocks of the Northwest Atlantic salmon fall within the competence of the NASCO (No. 69), and the highly migratory species of tuna within that of the International Commission for the Conservation of Atlantic Tunas (ICCAT, NO.64).

NAFO is charged with the management and conservation of fishery resources within the "regulatory area", i.e., the area beyond 200 miles, and - unlike NEAFC (No. 68) - has no regulatory powers within the 200 miles. In contrast to IBSFC, NEAFC and NASCO (Nos. 65,68,69), which rely on scientific advice by the International Council for the Exploration of the Sea (ICES), NAFO depends on in-house scientific expertise provided by its Scientific Council. The two other main bodies of NAFO are the General Council and the Fisheries Commission. The General Council and Scientific Council are competent in co-operative action for the whole of the NAFO area, while the Fisheries Commission may only make regulatory proposals for fishing in (regulatory) areas beyond 200 miles.

Cuba - which also was a party to the 1949 ICNAF Convention - remains the only developing country among the NAFO members, although its nominal catches and hence minor budget contributions are higher than those of some industrialized NAFO members.

Some ten years after its adoption, implementation of the NAFO Convention turned into one of the most controversial instances of recent practice involving fisheries organizations. The major difficulties encountered by NAFO occurred both between Parties and with non-Parties. Severe conflicts thus arose between Canada and the EC over fishing operations by the fleets of Spain and Portugal, whose requests for quotas from overfished EC waters the Community attempted to accommodate in the NAFO area. This led to a critical situation, with the EC opting out of NAFO regulatory measures, and even threatening to withdraw from NAFO altogether. Simultaneously, serious difficulties resulted from increased fishing efforts on the limited stocks in the NAFO regulatory area by new non-Party entrants, in particular the United States, the Cayman Islands, United Kingdom, and eight developing countries - Chile, Malta, Mauritania, Mexico, Panama, the Republic of Korea, St. Vincent and the Grenadines, and Venezuela.

In spite of various attemps at resolving both conflicts within and outside NAFO, the fishing effort in the NAFO Convention area remains high. If no satisfactory resolution to the present conflicts is achieved, domestic pressures may increase in coastal States to extend authority unilaterally beyond 200 miles to protect the stocks in question.

Participation

Unlike the NEAFC and NASCO Conventions (Nos. 68,69), the NAFO Convention does not refer explicitly to the EC, nor is there in its provisions any distinction between member States and the Community. The Convention only refers to Contracting Parties. Accordingly, the Convention does not extend any special status to the Community. The EC, as other parties, has one vote, the same rights concerning representation in the various organs of NAFO, and its contribution to the budget is calculated on the basis of the same formula as for other Parties.

While the NAFO Convention does not provide for reservations, the Eastern European States did enter objections to EC membership.

Since the NAFO Convention does not contain provisions on accession by other States, such accession - according to the existing rules of international law as codified in the Vienna Convention on the Law of Treaties - is subject to the approval of the Contracting Parties. In spite of difficulties caused by the fishing conduct of non-Party new entrants in the NAFO regulatory area, the non-Parties concerned have so far shown no interest in acceding to the Ottawa Convention. The Parties to the NAFO Convention (followed in this respect by the Parties to the NASCO Convention, No. 69) committed themselves to invite attention to any non-Party in matters related to its fishing activities in the NAFO regulatory area which "appear to affect adversely the attainment of the objectives of this Convention". They also agreed to consult when appropriate upon the steps to be taken against such adverse effects, co-ordinated initially within the NAFO Working Group and now the Standing Committee on Non-Contracting Parties' Fishing Activities (STACFAC). In this connection, it was emphasized that, nothwithstanding the limited fishery resources in the regulatory area, NAFO is formally open to accession by other States.

Implementation and information

No dispute settlement clause is contained in the Convention. Bilateral fishery agreements between the NAFO Parties usually provide for carrying out periodic bilateral consultations regarding their implementation. The 1972 Canada/France (St. Pierre and Miquelon) Agreement Concerning Their Mutual Fishing Relations off the Atlantic Coast of Canada provided for submitting any disputes to binding arbitration, and became the basis for the <u>Canada/France Filleting within the Gulf of St. Lawrence</u> arbitration. In its 1986 award in this case, the arbitral tribunal decided that the 1972 Agreement did not entitle Canada to forbid the French trawlers registered in St. Pierre and Miquelon to fillet their catch in the Gulf of St. Lawrence. The arbitration clause of the 1972 Agreement was also resorted to for the purpose of the presently pending <u>Canada/France (St. Pierre and Miquelon) Maritime Areas Delimitation</u> arbitration, which is to delimit the 200 mile zones and other maritime areas of both states.

The Scientific Council provides advice to coastal States, upon their request, on any matter pertaining to the scientific basis for the management and conservation of fishery resources in waters under the fisheries jurisdiction of these States; and to the Fisheries

Commission, either on the Council's initiative or on the Commission's request, taking into account the terms of reference specified by the Commission. The Parties are obliged to furnish to the Scientific Council any available data it requests. The Convention area is divided into scientific and statistical subareas and divisions, which may be modified by the General Council on the request of Scientific Council, provided that each coastal State exercising fisheries jurisdiction in any part of the area affected concurs with such action. The General Council, on the request of the Fisheries Commission and on the basis of advice of the Scientific Council, may also divide the regulatory area into divisions and subdivisions for fishery management purposes. The scientific and statistical subareas, divisions and subdivisions are defined in Annex III to the NAFO Convention, as modified by the Amendment on Boundaries of Subareas 0 and 1, which was adopted by Resolution of General Council of 7 June 1979 and entered into force on 1 January 1980. The Scientific Council reports on each of its annual meetings on data concerning particular stocks in various divisions. The tasks of the Scientific Council may, where appropriate, be carried out in cooperation with other public or private organizations having related objectives. The Council cooperates with ICES, as evidenced by, e.g., the Joint NAFO/ICES Study Group on Red Fish in Greenland, or the recent Joint NAFO/ICES Working Group on Harp and Hooded Seals, as well as with private institutions.

Membership in the NAFO Fisheries Commission (which is authorized to adopt regulatory measures only in the areas beyond 200 miles) is determined and reviewed by the General Council at its annual meetings. This membership is limited to Parties which participate in the fisheries of the regulatory area, and which have provided evidence satisfactory to the General Council that they expect to participate in these fisheries in the near future. Any Party that is not a Commission member may attend meetings as an observer (without the right to vote). The Fisheries Commission, in which each member has one vote, takes its decisions - as the General Council - by majority vote, provided there is a quorum of two-thirds of the Commission members. Measures adopted by the Commission enter into force after an opting-out procedure that prevents any Commission member from being bound by a measure to which it objects. If objections are entered by a majority of Commission members, the proposal shall not become a binding measure, unless any or all of the Commission members nevertheless agree among themselves to be bound by it. The Commission members may withdraw from a measure at any time after one year from its entry into force (withdrawals becoming effective one year after the Executive Secretary has been notified to this effect).

The Fisheries Commission is empowered - based on advice from the Scientific Council - to take regulatory measures with respect to fisheries beyond the 200 mile limits (whether entirely beyond 200 miles or associated with stocks within 200 miles), including proposals for joint action by the Parties aimed at optimum fishery utilization and international measures of control and enforcement. It may also invite the attention of Commission members to any matters related to the objectives of the NAFO Convention. The Fisheries Commission is obliged to "seek to ensure" consistency between its measures concerning fish stocks in the regulatory area beyond 200 miles and measures taken by a coastal State with regard to such stocks within its 200 mile zone. Both the coastal State and the Commission are thus obliged to promote the co-ordination of such measures, each coastal State having a duty to keep the Commission informed of its own measures.

The Parties to the NAFO Convention are obliged to take implementing legislative and enforcement measures, which they must report to the Fisheries Commission annually. The NAFO Convention maintained the ICNAF scheme of joint international enforcement with regard to the NAFO regulatory area. The technical NAFO Conservation and Enforcement Measures are periodically reviewed.

The NAFO Convention was concluded in English, which is the official language of NAFO. NAFO regularly publishes its Annual Reports (including those of its General Council, Scientific Council and Fisheries Commission), Annual Proceedings of the three main bodies, and NAFO Conservation and Enforcement Measures. Other publications include: the NAFO Handbook, published in 1984, containing the basic texts; NAFO Statistical Bulletin, published annually and containing complete catch and effort statistics on the commercial fisheries of the Northwest Atlantic region (continuing the previous ICNAF series, the first NAFO volume being Vol. 29, published in July 1981); NAFO List of Fishing Vessels, published every three years and containing a list of vessels over 50 gross tons fishing in the regulatory area (the first such 1980 NAFO List was published in March 1983); NAFO Sampling Yearbook, published annually and containing a list of available length and age sampling data from research and commercial catches and landings of major commercial species, collected by research personnel of the NAFO parties; NAFO Journal of Northwest Atlantic Fishery Science, published annually and providing a medium for the dissemination of the results of investigations on various aspects of the Northwest Atlantic fisheries; NAFO Circular Letter; as well as NAFO Scientific Council Studies, containing various research documents (SCR) and summary documents (SCS).

NAFO's numerous recommendations binding on its members are published as legislative acts (decrees, ordinances, etc., and EEC Council Regulations) in national official gazettes (and in the Official Journal of the European Communities [OJEC], e.g., the 1988 NAFO Joint International Inspection Scheme, implemented by EEC Council Regulation No. 2868/88).

Operation, review and adjustment

In contrast to NEAFC (No. 68) and some other fishery organizations, the organizational structure of NAFO is rather complex and comprises three main bodies and the Secretariat. Of the three bodies - the General Council, the Scientific Council, and the Fisheries Commission - the first two comprise all Parties, while the third comprises only those which participate or intend to participate in fisheries in the NAFO regulatory area. The Chairman of the General Council is the President of NAFO and its principal representative. He convenes regular annual meetings of NAFO, as well as any other meetings upon the request of a NAFO Party with the concurrence of another Party.

The three main bodies may establish subsidiary committees and subcommittees for the exercise of their functions. These include: for the General Council, the Standing Committee on Finance and Administration (STACFAD) and the Standing Committee on Fishing Activities of Non-Contracting Parties (STACFAC - created in 1990); for the Fisheries Commission, the Standing Committee on International Control (STACTIC); and for the Scientific Council, the Standing Committee on Fisheries Science (STACFIS), the Standing Committee on Research Coordination (STACREC), and the Standing Committee on Publications (STACPUB). Working Groups are established for specific tasks, as was the case with the Working Group on Joint International Enforcement in the Regulatory Area, or the one which preceded establishment of STACFAC.

The three main bodies and their subsidiary bodies adopt, and amend as necessary, their rules of procedure, while those of the Secretariat are determined by the General Council. The General Council also adopts the NAFO Annual Budget. Each Party pays the expenses of its own participation in all NAFO meetings. Contributions to the budget are made according to the following formula: 10% of the budget is divided among the coastal States in proportion to their nominal catches in the Convention area (in the year ending two years before the beginning of the budget year); 30% of the budget is divided equally among all eleven Parties; and 60% of the budget is divided among all Parties again in proportion to their nominal catches. The species taken into account in determination of nominal catches are listed in Annex I to the NAFO Convention. As in the case of NASCO (No. 69), a Party which has not paid its contributions for two consecutive years shall neither be entitled to vote nor present objections under the NAFO Convention until it has fulfilled its obligations, unless the General Council decides otherwise. The 1990 NAFO budget amounted to Canadian $864,830.

(67) South Pacific Forum Fisheries Convention
(Honiara, 10 July 1979), and related agreements

The Convention reflects the concerns of the peoples of the South Pacific for the conservation and management of the region's tuna resources, in their newly acquired exclusive economic zones. According to the Preamble to the Convention, the member countries have a "common interest" in the conservation and utilization of the living resources in particular tuna; a desire to "promote regional cooperation" and coordination in fisheries policies; a desire to "secure maximum benefits from the living marine resources" and to "facilitate " the collection of, analysis, evaluation and dissemination of relevant statistical, scientific and economic information". The member countries recognized at the outset that the conservation and optimum utilization of the regions tuna resource was of paramount importance to them and therefore, in order to secure maximum benefits from the resource they would need to co-operate and coordinate their fisheries policies.

The geographic area of application of the Convention is not precisely defined, but is understood to encompass the South Pacific and the Western Pacific. This area exceeds 30 million square kilometres, and no limitation exists on the species to which the Convention applies, but it focuses mostly on highly migratory species, due to their economic significance.

Membership in the 1979 Honiara Convention is restricted to the independent and self-governing territories of the South Pacific, which excludes the non-self-governing French and United States dependencies as well as distant-water fishing States. The 16 Parties to the 1979 Convention thus include 14 developing countries as well as Australia and New Zealand. The South Pacific Forum Fisheries Agency (FFA) established by this Convention is headquartered in Honiara, Solomon Islands.

The independent and self-governing States of the South Pacific established the FFA with the objective of presenting a common front vis-à-vis the distant-water fishing States seeking access to the highly migratory species in the exclusive economic zones in the region.

The FFA functions as an advisory and coordinating agency. It does not have regulatory powers. The Convention is implemented through the Parties and the FFA's two organs, namely, the Committee, in which all Parties to the Convention are represented, and the Secretariat.

The Committee gives guidance and provides a forum for consultation on fisheries, and promotes inter-regional coordination and cooperation related to the harmonization of policies with respect to fisheries management, relations with distant-water fishing countries, surveillance and enforcement, onshore fish processing, marketing and access to the 200 nautical mile zones of the Parties.

In addition to contributions from member countries, a large proportion of the Agency's programmes is now funded by extra-budgetary sources, which means that programmess become affected when aid donors discontinue their support. The main sources of extra-budgetary support have been the International Center for Ocean Development (ICOD), Canadian International Development Agency (CIDA), European Community (EC), Australian Bureau for International Development (AIDAB), Commonwealth Fund for Technical Cooperation (CFTC) and the United States Agency for International Development (USAID).

The FFA keeps a Regional Register of Foreign Fishing Vessels, which is the basis for the plan on harmonization and coordination of fisheries regimes and access agreements adopted by the FFA Committee in 1983. The Register is kept on the basis of the information submitted by vessels in compliance with uniform reporting requirements, and seeks to enable the State Parties to grant licenses only to those foreign vessels which are accorded "good standing" status on the Register, and not to those which have been "blacklisted".

The FFA Secretariat has the function to collect, analyze, evaluate and disseminate to the Parties information concerning statistical and biological aspects of the marine living resources, concerning procedures, legislation and agreements adopted by other countries within or beyond the region, and on prices, shipping, processing and marketing of fish and fish products. Upon request of a Party, it provides technical advice, information and assistance in the development and implementation of fisheries policies and access agreements. The Parties are to supply the Secretariat with information on catch and effort statistics by their vessels, and relevant biological and statistical data.

The FFA Secretariat also operates an information service, coordinates tuna development research, conducts industry and market studies, participates in fisheries development planning projects, and collects and analyzes data on fishing patterns.

The FFA Secretariat implements the Convention by engaging in numerous projects, some of which led to the adoption of the 1982 Nauru Agreement and the 1989 Wellington Driftnets Convention. It was also instrumental in the 1980 and 1984 agreements concluded by some of the FFA's members and the American Tuna Boat Association, and later in the conclusion of the 1987 Port Moresby Treaty. In that framework, the Secretariat has distributed certificates of access, received and held fees and reported to the participating States.

(a)   The Nauru **Agreement Concerning Co-operation in the Management of Fisheries of Common Interest** was signed on 11 February 1992 and entered into force on 23 April 1983. Its objective is to co-ordinate fisheries manaegment with regard to common stocks (mainly tuna) in the national jurisdiction zones of the Parties, and to harmonize the licensing requirements applicable in the FFA region to foreign vessels. Though separate from the Honiara Convention, the Nauru Agreement uses the secretariat services provided by the FFA.

The Parties to the 1982 Nauru Agreement are 8 developing countries (Federated States of Micronesia, Kiribati, Marshall Islands, Nauru, Palau, Papua New Guinea, Solomon Islands and Tuvalu); it is open to the accession of other States with the approval of all Parties.

The Parties agreed to establish a coordinated approach to foreign vessels participating in the fishery for common stocks, on the basis of the following points:

(i)   Vessels from the Parties are to be granted priority over vessels applying for access from other States;

(ii)   Minimum uniform licensing requirements for foreign vessels are to be established;

(iii)   All foreign vessels are to apply for and possess a licence;

(iv)   Observers shall be placed on foreign fishing vessels;

(v)   Standardized log books are to be kept;

(vi)   Timely reporting of activities by foreign fishing vessels to local authorities and standardized identification of foreign fishing vessels;

(vii)   The payment of access fees to be calculated on the basis of principles established by the Parties;

(viii)   The requirement to submit to the authorities complete catch and effort data, and;

(ix)   The inclusion of the requirement that the flag State take the necessary measures to ensure compliance with the regulations established.

The Parties also seek to standardize their licensing procedures and explore the possibilities of establishing a centralized licensing system. The Parties are to coordinate their surveillance activities, by arranging for the rapid exchange of information, and reciprocal enforcement.

The FFA Secretariat functions as secretariat to the Nauru Agreement, providing administrative support and assisting the Parties for their annual meetings and administrative arrangements, for the exchange and analysis of statistical data concerning the fisheries and information on vessels.

(b)   On 2 April 1987, after two years and 13 rounds of negotiations, and with the technical and research assistance of the FFA staff, the **Treaty on Fisheries Between the Governments of Certain Pacific Island States and the Government of the United States of America** was signed at Port Moresby.

The signatories of the Port Moresby Treaty are the same Island States which are Parties to the 1979 Honiara Convention.

The stated purpose of the Treaty, according to its Article 2, is for the United States Government to co-operate with the Pacific Island States, through the provision of technical and economic support, for them to maximize benefits from the development of their fisheries resources, from the operations of licensed US fishing vessels. Access of those licensed vessels constitutes the larger part of the reciprocal benefit granted to the United States by the Island States.

The 5-year Treaty (which is expected to be extended by the Parties after 1993) applies to all waters, except the waters subject to the jurisdiction of non-Party States, North of 60 degrees South latitude, East of 90 degrees East longitude and bounded on the Western and Northern side by specified coordinates. It is applicable to the exploitation of different highly migratory species, and it amounts to the institution of uniform licensing conditions and procedures for US vessels, and the payment of license fees and granting off technical assistance by the United States. The licensing system is managed by the FFA Director as Administrator of the Treaty.

Flag State responsibility provisions in the Treaty are new in access agreements. The United States undertakes to investigate and prosecute offences by its vessels, applying its own laws and those of the Island States concerned, and turn over to them the total value of the fines, forfeiture or penalties collected. In many ways, the United States acts as an enforcement agent for the island counties.

Aside from the Treaty with the United States, a dozen other countries have secured access through negotiated licensing agreements with the FFA Island States. In 1987 and 1988, the agency's members were considering initiatives for a multilateral fisheries arrangement with Japan.

(c)   Partly as a result of informal scientific meetings in the South Pacific Albacore Research Group (SPAR), followed by the official Tarawa Declaration of July 1989 by the Heads of Government of the South Pacific Forum, a **Convention for the Prohibition of Fishing with Long Driftnets in the South Pacific** was concluded in Wellington on 23 November 1989. It applies to the high seas as well as to the areas under the jurisdiction of coastal States in the region. The Convention entered into force on 17 May 1991, after the ratification by four signatories (Cook Island, Federated States of Micronesia, New Zealand and Tokelau), all of which are South Pacific Forum members. However, some of the States most actively engaged in driftnet fishing in the South Pacific are not members, although the 1989 Convention provides for consultations with them, and the Parties are required to prohibit the landing, processing or importation of catches, not to assist or encourage non-Parties in the use of driftnets, and to restrict port access.

The Convention has two Protocols, adopted in Noumea on 20 October 1990, the first of which (signed by the United States on 26 February 1991) is open to those distant-water countries which fish in the South Pacific region, and through which they agree to prevent their nationals and vessels from fishing within it with driftnets; the second protocol, open to all countries in the Pacific rim, commits States with fisheries jurisdiction in waters adjacent to the Convention Area, to prohibit fishing within it with driftnets.

The UN General Assembly, by Resolution 44/225 of 22 December 1989, recommended first a moratorium on large-scale pelagic driftnet fishing by 30 June 1992, applicable to all areas of the high seas unless effective conservation and management measures are taken by concerned parties in a region. It also called for the cessation of large-scale pelagic driftnet fishing activities in the South Pacific region by 1 July 1991, as an interim measure until appropriate conservation and management arrangements can be made for South Pacific albacore tuna resources. Finally, it called for the cessation of the expansion of large-scale pelagic driftnet fishing in the North Pacific and all other high seas areas outside the Pacific Ocean, recognizing a special role for regional organizations in the conservation and management of the living resources of the high seas. However, although the problem of driftnet fishing has also been discussed at FAO's Committee on Fisheries, there is no single body involving all of the States concerned, either at the regional or global levels, with responsibility for the collection of appropriate scientific data, the assessment of that data and the formulation of standards for the control and regulation of driftnet fishing.

(d)   During consultation meetings held in Honiara and Noumea in March and October 1990, proposals were submitted for a new international convention for the conservation, management and optimum utilization of South Pacific Tunas, or alternatively for an arrangement relating to the management of South Pacific Albacore Tuna.

At the 19th meeting of the Forum Fisheries Committee (22-23 October 1990), a new draft treaty and a model subsidiary agreement for co-operation on fisheries surveillance and enforcement in the Pacific Island Region was presented (FFA Report 90/115, attachment D, annex 1) for further consideration by the FFA parties.

(68) Convention on Future Multilateral Co-operation in the North-East Atlantic Fisheries
(London, 18 November 1980)

Objectives and achievement

The 1980 London Convention establishing the North-East Atlantic Fisheries Commission (NEAFC) replaced the 1959 North-East Atlantic Fisheries Convention and an old NEAFC, which itself superseded the Permanent Commission set up under the precedent-setting 1946 Convention for the Regulation of the Meshes of Fishing Nets and the Size Limits of Fish. The new NEAFC Convention is to an important extent inspired by corresponding provisions of the 1978 Convention establishing the Northwest Atlantic Fisheries Organization (NAFO), on which negotiations began at the same time (in 1977, No. 66). The 1980 NEAFC Convention - as the 1978 NAFO Convention as well as the 1982 Protocol to the Convention establishing the International Baltic Sea Fishery Commission (IBSFC, No. 65) - introduces a new system which adapts fisheries management to the exclusivity of the coastal State rights within the 200 mile exclusive economic and fishery zones, and which allows for EC participation as a Contracting Party.

The NEAFC Convention aims to "promote the conservation and optimum utilization of the fishery resources of the North-East Atlantic area". To this end, the new NEAFC provides a cooperative forum for consultation and exchange of information on the fishery resources and management policies. It also has regulatory powers confined largely to fisheries beyond the 200 mile limit; within 200 miles NEAFC powers are significantly limited. Similar to the IBSFC and the North Atlantic Salmon Conservation Organization (NASCO, No. 69), the NEAFC has no explicit responsibilities with respect to scientific matters relying in this respect on the Advisory Committee on Fishery Management (ACFM) of the International Council for the Exploration of the Sea (ICES, No. 63).

The Convention covers all waters of the North-East Atlantic, including the North Sea and part of the Arctic Sea, but excluding the Mediterranean Sea as well as the Baltic Sea and the Belts. The Convention area coincides with most of FAO Statistical Area 27. The NEAFC Convention applies to all fishery resources, except marine mammals, sedentary species, and - insofar as they are dealt with by other treaties - highly migratory species and anadromous stocks.

The Contracting Parties, comprising all coastal and some distant-water fishing States, do not include developing countries. One such State - (distant-water fishing) Cuba was a member of an old NEAFC and signed the new NEAFC Convention upon its adoption in 1980, but has not ratified it.

In spite of its limited regulatory powers in the vast areas within 200 miles, the NEAFC continues to promote rational conservation and optimum utilization of the North-East Atlantic fisheries through the cooperative efforts of its members. NEAFC relies on scientific assistance by the ICES (No. 63), the adequateness of which depends in turn on the accuracy of data provided by the NEAFC members to ICES. Thus, the effectiveness of the system is heavily dependent on the quality of input (especially catch statistics) from the NEAFC members. Compared to NAFO (No. 66 above), NEAFC has in practice adopted far fewer regulatory measures. The fishery resources beyond the 200 mile limit in the North-East

Atlantic are rather limited and, therefore, no conflicts between coastal and distant-water fishing States have arisen in this region with respect to stocks that straddle the 200 mile zones and the adjacent high seas.

Participation

NEAFC currently has eight Contracting Parties, including the EC. While the EC has as one Party the same right of representation, vote and contribution, the NEAFC Convention avoids specification of the criteria for membership, simply listing the EC along with other Parties. In addition, while providing for accession by other States (upon approval by three-fourths of the parties) the Convention specifies that this does not relate to EC members, thus excluding accession by any international organization other than the EC.

The Convention provides for amendment procedures, but not for reservations. No dispute settlement clause is contained in the Convention. Bilateral fishery agreements between the NEAFC Parties usually provide for settling disputes by consultations.

Implementation and information

The procedural rules concerning regulatory powers of NEAFC differ for fisheries within and beyond the 200 mile limit. NEAFC is authorized to make recommendations related to fisheries in the regulatory area beyond 200 mile zones by a two-thirds majority vote, provided that no vote is taken unless there is a quorum of two-thirds of the parties. These recommendations enter into force through an opting-out procedure preventing a party from being bound by recommendations to which it objects. If three or more Parties have objected, a recommendation shall not become binding on any Party. Parties may withdraw from a recommendation at any time after it has entered into force (withdrawals becoming effective one year after the NEAFC has been notified to this effect).

In contrast to NAFO, there is in the NEAFC Convention an explicit reference to the regulatory and advisory powers of NEAFC with respect to fisheries within 200 mile zones of the Parties. Both recommendations and advice can only take place upon request of a Party to whose 200 mile zone they relate, and a recommendation must receive (as under the IBSFC Convention) an affirmative vote of that Party. Only Parties exercising fisheries jurisdiction within the zone may object to (opt-out of) a recommendation related to that zone, in which case the recommendation does not become binding on any Party. Similarly, only such a Party is authorized to withdraw from a recommendation related to its zone at any time after it has entered into force, in which event that recommendation ceases to be binding on any Party (withdrawals becoming effective 90 days after NEAFC has been notified to this effect).

In addition to these procedural rules, the impact of coastal Parties' rights within their 200 mile zones is apparent from the requirement that NEAFC must "seek to ensure" consistency between its recommendations concerning fish stocks beyond 200 miles and measures taken by a respective Party with regard to such stocks within its 200 mile zone. For this purpose, each Party is obliged to keep NEAFC informed of its measures.

NEAFC has no joint enforcement scheme, relying on individual enforcement of its members reported to it annually. Each Party also has a duty to inform NEAFC of its legislative measures and of any agreements (including foreign access) related to fishery conservation and utilization in the Convention area.

The NEAFC Convention was concluded in the English and French languages, both equally authentic and both forming working languages of the NEAFC. NEAFC publishes regularly Reports of its annual meetings and the Technical Conservation Measures Manual referred to above. Within its objective of facilitating the harmonization of measures applied by the Parties, the Manual is useful to fisheries administrators, particularly when reviewing their own country's technical measures. NEAFC also published in 1985 its Handbook of Basic Texts and issues various occasional publications.   The NEAFC's recommendations binding on its members are published as legislative acts (decrees, ordinances, etc., and the EC Council Regulations) in their national official gazettes.

Operation, review and adjustment

The organizational structure of the NEAFC is rather simple, the Commission consisting of all members, each having one vote, and a Secretariat (located in London, UK). This results from NEAFC's reliance on ICES for scientific advice, which eliminates the need for an in-house scientific committee. The NEAFC does, however, operate a Finance and Administration Committee.

NEAFC adopts its own rules of procedure, rules for the Finance and Administration Committee, and annual budget. Each Party to the NEAFC Convention pays the expenses of its own participation in NEAFC meetings. Contributions to the budget are made according to the following complex formula: one-third of the budget is divided equally among all the eight Parties; two-thirds of the budget is divided among all the Parties in proportion to their nominal catches in the Convention area on the basis of the ICES catch statistics; the annual contribution of any Party having a population of less than 300,000 inhabitants is limited to a maximum of 5% of the total budget, and when this contribution is so limited, the remaining part of the budget is divided among the other Parties in accordance with first two criteria. The limitation based on population, applying in practice to Denmark (for the Faroe Islands and Greenland) and Iceland, is subject to annual review of NEAFC and may be changed by a three-fourths majority decision. The three major contributors to the budget in accordance with the above formula are the EC, Norway and the USSR.

Contributions to the ICES amount to almost two-thirds of the NEAFC expenses.

(69) Convention for the Conservation of Salmon in the North Atlantic Ocean
(Reykjavik, 2 March 1982)

Objectives and achievement

The Convention for the Conservation of Salmon in the North Atlantic Ocean created the North Atlantic Salmon Conservation Organization (NASCO). According to Article 3, paragraph 2 of this Convention, "the objective of the North Atlantic Salmon Conservation Organization is to contribute through consultation and co-operation to the conservation, restoration, enhancement and rational management of salmon stocks subject to the Convention, taking into account the best scientific evidence available to it." The terms "restoration" and "enhancement," not used in other fishery treaties, relate to the cost-intensive measures required from the State of origin for the maintenance of the salmon stocks in adequate conditions. NASCO operates three regional Commissions for North America, West Greenland, and the North-East Atlantic, and relies on scientific advice by the Advisory Committee on Fishery Management (ACFM) of the International Council for the Exploration of the Sea (ICES, No. 63 above, also operating the North Atlantic Salmon Working Group).

Each regional Commission has agreed regulatory measures for fisheries which intercept salmon from another country. Since NASCO's inception in 1984 regulatory measures have been in force in, or agreed for, the following years:

West Greenland Commission	North-East Atlantic Commission	North American Commission
1984	1984	1986
1986	1987	(applied to subsequent
1987	1988	years by Canadian
1988	1989	legislation)
1989	1990	
1990	1991	
	1992	

In addition to these regulatory measures the Council of NASCO has addressed a number of issues which could adversely affect salmon conservation. These include the possible impacts of salmon aquaculture on the wild stocks, the impacts of acidification and the impacts of climate change. A number of actions have been agreed. In addition a number of databases have been established on laws, regulations and programmes relating to salmon conservation and management of all rivers containing salmon and of tag release information. A Tag Return Incentive Scheme to encourage the return of scientific tags for assessment purposes has also been established. No major conflicts with non-Party fishing States have occurred in the NASCO area. However, the question of a salmon fishery in the Norwegian Sea beyond 200 miles from the baselines by vessels reflagged in non-Parties (Panama and Poland), led to the adoption of a resolution by the NASCO Council calling for concerted diplomatic action by all NASCO members with a view to ending this fishery.

Participation

Participation is restricted. The Convention was open for signature by Canada, Denmark (in respect of the Faroe Islands), Iceland, Norway, Sweden, the USA and the European Community (EC). The Convention is open for accession, subject to the approval of the Council, by any other State that exercises fisheries jurisdiction in the North Atlantic Ocean or is a State of origin for salmon stocks subject to the Convention (Article 17, paragraph 3).

At present, there are 9 Parties, not including any developing countries. All Parties are represented in the Council, but the regional Commissions have restricted membership.

The Convention does not provide for reservations. No dispute settlement clause is contained in the Convention. Bilateral fishery agreements between the NASCO parties usually provide for settling disputes by consultations.

Implementation and information

Each Party shall ensure that such action is taken, including the imposition of adequate penalties for violations, as may be necessary to make effective the provisions of the Convention and to implement regulatory measures which become binding on it under Article 13. Each Party shall transmit to the Council an annual statement of the actions taken (Article 14).

Each Party shall provide to the Council available catch statistics for salmon, such other statistics for salmon stocks as required by the Council and any other available scientific and statistical information which the Council requires for the purposes of the Convention (Article 15).

Each year, each Party shall notify the Council of:

(a)   the adoption, or repeal since its last notification, of laws, regulations and programmes relating to salmon conservation, restoration, enhancement and rational management;

(b)   any commitments by the responsible authorities concerning the adoption or maintenance in force for specified periods of time of measures relating to salmon conservation, restoration, enhancement and rational management;

(c)   factors within its territory and area of fisheries jurisdiction which may significantly affect the abundance of salmon stocks (Article 15).

The Council's regulatory powers cover its authority to make recommendations concerning salmon stocks (including the enforcement of laws and regulations) to the Parties and the three Commissions, the scope of such recommendations being, however, importantly limited due to exclusion therefrom of the matters pertaining to salmon harvests within the 200 mile zones. Yet, and only upon the specific request of a Commission, the Council is authorized to make recommendations to that Commission on regulatory measures which the Commission may propose pursuant to the Reykjavik Convention.

The Council has agreed upon a format for submitting the annual returns required under Articles 14 and 15 of the Convention. A return is required by all Parties even if no new actions have been taken. These returns are presented to the Council in summary form. In addition, reports on the implementation of regulatory measures are presented to the appropriate regional Commission.

Each Party is obliged to take legislative and enforcement measures in its rivers and 200 mile zone for the purpose of implementing the Reykjavik Convention and NASCO's recommendations, such measures reported to the NASCO Council annually, with copies of respective measures being furnished to the Council upon its request.

Each Party is also committed to provide the Council with catch statistics for salmon taken in its rivers and 200 mile zone as well as with any other available scientific and statistical information which the Council may require for the purposes of the Convention. The most commonly adopted method of collecting catch statistics in the NASCO Convention area is to licence all fishermen and to require them to make catch returns, but various other methods are also used. All Parties have complied in making their annual returns.

The NASCO Convention was concluded in the English and French languages, both equally authentic and both forming the official languages of NASCO. NASCO regularly publishes reports of annual meetings of the Council and the three Commissions, biennial reports on its activities (so far published for 1983-84, 1985-86, 1987-88, and 1989-90) and technical papers. In 1988 NASCO published its Handbook of Basic Texts. Other tasks of the NASCO Council and its three regional Commissions in compiling and disseminating relevant information and scientific data are referred to in section C devoted to Implementation.

The recommendations of NASCO and its regional Commissions binding on their members are published as legislative acts (decrees, ordinances, etc., and the EC Council Regulations) in their respective official gazettes. A format for the provision by the Parties of copies of their respective laws, regulations and programmes was agreed by NASCO in 1985, and a computer-based database of such information has been established. Progress reports in this respect were reviewed by the NASCO Council in 1989 and 1990. The database, forming a unique record of laws and regulations relating to North Atlantic salmon, apart from its usefulness for NASCO's operation, is also available for individual use by the Parties.

Operation, review and adjustment

NASCO is composed of: the Council comprising all members, each having one vote; three regional Commissions for North America, West Greenland and the North-East Atlantic, in which each member also has one vote; and the Secretariat (located in Edinburgh, United Kingdom). Reliance by NASCO on the scientific advice of the ICES eliminates the need for an in-house scientific committee. Working Groups are established for dealing with specific issues as necessary (such as the Working Group on Salmonid Introductions and Transfers).

The Council and the Commissions meet annually, and may hold such other meetings as requested by a Party (member of a Commission) with the concurrence of another Party (member of a Commission). Parties may participate as observers in the deliberations of a Commission of which they are not members. The representatives of the ICES participate as observers in the meetings of both the Council and regional Commissions. The strong links between the two organizations are reflected by the ACFM of ICES reporting to the annual meetings of NASCO, and the NASCO Council formally requesting annual advice from ICES for each Commission area. In exercising their functions the Commissions shall take into account a number of factors including the advice from ICES (Article 9).

The annual budget (1990) was £278,660, financed by contributions from member parties according to the following formula: 30% divided equally among the Parties; 70%

divided among the Parties in proportion to their nominal catches in the calendar year ending not more than 18 months and not less than 6 months before the beginning of the financial year.

The Council has agreed that non-governmental organizations involved in salmon conservation and management may attend the meetings of the Council and may make statements at sessions designated as "Special Sessions". NASCO presently has fourteen non-governmental observers.

Any Party may propose amendments to the Convention. The adoption of an amendment requires unanimous approval.

(70) Agreement on the Network of Aquaculture Centres
in Asia and the Pacific
(Bangkok, 8 January 1988)

Objectives and achievement

The objective of this regional agreement, which entered into force on 11 November 1990, is to assist the member States in their efforts to expand aquaculture development. The regional experience so initiated could have an important bearing on similar cooperative efforts in other regions.

In the past, NACA has concentrated its effort on supporting aquaculture technology development in the developing countries of the Asia-Pacific region. NACA is currently preparing a programme to support countries of this region in taking a more holistic approach to aquaculture development, which would consider the wider environmental issues.

The membership of the agreements consists exclusively of developing countries.

As the agreement has only been operation for one year, evaluation of goal achievement would be premature. Organizational arrangements have proceeded on schedule.

Participation

Membership is limited regionally to the States invited to participate in the Conference of Plenipotentiaries at which the agreement was adopted. However, other States may accede to the agreement subject to prior approval by two-thirds of the members.

Reservations are not foreseen; no reservations have been entered.

All member states are developing countries from the Asia and Pacific region.While only developing countries are participating in programme activities, support is now being sought from interested donor countries following the phase-out of initial UNDP support for the "Network of Aquaculture Centers in Asia" at the end of 1989.

Implementation and information

The intergovernmental organization for the Network of Aquaculture Centers in Asia and the Pacific (NACA), established by the Bangkok agreement, shall consolidate the expanded network to share the responsibility of research, training and information exchange essential to aquaculture development in the region (article 3) and to conduct disciplinary and interdisciplinary research on selected aquafarming systems for the adaptation or improvement of technologies and for the development of new technologies.

Regional centres exist in China, India, the Philippines and Thailand.

Within NACA, an FAO/UNDP Regional Seafarming Development and Demonstration Project, operational since 1987, has been extended through 1991. Basically demonstrating the value and use of established and commercially viable seafarming systems and technology, it assists in the formulation of a regional seafarming information system providing data for planning and management.

Operation, review and adjustment

The Governing Council Meeting, attended by all participating governments is the supreme policy making body of NACA. The Governing Council Meeting is held annually. Costs for the meeting will, from 1992, be borne by participating Governments. Costs of functioning of the Secretariat and core activities are also borne by member Government contributions to NACA. The Secretariat, headed by a co-ordinator, is located in Bangkok.

Participating Governments have appointed senior governmental officials to act as the focus of NACA activities for all major programmes. The participation of these senior officials, who act as focal points for collation and dissemination of information at the national level, facilitates exchange of scientific knowledge and advice, and ensures effective participation of national authorities and agencies.

Codification programming

NACA cooperates with the Committee for the South China Sea of the Indo-Pacific Fishery Commission (No. 58 above). In addition, NACA cooperates with a range of regional and international organizations, among which are the Food and Agriculture Organization of the United Nations (FAO), International Center for Living Aquatic Resources Managment (ICLARM), Southeast Asian Fisheries Development Centre (SEAFDEC), Mekong Committee, Asian Institute of Technology, United Nations Environment Programme (UNEP) and Economic and Social Commission for Asia and the Pacific (ESCAP). As part of the new programme approach of NACA, the organization will establish cooperation with other agencies and organizations involved in aquatic resource management and conservation

STATUS OF RATIFICATIONS AS OF 1 JANUARY 1992

(57) <u>International Convention for the Regulation of Whaling</u> (Washington 1946)

Antigua & Barbuda	Netherlands
Argentina	New Zealand
Australia	Norway
Brazil	Oman
Chile	Peru
China	Republic of Korea
Costa Rica	Saint Lucia
Denmark	St. Vincent & the Grenadines
Ecuador	Senegal
Finland	Seychelles
France	South Africa
Germany	Spain
Iceland	Sweden
India	Switzerland
Ireland	USSR*
Japan	United Kingdom
Kenya	United States of America
Mexico	Venezuela
Monaco	

(58) <u>Agreement for the Establishment of the Indo-Pacific Fisheries Commission</u> (Baguio 1948)

Australia	Nepal
Bangladesh	New Zealand
Cambodia	Pakistan
France	Philippines
India	Republic of Korea
Indonesia	Sri Lanka
Japan	Thailand
Malaysia	United Kingdom
Myanmar	United States of America
	Viet Nam

(59) <u>Convention for the Establishment of an Inter-American Tropical Tuna Commission</u> (Washington 1949)

Costa Rica	Panama
France	United States of America
Japan	Vanuatu
Nicaragua	

(60) <u>Agreement for the Establishment of the General Fisheries Council for the Mediterranean</u> (Rome 1949)

Albania	Libya
Algeria	Malta
Bulgaria	Monaco
Cyprus	Morocco
Egypt	Romania
France	Spain
Greece	Syria
Israel	Tunisia
Italy	Turkey
Lebanon	Yugoslavia*

(61) <u>International Convention for the High Seas Fisheries of the North Pacific Ocean</u> (Tokyo 1952)

Canada
Japan
United States of America

(62) <u>Convention on the Organization of the Permanent Commission on the Exploitation and Conservation of the Marine Resources of the South Pacific</u> (Santiago 1952)

Chile
Ecuador
Peru

(63) <u>Convention for the International Council for the Exploration of the Sea</u> (Copenhagen 1964)

Belgium	Norway
Canada	Poland
Denmark	Portugal
Finland	Spain
France	Sweden
Germany	United Kingdom
Iceland	United States of America
Ireland	USSR*
Netherlands	

(64) <u>International Convention for the Conservation of Atlantic Tunas</u> (Rio de Janeiro 1966)

Angola   Japan
Benin   Morocco
Brazil   Portugal
Canada   Republic of Korea
Cape Verde   Sao Tome & Principe
Cote d'Ivoire   South Africa
Equatorial Guinea   Spain
France   USSR*
Gabon   United States of America
Ghana   Uruguay
Guinea   Venezuela

(65) <u>Convention on Fishing and Conservation of the Living Resources in the Baltic Sea and Belts</u> (Gdansk 1973)

Finland
Poland
Sweden
USSR*
EEC

(66) <u>Convention on Future Multilateral Co-operation in the Northwest Atlantic Fisheries</u> (Ottawa 1978)

Bulgaria   Norway
Canada   Poland
Cuba   Romania
Denmark   USSR*
Iceland   EEC
Japan

(67) <u>South Pacific Forum Fisheries Convention</u> (Honiara 1978)

Australia   Niue
Cook Islands   Palau
Fiji   Papua New Guinea
Kiribati   Samoa
Marshall Islands   Solomon Islands
Micronesia   Tonga
Nauru   Tuvalu
New Zealand   Vanuatu

(68) <u>Convention on Future Multilateral Co-operation in the North-East Atlantic Fisheries</u> (London 1980)

Bulgaria	Poland
Denmark	Sweden
Finland	USSR*
Iceland	EEC
Norway	

(69) <u>Convention for the Conservation of Salmon in the North Atlantic Ocean</u> (Reykjavik 1982)

Canada	Sweden
Denmark	United States of America
Finland	USSR*
Iceland	EEC
Norway	

(70) <u>Agreement on the Network of Aquaculture Centres in Asia and the Pacific</u> (Bangkok 1988)

Bangladesh	Myanmar
China	Nepal
Democr. People's Rep.	Pakistan
of Korea	Sri Lanka
Hong Kong	Viet Nam
Malaysia	

* Membership status subject to further clarification.

CHAPTER VI

TRANSBOUNDARY FRESHWATERS

Guillermo J. Cano

This chapter covers 24 multilateral agreements and instruments relating to transboundary freshwaters (Nos. 71 - 94), starting from the list previously submitted to the UNCED Preparatory Committee[1]; it should be noted that a number of the agreements listed actually concern a single freshwater basin.

Bilateral agreements on transboundary freshwaters are addressed in chapter XII below, using the River Plate Basin as an example. It is worth noting that in the case of the River Plate Basin, a survey of the environmental activities undertaken by the bodies responsible for the management of the basin[2] revealed that, although such activities were effective at the level of bilateral relations between countries forming part of the basin (and concerning sections of the basin), those undertaken by multilateral bodies responsible for the whole basin (No.80) were practically non-existent. This underscores the significance of bilateral agreements, which in some regions (e.g., in North America) are the main source of international law in this field.

Even though marine waters are addressed separately in this survey (in chapters IV and V), it is important also to recall the unity of the hydrological cycle. Estuaries and other coastal waters present a wide range of specific problems in the areas of both management and legislation and, in some cases, are covered by specific conventions[3]. These problems are due mainly to the large number of administrative jurisdictions involved and are particularly acute where environmental issues are concerned (variations in sea level, preservation of wildlife conservation).

"Transboundary" freshwaters, as considered in the present chapter, are (a) rivers and lakes which act as a boundary or political border ("contiguous"), and (b) rivers or lakes which cross a border ("successive"). It has been argued that sovereignty is shared in the case of contiguous rivers but not in the case of successive ones. To overcome this problem and to avoid describing successive rivers as "international", it was decided to describe them all as "transboundary".

The term also covers aquifers and other layers or deposits of groundwater which straddle a political border. It may also be said to include atmospheric waters, in the case of weather

---

[1] Doc. A/CONF.151/PC/79, appendix 1, Development of Legal Instruments for Transboundary Waters, Progress report by the Secretariat (1991).

[2] G. J. Cano, "La política ambiental en los tratados de la Cuenca del Plata", paper presented at the "Simposio sobre perspectiva ambiental para el año 90: evaluación de los estudios de impacto ambiental en América Latina, reunido en Sao Paulo, Brazil, 18-21 Febrero 1991", organized by the Fundación Memorial de América Latina and the Environment Secretariat of the State of Sao Paulo.

[3] See H. Smets "La protección del ambiente en las zonas costeras de interés turístico", Ambiente y Recursos Naturales: Revista de Derecho, Política y Administración, vol. IV-1 (March 1987), p. 52; and La gestión de las zonas costeras - Análisis de una recomendación de la OCDE, second SFDE symposium (1978), pp. 142-151.

modification (cloud seeding) and acid rain, although the latter are addressed separately in the present survey (in chapter III). The artificial diversion of waters from river basins may convert watercourses or bodies of water into "transboundary" waters when they would not naturally be so. This is the case with the Dominican Republic and Haiti where the Artibonito irrigation system is fed by the Dominican River Macasia-Caña, part of whose waters flow into Haiti[4]. Furthermore, connections between hydroelectric power stations located on different rivers and in different countries may mean that the facilities are of international interest, even though the waters do not meet. This is true of the River Lempa between Honduras and El Salvador[5].

The annotated list of multilateral agreements on transboundary freshwaters, as contained in part G of the annex to this volume, was prepared on the basis of information contained in document A/CONF.151/PC/79, appendix 1, and in the following works: International Environmental Law - Multilateral Treaties, (W. E. Burhenne ed., Berlin 1974-1992, Erich Schmidt Verlag in collaboration with the Environmental Law Center of the International Union for Conservation of Nature and Natural Resources); D. A. Caponera, The Legal Regime of International Water Resources, (Rome 1981, FAO Legislative Study No. 53); Systematic Index of International Water Resources Treaties, Declarations, Acts and Cases by Basin (Rome 1978, FAO Legislative Study No. 15); V. G. Arnaud, Derecho internacional ambiental - La contaminación de los ríos en el derecho internacional público, (Buenos Aires 1974, Publication No. 11 of the National Institute for Water Science and Technology); S. van Gelderen, "Tratados ambientales internacionales pertinentes a America Latina - su estado de aplicación", in Ambiente y Recursos Naturales: Revista de Derecho, Política y Administración (vol. V - 3, Sept. 1988, pp. 105-113); G. J. Cano, "Trends in international environmental law with particular reference to the western hemisphere", in The Future of the International Law of the Environment (R. J. Dupuy ed. Dordrecht, 1985, Hague Academy of International Law and United Nations University, pp. 414-416).

As with all environmental instruments, the process of negotiation and drafting provides important clues for subsequent evaluation[6]. A recent United Nations document on international river basins[7] highlights the impact of the negotiating process on the development of international instruments and their effectiveness.

In 1970, the UN International Law Commission was asked to codify the law of the non-navigational uses of international watercourses. It took 21 years to produce a first draft for submission to the General Assembly (see note 16 below). After many years of unsuccessful

---

[4] See Estudio para un proyecto de tratado entre las repúblicas Dominicana y de Haiti sobre sus recursos hídricos bajo régimen jurídico internacional, informe preliminar (Buenos Aires, 1991, INTAL), para. 18.

[5] See doc. E/CN.12/511, Preliminary Review of Questions relating to the Development of International River Basins in Latin America, para. 6.

[6] W. Lang, "Negotiations on the Environment", in: International Negotiation (San Francisco 1991, PIN: Process of International Negotiations Project) pp. 343-356.

[7] See United Nations, Institutional Issues in the Management of International River Basins: Financial and Contractual Considerations (New York, 1988, Natural Resources/Water Series No. 17, Sales No. E.87.II.A.16), pp. vi and 81.

negotiations in the Council of Europe, the United Nations Economic Commission for Europe (which also includes the United States and Canada) prepared a comprehensive regional convention on the protection and use of transboundary watercourses and international lakes, which was opened for signature on 18 March 1992 in Helsinki.

There are also relevant non-governmental sources which constitute what is known as "soft law". The best known example of this are the Helsinki Rules, adopted in 1966 by the International Law Association (ILA) and supplemented since then by various other provisions adopted by the same association[8], including rules relating to flood control (New York 1972), land-based marine pollution (New York, 1972), maintenance and improvement of navigable waterways separating or crossing various States (New Delhi, 1974), protection of water resources and waterworks in time of war (Madrid, 1976), administration of international water resources (Madrid, 1976), flow regulation and the interdependence between water and other natural resources (Belgrade, 1980), pollution of international river basins (Montreal, 1982), law on international groundwater resources (Seoul, 1986), and additional rules applicable to international water resources (Seoul, 1986). These have been adopted or recommended by Governments or regional governmental organizations[9], or invoked in legal judgements[10]. The Institut de Droit International[11], the Inter-American Bar Association[12], and the International Association for Water Law (IAWL)[13] may be added to the list.

It should be noted that the ILA documents have been widely accepted by Governments and in judicial decisions. But all this predates the emergence of the concept of sustainable development. The sustainability sought is not only physical and biological, but also economic, social, cultural and financial[14]; the concept therefore will have important implications also for the future development of international law in the field of transboundary water resources. Some of these new directions, and the related needs of further professional training in this field, have

---

[8]   Finnish Branch of the International Law Association, <u>The work of the ILA on the Law of International Water Resources</u> (Helsinki, 1988), eds. E. J. Manner and Veli-Martti Metsälampi.

[9]   Asian-African Legal Consultative Committee, text in doc. A/CN.4/274, vol.II.

[10]   Supreme Court of Argentina <u>in re</u> Provincia de La Pampa vs. Provincia de Mendoza por las aguas del río Atuel, Judgement of 3 December 1987, published in <u>Ambiente y Recursos Naturales</u>, vol. VI-4 (December 1989), p. 81 (preambular paras. XXIV, XXXII and XXXIV).

[11]   Institut de Droit International, resolutions adopted at Heidelberg (1887), Madrid (1911), Paris (1934), Salzburg (1961) and Athens (1979).

[12]   Inter-American Bar Association (IABA), Buenos Aires Declaration (1957) and resolutions of San José, Costa Rica (1967) and Caracas (1969).

[13]   International Association for Water Law (AIDA/IAWL), <u>Annales Juris Aquarum II</u> (Caracas, 1976) and <u>Annales Juris Aquarum III</u>, published under the title <u>La gestión de los recursos hídricos en vísperas del siglo XXI</u>, ed. Generalitat Valenciana, pp. 20 and 281.

[14]   G. J. Cano, "Introducción al tema del desarrollo sustentable y las ciencias políticas", <u>Anales de la Academia Nacional (Argentina) de Ciencias Morales y Políticas</u>, vol. XIX (1992).

already been addressed in two workshops organized by the United Nations University and the Hague Academy of International Law[15].

In many multilateral agreements, navigational uses are dealt with separately from the other uses: this is confusing and is one of the reasons why such agreements are less effective. It is true that navigation originally was the principal, and virtually the only, use of transboundary water resources when the Congress of Vienna was concluded in 1815. Legal regulation of navigational use was kept clearly distinct from that of other uses, and the work of the International Law Commission (ILC) is still confined to non-navigational uses. The Inter-American Convention proposed in Rio de Janeiro in 1965 took the same approach. This limitation seems too narrow, considering that navigational use, which does not consume resources, may conflict with other subsequently developed uses which do involve consumption (irrigation, local freshwater supply, industrial uses, mining), as well as with other uses not involving consumption such as hydroelectric power generation, where changes to the natural flow of the water may affect navigation. The author of the present paper has previously given detailed consideration to the development of the law of international water resources[16], with reference to the views of those ILC rapporteurs who advocated that legal regulation of navigational use should be consolidated with other uses. Similar views on the subject were expressed at an International Symposium on International Navigable Waterways held by UNITAR in 1970[17]. The negotiations in progress between the five Governments of the River Plate Basin, concerning the proposal to establish a waterway beginning in the Upper Paraguay River, continuing through the middle section of the Parana River and ending in the Uruguay River, have acknowledged the serious nature of the environmental problems connected with navigation, and efforts are being made to resolve them through the involvement of the United Nations Development Programme and the Inter-American Development Bank[18].

The methods of organization and operation of the agencies which manage international water basins have been examined at length on various occasions and the deficiencies encountered in some of these methods explain also why some international instruments have been delayed or are incomplete. The following is a brief review:

---

[15]   Hague Academy of International Law and United Nations University, The Future of International Law of the Environment (R. J. Dupuy ed., Dordrecht/Boston/Lancaster 1985) p. 411; and Hague Academy of International Law - Centre for Studies and Research on International Law and International Relations, Rights and Duties of Riparian States of International Rivers, (J. Barberis and R. Hayton eds., Dordrecht/Boston/London 1991). See also J. G. Lammers, Pollution of International Watercourses, (Boston/The Hague/Dordrecht/Lancaster 1984).

[16]   G. J. Cano, "The Development of the Law of International Water Resources and the Work of the International Law Commission", Water International, 14-4 (December 1989), p. 167; S.C. McCaffrey "The International Law Commission and Its Efforts to Codify the International Law of Waterways", Annuaire Suisse de Droit International, Vol. 47 (1990) pp. 32-55; and the 1991 Doman Colloquium on the Law of International Watercourses, in Colorado Journal of International Environmental Law and Policy, Vol. 3 No. 1 (1992), pp. 1-334.

[17]   UNITAR, Ríos y canales navegables internacionales - Aspectos jurídicos y financieros (Buenos Aires 1971). English version: International Navigable Waterways (New York, 1974).

[18]   Centro Ambiental de la Cuenca del Plata, Ecoprensa No. 2 (Montevideo, 1991), pp. 9 and 20.

(a)   In 1967, the United Nations Institute for Training and Research (UNITAR) convened in Quito (Ecuador) a Latin American regional seminar on the subject, which considered[19] both the institutional and legal aspects of water basin management, including legal aspects other than provisions of international water law that require settlement;

(b)   In 1969-1970, the United Nations convened a panel of experts on water policy which produced specific recommendations on international water resources and gave rise to the publication of a book which analyses them;[20]

(c)   In 1981, the United Nations organized in Dakar (Senegal) an Interregional Meeting of International River Organizations[21]. It analysed 20 instruments which had established agencies (of which only eight are bilateral). The following were the main recommendations on matters distinct from the principles of international water law: (i) in order to ensure international action, the powers which are normally assigned to a number of different governmental departments should be combined in a single body; (ii) there must be a sound institutional and legislative organization at the national level before the action taken by George Washington University, international bodies to which governments belong can be effective; (iii) experts must take precedence over diplomats in the negotiation and management of instruments, although the experts must work with the help or with the instructions of the diplomats; (iv) it is essential to have sufficient personnel with ad hoc training; (v) a suitable system for the interchange of physical, economic, social and legal information must be established;

(d)   In 1986, a workshop on disputes concerning international rivers[22] was convened by George Washington University, the International Institute for Applied Systems Analysis (IIASA) and other institutions in Laxenburg (Austria). The meeting did not discuss the legal aspects of the question but the political, economic and social implications. Its findings are essential reading for the evaluation of the results of the application of international instruments in the case studies examined (the Plata, Mekong, Senegal and Indus rivers), which constitute a significant sample of the world situation.

The financial and contractual aspects of international water basin management are examined in a later document, quoted in note 13, which emphasizes that the sharing of costs between governments does not always correspond with the sharing of benefits.

The desire to integrate the concepts of development and environmental protection (sustainable development) is derived from the Brundtland report (1987). There followed a series of governmental, technical and diplomatic meetings based on three major themes: (a) the

---

[19]   Corporaciones públicas multinacionales para el desarrollo y la integración de la América Latina, compiled by Marcos Kaplan for UNITAR (Fondo de Cultura Economica, Mexico City 1972), pp. 263-272.

[20]   United Nations, Management of International Water Resources: Institutional and Legal Aspects (New York 1975, Natural Resources/Water Series No 10).

[21]   United Nations, Experiences in the Development and Management of International River and Lake Basins (New York 1982, Natural Resources/Water Series No. 10).

[22]   The Management of International River Basin Conflicts, Proceedings of a workshop held in Laxenburg, Austria, in September 1986 (George Washington University, Washington/D.C. 1987), edited by Evan Vlachos and Anne C. Webb.

preservation of genetic diversity; (b) the global warming of the atmosphere and hence the global changes to be expected in the international, economic and social structure; and (c) finally, the very different other themes which are incorporated in Agenda 21 of UNCED, which have been discussed in numerous preparatory meetings for the Conference in Rio de Janeiro in June 1992. All this has given rise to a proliferation of meetings in different parts of the world, particularly in New York, Geneva, Nairobi and Beijing. Because of their number and the distances between them, the Governments of the less developed countries have found it impossible to attend all of them, for two reasons: (a) lack of sufficient trained and informed personnel; (b) lack of financial means to attend the meetings and to train sufficient personnel.

Non-governmental organizations also encounter these problems. The Brundtland report had assigned a major role to these organizations in the achievement of sustainable development, whether at the side of or even in opposition to governments. These groups comprise not only the traditional "roots" organizations but also others that are "popular" and less specialized. There are also the churches, entrepreneurs, workers' organizations, professional associations and the academic world (universities, scientific organizations, etc.). The problems confronting these non-governmental organizations are twofold: (1) the difference in the availability of financial resources between North and South which prevents organizations in the South from attending all meetings to which they are invited. They can attend meetings that are held near to their headquarters but this is rarely the case because nearly all the meetings are held in the North; (2) the difference of interests between the representatives of the North and the South.

In every country it is generally the local (state, province, prefecture or district) and municipal governments that have to apply what has been agreed in international instruments. They should therefore be consulted, and contribute to the negotiations leading to such instruments. Also, as we are dealing with international rivers, we should not forget that all international rivers are at the same time national rivers, and that the local and municipal authorities have a role to play in the management of them, or at least in some aspects of it.

In general, the treaties which establish a secretariat or some other type of body to monitor application, report periodically to the parties concerned and act as a repository for shared documentation are much more rigorously applied than those which do not. This is demonstrated by the study out of which arose the initiative submitted to the Organization of American States (OAS) of establishing an Inter-American System for the Protection of Nature[23]. The Convention signed in Washington on 12 October 1940 - which that initiative attempts to improve - does indeed lack such a body, and this is one of the main reasons why its execution has not been as fast and as vigorous as could be desired (see also chapter II).

There is also a lack of coordination, both at higher levels and on the ground, of the multilateral technical assistance provided to countries by international governmental bodies of a universal character, such as the United Nations and all its agencies, including UNDP, UNEP, and the World Bank; or by regional bodies (OAS, Inter-American Development Bank, NATO, CMEA, EEC, OECD, Organization of African Unity, Asian Development Bank, and so on). This topic is closely related to that of restructuring the United Nations system as it relates to the

---

[23]   V. H. Martinez, "Hacia la creación de un sistema interamericano para la conservación de la naturaleza", in Cuadernos de la Fundación Ambiente y Recursos Naturales No. 1 (Buenos Aires 1985), also published in a bilingual version (Spanish-English) by the Argentine Senate.

environment. The same may be said of the bilateral financial assistance offered with the same objectives, which it would be advisable to integrate and coordinate, as in some cases it is at a higher level than multilateral assistance.

When the Inter-American Development Bank laid down its environmental policy, it stated that some of its loans had been granted with no consideration being given to environmental effects, and that it had soon established missions to evaluate retroactively the environmental impact. It is now the practice to make this evaluation before the loans are granted[24]. In some countries, including the United States, it has become customary to draw up national laws with a fixed period of validity. This makes it necessary to review them periodically, and to produce progress reports. Such a practice could usefully be extended to international instruments. Reports on the implementation of treaties could be entrusted to agencies or persons, in the public or private sector, independent of Governments, as it would be unrealistic to expect Governments to be able to criticize themselves. Such a system of auditing by outsiders is commonplace in the business world.

The cooperation of the scientific community both in the negotiation and in the implementation of the international instruments under consideration here was strongly recommended at the ASCEND 21 Conference organized in Vienna in November 1991 by the International Council of Scientific Unions, in preparation for UNCED.

---

[24]   Inter-American Development Bank, "Procedimientos para clasificar y evaluar impactos ambientales en las operaciones del Banco", reprinted in <u>Ambiente y Recursos Naturales</u>, vol. VII-1 (1985), p. 107.

CHAPTER VII

HAZARDOUS SUBSTANCES

Wordsworth Filo Jones and Marceil D. Yeater

This chapter covers the following 10 agreements and instruments on hazardous substances, in chronological order:

(95)   The 1947 ECOSOC **Recommendations on the Transport of Dangerous Goods**, as revised;

(96)   The 1957 **European Agreement Concerning the International Carriage of Dangerous Goods by Road**, as amended;

(97)   The 1968 **European Agreement on the Restriction of the Use of Certain Detergents in Washing and Cleaning Products**, as amended;

(98)   The 1970 EFTA **Convention for the Mutual Recognition of Inspections in Respect of the Manufacture of Pharmaceutical Products**;

(99)   The 1972 **Convention on the Prohibition of the Development, Production and Stockpiling of Bacteriological (Biological) and Toxic Weapons, and on Their Destruction**;

(100) The 1981-1989 OECD **Recommendations on Mutual Acceptance of Data in the Assessment of Chemicals and Good Laboratory Practices**, and related instruments;

(101) The 1985 FAO **Code of Conduct on the Distribution and Use of Pesticides**, as amended;

(102) The 1987 UNEP London **Guidelines for the Exchange of Information on Chemicals in International Trade**, as amended;

(103) The 1989 Basel **Convention on the Control of Transboundary Movements of Hazardous Wastes and Their Disposal**; and

(104) The 1991 Bamako **Convention on the Ban of the Import into Africa and the Control of Transboundary Movements and Management of Hazardous Wastes within Africa**.

Agreements concerning nuclear materials are covered separately in chapter VIII, agreements concerning occupational hazards in chapter IX, and agreements concerning liability for damage in chapter X.

A list showing the status of ratifications as of 1 January 1992 is annexed (pages 334 - 338).

(95) Recommendations on the Transport of Dangerous Goods
(Geneva, 26 April 1957 7th edition 1990)

Objectives and achievement

These recommendations have been developed by the United Nations Committee of Experts on the Transport of Dangerous Goods and kept up to date in the light of technical progress, the advent of new substances and materials, the requirements of modern transport systems and, above all, the need to ensure the safety of people, property and the environment. They are addressed to governments and international organizations concerned with the regulation of the transport of dangerous goods. Amongst other aspects, the recommendations cover principles of classification and definition of classes, listing of the principal dangerous goods, general packing requirements, testing procedures, marking, labelling, placarding and shipping documents. They aim at presenting a basic scheme of provisions that will allow national and international regulations governing the various modes of transport to develop within it in a uniform fashion. It is expected that governments, intergovernmental organizations and other international organizations, when revising or developing regulations for which they are responsible, will conform to the principles laid down in these recommendations, thus contributing to worldwide harmonization in this field.

Participation

The recommendations are global in scope. They are not mandatory instruments. The only incentive to apply them are the intrinsic value to all who are directly or indirectly concerned with the transport of dangerous goods, i.e., benefits from increased safety and protection of the environment to be gained from the long experience of the UN experts, as well as facilitation of trade by applying uniform rules within a harmonized system.

The membership of the Committee is restricted to fifteen experts from countries particularly interested in the international transport of dangerous goods. According to rule 72 of the rules of procedure of the UN Economic and Social Council, other countries may participate in the work of the Committee as observers. There is now a desire to encourage the participation of developing countries and other non-member countries in the decision-making process for future work of the Committee.

Implementation and information

The Recommendations form the basis of the national regulations applicable to the transfer of dangerous goods in most industrialized countries. They are widely implemented through international agreements such as the European Agreement concerning the international carriage of goods by road (ADR), the Regulations concerning the International Carriage of Dangerous Goods by Rail (RID), and especially through globally accepted instruments such as the International Maritime Dangerous Goods Code (IMDG Code) and the technical Instructions for the Safe Transport of Dangerous Goods by Air (ICAO TI).

The worldwide acceptance of the IMDG Code and the ICAO TI is mainly due to the legal and technical assistance provided by IMO and ICAO through their training programmes, with financial help from UNDP. However, there is still a need to provide developing countries with such assistance with regard to the development of national rules and/or regional agreements regarding road and rail transport of dangerous goods.

The recommendations have been used for the determination of classes of wastes under the Basel Convention, and they formed one of the major bases for the International Labour Organization's effort to harmonize chemical classification internationally pursuant to its 1990 Convention on Safety in the Use of Chemicals at Work (No. 116 in the present survey). The hazard identification system of the recommendations (UN identification number plus placarding) has actually been implemented by most emergency services throughout the world.

The recommendations, known as the "orange book", are disseminated in all the official languages of the United Nations to the governments of member states, the specialized agencies, the International Atomic Agency and the other international organizations concerned. Recommendations on tests and criteria are published as a separate manual.

They include recommendations on the training of dangerous goods transport workers and may themselves be used for training purposes especially with regard to principles of classification, packing, marking, labelling of dangerous goods and to the use and interpretation of transport documents.

Operation, review and adjustment

Secretariat functions for the Recommendations are carried out by the Transport Division of the United Nations Economic Commission for Europe (ECE) in Geneva. The Committee of Experts meets biennially to review and update its recommendations which are adopted and published by resolution of the Economic and Social Council. (The subcommittee of Experts on the Transport of Dangerous Goods meets twice a year and held its most recent session in December 1991.)

In light of technical progress and the advent of new substances and materials, many suggestions have been made and are continuing to be made at the various sessions held by the Committee of Experts for the necessary adaptation of the recommendations to meet these changes. The principal areas of work are: classification of new substances; development of provisions for the transport of wastes or environmentally hazardous substances; definition of criteria; new types of packaging, most modes of transport; co-ordination of the work of various international organizations responsible for specific modes of transport, such as IMO, ICAO, UN/ECE, OCTI; co-operation with IAEA, ILO, UNEP, etc.

(96) European Agreement Concerning the International Carriage of Dangerous Goods by Road (ADR)

(Geneva, 30 September 1957) as amended

Objectives and achievement

The objectives of this transport agreement are to increase the safety of international transport by road and to replace the different conditions under which the international transport of dangerous goods was authorized prior to this agreement on the territories of different States according to their domestic legislation by agreed common conditions under which such transport should be authorized on the territories of all Member States.

The ADR provisions concerning classifications, packing and labelling of dangerous goods are based on the UN Recommendations on the Transport of Dangerous Goods, (No. 95 above) and therefore harmonized with those applicable to different modes of transport (rail, sea, air). ADR further lays down conditions as to the construction, equipment, and operation of vehicles carrying dangerous goods by road.

Although this agreement does not specially take into account the circumstances of developing countries, it has had an influence in both national and international practices including developing countries, as reflected in national legislation.

Participation

Membership in the Agreement is restricted to members of the United Nations Economic Commission for Europe and countries admitted to the Commission in a consultative capacity under paragraph 8 of the Commission's terms of reference.

Other countries that may participate in certain activities of the Economic Commission for Europe in accordance with paragraph 11 of the Commission's terms of reference, may become Contracting Parties to this Agreement. There were 20 parties as of January 1992, including one European developing country.

Article 16(2) provides that no reservations are possible to the Agreement except for those entered in the protocol of signature and those concerning dispute settlement (Articles 11 and 12).

Implementation and information

This is a regional binding agreement. In accordance with Article 7(1), the Agreement entered into force one month after the deposit of the fifth instrument of ratification on 20 January, 1968. The low number required for entry into force, the high degree of safety achieved as well as the benefits in trade facilitation resulting from a single set of internationally accepted rules for carriers accelerated its implementation.

The Contracting Parties have accepted commitments to ensure that certain dangerous goods are not accepted for international transport and that other goods be transported under conditions laid down in the annexes. However, Article 5 provides that transport operations to which this Agreement applies shall remain subject to national or international regulations applicable in general to road traffic, international road transport, and international trade.

Article 11 concerns the settlement of disputes about the interpretation or application of this Agreement. The Contracting Parties shall as far as possible settle disputes between them by negotiation. Any dispute which is not settled by negotiation shall be submitted to arbitration and the decision of the arbitration shall be binding on the parties to the dispute.

The official languages of the Agreement are English and French for the Agreement proper and French for the Annexes. An authoritative translation of the Annexes has been prepared in the English language, and a Russian version has also been published by the United Nations. Translations have been done at national level by most Contracting Parties and therefore the text is available in numerous languages.

Distribution of documents of the Inland Transport Committee and its subsidiary bodies is limited to governments, specialized agencies, and to intergovernmental and non-governmental organizations which take part in the work of the committee and of its subsidiary bodies.

A guide to the ADR has been published in English and French by the International Road Transport Union (IRU). The Annexes to the ADR contain practical operational provisions and therefore are used for shipper and driver training.

Operation, review, and adjustment

The Secretary General of the United Nations, who is the depositary of the Agreement, ensures its administration through the United Nations Economic Commission for Europe.

According to Article 13, three years after the entry into force of the Agreement, any Contracting Party may, by notification to the Secretary-General of the United Nations, request that a conference be convened for the purpose of reviewing the text of the Agreement. The Secretary General shall invite to any conference convened, all countries that are members of the Economic Commission for Europe and countries admitted to the commission in a consultative capacity. The Secretary General shall also invite countries which have become Contracting Parties under Article 6 (2).

At the most recent conference of the Working Party on Transport of Dangerous Goods in May 1991, the participating States proposed several amendments including improvement of vehicle safety, (i.e. vehicle stability, construction, and speed limit devices), provisions relating to training with special reference to driver training, improvement of the functioning of ADR, and relations with other international organizations. They also discussed, in particular, a draft by the European Community concerning the supervision and checking of transfers of wastes at community frontiers, which would take the Basel and Lome IV conventions into account.

Any Contracting Party or the Secretary General may propose amendments. Proposed amendments shall be submitted to the depositary who shall circulate them to all Contracting Parties and inform the other countries referred to in Article 6 (1). Any amendment adopted shall enter into force for all contracting parties in accordance with procedures set out in Article 14.

Codification programming

The annexes to the ADR are currently under review for inclusion of provisions relating to the carriage of environmentally hazardous substances (freshwater pollutants).

The annexes to this Agreement are closely harmonized, on the basis of the Recommendations of the UN Committee of Experts on the Transport of Dangerous Goods (No. 95 above), with the Regulations Concerning the International Carriage of Dangerous Goods by Rail (RID) (which are annexed to Appendix B of the Convention concerning International Carriage by Rail - COTIF).

(97) European Agreement on the Restriction of the Use of Certain Detergents in Washing and Cleaning Products
(Strasbourg, 16 September 1968)

Objectives and achievement

As noted in its preamble, the objectives of the European Agreement on the restriction of the use of certain detergents in washing and cleaning products are to protect the supply of water for the population, industry, agriculture and other business occupations, and the natural aquatic fauna and flora, in particular in so far as they contribute to human well-being, and to foster the unhindered enjoyment of places devoted to leisure and sport.

Participation

The Agreement was open for signature by the member States of the Council of Europe which take part in the activities in the field of public health under Resolution 59/23 of the Committee of Ministers and for accession by other member States and by non member States.

Reservations are not excluded by the Agreement.

Implementation and information

In accordance with the provisions of Article 4, the Agreement entered into force one month after the deposit of the third instrument of ratification, with the Secretary General of the Council of Europe on 16 February 1971, i.e., three years after signature.

Commitments accepted by the parties to this convention are:
- to legislate nationally so that washing or cleaning products containing one or more synthetic detergents are not put on the market unless the detergents are, as a whole, at least 80 percent susceptible to biological degradation (Article 1).
- to ensure that compliance with the above must not result in the use of detergents which, in normal use, might adversely affect human and animal health (Article 2).

The Secretary General of the Council of Europe shall convene meetings of multilateral consultations within the Council of Europe every five years or more frequently if requested by one of the Parties, for the purpose of revising or extending any of the provisions of this Agreement (Article 3).

The languages of the Agreement are English and French. The Secretary General of the Council of Europe transmits certified copies to each of the signatory and acceding states. It has been published with other multilateral treaties in the field of environmental protection, e.g. by UNEP.

Operation, review and adjustment

The Secretariat of the Council of Europe ensures the administration of the Agreement. Costs are covered by the general budget of the Council of Europe.

Periodic review and adjustment is a process governed by the provisions of Article 3 of this Agreement which are made in light of scientific and international developments. Based on this provision, a protocol amending this Agreement was adopted in Strasbourg on 25 October 1983 and entered into force on 1 November 1984.

(98) Convention for the Mutual Recognition of Inspections in Respect of the Manufacture of Pharmaceutical Products
(Geneva, 8 October 1970)

Objectives and achievement

The objective of this Convention is to contribute towards the removal of obstacles to international trade, establishment of strict national quality controls, i.e., official inspections and testing on the manufacture of drugs (especially those intended for export), exchange of information between parties regarding drug manufacturing inspections, and mutual acceptance of national inspections carried out in conformity with the convention.

Participation

The current membership of 16 Parties includes one European developing country. Though concluded within the framework of the European Free Trade Agreement (EFTA), several non-EFTA States have also become Parties. The admission of new member States occurs by invitation to accede and is limited to those countries with national arrangements necessary to apply an inspection system comparable to that referred to in this convention.

No mention is made of availability of reservations. No reservations have been entered.

The Convention provides for technical and scientific cooperation between Contracting Parties (exchange of information, inspections, covering product quality specifications, and production controls, etc.).

Implementation and information

In application of Article 9 (2), the Convention entered into force ninety days after the deposit of the fifth instrument of ratification on 26 May 1971.

Contracting Parties have accepted the following commitments:
- to provide information on both general and specific manufacturing practices of a particular firm (based on an official inspection) upon request from another Party (Articles 2 and 3)
- to communicate any potential dangers uncovered during an inspection (Article 5)
- to ensure inspections are conducted in accordance with certain procedures by adequately empowered agencies and competent inspectors (Part II)
- to meet at least annually to improve standards of good manufacturing practice, achieve better inspections, promote cooperation and mutual training of inspectors and improve implementation of the convention (taking into account current developments and work in other international organizations) (Part IV)

The Convention is based on mutual acceptance of the respective inspection systems of Contracting States.

There is no specific dispute resolution mechanism. Explanatory note 11 (annexed to the convention as an "integral part", Article 13) indicates that Parties should resolve their differences through informal discussions.

The languages of the Convention are English and French. The EFTA Secretariat has issued a bilingual text with explanatory notes and regularly issues updates lists of competent national authorities designated under Article 9. The annual reports by the committee of officials provide current information on the convention's implementation and are distributed to all signatories and acceding States.

Operation, review and adjustment

The Swedish government is the depositary for the Convention. Secretariat services have been provided by the EFTA Secretariat.

According to Article 8 (1), officials of the competent authorities shall meet whenever necessary but at least once a year. The committee's tasks are to exchange views on experience and methods of achieving effective inspections, to promote the training in common of inspectors, and to make recommendations on matters relating to the implementation of the convention. They also ensure that scientific knowledge is taken into account in policy-making decisions.

Officials of the competent authorities of Contracting Parties may propose amendments and make recommendations on any question relating to the implementation of this convention. No amendments are currently envisaged.

(99) Convention on the Prohibition of the Development, Production, and Stockpiling of Bacteriological (Biological) and Toxic Weapons and on their Destruction
(London, Moscow, Washington, 10 April 1972)

Objectives and achievement

According to its preamble, its objective is to prohibit the development of biological weapons and eliminate them, as a step towards general disarmament for the sake of all mankind.

Participation

Membership is open to all States. As of 1 January 1992, there were 117 Parties to the Convention including 84 from developing countries. No reservations are possible.

Subsequent negotiations on the biological weapons convention were conducted at the conference of the committee on disarmament (CCD) 1969-1978. Developing countries such as Argentina, Brazil, Iraq, Nigeria and others participated at this conference. Forty-five developing countries participated at the 3rd review conference of the convention held in Geneva in September 1991.

Implementation and information

In accordance with Article 14 (3), this Convention entered into force on 26 March 1975, after the deposit of instruments of ratification by twenty-two governments, including the governments designated as depositories of the convention.

Commitments imposed upon parties by the Biological Weapons Convention are as follows:

1. "Each State Party to this Convention undertakes to destroy, or to divert to peaceful purposes, as soon as possible but no later than nine months after the entry into force of the Convention, all agents, toxins, weapons, equipment and means of delivery specified in Article I of the Convention, which are in its possession or under its jurisdiction or control. In implementing the provisions of this Article all necessary safety precautions shall be observed to protect populations and the environment." Article II

2. "Each State Party to this Convention undertakes not to transfer to any recipient whatsoever, directly or indirectly, and not in any way to assist, encourage, or induce any State, group of States or international organizations to manufacture or otherwise acquire any of the agents, toxins, weapons, equipment or means of delivery specified in Article I of the Convention." Article III

3. "Each State Party to this Convention affirms the recognized objective of effective prohibition of chemical weapons and, to this end, undertakes to continue negotiations in good faith with a view to reaching early agreement on effective measures for the prohibition of their development, production and stockpiling and for their destruction, and on appropriate measures concerning

equipment and means of delivery specifically designed for the production or use of chemical agents for weapons purposes." Article IX

4.   "(1) The States Parties to this Convention undertake to facilitate, and have the right to participate in, the fullest possible exchange of equipment, materials and scientific and technological information for the use of bacteriological (biological) agents and toxins for peaceful purposes. Parties to the Convention in a position to do so shall also cooperate in contributing individually or together with other States or international organizations to the further development and application of scientific discoveries in the field of bacteriology (biology) for the prevention of disease, or for other peaceful purposes.

(2) This Convention shall be implemented in a manner designed to avoid hampering the economic or technological development of States Parties to the Convention or international cooperation in the field of peaceful bacteriological (biological) activities, including the international exchange of bacteriological (biological) agents and toxins and equipment for the processing, use or production of bacteriological (biological) agents and toxins for peaceful purposes in accordance with the provisions of the Convention." Article X

Problems relating to the objective or the application of the convention can be solved either by bilateral consultations or by consultations undertaken through "appropriate" international procedures within the framework of the United Nations and in accordance with its charter (Article 5)

Any State Party which has reason to believe that any other State Party is acting in breach of obligations deriving from the provisions of the convention, may lodge a complaint with the United Nations Security Council. Such a complaint should include all possible evidence confirming its validity. Each state party undertakes to cooperate in carrying out any investigation which the Security Council may initiate on the basis of the complaint. The Security Council shall inform the States Parties of the results of the investigation. (Article 6 [1] and [2])

The biological weapons convention has been adopted in English, Russian, French, Spanish, and Chinese. (Article 15)

Current information on the operation and implementation of this Convention is prepared by both the Secretariat and the United Nations Institute for Disarmament Research and distributed to States Parties, governments, and relevant international institutes and organizations.

Operation, review and adjustment

The secretariat for this Convention is provided by the Disarmament Affairs Division of the United Nations.

At any time after the entry into force of the Convention, any Contracting Party may propose amendments. If the majority of the State Parties accept the amendments, amendments shall enter into force for each Party accepting them and thereafter for each remaining State Party on the date of acceptance by it. (Article 11)

Pursuant to Article 12 of this Convention, review conferences are held every five years to ensure that the purposes of the Convention are being realized, taking into account new scientific and technological developments relevant to the Convention. Since this Convention came into force, three such review conferences have been held (in 1980, 1986, and 1991).

Codification programming

Currently under preparation is the drafting and negotiation of a complementary chemical weapons convention.

The remaining gaps that need to be covered by legal provisions include a system of safeguards concerning end-use; enhanced transparency and openness in the implementation of the Convention; confidence-building measures; a verification system as a means to improve the effectiveness of the Convention; improvement of the dispute resolution procedure and clearer definitions of certain terms in the Convention such as "biological agents" and "weapons, equipment or means of delivery" and "other peaceful purposes."

322

(100) OECD Recommendations on Mutual Acceptance of Data in the Assessment of Chemicals and Good Laboratory Practices
(1981 and 1989)

Objectives and achievement

Objectives are to encourage the generation and mutual acceptance of valid, high quality scientific data on the safety of chemicals by means of uniform testing guidelines and principles of good laboratory practice, protect public health and safety, increase ability to share information and thereby minimize costs, improve harmonization of chemicals control, and avoid technical barriers to trade.

The Recommendations do not refer to the special circumstances of developing countries.

Participation

These are regional instruments adopted by the Council of the Organization for Economic Cooperation and Development (OECD). Membership consists of 19 western European States, Australia, Canada, Japan, New Zealand, and the United States. None are developing countries. Reservations are possible, in the form of abstentions noted at the time of adoption; this possibility has been used with regard to several of the instruments listed below.

Implementation and information

By decision of 12 May 1981, the OECD Council recommended application of the OECD Guideline for the Testing of Chemicals set forth in Annex 1 of the Decision and the principles of Good Laboratory Practice (GLP) set forth in Annex 2 of the decision, followed by a Council Recommendation of 26 July 1983 concerning the mutual recognition of compliance with GLP, and a supplementary Council Decision Recommendation of 2 October 1989 which canceled and replaced the 1983 Recommendation.

The 1989 Decision Recommendation laid down in Part I the procedures to be followed relative to monitoring of compliance with the GLP principles. In essence, it states that member countries shall establish national procedures for monitoring compliance with GLP principles, designate an authority or authorities to discharge the functions required by the procedures for monitoring compliance, and require that the management of the test facilities issue a declaration that the test was carried out in accordance with Good Laboratory Practices.

The Council recommended further that in developing and implementing national procedures for monitoring compliance with GLP principles, member countries apply the "Guides for Compliance Monitoring Procedure for Good Laboratory Practice" and the "Guidance for the Conduct of Laboratory Inspections and Study Audits," set out respectively in Annexes I and II of this Decision-Recommendation.

A second part of the Council Act sets out decisions related to recognition of GLP compliance assurance among Member countries. Member countries are requested to designate authority for international liaison and to exchange information relevant to national compliance monitoring procedures.

OECD Council instruments are published in English and French, and distributed by the OECD Secretariat, which has also published comprehensive collections and monographs on environment-related instruments.

Operation, review and adjustment

The OECD Secretariat ensures the administration of these instruments, with guidance from the Environment Committee and the Chemical Management Committee. The costs of the international administration are covered by the general budget of OECD whereas the costs of national implementation measures are borne by Member States.

Part III of the decision of 2 October 1989 instructs the Management Committee of the Special Programme on the Control of Chemicals, in collaboration with the Chemicals Group of the Environment Committee, to ensure that the guidance materials in the Annexes are kept up to date. This committee also facilitates internationally-harmonized approaches to assure compliance with GLP practices through the Panel on GLP comprising representation of material monitoring authorities and reports periodically to the Council.

Related OECD Council Instruments include: Decision-Recommendation on Protection of the Environment by Control of Polychlorinated Biphenyls (1973); Decision on Minimum Pre-Marketing Set of Data in Assessment of Chemicals (1982); Decision-Recommendation on Further Measures for the Protection of the Environment by Control of Polychlorinated Biphenyls (1987); Decision-Recommendation on the Systematic Investigation of Existing Chemicals (1987); Decision-Recommendation on the Co-operative Investigation and Risk Reduction of Existing Chemicals (1991).

(101) International Code of Conduct on the Distribution and Use of Pesticides

(Rome, 19 November 1985) as amended in 1989

Objectives and achievement

The objective of the code is to promote practices which ensure efficient and safe use of pesticides while minimizing health and environmental concerns regarding such use, establish responsible and generally accepted trade practices, assist countries which have not established controls designed to regulate the quality and suitability of pesticide products needed in that country and to ensure that pesticides are used effectively for the improvement of agricultural production and of human, animal, and plant health.

Technical assistance can be provided to developing countries by pesticides exporting governments and international organizations to train personnel in the interpretation and evolution of test data regarding pesticides.

Participation

The Code establishes voluntary standards of conduct, and there is no membership. It addresses international organizations, governments of exporting and importing countries, industry, including manufacturers, trade associations, formulators and distributors, users, public-sector organizations such as environmental groups, consumer groups, and trade unions.

Developing countries have played a significant role in the development of the code through participation in meetings of expert panels, government consultations, and national and regional workshop held by FAO.

The incentives available to developing countries are the promotion of the safe and efficient use of pesticides through the implementation of bilateral and regional projects. Under these projects, countries receive training of personnel, expertise, and equipment for the effective control of pesticides. Under the prior informed consent clause, countries will receive information on pesticides that are banned or severely restricted.

Implementation and information

The code was adopted by the 23rd FAO conference in 1985 by consensus and adapted in 1989 to include the principle of prior informed consent (PIC). After the 25th conference, FAO and UNEP initiated a joint program on the implementation of PIC.

There is no actual compliance monitoring or enforcement, but implementation required a preparatory phase which involved the appointment of designated national authorities (DNA's) by their respective governments and development of a joint database on banned and severely restricted pesticides and other chemicals. Compliance with the code by governments and industry has been the subject of several surveys and reports both by the FAO secretariat (based on a questionnaire circulated to governments in 1986, with an analysis of responses published in 1989, FAO doc. AGP:GC/89/BP.1), and by non-governmental and industry organizations in 1987, 1988 and 1989.

The FAO and UNEP have established a joint expert group on prior informed consent. The function of the group is to provide advice and guidance for the implementation of PIC, to review Decision Guidance Documents (DGD) and other technical matters. Meetings of the group were held in December 1989, October 1990, June 1991 and February 1992.

The code has been published in the following languages: English, French, Spanish, Chinese, and Arabic. It has been distributed to all countries through their respective Embassies, through FAO representatives, and during meetings and workshops on pesticides held in various regions.

The current information on the operation and implementation of the code is made through reports to the FAO conferences and reports of meetings and workshops which are published and sent to various governments.

In the implementation of PIC, FAO jointly with UNEP has published "Guidance for Governments" document. In addition, FAO has published "Decision Guidance Document" for each pesticide in the PIC procedure, while UNEP has published similar documents on industrial and consumer chemicals. Information is also provided through training courses, workshops, and meetings.

Operation, review and adjustment

The provisions of the code are being implemented through FAO which is the Secretariat to the code, in close collaboration with other UN agencies including UNEP, WHO/IPCS and GATT, and with other organizations such as OECD, CEC, CEFIC, CMA, GIFAP, and IOCU. Implementation is also carried out through regional and bilateral projects in individual countries.

The annual (1990) costs of international administration is approximately U.S. 500,000 dollars. This is borne by FAO's regular budget. However, additional funds are available for technical assistance.

The main benefits from national participation is the effective implementation and use of pesticide control without significant adverse effects on people or the environments.

The provisions of the code and progress in its implementation are reviewed regularly by the various panels of experts appointed to deal with specific topics on pesticides. This also includes the joint FAO/UNEP panel of experts which specifically deals with PIC.

(102) UNEP London Guidelines for the Exchange of Information on Chemicals in International Trade
(adopted by UNEP Governing Council Decision 14/27 of 17 June 1987) as amended in 1989

Objectives and achievements

The Guidelines are addressed to governments with a view to assisting them in the process of increasing chemical safety in all countries through the exchange of scientific, technical, economic, and legal information on potentially harmful chemicals in international trade. Special provisions have been included regarding the exchange of information on banned or severely restricted chemicals in international trade, which call for co-operation between exporting and importing countries in the light of their joint responsibility for the protection of human health and the environment at the global level.

Although the Guidelines were not prepared specifically to address the situation of developing countries, they nevertheless provide a framework for the establishment of procedures for the effective use of information on hazardous chemicals in these countries.

The Guidelines have already affected and influenced national practice and the work of various international organizations (e.g. FAO, UNEP).

Participation

This set of Guidelines is addressed to all Governments. As of January 1992, 110 countries had indicated their intention to participate by appointing designated national authorities (DNA). Developing countries played a substantial role in both negotiating and amending the Guidelines. Financial incentives from both UNEP and some individual countries encouraged such participation.

Implementation and information

The Guidelines are global and non-mandatory. Under the general principles of the Guidelines, the participating countries accept the following commitments:
- to establish and strengthen their infrastructure dealing with chemicals control, e.g. creation of national registers of toxic chemicals;
- to participate in a general information exchange system on chemicals; and
- to participate in a notification procedure related to trade in banned or severely restricted chemicals (prior informed consent, PIC).

Implementation of the guidelines is the responsibility of the UNEP International Register of Potentially Toxic Chemicals (IRPTC) in Geneva, in co-operation with FAO, OECD and the organizations participating in the International Programme on Chemical Safety (ILO, WHO). FAO and UNEP have established a joint programme for the operation of the PIC procedure, which is also part of the related FAO International Code of Conduct on the Distribution and Use of Pesticides (No.101).

The Guidelines make provision for technical, scientific, and financial assistance to developing countries and to countries that are in need of improved systems for the safe management of chemicals. In co-operation with the United Nations Institute for Training and

Research (UNITAR), the UNEP/IRPTC secretariat has launched a training programme for implementation of the guidelines, starting in the Asia/Pacific Region, and to be extended to the Latin American/Caribbean and African regions. FAO in cooperation with other international organizations has held regional workshops in Thailand, Philippines, New Caledonia, Chile, and Ghana, which included modules and case studies on PIC. FAO and UNEP have been active in the training of country officials on the operation of the PIC procedure.

The Guidelines are published separately in the six UN languages and distributed to all Governments as well as to the industries and non-governmental organizations concerned.

Additional materials providing guidance for implementation of the PIC procedure are published by UNEP/FAO. A data base for the operation of PIC has been developed. In September 1991, the first six Decision Guidance Documents on Pesticides were distributed to all governments.

Operation, review and adjustment

The 1990 costs of administration by the UNEP/IRPTC secretariat were approximately U.S. 400,000 dollars.

The UNEP Governing Council at its 16th Session in May 1991 recommended that UNEP continue developing model national legislation to assist in the implementation of the amended Guidelines, and work on strengthening the legal basis of the Guidelines.

(103) Basel Convention on the Control of Transboundary Movements of Hazardous Wastes and their Disposal
(Basel, 22 March 1989)

Objectives and achievement

The objective of the Convention is to set up obligations for parties with a view to (a) reducing transboundary movements of wastes subject to the Basel Convention to a minimum consistent with the environmentally sound and efficient management of such wastes and controlling any permitted transboundary movement under the terms of the convention (b) minimizing the amount of hazardous wastes generated and ensuring their environmentally sound management (including disposal and recovery operations) as close as possible to the source of generation, and (c) assisting developing countries in environmentally sound management of the hazardous and other wastes they generate.

This convention, following the Cairo Guidelines and Principles of UNEP adopted by GC in 1987, for the Environmentally Sound Management of Hazardous Waste, recognizes the need to promote the transfer of technology particularly to developing countries. In respect of this convention, Decisions 14/16 and 15/33 of the Governing Council of UNEP also promote the transfer of environmental protection technology to developing countries.

Participation

Membership is open to States and political and/or economic integration organizations. As of 1 January 1992, 53 states and EEC had signed the convention. Eighteen countries had ratified, eleven of which were developing countries.

No reservations are possible. However, declarations have been made in certain ratification instruments in accordance with Article 26 (2).

Technical and scientific cooperation between Parties and co-operation between Parties and the competent international organizations are encouraged, for the purposes of exchange of information, planning, education, etc. Developing countries participated and played a prominent role in the drafting of this convention.

Implementation and information

In accordance with Article 25 (1), the convention shall enter into force on the 90th day after the date of deposit of the twentieth instrument of ratification; i.e. on 5 May 1992.

Commitments of Parties to the Convention include various general obligations of the Parties (under Article 4) such as the designation of a competent authority and focal point. The obligations also include a duty of the Parties to re-import, transmit certain information and cooperate with each other in order to improve and achieve environmentally sound management of hazardous wastes and other wastes.

Compliance monitoring and enforcement has not yet begun because the convention is not in force. Available compliance mechanisms include information and decisions taken at the conference of the parties, obligations of the Secretariat, and verification provisions (Article 15, 16 and 19).

Article 13 provides for transmission of information. This procedure serves as a compulsory reporting mechanism. The States Parties to the convention inform each other through the Secretariat of the measures they have adopted to ensure its application. The information is then transmitted to the Conference of the Parties established under Article 15 of the Convention.

Settlement of disputes should be done through negotiation or any other peaceful means of the choice of the parties to the dispute. If the dispute cannot be settled by such peaceful means, the dispute, if the Parties agree, shall be submitted to the ICJ or to arbitration under the conditions set out in annex IV on arbitration.

The capability of developing countries to implement the technical and financial aspects of this Convention is limited and therefore assistance in these areas will be essential.

Mechanisms and subsidiary bodies may become necessary taking into consideration the extremely specialized and technical nature of this Convention. Resolution 1 makes provision for the establishment of an Ad hoc working group to consider the necessity of establishing mechanisms for the implementation of this Convention.

The Convention has been published in all official UN languages and distributed to all governments. The interim Secretariat currently distributes current status information of the convention. Added obligations of the Secretariat are contained in the provisions of Article 16.

Additional material to provide guidance for the implementation of this Convention has been made available by UNEP by the publication of two booklets, summarizing the Convention and explaining its importance to African countries in particular. UNEP has also prepared draft model national legislation related to the convention. Training workshops on implementation of the Convention are being set up. The interim Secretariat is endeavoring to explain and describe the convention at various conferences and meetings with national officials.

Operation, review and adjustment

The Secretary General of the United Nations is the depositary of this Convention. UNEP currently administers the convention through the Secretariat in Geneva. The number of staff increased from 2 to 3 persons in 1991. Governments who signed the Final Act of the Basel Convention called upon themselves (Resolution 6) to provide UNEP with voluntary contributions to support the operation of the ISBC. The cost of administration in 1990 was US$ 691,305 using US$ 375,514 of voluntary contributions from individual countries and US$ 315,791 from the UNEP Environment Fund. The Parties' financial contributions will be established at the first Conference of the Parties to be held after the entry into force of the convention. The issue of a trust fund to assist developing countries in the event of a waste emergency should also be discussed at that time within the scope of both resolutions 1 and 3.

Article 15 provides the mechanism to ensure review and adjustment of the Convention requiring Conferences of the Parties. Any such adjustment or review must take scientific, technical, economic and environmental information into consideration.

Codification programming

The Basel Conference adopted a set of resolutions addressing the need to strengthen the Basel Convention regime through the adoption of additional legal instruments or strengthening already existing ones. The work undertaken for the implementation of these resolutions to be presented to the first Conference of the Contracting Parties can be summarized as follows:

-       Resolution I (Mechanism for the implementation of the Convention). This resolution was adopted at the Basel Conference in order to concretise the delegation set out in Article 15, paragraphs 5 (c) of the Convention by accelerating the implementation of this provision which allow the Conference of the Parties to establish such subsidiary bodies as one deemed necessary for the implementation of the Convention. Based on the replies received from the States in response to a letter addressed to them from the Executive Director of UNEP, a document containing a set of proposals will be considered by a meeting which will take place in Geneva from 24 to 26 February 1992. The meeting will recommend to the Conference of the States Parties the needed mechanisms and subsidiary bodies.

-       Resolution 2 (Relationship of the Basel Convention and the London Dumping Convention). The London Dumping Convention Consultative meeting, adopted since 1990. Several resolution containing measures to control and prevent the dumping of hazardous waste at sea in light of the provisions of the Basel Convention. By the adoption of these measures, Resolution 2 of the Basel Conference is considered to be implemented.

-       Resolution 3 (Liability and compensation). This resolution reflects the provision of Article 12 of the Convention which states that "The Parties shall co-operate with a view to adopting, as soon as practicable, a protocol setting out appropriate rules and procedures in the field of liability and compensation for damage resulting from the transboundary movement and disposal of hazardous wastes and other wastes".

        In order to implement this resolution, the Executive Director of UNEP has established an ad hoc working group which has finalized its work by recommending to the first meeting of the Conference of the Parties elements which might be included in a protocol on liability and compensation. Such elements provide for a comprehensive regime to ensure adequate and prompt compensation, promote the protection of human health and environment. A study on the establishment of a fund for compensation is at present undertaken by ISBC in order to be presented with the elements of the protocol to the first conference as requested by the Ad hoc Working Group.

-       Resolution 5 (Harmonization of the procedures of the Basel Convention and the code of practice for international transaction involving nuclear wastes). In order to implement this resolution, ISBC has been co-ordinating with the IAEA for the preparation of the code of practice. This code which was adopted in October 1990 by the General Conference of the IAEA affirms the general principles and objectives of the Basel Convention namely the sovereign right of every State to prohibit the movement of waste into, from or through its territory. The code requires that transboundary movements of radioactive waste should only take place in accordance with internationally accepted safety standards, with prior notification consent of the sending, receiving and transit states.

-       Resolution 7 (Co-operation between IMO and UNEP in the review of existing rules, regulation and practices with respect to transport of hazardous wastes at sea). IMO subcommittees on the carriage of dangerous goods and on containers and cargoes, in consultation with ISBC, have taken additional measures in respect of reviewing the existing rules, regulations and practices with respect to the transport of hazardous wastes by sea in the light of the Basel Convention. Also the amendment of the IMDG code is envisaged in order to ensure that the provisions of the Basel Convention are being taken adequately into account.

- <u>Resolution 8</u> (the elaboration of technical guidelines for the environmentally sound management of wastes subject to the Basel Convention). Work is also undertaken on the preparation of technical guidelines for the environmentally sound management of wastes. A set of principles, parameters and matrixes with commentaries have been developed by an informal consultative group in co-operation with the ISBC Secretariat. Their aim is to provide guidance to the competent authority in evaluating the environmental soundness of the disposal option(s) presented in the notification form (as called in the Basel Convention) and in making of the decision to consent to or reject a transboundary movement.

This set of principles, parameters and matrixes should be finalized in a meeting to be held in February 1992 in order to be presented to the first meeting of the contracting Parties of the Basel Convention. Also elements of possible international strategy and action programme for the environmentally sound management of hazardous waste was prepared by ISBC Secretariat and was considered by an <u>ad hoc</u> meeting of Government designated experts in December 1991.

Co-ordination is also taking place with UNEP Regional Seas Programme, Antarctic Convention, UNCED and GATT on trade issues.

(104) Convention on the Ban of the Import into Africa and the Control of Transboundary Movements and Management of Hazardous Wastes within Africa
(Bamako, 30 January 1991)

Objectives and achievement

The objective of the Convention is to prohibit the import of all hazardous wastes, for any reason, into Africa and to control the transboundary movement of such wastes generated in Africa. (Article 4)

This Convention takes into account the special circumstances of developing countries in Africa.

Participation

The Convention is open to member States of the Organization of African Unity (OAU). The OAU is made up of fifty-one African states and all are developing countries. The African Heads of States, the OAU Council of Ministers, and their representatives and delegates have played a prominent role in the drafting of, and the participation in the convention.

No reservations may be made to this Convention. (Article 26)

Implementation and information

In accordance with Article 25 (1), the Convention shall enter into force on the 19th day after the date of deposit of the tenth instrument of ratification from Parties signatory to this Convention. It is still not in force.

Commitments of Parties to the Convention include various general obligations including the adoption of precautionary measures which entail, inter alia, prevention of the release into the environment of substances which may cause harm to humans or the environment, without waiting for scientific proof regarding such harm. These precautionary measures also include the application of clean production methods (Article 4) which means "production of industrial systems which avoid, or eliminate the generation of hazardous wastes and hazardous products in conformity with Article 4, section 3 (f) and (g) of this convention."

Further obligations are the designation of a competent authority, focal point and a dumpwatch (Article 5), transboundary movement and notification procedures (Article 6), duty to re-import (Article 8), inter-Africa and international cooperation (Article 10 and 11).

Article 13 provides for transmission of information. This procedure serves as a compulsory reporting mechanism. Furthermore, the States Parties to the Convention inform each other through the Secretariat of the measures they have adopted to ensure its application. The information is then transmitted to the Conference of the Parties established under Article 15 of the Convention.

Compliance monitoring and enforcement has not yet begun because the convention is not yet in force.

Article 20 of the convention concerns the settlement of disputes about the interpretation or application or compliance with this convention, through negotiations and subsequent submission to the International Court of Justice or arbitration to be carried out under the procedure set out in Annex V of the Convention.

Although this Convention is not yet in force, factors such as financial resources, technical assistance, scientific resources, and the role of parliaments, industries, NGOs and public opinion are likely to influence its implementation.

The languages of the Convention are Arabic, English, French, and Portuguese.

The Secretariat distributes to the Parties reports and current status information on the convention. After entry into force, the Secretariat has additional obligations found in Article 16 of the Convention including the preparation and transmission of reports. The interim Secretariat now provides information and guidance on specific questions from countries.

Operation, review and adjustment

The Secretary-General of the Organization of African Unity, who is the depository of the convention, ensures its administration, through the ESCAS department which is acting as its interim Secretariat in Addis Ababa. The cost is covered by the budget of the OAU.

The scale of financial contributions to the convention by the Parties will be established at the first Conference of the Parties held after entry into force of this convention. The issue of a revolving fund, to assist in the event of waste emergencies, and the funding for the establishment of centers for training and technological transfers regarding the management of hazardous wastes and the minimization of generation will also be discussed at that time. (Article 14)

In accordance with Article 15 of the Convention, future review of the Convention by the Conference of the Parties must take into consideration available, scientific, technical, economic and environmental information.

STATUS OF RATIFICATIONS AS OF 1 JANUARY 1992

GLOBAL INSTRUMENTS   (Treaty numbers see page 309)

Parties	98	99	103
Afghanistan		x	
Albania			
Algeria			
Angola			
Antigua & Barbuda			
Argentina		x	x
Australia		x	
Austria	x	x	
Bahamas		x	
Bahrain		x	
Bangladesh		x	
Barbados		x	
Belarus*		x	
Belgium	x	x	
Belize		x	
Benin		x	
Bhutan		x	
Bolivia		x	
Botswana			
Brazil		x	
Brunei Darussalam		x	
Bulgaria		x	
Burkina Faso		x	
Burundi			
Cambodia		x	
Cameroon			
Canada		x	
Cape Verde		x	
Central African Republic			
Chad			
Chile		x	
China		x	x
Colombia		x	
Cook Islands			
Comoros			
Congo		x	
Costa Rica		x	
Cote d'Ivoire			
Cuba		x	
Cyprus		x	
Czech & Slovak Fed. Rep.		x	x

Parties	98	99	103
Democr. People's Rep. of Korea		x	
Denmark	x	x	
Djibouti			
Dominica			
Dominican Republic		x	
Ecuador		x	
Egypt			
El Salvador			x
Equatorial Guinea		x	
Estonia*			
Ethiopia		x	
Fiji		x	
Finland	x	x	x
France		x	x
Gabon			
Gambia			
Germany	x	x	
Ghana		x	
Greece		x	
Grenada		x	
Guatemala		x	
Guinea			
Guinea-Bissau		x	
Guyana			
Haiti			
Holy See			
Honduras		x	
Hungary	x	x	x
Iceland	x	x	
India		x	
Indonesia			
Iran (Islamic Republic of)		x	
Iraq		x	
Ireland	x	x	
Israel			
Italy	x	x	
Jamaica		x	
Japan		x	
Jordan		x	x
Kenya		x	
Kiribati			
Kuwait		x	
Lao People's Democratic Rep.		x	
Latvia*			

Parties	98	99	103
Lebanon		x	
Lesotho		x	
Liberia			
Libyan Arab Jamahiriya		x	
Liechtenstein	x	x	
Lithuania*			
Luxembourg		x	
Madagascar			
Malawi			
Malaysia			
Maldives			
Mali			
Malta		x	
Marshall Islands			
Mauritania			
Mauritius		x	
Mexico		x	x
Micronesia			
Monaco			
Mongolia		x	
Morocco			
Mozambique			
Myanmar			
Namibia			
Nauru			
Nepal			
Netherlands		x	
New Zealand		x	
Nicaragua		x	
Niger		x	
Nigeria		x	x
Niue			
Norway	x	x	x
Oman			
Pakistan		x	
Palau			
Panama		x	x
Papua New Guinea		x	
Paraguay		x	
Peru		x	
Philippines		x	
Poland		x	
Portugal	x	x	
Qatar		x	

Parties	98	99	103
Republic of Korea		x	
Republic of Yemen		x	
Romania	x	x	x
Rwanda		x	
St. Kitts & Nevis		x	
St. Lucia		x	
St. Vincent & the Grenadines			
Samoa			
San Marino		x	
Sao Tome & Principe		x	
Saudi Arabia		x	x
Senegal		x	
Seychelles		x	
Sierra Leone		x	
Singapore		x	
Solomon Islands		x	
Somalia			
South Africa		x	
Spain		x	
Sri Lanka		x	
Sudan			
Suriname			
Swaziland		x	
Sweden	x	x	x
Switzerland	x	x	x
Syrian Arab Republic			x
Thailand		x	
Togo		x	
Tonga		x	
Trinidad & Tobago			
Tunisia		x	
Turkey		x	
Tuvalu			
Uganda			
Ukraine*		x	
Union of Soviet Socialist Rep.*		x	
United Arab Emirates			
United Kingdom	x	x	
United Republic of Tanzania			
United States of America		x	
Uruguay		x	x
Vanuatu			
Venezuela		x	
Viet Nam		x	

Parties	98	99	103
Yugoslavia*		x	
Zaire		x	
Zambia			
Zimbabwe		x	

* Membership status subject to further clarification.

REGIONAL INSTRUMENTS

(96) <u>European Agreement Concerning the International Carriage of Dangerous Goods by Road</u> (Geneva 1957)

Austria
Belgium
Czech & Slovak Fed. Rep.
Denmark
Finland
France
Germany
Greece
Hungary
Italy

Luxembourg
Netherlands
Norway
Poland
Portugal
Spain
Sweden
Switzerland
United Kingdom
Yugoslavia*

(97) <u>European Agreement on the Restriction of the Use of Certain Detergents in Washing and Cleaning Products</u> (Strasbourg 1968)

Belgium
Denmark
France
Germany
Italy

Luxembourg
Netherlands
Spain
Switzerland
United Kingdom

CHAPTER VIII

NUCLEAR SAFETY

<u>Maria Rita Mazzanti</u>

This chapter covers the following agreements and instruments on nuclear safety, in chronological order:

(105)   1955 UNGA Resolution 913 (X) establishing the **Scientific Committee on the Effects of Atomic Radiation** (UNSCEAR);

(106)   the 1963 Moscow **Treaty Banning Nuclear Weapon Tests in the Atmosphere;**

(107)   the 1967 Tlatelolco **Treaty for the Prohibition of Nuclear Weapons in Latin America;**

(108)   the 1985 **South Pacific Nuclear-Free Zone Treaty;** and

(109)   the 1986 IAEA **Conventions on Early Notification of a Nuclear Accident,** and on **Assistance in the Case of a Nuclear Accident or Radiological Emergency.**

Agreements concerning liability for nuclear damage and bilateral agreements regarding nuclear emergencies are addressed in chapters X and XII.

A list showing the status of ratifications as of 1 January 1992 is annexed (pages 357-361).

(105) United Nations General Assembly Resolution 913 (X) Establishing the Scientific Committee on the Effects of Atomic Radiation (UNSCEAR)
(3 December 1955)

Objectives and achievements

The basic objective of the Resolution is to collect and interpret all available scientific data on the effects of ionizing radiation on man and his environment, including assessment of radiation levels and exposures from both natural and man-made sources, and to report on these evaluations to the General Assembly and the world community.

The Resolution is global in scope. There is no reference to the special circumstances of developing countries.

In compliance with its mandate, UNSCEAR has reviewed the radiation levels to which the world population is or may be exposed and on the effects and risks that could derive from such exposures; based on reports received from Member States of the United Nations and from specialized agencies. Between 1958 and 1988 the Committee prepared ten reports, namely 1958, 1962, 1966, 1969, 1972, 1977, 1982, 1986 and 1988 Reports. The reports are developed at annual sessions of the Committee based on working papers prepared by the Secretariat. Consultants appointed by the Secretary-General assist in the preparation of the text of the reports and scientific annexes.

Participation

The Scientific Committee originally consisted of the following countries: Argentina, Australia, Belgium, Brazil, Canada, Czechoslovakia, Egypt, France, India, Japan, Mexico, Sweden, the United Kingdom, the United States and the Union of Soviet Socialist Republics. Each country is represented by one scientist designated by the respective Government.

The membership of the Committee was subsequently enlarged by the U.N. General Assembly in its resolution 3154 (XXVII) to include Germany, Indonesia, Peru, Poland and Sudan. By resolution 41/62B the General Assembly further increased the membership of the Committee to a maximum of 21 and invited the People's Republic of China to become a member.

Specialist scientists of 21 States, including 9 developing countries attended the sessions of the Committee between 1977 to 1991.

According to its mandate, UNSCEAR shall:
a) receive and assemble reports on observed levels of ionizing radiation and on scientific observations relevant to the effects of ionizing radiation on man and environment provided by the States Members of the United Nations or members of the specialized agencies;
b) recommend uniform standards with respect to procedures for sample collection etc.;
c) compile and assemble in an integrated manner the various reports
d) review and evaluate national reports
e) make yearly progress reports and develop a summary report
f) transmit from time to time the documents and evaluations to the Secretary-General.

All States and specialized agencies are called upon to co-operate in making information and data available.

Implementation and information

Reports have been officially transmitted by Governments to the Committee. Between 1977 and 1988, the Committee received reports from the following countries: Argentina, Belgium, France, Germany, Japan, Switzerland, the USSR, the United Kingdom and the United States. In 1990 the Committee decided that it would no longer be necessary to maintain the system of official reports since the reports were now more generally available.

The main text of the Committee's reports is submitted to the UN General Assembly and published in the Official Records of the General Assembly in the UN six official languages. The full reports, including the scientific annexes, are issued as United Nations sales publications. This practice is intended to achieve wider dissemination of the Committee finding.

The following reports have been published to date:
- Ionizing Radiation: Levels and Effects, 1972, E.72.IX.17 & 18;
- Sources and Effects of Ionizing Radiation, 1977, E.77.IX.1;
- Ionizing Radiation: Sources and Biological Effects, 1982, E82.IX.8;
- Genetic and Somatic Effects of Ionizing Radiation, 1986, E.86.IX 9;
- Sources, Effects and Risks of Ionizing Radiation, 1988, E.88.IX.7;
- Radiation: Doses, Effects, Risks, UNEP: Blackwell 1991.

Operation, review and adjustment

The UNSCEAR Secretariat is located in Vienna and since 1974 has been linked administratively with the United Nations Environment Programme (UNEP). Costs are covered by the regular U.N. budget. Estimated requirements for the biennium 1992-1993 are US$ 1 million. Additional assistance and financial support for the preparation of some of the scientific annexes were offered to the Committee by various international and national organizations.

The work of the Committee is carried out in meetings of specialists scientists, who, in their capacity of official representatives or scientific advisers of national delegations, consider the papers prepared by the Secretariat. There are no possibilities to reduce the participation costs of developing countries.

Codification programming

The sessions of the Committee are attended by representatives of UNEP, WHO, FAO, IAEA, ICRP (International Commission of Radiological Protection) and ICRU (International Commission on Radiation Units and Measurements).

UNSCEAR has also contributed to the drafting of informal non-mandatory instruments, through its recommendations on international co-operation in developing safety regulations for handling, storing and transporting radioactive material.

342

(106) Treaty Banning Nuclear Weapon Tests in the Atmosphere, in Outer Space and Under Water
(Moscow, 5 August 1963)

Objectives and achievements

The Treaty prohibits all nuclear explosions, military or peaceful, in any environments - in the atmosphere, in outer space or under water - where an explosion could cause radioactive debris to be present outside the territory of the country conducting it. The Treaty does not cover underground testing, unless such explosions cause radioactive contamination.

The Treaty is global in scope. There is no reference to special circumstances of developing countries.

Although France and China are not parties to the Treaty, France announced in 1974 that it would refrain from conducting further atmospheric tests; China conducted its last atmospheric test in 1980; in March 1986, it confirmed that it would not conduct atmospheric tests in the future.

Participation

Article III paragraph 1 provides that the Treaty shall be open to all States. There are no provisions on reservation.

The Treaty was negotiated by the Soviet Union, the United Kingdom and the United States (the "Original Parties"). It was signed in Moscow on 5 August 1963 by the foreign ministers of these three States designated as depositaries of the Treaty. As of January 1992, 117 States were Parties to the Treaty, including 85 developing countries.

These are no special incentives to promote participation in the Treaty. Public opinion has been a major factor.

Implementation and information

Article III paragraph 3 provides that the Treaty shall enter into force after its ratification by the "Original Parties". The three "Original Parties" ratified the Treaty on 10 October 1963.

Each Contracting Party undertakes to prohibit, prevent and not to carry out any nuclear test explosion, or any other nuclear explosion, at any place under its jurisdiction or control:
a) in the atmosphere, beyond its limits, including outer space, or under water, including territorial waters or high seas; or
b) in any other environment if such explosion causes radioactive debris to be present outside the territorial limits of the State under whose jurisdiction or control such explosion is conducted (Article I).

The Treaty can be verified by national technical means without any need for on-site inspection. No nuclear tests in the atmosphere, in outer space or under water have been carried out by the Soviet Union, the United Kingdom and the United States since 1963. It is estimated that from 1963 to the end of 1990 the United States conducted 598 underground tests, the Soviet Union 464, and the United Kingdom 20.

There are no specific requirements of data supply. The Treaty does not contain any provision referring to settlement of disputes.

The original text is available in English and Russian (Article V). Texts, translations into other languages and related information material have been widely distributed, e.g., through the United Nations Department of Disarmament Affairs.

Operation, review and adjustment

The United Nations Department of Disarmament Affairs, at the request of the Parties, has provided <u>ad hoc</u> secretariat services in connection with the 1991 amendment conference. The costs of the amendment conference and the meeting for the organization of the conference were paid by all Parties on a cost-sharing basis.

While there are no provisions for participation in follow-up activities or periodic review, Article II provides that :
"1.   Any State may propose amendments to this Treaty. The text of any proposal shall be submitted to the Depositary Governments, which shall circulate it to all Parties to (the) Treaty. Thereafter, if requested to do so by one-third or more of the Parties, the Depositary Governments shall convene a conference, to which they shall invite all the
Parties, to consider such amendment."

Codification programming

At the request of one-third of the parties, the depositary Governments, in accordance with Article II, convened an amendment conference in New York from 7 to 18 January 1991 for the purpose of widening the scope of the treaty to include underground testing and compliance controls.   Of the 117 Parties, 100 (including 70 developing countries) participated. No amendments were adopted. Instead, a draft decision was submitted by Indonesia, Mexico, Nigeria, Peru, Philippines, Sri Lanka, United Republic of Tanzania, Venezuela and Yugoslavia (subsequently co-sponsored by Senegal). The Conference adopted the draft decision as orally revised by Mexico on behalf of the sponsors with 74 votes in favour, 2 against (United Kingdom and United States) and 19 abstentions, as follows;

"Acknowledging the complex and complicated nature of certain aspects of a comprehensive test-ban treaty, especially those with regard to verification of compliance and possible sanctions against non-compliance, the States parties were of the view that further work needed to be undertaken. Accordingly, they agreed to mandate the President of the Conference to conduct consultations with a view to achieving progress on those issues and resuming the work of the Conference at an appropriate time." (PTBT/CONF.13/Rev.1).

(107) Treaty for the Prohibition of Nuclear Weapons in Latin America
(Tlatelolco, 14 February 1967).

Objectives and achievement

The basic objectives of the Treaty are both regional and global. On the one hand, the Treaty was conceived to strengthen peace and security in the region, to prevent the possibility of nuclear-weapons race in the region and to protect the parties against possible nuclear attacks. On the other, it was designed to contribute to the prevention of the proliferation of nuclear weapons and as an important factor for general disarmament.

The Treaty consists of the Treaty proper and Additional Protocols I and II. Additional Protocol I refers to States outside Latin America which have de jure or de facto jurisdiction over territories within the limits of the geographical zone established in the Treaty. Additional Protocol II calls for all five nuclear weapons States to respect the statute of denuclearization of Latin America in respect of warlike purposes.

There is no reference to the special circumstances of developing countries.

Under Article 28 the Treaty enters into force when it has been signed and ratified by all States for which it is open, when Protocols I and II have been signed and ratified by all States concerned and when safeguards agreements have been concluded between the IAEA and the parties. As of 31 December 1990, safeguards agreements had been concluded between the IAEA and 19 States party to the Treaty, and with two States party to Additional Protocol I.

At present, only two agreements have been concluded solely on the basis of the Treaty of Tlatelolco; the other States party to the Treaty of Tlatelolco have concluded agreements pursuant to both the Non-Proliferation Treaty (NPT) and the Treaty of Tlatelolco. Two States with de jure or de facto international responsibility for territories within the zone of application of the Treaty have also concluded safeguards agreements, one of which is based solely on the Treaty of Tlatelolco, and the other concluded pursuant to both the NPT and the Treaty.

Participation

Membership is geographically restricted. Article 21 provides, inter alia, that the Treaty shall be open for signature by a) all the Latin American Republics and b) all other sovereign States situated in their entirety south of latitude 35 north in the western hemisphere.

The Treaty specifically stipulates that it "shall not be subject to reservation" (Article 27). However, the United Kingdom and the United States have reserved their right to reconsider their obligations with regard to a State in the nuclear-weapons-free zone in the event of any act of aggression or armed attack by that State, carried out with the support or assistance of a nuclear-weapon State. The USSR has made a similar reservation with regard to a party to the Treaty committing an act of aggression with the support of, or together with, a nuclear-weapon State.

The Treaty has been signed by 27 Latin American States, all of which are developing countries. Of these States, Argentina, which has signed the Treaty, has not yet ratified it, while Brazil and Chile, which have signed and ratified the Treaty, are not yet Parties to it as they have not so far made the declaration provided in Article 28, paragraph 2.

Additional Protocol I has been signed by all four countries which are, <u>de jure</u> or <u>de facto</u>, internationally responsible for territories which lie within the limits of the geographical zone established by the Treaty (France, the Netherlands, UK, USA). Three of them (the Netherlands, UK, USA) have also ratified this Protocol. All nuclear weapons States (China, France, UK, USSR, USA) have ratified Protocol II.

The proposal to establish a nuclear-weapon-free zone in Latin America had been initiated by Bolivia, Brazil, Chile and Ecuador at the 17th Session of the UN General Assembly in 1962, was elaborated by a preparatory commission of Latin American States and was the subject of subsequent resolutions of the General Assembly. All Latin American countries were involved in the drafting process.

Continuous diplomatic efforts have been made to promote wider participation in the Treaty. Public opinion in the region has played an important role in this respect.

Implementation and information

The Treaty enters into force, for those States which have ratified it, subject to the requirements set out in Article 28, paragraph 1, namely, that all the States included in the zone have acceded to the Treaty, that all the States concerned have acceded to the Additional Protocols and that safeguards agreements have been concluded with the IAEA. However, since these requirements might considerably delay the zone from coming into being, paragraph 2 of the same Article allows signatory States to waive there requirements, wholly or in part. Most signatories have actually done so.

The main obligations of the parties to the Treaty are defined in Article 1. The contracting parties undertake to use exclusively for peaceful purposes the nuclear material under their jurisdiction and to prohibit and prevent in their respective territories:

a)   the testing, use, manufacture, production or acquisition by any means of any nuclear weapon, by the parties themselves directly or indirectly, on behalf of anyone else, or in any other way;

b)   the receipt, storage, installation, deployment and any form of possession of any nuclear weapon, directly or indirectly, by the parties themselves directly or indirectly, on behalf of anyone else, or in any other way.

The Contracting Parties also undertake to refrain from engaging in, encouraging or authorizing, directly or indirectly, or in any way participating in the testing, use, manufacture, production, possession or control of any nuclear weapon. Further, Article 13 of the Treaty provides that "each Contracting Party shall negotiate ... agreements with the International Atomic Energy Agency for the application of its safeguards to its nuclear activities".

Under Protocol I the countries have agreed to undertake to apply the statute of denuclearization in respect of warlike purposes as defined in Article 1,3, 5 and 13 of the Treaty in territories for which, de jure or de facto, they are internationally responsible, and which lie within the limits of the geographical zone established in the Treaty.

Under Protocol II nuclear weapons States have agreed that:

a)   the statute of denuclearization of Latin America in respect of warlike purposes, as defined, delimited and set forth in the Tlatelolco Treaty shall be fully respected in all its expressed aims and provisions;

b)   they undertake not to contribute in any way to the performance of acts involving a violation of the obligations of Article 1 of the Treaty in the territories to which the Treaty applies;

c)   they undertake not to use or threaten to use nuclear weapons against the contracting parties of the Tlatelolco Treaty.

According to Article 14 of the Treaty, the Contracting Parties undertake to:

a)   submit to OPANAL and to the IAEA, for their information, semi-annual reports, stating that no activities prohibited under the Treaty has occurred in their respective territories;

b)   transmit simultaneously to OPANAL a copy of any report that they may submit to the IAEA which relates to matters that are subject to the Treaty and to the application of safeguards.

Further, Contracting Parties undertake to transmit to the Organization of American States, for its information, any report that may be of interest to it, in accordance with the obligations established by the Inter-American System. The Secretary General, with the authorization of the Council, may further request any Contracting Party to provide OPANAL with complementary or supplementary information (Article 15 paragraph 1).

Under the safeguards agreements signed with the IAEA, States party to the Treaty are required to provide IAEA with information concerning nuclear material subject to safeguards and the features of the facilities relevant to safeguarding such material. The IAEA requires only the minimum amount of information and data consistent with carrying out its responsibilities under the agreement.

According to Article 18, paragraphs 2 and 3, in case of nuclear explosions for peaceful purposes, States Parties undertake to notify OPANAL and IAEA of the date of the intended explosion; the nature of the nuclear device and the source from which it would be obtained; the place and purpose of the planned explosion; the proposed procedures for observation by OPANAL and IAEA; the expected force of the device and the fullest possible information on any radioactive fall-out that may result from the explosion, as well as other measures to be taken to avoid danger to the population, flora, fauna and territories of any other Party or Parties.

Articles 12, 13, 14, 15, 16 and 18 of the Treaty establish a strict control system, involving various organs of the permanent agency set up to insure strict compliance with the Treaty, the Agency for the Prohibition of Nuclear Weapons in Latin America (OPANAL), and the IAEA through the system of safeguards provided for in Article 13.

To promote compliance with the Treaty, three organs have been established:

a)   the General Conference, in which all the States Parties are represented and which meets every two years;

b)   the Council, composed of representatives of five States Parties, which meets continuously in Mexico City, the OPANAL Headquarters, at regular two-monthly intervals; and

c)   a Secretariat, which is responsible for coordinating the work of the two above-mentioned organs, for liaison, and for the distribution and exchange of information among member States.

The Treaty also creates a system of inspection to deal with suspected cases of violation of its provision and measures to be taken in the event of violation (Article 16).

In case of nuclear explosions for peaceful purposes, the General Secretary of OPANAL and the technical personnel designated by the Council of OPANAL and IAEA have unrestricted access to any area in the vicinity of the site of the explosion in order to ascertain whether the device and the procedure followed during the explosion are in conformity with the information supplied and the provisions of the Treaty (Article 18 paragraph 3).

Article 24 of the Treaty provides that unless the Parties agree on another mode of peaceful settlement, any questions or disputes concerning the interpretation or application of the Treaty shall be referred to the International Court of Justice.

The texts of the Treaty are available in Spanish, Chinese, English, French, Portuguese, and Russian. Information on the operation and implementation of the Treaty is made available to Governments by OPANAL and IAEA through official documents.

Further, in accordance with Article 19 paragraph 1 of the Treaty, OPANAL and IAEA concluded a co-operation agreement in 1972. The agreement refers, inter alia, to an exchange of information, publication and documents relating to matters of common interest. One example for the implementation of this agreement are the consultations and the exchange of information between both agencies with regard to the IAEA's Regional Co-operation Programme to Promote Nuclear Science and Technology in Latin America (ARCAL). IAEA training courses and seminars refer to IAEA activities in connection with the Treaty of Tlatelolco (such as ARCAL).

Operation, review and adjustment

Article 8 establishes as special organs of the OPANAL a General Conference, a Council and a Secretariat. According to Article 9 paragraph 3 the General Conference of OPANAL shall adopt the Agency's budget and fix the scale of financial contributions to be paid by Member States, taking into account the systems and criteria used for the same purpose by the UN.

There are no mechanisms for scientific advisory work. Participation of national authorities is through OPANAL.

Article 6 provides that a meeting of all the Signatories may be convened upon request of any of the signatory States or OPANAL to consider question which may affect the very essence of the Treaty, including possible amendments. Further, Article 29 provides that each Contracting Party may propose amendments to the Treaty. The proposal shall be submitted by the Party to the Council of OPANAL through the General Secretary, who shall transmit the proposal to all other Contracting Parties and other signatories in accordance with Article 6. A Special session of the General Conference of OPANAL is then convened to examine the proposal, for the adoption of which a two-third majority of the Contracting Parties present and voting is required. No review or amendment meetings have been held to date.

(108) South Pacific Nuclear-Free Zone Treaty

(Raratonga, 8 August 1985)

Objectives and achievement

The Treaty establishes a nuclear-free zone in the South Pacific. The zone covers a vast area extending to Australia in the West and to the Equator in the North. In the East it is adjacent to the area of application of the Treaty of Tlatelolco (No. 107 above) and, in the South, to the Antarctic Treaty (No. 14). The basic objectives of the Treaty are to keep the region free of the stationing of nuclear weapons, nuclear testing and environmental pollution by radioactive waste. Furthermore, the Treaty prohibits all types of nuclear explosions. There are three additional Protocols to the Treaty related to the five nuclear weapons states (China, France, United Kingdom, United States and Soviet Union). Protocol 1 invites France, the United States o America and United Kingdom to apply key provisions of the Treaty to their South Pacific territories. Protocols 2 and 3 respectively invite the five nuclear weapon States not to use or threaten to use nuclear weapons against Parties to the Treaty and not to test nuclear explosive devices within the zone.

Because of the very substantial size of the zone, the Treaty could have an important bearing on the global environment if applied by all countries in the region and by all States with territories within the zone for which they are internationally responsible. There are no provisions specifically referring to developing countries.

The basic objectives of the Treaty have been met as far as concerns the obligations of the States Parties. With regard to the application to peaceful nuclear activities of safeguards by IAEA as provided in Article 8, of the ten States Parties to the Treaty, two (Australia and New Zealand) are IAEA Member States. Eight (Australia, Fiji, Kiribati, Nauru, New Zealand, Solomon Islands, Tuvalu and Western Samoa) are Parties to the Treaty on Non-Proliferation of Nuclear Weapons (NPT), all having concluded an NPT safeguards agreement with the IAEA. One signatory State which has not yet ratified the Raratonga Treaty (Papua New Guinea) is not an IAEA Member State but is a Party to the NPT as well and has concluded an NPT safeguards agreement with the IAEA.

Participation

Article 12 of the Treaty provides that the Treaty shall be open for signature by any Member of the South Pacific Forum (see No. 67). The Treaty is not subject to reservations (Article 14).

Eleven of the South Pacific Forum countries have signed the Raratonga Treaty, and ten have ratified, eight of which are developing countries.

In a communiqué issued in 1975, the Heads of Government of the State members of the South Pacific Forum had emphasized the importance of keeping the South Pacific region free from the risk of nuclear contamination and involvement in a nuclear conflict. In a letter to the Secretary-General of the UN dated 15 August 1975 Fiji and New Zealand requested the inclusion in the Agenda of the thirtieth session of the General Assembly of an item entitled "establishment of a nuclear-weapon-free zone in the South Pacific". On the basis of this initiative, on 11 December 1975 the General Assembly adopted a resolution 3477 (XXX) on the establishment of a nuclear-weapon-free zone in the South Pacific. In 1983 the proposal was reiterated by Australia at the fourteenth meeting of the South Pacific Forum in Canberra. In August 1984 the South Pacific Forum, meeting at Funafuti, Tuvalu, endorsed a set of principles proposed by Australia and appointed a working group to prepare the text of the Treaty. The forum met again in Raratonga, Cook Islands, in August 1985 and considered and adopted unanimously the Treaty that had been drafted by the working group. All countries of the South Pacific Forum contributed to the work on the draft text on the Treaty.

Participation in the treaty was mainly motivated by the consensus of the countries of the South Pacific region that the nuclear-free zone would contribute to their security and welfare and minimize risks to their health and environment.

Implementation and information

Pursuant to Article 15, paragraph 1, the Treaty entered into force on 11 December 1986, following the deposit of the eighth ratification. Protocol 2 and 3 have been signed and ratified by China and the USSR. The USA and the UK have indicated their willingness to abide by the provisions of the Treaty and its Protocols but have refrained from signing the two Protocols, as has France, which considers that the provisions relating to nuclear testing discriminate against its rights in French territories.

Each Party undertakes:

a)   that it will not develop, manufacture, acquire, receive from others any nuclear explosive device by any means anywhere inside or outside the South Pacific Nuclear Free Zone (Article 3);

b)   that all nuclear activities in the region, including the export of nuclear material, will be conducted under strict safeguards to ensure exclusively peaceful, non-explosive use (Article 4);

c)   that it will prevent in its territory the stationing of any nuclear explosive device (Article 5);

d)   that it will prevent in its territory the testing of any nuclear explosive device (Article 6);

e)   that it will take measures against the dumping at sea in the region of radioactive waste and support the conclusion of the Convention for the Protection of the Natural Resources and Environment of the South Pacific Region (No. 55).

Under the safeguards agreements signed with the IAEA, States party to the Treaty are required to provide IAEA with information concerning nuclear material subject to safeguards and the features of the facilities relevant to safeguarding such material. The IAEA requires only the minimum amount of information and data consistent with carrying out its responsibilities under the agreement.

Further, Annex 4 paragraph 6 of the Treaty (complaints procedure) provides that each Party shall give to special inspectors appointed by the Consultative Committee full and free access to all information and places within its territory, which may be relevant to enable the work of the special inspectors.

The Treaty provides for a control system for the purpose of verifying compliance by State Parties (Article 8). The control system is composed of:

a)   exchange of information in case of detection of any significant event that may affect the implementation of the Treaty;

b)   consultations on any matter arising in relation to the Treaty;

c)   the application to peaceful nuclear activities of safeguards by the IAEA, and

d)   a complaints procedure as provided in Annex 4.

The Parties to the Treaty agreed that the safeguards agreement to be concluded with IAEA should be equivalent to NPT safeguards agreements based on document IAEA INFCIRC/153. Existing nuclear activities in the countries are, in fact, already covered by safeguards agreements concluded pursuant to NPT.   Safeguards agreements have been concluded with Australia, Fiji, Nauru, New Zealand, Cook Islands, Niue (both covered by New Zealand agreement), Papua New Guinea and Western Samoa. Agreements with Kiribati and Tuvalu have been approved by the IAEA Board of Governors and sent to their Governments for signature in October and July 1990 respectively. The reports of inspections under the safeguards agreements are confidential information.

According to Annex 4, if there are reasons for a complaint that another Party is in breach of its obligations under the Treaty, a Party may bring the matter to the attention of the complained Party with a view to finding an amicable solution. If, however, the matter is not resolved, the complaint Party may bring the complaint to the Director of the South Pacific Bureau for Economic Cooperation with a request that a Consultative Committee be convened to consider it. The Committee may then decide to carry out an inspection in the territory of the complained Party or elsewhere.

The original text exists in English only. Article 16 provides that the depositary shall transmit certified copies of the Treaty and of its Protocols to all Members of the South Pacific Forum and all States eligible to become Party to the Protocols. The texts of the Treaty and the Protocols were also published in IAEA official documents (INFCIRC/331 and INFCIRC/331 Add.1) and were circulated to all Member States of the IAEA. The documents are available in all six official languages of the United Nations.

Information on IAEA's role under the Treaty was published in document GOV/INF/528 (Role of the Agency under the South Pacific Nuclear Free Zone Treaty). The document was then discussed at the IAEA's Board of Governors meeting on 17 September 1987. All safeguards agreements negotiated by the IAEA in connection with the Treaty are submitted to the IAEA Board of Governors for its approval (GOV/INF/528 para. 4). Notice of the agreements are published in IAEA official documents (INFCIRCs) and distributed to all Member States. Information related to the implementation of the Treaty is formally communicated to the Director General of the IAEA by the Director of the South Pacific Bureau for Economic Co-operation as well as by States Parties to the Treaty.

Operation, review and adjustment

Article 10 provides that the Director of the South Pacific Bureau for Economic Co-operation, at the request of any Party, shall convene meetings of the Consultative Committee for consultation and co-operation on any matter related to the Treaty or for reviewing its operation. Article 11 provides that the Consultative Committee shall consider amendments proposal presented by the Parties and circulate them to the parties. The proposals that are accepted by the Committee by consensus shall then be communicated to all Parties for acceptance. Amendments shall enter into force thirty days after the depositary has received acceptances from all Parties. No review or amendment meetings have been held to date.

Codification programming

There have also been a number of proposals for international agreements on nuclear-free zones in other regions:

-       The United Nations General Assembly, at its twentieth session, endorsed the Declaration on the <u>Denuclearization of Africa</u> issued by the Heads of States and Governments of African Countries by its resolution 2033 (XX) of 3 December 1965 and called upon all States to refrain from testing, manufacturing, using or deploying nuclear weapons on the continent of Africa as well as from transferring such weapons, scientific data or technical assistance, either directly or indirectly, in any from which might be used to assist in the manufacturing or use of nuclear weapons in Africa.

-       The question of the <u>establishment of a nuclear-weapon-free zone in South Asia</u> was discussed at the twenty-ninth session of the General Assembly on 9 December 1975 at the request of Pakistan. Since 1976 fifteen resolutions have been adopted on the question. On 13 December 1990 the General Assembly by resolution 45/53 took note of a proposal to convene under the auspices of the United Nations a conference on nuclear non-proliferation in South Asia as soon as possible, with the participation of the regional and other concerned States, and requested the Secretary General to communicate with the States of the region and other concerned States and to promote consultations among them.

A historical summary of proposals for regional nuclear-weapon-free zones and zones of peace has been prepared by the UN Department of Disarmament Affairs (<u>The United Nations and Disarmament: A Short History</u>, 1988).

(109) Convention on Early Notification of a Nuclear Accident
(hereafter Notification Convention), and
Convention on Assistance in the Case of a Nuclear Accident or a Radiological Emergency
(hereafter Assistance Convention), (Vienna, 26 September 1986).

Objectives and achievement

The Notification Convention creates a mechanism to provide information as early as possible in order to minimize the transboundary environmental, health and economic consequences of a nuclear accident. The Assistance Convention sets out an international framework aimed at facilitating the prompt provision of assistance in the event of a nuclear accident or radiological emergency, directly between States Parties, through or from the International Atomic Energy Agency (IAEA), and from other international organizations.

The conventions are global in scope.

Article 7 of the Assistance Convention provides that a State Party may offer assistance to another State Party without reimbursement taking into account, inter alia, the needs of the developing countries and the particular needs of countries without nuclear facilities. While the Notification Convention contains no provision referring to the special needs of the developing countries, it may be noted that during the meeting of Governmental Experts convened to draft the text of the Convention, the representative of Nigeria proposed that the IAEA should assist States which do not have nuclear activities themselves but which border other States having an active nuclear programme (South Africa) but not party to the Convention. The IAEA was called upon to conduct investigations into the feasibility and establishment of an appropriate radiation monitoring system for the benefit of the said State. The so-called Nigerian proposal was then reflected in the present Article 8 of the Convention.

The two conventions were prompted by the nuclear accident at Chernobyl (USSR). To date, there have been no other major accidents requiring recourse to the conventions, and no notifications except for a communication from the USSR circulated by IAEA in 1988 (INFCIRC/357).

Participation

Membership is open to all States and international organizations and regional integration organizations constituted by sovereign States which have treaty-making competence in matters covered by the Conventions.

Reservations are possible to the dispute settlement procedures provided in both conventions, and to specified provisions on privileges, immunities and claims settlement under the Assistance Convention. A total of 40 States entered reservations, three of which were subsequently withdrawn.

Of the 82 Parties to both conventions, 15 are from the African region; 10 from Latin America; 40 from Middle East and Europe; 15 from the Asia and Pacific and 2 from North America. 47 are developing countries.

On 21 May 1986 the IAEA Board of Governors had decided to establish an expert working Group to consider additional measures to improve co-operation in the field of nuclear safety, and to convene, under IAEA auspices, a conference of Governmental representatives to draft international instruments on the early notification and assistance in the event of a nuclear accident. Pursuant to this decision, a group of governmental experts met at the IAEA's Headquarters, in Vienna, from 21 July to 15 August 1986. Experts from 62 IAEA Member States (including 30 developing countries) participated in the meeting, which prepared the two conventions.

So far, no technical assistance to developing countries has been provided, under Article 7 of the Assistance Convention or Article 8 of the Notification Convention.

Both conventions were adopted as a direct response to the accident of Chernobyl. The accident received very high attention in public opinion, the press, NGOs, parliaments and governments, which certainly influenced participation in the conventions.

Implementation and information

Both conventions required only three ratifications to enter into force, which accelerated their implementation.

Under the Notification Convention, a State Party, in the event of a nuclear accident with actual or potential transboundary effects involving its facilities or activities, is required to notify other States, which may be physically affected, directly or through the IAEA itself, of the nature of the accident, its location and the time of its occurrence. That State Party is required to provide other States and IAEA promptly with specified information relevant to minimizing the radiological consequences in those States (Article 2). Pursuant to Article 3, State Parties may voluntarily notify accidents relative to military nuclear activities, with a view to minimizing the radiological consequences of the nuclear accident. All five nuclear-weapon States have declared their intention to make such notifications. In addition, State Parties are also required to respond to a request by an affected State for additional information or consultation (Article 6). Further, pursuant to Article 7, each State Party shall make known its competent authorities or point of contact responsible for issuing and receiving the notification and information referred above.

Under the Notification Convention, States Parties report to the IAEA through the competent authorities and points of contact. Article 4 of the Convention provides that IAEA shall inform States Parties, Member States and other States which are or may be physically affected by the nuclear accident and international intergovernmental organizations of a notification received pursuant to Article 2 (a). The information is published in IAEA official publications and is issued in all the six official languages of the United Nations. On 28 September 1988, IAEA circulated a communication at the request of the Resident

Representative of the Union of Soviet Socialist Republics (INFCIRC/357). There are no reporting obligations under the Assistance Convention unless a nuclear accident or radiological emergency occurs, which has not been the case since 1986.

Article 5 of the Notification Convention provides that in case of a nuclear accident, the information to be provided shall comprise the following data:

" ...   a)   the time, exact location where appropriate, and the nature of the accident;

b)   the facility or activity involved;

c)   the assumed or established cause and the foreseen development of the nuclear accident relevant to the transboundary release of the radioactive material;

d)   the general characteristics of the radioactive release, including, as far as practicable and appropriate, the nature, probable physical and chemical form and quantity, composition and effective height of the radioactive release;

e)   information on current and forecast meteorological and hydrological conditions, necessary to forecasting the transboundary release of the radioactive materials;

f)   the results of environmental monitoring relevant to the transboundary release of the radioactive materials;

g)   the off-site protective measures taken or planned;

h)   the predicted behaviour over time of the radioactive release. "

Pursuant to paragraph 2 of Article 5 the information referred above shall be supplemented by further relevant information on the development of the emergency situation with the inclusion of its foreseeable and actual termination. Information may be used without restriction except when such information is provided in confidence by the notifying State Party (Art. 5 paragraph 3).

Pursuant to Article 2 paragraph 2 of the Assistance Convention, a State Party requesting assistance shall provide the assisting State "with such information as may be necessary for that party to determine the extent to which it is able to meet the request". Article 2 paragraph 4 provides that State Parties shall notify the IAEA of experts, equipment and materials which could be made available in case of a nuclear accident or radiological emergency. Confidential information that may become available to either the requesting or the assisting State in connection with the assistance provided shall be kept confidential and shall be used exclusively for the purpose of the assistance agreed upon (Article 6 paragraph 1). No compliance controls are provided.

Article 11 of the Notification Convention and Article 13 of the Assistance Convention provide that in the event of a dispute between the States Parties, or between a State Party and the IAEA, concerning the interpretation and application of the Convention, the parties shall consult with a view to settle the dispute by negotiation or by any other peaceful means. If, however, the dispute cannot be settled within one year from the request of consultation, the dispute shall be submitted to arbitration or referred to the International Court of Justice for decision. Pursuant to paragraph 3, States Parties may declare that they do not consider themselves bound by either or both the above dispute settlement procedures.

Factors that have influenced implementation include the ongoing technical assistance provided by IAEA (which is also referred to in Article 5 of the Assistance Convention).

Authentic texts of the conventions are available in all the six official languages of the United Nations. All information on implementation of the conventions is made available directly to Governments and the competent authorities designated. In addition, IAEA issues a wide range of public information materials relating to the conventions. At national level, designated national authorities are responsible for issuing and receiving notifications and information.

The above-mentioned material is also used in training courses and seminar organized by IAEA and by member States.

Operation, review and adjustment

The IAEA Secretariat in Vienna is in charge of administering the conventions. Costs are covered by the regular IAEA budget. No meetings have taken place so far.

IAEA does not finance the participation costs of experts from developing countries. No long-term scientific advisory functions or participation from NGOs or industry are foreseen.

Article 14 of the Notification Convention and Article 16 of the Assistance Convention provide that Parties may propose amendments to the Convention. If a majority of the Parties request the depositary to convene a conference to consider the proposed amendments, the depositary shall invite the Parties to attend a conference. Any amendment adopted at the conference by a two-thirds majority of Parties shall be laid down in a protocol for signature by Parties to the Convention. No amendments have been proposed to date.

Codification programming

In addition to legally binding agreements in the field of nuclear safety and liability (see No. 94), IAEA has also developed, in co-operation with the non-governmental International Commission on Radiological Protection (ICRP) and other organizations concerned, a series of non-mandatory instruments, including Nuclear Safety Standards (NUSS, comprising sixty volumes in the form of five codes of practice accompanied by safety guides), Basic Safety Standards for Radiation Protection (IAEA Safety Series No. 9), Regulations for Safe Transport of Radioactive Material (IAEA Safety Series No. 6), and a Code of Practice on the International Transboundary Movement of Radioactive Waste, adopted by the IAEA General Conference in 1990 (INFCICR/386).

At its 35th session in September 1991, the IAEA General Conference decided to intitiate preparations for a nuclear safety convention, taking into account the activities and roles of other relevant international bodies. Among the elements to be considered for inclusion in the convention are the obligations of States relating to:

(a) the legislative framework for the regulation of civil nuclear facilities and activities of the nuclear fuel cycle;

(b) appropriate education and training of manpower;

(c) emergency plans to cope with accident situations;

(d) safety of facilities (including siting, design, construction, commissioning and decommissioning);

(e) safe operation and maintenance of facilities;

(f) continuous safety surveillance and additional periodic reassessments of facilities;

(g) safe management and disposal of radioactive waste;

(h) sharing of certain information as agreed in the convention.

STATUS OF RATIFICATIONS AS OF 1 JANUARY 1992

GLOBAL INSTRUMENTS (Treaty numbers see page 339)

Parties	105	106	109
Afghanistan		x	
Albania			
Algeria			
Angola			
Antigua & Barbuda		x	
Argentina	x	x	x
Australia	x	x	x
Austria		x	x
Bahamas		x	
Bahrain			
Bangladesh		x	x
Barbados			
Belarus*		x	x
Belgium	x	x	
Belize			
Benin		x	
Bhutan		x	
Bolivia		x	
Botswana		x	
Brazil	x	x	x
Brunei Darussalam			
Bulgaria		x	x
Burkina Faso			
Burundi			
Cambodia			
Cameroon			
Canada	x	x	x
Cape Verde		x	
Central African Republic		x	
Chad		x	
Chile		x	
China	x		x
Colombia		x	
Cook Islands			
Comoros			
Congo			
Costa Rica		x	x
Cote d'Ivoire		x	
Cuba			x
Cyprus		x	x
Czech & Slovak Fed. Rep.	x	x	x

Parties	105	106	109
Democr. People's Rep. of Korea			
Denmark		x	x
Djibouti			
Dominica			
Dominican Republic		x	
Ecuador		x	
Egypt	x	x	x
El Salvador		x	
Equatorial Guinea		x	
Estonia*			
Ethiopia			
Fiji		x	
Finland		x	x
France	x		x
Gabon		x	
Gambia		x	
Germany	x	x	x
Ghana		x	
Greece		x	x
Grenada			
Guatemala		x	x
Guinea			
Guinea-Bissau		x	
Guyana			
Haiti			
Holy See			
Honduras		x	
Hungary		x	x
Iceland		x	x
India	x	x	x
Indonesia	x	x	
Iran (Islamic Republic of)		x	
Iraq		x	x
Ireland		x	x
Israel		x	x
Italy		x	x
Jamaica			
Japan	x	x	x
Jordan		x	x
Kenya		x	
Kiribati			
Kuwait		x	
Lao People's Democratic Rep.		x	
Latvia*			

Parties	105	106	109
Lebanon		x	
Lesotho			
Liberia		x	
Libyan Arab Jamahiriya		x	
Liechtenstein			
Lithuania*			
Luxembourg		x	
Madagascar		x	
Malawi		x	
Malaysia		x	x
Maldives			
Mali			
Malta		x	
Marshall Islands			
Mauritania		x	
Mauritius		x	
Mexico	x	x	x
Micronesia			
Monaco			x
Mongolia		x	x
Morocco		x	
Mozambique			
Myanmar		x	
Namibia			
Nauru			
Nepal		x	
Netherlands		x	x
New Zealand		x	x
Nicaragua		x	
Niger		x	
Nigeria		x	x
Niue			
Norway		x	x
Oman			
Pakistan		x	x
Palau			
Panama		x	
Papua New Guinea		x	
Paraguay			
Peru	x	x	
Philippines		x	
Poland	x	x	x
Portugal			
Qatar			

Nuclear Safety

Parties	105	106	109
Republic of Korea		x	x
Republic of Yemen		x	
Romania		x	x
Rwanda		x	
St. Kitts & Nevis			
St. Lucia			
St. Vincent & the Grenadines			
Samoa		x	
San Marino		x	
Sao Tome & Principe			
Saudi Arabia			x
Senegal		x	
Seychelles		x	
Sierra Leone		x	
Singapore		x	
Solomon Islands			
Somalia			
South Africa		x	x
Spain		x	x
Sri Lanka		x	x
Sudan	x	x	
Suriname			
Swaziland		x	
Sweden	x	x	x
Switzerland		x	x
Syrian Arab Republic		x	
Thailand		x	x
Togo		x	
Tonga		x	
Trinidad & Tobago		x	
Tunisia		x	x
Turkey		x	x
Tuvalu			
Uganda		x	
Ukraine*		x	x
Union of Soviet Socialist Rep.*	x	x	x
United Arab Emirates			x
United Kingdom	x	x	x
United Republic of Tanzania		x	
United States of America	x	x	x
Uruguay		x	x
Vanuatu			
Venezuela		x	
Viet Nam			x

Parties	105	106	109
Yugoslavia*		x	x
Zaire		x	
Zambia		x	
Zimbabwe			

REGIONAL INSTRUMENTS

(107) <u>Treaty for the Prohibition of Nuclear Weapons in Latin America</u> (Tlatelolco 1967)

Antigua & Barbuda
Bahamas
Barbados
Bolivia
Brazil**
Chile**
Colombia
Costa Rica
Dominican Republic
Ecuador
El Salvador
Grenada
Guatemala

Haiti
Honduras
Jamaica
Mexico
Nicaragua
Panama
Paraguay
Peru
Suriname
Trinidad & Tobago
Uruguay
Venezuela

<u>Protocol I</u>

Netherlands
United Kingdom
USA

<u>Protocol II</u>

China
France
USSR*
United Kingdom
USA

(108) <u>South Pacific Nuclear-Free Zone Treaty</u> (Raratonga 1985)

Australia
Cook Islands
Fiji
Kiribati
Nauru

New Zealand
Niue
Samoa
Solomon Islands
Tuvalu

---

* Membership status subject to further clarification.
** Not in force (see page 344)

CHAPTER IX

WORKING ENVIRONMENT

Virginia A. Leary

This chapter covers the following seven international agreements on the working environment, in chronological order:

(110) the Convention concerning the Protection of Workers against Ionising Radiations (ILO Convention 115, Geneva, 22 June 1960)
(hereafter, **Radiation Protection Convention**, 1960);

(111) the Convention concerning Protection against Hazards of Poisoning Arising from Benzene (ILO Convention 136, Geneva, 23 June 1971)
(hereafter, **Benzene Convention**, 1971);

(112) the Convention concerning Prevention and Control of Occupational Hazards caused by Carcinogenic Substances and Agents (ILO Convention 139, Geneva, 26 June 1974)
(hereafter, **Occupational Cancer Convention**, 1974);

(113) the Convention concerning the Protection of Workers against Occupational Hazards in the Working Environment Due to Air Pollution, Noise and Vibration (ILO Convention 148, Geneva, 20 June 1977)
(hereafter, **Working Environment (Air Pollution, Noise and Vibration) Convention**, 1977);

(114) the Convention concerning Occupational Safety and Health and the Working Environment (ILO Convention 155, Geneva, 22 June 1981)
(hereafter, **Occupational Safety and Health Convention**, 1981);

(115) the Convention concerning Safety in the Use of Asbestos (ILO Convention 162, Geneva, 22 June 1986)
(hereafter, **Asbestos Convention**, 1986); and

(116) the Convention concerning Safety in the Use of Chemicals at Work (ILO Convention 170, Geneva, 24 June 1990)
(hereafter, **Chemicals Convention**, 1990).

A list showing the status of ratifications as of 1 January 1992 is annexed (pages 388 - 391).

The conventions on the working environment examined here have all been adopted by the International Labour Organization (ILO) under ILO procedures. They thus share many common aspects including the method of drafting and adoption, provisions regarding reservations, the number of ratifications required for entry into force and measures of implementation. For the most part, they will, therefore, be considered collectively rather than individually in this study. Where the material warrants, reference will be made to individual conventions.

Two important factors relating to the evaluation of the effectiveness of these conventions (and which distinguish them from other environmental instruments) should be noted at the outset:

(1) Their adoption and implementation within the context of the entire work of the International Labour Organisation; and

(2) the participation of non-governmental actors, namely, employers' and workers' organizations, in their adoption and implementation (referred to as "tripartism").

Standard setting in social and labour matters has been a major aspect of the work of the ILO since its founding in 1919 and a highly sophisticated system of supervision of the implementation of conventions has been developed over more than 60 years by the ILO. Although the conventions on the working environment are among the newer ILO conventions, they are subject to the same long-developed system of supervision as other ILO conventions. It was unnecessary to create new systems of implementation for them as has often been necessary for other recent environmental conventions. The implementation of these conventions under the general ILO supervisory system is discussed in Section C below.

As technical assistance became an increasingly important ILO activity, an effort was made to relate the technical assistance activities to the standard-setting work. In the area of occupational safety and health, with which these conventions are concerned, there has been an especially close link developed between ILO technical assistance programs and convention implementation. This linkage is explained in several of the later portions of this study.

Tripartism is a well-known feature of the International Labour Organisation. Unlike other international organisations, non-governmental organisations are fully integrated into the totality of the work of the ILO. Workers' and employers' organisations participate in the work of drafting ILO conventions and are notably active participants in the supervision of implementation of ILO conventions. The roles of workers and of employers are obviously of considerable importance in the improvement of the working environment; hence, the importance of tripartism in any evaluation of conventions on the working environment.

Objectives and Achievement

1. OBJECTIVES

The basic objective of each of the seven conventions studied here is the improvement of the working environment--the protection of the health and safety of the worker in his or her work place. The conventions concern protection of the worker from hazards to health arising from the use of radiation, benzene, asbestos, carcinogenic substances and chemicals, as well as hazards from air pollution, noise and vibrations. The Occupational Safety and Health Convention, 1981, differs somewhat from the other six conventions, since it does not concern a specific hazard to health but requires States Parties to take steps to formulate and implement a "coherent national policy on occupational safety, occupational health and the working environment."

Detail concerning the content of each of the seven conventions is provided in the section on Implementation and Information.

An indirect objective of the conventions on the working environment is the protection of the general environment. The protection of the working environment "enhances the protection of the general public and the environment" as expressed in the Preamble to the Chemicals Convention, 1990. It suffices to cite the Bhopal, Seveso and Basel disasters to note the relation between the protection of the working environment and the protection of the general environment.

2. INTEGRATION OF ENVIRONMENT AND DEVELOPMENT

The concept of development is no longer considered as relating solely to economic development but encompasses social aspects as well. "The satisfaction of human needs and aspirations is the major objective of development" (Bruntland Report, p. 43). The protection of life must be regarded as a basic objective of development. Economic development which causes hazards to the health of the working population--and possibly to other groups of the population as well--cannot be considered sustainable development. The aim of these conventions is to ensure that economic development is not carried out at the expense of the more vulnerable groups of the population. The Bruntland Report pointed out that "the distribution of power and influence within society lies at the heart of most environment and development challenges. Hence new approaches must involve programmes of social development....to protect vulnerable groups, and to promote local participation in decision making." (p. 38).

The protection of the safety and health of the vulnerable group of industrial and agricultural workers is an obvious aim of the conventions, but the conventions also provide for local participation, even at the individual enterprise level, in decisions regarding the working environment. Article 18 of the Chemicals Convention, for example, provides that workers and their representatives shall have the right to information on the identity of chemicals used at work and the hazardous properties of such chemicals. It gives workers the right to remove themselves from danger resulting from the use of chemicals which they reasonably believe may endanger their safety or health. This is a striking example of local participation in environmental decisions.

3. TAKING INTO ACCOUNT SPECIAL CIRCUMSTANCES OF DEVELOPING COUNTRIES

Article 4, paragraph 1 of the Occupational Safety and Health Convention, 1981 (No. 155) calls upon each member to "formulate, implement and periodically review a coherent national policy on occupational safety, occupational health and the working environment". Article 2, paragraph 1 permits exclusion from the application of the Convention of limited categories of workers in respect of which there are particular difficulties.

Paragraph 3 requires the Government to indicate in future reports any progress towards wider application and at the ILO organised Asian Regional Tripartite Seminar on Occupational Safety and Health Policies, Bangkok, January 1985, it was pointed out that the promotional nature of the Occupational Safety and Health Convention, 1981 was "significant for the developing countries in the Asian region" because it did not necessarily call for immediate action but permitted progressive application to sectors or industries where such application was possible. See <u>Proceedings</u> of the Seminar, ILO, International Programme for the Improvement of Working Conditions and Environment (PIACT).

Moreover, the conventions also contain provisions which attempt to take into account special circumstances of any ratifying country and, hence, may be used by developing as well as developed countries. For example, the Occupational Safety and Health Convention, 1981, provides in Article 1(2) that

> A Member ratifying this Convention may, after consultation at the earliest possible stage with the representative organisations of employers and workers concerned, exclude from its application, in part or in whole, particular branches of economic activity, such as maritime shipping or fishing, in respect of which special problems of a substantial nature arise.

This provision and similar provisions in other working environment conventions permit some flexibility in the application of the Conventions. The Benzene Convention, 1971, and the Asbestos Convention, 1986, permit temporary derogations from the provisions of the Convention, under certain circumstances.

The Chemicals Convention, 1990, contains a provision which, while not referring to developing countries specifically, takes into account their special circumstances; the provision requires states exporting hazardous chemicals to inform importing countries of the hazards. Developing countries frequently lack the requisite technical knowledge necessary to determine the hazardous nature of chemicals they may be importing. Article 19 of the Convention reads,

> When in an exporting member State all or some uses of hazardous chemicals are prohibited for reasons of safety and health at work, this fact and the reasons for it shall be communicated by the exporting member State to any importing country.

ILO conventions are normally supplemented by the adoption of a recommendation on the same topic simultaneously with the adoption of the convention. The conventions are usually drafted in general terms which will make ratification possible for the widest number of states, including developing countries. Recommendations, which are not legally binding instruments, often contain more detailed provisions which can be implemented by countries capable of more advanced implementation or detailed regulations not suitable for a convention. Some of the provisions of the recommendations, which should be considered in conjunction with the conventions, contain provisions which take into account the special problems of developing countries.

In the Recommendation concerning Prevention and Control of Occupational Hazards Caused by Carcinogenic Substances and Agents (supplementing Occupational Cancer Convention, 1974) reference is made to international assistance which could be utilized to assist in carrying out the record keeping and dissemination of information required by this instrument (Paragraphs 15(2) and 16(1)). Such assistance is available from the ILO. The Organisation carries out extensive technical assistance programmes in occupational safety and health to assist developing countries in implementing conventions and improving occupational safety and health generally.

In 1990, the ILO published a brochure entitled <u>International Labour Standards for development and social justice</u>, which emphasized the complementarity between ILO standard-setting and technical co-operation activities; two important means of action to achieve ILO objectives.

Developing countries have been particularly concerned about the role and responsibilities of multinational enterprises within their countries. In 1977, the ILO adopted the Tripartite Declaration of Principles concerning Multinational Enterprises and Social

Policy. Paragraphs 36 to 39 of the Declaration relate to safety and health and multinational enterprises. Paragraph 36 states that governments should ensure that both multinational and national enterprises provide adequate safety and health standards for their employees and urges governments to ratify the ILO Conventions on the working environment then adopted up to that time. The following Paragraph provides that multinational enterprises should maintain the highest standards of safety and health in conformity with national requirements, bearing in mind their relevant experience within the enterprise as a whole. It also provides that the enterprise should make available to representatives of workers and employers information on the safety and health standards relevant to their local operations.

A link is established between the conventions and recommendations discussed in this study and the Tripartite Declaration; Paragraph 39 of the Recommendation concerning Safety in the Use of Asbestos, 1986 reads,

> In accordance with the Tripartite Declaration of Principles concerning Multinational Enterprises and Social Policy, adopted by the Governing Body of the International Labour Office, a national or multinational enterprise with more than one establishment should be required to provide safety measures relating to the prevention and control of, and protection against, health hazards due to occupational exposure to asbestos, without discrimination, to the workers in all its establishments regardless of the place or country in which they are situated.

An identical provision is included in Paragraph 12(2) of Recommendation 177 concerning Safety in the Use of Chemicals at Work, 1990.

The flexibility provided in many of the conventions on the working environment, as well as the provisions for progressive implementation and the fact that the conventions are generally drafted in general terms and supplemented by non-binding recommendations appears to respond to criticisms made by developing countries regarding the drafting of some ILO conventions. The ILO Director-General's Report to the 70th Session of the International Labour Conference, 1984, pointed out that spokesmen for governments of developing countries

> have stressed the importance of drafting instruments in a sufficiently flexible manner, and of ensuring that Third World countries enjoy adequate opportunities to make known their views at the preparatory stages and in the course of the Conference discussions. These various concerns were recalled, for instance, by the Union Minister for Labour and Rehabilitation of India in his address to the Conference in 1983, in which he welcomed the trend in recent years towards greater flexibility in ILO standards...[1]

4. MEETING BASIC OBJECTIVES; MEASURING GOAL ACHIEVEMENT

The basic objectives of the conventions on the working environment are the improvement of safety and health in the workplace. Meeting these objectives is an on-going process which has begun through the adoption, ratification and supervision of conventions concerning some of the well-known major hazards to health in the workplace. Issues relating to measuring goal achievement are discussed later in this study under Section C on Implementation.

---

[1].Extract from the Report of the Director-General to the International Labour Conference, 70th Session, 1984, International Labour Office, Geneva, p. 5

Participation

1. RATIFICATION

The conventions on the working environment are open for ratification only by member States of the International Labour Organisation (numbering 150 as of 1 January 1992). However, since the number of members of the ILO is only slightly less than the number of members of the UN and of the total number of States in the world, membership is almost open-ended.

Most ILO conventions, including the conventions on the working environment, come into force twelve months following ratification by two member States. This is an unusual provision in international conventions which generally require far more ratifications for entry into force. ILO conventions are intended for internal application in ratifying states and it has been pointed out that there is no intrinsic reason why ILO conventions could not enter into force upon one ratification only, bringing into play the ILO supervisory machinery for the one state which has ratified.

According to the final articles, the conventions may be denounced by a ratifying member after the expiration of ten years from the date on which the Convention first comes into force and at each succeeding ten year period. The denunciation takes effect one year after the date on which it is registered.

Provision is also made in the final articles for the replacement of the Convention by a new Convention revising the former Convention. The final articles of these treaties provide that, should the ILO Conference adopt a new Convention revising a Convention in whole or in part, unless the new Convention otherwise provides, the ratification by a member of the revising Convention ipso jure involves the immediate denunciation of the previous Convention. As soon as the new Convention comes into force, the former Convention ceases to be open to ratification.

2. RESERVATIONS

No reservations are permitted to these conventions nor to any ILO conventions. As mentioned previously, conventions are often drafted in general terms in order to permit as wide ratification as possible. More detailed provisions and higher standards are usually included in the non-binding recommendations. In addition, certain flexibility provisions of these conventions, pointed out earlier in Section A (3), permit special circumstances of ratifying states to be taken into account.

3. GEOGRAPHIC DISTRIBUTION OF MEMBERSHIP

The seven conventions considered in this study are all relatively recent ILO conventions: the earliest was adopted in 1960 and the most recent in 1990. All are in force except the Chemicals Convention, 1990. One hundred and forty-two ratifications have been registered for the six conventions on the working environment now in force. Seventy-six of those ratifications have been made by developing countries--somewhat more than 50% of the total number of ratifications (as listed in the Annex).[2] The geographic distribution of those ratifications for the totality of the conventions is as follows:

    Region   No. of Ratifications (as of 1 January 1992)

Latin and Central America   37

Africa   18

Middle East   11 (includes 1 by Israel)

Asia   6 (includes 2 by Japan)

Europe   70 (includes 7 by developing countries)

        Total   142

It is apparent from the preceding figures that these conventions have attracted the fewest number of ratifications from Asian countries.

The figures for ratification of the individual conventions by developing countries are as follows:

Convention	Total Ratifications (as of 1 January 1992)	Total Developing Country Ratifications (as of 1 January 1992)
Radiation Protection Convention, 1960	39	18
Benzene Convention, 1971	28	18
Occupational Cancer Convention, 1974	25	14
Working Environment Convention, 1977	25	13
Occupational Safety & Health Convention, 1981	15	7
Asbestos Convention, 1986	10	7
Chemicals Convention, 1990	Not yet in force	

---

[2]. Around 2/3 of the ratifications of all 172 ILO conventions have been made by developing countries. Nineteen developing countries have ratified more than 50 ILO conventions. International Labour Standards for Development and Social Justice, ILO, Geneva, 1989.

4. ACTUAL PARTICIPATION BY DEVELOPING COUNTRIES: NEGOTIATION AND DRAFTING

All ILO conventions are negotiated and drafted in a similar manner. Topics for possible new instruments are suggested by the ILO Governing Body, usually following suggestions from governments or employers' or workers' organisations. The Office (ILO secretariat) then prepares a study of the law and practice of ILO member States on various aspects of a suggested new standard as well as a questionnaire which is sent to all member States relating to the desirability of a new standard, the form it should take (convention or recommendation) and possible content. This report is sent to States 12 months before the first discussion of the new instrument at the International Labour Conference. A second report is then prepared summarizing the replies of member States and including a draft proposal for a convention and/or recommendation based on the replies of member States. This second report is sent to member States four months before the discussion of the convention at the Conference. The proposed convention and/or recommendation are discussed at two succeeding sessions of the annual International Labour Conference. (Article 39, Standing Orders of the Conference). At the second session, the Convention and/or Recommendation is adopted.

Developing states have participated actively in the negotiation and drafting of the seven ILO conventions under consideration in this study. Two examples may be given of this participation: the adoption of the Chemicals Convention, 1990 and the Asbestos Convention, 1986.

At its November 1987 Session, the ILO Governing Body decided to place on the agenda of the 1989 Session of the International Labour Conference the question of safety in the use of chemicals at work. This decision resulted from the conclusions of the Meeting of Experts on Harmful Substances in Work Establishments which was held in May 1987 to advise the Office on the appropriateness of placing such an item on the agenda of the 1989 Session of the Conference. Twenty-one experts representing governments, employers and workers as well as a number of observers attended this Meeting. Eight of the 21 experts, including the Chairman, were from developing countries.[3]

The preliminary report prepared by the Office on the possible adoption of instruments on safety in the use of chemicals at work contains a chapter on the law and practice in various countries obtained, inter alia, from information provided by member States of the ILO. The law and practice of 33 countries was summarized. Sixteen of the 33 are developing countries.[4]

This report also contained a general questionnaire relating to the issue and requested replies of member States regarding the adoption of a convention or recommendation and the possible content of such instruments. A request was made to all member States for replies to the questionnaire. At the time the second report was prepared on the use of chemicals at work, 74 replies had been received from member States on the questionnaire. Forty-one of

---

[3]. Safety in the Use of Chemicals at Work, Working Document and Report of a Meeting of Experts, Geneva, 5-13 May 1987, ILO, Geneva.

[4]. International Labour Conference, 76th Session, 1989, Report VI (1), Safety in the use of chemicals at work, Ch. II, p. 10.

these <u>74</u> replies were from developing countries.[5] The adoption of the Convention was then discussed at the annual Conferences in 1989 and 1990 and the Convention was adopted in 1990.   The adoption of the Convention and Recommendation were discussed at the Conference by Committees in which developing countries as well as developed participated fully.

Similar participation by developing countries was also evident in the negotiation and drafting of the Convention and Recommendation concerning Safety in the Use of Asbestos in 1986. At the time the second report was drawn up, the Office had received replies from <u>76</u> member States, of whom <u>51</u> were developing countries.[6] Delegates from developing countries also participated fully in the Committee which adopted this Convention in 1986.

5. FACTORS INFLUENCING THE PARTICIPATION OF DEVELOPING COUNTRIES

Developing countries are participating substantially in the drafting, adoption and ratification of conventions on the working environment, as shown by the information in the preceding section.   Nevertheless, member States of the ILO have reported on certain difficulties in improving occupational safety and health affecting their participation in these conventions. The most important inhibiting factors are lack of economic resources and lack of trained manpower (for labour inspection, training of employers and workers, etc). The lack of resources makes it difficult for governments to effectively enforce safe working conditions and for the private sector to comply with safety requirements. The shortage of trained manpower in the field of workplace safety has frequently been noted as a problem in developing countries.

In most developing countries, economic pressures arising from international competition, lack of capital and insufficient technologies take precedence over concern for improving working conditions. There may be a low level of consciousness of the relationship between economic efficiency and the promotion of safety and health conditions. Adequate statistics concerning hazards in the workplace are frequently lacking. The generation of employment is given priority over the improvement of conditions of work. Widespread unemployment and underemployment often result in substandard conditions of work. Improved productivity in agricultural work and on plantations through the use of pesticides and fungicides may be given priority over the health of workers.

Workers are sometimes informed that they must choose between higher wages or improved safety and health conditions at work. In some cases, safety and health issues are not considered as an issue for collective bargaining. Small and medium size firms in developing countries frequently lack the funds and technical expertise to improve working conditions. Large firms, which are usually subsidiaries of multinational enterprises, are in a better position to do so, but are sometimes charged with failing to inform their subsidiaries of dangers of chemicals or other material imported into the country or using outdated equipment no longer employed in the home country. Lack of knowledge of the danger of certain products is a problem. Small and medium size firms usually know chemicals only by

---

[5]. International Labour Conference, 76th Session, 1989, Report VI (2), <u>Safety in the use of chemicals at work,</u> p. 1.

[6]. International Labour Conference, 71st Session, 1985, Report VI (2), <u>Safety in the Use of Asbestos,</u> p.1.

their trade names and very few have material safety data sheets supplied when they have purchased chemicals.[7]

6. MEASURES TO PROMOTE PARTICIPATION OF DEVELOPING COUNTRIES

The ILO has undertaken a substantial number of programmes to assist developing countries in overcoming the above-described obstacles. The poverty of developing countries, due to factors beyond the control of the ILO, is clearly one of the most important obstacles to improvement in this field. In countries with economic constraints, the resources allocated for safety and health promotion were reduced or remained static in the 1980s. The ILO has assisted such countries to carefully formulate national policies which enabled them to identify safety and health problems that required priority attention, to initiate mutually supportive measures and to take appropriate action to avoid duplication.

Measures to promote the participation of developing countries in the operation and implementation of the agreements on the working environment may be carried out under

(a) ILO measures to promote participation in the operation and implementation of ILO conventions in general or

(b) may be undertaken as part of the ILO programme in Occupational Safety and Health relating specifically to conventions on occupational safety and health.

(a) ILO measures to promote participation of developing countries in operation and implementation of all conventions.

On request and to the extent of available resources, the International Labour Office provides assistance to the administrative services of developing countries responsible for questions relating to international labour standards. This assistance is provided to enable the country to ensure the participation of its representatives in the adoption of international conventions and recommendations, to assist national ministries to understand the procedures for supervision of implementation of standards and to check that various procedures concerning standards have been completed (particularly reporting procedures). The assistance is provided by

-- the organization of courses by the Standards Department of the ILO in Geneva relating to various aspects of drafting, ratifying and implementing standards, to which government officials are invited.

--the appointment of ILO regional advisers on standards available for visits to member States to familiarize them with various aspects relating to standards.

--the organization of regional and international tripartite seminars on standards in general or on specific subjects related to certain standards.

--by organizing, on occasion, direct contact missions for particularly complex cases.[8]

---

[7]. A number of the problems of Asian countries in particular in the field of occupational safety and health are discussed in Proceedings, Asian Regional Tripartite Seminar on Occupational Safety and Health Policies, Bangkok, January 1985, ILO, International Programme for the Improvement of Working Conditions and the Environment (PIACT), pp. 151, 163, 167 and 186.

[8]. International Labour Standards for Development and Social Justice, ILO, Geneva, pp. 16-17.

(b) ILO assistance to developing countries relating specifically to conventions on the working environment

In the Introduction it was pointed out that conventions on the working environment adopted by the ILO must be considered within the context of the totality of the work of the ILO. This is true particularly of the conventions on the working environment which are an important part, but only a part, of the ILO programme on Occupational Safety and Health. This programme consists of the adoption of conventions and recommendations (standard-setting) but also of a regular programme of work and technical co-operation activities. These three aspects are inter-related. The conventions and recommendations provide standards which all member States should aim to achieve; the programme of work and technical co-operation provides assistance, particularly to developing countries, to support national efforts to move towards implementation and ratification of those standards.

(i). The International Programme for the Improvement of Working Conditions and the Environment (PIACT)

ILO activities to stimulate national action on the working environment are promoted through PIACT, the International Programme for the Improvement of Working Conditions and Environment, launched in 1976. PIACT assists developing countries by providing the assistance of regional advisers on safety and health issues, sending missions of experts to advise on particular problems and organizing seminars and workshops on subjects related to the working environment.[9]

Recent seminars and workshops organized by PIACT include
--Regional Technical Workshop on Occupational Safety and Health for Asia and the Pacific for Chiefs of National Safety and Health Administrations (Kuala Lumpur, Malaysia, July 1988)
--Meeting of Experts on Harmful Substances in Work Establishments, (Geneva, May 1987)
--Workshop on Safety and Health Information Dissemination for Selected Asian and Pacific countries, (Bangkok, October 1987)
--Workshop on Safety and Health Information Dissemination for African Countries (Blantyre, October 1989)
--Asian Regional Tripartite Seminar on Occupational Safety and Health Policies (Bangkok, January 1985)

The last-mentioned seminar is of particular interest in the context of this study since it focused specifically on promoting the principles of Occupational Safety and Health Convention, 1981, and its accompanying Recommendation. Nineteen participants from ten Asian countries (seven from governments and six each from employer and worker circles) attended the seminar. It was an important seminar for developing countries since this Convention, which lays down standards aimed at the formulation, implementation and periodic review of a coherent national policy for the protection of workers from occupational

---

[9]. ILO, Tripartite Advisory Meeting on the Evaluation of the International Programme for the Improvement of Working Conditions and Environment (PIACT), Review of Activities (1976-1981) and future orientation, Appendix II, TAMPE/1982/1, ILO, Geneva, 1981.

accidents and diseases, does not necessarily call for immediate action by member States but encourages a positive approach of progressive application to sectors or industries where such application is made possible.

The ILO collaborates with other international organizations on projects of common concern such as the International Programme on Chemical Safety, a co-operative venture between the ILO, the World Health Organisation (WHO) and the United Nations Environment Programme (UNEP).

The extensive activity of the ILO Occupational Safety and Health Programme in information dissemination, training and educational programmes is explained in Section D below.

(ii) Technical Cooperation

The ILO reported in 1987 that over 60 countries had received technical assistance under the Occupational Safety and Health programme, including the provision of experts to assist member States to set up systems of technical and medical inspection, industrial hygiene laboratories or centres, the award of grants for study and further training, the provision of necessary equipment and training to qualified staff and the establishment of major hazard control systems.[10]

Following the Bhopal tragedy in India in 1984, the ILO held a Tripartite Ad Hoc Meeting of Consultants on Methods of Prevention of Major Hazards in Industry in order to discuss recent developments in major hazard control methods and future action to avoid the occurrence of major accidents. It organized a regional workshop in Bombay to assist ILO member States in developing policies for avoiding industrial accidents, including identification of major hazards, control systems and information exchange.[11]

Each project consists of basically three elements: provision of expert services, the supply of equipment and the organisation of fellowship and in-service training programmes. Funding for technical cooperation has been provided by the ILO budget, UNDP funding, development banks and multi-bilateral assistance from industrialised country members of the ILO.

Implementation and information

Member States of the ILO which ratify the conventions on the working environment evaluated in this study are subject to the same supervisory system which has been established for all ILO conventions. The obligation of reporting on ILO conventions is established by provisions of the ILO Constitution and ratifying States report to the same supervisory bodies concerning all conventions. The ILO has developed procedures for promoting compliance with ratified conventions as well as mechanisms for dealing with disputes concerning implementation of conventions that are common for all conventions. The individual conventions on the working environment, thus, do not contain provisions establishing supervisory systems since they are subject to the general supervisory system applying to all

---

[10]. Safety in the Use of Chemicals at Work, Working Document and Report of a Meeting of Experts, Geneva, May 1987, PIACT/1987/1, p. 25.

[11], Ibid.

ILO conventions. Except where specifically stated, the following discussion on implementation is not unique for the conventions on the working environment but is applicable to all ILO conventions.

As was pointed out earlier in this study, most ILO conventions enter into force 12 months after the second ratification, unlike nearly all other multilateral treaties which generally require a much larger number of ratifications for entry into force. Entry into force brings into play the ILO supervisory system for the implementation of the conventions. Provisions regarding entry into force of these conventions, therefore, accelerate the implementation of the agreements.

1. COMMITMENTS IMPOSED ON RATIFYING STATES BY THE AGREEMENTS ON THE WORKING ENVIRONMENT

(a) Obligations relating to national law and practice:

> States ratifying international agreements are obliged under international law to bring their national law and practice into conformity with their international obligations. Hence, all States ratifying the agreements on the working environment are obligated to conform their internal law and practice to the substantive provisions of the agreements. The agreements, however, may specify whether such conformity must be immediate or may be progressive over time. The ILO conventions on the working environment have varying provisions regarding this time element, as pointed out under each convention in the material following.
> The substantive obligations of each of the conventions on the working environment are summarized below; the summaries are indicative of the contents of the conventions but are not intended to include reference to each and every provision.

> --The Radiation Protection Convention, 1960, contains 15 substantive articles requiring, inter alia, that ratifying States make every effort to restrict the exposure of workers to ionising radiations to the lowest practicable level, to fix maximum permissable doses of ionising radiations which may be received from sources external or internal to the body, to provide appropriate warnings to indicate the presence of hazards from ionising radiations, to monitor workers in order to measure their exposure to ionising radiations, to provide appropriate medical examinations of workers and to provide appropriate inspection services for the purpose of supervising the application of its provisions.
> The Convention requires ratifying states to give effect thereto by means of laws or regulations, codes of practice of other appropriate means. Article 3 (3) (b) requires ratifying States to modify 'as soon as practicable' measures adopted by it prior to the ratification of the Convention, and hence provides some lag-time for Governments to catch up with the latest detailed standards which reflect development in scientific knowledge on ionising radiations which is referred to in Article 3 (1).
> --The Benzene Convention, 1971, contains 13 substantive articles providing, inter alia, that whenever harmless or less harmful substitute products are available, ratifying States should use such substitutes instead of benzene, that the use of benzene products shall be prohibited in certain work processes to be specified by national laws or regulations, that occupational hygiene and technical measures should be taken to ensure effective protection of workers exposed to benzene, that necessary measures

should be taken to prevent the escape of benzene vapour into the air, that work processes involving the use of benzene or of products containing benzene should, as far as practicable be carried out in an enclosed system, that appropriate medical examinations should be provided for workers employing benzene products and that pregnant and nursing mothers and young persons under 18 years of age should not be employed in work processes involving exposure to benzene and that benzene products should be clearly labeled. It further provides that appropriate inspection services for the purpose of supervising the application of the convention should be established.

--The <u>Occupational Cancer Convention, 1974</u>, contains 6 substantive articles which provide that ratifying States shall periodically determine the carcinogenic substances and agents to which occupational exposure shall be prohibited or made subject to authorisation or control (consideration to be given to the latest information contained in ILO codes of practice or guides), that every effort should be made to replace carcinogenic substances to which workers may be exposed by non-carcinogenic substances, that ratifying States should prescribe measures to be taken to protect workers against the risks of exposure to carcinogenic substances and take steps so that workers who have been or are likely to be exposed to carcinogenic substances be provided with all available information on the dangers involved and measures to be taken, and to take measures to ensure appropriate medical examinations. It requires ratifying States to provide appropriate inspection services for the purpose of supervising the application of the Convention.

--The <u>Working Environment (Air Pollution, Noise and Vibration) Convention, 1977,</u> contains 16 substantive articles. It permits ratifying States to accept the obligations of the Convention separately in respect of air pollution, noise and vibration. It provides, <u>inter alia,</u> that national laws or regulations shall prescribe the measures to be taken for the prevention and control of, and protection against, occupational hazards in the working environment due to air pollution, noise and vibration, imposes requirements on employers and workers to conform to safety measures, requires the establishment of criteria for determining the hazards due to exposure to air pollution, noise and vibration, requires the working environment to be kept as free as possible from any hazard due to these three aspects and for supervision of the health of workers exposed to such hazards. It also provides for appropriate inspection services.

--The <u>Occupational Safety and Health Convention, 1981,</u> provides that each ratifying State shall formulate, implement and periodically review a coherent national policy on occupational safety, health and the working environment. The aim of the policy should be to prevent accidents and injury to health by minimising hazards in the workplace. It provides that the policy shall take into account such matters as the design, testing, arrangement and use of material elements of work, relationships between the material elements of work and the persons who carry out and supervise the work, training necessary for the achievement of adequate standards of safety and health and the protection of workers from disciplinary measures as a result of actions taken to protect health.

As mentioned in A.3 this Convention is of a promotional nature.

--The <u>Asbestos Convention, 1986</u>, has 22 detailed articles dealing with protection of workers due to occupational exposure to asbestos. It prohibits the use of certain products and spraying of all forms of asbestos, care in demolition of structures in which asbestos has been used, measures concerning workers' clothing which may be contaminated with asbestos, and information and education regarding hazards relating to asbestos and a number of other specific provisions to control danger to the health of workers from asbestos exposure. It requires that the enforcement of the laws and regulations adopted to protect workers from health hazards due to exposure to asbestos should be secured by an adequate system of inspection.

The Preamble to the Convention refers to the Code of Practice on Safety in the Use of Asbestos published by the ILO in 1984.

--The Chemicals Convention, 1990, contains 19 substantive articles which provide for the classification of chemicals according to 'the type and degree of' their intrinsic health and physical hazards, for the marking of all chemicals and labelling of hazardous chemicals, for employers to maintain chemical safety data sheets containing essential information regarding their identity, supplier, classification, hazards and safety precaution, for responsibilities of suppliers, for proper disposal of chemicals, for duties of workers and rights of workers to remove themselves from danger resulting from the use of chemicals. It contains an important provision stipulating that when, in an exporting member State, all or some uses of hazardous chemicals are prohibited for reasons of safety and health at work, this fact and the reasons for it shall be communicated by the exporting state to any importing country.

Comments:

In addition to the substantive provisions of these conventions, other provisions are of interest:

(1) Reference to international or scientific criteria, programmes or guidelines are contained in a number of the conventions. The Chemicals Convention, 1990, refers in the Preamble to the International Programme on Chemical Safety of the ILO, UNEP, WHO, FAO and UNIDO and notes the relevant instruments, codes and guidelines promulgated by these organisations. Reference also is made in the Preamble to the list of occupational diseases, as amended in 1980, appended to the ILO Employment Injury Benefits Convention, 1964. Several articles of the Convention refer to international standards regarding the use of chemicals.

The Asbestos Convention, 1986, refers in the Preamble to the Code of practice on safety in the use of asbestos published by the ILO in 1984. Several articles of the Convention provide that national laws and regulations should be periodically reviewed in the light of technical progress and advance in scientific knowledge.

The Preamble to the Occupational Cancer Convention, 1974, states that, in drafting the Convention, account has been taken of the relevant work of other international organisations, and in particular of the World Health Organisation and the International Agency for Research on Cancer.

(2) Consultation with Employers' and Workers' Organisations is frequently mentioned in these conventions. In the Introduction to this study, it was pointed out that the ILO is a tripartite organisation involving not only government representatives, but also employers' and workers' organisations. Each of the conventions on the working environment contains a number of provisions requiring ratifying States to consult with these organisations. Article 3 of the Chemicals Convention, 1990, for example, provides that "The most representative organisations of employers and workers concerned shall be consulted on the measures to be taken to give effect to the provisions of this Convention." Conventions which permit the exclusion of particular branches of the economy or temporary derogations from their provisions invariably require consultation with employers' and workers' organisations.

(3) <u>Labour Inspection.</u> Provisions on labour inspection in the conventions have been cited earlier, but their importance in connection with these conventions warrants emphasis. Specific provisions on the obligation of the ratifying state to provide inspection services for the purpose of supervising the application of the Convention are included in most of these conventions on the working environment.

The extent of compliance of States with their obligations under the conventions on the working environment regarding implementation in national law and practice are discussed in sub-section 3 below.

(b) Obligations to report to international supervisory bodies

Article 22 of the ILO Constitution requires member States which have ratified conventions to report on their application of these conventions. At present, as a rule States are required to report on the position of their law and practice applying the convention every four years. Report forms sent by the Office on each Convention provide guidance on the information to be included in the report.

States which have ratified one of the seven conventions on the working environment evaluated in this study must, therefore, as a rule report to the ILO on the status of their law and practice with regard to the Convention every four years. The reports are given a legal examination by the ILO Committee of Experts on the Application of Conventions and Recommendations. The role of that Committee and the over-all ILO supervisory system is explained in the following section. When the Committee of Experts observes serious and persistent divergencies between the obligations of the Convention and the law and practice of a particular State, it may request governments to report in detail in the intervening period of the four-year reporting cycle.

In addition to these general obligations to report, the conventions on the working environment contain other specific reporting obligations. A number of these conventions require the State to notify the ILO if it has chosen, in accordance with the terms of the Convention, to exempt certain branches of the economy from the obligation of the Convention or to derogate temporarily from the provisions of the Convention. The reasons for exclusion of branches are required to be reported on and the position of the State's law and practice in respect to the excluded branches must also be contained in future reports. The Working Environment (Air Pollution, Noise and Vibration) Convention, 1977, provides that a ratifying State which wishes to exclude from the obligations of the Convention one or more of the categories of hazards shall so specify in its ratification, but must also give the reasons for doing so in its first report and subsequent reports must provide the position of its law and practice concerning the excluded branches.

States which have not ratified ILO conventions may be called upon, in accordance with Article 19 of the ILO Constitution, to provide information regarding their law and practice in relation to a particular convention and the difficulties which prevent ratification. On the basis of these reports and the reports which are simultaneously requested from ratifying States, the Committee of Experts regularly prepares a General Survey on the state of implementation of certain conventions. In 1987, a General Survey was prepared on the Working Environment Convention (Air Pollution, Noise and Vibration) Convention, 1977, and its accompanying Recommendation.[12] The Survey is discussed in a later section of this study.

Implicit in the obligation to report is the obligation of States to reply to questions directed to them by the ILO supervisory bodies, particularly the Committee of Experts on the Application of Conventions and Recommendations.

The extent of compliance of States with reporting obligations is discussed below in the subsection dealing the extent of compliance.

2. MONITORING AND MEASURING COMPLIANCE: THE ILO SUPERVISORY SYSTEM

The conventions on the working environment are examined under the ILO general supervisory system; the system described in this section, therefore, is the system used to monitor and measure the compliance of ratifying States with the obligations imposed by the agreements on the working environment evaluated in this study.

The ILO system of supervision of reports is referred to as the "regular system of supervision". As a rule the reports on ratified conventions, as mentioned previously, are due every four years. They are to be sent to the ILO by 15 October, covering the period up to 1 June of that year and are scheduled for examination by the ILO Committee of Experts in March of the following year. A very large number of reports are received on the 172 ILO conventions each year. In 1991, 1,409 reports covering the period up to 1 June 1990, were received.

(a) Role of ILO officials

ILO officials in the International Labour Standards Department are assigned to make a preliminary examination of the conformity of the law and practice of States with the conventions they have ratified, since it would be impossible for the Committee of Experts to examine all the reports in the two weeks of their meetings without these preliminary examinations.   Each ILO official who carries out these examinations is specialized in a particular group of conventions. One ILO official is assigned the preliminary examination of the conventions on the working environment, as well as other occupational safety and health conventions.

Employers' and workers' organisations are invited by the ILO to provide observations on the application of conventions in their countries. In 1991, 183 such observations were received--56 from employers' organisations and 127 from workers' organisations. ILO officials charged with the preliminary examination of reports on ratified conventions may also call upon the technical branches of the ILO (such as the Occupational Safety and Health Branch) for any comments or contributions they may have on the application of conventions and conduct their own research on the law and application of ratifying countries, including obtaining information objectively verifiable which is not included in the reports.

(b) Legal examination by Committee of Experts

The system of examination of the reports is two-tiered. The first is a legal

---

[12]. The General Survey also covered another ILO convention, the Guarding of Machinery Convention, 1963.

examination by a quasi-judicial body, the 20-member ILO Committee of Experts, in March of each year; the second examination is by the tripartite Committee on Application of Standards at the annual Conference in June of each year.

The two examinations are quite different. The 20 members of the Committee of Experts are prominent judges, professors, and labour law experts from selected geographic areas who have been named by the ILO tripartite Governing Body on the nomination of the Director-General. They serve in their independent capacity and carry out their examination in a closed session, without the presence of representatives of States. Their examination is legal, focusing on the law and practice as reported by the States and examined by ILO officials. States are not represented before the Committee. The Committee has acquired a reputation for competence, independence and objectivity based on its more than sixty years of experience.

(c) Comments on compliance directed to States: "Observations" and "Direct Requests"

The Committee of Experts directs questions to individual States concerning the application of conventions. "Observations" concern more long-standing or important failures to implement conventions and are printed in the annual Report of the Committee which is published before the June Conference.[13] Less important discrepancies, or discrepancies noted for the first time, are referred to in "direct requests" and are sent to the States concerned but are not published, although reference is made to them in the published report. The Committee's report also publishes the names of States which have failed to send in reports. In addition to the observations and direct requests addressed to individual states, the Committee also occasionally makes a General Observation concerning a convention which is intended for information and guidance of all states which have ratified the convention.

The Committee does not 'condemn' States for 'violations', but directs comments or questions to a government in the most polite terms when it finds that a convention is not being fully implemented. It may note "with regret" the failure of a State to bring its law and practice into conformity with a convention. The Committee also, on occasion, notes "with satisfaction" action which has been taken by a particular State to adopt legislation or change practices which have previously been subjected to criticism by the Committee. On occasion, it also requests a State to furnish another report the following year when it is not satisfied with the information provided in the report and does not wish to let the matter wait until the following report due in four years. It also publishes each year a General Survey on a particular convention or group of conventions.

The Committee is persistent in its efforts to ensure conformity with conventions. On many occasions, it makes similar comments year after year as a means of continuing pressure on a State.

(d) Consideration by tripartite Conference Committee

The Conference Committee on Standards which also considers the reports of ratifying States, based on the analyses by the Committee of Experts, is comprised of members of the

---

[13]. In 1991, the Committee's Report consisted of 523 pages.

delegations of States, including representatives of employers' and workers' organisations, attending the annual Conference. In 1991, the Conference Committee was composed of 192 members. It is regarded as one of the most important Committees of the Conference. At each annual Conference, the Conference Committee chooses some of the more serious cases raised by the Committee of Experts for discussion in public sessions. States' representatives appear before the Conference Committee to reply to questions. Members of the Conference Committee are not limited in their questioning to points raised in the Committee of Experts' report, but may raise other issues or facts as well.

Two aspects of the ILO Conference Committee procedure are particularly worthy of note: (a) the active, and critically important, participation of employer and worker representatives in addition to government delegates, and (b) the reference in the Committee's report in some years to certain governments which have failed to implement ratified conventions or failed consistently to provide reports. The Committee report states, when appropriate, that in some countries there has been continued failure fully to implement conventions, that the Committee notes this with grave concern, and that such cases will be discussed in subsequent paragraphs of the report. It may also indicate other less serious problems encountered. A complete record of discussion leading to the conclusion is also included in the report.

Although such mention may seem a minor sanction, the reaction of governments is evidence that such publication as a means of 'mobilizing shame' is a sensitive matter and one which governments do not lightly ignore. Ministry of labour officials have stated that public citation of their government for failure to implement conventions has had positive results, on occasion, by drawing the attention of other ministries and the legislative branch to the need for changes previously urged without effect by labour officials.

3. EXTENT OF COMPLIANCE WITH CONVENTION OBLIGATIONS

(a) Compliance with reporting obligations:

As the following statistics covering the last five years demonstrate, there has been a high degree of compliance by ratifying States with the obligation to report to the ILO at four year intervals on the application of conventions on the working environment.[14]

Convention	Year reports due	No. of Ratifications	Number of Reports not rec'd
Radiation Protection, 1960	1991	39	5
"	1987	38	4
Benzene, 1971	1988	26	2
Occ. Cancer, 1974	1988	22	2
Working Environment, 1977	1987	17	0
"	1990	24	5
Occ, S & Health, 1981	1990	12	2

---

[14]. The statistics are taken from the annual reports of the ILO Committee of Experts on the Application of Conventions and Recommendations, 1987-1991.

The Asbestos Convention, 1986, came into force only in 1989 and reports were not yet due by October 1990. The Chemicals Convention, 1990, is not yet in force.

Among the 20 reports on these conventions which were not received, 15 were from developing countries. It should be noted, however, that some were due from countries experiencing serious problems (Afghanistan, Lebanon and Nicaragua) during this period.

(b) Compliance with substantive obligations; Comments directed to States by Committee of Experts:

In the past five years, the Committee of Experts has addressed a number of comments to States which have ratified conventions on the working environment relating to their application of the conventions. The number of observations and direct requests addressed to governments under each convention reported in the annual Committee reports are summarised below. It will be recalled that "observations" are published and relate to more persistent or serious failures to implement conventions, although they may also express "interest" or "satisfaction" resulting from improvement in implementation in response to Committee comments. Direct requests are referred to in the Committee's report but are not published. They normally relate to less serious and less persistent failures to implement.

Summary of Committee Comments 1987-1991

Convention	No. of Observations	No. of Direct Requests
Radiation, Protection, 1960	5	33
Benzene, 1971	6	29
Occupational Cancer, 1974	5	34
Working Environment, 1977	10	25
Occupational Safety & Health, 1981	3	16
Totals	29	137

Among the 29 observations were six which noted with satisfaction the adoption of legislation or practices following Committee comments. In addition, two comments "noted with interest" pending efforts to adopt legislation or change practices to improve implementation following Committee comments. It thus appears that 21 of the comments related to substantive problems with implementation. Several of these were strong comments repeated to the same governments over succeeding years, referring to repeated failure to reply to the Committee's questions or to implement satisfactorily the convention.

It appears, nevertheless, that the Committee uncovered relatively few serious problems with the implementation of the conventions (given the number of observations concerning the five conventions over a five year period) but did note a substantial number of lesser failures to implement or less persistent failures.

During this same five year period, no government was cited in special paragraphs of the Conference Committee reports for especially serious failures to implement conventions on the working environment. Only four times during this period did the Committee call on government representatives to appear before it to discuss issues regarding implementation of the conventions.

4. MEASURES TO PROMOTE COMPLIANCE

(a) Comments of supervisory bodies.

The most important element in the promotion of implementation of these conventions has been the persistence of comments by the Committee of Experts and the calling of representatives of the government to appear before the Conference Committee to reply to questions regarding application of the Convention. Although, as mentioned immediately above, discussion of these conventions has been rare in the Conference Committee, it has appeared to promote compliance in the case referrred to in the following section. Analysis of the comments made over the years by the Conference Committee on these conventions has shown that persistence in observations to governments has been effective in improving implementation.

(b) Technical assistance provided by the ILO

Reference has been made earlier in this study to the varieties of technical cooperation to assist in the area of occupational health and safety. On several occasions, the Committee of Experts has recommended that governments call upon the ILO for technical assistance in implementing conventions.

In 1989, the Committee recommended to the government of Guinea, in an observation, that it request technical assistance from the Office in implementing the Occupational Cancer Convention, 1974. At the 1989 Conference, a government representative of Guinea was asked to appear before the Committee to discuss implementation of the Convention. In an observation in 1990, the Committee of Experts "noted with interest" that during the discussion concerning the application of this Convention in the 1989 Conference Committee, the government expressed the wish for technical assistance with a view to drawing up as quickly as possible an adequate legal framework for protection against occupational cancer. In April and May 1990, the official of the International Labour Standards Department charged with the responsibility for this Convention and an expert from the Occupational Safety and Health Branch undertook a mission to Guinea, during which a text was drafted with Guinea officials, which permitted implementation of the Convention.

(c) General Survey, 1987, on the Working Environment (Air Pollution, Noise and Vibration) Convention, 1977

The Committee of Experts regularly examines in depth a particular convention or group of conventions and publishes a General Survey on the Convention. These General Surveys are helpful both to States considering ratification and States which have already ratified the Convention. They contain extensive explanations concerning the meaning of terms in the Convention, the content of various provisions and problems that have been experienced in ratifying and implementing the convention or conventions.

In 1987, the Committee of Experts prepared a General Survey on the implementation of the Working Environment (Air Pollution, Noise and Vibration) Convention, 1977.[15] In accordance with Article 19 of the ILO Constitution, reports were requested not only from States which had ratified the Convention, but also from States which had not ratified it asking them to explain their reasons for non-ratification and plans for possible ratification. The Survey appeared to have a positive influence on ratification, since the following year six new ratifications of the Convention were registered. All 17 States which had ratified the Convention to this time provided reports.

This was the first time that such a General Survey was made of occupational safety and health conventions by the Committee. The 230 page report, entitled Safety in the Working Environment, examines many of the important issues relating to ratification and implementation of this Convention. It discusses in detail the scope of the instruments, general measures for protection of the working environment, establishment of criteria and exposure limits, preventive and protective measures, supervision of the health of the workers. It will serve as a useful guide to States ratifying the Convention in the future and to those looking for guidance as to the implications of the various provisions of the Convention.

5. MECHANISMS TO DEAL WITH DISPUTES OVER IMPLEMENTATION

A number of mechanisms are available to deal with disputes over implementation of ILO conventions. With one exception, noted below, these mechanisms have not been used as yet in connection with conventions on the working environment. Conflicts over the interpretation or application of ILO conventions may be submitted to the International Court of Justice. However, except for a period in the early history of the ILO when interpretations were requested from the Permanent Court of International Justice, no conflicts or requests for interpretation have been submitted to the Court.

The ILO Constitution also permits the bringing of complaints or representations concerning the application of ILO conventions. Articles 24-26 of the ILO Constitution provide procedures for the filing of complaints against States for failing to implement ratified conventions and for the establishment of Commissions of Inquiry in particular cases.

---

[15]. The Survey also related to the Guarding of Machinery Convention and the accompanying Recommendation. Safety in the Working Environment, General Survey by the Committee of Experts on the Application of Conventions and Recommendations, International Labour Conference, 73rd Session, 1978.

Article 26 of the Constitution provides that a State which has ratified a particular convention may file a complaint that another ratifying State is not effectively observing the provisions of the Convention. The same Article provides that the Governing Body may appoint a Commission of Inquiry to investigate the complaint if it sees fit. The Governing Body may also appoint Commissions of Inquiry on its own motion or on receipt of a complaint from a delegate of the Conference.

Article 24 of the Constitution provides that industrial associations of employers or workers may make "representations" that a member State has failed to observe a convention. Representations are examined by a tripartite committee appointed by the Governing Body from among its members and the representation and the government's reply may be published if the Governing Body so decides. In 1987, the Oil, Chemical and Atomic Workers International Union, AFL-CIO, invoking Article 24 of the ILO Constitution, submitted a representation alleging non-observance by the Government of the Federal Republic of Germany of the Occupational Cancer Convention, 1974 (no. 139), as well as other conventions not relating to occupational safety and health. The allegations related to practices and activities within the United States of BASF A.G. Corporation, headquartered in the Federal Republic of Germany, and its wholly owned subsidiaries. The representation was declared "not receivable" since the activities and practices in question had not occurred "within the jurisdiction of the Federal Republic of Germany for the purposes of the procedure for examination of representations under Article 24 of the Constitution...", (GB.235/17/11, Geneva, 2-6 March 1987).

These various mechanisms have been used on a number of occasions, but only once, as mentioned previously, in connection with any of the conventions on the working environment.

The text of the conventions on the working environment are, similarly to all ILO conventions, published and disseminated in seven languages: English, French, Spanish, Arabic, Chinese, German and Russian. The English and French versions of the text of the Conventions are equally authoritative.

All ILO member States are required to submit newly adopted ILO conventions to the competent authorities of the State for consideration within the time-limit of 12 to 18 months following adoption. They are to report to the ILO on steps taken to do so. The purpose of this submission requirement is to be certain that the Convention is available to competent authorities and to the public in the member States. This is an unusual requirement regarding international conventions.

Current information on the operation and implementation of international agreements and instruments are provided in the annual reports of the Committee of Experts which are sent to the member States of the ILO, in the annual Record of Proceedings of the Conference which includes the Report of the Conference Committee on the Application of Standards, and on numerous other publications of the ILO, including the General Surveys which appear regularly. The General Survey on the Working Environment Convention, 1977, referred to in the preceding section is an excellent method of informing the government concerning details required for implementation of the Convention.

The ILO regularly publishes the Proceedings of the numerous workshops and seminars dealing with occupational safety and health which it organises, particularly in developing countries.

The ILO also maintains an International Occupational Safety and Health Information Centre (CIS) which publishes and disseminates numerous documents concerning the working environment. It circulates widely a brochure listing all its publications on occupational safety and health.

A Training Manual on Safety-Health and Working Conditions, particularly directed to developing countries, has been prepared by the ILO in collaboration with the Swedish Joint Industrial Safety Council. In June 1991, the first issue of the African Newsletter on Occupational Health and Safety was published. The Newsletter is supported by collaboration between the ILO and the Finnish International Development Agency.

Operation

I. Institutional Arrangements and Costs of International Administration

As pointed out throughout this study, the conventions on the working environment are administered as part of the general ILO program of drafting, adoption and supervision of ILO conventions. A number of departments and branches of the International Labour Office are concerned in the administration of these conventions. During the period of drafting of the conventions on the working environment, the Occupational Safety and Health Branch and the Legal Department have important roles. The International Labour Standards Department is responsible for issues concerning the implementation of the conventions and acts as the secretariat for the Committee of Experts and the Conference Committee on the Application of Conventions and Recommendations in their work of supervision. Departments and branches of the Office concerned with technical cooperation, particularly the International Programme for the Improvement of Working Conditions and Environment (PIACT) may provide assistance to developing countries in issues relating to implementation of conventions. The International Occupational Safety and Health Information Centre provides documentation and publications concerning issues of the working environment.

The costs of international administration of these conventions is part of the general budget of the ILO. Technical cooperation provided to assist developing countries in implementing these conventions may be provided through UNDP funding, development banks or multi- bilateral assistance as well as from the ILO regular budget. Given the number of ILO departments, branches and programmes involved in the international administration of these conventions, it is exceptionally difficult, if not impossible, to separate out the costs of all these departments, branches and programmes as they relate to the administration of these seven conventions.

2. Mechanisms to ensure that scientific knowledge and advice is taken into account in policy-making decisions under these agreements

A number of provisions of the conventions on the working environment provide for reference to current scientific knowledge. Article 3 (1) of the Radiation Protection Convention, 1960, provides that all appropriate steps shall be taken to ensure effective protection of workers "in the light of knowledge available at the time." The Committee of Experts noted in a General Observation in 1991 that in assessing compliance with the Convention, it had frequently referred to current knowledge as embodied in the 1977 recommendation of the International Commission on Radiological Protection (ICRP) and other international reference sources based on the same recommendations. It pointed out that developments in the last few years had induced the ICRP to prepare a completely new set of recommendations to take account of new biological information. It stated that since these recommendations were about to be issued at the time of the Committee's 1991 Session it would defer commenting on the application of the Convention.[16]

Codification programming

On two occasions recently, in 1979 and in 1987, the ILO Governing Body has reviewed the classification of existing ILO Conventions and Recommendations, examined the need for revision of existing conventions and considered possible subjects for the adoption of new standards, including in the field of occupational safety and health.[17]

The 1979 examination by the Governing Body had listed the Radiation Protection Convention, 1960, as an instrument to be revised. The 1987 examination pointed out that the problem involved in the meantime had been taken into account by ILO supervisory bodies and activities in the field had also been developed by the International Atomic Energy Agency. (See section E.2 for the most recent Committee of Experts General Observation on this Convention). The 1987 study concluded that, in these circumstances, the adoption of revised standards on ionising radiations was no longer appropriate.[18]

Six new items were listed as possible subjects for new instruments in the field of occupational safety and health: (1) harmonisation of procedures for notification and registration of occupational accidents and diseases, (2) prevention of accidents arising out of the production and storage of dangerous substances, (3) fire prevention in commercial and similar establishments, (4) non-ionising radiation, (5) identification, transport, handling and use of harmful substances, and (6) use of agrochemicals in agriculture. In 1990, the Chemicals Convention, was adopted in response to the second item above.

The ILO Advisory Committee on Salaried Employees and Professional Workers had suggested in 1985 that intensive research should be undertaken into the potential health hazards of work with visual display units. The Office continues to follow the subject but believes it premature to envisage the adoption of standards on the question by the Conference.[19]

Procedures have begun for the adoption of new ILO standards on the subject of Prevention of Industrial Disasters. The Office has prepared a world-wide study of law and practice on the subject of major hazard control and sent a questionnaire to member States concerning the possible adoption of a convention and/or recommendation at the 1993 Conference. The questionnaire reflects the guidance contained in the ILO Code of practice on the prevention of major industrial accidents approved by the Governing Body in 1990.

---

[16]. Report of the Committee of Experts on the Application of Conventions and Recommendations, Report III (Part 4 A), International Labour Conference, 78th Session 1991, p. 403.

[17]. See Report of the Working Party on International Labour Standards and Decisions of the Governing Body, ILO Official Bulletin, Special Issue, Vol. LXX, 1987, Series A.

[18]. Ibid., Appendix III, para. 27, p. 45.

[19]. Ibid., Appendix III, para. 29, p. 45.

The first discussion of the adoption of the standards will be held at the 1992 International Labour Conference.

The ILO has found that mechanisms other than formal agreements contribute to the development of international law in the field of occupational safety and health. Reference has been made in various parts of the study to the usefulness of Recommendations, which are non-binding instruments, in addition to conventions. In the area of protection of the working environment, the ILO has drafted not only conventions and recommendations but also codes which may serve as guides to action by member States. The Code of practice on the prevention of major industrial accidents is referred to in the preceding paragraph. There is also a Code of practice on safety in the use of asbestos, Code of Practice on Radiation Protection, the ILO Practical Guide to the Protection of Workers against Noise and Vibrations in the Workplace and the various subjects covered in the Occupational Safety and Health Series, including Series No. 39 on Occupational Cancer: Prevention and Control. In addition, the list of occupational diseases, as amended in 1980, appended to the ILO Employment Injury Benefits Convention, 1964, has been referred to as a useful guide in the Chemicals Convention, 1990.

STATUS OF RATIFICATIONS AS OF 1 JANUARY 1992

(Treaty numbers see page 362)

Parties	110	111	112	113	114	115	116
Afghanistan			x				
Albania							
Algeria							
Angola							
Antigua & Barbuda							
Argentina	x		x				
Australia							
Austria							
Bahamas							
Bahrain							
Bangladesh							
Barbados	x						
Belgium	x						
Belize	x						
Benin							
Bhutan							
Bolivia		x				x	
Botswana							
Brazil	x		x	x		x	
Brunei Darussalam							
Bulgaria							
Burkina Faso							
Burundi							
Byelorussia*	x						
Cambodia							
Cameroon						x	
Canada						x	
Cape Verde							
Central African Republic							
Chad							
Chile							
China							
Colombia		x					
Cook Islands							
Comoros							
Congo							
Costa Rica				x			
Cote d'Ivoire		x					
Cuba		x		x	x		
Cyprus					x		
Czech & Slovak Fed. Rep.	x	x	x	x	x		

Parties	110	111	112	113	114	115	116
Democratic People's Rep. of Korea							
Denmark	x		x	x			
Djibouti	x						
Dominica							
Dominican Republic							
Ecuador	x	x	x	x		x	
Egypt	x		x	x			
El Salvador							
Equatorial Guinea							
Estonia*							
Ethiopia					x		
Fiji							
Finland	x	x	x	x	x	x	
France	x	x		x			
Gabon							
Gambia							
Germany	x	x	x				
Ghana	x			x			
Greece	x	x					
Grenada							
Guatemala						x	
Guinea	x	x	x	x			
Guinea-Bissau							
Guyana	x	x	x				
Haiti							
Holy See							
Honduras							
Hungary	x	x	x				
Iceland			x		x		
India	x	x					
Indonesia							
Iran (Islamic Republic of)							
Iraq	x	x	x	x			
Ireland							
Israel		x					
Italy	x	x	x	x			
Jamaica							
Japan	x		x				
Jordan							
Kenya							
Kiribati							
Kuwait		x					
Lao People's Democratic Rep.							
Latvia*							
Lebanon	x						

Parties	110	111	112	113	114	115	116
Lesotho							
Liberia							
Libyan Arab Jamahiriya							
Liechtenstein							
Lithuania*							
Luxembourg							
Madagascar							
Malawi							
Malaysia							
Maldives							
Mali							
Malta		x		x			
Marshall Islands							
Mauritania							
Mauritius							
Mexico	x				x		
Micronesia							
Monaco							
Mongolia							
Morocco		x					
Mozambique							
Myanmar							
Namibia							
Nauru							
Nepal							
Netherlands	x				x		
New Zealand							
Nicaragua	x	x	x				
Niger							
Nigeria							
Niue							
Norway	x		x	x	x		
Oman							
Pakistan							
Palau							
Panama							
Papua New Guinea							
Paraguay	x						
Peru			x				
Philippines							
Poland	x						
Portugal				x	x		
Qatar							
Republic of Korea							
Republic of Yemen							
Romania		x					

Parties	110	111	112	113	114	115	116
Rwanda							
St. Kitts & Nevis							
St. Lucia							
St. Vincent & the Grenadines							
Samoa							
San Marino				x			
Sao Tome & Principe							
Saudi Arabia							
Senegal							
Seychelles							
Sierra Leone							
Singapore							
Solomon Islands							
Somalia							
South Africa							
Spain	x	x		x	x	x	
Sri Lanka	x						
Sudan							
Suriname							
Swaziland							
Sweden	x		x	x	x	x	
Switzerland	x	x	x				
Syrian Arab Republic	x	x	x				
Thailand							
Togo							
Tonga							
Trinidad & Tobago							
Tunisia							
Turkey	x						
Tuvalu							
Uganda						x	
Ukraine*	x						
Union of Soviet Socialist Rep.*	x			x			
United Arab Emirates							
United Kingdom	x			x			
United Republic of Tanzania				x			
United States of America							
Uruguay		x	x	x	x		
Vanuatu							
Venezuela			x		x		
Viet Nam							
Yugoslavia*		x	x	x	x		
Zaire							
Zambia		x		x			
Zimbabwe							

* Membership status subject to further clarification.

CHAPTER X

LIABILITY FOR ENVIRONMENTAL DAMAGE

Günther Doeker and Thomas Gehring

This chapter covers the following international agreements on liability for environmental damage:

I.   Liability for nuclear damage

(117) The 1960 Paris **Convention on Third Party Liability in the Field of Nuclear Energy**, and related instruments;

(118) the 1963 Vienna **Convention on Civil Liability for Nuclear Damage**, and related instruments;

(119) the 1971 Brussels **Convention Relating to Civil Liability in the Field of Maritime Carriage of Nuclear Material**;

(120) the 1962 Brussels **Convention on the Liability of Operators of Nuclear Ships**;

II.   Civil liability for pollution damage caused by maritime transport of oil

(121) the 1969 Brussels **Convention on Civil Liability for Oil Pollution Damage**, and related instruments;

(122) the 1971 Brussels **Convention on the Establishment of an International Fund for Compensation of Oil Pollution Damage**, and related instruments;

III.   Civil liability for pollution damage caused by offshore operations

(123) the 1977 London **Convention on Civil Liability for Oil Pollution Damage Resulting from Exploration for and Exploitation of Seabed Mineral Resources**;

IV.   Civil liability for damage caused by inland transport of dangerous substances

(124) the 1989 Geneva **Convention on Civil Liability for Damage Caused During Carriage of Dangerous Goods by Road, Rail and Inland Navigation Vessels.**

V.   Other developments concerning liability for environmental damage

Reference is also made to current drafting work towards (a) a Protocol to the 1989 Basel Convention (No. 103) on liability and compensation for damage resulting from the transboundary movement and disposal of hazardous wastes; (b) a Council of Europe draft convention on civil liability for damage resulting from activities dangerous to the environment; and (c) related work in the U.N. International Law Commission.

A list showing the status of ratifications as of 1 January 1992 is annexed (pages 431-435).

International environmental conventions generally focus on so-called "ultra-hazardous" activities which have a number of characteristics in common:

-   Activities (e.g., maritime transport of large quantities of oil, peaceful use of nuclear energy) are considered benign and economically advantageous. But they involve high risks of accidental damage. High risk implies comparatively low probability to cause relatively high damage (in contrast to high probability to cause relatively minor damage).
-   In view of the complexity of technologies involved or for other reasons, the risk to cause damage may be minimized, but not entirely avoided. Any attempt to avoid such risks would result in the termination of the risk-creating activity.
-   As long as activities are carried out, a certain economic risk of (large-scale) damage remains which has to allocated.

Against this backdrop, international liability conventions try to balance two conflicting goals: (a) to relieve third-party victims of damage caused by risk-creating activities; and (b) to relieve operators of unnecessary obstacles in carrying out such activities.

As a consequence, liability conventions distribute economic risks between risk-creator (e.g. operators or owners), third parties suffering damage, and the public; and they provide an internationally uniform legal framework for the regulation of liability for damage arising from certain activities.

The balance between these goals varies, of course, depending upon the specific contexts in which conventional regimes are moulded.

Generally, liability regimes are determined by five principles:
(i)   Strict or absolute liability (liability regardless of fault);
(ii)   limited liability;
(iii)   channelling liability to a single clearly identifiable person;
(iv)   compulsory insurance or other financial securities limited in amount;
(v)   procedures for civil claims in competent national courts.

These principles indicate that liability conventions are construed to allocate economic risks. To the extent that they allocate economic costs of activities to risk-creators, they reflect the Polluter-Pays Principle. Generally, the principle of (strict) liability provides an incentive to minimize risks; liability regimes therefore seem to have an immediate impact on environmental protection. In so far as they remove legal and economic constraints from industrial activities that are generally considered benign, they also have a direct impact on development. In balancing the two goals, they attempt to integrate the two important elements of environment and development.

Basically, the approach of the liability regimes reviewed here provides (a) an inter-governmentally adopted and domestically implemented legal framework; and (b) regular settlement of claims below the inter-governmental level between bearers of liability, insurers and victims, supervised by national courts.

I. Liability for Nuclear Damage

The Conventions on liability for nuclear damage balance the promotion of economic activities on the one hand and economic relief for victims of damage caused by such activities on the other. They emphasize the promotion aspect, considering that international law concerning nuclear liability was developed during the early 1960s, at a time when peaceful use of nuclear energy was at its beginnings and far from being an economically powerful industrial sector. The international instruments concerning nuclear liability law are closely interrelated.

1. The Paris/Brussels Conventional Regime

The regional Paris/Brussels conventional regime was prepared within the Organisation for Economic Co-operation and Development (OECD). It consists of the following instruments:

(117) Convention on Third Party Liability in the Field of Nuclear Energy, Paris 1960 (Paris Convention);

(a)   Additional Protocol to the Convention on Third Party Liability in the Field of Nuclear Energy, Paris 1964;

(b)   Protocol to Amend the Convention on Third Party Liability in the Field of Nuclear Energy of 29 July 1960, as Amended by the Additional Protocol of 28 January 1964, Paris 1982;

(c)   Convention Supplementary to the Paris Convention of 29 July 1960 on Third Party Liability in the Field of Nuclear Energy, Brussels 1963 (Brussels Supplementary Convention);

(d)   Additional Protocol to the Convention of 31 January 1963 Supplementary to the Paris Convention of 29 July 1960 on Third Party Liability in the Field of Nuclear Energy, Paris 1964;

(e)   Protocol to Amend the Convention of 31 January 1963 Supplementary to the Paris Convention of 29 July 1960 on Third Party Liability in the Field of Nuclear Energy as Amended by the Additional Protocol of 28 January 1964, Paris 1982.

(f)   Joint Protocol Relating to the Application of the Vienna Convention and the Paris Convention, Vienna 1988.

Objectives and achievement

The objectives of the Paris Convention, based upon the intention to elaborate and harmonize legislation related to nuclear energy concerning third party liability, are (a) to ensure adequate and equitable compensation for persons suffering nuclear damage; and (b) to ensure that the development, the production and uses of nuclear energy are thereby not precluded. Unlike the regimes concerning carriage of dangerous substances and oil pollution (Nos. 97-98 and 100 below), the Paris Convention emphasizes the priority to develop nuclear energy production as compared to the relief of victims. Accordingly, it provides the following liability regime:

- The operator of a nuclear installation shall be strictly and exclusively liable for nuclear damage (Art. 3). All other persons involved, e.g. suppliers or carriers, are relieved from any liability whatsoever (Art. 6).
- Liability of the operator shall be covered by insurance or financial security (Art. 10).
- Liability is limited in time to ten years from the occurrence of an incident (Art. 8) and in amount to 15 million European Units of Account (EUA, equivalent to gold-based US dollars) (subsequently amended) per incident (Art. 7). Domestic laws may provide other limits, but the amount may not fall below 5 million EUA (later amended) (Art. 15).
- Action shall be brought in a competent court in the state in which the installation is situated (Art. 13).
- Parties may adopt additional measures concerning various aspects.

Within the limits relating to time and amount of compensation, the regime establishes a victim-oriented liability regime, while at the same time channelling economic risks to one easily identifiable person and relieving industry from covering multiple risks by insurance. However, amounts of compensation are in no way related to anticipated costs caused by severe nuclear incidents. To stabilize the "channelling" rule and the exclusive liability of the operator of a nuclear installation, additional funds had to be provided.

The sole objective of the Brussels Supplementary Convention is to supplement the measures adopted in the Paris Convention by increasing the amounts of compensation available (cf. preamble). The Supplementary Convention establishes a three-tier compensation system:

- The basis is provided by the operator's liability according to national legislation and the Paris conventional regime. Compensation must not be less than EUA 5 million (subsequently amended).
- An additional layer raises the amount available for compensation up to a total of EUA 70 million (subsequently amended). It is financed from public funds of the Party in the territory of which the damage-prone installation is situated.
- A third layer brings the compensation available up to a total of EUA 120 million (subsequently amended). It is financed by public funds through the community of Contracting Parties (Art. 8).
- Public funds of the second and third layers are subject to the same claims procedures as private funds; in practice, the court competent under the Paris Convention allocates funds available under the Brussels Supplementary Convention (Art. 9).

\-   Contributions to the third layer are calculated in proportion to gross national products of the Parties (50%) and in proportion to the aggregate thermal power of reactors situated in the territory of Parties (Art. 12).

The 1964 Protocols do not in substance modify the interrelated regime. It was the objective of the 1964 Additional Protocol to the Paris Convention to adapt the regional Paris Convention to the regime of the global Vienna Convention, adopted in 1963 within IAEA (see No. 118 below) to allow simultaneous participation in both instruments. Similarly, the 1964 Additional Protocol to the Brussels Supplementary Convention adapts the latter instrument to a slightly modified Paris Convention.

The 1982 Protocols incorporate a number of interpretations adopted by the Contracting Parties and introduce two modifications of the regime. They replace the European Unit of Account, which was based on the gold-based US-dollar, by the Special Drawing Right (SDR) of the International Monetary Fund as principal unit of account. Accordingly, the 1982 Protocol to the Paris Convention adjusts the amount of liability on behalf of the operator at SDR 15 million, but not less than SDR 5 million. At the same time, the 1982 Protocol to the Brussels Supplementary Convention raised the compensation limits of the second and third layers to SDR 175 million and SDR 300 million respectively.

The Paris/Brussels regime integrates environmental and developmental aspects of the peaceful use of nuclear energy, although priority is placed upon the latter. Due to low limitation amounts (as compared to the anticipated costs of a major incident), it might have only an indirect influence on environmental protection. Moreover, it does not provide for compensation for measures designed to prevent damage.

Participation in the Paris/Brussels regime is currently limited to Western Europe. It does not take into account the special situation of developing countries. Nevertheless, since it was the first international regime on liability for nuclear damage, the Paris Convention heavily influenced the development of domestic laws concerning nuclear liability all over the world. Its general approach was incorporated, with only minor modifications, into the global Vienna Convention (No. 94). Accordingly, it introduced internationally applied standards concerning liability for a type of ultra-hazardous activities.

One objective of the Conventions, namely the creation of a uniform law of liability for nuclear damage, has been achieved far beyond their regional territorial application. The intention to provide uniformity of law to remove obstacles for the development of new sources of energy proved to be successful. There has been no serious attempt to modify the basic principles of the Paris/Brussels conventional regime.

As far as the provision of "adequate and equitable" compensation is concerned, the result is more ambiguous. No serious nuclear incident has occurred in the territorial jurisdiction of the Conventions to test the compensation mechanism. There is no doubt that compensation limits are low. They were not increased in light of growing economic risks involved in the exploitation of nuclear energy for peaceful purposes, or growing economic capabilities of nuclear and insurance industries in Western Europe. As a consequence of modifications introduced by the 1982 Protocols, the part of compensation financed by public funds increased significantly, while the part of privately financed compensation was allowed to decrease. In proportion many Contracting Parties provide by domestic law compensation far beyond the limits of the first two layers of the interrelated regime; e.g., Germany provides for unlimited operators' liability, with

DM 500 million (approximately SDR 200 million) to be covered by private insurance and insurance pools, and another DM 500 million provided by public funds. The OECD Steering Committee for Nuclear Energy recommended in 1990 to adjust operators' liability to SDR 150 million, ten times that provided for by the Paris Convention[1]. As a consequence, the authority of the Paris Convention as reliable guide in matters of nuclear liability seems at risk of being gradually undermined, while the Brussels Supplementary scheme may lose its relevance owing to high national standards.

Participation

The Paris Convention is regional in scope. It was elaborated within OECD (then OEEC). The first paragraph of the preamble expressly mentions as signatories to the Convention seventeen European members of OECD. Other member countries of OECD and States associated with that organization may join the Convention. However, States that are neither signatories nor members of or associated with OECD may become members by unanimous assent of the Contracting Parties (in fact, the USSR was invited to join, in the course of a G-7 meeting in Tokyo). Participation in the Brussels Supplementary Convention depends upon participation in the Paris Convention. Yet, non-signatories to the Brussels Supplementary Convention may accede only upon unanimous assent of Contracting Parties. The various Protocols do not introduce other procedures.

Under both the Paris and Brussels Supplementary Conventions, reservations to one or more provisions may be made by a Party at any time prior to its ratification or accession. Yet, reservations are admissible only in case they have been expressly accepted by the Signatories. The Paris Convention, as amended, is accompanied by five accepted reservations, which are applicable to several Parties.

The Paris Convention is in force for 14 Parties which are exclusively European members of OECD. 11 of these States are also members of the Brussels Supplementary Convention. Developing countries neither attended negotiations nor joined the Conventions at a later date. In light of the existence of the Vienna Convention (No. 118), there has been no attempt to encourage developing countries to participate.

Participation of countries in the Paris Convention was, without doubt, influenced by the conviction that the limits of compensation provided were insurable and could be covered by operators. With respect to private operators, States would not incur any costs.

The decision to participate in the Brussels Supplementary Convention was primarily based on the desire to remove possible obstacles to the development of nuclear power, provided that compensation by public funds was limited to a reasonable amount. US-based suppliers of nuclear technology had indicated they might stop supply due to compensation amounts that were too low to preclude claims under regular (i.e. non-nuclear) US liability laws. Therefore, it appears that the decision to participate may to a significant degree be attributed to the influence of industrial non-governmental organizations.

---

[1] See (OECD) Nuclear Law Bulletin No. 45/1990, p. 75.

Reservations contributed to flexibility without over-burdening the treaty regime with exemptions of interest only to a limited number of Parties concerned. However, since reservations cannot be made unilaterally, they are subject to negotiation and form part of the overall compromise commonly adopted.

Implementation and information

The Paris Convention entered into force upon deposit of the fifth ratification, in April 1968. However, as its primary purpose was the unification of national laws on nuclear liability, its incorporation into domestic legal systems did not depend upon its formal entry into force. The Brussels Supplementary Convention required six ratifications. It seems evident that fund schemes require a minimum participation number to become operative in order to distribute the economic risks involved. Despite the late entry into force of the Brussels Supplementary Convention (December 1974), the requirement appears not to have been overly restrictive.

The 1964 Protocols provide for simultaneous ratification of Conventions and their respective Protocols. They were thus incorporated into the regular ratification process. According to the Paris Convention, the 1982 Protocol entered into force in October 1988 upon ratification by two-thirds of the Parties. However, according to the Brussels Supplementary Convention, amendments require "agreement" by Parties, i.e., the 1982 Protocol required ratification by all Parties to the Convention. The fact that the Protocol entered into force only in August 1991 may be attributed to this strict requirement. Both Protocols of 1982 stipulate that Parties are under an obligation to undertake ratification of the respective instruments as soon as possible. While the intention of the clause seems to be clear, its effect remains doubtful.

Under the Paris Convention, Parties are primarily obliged to implement the regime on nuclear liability into national law. It includes provisions for jurisdiction of courts, enforcement of judgements of foreign courts, and application of the Convention without discrimination as to nationality or residence. Likewise, Parties to the Brussels Supplementary Convention are primarily obliged to incorporate regulations concerning additional compensation into domestic law.

Compliance concerning obligations of the interrelated conventional regime can only be monitored by assessment of domestic laws on nuclear liability. While the Conventions do not provide for supervisory mechanisms, the OECD Nuclear Energy Agency (NEA) as responsible parent organization for the Paris Convention carefully follows up and provides information on developments in domestic nuclear laws.

According to the Brussels Supplementary Convention, Parties shall submit a list of all installations for peaceful uses of nuclear energy and update these lists as appropriate. Moreover, in case of nuclear incidents, Parties shall communicate early information about the incident and have to make available public funds for compensation. Yet, as of now, no such incident has occurred. No other obligations as to data disclosure exist.

Promotion of compliance largely depends upon consultations within the NEA-Steering Committee on Nuclear Energy. The Steering Committee also promotes rapid ratification of instruments that are adopted and signed.

Beside informal consultation in the Steering Committee, the Brussels Supplementary Convention institutes a formal procedure with regard to objections concerning lists of nuclear installations submitted by the Parties. Parties may notify such protests to the depositary (the Belgian Government) within three months upon submission of the list concerned. Any (other) disputes arising between two or more Parties to either of the Conventions shall be submitted to the European Nuclear Energy Tribunal. However, as of now, no dispute has been brought before the Tribunal.

The texts of all instruments are widely disseminated in English and French by OECD. The principal vehicle for the dissemination of information on the operation and implementation of Conventions, as well as on domestic laws or nuclear third party liability in general, is the Nuclear Law Bulletin published twice a year by NEA in the working languages of OECD. It closely follows law-making and implementation processes and reproduces texts of new instruments, decisions and recommendations prepared and adopted by the OECD/NEA Steering Committee, etc. Decisions and recommendations of the Steering Committee interpreting the Paris Convention have been compiled in a bilingual booklet re-issued in 1990. Most recently, OECD/NEA issued a study of domestic and international nuclear liability laws under the title "Nuclear Legislation: Third Party Liability" (Paris 1990).

NEA and OECD have also repeatedly organized symposia addressing specific issues of international nuclear liability laws. The proceedings are published.

Operation, review and adjustment

While the OECD performs depositary functions for the Paris Convention, the Belgian Government performs depositary functions for the Brussels Supplementary Convention. Neither the Paris nor the Brussels Supplementary Conventions or any of the Protocols establish a separate institutional mechanism, but instead rely on the institutional mechanism of the parent organization. Within the framework of OECD/NEA, there exists a Steering Committee for Nuclear Energy composed of government representatives, which meets regularly, and which has established a permanent subsidiary body, the Group of Governmental Experts on Third Party Liability in the Field of Nuclear Energy. Through these bodies, the provisions of the Paris Convention are subject to continuous review and interpretation. Although the institutional mechanism of NEA is not formally responsible for the Brussels Supplementary Convention, in fact it fully includes the latter instrument in its monitoring and review process.

There are no institutionalized mechanisms for bringing scientific and technical advise into the decision-making process. With regard to the Paris regime, co-operation between States and industries concerned has been, and still is, close, especially with associations representing insurers and electric power producers. By contrast, there is no participation of environmental NGOs in relevant international fora, in particular in the Steering Committee and its subsidiary body.

The Paris Convention provides for a review conference five years after entry into force. In the Brussels Supplementary Convention there is no provision for such a review. In practice, however, both instruments are under continuous review within the Steering Committee and the Group of Governmental Experts.

Neither Convention stipulates provisions for regular review of compensation limits and their adaptation to changing conditions. Each modification of compensation figures is subject to a time-consuming ad hoc amendment and ratification process.

Codification programming

Currently, no drafts or revisions of existing instruments are under preparation at the regional level. Future work by Paris/Brussels Convention Parties within the framework of NEA/OECD has to be closely coordinated with parallel work proceeding within IAEA. It may be expected that the Paris/Brussels regime will have to be adapted to results achieved at the global level.

Co-ordination between the regional and the global level is accomplished by close co-operation between the two secretariats concerned (NEA and IAEA), and by participation of Paris/Brussels Convention Parties in proceedings at the global level. In fact it has been attempted to integrate the two parallel liability regimes through adoption of a Joint Protocol (see No. 94/b below).

Two principal gaps exist in the Paris/Brussels scheme. The regime lacks institutional flexibility, whereas more recently adopted instruments concerning other ultra-hazardous activities frequently contain simplified amendment procedures for rapid adaptation of provisions to changing circumstances. This is particularly relevant with respect to changes of amounts of liability and compensation.

The Paris/Brussels regime does not compensate for expenditures incurred for preventive measures. Since compensation depends on clear causal evidence, successful preventive measures may interrupt the causal chain. The "Chernobyl" incident made clear that beyond the borders of the country in whose territory an incident occurs, costs arise primarily with regard to preventive measures. Ways of incorporating such measures into the compensation scheme are now being considered.

Due to the institutional inflexibility of the Paris/Brussels regime, decisions or recommendations of the NEA Steering Committee or the OECD Council gain relevance for the development of internationally co-ordinated nuclear liability laws. If implemented into domestic laws, they may - to a certain extent - replace amendments of formal legal instruments.

2.   The Vienna Convention

The regime consists of three instruments:

(118)   the Vienna Convention on Civil Liability for Nuclear Damage, 1963;
- (a)   the Optional Protocol Concerning the Compulsory Settlement of Disputes, Vienna 1963;
- (b)   the Joint Protocol Relating to the Application of the Vienna Convention and the Paris Convention, Vienna 1988.

Objectives and achievement

The Vienna Convention, which is global in scope, primarily establishes minimum standards providing financial protection against damage resulting from nuclear installations. In this way, the Convention was intended to contribute to the development of friendly relations between countries with differing constitutional and social systems (preamble). Unlike the Paris Convention (No. 117 above), it does not address the issue of adequacy or equitableness of compensation. However, the liability regime of the Vienna Convention resembles closely that of the regional Paris Convention:

- Operators of nuclear installations shall be absolutely and exclusively liable for nuclear damage (Arts. II, IV).
- They shall cover their liability by financial security, e.g., insurance. However operators that are States or their constituent parts (regional entities) shall not be required to hold insurance cover. Licensing States shall ensure payment of compensation beyond the yield of insurance (Art. VII).
- Liability may be limited in amount, but to no less than gold-based US$ 5 million, and in time to no less than 10 years from the occurrence of an incident (Art. V).
- Action shall be brought in a competent court in the installation state (Art. XI).

An important objective of the Vienna Convention was to facilitate the development of nuclear programmes, i.e., of ultra-hazardous activities, in member countries. The Convention balances the promotion of industrial development (developing a uniform and widely recognized law of liability for nuclear damage) and environmental protection (relieving victims from economic costs of nuclear damage).

The Convention does not expressly address the special situation of developing countries. However, the cost-effective element of the regime, i.e. the minimum amount of compensation, has been adjusted in view of the participation of developing countries at a lower figure as compared to the Paris/Brussels regime (No. 117 above) and to the Nuclear Ship Convention (No. 120 below).

The Vienna Convention has, as a concomitant to the Paris Convention, contributed to promoting uniform laws on liability for nuclear damage. However, its effect remained limited because only 14 States are party to the Convention, several of which do not have any nuclear programme. At present, the Convention is applicable only to 8 existing reactors and four under construction, whereas the Paris Convention applies to 153 existing installations and 13 under construction[2].

Participation

The Vienna Convention is open for signature and subsequent ratification by States represented at the International Conference on Civil Liability for Nuclear Damage, Vienna 1963. Accession is possible for the members of the United Nations, its specialized agencies or the IAEA.

The Convention does not address the issue of reservations.

Currently[3], the Convention is in force for 14 countries, namely Argentina, Bolivia, Cameroon, Chile, Cuba, Egypt, Hungary, Mexico, Niger, Peru, Philippines, Poland, Trinidad & Tobago and Yugoslavia. No member of the Paris Convention as of now has ratified the Vienna Convention.

The Convention was prepared by an Intergovernmental Committee attended by representatives from seven Western industrialized countries (four European, three others), three Eastern European industrialized countries, and four developing countries (Argentina, Brazil, India and Egypt). The Diplomatic Conference that adopted the Convention was attended by 58 delegations of which 29 were from industrialized countries (18 from Western Europe, 6 from Eastern Europe, and 5 others), whereas 25 represented developing countries (9 from Asia, 10 from America, 3 from Africa, and 4 from Europe); two additional developing countries were represented by observers[4].

No regular meetings or programme activities are envisaged. However, within the framework of IAEA, a Standing Committee on Civil Liability for Nuclear Damage was established that met occasionally to discuss issues relevant to the Convention. It was composed of 15 States, including 5 developing and 10 industrialized countries. Limitations concerning participation were removed as the Committee was transformed into an open-ended negotiation forum with a broader mandate. Currently, about sixty delegations from both developing and industrialized countries as well as non-governmental organizations attend its sessions.

The principal benefit for all countries participating in the Convention, including developing countries, is the right of their nationals to claim compensation in case of nuclear damage caused by installations situated in a Contracting Party. Currently, the minimum amount of compensation is subject to review and subsequent adaptation; the benefit may be expected to substantially increase in the near future.

---

[2] Figures from Status of nuclear installations as of 31 December 1990; IAEA Bulletin 1/1991, p. 43.

[3] As of 1 January 1992.

[4] Figures from: International Conventions on Civil Liability for Nuclear Damage, IAEA Legal Series No. 4, Vienna 1976.

Participation in the Convention does not depend on technical and scientific assistance. However, IAEA may provide legal assistance if requested. In case of countries without nuclear programmes, participation does not imply any financial obligations.

Implementation and information

The Convention entered into force three months after the deposit of the fifth instrument of ratification (Article XXXII). This requirement appears not to have been overly ambitious, even though it took 14 years until the Convention entered into force on 12 November 1977.

Obligations imposed upon Parties extend primarily to implementation of the regime set out in the Convention. States Parties ensure the payment of compensation in case they do not provide for insurance of the operator or beyond the yield of such insurance and up to the operator's liability. Parties shall provide for necessary jurisdictional competences, and recognize final judgements entered by foreign courts in accordance with the Convention. They shall not invoke immunities in legal proceedings under the Convention. There is no systematic monitoring of implementation. Parties do not regularly report about implementation and do not have to disclose or supply data.

While the Convention has no rules concerning the settlement of disputes, the 1963 Conference adopted a Protocol Concerning Compulsory Settlement of Disputes. The Protocol is optional and subject to ratification. It enters into force upon the second ratification. As of now, only one ratification has been deposited.

The Convention was drafted and published in four languages, English, French, Spanish, and Russian[5]. Travaux préparatoires have been published in English[6], French, Spanish and Russian.

Operation, review and adjustment

The Director-General of IAEA is the depositary. The Convention does not provide for institutional or administrative arrangements. There are no regular meetings and programmes. In consequence, no costs of attendance or administration are incurred by Parties under the Convention.

While there are no separate mechanisms under the Convention for the regular review of provisions or consideration of scientific and technical information, the Board of Governors of IAEA may decide, and has decided, specific minor technical issues. Pursuant to Article XXV, a review conference shall be convened by the Director General of IAEA upon request by at least one-third of the Contracting Parties any time after the expiry of five years from entry into force of the Convention (i.e. since 1982). As of now, no such conference has taken place, but a review conference may be called in 1992.

---

[5] International Conventions on Civil Liability for Nuclear Damage, IAEA Legal Series No. 4, Vienna 1966.

[6] Civil Liability for Nuclear Damage, Official Records, International Conference, Vienna, 29 April - 19 May 1963, IAEA Legal Series No. 2, Vienna 1964.

Beside the arrangements provided for under the Convention, the IAEA Standing Committee on Civil Liability for Nuclear Damage provided an arena for deliberations concerning the Convention. With respect to the current review of the Vienna Convention, the mandate of the Committee, renamed "Standing Committee on Liability for Nuclear Damage", was extended to include international liability matters.

Codification programming

The Chernobyl incident dramatically demonstrated that neither the regime of the Vienna Convention nor its geographical scope are satisfactory. Since 1987, a review of all aspects of international law on liability for nuclear damage has been instituted within the framework of the IAEA. The first stage of this work led to the adoption in 1988 of the Joint Protocol Relating to the Application of the Vienna Convention and the Paris Convention. With regard to the revision of the Vienna Convention, major issues under consideration concern the following: a revision of the limitations of liability of the Vienna Convention, with regard to the minimum amount of compensation, the period of time within which compensation may be claimed, and the exclusion of compensation for preventive measures. The Standing Committee has also addressed an evaluation of possibilities for introducing additional compensation, such as the compensation provided by the Brussels Supplementary Convention in addition to liability of the operator under the Paris Convention (No. 93). Supplementary layers of compensation may either be incorporated into the Vienna conventional regime or in a new draft instrument. Issues of State responsibility and liability are also under consideration.

The review and revision process of the Vienna Convention, and the drafting of some possible new mechanism has to be closely related to developments proceeding within OECD/NEA in respect of the Paris/Brussels conventional regime. Drafting is coordinated through close relations between the two international organizations, i.e. OECD/NEA and IAEA, and through participation of Paris/Brussels Convention Parties in the current deliberation process within IAEA. Measures adopted at the global level may require subsequent adaptation of the regional Paris/Brussels conventional regime.

Developments in international law have been influenced by developments at the domestic level. Domestic laws extend the scope of liability far beyond the minimum standards contained in international conventions. Therefore, the current revision of the Vienna Convention attempts to re-establish a higher degree of international uniformity of nuclear liability laws.

3. The Joint Protocol relating to the Application of the Vienna Convention and the Paris Convention, Vienna 1988.

Objectives and achievement

Third party liability for nuclear damage from stationary sources is governed by two regimes that are, even though similar in approach, independent from each other. One lesson that can be drawn from "Chernobyl" accident is that the two regimes should be merged. Accordingly, the objective of the Joint Protocol is to establish a link between the Vienna and Paris Conventions. Such an approach appears to be unique. A single Protocol, signed by the Parties to both regimes, is intended to amend both Conventions at the same time. It provides that an operator situated in a country participating in the Paris Convention shall be liable (also) for damage suffered in the territory of a Party to the Vienna Convention, if it has acceded to the Joint Protocol; and vice versa.

Since the Joint Protocol has been adopted only recently (1988), it is not yet clear whether it will meet its objective. To a large extent, its success will depend upon increasing acceptance of the Vienna Convention by Eastern European countries having nuclear programmes. The number of ratifications, in particular by countries with nuclear installations, will indicate its success.

Participation

Participation is limited to Parties to the Paris and Vienna Conventions.

Currently, 22 States have signed the Joint Protocol, including 14 Parties and one additional signatory to the Paris Convention (Western Europe) and 6 Parties to the Vienna Convention (5 developing countries and one East European country). As 0of now[7] 10 countries have deposited their instruments of ratification, accession or approval, including 5 participants of the Paris Convention, and 5 participants of the Vienna Convention, among them two East European industrialized States and 3 developing countries.

The issue of reservations is not addressed in the Protocol.

Negotiations proceeded within IAEA and were open to all countries. At the time of negotiations (1987), developing countries were the only Contracting Parties of the Vienna Convention.

Implementation and information

Having received the required ten ratifications (five from each Convention), the Joint Protocol will enter into force on 27 April 1992.

Obligations imposed upon Parties extend to a revision of their domestic nuclear liability laws. The Protocol does not include any reporting obligation. There is no provision on supervision.

---

[7] 1 January 1992.

Promotion of compliance and dispute settlement depends upon the institutional mechanisms of the two Conventions and their respective parent organizations.

While the Joint Protocol does not address the Brussels Supplementary Convention compensation scheme, the territorial extension of the operators' private liability under the Paris Convention may result in earlier application of the additional compensation scheme. Implementation by Parties to the Paris Convention that are also Parties to the Brussels Supplementary Convention may therefore also depend upon accommodation of obligations between the Contracting Parties of the latter Convention.

The Protocol was issued in the six working languages of the United Nations; it has been widely disseminated in English and French through the Nuclear Law Bulletin. No additional information is available except that produced and disseminated under the two conventional regimes.

Operation, review and adjustment

The Joint Protocol is deposited with the Director General of the International Atomic Energy Agency. It does not provide for any secretariat, administration or regular meetings.

The Protocol has no mechanism for review, nor does an amendment clause exist. Policy-making and review functions will be discharged under the two Conventions.

Codification programming

Within the current process of reviewing and revising of the Vienna Convention, one or more additional systems of compensation supplementary to the private liability of the operator of a nuclear installation may be introduced. In consequence, the Paris and Vienna Conventions may be supplemented by a single regime of additional compensation in the future.

However, the Joint Protocol emphasizes that policy-making in either of the two regimes is of concern for Parties to the other regime. Until formal institutional structures are developed, mutual participation and close cooperation are of major importance.

4. Maritime Transport of Nuclear Material

(119) Convention Relating to Civil Liability in the Field of Maritime Carriage of Nuclear Material, Brussels 1971.

Objectives and achievement

Both the Paris and the Vienna Convention "channel" liability for nuclear damage to operators of nuclear installations. Damage occurring during transport is usually attributed to the sending and, in some cases, to the receiving installation. However, both Conventions do not interfere with existing conventions of traditional maritime law. Accordingly, during maritime carriage of nuclear material parallel liabilities may arise: strict but limited liability of the operator of the nuclear installation concerned under nuclear law, and traditional fault liability of the carrier under maritime law. In certain cases, this latter liability may be unlimited. In consequence, maritime insurers did not cover nuclear risks, and maritime carriers refused to accept nuclear cargo.

The objective of the Maritime Carriage Convention is to ensure that operators of nuclear installations are exclusively liable for nuclear damage caused during maritime transport of nuclear material. It provides that any person that might be liable under national or international maritime law shall be exonerated from liability if the operator of a nuclear installation is liable either under international nuclear law (Paris or Vienna Conventions, Nos. 93 and 94 above), or under national nuclear law provided that national law is in all aspects as favourable to victims as the relevant international conventions.

Like the Joint Protocol, the Maritime Carriage Convention bridges an existing gap between parallel legal systems. It does not establish an independent liability regime.

The underlying objective of the Convention, namely the removal of obstacles to maritime carriage of nuclear material, has been successful only to a limited degree. Most ratifications have been deposited by Western European States, i.e. Paris Convention States. Generally, interest in the Convention remained low. The general principle, however, namely the separation of nuclear and maritime liability, gradually enters instruments of maritime law.

Participation

Participation follows the "Vienna formula", i.e. participation is limited to members of the United Nations, its specialized organizations, IAEA and the Statute of the ICJ.

Reservations are possible upon ratification, accession or approval in case they have been made according to the requirements of the Paris and Vienna Conventions. Of the 13 Contracting Parties, only Germany made a reservation.

The current membership is as follows: 10 Parties from Western Europe, and 4 Parties that are developing countries.

Whereas the instrument was prepared within OECD/NEA and the Comité Maritime International (CMI), an association of shipping interests, it was drafted within the IMCO Legal Committee and adopted by an IMCO Diplomatic Conference. The IMCO meetings were attended by a considerably higher number of delegations, including developing countries. 38 States were represented at the Diplomatic Conference that adopted the Convention, including 19 from developing countries (6 from America, 6 from Asia, 5 from Africa, and 2 from Europe), and 19 industrialized countries (15 from Western Europe and 4 Others). In addition, five developing countries were represented by observer delegations[8].

The Maritime Carriage Convention is in fact an instrument for joint amendment of nuclear liability conventions and several maritime liability conventions; no other programme activities are therefore foreseen. Two groups of States benefit from participation: States with nuclear power programmes benefit from being able to transport nuclear material by sea; and maritime countries enable their commercial fleet to accept nuclear cargo.

Implementation and information

The Convention required the deposit of five ratifications, accessions or approvals for its entry into force, on 15 July 1975.

The Convention obliges Parties to implement relevant provisions into national nuclear and maritime law. It does not provide for organized monitoring or data reporting. However, despite its being part of international maritime law, it is of interest primarily for the development of nuclear energy. It is, therefore, subject in particular to NEA nuclear law supervisory activities.

There are no institutional mechanisms for the promotion of compliance or for the settlement of disputes.

The text of the Convention has been published by IMO in four languages (English, French, Russian, and Spanish), accompanied by the Final Act of the relevant Conference.

Although it is administered by IMO, information largely relies upon NEA activities, including reports in the Nuclear Law Bulletin.

Operation, review and adjustment

The Secretary-General of IMO performs depositary functions under the Convention. The Convention does not provide for the establishment of a secretariat or the conduct of regular meetings or programme activities.

The depositary organization shall call a conference for revision of the instrument upon request of one third of the Parties. This provision has not been applied so far. Since the Convention does not establish an independent liability regime, it does not require continuous adaptation to changing circumstances.

---

[8] Final Act of the International Legal Conference on Maritime Carriage of Nuclear Substances 1971.

Codification programming

As far as the international regulation of maritime carriage of nuclear material is concerned, new draft instruments or draft revisions are not under consideration. However, the concept of separation of nuclear and maritime liability is incorporated in an ongoing process of continuous incorporation into revised or new instruments of international maritime law, e.g., the Convention on Limitation of Liability for Maritime Claims, London 1976.

5.   Liability of Operators of Nuclear Ships

(120) Convention on the Liability of Operators of Nuclear Ships, Brussels 1962.

Objectives and achievement

The launching of the first nuclear-powered freighter made it apparent that commercial competitiveness relied on the principle that coastal states generally accept the calling of such ships in ports under their territorial jurisdiction. At the same time, an increasing number of nuclear-powered ships, including warships, raised the risks of large-scale (nuclear) damage, for which commercial shipping was liable according to traditional maritime law.

The objective of the Nuclear Ship Convention is, therefore, to determine by agreement uniform rules concerning the liability of operators of nuclear ships (preamble). For this purpose, the Convention establishes the following regime:
-    The operator shall be absolutely liable for nuclear damage caused by the operation of a nuclear ship. Other persons shall be exonerated from any liability that might arise under any other law (Art. II).
-    Liability shall be limited to 1500 million gold-based francs (approximately gold-based US$ 100 million) (Art. III).
-    The licensing State shall determine the amount up to which the operator shall be obliged to cover his liability by insurance. The licensing State shall ensure the availability of the full amount of compensation by providing the necessary funds beyond the yield of such insurance (Art. III).
-    The regime extends to any nuclear-propelled ship, including warships (Art. I).
-    Action for compensation may be brought in a court of the licensing State or of any Contracting Party in whose territory damage is sustained. However, in case the limitation amount does not satisfy all claims, or the ship causing nuclear damage is a warship, the competent court shall be that of the licensing State (Arts. X, XI).

With reference to the operation of nuclear-propelled ships being commercially used, the Convention attempts to effectively integrate environmental and developmental aspects. Without the existence of a sufficiently effective liability regime, coastal States would not accept the entrance of nuclear-propelled vessels in their waters and ports. With regard to economic risks involved in new and ultra-hazardous industrial activities, the responsibility of Parties creating and being in a position to minimize such risks (i.e., operators and licensing states), protects possible victims and removes obstacles to such activities.

The Convention has not been successful as it never entered into force. Two factors contributed to its failure: States with nuclear-propelled warships refused to accept the application of a conventional regime based on private-liability to warships, and nuclear propulsion turned out not to be economically competitive.

Participation

The Convention is open for signature and subsequent ratification by States having attended the 1962 Diplomatic Conference on Maritime Law. Members of the United Nations, its specialized agencies and the IAEA may accede to it.

The Convention has been signed by 15 States, including five European industrialized countries and ten developing countries (6 Asian, 2 African, 1 American, 1 European). It has been ratified by two West-European States and acceded to by 2 developing countries[9].

The Convention had been prepared within the Comité Maritime International, the private association of shipping interests on maritime law, and the IAEA. The relevant CMI session was not attended by any national shipping association from developing countries and only one from Eastern Europe[10]. The IAEA "Panel of Legal Experts" was attended by members from the following regional groups: Western Europe (10), Eastern Europe (5); other industrialized countries (3); developing countries (4), of which three from Europe plus India[11]. The eleventh session of the Diplomatic Conference on Maritime Law (first phase) was attended by delegations from 49 countries, including 30 from industrialized countries (18 West-European, 7 East-European, 5 others) and 19 from developing countries (8 Asian, 4 African, 3 American, 4 European) plus 8 observer delegations from developing countries. Of the 50 delegations that attended the second phase of the Conference, 28 represented industrialized countries (17 West-European, 7 East-European, 4 others) and 22 developing countries (8 Asian, 4 African, 6 American, 4 European). Out of five observer delegations, three represented developing and two industrialized countries[12].

Until nuclear propulsion of commercial ships becomes more widespread, or until States operating nuclear-propelled ships accept application of a civil liability regime to ships in non-commercial service, including warships, no incentive for further participation is apparent.

Implementation and information

To enter into force, the Convention requires the deposit of two ratifications, including at least one ratification by a licensing state. The requirement reflects the very minimum condition making the conventional regime applicable at least between two States and for at least one nuclear-propelled ship. However, to date no licensing State ratified the Convention.

---

[9] Cf. Nuclear Law Bulletin 13/1974, p. 32-33.

[10] International Maritime Committee XXIVth Conference - Rijeka 1959.

[11] Liability of Operators of Nuclear Ships, Report of the Panel of Legal Experts; Doc. No. 3, Diplomatic Conference on Maritime Law, Brussels 1961. Panel members were mostly governmental experts, but acted in a personal capacity.

[12] Cf. Royaume de Belgique, Ministère des affaires étrangères et du commerce extérieur: Conférence Diplomatique de Droit Maritime, Onzième Session, Bruxelles 1961, Brussels 1962; and Royaume de Belgique, Ministère des affaires étrangères et du commerce extérieur: Conférence Diplomatique de Droit Maritime, Onzième Session (2e phase), Bruxelles 1962, Brussels 1963.

Obligations imposed upon Parties extend primarily to incorporating the liability regime into domestic legislation. The regime includes provisions for the supply by licensing States of public funds beyond the yield of private insurance of operators in case of nuclear damage, necessary jurisdictional provisions, the waiving of immunity as far as the conventional regime is concerned, and the undertaking of appropriate measures to prevent nuclear ships from flying flags of Contracting States without their licence or authority.

The Convention does not provide for monitoring. There are no obligations as to data reporting, compliance and follow-up on non-compliance. Disputes between two or more Parties shall be submitted to arbitration, if they cannot be settled by negotiation. If, within six months, the Parties concerned are unable to agree on arbitration procedures, any one of them may refer the dispute to the International Court of Justice. Upon signature, ratification or accession, a Party may declare that it does not consider itself bound by the dispute-settlement mechanism. The mechanism has not been used.

The text of the Convention was drafted in four languages, English, French, Russian, and Spanish. Proceedings of the 11th Session of the Diplomatic Conferences on Maritime Law were published by the depositary, the Government of Belgium. The published proceedings reproduce documents in English and French, as submitted, and other documents in (French) translation.

Operation, review and adjustment

The Convention is deposited with the Belgian Government. It does not provide for institutional mechanisms, nor is it related to an existing international organization. The Depositary Government shall convene conferences for the purpose of revising the Convention five years after its entry into force or upon request of one-third of the Contracting Parties.

Codification programming

Currently no draft instruments or draft revisions of the Convention are in preparation. Unless nuclear-propelled and commercial vessels become operative and economically competitive, the international legal regime on liability for nuclear damage caused by these ships does not have much relevance.

Although the Convention did not enter into force, its liability regime served as model for a number of bilateral port-visit arrangements concerning two nuclear-powered carriers, namely Savannah (USA) and Otto Hahn (Germany). To facilitate and to guide time-consuming bilateral negotiations, the OECD- Nuclear Energy Agency elaborated a "Model for Bilateral Agreements on the Visits of Nuclear Ships"[13], which contributed to the development of international law concerning liability of operators of nuclear ships.

---

[13]   Cf. Nuclear Law Bulletin 12/1973, pp. 31-37.

II. Civil Liability for Pollution Damage Caused by Maritime Transport of Oil

The regime concerning civil liability for pollution damage caused by maritime transport of oil consists of the following interrelated instruments:

(121) **the International Convention on Civil Liability for Oil Pollution Damage,** Brussels 1969 (CLC);

  (a) the Protocol to the International Convention on Civil Liability for Oil Pollution Damage, London 1976 (1976 CLC Protocol);

  (b) the Protocol of 1984 to amend the International Convention on Civil Liability for Oil Pollution Damage, London 1984 (1984 CLC Protocol);

(122) **the International Convention on the Establishment of an International Fund for Compensation of Oil Pollution Damage,** Brussels 1971 (Fund Convention);

  (a) the Protocol to the International Convention on the Establishment of an International Fund for Compensation of Oil Pollution Damage, London 1976 (1976 Fund Protocol); and

  (b) the Protocol to amend the International Convention on the Establishment of an International Fund for Compensation of Oil Pollution Damage, London 1984 (1984 Fund Protocol).

Objectives and achievement

The oil pollution liability regime must be seen in the context of traditional maritime liability law regulating the relationship among different parties directly involved in maritime transport (e.g. ship-owners, freight-owners, ports, salvors). Maritime pollution liability relates maritime transport with third parties, including coastal states, which are not directly involved and do not directly benefit from these economic activities.

In order to balance these interests related to maritime transport of oil and victims' interests, the CLC stipulates two basic objectives: (a) to ensure that adequate compensation is available to persons suffering from pollution damage through oil escaping during its maritime transport by ship, and (b) to adopt uniform regulations on liability and compensation for oil pollution damage (cf. preamble).

To meet these objectives, the Convention establishes a uniform liability regime with the following basic features:

- The owner of an oil tanker is liable for pollution damage caused by oil regardless of fault or negligence, except for some exonerations (Art. IV). The regime therefore clearly identifies an addressee against whom claims must be brought without, however, denying the owner's right of recourse under domestic law (Art. III).

- The owner has to cover his liability by insurance or other financial instruments (Art. VII). Bankruptcy or the dissolution of the company will therefore not preclude compensation.

-        The owner may limit his liability depending upon the tonnage of the ship, but not exceeding the amount of 210 million gold-based francs (Art. V, subsequently amended). In practice, the limits have been set with reference to the structure of the insurance market.

-        The right to limit liability is based upon the establishment of a fund with a competent court or authority within the territory of any one of the Contracting Parties in which action has been brought.

-        The fund is exclusively established for paying out claims in compensation for pollution damage occurring in the territory or territorial sea of a Contracting Party and for measures to prevent such damages.

-        The Convention does not apply to warships and other state-owned ships not engaged in commercial activities (Art. XI).

The 1971 Fund Convention tries to cover the remaining economic risks. Its basic objectives are (a) to provide for a compensation system, supplementing that of the CLC, in order to ensure full compensation of victims; and (b) to distribute the economic burden between shipping and cargo interests (cf. preamble).

The Fund Convention establishes an International Oil Pollution Compensation Fund:

-        The Fund provides compensation up to a flat-rate ceiling to victims above the compensation provided under the CLC, as well as in case ship-owners are financially incapable to pay, or are exonerated (Art.4).

-        The Fund also covers part of the liability imposed upon the ship-owner (Art. 5, later amended).

-        Fund compensation for a single incident is limited to 950 million gold-based francs, including the amount paid under the CLC (later amended).

-        The Fund is financed by contributions from companies ("persons") residing in the territory of Contracting Parties and receiving oil which has been subject to maritime transport. Contributions are determined in proportion to the amount of oil received above a specific minimum quantity which remains unassessed (Art. 10).

The 1976 Protocols have the objective to replace the gold-based unit of accounts by Special Drawing Rights (SDR) of the International Monetary Fund. Figures for ceilings were accordingly adjusted to SDR 14 million (CLC) and SDR 60 million (Fund).

The objectives of the 1984 Protocols are (a) to draw conclusions in the context of past legal and Fund practice without, however, changing the principles of the existing liability and compensation regime; and (b) to adapt the ceilings to inflation and increased economic risks involved in maritime transport of oil. Ceilings were thus raised to SDR 59.7 million for owners' liability under the revised CLC (Art. 6, CLC-Protocol, applicable to large tankers), and to SDR 135 million for compensation with respect to the revised Fund (including the amount paid under CLC); this amount is to be increased to SDR 200 million in case certain major contributors join the Fund Convention as revised by the Protocol (Art 6, Fund Protocol). The 1969 CLC and its 1984 Protocol, as well as the 1971 Fund Convention and its 1984 Protocol are to form single instruments.

Due to the rapid growth of large-size oil tankers, the combined CLC/Fund regime did in fact reset the traditional balance between promotion of an economic activity and protection of third-party interests, including protection of the coastal environment, fish stocks etc.

The CLC achieved to a large extent its objective concerning the introduction of a uniform regime on oil pollution liability into the body of traditional maritime law. The success of the uniform regime for oil pollution liability can be measured in terms of participation. Following its entry into force in June 1975, the CLC was ratified or acceded to by 71 States[14]. The liability regime today is accepted by most maritime and coastal States concerned.

With regard to the objective to ensure adequate compensation to victims including coastal States, the effect of the regime is more ambiguous. At the time of its adoption, the compensation available under the CLC was adequate to meet the costs of oil spills. The disastrous Torrey Canyon casualty caused costs of about French francs 78 million, that is, well below the ceiling. Yet, over time the rate to which damage from major accidents could be compensated by the funds made available under CLC steadily decreased[15].

For major incidents, the International Oil Pollution Compensation Fund provides a necessary supplementary compensation. The Fund Convention establishes an unprecedented system of compensation by which a sector of the economy has to bear its share of the economic burden of risks involved in maritime transport of oil. Although it had attracted considerably less members as compared to the CLC, the Fund Convention must be deemed to be a highly successful international legal instrument. Since its entry into force in October 1978, 47 countries joined the scheme[16]. Yet, due to the limitation of funds available, and due to inflation and increase in costs, it was not possible in any case to ensure that full compensation was paid[17].

The 1976 Protocols, on the other hand, attracted a considerably lower rate of participation; the Fund Protocol (1976) did not even come into force. But the objective of the Protocols has been largely met as the Special Drawing Right has replaced the former gold-based standard on a interim basis.

The 1984 Protocols revise slightly the generally successful interconnected regime and try to solve its major drawback, namely the low fixed ceilings for compensation. However, they have not yet come into force.

Participation

The CLC (1969) is open to members of the United Nations system (UN, Specialized Agencies, IAEA and ICJ). Due to its provision of an additional layer of compensation, participation in the Fund Convention (1971) depends upon ratification of the CLC (1969). Accordingly, withdrawal from the CLC is considered as simultaneous withdrawal from the Fund Convention.

---

[14]   Status as of 1 January 1992.

[15]   Cf. OECD: Combating Oil Spills, Paris 1982.

[16]   Status as of 1 January 1992.

[17]   Out of about 60 cases in which the Fund has so far been involved, in one case it had not been possible to fully compensate damage. A second case in which claims may exceed the ceiling is still pending. (Information provided by the Secretariat of the Oil Pollution Compensation Fund.)

The admissibility of reservations is not addressed in any of the various instruments. With regard to the CLC, two States (the former USSR and German Democratic Republic) submitted reservations concerning a general waiver of State immunity in case of oil tankers being commercially used but State-owned. Several States declared that they were unable to accept that reservation[18].

According to the 1976 Protocols, changing the basis of the unit of account from gold-based franc to SDR, States that are not members of IMF can declare that they continue to use the gold-based franc. No State made such a declaration. No similar clauses were inserted into the 1984 revisions.

Of the currently 71 Parties to the CLC (1969), 47 are developing countries (17 Asian [including Pacific], 11 American [including Caribbean], 16 African, and 3 European [including Cyprus]), and 24 industrialized countries (17 West European, 2 East European, 5 others). Of the 38 Parties to the 1976 CLC Protocol, which entered into force in 1981, 19 are developing countries (11 Asian, 4 American, 2 African, 1 European), and 19 industrialized countries (15 West European, 2 East European and 2 others). Of the current 7 Parties to the 1984 CLC Protocol, which has not yet entered into force, 2 are developing countries (both from South America), and 5 are industrialized countries (3 West European and 2 others).

Of the currently 47 countries that are Parties to the 1971 Fund Convention, 29 are developing countries (12 from Asia, 1 from America, 13 from Africa, and 3 from Europe), and 18 industrialized countries (14 from West Europe, 2 from East Europe, and 2 others). Of the 19 Parties to the 1976 Fund Protocol, which has not yet entered into force, 6 are developing countries (2 Asian, 1 American, 1 African, 2 European), and 13 industrialized countries (11 West European, 2 East European). So far only two 2 Parties from West Europe have ratified the 1984 Fund Protocol which has not yet entered into force.

Many developing and industrialized States participated in the preparation of the various legal instruments of the regime. The 1969 International Legal Conference on Marine Pollution Damage, which adopted the CLC, was attended by 48 delegations, including 21 from developing countries (9 from Asia, 4 from America, 6 from Africa, and 2 from Europe), and 27 from industrialized states (17 from Western Europe, 4 from Eastern Europe and 6 others). In addition, six more countries were represented by observers, including four developing countries[19]. The 1971 Conference on the Fund Convention was attended by 49 delegations, of which 26 were from developing countries (8 from Asia, 8 from America, 8 from Africa, 2 from Europe), and 23 from industrialized countries (16 West European, 3 East European and 4 others)[20]. Among the 69 countries represented at the 1984 Diplomatic Conference, which adopted 2 Protocols to amend the CLC and the Fund Convention, 43 were developing countries (11 from Asia, 16 from

[18]   No State did, however, refuse the entry into force of the Convention between itself and those having deposited reservations.

[19]   Figures from IMCO: Official Records of the International Legal Conference on Marine Pollution Damage 1969, London 1973.

[20]   IMCO: Official Records of the Conference on the Establishment of an International Compensation Fund for Oil Pollution Damage 1971, London 1978.

America, 13 from Africa, and 3 from Europe) plus 2 additional observer delegations from developing countries, and 26 industrialized countries (16 West European, 5 East European, and 5 others)[21].

The integrated regime offers benefits for both coastal and maritime shipping States. For coastal States it ensures, in case of oil spills from maritime transport of oil, access to resources for financing preventive measures and rehabilitation of the environment, and for compensation of victims. Maritime States benefit from unified liability systems facilitating international shipping.

Participation in the regime requires financial commitments, in the case of the CLC by owners of oil tankers, in the case of the Fund Convention by oil recipients. However, incremental costs are comparatively low. The first Director of the Fund estimated for 1980, a year with high damage due to oil pollution, an incremental cost of about £ 0.027013 per ton of crude oil and heavy fuel oil[22]. Likewise, coverage of risk in terms of civil liability for pollution damage under the CLC is, in fact, only a small portion of total insurance costs[23]. While adoption of the CLC results in promotion of maritime shipping, the Fund constitutes an insurance system as such. Participation involves regular contributions in exchange for a reduction of coastal States' economic risks.

Except for general legislative and administrative capacity, neither technical nor scientific assistance is required to implement the Conventions. The Secretariat of the Fund offers assistance and information concerning the legal implementation of the regime.

As far as participation is concerned, a number of factors are noteworthy. First, the liability regime focuses on damage that is geographically confined and occasionally catastrophic, i.e., oil spills (as compared to the quantitatively more important voluntary release of oil by tankers and other ships). Negotiations leading both to the 1969/1971 regime and to its 1984 revisions were prompted by incidents that attracted major press coverage, i.e., the 1967 Torrey Canyon accident, and the 1978 Amoco Cadiz accident.

The regime is of particular importance to a globally trading industry, i.e., maritime carriage of oil. The industry, through the International Maritime Committee (CMI), played an active role in the preparation of the CLC and its 1984 revision. Since the CMI is made up of national committees, and members of national committees also participated in several delegations during the negotiations, it may be assumed that the shipping industry also influenced the decision and implementation process at the domestic level in several countries.

The influence of the oil processing industry is also relevant. Oil companies, organized in the Oil Companies' International Marine Forum (OCIMF), have generally accepted to bear

---

[21] IMO: International Conference on Liability and Compensation for Damage in Connexion with the Carriage of Certain Substances by Sea 1984, Final Act.

[22] Reinhard Ganten: International System for Compensation for Oil Pollution Damage, Oslo 1981, p. 17.

[23] Henri Smets: Oil Spill Risk: Economic Assessment and Compensation Limit, 14 Journal of Maritime Law and Commerce 1983, p. 33, gives the following rates for a typical West European supertanker on a Gulf-Rotterdam itinerary: 7 Ffrs./DWT (Dead Weight Ton) for the hull; 7 Ffrs./DWT for the cargo; and 1,2 Ffrs./DWT for civil liability, 10% of which accounting for oil pollution damage. Doubling the latter portion would therefore increase insurance costs of 15,6 Ffrs by another 0,16 Ffrs.

a share of economic risks in order to avoid the negative implications of unilateral measures for the business of large-scale maritime transport of oil. During the period of inter-governmental negotiations establishing the CLC, they adopted in 1968 the "Tanker Owners Voluntary Agreement Concerning Liability for Oil Pollution" (TOVALOP) which provides for owners' liability parallel to that under the CLC. TOVALOP entered into force in 1969 and within a short period of time covered nearly 90% of the world tanker fleet. Likewise, during the negotiations on the Fund-Convention, companies adopted the "Contract Regarding an Interim Supplement to Tanker Liability for Oil Pollution" (CRISTAL) which is similar to the Fund and provides compensation supplementary to TOVALOP. Like the Fund, CRISTAL is financed by cargo interests. Both voluntary agreements have been revised and adapted to their intergovernmental corollaries. The revised agreements apply regardless of whether or not the CLC or the Fund Convention apply to the incident. TOVALOP applies virtually to all tankers, CRISTAL covers approximately 80% of all cargoes of oil carried by sea[24].

As to reservations, the 1976 Protocols stipulate that Parties that are not members of the IMF may declare that they continue to use the gold-based unit of account. This clause is of interest predominantly for East-European countries. Yet, the clause was never used and did not gain practical relevance for the regime.

Implementation and information

The CLC and its 1976 Protocol entered into force after ratification, accession or approval by 8 States, including 5 States having at least one million units of gross tanker tonnage. The CLC came into force in June 1975 for 14 Parties, almost six years after its adoption; the tonnage requirement clearly delayed entry into force. Likewise, the 1976 Protocol to the CLC entered into force in April 1981 for 9 Parties; here again, the tonnage requirement was a constraint. The 1984 Protocol to the CLC increased minimum requirements to 10 ratifications, including 6 by States having at least a million units of gross tanker tonnage. However, since one of the objectives of the CLC is to provide uniform law, not least to avoid competitive disadvantages to early participants, such a requirement covering ratifications and tanker tonnage appears appropriate.

The Fund Convention and its 1976 Protocol were to enter into force after ratification, accession or approval by at least 8 states, and a minimum representation of 750 million tons of contributing oil. Moreover, the Fund Convention was not to enter into force prior to entry into force of the CLC. While the Convention entered into force for 15 Parties almost seven years after its adoption in October 1978, the 1976 Fund Protocol, with currently 19 ratifications, has not been able to secure the requirement as these Parties represent only approximately two-thirds of the amount of contributing oil required. In both cases, the minimum requirement concerning provisions of oil has considerably constrained entry into force.

Since the Fund is principally an insurance pool, a minimum of contributing oil appears to be essential for its operation, because it ensures a minimum distribution of risks. After all, the Fund Convention provides a limit for compensation for each single incident but the actual

---

[24] Copies of TOVALOP and CRISTAL may be obtained from the International Tanker Owners Pollution Federation, London.

amount of annual contributions is not limited as it depends on the number and gravity of incidents which have to be compensated.

The 1984 Fund Protocol provides rules for accelerated entry into force, i.e., eight ratifications, accessions or approvals representing 600 million tons of contributing oil. However, Parties may declare that participation will become effective only upon joint withdrawal from the CLC (1969) and Fund (1971) Conventions as soon as at least 750 million tons of contributing oil are represented. Moreover, the Fund Protocol of 1984 shall not enter into force prior to the entry into force of the CLC Protocol of 1984.

The requirement to pay high initial contributions immediately upon ratification, which may have been an obstacle to early ratification[25], was dropped. Moreover, entry into force was implicitly eased by another provision which is not part of the final clauses. The Fund (1984) enters into force with a compensation limit of SDR 135 m. In case, however, that three member States combine 600 million tons of contributing oil, the limit automatically increases to SDR 200 million. In practice, the fulfillment of this condition depends upon participation by the USA (either in combination with Japan, or with Italy and France, or with Italy and the Netherlands)[26]. The Fund may enter into force without participation by the USA, but it will only operate to full capacity upon participation by the largest consumer of oil carried by sea.

The CLC establishes a civil liability regime for oil pollution damage. The main commitment imposed on Contracting States is to implement the regime in domestic law, while actual liability arises exclusively for owners of oil tankers. Contracting States have to perform some auxiliary duties. They shall ensure that competent authorities attest and certify that ship owners cover oil pollution risks by appropriate insurance. They shall mutually accept certificates issued by Contracting States. They shall ensure that oil tankers, wherever registered (e.g. in non-contracting states), do not enter or leave ports or offshore installations situated in their territory or territorial sea without such a certificate. Parties shall ensure that courts have the necessary competences, and they shall recognize judgements of courts competent under the Convention. Finally, Contracting Parties shall waive immunity with regard to ships that are State-owned but involved in commercial trading. The 1984 CLC Protocol does not impose any substantially different commitments upon Parties.

Institutionalized monitoring of the implementation of these duties or reporting obligations do not exist. However, the cost-effective part of the CLC liability regime, the coverage of economic risk by insurance, is subject to decentralized control by port States.

The Fund Convention imposes on Contracting Parties primarily the obligation to implement the rules concerning contributions to the Fund into domestic law. States do not guarantee contributions; and normally they do not contribute. But they shall ensure that contributions are paid, e.g., by imposing sanctions. They shall ensure that the Fund is recognized as a legal person entitled to sue oil-receiving persons. They shall ensure that the Fund has a right to intervene in case of Fund incidents in legal proceedings concerning CLC

[25] Cf. Reinhard Ganten: Oil Pollution Liability. Amendments Adopted to Civil Liability and Fund Conventions; 2 Oil & Petrochemical Pollution 1985, p. 102.

[26] Cf. Reinhard Ganten: Oil Pollution Liability. Amendments Adopted to Civil Liability and Fund Conventions; 2 Oil & Petrochemical Pollution 1985, p. 100 and note 30.

liability, since judgements on CLC liability may have an impact on additional Fund compensation. In case Contracting Parties declare that they will contribute in the place of their nationals, they have to waive their immunity in that respect. Finally, Parties shall communicate annually a list of oil-receiving persons under their jurisdiction and the amount of oil received by each person. Although this list is indispensable for the assessment of contributions by the Fund Secretariat, late submission was frequent during the initial period. The 1984 Fund Protocol provides for a modest sanctioning mechanism, as it holds States liable for any financial losses of the Fund due to late submission of their annual lists. Apart from this slight modification, the 1984 Protocol does not impose any substantially different commitments upon States.

Like the CLC, the Fund Convention does not provide for organized monitoring of implementation. However, the most cost-effective part of obligations, i.e., regular contributions on the part of persons receiving oil above a certain quantity, as well as the only regular obligation of Contracting States, i.e. the annual submission of lists of contributing persons, are closely monitored by the Fund Secretariat. Moreover, the Fund Secretariat is fairly well informed about relevant national law and maintains close informal relations with administrative units of Contracting Parties that are responsible for implementation of the regime. As a consequence, the implementation process is promoted by informal consultations. So far, the Fund did not have to sue any non-contributing, financially capable person. The Assembly of Contracting Parties to the Fund Convention does not play a major role in the promotion of implementation.

Once the decision to join one or more of the instruments of the CLC/Fund regime is taken, implementation generally does not seem to have raised major problems. This may be due to the fact that the cost-effective parts of commitments are to some degree self-enforcing and removed from the intergovernmental level. Also, the Secretariat also provides training and assistance for implementation, especially for developing countries.

The IMO (former IMCO) Secretariat publishes Final Acts of diplomatic conferences. Texts of agreements are disseminated primarily in English and French. Since international conventions on maritime law are frequently used in legal proceedings, the International Maritime Organization published the Official Records of the Diplomatic Conferences of 1969 (CLC) and 1971 (Fund Convention) in English. Fund practice is reported to the biennial meetings of the Assembly of Contracting Parties. The Fund Secretariat has issued a number of papers facilitating implementation of the regime and the submission of claims, including a non-technical "Claims Manual" for the information of victims about claims procedures, etc. For a broader public, current developments are reported in regular IMO publications (e.g., IMO Newspaper).

Operation, review and adjustment

The Secretary-General of IMO (former IMCO) performs depositary functions for both the CLC and the Fund Conventions.

Except for a decentralized port State control system, the CLC does not have its own institutional apparatus, e.g. a regular conference of Parties. Commitments are not regularly reviewed. However, IMO, as depositary organization, shall convene a conference of Contracting Parties if so desired by at least one-third of the Parties. Such a conference was called twice for the adoption of Protocols: in 1976 and in 1984. In fact, the IMO Legal Committee, initially established as an <u>ad hoc</u> forum for the preparation of CLC and Fund Conventions, has assumed the role of a deliberation forum, responsible for general supervision and review of the CLC.

The 1984 Protocol designates the IMO Legal Committee, expanded by those Contracting Parties that are not members of IMO, as a forum for discussion and decision-making about amendments of limitation amounts according to simplified procedures. Because IMO provides the deliberation forum and the necessary servicing functions, separate secretariat and administrative costs do not arise under the CLC.

By contrast, the Fund Convention established a comprehensive institutional apparatus. A secretariat, led by the Fund Director, is responsible for the conduct of business, including collection of contributions and most final settlements. The 1971 Fund Convention establishes two decision-making bodies, the Assembly of Contracting Parties which meets annually, and the Executive Committee comprising one third of Parties and meeting at least annually. However, because of annual rotation in membership of the Executive Committee, the supervisory structure did not work satisfactorily. Under the 1984 Protocol, the Executive Committee is not re-established. Instead, the Assembly as the principal policy-making body controls the Fund and its Secretariat and may establish technical working groups for the supervision of financial settlements for particular incidents[27].

Despite regular meetings of the Assembly of Parties, amendments of compensation limits according to simplified procedures under the 1984 Fund Protocol are to be deliberated and decided within the IMO Legal Committee in order to co-ordinate changes in the limitation amounts of both Conventions by a single decision-making body.

Annual Secretariat costs amount to £ 500,000 - 600,000. Expenses are paid from the Fund, i.e., by contributing persons and not by Contracting States. Expenses for delegations, travel etc. are paid by Contracting Parties.

The CLC/Fund regime has no system or rules by which scientific and technical knowledge are incorporated into the decision-making process. As the regime is primarily concerned with allocation of economic risks involved in maritime transportation of oil, the input of scientific and technical knowledge plays a minor role in the decision-making process.

The Fund Secretariat, the Assembly and the Executive Committee, all play a role in the evolution of the legal regime. In particular, financial settlements provide some "case law" as to the authoritative interpretation of the two conventions.

---

[27] On the reasons for this revision, see Reinhard Ganten: Oil Pollution Liability. Assessment of Possible Revisions; Oil & Petrochemical Pollution 1983, pp. 21-22.

Limitation amounts have to be regularly adapted to increasing risks and inflation. The 1969 CLC does not contain any provision in this regard. The 1971 Fund Convention allows an increase of compensation limits up to 100% by Assembly decision. In 1979, following the Amoco Cadiz accident, the Assembly increased the limit by 50% (from SDR 30 to SDR 45 million), in 1987 up to the limit of SDR 60 million. In both 1984 Protocols, provision is made for a simplified amendment procedure concerning limitation amounts that is applicable under several restrictions. Amendments are deliberated within the IMO Legal Committee and decided upon by a two-thirds majority of Parties. Amendments enter into force after a period of 18 months unless at least one quarter of Parties submit objections within that period. Amendments adopted under this procedure are binding upon all Parties.

Codification programming

With regard to liability for damage caused by maritime transportation of oil, no revisions beyond the 1984 Protocols are currently pending. However, preparations for a separate Convention on Liability and Compensation in Connexion with the Carriage of Noxious and Hazardous Substances by Sea (HNS Convention) have been resumed within IMO.

Work in the two fields of liability for pollution caused by maritime carriage of dangerous substances proceeds within the Legal Committee of IMO. Co-ordination is thus facilitated by the uniformity of the negotiation forum. Co-ordination of the HNS project negotiated within IMO with its corollary addressing liability for damage during inland transport of dangerous substances negotiated within ECE (No. 124 below) has been accomplished by avoidance of simultaneous preparation of instruments. When adoption of the Draft HNS Convention failed in 1984, the project was abandoned until the ECE corollary was virtually finalized.

With respect to liability for damage from maritime carriage of dangerous substances, the HNS Convention under consideration will bridge a major gap existing in international maritime law on third party liability. As far as damage from maritime carriage of oil is concerned, some risks remain uncovered by the CLC/Fund regime, including damage other than pollution damage, e.g., resulting from explosion of tankers, and oil pollution damage from unidentified sources, e.g., caused by deliberate release of oil residues. Finally, if the oil business is considered as an integrated industry, risks of oil pollution and other damage not arising from maritime carriage of oil, but e.g., from offshore operations, are not yet covered by globally applicable international regulations on liability (see No. 123 below).

International law concerning liability for oil pollution damage arising from maritime carriage of oil has been developed in close collaboration with major oil companies. It has been influenced by TOVALOP and CRISTAL, the voluntary liability and compensation contracts agreed upon by oil companies. The CLC/Fund legal regime is continuously developed by Fund practice in respect of the settlement of claims, and through joint authoritative interpretation by the Fund Assembly.

III. Civil Liability for Pollution Damage Caused by Offshore Operations

(123) **Convention on Civil Liability for Oil Pollution Damage Resulting from Exploration for and Exploitation of Seabed Mineral Resources,** London 1977.

Objectives and achievement

The major oil spill off the coast of Santa Barbara, California, in 1972 and the beginning exploitation of oil resources in the North Sea continental shelf area brought attention to the importance of large-scale accidental oil spills caused by offshore operations. Responding to this development, the regional London Convention concerning offshore operations pursues two objectives: (a) to ensure that adequate compensation is available for victims of oil pollution from offshore operations, and (b) to provide uniform rules and procedures for determining questions of liability and compensation (preamble). The Convention establishes the following regime:

- Operators shall be strictly liable for oil pollution damage caused by offshore installations and for costs of measures for the prevention of such damage (Art. 3); they shall have a right of recourse according to national law.
- Liability shall be limited per incident to SDR 30 million; this amount shall automatically increase to SDR 40 million after a period of five years from the opening of the instrument for signature (Art. 6).
- Liability shall be covered by insurance or financial security up to SDR 22 million, to be increased automatically to SDR 35 million after the same five year period (Art. 8). These amounts seemed to be the limits for which insurance cover was obtainable.
- In case of an accident, legal action shall be brought in courts of any Contracting State in which damage occurred or of the licensing State. The operator shall establish a limitation fund in one of these courts which shall, in turn, be competent to decide on matters of compensation (Art. 11).
- Contracting Parties may provide for higher limits or unlimited liability (Art. 15).

The Convention intends to make operators liable for dangerous, but generally beneficial commercial activities involving economic risks. It thus directly integrates industrial development and environmental aspects.

The territorial applicability of the Convention is restricted to the areas of the North Sea, the Baltic Sea and the North Atlantic, adjacent to the European coastline. Although the Convention does not have an immediate bearing on global environmental protection and sustainable development, it is apt to serve as a precedent for the negotiation of similar liability regimes balancing developmental and environmental aspects of dangerous activities in offshore areas of other regions or regional seas. Since the Convention focuses exclusively on Western Europe, it does not take into account the special situation of developing countries.

If achievement is measured in terms of the number of States which have ratified the Convention and implemented the regime, the Convention did not achieve its objectives; it did not receive any ratification so far. Nevertheless, the negotiation process caused the establishment of a voluntary compensation scheme by oil companies involved in North Sea offshore operations ("Oil Pollution Liability Agreement", OPOL) providing, in its current version, for compensation up to US$ 100 million[28]. In connection with domestic laws of liability, OPOL provides a better claims situation for victims than the Convention would have done. Hence, while the Convention has not met its objective of providing uniform rules and procedures, it has, in an indirect way, ensured the availability of adequate compensation for victims.

Participation

The Convention is restricted to the group of countries having been invited to the Intergovernmental Conference which adopted the Convention. The Conference was attended by nine West-European States. The Contracting Parties may, however, by unanimous agreement invite other States having coastlines on the North Sea, the Baltic Sea, or the Atlantic Ocean north of 36°N (i.e., European coastlines).

No reservations may be made under the Convention.

The major reason for non-ratification by interested countries has been the existence of the above-mentioned Oil Pollution Liability Agreement.

Implementation and information

The Convention requires four ratifications to enter into force. The principal commitment imposed on Parties is domestic legal implementation of the regime set out in the Convention. This commitment includes provision of necessary jurisdictional competences and waiving of immunities in case of a State Party itself being operator of offshore activities. No obligations exist as to reporting or data supply. Implementation has to be monitored decentralized, that is, by Parties and NGOs, e.g., oil companies concerned.

The Convention does not contain any provision addressing the promotion of implementation or dispute settlement.

The United Kingdom Government published the Convention and the Final Act of the 1977 Diplomatic Conference in English.

Operation, review and adjustment

The Government of the United Kingdom performs depositary functions. There are no institutional arrangements as to the establishment of a secretariat or regular meetings.

While mechanisms for regular review of provisions do not exist, the Convention sets out a mechanism for accelerated adaptation of limitation figures. Under the Convention a Committee composed of one representative of each Contracting Party is established and shall be convened if a Party considers limitation figures no longer adequate. The Committee may, by a majority of three-quarters of the Parties, adopt a recommendation on the modification of these figures. Figures recommended enter into force upon acceptance by all Parties. Parties not responding within six months are deemed to have accepted the modification. If a Party objects within six months, amounts recommended shall enter into force for all other Parties.

---

[28]   Copies may be obtained from The Offshore Pollution Liability Limited, Ewell, Surrey, United Kingdom.

Codification programming

At present no specific draft revisions or new draft instruments are discussed, although some States concerned closely monitor the situation with a view to revising the Convention in terms of imposing unlimited and strict liability of operators.

IV. Civil Liability for Damage Caused by Inland Transport of Dangerous Substances

(124) Convention on Civil Liability for Damage Caused During Carriage of Dangerous Goods by Road, Rail and Inland Navigation Vessels (CRTD), Geneva 1989.

Objectives and achievement

The Convention covers risks involved in inland transport of dangerous goods. The objective of the Convention is to establish uniform rules ensuring adequate and speedy compensation for damage during inland carriage of dangerous goods (preamble). It creates the following liability regime:

- The carrier, i.e., the registered owner or other person controlling a road vehicle or an inland navigation vessel or the operator of a railway line, is liable for damage caused during transport of dangerous goods (Art. 5). Damage extends to loss of life or personal injury, loss or damage of property, loss or damage by contamination to the environment, including reasonable measures for the reinstatement of the environment, and the costs of preventive measures (Art. 1).
- The carrier's liability shall be covered by insurance or financial security (Art. 13), except that carriers being States or their constituting parts do not require insurance cover (Art. 16).
- The carrier may limit his liability per incident, in case of a road or rail carrier to SDR 18 million for claims concerning loss of life or personal injury and to SDR 12 million with respect to other claims, and in the case of inland navigation vessels to SDR 8 million and SDR 7 million respectively (Art. 9).
- No claim may be made beyond the regime against the carrier or any person engaged in the transport operation or in related salvage activities (Art. 5).
- Action may be brought in courts of Contracting Parties in which either the incident has occurred, or damage was sustained, or preventive measures were undertaken, or the carrier has his habitual residence (Art. 19). The carrier may establish a limitation fund in one of the courts where action has been brought. The court at which the fund has been established will be responsible to decide about distribution of compensation.

The Convention intends to integrate development and environment by balancing the prerequisites of a generally benign activity, i.e. transportation of dangerous substances, and its adverse effects and inherent economic risks of causing damage to the environment and to third parties.

The Convention refers to locally confined incidents of accidental damage. Even though it was prepared under the auspices of the UN Economic Commission for Europe (ECE), its possible impact is not limited regionally. It may be joined by States beyond the membership of ECE and it may serve as a precedent for conclusion of similar agreements applicable to other regions, although the principal territorial focus is Europe and some neighboring States.

The Convention does not specifically take into account the circumstances of developing countries.

Since the Convention was adopted only in October 1989, little can be said about the degree of achieving its objectives. However, its success may be measured both in terms of the number of States accepting and implementing the regime, and in terms of the amount of compensation available under the Convention as compared to the costs caused by incidents.

Participation

Although adopted in a regional forum (ECE), membership is open to all States. Reservations may be made on three specified points relating to higher standards for the protection of victims. Reservations other than those specified are not possible.

The Convention has not yet entered into force. While two countries, including one non-European developing country, have signed the Convention, no instrument of ratification has been submitted so far.

The Convention was drafted by the International Institute for the Unification of Private Law (UNIDROIT) and negotiated within the Inland Transport Committee of ECE. These fora generally address a European membership. There are no particular incentives for the encouragement of participation by developing countries. Measures for the promotion of participation by developing countries have not been
adopted.

Implementation and information

The Convention enters into force after five instruments of ratification, approval, acceptance or accession have been deposited.

Parties are primarily under the obligation to implement the legal regime set out in the Convention. It includes the necessary jurisdictional competences, the designation of one or more authorities for issuing certificates of insurance, the designation of the authority for issuing or receiving communications related to compulsory insurance, the waiving of immunity in case a State or constituting part thereof is a carrier.

The Convention does not require Parties to regularly report implementation or supply and disclose data. However, Parties having made reservations to the Convention shall notify the depositary of the contents of their national law.

No mention is made in the Convention of measures to enhance compliance, of reactions to non-compliance, or of the settlement of disputes.

The Convention has been disseminated by ECE as a UN document in English, French and Russian. Publication of the Convention was accompanied by an explanatory report providing guidance for the interpretation and implementation of the regime.

Operation, review and adjustment

Depositary functions under the Convention are performed by the Secretary General of the United Nations. The Convention does not provide for the establishment of a separate institutional mechanism. However, the Inland Transport Committee of ECE provides the standing forum for deliberations in matters concerning the Convention. Upon request of one third of, but at least three Parties, the Inland Transport Committee shall convene a Conference of Parties for revising or amending the Convention. Moreover, the Inland Transport Committee shall convene, upon request of one quarter of, but at least three Parties, a Committee constituted of one representative from each Contracting Party for amending compensation amounts according to simplified amendment procedures.

The Convention does not provide for regular meetings or programme activities, nor for a secretariat.

There are no mechanisms for regular or periodic review of the regime. Nevertheless, the Convention provides for simplified procedures for amendment of compensation figures. Requests for such amendments shall be supported by one quarter of, but at least three Parties. Requests are considered by the Committee of the Parties which adopts amendments of limitation figures by a two-thirds majority. An amendment is deemed to have been accepted if within a period of 18 months not at least a quarter of Parties has communicated its non-acceptance. Amendments accepted are binding for all Parties. In deciding, the Committee shall take into account past experience with incidents, changes in monetary value, and the anticipated impact of an amendment on insurance costs.

Codification programming

No drafts or draft revisions are currently under consideration with regard to inland transport of dangerous substances. A related instrument addressing liability for damage from maritime transport of dangerous substances is currently being prepared within IMO (see section II above), and an instrument addressing liability for dangerous activities is under consideration within the Council of Europe.

V. Other Developments Concerning Liability for Environmental Damage

Apart from the above-mentioned projects concerning liability for hazardous activities referring to maritime carriage of noxious and hazardous substances (IMO) and nuclear damage (IAEA), a number of other specific liability regimes are currently under preparation.

1.   Liability for environmental damage in the framework of comprehensive instruments

Preparation of detailed rules on liability for environmental damage is being considered, or such rules are currently being prepared, as part of several comprehensive international treaty systems addressing specific hazardous activities:

-      Within the framework of the United Nations Environment Programme (UNEP), a protocol on liability and compensation for damage resulting from the transboundary movement and disposal of hazardous wastes, to supplement the 1989 Basel Convention on the Control of Transboundary Movements of Hazardous Wastes and their Disposal (No. 103), is being negotiated. An Ad Hoc Working Group of Legal and Technical Experts has elaborated some "elements for a protocol" to be submitted to the first meeting of the Contracting Parties to the Convention. The meeting will be convened upon entry into force of the Convention which is expected to take place in 1992. The purpose of the draft protocol is to provide a comprehensive regime to ensure adequate and prompt compensation for damage from transboundary movement and disposal of hazardous wastes and other wastes, to deter violations of the Basel Convention and to enable restoration of the environment. The "elements" suggest to supplement private liability of operators either by an international fund, or by state liability, or by a combination of both concepts. Drafting is to be closely co-ordinated with the Draft Convention on Civil Liability for Damage Resulting from Activities Dangerous to the Environment, which is currently under preparation in the Council of Europe (see below). It should also be coordinated with any future regulations on liability for damage from ocean dumping within the framework of the 1972 London Convention on the Prevention of Marine Pollution by Dumping of Wastes and other Matter (No. 35). Consideration of such regulations, however, have been postponed for the time being (see below).

-      Within the framework of the Antarctic Treaty System (No. 14), the 1991 Protocol on Environmental Protection to the Antarctic Treaty, envisages the development of and annex on "rules and procedures relating to liability for damage arising from activities taking place in the Antarctic Treaty area and covered by this Protocol"[29]
No further action has been taken so far.

-      Within the framework of IMO, the question has been raised whether to prepare an instrument on liability for damage arising from ocean dumping of wastes, supplementing the Convention on the Prevention of Marine Pollution by Dumping of Wastes and Other Matter, London 1972 (No. 35). Drafting has been postponed in order to facilitate co-ordination with two other projects addressing matters of liability for damage from waste management, i.e., the above-mentioned UNEP Protocol on Liability and Compensation

---

[29] Article 16, as adopted in Madrid on 4 October 1991.

for Damage Resulting from the Transboundary Movement and Disposal of Hazardous Wastes and the Draft Convention on Civil Liability for Damage Resulting from Activities Dangerous to the Environment (Council of Europe, see below).

- Within the framework of the 1982 UN Convention on the Law of the Sea (No. 38), the Preparatory Commission for the International Sea-Bed Authority and the International Tribunal for the Law of the Sea drafts specific rules on liability for damage caused by deep sea-bed mining activities, as part of a comprehensive set of Draft Regulations on the Protection and Preservation of the Marine Environment from Activities in the Area.

2. Liability for dangerous activities (Council of Europe)

Responding to the "Sandoz" incident which heavily polluted the Rhine River, a Draft Convention on Civil Liability for Damage Resulting from Activities Dangerous to the Environment is currently being prepared within the Council of Europe. The draft elaborated by a Committee of Experts has been published in July 1991 with a view to organizing consultations with interested (e.g., non-governmental) actors. The project is regional in scope. Its objective is to ensure adequate compensation and to provide means for the prevention of damage and the reinstitution of the environment. It channels liability to the operator of a dangerous activity and provides for some institutional arrangements, including a Standing Committee. The Draft Convention addresses a broad range of dangerous activities, including the production and handling of dangerous substances and genetically modified organisms or dangerous micro-organisms, technologies producing dangerous non-ionising radiations, the incineration, handling, treatment or recycling of wastes, and the operation of sites for the permanent disposal of wastes. Drafting has to be closely co-ordinated with all existing liability regimes and current developments in various areas of liability for environmental damage, including liability for nuclear damage (OECD/NEA, IAEA), maritime carriage of dangerous substances and oil (IMO), inland carriage of dangerous substances (ECE), and transboundary movement and disposal of hazardous wastes and other wastes (UNEP).

3. International liability for injurious consequences arising out of acts not prohibited by international law (International Law Commission)

The most comprehensive, and therefore most general, project is currently under discussion in the UN International Law Commission (ILC). While its primary focus is on international, i.e., inter-governmental, liability for activities involving risks and activities with harmful effects, it recently extended to civil liability matters as well.

As the project extends to dangerous activities for which liability conventions are existing or under preparation, drafting has to be coordinated with developments concerning all other liability regimes now in the process of drafting. While there have been some co-ordinating efforts with regard to law-making projects under preparation within IAEA and the Council of Europe, the special rapporteur of the project was (as Chairman) personally involved in the UNEP Ad Hoc Working Group of Legal and Technical Experts for the elaboration of elements to be included in a Protocol on Liability and Compensation for Damage Resulting from the Transboundary Movement and Disposal of Hazardous Wastes and other Wastes. Co-ordination basically depends upon members of the ILC, in particular upon the special rapporteur, and on the annual deliberations in the Sixth Committee of the UN General Assembly to which the Commission annually reports.

STATUS OF RATIFICATIONS AS OF 1 JANUARY 1992

GLOBAL INSTRUMENTS   (Treaty numbers see page 392)

Parties	118	119	120	121	122
Afghanistan					
Albania					
Algeria				x	x
Angola					
Antigua & Barbuda					
Argentina	x	x			
Australia				x	
Austria					
Bahamas				x	x
Bahrain					
Bangladesh					
Barbados					
Belarus*					
Belgium		x		x	
Belize				x	
Benin				x	x
Bhutan					
Bolivia	x				
Botswana					
Brazil				x	
Brunei Darussalam					
Bulgaria					
Burkina Faso					
Burundi					
Cambodia					
Cameroon	x			x	x
Canada				x	x
Cape Verde					
Central African Republic					
Chad					
Chile	x			x	
China				x	
Colombia				x	
Cook Islands					
Comoros					
Congo					
Costa Rica					
Cote d'Ivoire				x	x

Parties	118	119	120	121	122
Cuba	x				
Cyprus				x	x
Czech & Slovak Fed. Rep.					
Democr. People's Rep. of Korea					
Denmark		x		x	x
Djibouti				x	x
Dominica					
Dominican Republic				x	
Ecuador				x	
Egypt	x			x	
El Salvador					
Equatorial Guinea					
Estonia*					
Ethiopia					
Fiji				x	x
Finland		x		x	x
France		x		x	x
Gabon		x		x	x
Gambia				x	x
Germany		x		x	x
Ghana				x	x
Greece				x	x
Grenada					
Guatemala				x	
Guinea					
Guinea-Bissau					
Guyana					
Haiti					
Holy See					
Honduras					
Hungary	x				
Iceland				x	x
India				x	x
Indonesia				x	x
Iran (Islamic Republic of)					
Iraq					
Ireland					
Israel					
Italy		x		x	x
Jamaica					
Japan				x	x

Parties	118	119	120	121	122
Jordan					
Kenya					
Kiribati					
Kuwait				x	x
Lao People's Democratic Rep.					
Latvia*					
Lebanon			x	x	
Lesotho					
Liberia		x		x	x
Libyan Arab Jamahiriya					
Liechtenstein					
Lithuania*					
Luxembourg				x	
Madagascar			x		
Malawi					
Malaysia					
Maldives				x	x
Mali					
Malta				x	x
Marshall Islands					
Mauritania					
Mauritius					
Mexico	x				
Micronesia					
Monaco				x	x
Mongolia					
Morocco				x	
Mozambique					
Myanmar					
Namibia					
Nauru					
Nepal					
Netherlands		x	x	x	x
New Zealand				x	
Nicaragua					
Niger	x				
Nigeria				x	x
Niue					
Norway		x		x	x
Oman				x	x
Pakistan					

Parties	118	119	120	121	122
Palau					
Panama				x	
Papua New Guinea				x	x
Paraguay					
Peru	x			x	
Philippines	x				
Poland	x			x	x
Portugal			x	x	x
Qatar				x	x
Republic of Korea				x	
Republic of Yemen		x		x	
Romania					
Rwanda					
St. Kitts & Nevis					
St. Lucia					
St. Vincent & the Grenadines				x	
Samoa					
San Marino					
Sao Tome & Principe					
Saudi Arabia					
Senegal				x	
Seychelles				x	x
Sierra Leone					
Singapore				x	
Solomon Islands					
Somalia					
South Africa				x	
Spain		x		x	x
Sri Lanka				x	x
Sudan					
Suriname			x		
Swaziland					
Sweden		x		x	x
Switzerland				x	
Syrian Arab Republic			x	x	x
Thailand					
Togo					
Tonga					
Trinidad & Tobago	x				
Tunisia				x	x
Turkey					

Parties	118	119	120	121	122
Tuvalu				x	x
Uganda					
Ukraine*					
Union of Soviet Socialist Rep.*				x	x
United Arab Emirates				x	x
United Kingdom				x	x
United Republic of Tanzania					
United States of America					
Uruguay					
Vanuatu				x	x
Venezuela					
Viet Nam					
Yugoslavia*	x			x	x
Zaire			x		
Zambia					
Zimbabwe					

* Membership status subject to further clarification.

REGIONAL INSTRUMENTS

(93) <u>Convention on Third Party Liability in the Field of Nuclear Energy</u> (Paris 1960)

Belgium
Denmark
Finland
France
Germany
Greece
Italy

Netherlands
Norway
Portugal
Spain
Sweden
Turkey
United Kingdom

CHAPTER XI

ENVIRONMENTAL DISPUTES

Profullachandra N. Bhagwati

The United Nations General Assembly stated in its Resolution 44/228 of 22 December 1989, that UNCED should have as one of its objectives "to assess the capacity of the United Nations system to assist in the prevention and settlement of disputes in the environmental sphere and to recommend measures in this field, while respecting existing bilateral and international agreements that provide for the settlement of such disputes".

The Executive Director of the United Nations Environment Programme (UNEP) pointed out in his introductory report to the 16th session of the Governing Council of UNEP in 1991 that "recent years have witnessed a sharp increase in the number and range of environmental conflicts", meaning not only "disputes between States but any controversy over natural resources and/or impacts of environmental harm". The Executive Director added: "A characteristic of environmental conflicts is a divergence of interests between neighbouring States or between an individual State and the international community as a whole. Among the more prevalent types of current environmental conflicts are those touching on the impacts of: (1) transboundary air pollution, including acid rain; (2) trans-boundary water pollution; (3) overuse or misuse of such shared natural resources as lakes, rivers, underground aquifers, forests; (4) transboundary movements of hazardous wastes; and (5) the impacts of global interenvironmental problems - climatic change, ozone depletion and loss of biodiversity -on those who are not necessarily their main cause. Such conflicts, some with potentially explosive political contents, have brought into sharp focus the urgent need for specific measures for their prevention or resolution".

The Group of Legal Experts of the World Commission on Environment and Development had already noted in 1987 that "Many disputes can be avoided or more readily resolved if the principles, rights and responsibilities cited earlier are built into national and international legal frameworks and are fully respected and implemented by many States. Individuals and States are more reluctant to act in a way that might lead to a dispute, when, as in many national legal systems, there is an established and effective capacity as well as ultimately building procedures for settling disputes. Such a capacity and procedures are largely lacking at the international level, particularly on environmental and natural resource management issues".

It will be seen that there is thus all round recognition of the need to review existing procedures and evolve new approaches and strategies for prevention and settlement of international environmental disputes.

I. DISPUTE PREVENTION

It can hardly be disputed that prevention is better than cure and it would be eminently desirable to devise procedures which prevent environmental disputes from arising rather than allow environmental disputes to arise and then provide mechanisms for their settlement. The surest way to avoid environmental disputes is to ensure efficient implementation of the obligations undertaken under international environmental instruments. The following are some of the procedures which can help to secure effective implementation of the obligations under international environmental instruments and thereby prevent environmental disputes.

Prior Consultation

One of the procedures for avoidance of international environmental disputes recommended by the Meeting of Senior Legal Advisers convened by UNEP in Nairobi in September 1991, was "prior notification and consultation concerning planned measures that may have extra-territorial impacts". This legal concept of prior consultation is well-entrenched in international law and is especially important in the development of effective international law governing environmental problems, because it operates pro-actively before an environmental problem occurs, rather than merely reactively after the problem has become a reality and culminated in an environmental dispute. A State ought to consult another State when it is contemplating an action that may adversely affect such other State, even though such action may not be in violation of prevailing international law. Even if there is no obligation under treaty or custom, a practice of prior consultation is valuable, particularly because international opportunities for conciliation, arbitration and adjudication may sometimes be non-existent and even when they exist, they may not be easy to avail. State practice in regard to prior consultation has been evident in certain areas such as international watercourse systems, air basins, partially enclosed seas and areas or resources beyond the jurisdiction of any national State such as the ocean and outer space.

Consultation among States or by States with international organizations or bodies is not uncommon. The practice reflects the fundamental legal principle that the abuse of rights is contrary to law or the principle that the owner of property rights must observe the limitations expressed in the maxim sic utero tuo ut alienum non laedas. Although there is no universal requirement of international law that a State must consult other States or international organization because a contemplated unilateral act may adversely affect the interest of another State or States, present international law does recognize, in particular circumstances, a duty to take account of the interests of other States (e.g., the 1982 UN Convention on the Law of the Sea, No. 38). The practice of prior consultation is also a characteristic of a growing number of international organizations.

Instances where the obligation of prior consultation has been recognized by arbitral or judicial decisions in certain situations may be found in the observations of the International Court of Justice in the North Sea Continental Shelf cases and the Fisheries Jurisdiction Case and in the 1957 award of the arbitral tribunal in the Lake Lanoux Case between France and Spain. Other instances in treaties may be found, inter alia in Article 9 of the 1974 Paris Convention for the Prevention of Pollution from Land Based Sources (No. 45), Article 12 of the 1980 Athens Protocol to the 1976 Barcelona Convention for the Mediterranean Sea (No. 46), Article 3 of the 1980 Memorandum of Intent concerning Transboundary Air Pollution between the United States and Canada, Article 5 of the 1979 Convention on Long-range Transboundary Air Pollution (No. 31), Article 5 of the 1991 Convention on Environmental Impact Assessment in a Transboundary Context (No. 11), and several other treaties. It may be noted that a norm has now developed requiring a State to consult another when it is contemplating a potentially polluting project close to a common border. The doctrine of prior consultation needs to be developed to extend to all situations of transboundary pollution and may usefully be included in bilateral or multilateral treaties and instruments in the area of environment. It will go a long way in averting environmental disputes and preventing their emergence.

Reporting Procedure

There is a close inter-connection between effective enforcement of the obligations undertaken under international environmental instruments and the arising of environmental disputes for breach of such obligations. If there is effective enforcement, the possibilities of environmental disputes will be reduced, if not altogether eliminated and the procedures of effective enforcement should, therefore, necessarily include procedures for avoidance of environmental disputes. One of the procedures recommended by the UNEP Meeting of Senior Legal Advisers held in Nairobi in September 1991 for this purpose is "the regular exchange of data and information concerning the subject matter" of the particular instrument and this can best be achieved by incorporating reporting obligations in the instrument.

Periodic reports on implementation in law and practice of the obligations undertaken by States under international environmental instruments ratified by them would make available to the international secretariats established under such instruments, and through such international secretariats or directly to UNEP, full data and information concerning compliance with such obligations. If there is non-compliance with any of the obligations, it would be immediately brought to the notice of UNEP through the periodic reports. The periodic reports would help avert environmental disputes likely to arise from non-compliance, because they would convey timely intimation which could be utilized by the UNEP Governing Council or any subsidiary Committee set up by it, to take adequate measures, by negotiation and persuasion with the non-complying State, to secure compliance with the obligation and thus avoid environmental disputes with the State or States likely to be affected by such non-compliance or with the international community where the obligation is owed to the international community.

The reporting procedure followed under the Constitution of the International Labour Organization (ILO) can furnish a very good model which could be adapted in the case of international environmental instruments by member States. This procedure has worked extremely well over more than 60 years. Under Article 22 of the ILO Constitution, every member State which has ratified a convention, has to make a periodic report to ILO in regard to the effect given in law and practice to the conventions ratified by it. Since the conventions now run into a large number - at present there are over 150 (see Nos. 110-116 of the present survey) - the Governing Council has laid down the period of reporting at two year intervals in case of certain important conventions and four year intervals in case of others. Before transmitting their periodic reports to ILO, Governments are required to send copies to the most representative organizations of employers and workers in the country. These organizations may then address comments on the effect given to the convention concerned either directly or through the Government. There is a Committee of Experts constituted by the Governing Council which consists of 20 distinguished jurists drawn from different parts of the world solely on the basis of their legal expertise. The Committee of Experts scrutinizes the reports and any comments thereon and it may then decide that law and practice are satisfactory and no further action is required. Alternatively, it may do one or both of two things: (1) it may call for further information by addressing a direct request to the member State; and/or (2) it may make an observation on the effect given to the Convention in that country. The report of the Committee of Experts is used as the basis for discussion at the Conference Committee on the application of Conventions and Recommendations where selected Governments are requested to appear in order to discuss the matters which have been raised by the experts in their report. The Conference Committee reports back to the Conference as a whole. Its report summarizes the debate in the Committee and may single out particularly serious or persistent breaches of ratified conventions. This is a serious step and one which member States are generally extremely anxious to avoid.

In addition to its examination of periodic reports on ratified conventions, each year the Committee of Experts carries out a general survey of law and practice among all member States in relation to a particular convention or group of conventions. For this purpose, every member State is required by Article 19 of the ILO Constitution to submit a detailed report on national law and practice in relation to the convention or group of conventions, even if the member State has not ratified them.

This procedure adopted by ILO is highly distinctive and has proved to be exceedingly effective and authoritative. It may be mentioned that similar reporting procedures are also provided in some of the international human rights instruments such as the International Covenant on Civil and Political Rights and the International Covenant on Economic, Social and Cultural Rights under which the Human Rights Committee and the Committee on Economic, Social and Cultural Rights receive national reports and monitor performance. The conventions on discrimination against women, against racial discrimination and against torture have also broadly equivalent reporting mechanisms.

This reporting procedure could be adapted usefully and with great advantage in the case of international environmental instruments, and monitoring mechanisms consisting of independent experts could be set up under each international environmental instrument to ensure effective implementation of the obligations undertaken under such instrument; or a common monitoring mechanism could be set up for several instruments. This would help considerably in preempting environmental disputes arising from non-compliance with obligations under international environmental instruments. It may be pointed out that the reporting procedure has been incorporated in a few international environmental instruments, including the draft convention on biodiversity. See, for example, the London Convention for the Prevention of Marine Pollution by Dumping of Wastes and other Matter (No. 35), the Convention on International Trade in Endangered Species of Wild Fauna and Flora (No. 18), the Convention on Long-range Transboundary Air Pollution (No. 31), the Basel Convention on the Control of Transboundary Movements of Hazardous Wastes and their Disposal (No. 103), the Vienna Convention for the Protection of Ozone Layer (No. 33) and its Montreal Protocol on Substances That Deplete the Ozone Layer.

Fact-finding

A third procedure recommended by the UNEP Meeting of Senior Legal Advisers held in Nairobi in September 1991 is fact-finding with regard to matters relating to obligations under the relevant instruments, even when no difference or dispute has yet arisen between the parties. The fact-finding may take various forms and contemplate various procedures, all of which would help to avert environmental disputes:

(a)   States planning to carry out or permit activities which may entail a significant risk of interference with the reasonable and equitable use of a transboundary natural resource, or a transboundary environmental interference causing harm in an area under national jurisdiction of another State or in an area beyond the limits of any national jurisdiction, shall give timely notice to the States concerned. They shall also, on their own initiative or upon request by the other State concerned, provide such relevant information as will permit those other States to make an assessment of the probable effects of the planned activities. The communication of the relevant data and information in regard to the activities before they are undertaken would help prevent the commission of unlawful transboundary interferences and thereby avoid environmental disputes. The obligation to give prior notice of planned activities appears, inter alia, in many treaties concerning the use of international water-courses; for example, the 1971 Act of Santiago between Argentina and Chile concerning Hydrologic Basins, the 1963 Niamey Act regarding Navigation and Cooperation between the States of the Niger Basin (No.77), the 1960 Indus Water Treaty and many other treaties. Treaty provisions, requiring prior notice are also found for planned activities possibly entailing trans-frontier radioactive contamination and in the case of weather modification; for example, in the 1975 Agreement between Canada and the U.S. on the Exchange of Information on Weather Modification Activities. Information on planned activities which may cause transboundary environmental interference is also usually given even in the absence of existing treaty obligations to that effect. The obligation to give prior notice and to provide relevant information to the States likely to be affected could usefully be incorporated in international environmental instruments as a provision calculated to avoid environmental disputes.

(b)   It would be useful to incorporate a provision that in order to maintain or attain a reasonable and equitable use of a transboundary natural resource or to prevent transboundary environmental interferences, the States concerned may establish coordinated or unified networks for the collection of data relating to the transboundary natural resource or for regular observation of transboundary environmental interferences and coordinate, and where appropriate, jointly undertake scientific and technical studies to that effect. The States concerned may set up coordinated or unified monitoring mechanisms and programmes of evaluation. They may also establish by common agreement specific environmental standards in various forms such as environmental quality standards or emission standards. This would also help in avoiding environmental disputes by providing for acceptance of agreed data information and standards and coordinated or unified monitoring mechanisms.

(c) Verification of the implementation of international environmental instruments is another facet of fact-finding which by ensuring implementation helps to avoid environmental disputes. This procedure has been stressed in 1991 in the introductory report of the Executive Director to the 16th session of the Governing Council of UNEP. "Verification carried out by the Contracting Parties", says the Executive Director, "through the creation of special monitoring institutions is another common material. There are numerous treaties on river and lake protection and wildlife protection and other subjects under which international commissions or implementation committees have been established, a recent example being the Implementation Committee set up under the non-compliance procedure adopted by the Second Meeting of the Parties to the Montreal Protocol". There are also precedents for entrusting international organizations, such as the Commission of the European Communities (EC) and the International Atomic Energy Agency (IAEA) with verification responsibilities, but, as pointed out by the Executive Director of UNEP, an important requirement would be the competence of the organization in the relevant field. Another variation would be an integrated verification responsibility both of the body created under the particular instrument and of one of the main organs of the United Nations system.

(d) The model for fact-finding provided in Articles 26 to 29 of the ILO Constitution also deserves consideration and adoption. Article 26 provides that any member State may file a complaint with ILO if it is not satisfied that any other member State is securing the effective observance of any Convention which both have ratified. The Governing Council may, if it thinks fit, communicate the complaint to the Government in question and invite that Government to make such statement as it thinks proper. If the Governing Council does not think it necessary to communicate the complaint to the Government in question, or if, when it has made such communication, no statement in reply has been received within a reasonable time which the Governing Council considers satisfactory, the Governing Council may appoint a Commission of Inquiry to consider the complaint and to report on it. The Governing Council can adopt the same procedure either <u>suo motu</u> or on receipt of a complaint from a delegate to the conference. When this matter is being considered by the Governing Council, the Government in question would be entitled to send a representative to take part in the proceedings of the Governing Council. Article 27 requires the member State to place at the disposal of the Commission of Inquiry all the relevant information in their possession. It is provided by Article 28 that when the Commission of Inquiry has fully considered the complaint, it shall prepare a report embodying the findings on all questions of fact relevant to determining the issue between the parties and containing such recommendations as it may think proper as to the steps which should be taken to meet the complaint and the time within which such steps should be taken. The report of the Commission of Inquiry is then required by Article 29 to be sent to the Governing Council and to each of the Governments concerned in the complaint and has also to be published. Each of the Governments has then to inform the Director-General within three months whether or not it accepted the recommendations contained in the report of the Commission of Inquiry and if it does not, it must refer the complaint to the International Court of Justice.

This procedure has worked quite well in the ILO and it could be appropriately adapted in relation to the international environmental instruments. The factual situation in regard to non-compliance with the obligations undertaken under international environmental instruments could be investigated by a Commission of Inquiry to be appointed by the Governing Council of UNEP on the complaint of a member State or a credible and responsible non-governmental organization. The Commission of Inquiry would obviously have to be composed of "experts having special competence on legal and substantive aspects of environmental protection, natural resources managements and sustainable development". They could be drawn from a pool of experts maintained by the Governing Council of UNEP. This may be regarded both as a method of prevention and also a method of settlement of environmental disputes, which could be introduced through the adoption of a legal instrument.

Hexagonale Proposal

One other proposal which bears close examination in this connection is that submitted by the six countries at the UNCED Preparatory Committee in 1991 (A/CONF.151/PC/L.29), hereinafter referred to as the "Hexagonale proposal". It urges all States where situations originating on their territory are likely to lead to disputes with other States concerning the environment, to provide adequate information to those other States, which on their part would equally be entitled to request and to receive such information. It recommends that States whose territory is likely to be impaired by transboundary environmental effects of activities or omissions on the territory of other States may request at any time the establishment of an Inquiry Commission to clarify and establish the factual issues of the situation. It then calls upon the Executive Director of UNEP to initiate negotiations on a legal instrument providing for a mechanism for dispute prevention concerning the environment, containing inter alia the following elements:

(a)   The request to establish an Inquiry Commission should be conveyed by the State which originally requested information on a given situation, to the State on whose territory the situation originates. It should also be notified to the Executive Director of UNEP. The members of the Inquiry Commission should be drawn from a pool of experts maintained by the Executive Director of UNEP on the basis of nominations received from the States.

(b)   The Inquiry Commission should consist of three members, one to be nominated by each of two States concerned and the third to be chosen by the two initial members and failing agreement amongst them, by the Executive Director of UNEP.

(c)   The Inquiry Commission should clarify and establish the factual issues of the situation and submit a report within six months of its establishment. The report should be deposited with the Executive Director of UNEP and transmitted to the States concerned.

(d)   The expenses of the Inquiry Commission should be borne by the interested parties but so far as the Least Developed Countries are concerned, in order to facilitate the use of this mechanism by them, they should be entitled to financial assistance from the UNEP Environment Fund.

It may be noticed that this proposal is very much akin to the ILO model discussed in the preceding section. The Inquiry Commissions are fact-finding commissions, with the ILO model having also power to make recommendations in regard to the steps to be taken to meet the complaints relating to the apprehended transboundary environmental interference or harm. Either of these two models may be adopted or there may be an amalgam of the two models. Whatever the model adopted, it will help considerably to avoid international environmental disputes.

II. DISPUTE RESOLUTIONS

Having considered the various procedures which may be adopted for prevention of environmental disputes, attention may now be focussed on methods for resolution of such disputes when they have arisen.

While so far, in this study, the expression "international environmental disputes" has been used, this may not be an appropriate term to describe the different kinds of environmental disputes that may arise. The expression "international environmental disputes" seems to be limited to inter-governmental disputes, usually described as a disagreement or conflict of views or interests <u>between States</u> relating to the alteration, through human intervention, of natural environmental systems. But this limitation to intergovernmental disputes is too narrow, because disputes may and often do arise between industrial pollution victims on the one hand and a State or non-State actor on the other. It would, therefore, be preferable to use the expression "transnational" to cover both these categories of environmental disputes.

There is another classification of environmental disputes which may be made on the basis of the legal relationship out of which they arise. It has been pointed out that the bulk of environmental conflicts occur between specific victims (e.g. of pollution) and specific villains (e.g. polluters) - in legal terms these may be classified as disputes over reciprocal obligations. On the other hand, a growing number of environmental problems are typically not concerned with obligations <u>vis à vis</u> particular States or individuals, but with collective obligations owed to the international community and to mankind as a whole[1]. The former category of environmental disputes comprises disputes between States or between individual victims in one State and another State or non-State actor in another State arising out of activities or omissions occurring on the territory of one State or in areas outside the limits of national jurisdiction, which have transboundary environmental effects in the territory of another State; while the latter

---

[1]   P.H. Sand, "New Approaches to Transnational Environmental Disputes", <u>International Environmental Affairs</u>, vol. 3 (1991), pp. 193-206.

category comprises disputes arising out of activities or omissions occurring in one State or in areas not under any national jurisdiction which have transboundary environmental effects outside the limits of any national jurisdiction. The environmental disputes which need resolution machinery are not only disputes in which the offending activities or omissions have already taken place but also those where announced or proposed activities give rise to concern, prior to the occurrence of such activities or omissions.

There are a large number of environmental treaties and other arrangements dealing with issues relating to environment, and most of them contain provisions for dispute settlement of varying nature, including in some cases highly elaborate arbitration procedures and references to the International Court of Justice. But closer analysis reveals that in quite a number of instruments these provisions can usually not be invoked unilaterally at the request of any one State concerned but they make third-party adjudication dependent on common agreement by the parties to the dispute and, therefore, they do not provide for mandatory arbitration or adjudication. It has been the general trend to provide for optional dispute settlement, the formula of which was introduced in the Vienna Convention for the Protection of the Ozone Layer (No. 33), and such a clause is also to be found in Article 20 of the Basel Convention on the Control of Transboundary Movements of Hazardous Wastes and their Disposal (No. 103) and various other international environmental agreements. It has been noted that Governments have tended to avoid judicial and liability-based methods of dealing with these questions[2]. There is a widespread belief that <u>binding</u> third party mechanisms have not succeeded in satisfactorily dealing with environmental disputes in reasonable time and often by reason of the very nature of the mechanisms, they are tied up with the adversarial model and do not allow a variety of interests to be represented and heard and participate in the resolution. The sheer inertia of the proceedings under binding third party mechanisms is sometimes a negative factor which acts as a deterrent. For example, as has been pointed out, both the Trail Smelter case and the Gut Dam case took a solid 15 years from the first claims to the final arbitral award - a time-cost few environmental problems to-day can afford. It would, therefore, be desirable to evolve voluntary and non-binding mechanisms for the resolution of transnational environmental disputes; i.e., mechanisms with "non-compulsory" outcomes.

The first and primary voluntary and non-binding mechanism for resolution of transnational disputes is the procedure of direct negotiations. This is usually the first approach used to resolve transnational disputes, and almost every bilateral or multi-lateral environmental treaty contains a provision that in case a dispute arises concerning the interpretation or application of the treaty, the parties are expected to settle the dispute by negotiations. The Hexagonale proposal for settlement of international disputes concerning the environment (A/CONF.151/PC/WG.III/L.1) also provides in paragraph (1) of Annex 2 that "in the event of a dispute between States concerning transboundary environmental effects which activities or omissions occurring on the territory of one State have or may have on the territory of another State, the parties concerned shall, without undue delay and in good faith, consult among themselves with a view to settle the dispute through negotiation or any other means of their own choice"; and "when the dispute arises for damages to the global or regional environment caused

---

    [2]   R. Bilder, "The Settlement of Disputes in the Field of the International Law of the Environment", <u>Recueil des Cours: Collected Courses of the Hague Academy of International Law</u>, vol. 144 (1975-I), pp. 139-239.

by activities or omissions having occurred under the responsibility of one State in areas not under national jurisdiction, any State party of the relevant treaties shall be entitled to initiate consultation for the settlement of the dispute". The procedure of direct negotiations is recognized as the first and foremost mechanism for settlement of transnational disputes. But this approach would be appropriate only when the dispute is inter-governmental, that is, between States where the States can carry out negotiations. Where, however, the transnational dispute concerns the claims of nationals of one State against another State, or against a non-State actor in such other State for compensation or their properties on account of transboundary environmental effects of activities or omissions on the territory of such other State, this approach may not be feasible unless the State whose nationals have suffered loss or damage espouses the cause of its nationals and negotiates directly with the State from whose territory the activities or omission causing the loss or damage have originated.

It may be necessary, sometimes, for the purpose of assisting in negotiations and effectively bringing about a settlement of the environmental dispute, to bring in non-governmental interests as full participants and in such a case, it would be desirable to develop "a cooperative model in which the good offices of an international organization or another respected independent third party" can make it possible to bridge some of the difficulties and gaps in the direct negotiation process. International environmental instruments could profitably include a provision for such a cooperative model, which would help considerably in bringing about a smooth and effective settlement of transnational environmental disputes.

It has been pointed out that a large number of environmental disputes in post-war Europe have been settled -- usually with little more than local publicity- at the inter-administrative level in the border regions concerned, by way of direct ad hoc negotiations or through standing transboundary commissions. The negotiations may be assisted or facilitated through the intervention of a mediator chosen by the parties. This kind of mediation has been extensively used in the United States to bring about settlement of intra-State environmental disputes and it could appropriately be extended to cover transnational environmental disputes. The task of acting as a facilitator in the resolution of environmental disputes could also be usefully performed by UNEP. This task, as pointed out in the introductory report of the Executive Director to the 16th session of the Governing Council of UNEP in 1991, is "nothing new to UNEP". The Executive Director states in his Report: "The UNEP regional seas programme is designed not only to protect the environment of a given regional sea, but also to prevent environmental disputes between 'co-owners' of that sea. Moreover, there have been several instances where UNEP has acted, upon request, as mediator or facilitator in environmental disputes. Just recently, at the request of the two Governments concerned, UNEP sent an expert team to examine the conflicting claims of two European States concerning transboundary air pollution. The UNEP team studied the situation, ascertained the facts and formulated a cooperative scheme between the two Governments to solve the problem and enhance the environment - for the benefit of all concerned".

This is clearly an approach to conflict resolution that could be very useful, namely that UNEP, at the request of a Government, would act as a facilitator to assist the Governments to work together to structure a problem, to identify its scientific aspects and propose alternative solutions. The Governments would themselves be then responsible for deciding on how they wish to address the problem. The Governing Council of UNEP could carry out this task of facilitating resolution of environmental disputes by acting as a mediator and using its good offices; this task could be carried out by the Governing Council directly or through a subsidiary body or by mandating the Executive Director in specific cases, upon the request of a Government. The procedure of direct negotiations or negotiations facilitated or assisted by UNEP or by any transboundary commission or organization or mediator could help considerably in bringing about settlement of environmental disputes, without the States or the parties affected by environmental interference having to go to a third-party binding mechanism or even to a third-party binding mediation. Even where the environmental interests of the international community as a whole, comprising present and future generations, are affected, the Governing Council of UNEP could either directly or through a subsidiary body or through the Executive Director initiate negotiations with the State where the environmental interference originated and bring about resolution of the problem.

But if the parties are unable to reach settlement of the environmental dispute through the procedure of direct negotiations or structured negotiations with the good offices of a third party or a mediator, either party could adopt the procedure of compulsory resort to conciliation or mediation by a person or persons drawn from an expert panel maintained by UNEP; but the report and recommendations of such conciliator or mediator would not have the effect of a binding decision and they could form the basis for renewed consideration of the matter by the parties concerned. This procedure has been adopted in some environment-related treaties such as the Agreement for the Establishment of a General Fisheries Council for the Mediterranean (No. 60), the amended Agreement for the Establishment of the Indo-Pacific Fisheries Commission (No. 58) and the Vienna Convention for the Protection of the Ozone Layer (No.33), amongst others.

What is to happen if this mode of resolution of environmental dispute fails? Under a number of recent environmental agreements, each State, when signing, ratifying, accepting, approving or acceding to the agreement or at any time thereafter, may declare in writing that it accepts as compulsory one or both of the following means for the settlement of environmental disputes:

(a)   submission of the dispute to arbitration in accordance with the procedure established under the treaty, where the arbitral decision would be binding;

(b)   submission of the dispute for the binding decision of the International Court of Justice.

One or the other and at times both these modes of settlement of environmental disputes have been provided in some environmental instruments such as the Antarctic Treaty and the Convention on the Conservation of Antarctic Marine Living Resources (under No. 14, where both modes are provided), Convention on International Trade in Endangered Species of Wild Fauna and Flora (No. 18, where mode 'a' is provided), the Convention on the Conservation of Migratory Species of Wild Animals (No. 22, where mode 'a' is provided), the International Convention for the Prevention of Pollution from Ships (No. 36, where mode 'a' is provided), the Convention on the Prevention of Marine Pollution from Land-Based Sources (No. 45, where mode 'a' is provided), the Convention for the Protection and Development of the Marine Environment of the Wider Caribbean Region (No. 52, where mode 'a' is provided), and the optional Protocol in the Vienna Convention on Civil Liability for Nuclear Damage (under No. 118, where mode 'b' is provided), amongst others.

The meeting of the Senior Legal Advisors held by UNEP in September 1991 recommended that international instruments may, where appropriate, include optional declaration in writing to the depositary that a party accepts as compulsory one or both of the following means of dispute settlement: (i) binding arbitration, in accordance with procedures under the instrument; (ii) judicial settlement, by submission of the dispute to the International Court of Justice. The Vienna Convention for the Protection of the Ozone Layer (No. 33) provides a model for such a clause. It may be noted that an identical recommendation has been made in paragraph 4 of Annex 2 to the Hexagonale proposal for settlement of international disputes concerning the environment. The arbitral tribunal, according to this recommendation, would decide the dispute on the basis of international law and would have the power to prescribe any provisional measures which it considered appropriate under the circumstances to preserve the respective rights of the parties to the dispute or to prevent serious harm to the environment, pending the final decision. In case of submission of the environmental dispute to the International Court of Justice, such provisional or interim measures could be adopted by the International Court of Justice in accordance with Article 41 of its Statute. The recommendation also suggests that any decision rendered by the Arbitral Tribunal shall be final and binding on the parties, but such decision shall have no binding force except between the parties and in respect of that particular dispute, as in the case of decisions of the International Court of Justice in accordance with Article 5 of the Statute of the Court. These should be the elements, according to the Hexagonale proposal, of the procedure for settlement of environmental disputes to be included in international instruments.

Where the environmental interests of the international community as a whole are affected, UNEP could play a significant role. This includes cases where environmental obligations concerning global commons and common heritage resources are owed to the international community as a whole, including future generations. Where environmental obligations of this kind are involved, a non-compliance complaint may be initiated even by a State which is not directly victimized and in whose territories the effects of non-compliance are not felt. This non-compliance procedure was adopted by the Parties to the Montreal Protocol on Substances That Deplete the Ozone Layer (under No. 33) at their London Conference in June 1990 where it was provided that any Party may, through the Secretariat, submit "reservations regarding another Party's implementation of its obligations under the Protocol" to an Implementation Committee reporting to the Conference of the Parties. It has been pointed out that even though this procedure was cautiously defined as non-judicial and non-confrontational, its general approach (not requiring any injury or other condition of standing for the Party submitting the complaint) resembles that of a "class action" in the interest of all Parties. This procedure giving a right of complaint even to a non-affected State could be included in international instruments creating collective obligations to the international community as a whole. It may be well worth considering whether a similar right of complaint should also be accorded to recognized environmental groups which are functioning as non-governmental organizations in the area of environment, following the practice which has developed under the 1957 Rome Treaty establishing the European Community (EC, as amended by the 1986 Single European Act, No.9).

Article 155 of the 1957 Rome Treaty makes the EC Commission the guardian of the Treaty's implementation, and Article 169 empowers it to initiate proceedings against any member State in case of infringements, sanctioned, if necessary, by formal action in the European Court of Justice at Luxembourg. It has been noted that over the past ten years, this "custodial" procedure has become one of the most important means of enforcing EC environmental standards. The EC infringement proceeding comprises three stages. As a first step, the Commission sends "letters of formal notice" to member States that fail to enact or apply a Community directive, or to report on its enactment or application. After giving the member State an opportunity to respond, the Commission then proceeds to render a reasoned opinion confirming the infringement in the light of all the facts gathered. If the member State still does not comply, the Commission may then refer the matter to the European Court of Justice. This procedure has been extensively used and over the years, a new feature has evolved gradually during its implementation, as the Commission has been initiating infringement proceedings against member States not only on the basis of its own monitoring obligation but also on citizens complaints - from private individuals, associations or municipalities. As a result of public information on the complaints procedure and the establishment of a complaints registry within the Commission Secretariat in Brussels, the number of environmental complaints has risen dramatically over the years. While complaints are usually based on local non-compliance with EC standards, in some cases they have had wider effects. For example, a single complaint by a resident in the United Kingdom with regard to EC directive 80/779 of 15 July 1980 triggered a Commission investigation that led to infringement proceedings against seven member States. The EC Commission has no powers of enforcement of its own decisions or of the decisions of the European Court of Justice in environmental infringement proceedings, comparable to those of a national Government. However, the mere initiation of EC action can have international political and economic consequences in member States. The custodial action procedure of the EC Commission has thus evolved from a three-stage to a four-stage process, the first stage in most cases being a citizen's complaint. The role of the EC Commission in this field has been described as that of a "European Environmental Ombudsman". This procedure could be profitably adapted for use in international environmental instruments.

With regard to transnational environmental disputes arising from claims made by persons detrimentally affected by interference with their use of a trans-boundary natural resource, or by a transboundary environmental interference, lower-level remedies such as local legal remedies and private law proceedings would be preferable and these remedies should be strengthened. International environmental instruments should provide for such matters as the jurisdiction of the domestic, civil and administrative courts, the applicable law and the enforcement of administrative and judicial decisions or such provision could be made in separate instruments and States invited to accept and ratify it. One major advantage of settling transnational environmental disputes privately between polluters and victims through private law proceedings in domestic courts is the recognition of the "polluter-pays" principle, which leads to cost internationalization at source. But, unless uniformity and enforceability of private law remedies are brought within an international legal regime in the manner suggested above, they will remain in the realm of uncertainty and unpredictability and fail to provide relief to the victims of transnational interference. The Bhopal disaster illustrates vividly how victims of transnational pollution accidents encounter serious difficulties in obtaining relief and redress. There, as the gravity of transnational pollution problems has become evident, it is increasingly felt and there is a growing demand that domestic courts should become the avenue for redress. There is accordingly great need to make appropriate provision for the victims of transnational pollution to obtain relief through the domestic courts in private law proceedings instead of depending on the exercise of diplomatic protection by their State.

In the first place, States of origin, that is, States where a transboundary environmental interference originated, should grant to foreign victims equivalent access to and treatment in the same administrative and judicial proceedings as are available to persons within their own jurisdiction who have been or may be similarly affected. This principle allows the victims to take action proprio motu for the protection of their interests instead of waiting until action is taken by their Government, which in many cases, particularly in the case of developing countries, may be difficult, if not impossible, for various diplomatic or political reasons. There are some countries where the administrative authorities and/or courts take the view that the scope of the applicable law is strictly territorial, so that foreign interests are not considered to be legally affected nor protected by that law, with the consequence that the foreign complainants are denied locus standi. By contrast, there are several countries where affected foreign victims - even potentially affected victims - are given locus standi before the administrative authorities or courts of those countries. Reference may also be made, inter alia to the 1974 Nordic Environmental Protection Convention (No. 2), some of the OECD Council recommendations concerning transfrontier pollution (No. 3), the 1982 UNEP Guidelines Concerning the Environment Related to Off-shore Mining and Drilling within the Limits of National Jurisdiction (No. 37) and the 1978 UNEP Principles of Conduct Concerning Shared Natural Resources (No. 6), which provide for, recognize or recommend a right of access (equal or equivalent to the right possessed by nationals of the State of origin) to the administrative or judicial authorities of the State of origin, without however affecting the possibility, where previously existing, to start proceedings before the administrative or judicial authorities of the (potentially) affected State. There are also certain conventions dealing with liability for nuclear damage which provide for jurisdiction only in the courts of the Party in whose territory the nuclear incident occurred or when the incident occurred outside the territory of a Party or the place of nuclear incident cannot be determined with certainty, then, in the courts of the Party in whose territory the nuclear installation is situated - as under the 1960 Paris Convention on Third Party Liability in the Field of Nuclear Energy (No. 117) and the 1963 Vienna Convention on Civil Liability for Nuclear Damage (No. 118). This brief resume shows that it is necessary and possible to remove impediments, wherever they exist, in regard to the jurisdiction of the courts and administrative authorities of the States of origin.

With regard to the administrative authorities and courts of the State in which the harmful consequences of a transboundary environmental interference are sustained or likely to be sustained, resort to them is usually difficult, because of jurisdictional problems and the applicable national rules of private international law under which civil proceedings can sometimes be brought only in the State of origin. But there are certain international agreements which make it possible for proceedings to be brought in the administrative authorities and courts of the affected state. For example, the 1968 EC Convention on Jurisdiction and Enforcement of Judgements in Civil and Commercial Matters allows tort proceedings to be filed not only before the courts of the State of origin but also before the courts of the affected State. Another example may be found in the 1969 Brussels International Convention on Civil Liability for Oil Pollution Damage (No. 121) under which an action for compensation can be brought only before the courts of the State in whose territory including the territorial sea, the pollution damage has been caused. The 1977 London Convention on Civil Liability for Oil Pollution Damage Resulting from Exploration for and Exploitation of Seabed Mineral Resources (No. 123) provides that action for compensation under the Convention may be brought only in the courts of a State where pollution damage was suffered as a result of an incident or in the courts of the so-called controlling State.

But where an action can be brought in the courts of the State in which the harmful consequences of a transboundary interference or pollution are sustained or are likely to be sustained, a difficulty may arise as to how a judgement rendered in favor of the plaintiff can be enforced. Such a judgement would be meaningless and futile unless the plaintiff can have the judgement enforced in the State where the cause of the transboundary interference or the polluting activity is located or the defendant possesses assets. This was a problem encountered in the Bhopal case. There can be several obstacles in the way of enforcement by one State of a judgement rendered by the courts of another State. Some obstacle may be that the court which rendered the judgement was, according to the standards of the State considering enforcement, not competent to decide the case. Another obstacle to enforcement may be that the reciprocity requirement is not satisfied or that the judgement is regarded as incompatible with the public policy of the State in which enforcement is sought. One other factor which is required to be kept in mind is whether and if so, to what extent, the authorities of the State considering enforcement of a foreign judgement will reconsider the merits of the case. These difficulties would be considerably reduced if the States concerned enter into a convention regulating the reciprocal recognition and enforcement of the judgements of their courts. Here again the example of the 1968 EC Jurisdiction and Enforcement of Judgements Convention is extremely relevant. Under this Convention, a contracting State can refuse enforcement of a judgement rendered in another contracting state only on a limited number of grounds, the principal amongst these grounds being that the decision shall not be contrary to the public policy of the State in which the enforcement is sought.

It would therefore be desirable that international environmental instruments themselves provide which shall be the State, whether the State of origin or the affected State, whose administrative authorities and courts shall be competent to grant relief to persons detrimentally affected by a transboundary interference or pollution. It would be more convenient to the affected persons if competence were granted to the administrative authorities or courts of the State in which the harmful consequences of transboundary interference or pollution are suffered by the persons affected. But, in that event, a provision would have to be included for enforcement by one contracting State of a judgement rendered by another contracting state, so that a judgement rendered by a court of the State in which the harmful consequences have been suffered, can be enforced by the plaintiff in the State in which the transboundary interference or the polluting activity has occurred. If, however, competence is granted to the courts of the State of origin, there should be a specific provision included in the international environmental instrument concerned that the courts of the State of origin shall grant to foreign victims equivalent access to and treatment in the same administrative and judicial proceedings as are available to persons within their own jurisdiction who have been or may be similarly affected.

Another problem which requires to be addressed in cases of this kind and is in regard to the applicable law by which the proceedings are to be governed. This problem has been dealt with in some international instruments. The 1974 Nordic Environmental Protection Convention (No. 2) provides in Article 2 that the permissibility of environmental harmful activities shall be determined by the law of the State of origin. The question of compensation, however is to be judged, according to article 3 (2), by rules not less favourable to the injured party than the rules of compensation of the State of origin, thus leaving open the possibility of applying a more favorable law of the State where the harm has been caused. Reference may also be made to the 1974 OECD Principles Concerning Transfrontier Pollution (No. 3) which provide that States of origin should grant foreign victims "no less favorable" treatment than accorded to person affected by similar pollution in the State of origin. "Equivalent treatment" and "the same remedies" have also been recommended in the 1978 UNEP Principles of Conduct on Shared Natural Resources (No. 6). It will be seen that these provisions do not prescribe the applicable law but purport to lay down a certain minimum standard for the treatment to be accorded to foreign victims. A more favorable treatment or rule of compensation which may be prevailing in the State where the harm has been caused could certainly be applied in granting relief to foreign victims. There is in fact a tendency towards a more flexible approach to the choice-of-law problem, as exemplified by the 1957 Poro Case (W. Poro v. Houillières du Bassin de Lorraine, judgement of 22 October 1957 by the Court of appeals of Saarbrücken) where a German court resolved a Trail Smelter type of situation by applying the (French) national law "most favorable to the plaintiff".

There is also another procedure by which "transnational handicaps" may be eliminated substantially, if not altogether, in so far as claims for relief by persons affected by transboundary interference or pollution are concerned. The claims settlement procedure adopted in 1967 by the Austro-German Boundary Airport treaty provides that the German Government shall substitute its own liability for the civil liability of Austrian authorities as regards specified claims for damages or taking of property on German territory caused by the establishment or operation of the Salzburg airport and shall subsequently be reimbursed by the Austrian Government. It has been noted that this procedure actually reverses the traditional process of international claims settlement, where lump sum deals are first transacted between Governments and then distributed to individual claimants. The procedural fiction of "substitution" has also been used in claims for noise and sonic-boom damage caused by NATO military aircraft in Western Europe pursuant to Article VIII (5) of the 1951 Status of Forces Agreement (SOFA). In fact, a large number of claims for noise damage by foreign military aircraft have been settled locally under this provision as if they contained no transnational elements at all. This is a useful procedure which could conveniently be adapted for satisfactory and effective settlement of the claims of persons affected by transboundary environmental interference or pollution.

The Hexagonale proposal for the settlement of international disputes concerning the environment has recommended another procedure for the settlement of claims of nationals of one State against another State regarding compensation for losses or damages suffered by those nationals or their properties from transboundary environmental effects of activities or omissions on the territory of that State. The recommendation is for setting up Mixed Claims Commissions, following, <u>inter alia</u>, the elements set forth in Annex 1 to the proposal. That Annex sets out the details of the procedure to be followed in referring claims to the Mixed Claims Commission, and provides that all decisions of the Mixed Claims Commission shall be final and binding and shall be enforceable against non-State parties as if they were judgements of a court of the State in which enforcement is sought.

These are some of the procedures which have been suggested from time to time for the purpose of settlement of environmental disputes concerning claims of nationals of one State against another State or nationals of such other State regarding compensation for losses or damages suffered by those nationals or their properties from transboundary environmental harm or injury caused by activities or omissions on the territory of such other State. It would be desirable if any one of these procedures, which may be considered appropriate, were specifically included in international environmental instruments. It is only if a proper and effective remedy is provided by adopting any one or more of these procedures that foreign victims will be able to claim adequate relief against transboundary environmental interference or pollution which causes or is likely to cause harm or injury to them.

CHAPTER XII

SAMPLE BILATERAL INSTRUMENTS

Alexander Borg Olivier

This chapter considers the following 6 samples of bilateral agreements and instruments:

I. Atmosphere (North America):
    the 1991 **Canada-USA Agreement on Air Quality;**

II. Nuclear Emergencies (Europe):
    the 1987 **Finland-USSR Agreement on Early Notifications of a Nuclear Accident and on Exchange of Information relating to Nuclear Facilities;**

III. Freshwaters (South America):
    the 1973 **Argentina-Uruguay Agreement concerning the River Plate,** and related instruments;

IV. Marine Living Resources (Africa):
    the 1979 **EEC-Senegal Agreement on Fishing off the Coast of Senegal,** and related instruments;

V. Wildlife Protection (Asia):
    the 1981 **China-Japan Treaty for the Protection of Migratory Birds and Their Habitats;**

VI. General Environmental Co-operation (North-South):
    the 1980 **Memorandum of Understanding on Environmental Protection Between the United States Environmental Protection Agency and the Federal Ministry of Housing of Nigeria,** and related instruments.

454

I. ATMOSPHERE

Currently, there exist few bilateral agreements whose purposes are directed at combatting atmospheric pollution, either in respect to the conservation and harmonious utilization of natural resources shared by two or more states or in regard to transboundary pollution precedents and norms. Similarly, few bilateral instruments address either individual aspects of air pollution—such as protection of the ozone layer—or certain types of pollution—such as motor vehicles. Most instruments which address individual air quality issues are of a regional dimension, and important progress can be seen within Europe and North America, in particular. Nevertheless, the principles and provisions contained in many of these regional instruments have tended to assure a harmonization of bilateral agreements in the field of air quality, placing emphasis on prevention through consultation and information sharing.

In the field of bilateral regulation, several agreements between the United States and Canada addressing forms of atmospheric pollution can be traced as far back as 1935, when the Ottawa Convention for the Establishment of a Tribunal to Decide Questions of Indemnity Arising from the Operation of the Smelter at Trail, British Columbia (Trail Smelter) was signed[1]. The decision of the tribunal in that case remains a seminal basis for air quality regulation. More recently, the efforts of these two countries in the area of air toxics deposition in the Great Lakes region are addressed in the United States - Canada Great Lakes Water Quality Agreement (GLWQA), as amended in 1987. Annex 15 to the Agreement builds upon existing bilateral co-operation between these two States concerning "wet-air" deposition (e.g. phosphorus, nitrogen) affecting the lakes[2]. The GLWQA Integrated Atmospheric Deposition Network, outlined in Annex 15, is of particular importance to current US-Canadian efforts regarding practical approaches to monitor and control airborne toxic pollution.

Both Canada and the United States thus are Parties to the 1979 Geneva Convention on Long-range Transboundary Air Pollution (No. 31 in the present survey) and its 1988 Sofia Protocol Concerning the Control of Emissions of Nitrogen Oxides or their Transboundary Fluxes, and have both signed the 1991 Geneva Protocol Concerning the Control of Emissions of Volatile Organic Compounds or Their Transboundary Fluxes. However, while Canada also is a Party to the related 1985 Helsinki Protocol on the Reduction of Sulphur Emissions or Their

---

[1] See International Environmental Law: Basic Instruments and References (E.B. Weiss, D.B. Magraw & P.C. Szasz, Transnational Publishers 1992). The assistance of Mr. Paul Szasz in making an advance list of this comprehensive treaty collection available is gratefully acknowledged.

[2] Telefax communication, official of the Office of International Activities, United States Environmental Protection Agency (11 February 1992).

Transboundary Fluxes by at least 30%, the United States is not.

The basic air quality objectives outlined in the Canada-United States Agreement on Air Quality (signed in Ottawa on 13 March 1991) address the shared concerns of both countries regarding the negative effects of transboundary air pollution and require that each State establish measures to limit emissions and air pollutants. The main text of the agreement situates a framework for dealing with a variety of transboundary air pollution problems, such as acid rain, urban smog and single plant emissions. However, specific obligations are imposed only for reduction or limitation of acid-rain-causing emissions (Annex 1), and each Party is free to adopt the programmes and other measures it deems necessary to implement its objectives.

The specific air quality objectives contained in Annex 1 endeavour to permanently cap sulphur dioxide emissions in both countries; require scheduled reductions in emissions of nitrogen oxides from factories and power plants; impose stricter emission standards for new motor vehicles; require that emissions of sulphur dioxide and nitrogen oxides be closely monitored; and impose actions to be taken to protect both countries' wilderness areas from transboundary air pollution.

The Clean Air Act Amendments of 1970 form the original core of United States' efforts in controlling airborne pollution. In brief, the 1970 legislation required that the US Environmental Protection Agency (EPA) establish national ambient air quality standards to define the minimum levels of air quality to be achieved[3]. Specific air quality concerns were not addressed. Under the terms of the Amendments, each State was to base source-emission limitations on EPA standards. The regulatory regime thus established created a federal-state partnership governing air quality control; a "command-and-control" scheme that dominated US air quality regulation through two decades.

In 1990, in response to the intensive efforts of environmental groups to draw attention to the need to address specific air quality concerns, such as acid-rain, the US Congress passed additional amendments to the Clean Air Act, which greatly expanded existing regulatory air quality controls. The Congress also created the Acid-Rain Control Programme (in anticipation of the US-Canadian Agreement on Air Quality) as the first major programme designed to use market forces to achieve Clean Air Act objectives[4].

The 1990 Programme has been hailed by the US Government as a bold departure from the facility by facility command-and-control regulatory schemes established under the 1970 amendments. In apparent deference to scientific inroads made in determining the causes of acid rain, the 1990 Amendments resolve to cut US sourced sulphur dioxide emissions by one half by the year 2000. The 1990 Amendments also provide for the adoption of programmes referred to in Annex 1 of the US-Canadian Air Quality Agreement for reducing and eventually limiting acid-rain causing emissions.

The Parties have reserved for themselves a general right of mutual consent regarding all activities to be undertaken by each across the entire implementation, review and settlement spectrum. To this end, consultation and negotiation are the appropriate means reserved for

---

[3] The National Law Journal, Monday, 10 February 1992 at 28.

[4] See id. at 29.

resolving conflict over or modification of any matter within the scope of the agreement.

The methods by which current information on the operation and implementation of its provisions is to be made available to concerned other parties or the public are contained in Articles VII through IX.

Article VII, entitled Exchange of Information, states that:

"1.   The Parties agree to exchange, as a regular basis and through the Air Quality Committee established under Article VIII, information on:
(a) monitoring;
(b) emissions;
(c) technologies, measures and mechanisms for controlling emissions;
(d) atmospheric processes; and
(e) effects of air pollutants, as provided in Annex 2.

2.   Notwithstanding any other provisions of this Agreement, the Air Quality Committee and the International Joint Commission (referred to in Article IX) shall not release, without the consent of the owners, any information identified to them as proprietary information under the laws of the place where such information has been acquired."

Article VIII establishes the Air Quality Committee and defines its responsibilities:

"1. ...
2. ...
(a) reviewing progress made in the implementation of this agreement, including its general and specific objectives;
(b) preparing and submitting to the Parties a progress report within a year after entry into force of this Agreement and at least every two years thereafter;
(c) referring each progress report to the International Joint Commission for action in accordance with Article IX of this Agreement; and
(d) releasing each progress report to the public after its submission to the Parties."

The Committee was established in 1991, and met for the first time in November, 1991. The Committee has nine members from each Government, and is co-chaired by the US State Department and Environment Canada. The Committee has two sub-committees -- one on programme monitoring and reporting, and one on scientific co-operation. The two sub-committees also met in November 1991.

The initial emphasis of the Air Quality Committee and the two sub-committees was assessing ongoing bilateral air activities between the two countries, and to identify areas of future co-operation in light of the provisions of the Air Quality Agreement.

Improvements in air quality are measured through national networks of disposition and air concentration monitoring. In the case of acidic deposition, for example, both countries measure wet and dry deposition of sulphates and nitrates. Both countries also measure sulphur dioxide concentrations for health reasons, and the United States measures sulphate concentrations in the context of visibility monitoring programmes. Both countries conduct forest monitoring programmes, although the relationship between acidic deposition and forest damage is not as clear as the relationship between acidic compounds and surface water chemistry. In the United States, there is an active and expanding programme of visibility monitoring.

The Air Quality Agreement calls for the publication of a progress report on the implementation of the Agreement within one year of signing of the Agreement, and every two years thereafter. These progress reports will be made available to the public, and the International Joint Commission has an important role in soliciting public comments on the report and reporting back to the Parties.

The two Governments are currently in the process of compiling the first progress report, expected to be completed in March 1992. The report will contain information on the history of the agreement, progress in implementing acidic deposition control programmes in the two countries, compliance monitoring, prevention of significant deterioration and visibility, emission inventories, atmospheric modelling, deposition and air concentration monitoring, effects research and monitoring, and market-based incentives for environmental protection. Acidic deposition is the area that is focused on in the first report.

The Agreement has been a positive experience so far in that it has strengthened existing lines of communication and provided the opportunity for new lines of communication on a variety of subjects related to air quality research, monitoring, programme development and programme implementation. For example, the two countries are working together to strengthen and enhance co-operation on the compilation of emission inventories, which are important in the analysis and management of air quality problems. Also, the two countries formally and informally exchange information and ideas on the use of market-based mechanisms as a way to achieve more cost-effective emissions reductions.

The two Governments are absorbing the costs of conducting business under the Air Quality Agreement under various operating budgets -- e.g., funds allocated for acid rain control programmes, deposition monitoring, effects research.

Disputes concerning implementation of the Agreement regarding any proposed action, activity or project subject to assessment under Article V, paragraph 1, or under Article XIV, shall be handled in accordance with provisions contained in Articles XI, XII, and XIII.

Article V provides that:

"1.   Each Party shall ... assess those proposed actions, activities and projects within the area under its jurisdiction that, if carried out, would be likely to cause significant transboundary air pollution, including consideration of appropriate mitigation measures."

Article XI requires that the Parties shall consult, at the request of either Party, on any matter within the scope of the Agreement. (Matters within the scope of the Agreement are identified in Article X, paragraph 3(b), as existing policies, programmes or measures that would be likely to affect significantly transboundary air pollution). No disputes have arisen to date. Disputes would first be referred to the Air Quality Committee for discussion and further action.

If, after consultations in accordance with Article XI, an issue remains concerning a proposed or continuing action... the Parties may refer the matter to an appropriate third party (Article XII). "The Parties shall consider whether to submit... that dispute to the International Joint Commission [I.J.C.] or... to submit to another form of dispute resolution." Article IX, paragraph 1(a) provides that fact finding procedures are available to the Commission in the implementation of the Agreement and, according to the I.J.C., are also available in dispute settlement situations as well[5]. No dispute settlement test case has as of this writing, however, been presented to the Commission for binding resolution in the area of air quality. In other areas covered by the 1909 Treaty, the US and Canada have traditionally asked for the Commission's assistance and non-binding recommendations under Article IX. This practice should likely continue in the air quality field.

The International Joint Commission was established in 1909 pursuant to the Boundary Waters Treaty entered into between Great Britain (on behalf of Canada) and the United States, in an effort to resolve US/Canadian cross-border water-allocation disputes then prevalent between the two States. Today the I.J.C. deals with cross-border problems generally and no longer just water allocation rights; its longevity in large part attributed to the success of the original dispute settlement mechanism. For this reason the I.J.C. has continued to play a useful role.

The dispute settlement mechanism of the 1909 Treaty provided that six commissioners, three from each country, would be appointed members of the I.J.C. to investigate water disputes referred by either government, with particular regard to the wrongful diversion or allocation of waters flowing across common borders. Today, the three United States commissioners are appointed by the President, with the advice and consent of the Senate, and have no fixed-terms. The three Canadian commissioners are appointed by Canada's Prime Minister for terms ranging from 6 months to 5 years[6]. Together, the commissioners are free to appoint investigative as well as technical bodies, whose memberships are drawn from both States' governmental and nongovernmental agencies. Board members have traditionally included among their membership experts who have first-hand knowledge of the particular issues at hand[7]. These I.J.C. bodies also oftentimes serve as a mechanism to establish bipartisan advice, even when critical of either or both countries' activities. Board recommendations, nonetheless, are always officially made through the I.J.C. and political infighting is rare. Although there is apparently no illusion on either side that in 1909 environment protection was merely an afterthought, rational water-project-development along the Canadian and US borders flourished in large part due to the work of these bodies.

Other factors as well have contributed to the success of the I.J.C. and continue to be of significance in the context of air quality. Most interesting is the belief that because rivers flowing across the frontier travel in both directions, extreme views are discouraged by the

---

[5] Telephone communication, official of the International Joint Commission, Washington, D.C. (5 February 1992).

[6] See id.

[7] Working paper, Mr. Pete Christich, North American Programmes Officer, Office of International Activities, United States Environmental Protection Agency (8 October 1991).

I.J.C.'s dispute settlement mechanism[8]. Each party in other words is encouraged to cooperate and not appear to reject the Commission's authority. In addition, because the commissioners are all executive branch appointees, they are considered to be largely free of political pressures in exercising their duties; lines of communication therefore remain clear. Lastly, and perhaps most important, once problems are referred to it the Commission is capable of exercising coercive powers in seeing that each party lives up to agreements reached in the dispute settlement process. In the United States, documents may be subpoenaed and information found therein used by the Commission in the fulfillment of its mandate. Though the subpoena power has never been utilized in a cross boundary dispute, it is nevertheless still available.

In the past, the I.J.C. has exercised its independence by producing written bipartisan criticisms of both countries' policies regarding pollution control and reduction goals in the boundary waters area. The reports, issued every two years, are called "report cards"[9] by the public in both States, and are widely respected. These reports shall likely continue their effectiveness in the future regarding the Commission's new air quality responsibilities.

---

[8] Telephone communication, Mr. Pete Christich; see id., (6 February 1992).

[9] Working paper, see note 7 at 2.

II. NUCLEAR EMERGENCIES

Current bilateral regulation in the field of nuclear energy is much more prevalent than we found in the field of air quality. Bilateral arrangements to promote, facilitate, and encourage co-operation between states in anticipation of emergency situations are understandably of high political importance.

Characteristically, a great deal of bilateral regulation in this area has been the result of heightened awareness of the dangers of nuclear emergencies caused by the Chernobyl nuclear accident of April, 1986. Nevertheless, a relatively large number of bilateral instruments dealing with the peaceful uses of nuclear energy, emergencies, and the handling of radioactive waste had already been in effect before. Environmental emergency agreements of other types have also been around for years, including those dealing with oil pollution, natural disasters, and accident assistance generally. Examples of two such agreements include the USA-Canada Agreement Relating to the Establishment of Joint Pollution Contingency Plans for Spills of Oil and Other Noxious Substances, done at Ottawa, 19 June 1974; and the Convention between the Federal Republic of Germany and the Grand Duchy of Luxembourg on the Exchange of Information in Case of Accidents which could have Radiological Consequences, 2 March 1978, dealing with oil spills and mutual assistance, respectively. The basic objective of these agreements is similar to that in the field of nuclear emergencies, namely to ensure a qualified co-ordinated response in the event of a significant pollution threat or other serious accident occurring within the jurisdiction of either state.

Like air quality, current bilateral regulation in the field of nuclear energy demonstrates a preference for prevention of harm as opposed to liability and reparations for damage. The essential obligations which bilateral agreements in this field impose on states take their lead from customary international law. Generally, participants of both multilateral and bilateral regimes are obliged to recognize a primary duty or obligation to inform other states which may be affected by any accidental deterioration of the environment and to rapidly furnish pertinent available information in order to limit as much as possible the radioactive consequences in other countries. In the area of emergency situations, two sorts of measures are anticipated: those to be taken prior to potential accidents and those which should be undertaken when the situation is actually presented[10].

The obligation to notify can range from accidents arising from activities involving any nuclear reactor, any nuclear fuel cycle facility, radioactive waste management facility, the transport and storage of nuclear fuels, as well as any operation involving the manufacture, use, storage, disposal or transport of radioisotopes, including the use of nuclear-powered

---

[10] A.C. Kiss and D. Shelton, International Environmental Law, (Transnational Publishers 1991), at 336.

spacecraft[11].   The types of information to be furnished must often include: the exact time, location, and nature of the accident, the installation or activity concerned, the presumed or understood cause, the likely evolution of the accident, and the general characteristics of the discharge[12].

Pre-Chernobyl bilateral instruments in the field of nuclear emergencies include: the Belgium-France Agreement on Radiological Protection concerning the Ardennes nuclear power plant (7 March 1967); the Germany-Luxembourg Agreement on the Exchange of Information in the Case of Accident which could have Radiological Consequences, 2 March 1978; the Germany-Switzerland Agreement on Radiation Protection in Case of Emergency, 31 May 1978; the France-Switzerland Agreement on the Exchange of Information in Case of Accident which could have Radiological Consequences, 18 October 1979; and the Japan-USA: Agreement Concerning Severe Nuclear Accident Research, 1 October 1984.

After the Chernobyl accident, and supplementing the global 1986 IAEA Conventions (No. 109 in the present survey), the Scandinavian countries concluded several bilateral agreements on the exchange of information and reporting relative to nuclear plants and nuclear events, with each other (Sweden-Denmark, 21 October 1986; Finland-Sweden, Finland-Denmark and Finland-Norway, 25 February 1987) and with the USSR (Norway 1988, Sweden 1988).

The basic objective of the Agreement between the Government of the Republic of Finland and the former Government of the Union of Soviet Socialist Republics on the early notification of nuclear accidents and the exchange of information on nuclear facilities is to establish a regime to ensure the safe use of nuclear energy, in order to limit the transboundary consequences of possible releases of radioactive substances.   The scope of application of the Agreement refers to non-military facilities generally.   Application requires notification of nuclear accidents and pre and post accident exchange of information which may be used by an affected Party when assessing the consequences of a nuclear accident threatening its borders.

The objectives identified above shall be implemented and their achieved goals measured in accordance with the terms of Article 3.   The Finnish Centre for Radiological and Nuclear Safety and the former Soviet Ministry of Atomic Power were the authorities responsible for implementation of goal achievement provisions.   The Government of the new Russian Federation has indicated that the Russian Federation Ministry of Atomic Energy continues to perform the information exchange functions laid down in the bilateral agreement and revisions to that part of the agreement are contemplated.

According to Article 2, information transmitted under the provisions concerning the regime for monitoring the operation of nuclear facilities, may be used only for purposes of 1) assessing the consequences in the country receiving the information in the event of accident; and 2) when formulating measures for the protection of its population.

In addition, the Parties have expressly reserved that implementing legislation may limit the obligations to provide information (Article 8), and that the Agreement shall not affect the rights and duties of each Party deriving from agreements concluded by them earlier.

---

[11]   See id. at 335.

[12]   See id. at 334.

Amendments to the Agreement shall require the consent of the Parties (Article 11).

Information on the operation and implementation of the Agreement may be released, currently, only through the governmental channels identified in Article 3. As the Agreement requires merely that each Party shall inform or notify the other of activities designed to ensure the safe use of nuclear energy within the territorial limits set out in Article 2, practical measures have to be defined that will allow fulfillment of these obligations. Unless otherwise agreed, however, information eventually released to the public may only be used for the two purposes identified in Article 2.

Despite changes in the former Soviet Union, it has been possible for the Parties to nevertheless maintain contacts on a continuous basis, and implementation of the Agreement on practical matters continues between the Finnish Centre for Radiological and Nuclear Safety and the Atomic Energy Ministry of the Russian Federation[13]. Reports on the experiences of the use of the nuclear facilities have been exchanged annually since the Agreement's entry into force. The competent authorities of both Parties continue to acknowledge that under the Agreement they are to meet twice a year, the next meeting being scheduled for March, 1992. Informal contacts and co-operation proceed regularly between the respective nuclear authorities, and include visits and training programmes concerning nuclear safety.

Compliance by the Parties with their obligations under this Agreement shall be monitored in accordance with the terms of legislation enacted in Article 3, paragraph 2, and Article 12. Internal mechanisms perform the monitoring duties envisaged in the terms of Articles 3 and 5.

Regardless of the assigned monitoring body, compliance relies largely on the data supplied and disclosed by the nuclear agencies of each State, as well as the information supplied by operators. The scientific requirements of data supply and disclosure, as contained in Articles 2 and 6, anticipate two sorts of measures, as mentioned. Those are: those measures to be taken before an accident occurs, (information exchange) and those which should be undertaken when the situation is presented (notification of nuclear accidents). Again, however, legislation defines the specific requirements of data supply and monitoring in this instance, and should be consulted.

Disputes arising concerning interpretation or application of the Agreement, shall be settled by negotiations between the Parties (Article 10).

---

[13] Briefing document, Permanent Mission of Finland to the United Nations, (6 February 1992); and communication from the Permanent Mission of the Russian Federation to the United Nations (14 February 1992).

III. FRESHWATERS

Transboundary freshwater resources have been the subject of international legal instruments for several centuries, and there are currently more than 2000 bilateral and multilateral agreements in existence in this field[14]. International codification efforts are progressing both at the global and at the regional level (see UNCED document A/CONF.151/PC/79), and the relevant legal instruments concerning the Plate River (Rio de la Plata) basin are also addressed in Chapter VI.

While Argentina and Uruguay are Parties to several regional and bilateral agreements applicable to the Plate River basin, the present analysis will focus on the Treaty Concerning the Rio de la Plata and the corresponding Maritime Boundary, entered into by the Governments of Uruguay and Argentina on 19 November 1973. Its basic objective is the resolution of long-standing issues existing between the two States that, once resolved, will allow each to fully use and exploit the resources of the river within existing maritime boundaries. Accordingly, the scope of the Agreement is quite broad and affects issues regarding navigation and works, pilotage, port facilities, unloading and additional loading, safeguarding human life, salvaging, mineral resources and mining, islands, pollution, fishing, research and defence. In terms of effective integration of environmental regulation and development, the Agreement attempts to lay the bases for broader co-operation between the two countries, within the context of respect for the sovereignty and respective rights and interests of each. The Agreement's actual and potential bearing on freshwater protection and sustainable development is, therefore, understandably great.

In setting out the specific rights and duties of each Party regarding the resources provided by the river ecosystem, the Agreement is divided into two parts. Part I, Chapter I contains a jurisdictional overview designed to guide the Parties' economic activities along their respective halves of the river. Of concern to us in this first Part are the provisions contained chiefly in Chapters VIII, IX, X, XI and XII.

The basis of Chapter VIII is the establishment of a nature reserve for the conservation and preservation of indigenous fauna and flora on Martin Garcia Island, currently under Argentine jurisdiction.

Chapter IX sets forth the purposes of the Agreement , insofar as it is directed at combatting water pollution. Interestingly, pollution is defined therein as any indirect or direct introduction by man into the "aquatic environment" of substances ... which have harmful effects. This definition serves to assure that the Parties have agreed to act to preserve and protect the entire river ecosystem, and not merely certain features of it.

---

[14] FAO Legislative Study No. 15, Systematic Index of International Water Resources Treaties, Declarations, Acts and Cases by Basin, 1978.

Chapter X governs fishing activities on the river, with particular regard to preserving its living resources, with the exception of marine mammals (Chapter XVI.) Chapter XI permits each Party to undertake scientific research. Finally, Chapter XII sets out the parameters for the creation of the Administrative Commission of the Rio de la Plata, the functions of which, as they relate to the environment, are defined in Article 66.

The Administrative Commission shall perform the following environmental functions:

(a) Promote the joint conduct of scientific studies and research, with special reference to the evaluation, conservation, preservation, and rational exploitation of living resources and the prevention and elimination of pollution and other harmful effects which may derive from the use, exploration and exploitation of the waters of the river;

(b) Enact rules regulating fishing activities in the river with regard to the conservation and preservation of living resources;

...

(i) Transmit as soon as possible to the Parties any communications, consultations, information and notifications which they may send one another in accordance with Part I of this Treaty.

The basic objective of Part II of the Agreement is to delimit the maritime lateral limits within which the laws of each State are to apply across the spectrum of issues identified in Part I. Of particular significance to our review regarding the identification of objectives are provisions in Part II regarding fishing, contained in Chapter XVI; Pollution, Chapter XVII; Research, Chapter XVIII; and creation of a Joint Technical Commission, with authority directed at regulating catch-volumes, Chapter XIX.

For ease of reference, it is necessary to note here that the areas identified in the second Part of the Accord merely establish zones within which each Party is permitted or forbidden to engage in certain activities.

In the common fishing zone the Parties jointly exploit and jointly regulate access to and conservation of the maritime fisheries resources. The broad policy objectives to be pursued in the common fishing zone are as contained in Part I, while their implementation is to take place through the Joint Technical Commission and through decisions taken by the Parties in accordance therewith.

The Agreement provides that within the common fishing zone vessels flying the flag and registered by either Party may engage in the exploitation of the marine living resources (Art. 73). The Parties are to exchange lists of vessels flying their flag and engaged in fishing activities in the fishing zone (Art. 76). Catch quotas are determined per species and divided between the Parties on an equitable basis in proportion to the fishing resources contributed by each of them on a scientific and economic basis (Art. 74). Control and surveillance functions are conducted by each Party on its side of the lateral maritime boundary of the fishing zone, the manner of which is coordinated by the Parties (Art. 76).

Current information on the operation and implementation of Part I of the Accord is made available to concerned outside parties through the procedures outlined in Articles 66 and 67. It is the primary responsibility of the Administrative Commission to "Promote the joint conduct of scientific studies and research, with special reference to the evaluation, conservation, preservation, and rational exploitation of living resources and the prevention and elimination of pollution and other harmful effects which may derive from the use, exploration and exploitation of the water of the river" (Article 66(a)). The Commission reports its findings periodically to the "Governments of both Parties on the progress of its activities" (Article 67). There are no provisions in Part I allowing direct dissemination of any information otherwise derived to any other Parties.

In Part II, the Joint Technical Commission performs a similar function and, too, is confined in its ability to disclose findings to outside parties. The Commission conducts studies, adopts and coordinates plans and measures relevant to conservation, preservation and the rational use of living resources and protection of the common fishing zone (Art 80).

Compliance by the Parties with their obligations under the Agreement is monitored in Part I by the Administrative Commission; in Part II by the Joint Technical Commission. Each State has, therefore, relinquished its reporting obligations in large measure to the independent delegations they've established.

The Joint Technical Commission is composed of two delegations, each consisting of five members. For the purpose of carrying out its tasks the Commission may establish permanent or ad hoc sub-committees which may have an investigatory or advisory function ((Art 13, Rules of Procedure of the Commission). Each delegation has one vote and decisions are taken by a concurring vote of both delegations. Voting may take place if at least three members of each delegation are present (Art. 14, Statute of the Commission). The Commission meets in ordinary sessions once a year and in extra-ordinary sessions whenever either delegation so requests (Art. 7, Rules of Procedure of the Commission). During the most recent meeting of the Commission, the Parties did not recommend modification of any of the Agreement's terms[15].

Any disputes arising between the Parties concerning a failure of either or of the Commissions to comply with data collection and disclosure mandates may be settled through negotiations or eventual referral to the International Court of Justice (Articles 69 and 87, respectively).

Procedures for the settlement of disputes between the Parties require that they first submit to conciliation (Article 68). If after 120 days they are unable to arrive at an agreement, direct negotiations follow (Article 69). Ultimately, any dispute which cannot be settled by either of these means may be submitted to the International Court of Justice (Article 87).

---

[15] Briefing document, Permanent Mission of Argentina to the United Nations, (10 February 1992).

466

IV. MARINE LIVING RESOURCES

Like regulation of freshwater resources, regulation of the marine environment in the area of marine fisheries presents many situations whereby the rules applicable to them will require that measures be taken at both the regional and global level. Legal norms in this area are therefore necessarily flexible and borrow from the regulatory practices governing other traditional uses of the sea.

As a traditional use of the sea, fishing has witnessed unequalled growth in recent years. Overfishing is a major cause for concern, threatening the preservation of marine wildlife. In addition, marine pollution impacts severely on fisheries. It is thus necessary when considering agreements protecting marine fisheries and the goals they are intended to reach, that we not only identify the causes of stress which affect fisheries and motivations behind protection of fish stocks, but also consider the variety of oceans which exist and the uses made of them.

The Agreement between the Government of the Republic of Senegal and the European Economic Community (EEC) on fishing off the coast of Senegal, signed (with an additional Protocol), at Brussels on 15 June 1979 has as its basic objective the establishment of principles and rules which will govern the fishing activities of vessels flying the flags of Member States of the European Economic Community, in waters over which the Republic of Senegal has sovereignty or jurisdiction in resect of fisheries (Article 1). As in the case of similar EEC agreements concluded with other African States (e.g., with Guinea Bissau on 27 February 1980), this agreement superseded agreements previously entered into between the Government of Senegal and individual member-states of the Community concerning fishing rights in West African waters. Examples of these previous agreements are the Convention between the French Republic and the Republic of Senegal concerning the relations between the two States regarding maritime fishery, 16 September 1974; the Agreement between the Government of the Republic of Italy and the Government of the Republic of Senegal concerning maritime fishing, 17 January 1975; the Fishery Convention between the Government of the Republic of Guinea-Bissau and the Government of the French Republic, 20 January 1977; Convention between the Spanish Government and the Government of the Republic of Senegal concerning maritime fishery, 15 May 1975; Convention concerning maritime fishery between the Government of the French Republic and the Government of the Republic of Dahomey, 27 February 1975.

Conservation and optimum utilization of fish stocks in the Central-East Atlantic are primary goals the Parties hope to ensure by entering into the Agreement. Insofar as the Agreement seeks to regulate the impact of marine pollution in the area under consideration, the Parties undertake to concert action, either directly or within international organizations, to ensure the management and conservation of the living resources ...and to facilitate relevant scientific research (Article 6).

All the above-mentioned West African agreements contained provisions to ensure the preservation and conservation of fish resources. Most of them also undertook to coordinate scientific co-operation through research and dissemination and endorsed increased international co-operation safeguards (particularly, Spain-Senegal).

The potential bearing that the present EEC-Senegal Agreement has on protection and sustainable development of commercial fish stocks is best revealed by the care with which the Parties have delimited the conditions by which the pursuit of fishing activities may be undertaken. The provisions contained in Annex 1 outline application procedures for licenses enabling vessels to fish in Senegalese waters; provisions for the presentation of a statement of catch to the relevant Senegalese authority after each trip; landing of catch provisions, training grants, and specific rules regarding use of waters under Senegalese jurisdiction. Such careful delimitation suggests that the Agreement should achieve a high level of success in the rational management and conservation of targeted fish stocks. Goal achievement will be measured accordingly by the degree of success the Parties have in maintaining at current levels the number of "fishing opportunities" available to licensees. The earlier agreements reflected a similar concern.

The actual bearing that the Accord has on integrating environmental and developmental concerns is set out in Article 9. In that article it is provided that in return for the fishing opportunities accorded under the Agreement, compensation will be paid by EEC Member States and used specifically by Senegal to finance projects and services of a rural nature, particularly as they relate to sea-fishing. This compensation, which shall be paid without prejudice to other financing accords existing between the Parties, shall be mobilized in accordance with the procedures described in the Protocol to the Agreement. Annex I.D. of the main Agreement also includes provision for training and study grants, which are considered therein an "essential condition for the success of" the Parties' developmental concerns. The grants shall allow for improved technical, scientific and economic skills training connected with fisheries. In regards thereto, it is also stated that "the Community shall make it easier for Senegalese nationals to find places in establishments in its Member-States" in order to improve the over-all competence of Senegalese fisheries personnel.

According to the most recent revision of the Protocol (normally concluded for a two-year period), which will be up for renewal in May 1992, EEC funding under the Agreement currently amounts to ECU 15 million per year, including 14.375 million as straight compensation, 0.4 million for scientific research in marine fishery, and 0.225 million for training and study grants.

The two Annexes to the Agreement form an integral part of the Agreement and, unless otherwise specified, a reference to the Agreement constitutes a reference to its Annexes (Article 16). In this regard, Article 12 allows that "should the authorities of Senegal decide, as a result of an unforeseeable change in the state of the fish stocks, to take new conservation measures which, in the opinion of the Community, have a considerable effect on the fishing activities of Community vessels, consultations must be held between the Parties in order to adapt Annex 1 and the Protocol referred to in Article 9."

Senegal's willingness to allow the regulation of fishing within its territorial waters was, in particular, the result of an attractive compensation regime established pursuant to Article 9 and the additional Protocol. The establishment of a Joint Committee under Article 11 which ensures each Parties' compliance with provisions outlined in the Agreement, is another important factor reflecting joint participation in this regulatory field. The most recent meeting of the Committee was held in February 1991.

The Senegalese Ministry of Rural Development monitors compliance with the provisions set out in Annex 1. Additional compliance monitoring mechanisms relating to the license application and issuing functions of Annex 1 are handled through the Direction de l'Oceanographie et des Peches Maritimes and the Delegation of the Commission of the European Communities at Dakar. Whereas, in the earlier West African agreements superseded by the provisions of the 1979 accord, compliance monitoring rules were governed by internal Senegalese laws, and local authorities were responsible for their implementation, the EEC Commission now follows closely the granting of fishing licenses by Senegal, as import data for renewal of the biennial Protocol.

Maintaining and developing statistics on the taking of fish is made difficult, generally, by the unorganized character of fishing activities, especially in rural areas, in which a large number of individuals oftentimes participate independently. Compliance monitoring mechanisms, particularly licensing data, provide information on the allowable quota of fish that may be taken but not necessarily the actual numbers gathered.

The EEC-Senegal Agreement provides that the order of magnitude of fish catches shall be ascertained by data collected from strict disclosures made in accordance with Annex 1. Specific provisions of Annex 1 require that under the terms of the licenses issued to individual vessels, vessel owners are required to report their catches regularly, thereby easing governmental reporting, data supply and data disclosure obligation. Under Section B of Annex 1: "Statement of Catch," all vessels authorized to fish in Senegalese waters ...shall be obliged to forward to the Direction de l'Océanographie et des Peches Maritimes a statement of their catch .... In addition, "a statement of catch must be presented after each trip for wet vessels or every month for freezer vessels, and in this case before the end of the month."

Under Section C: "Landing of Catch," vessels authorized to fish in Senegalese waters under the Agreement shall be obliged to land part or all of their catch, depending on the type of fishing practiced ....Any failure to comply with the obligation to land catches shall render the shipowner liable to (fine or withdrawal of license).

Disputes arising during the license application or renewal portions of Annex 1 shall be resolved through consultations to be held between the representatives of the Parties (Article 10). The procedure for the settlement of disputes otherwise arising is found in Annex II. Annex II prescribes that within two months of the date on which either Partly requests arbitration of a dispute, each Party shall appoint one member of the arbitration tribunal; these two will agree within three months on the appointment of a third arbiter from a another state. The cost of this binding arbitration procedure is born by both Parties equally. Decisions are reached by a majority in accordance with the Agreement and customary rules of international law.

An important recent development was the signature of a new regional **Convention on Fisheries Co-operation among African States Bordering the Atlantic Ocean** in Dakar (Senegal) on 5 July 1991, (text in UN Law of the Sea Bulletin 1991/No. 9), applicable to the fisheries areas covered by the present EEC Agreements. Under the auspices of the Food and Agriculture Organization of the United Nations (FAO), regional institutions including a Conference of Ministers, a Bureau, a Secretariat, and a regional fisheries development fund are to be established to promote co-operation in fisheries management and development in the region.

V. WILDLIFE PROTECTION

Comparable to fisheries and freshwater resources, but unlike air quality--particularly as it relates to climate change--the reason for the existence of international norms in the area of wildlife protection emanates from the realization that wild animals and plants constitute a common heritage of mankind, sharing with the deep-sea bed and its mineral resources a virtually singular recognition that the long-term survival of all species is indispensably linked to the health of wildlife in naturally occurring ecosystems. By this idea, habitat protection is in itself the focal point of wildlife regulation, and not merely the recognition of a need to preserve single species. This was not always the case, though.

Early environmental regulation aimed at protecting wild animals was oftentimes motivated solely by economic considerations and the desire to assure future exploitation of certain species. As mentioned in Part IV, this is still the primary motivation with regard to fisheries.

The common principles and techniques used in bilateral instruments which recognize that diverse wildlife populations constitute an important element of our common heritage, and not merely an economic source, generally attempt to regulate and maintain essential ecological processes necessary to support wild life; preserve the genetic diversity of individual species; and allow sustainable utilization by humans of species located within individual ecosystems. International agreements for the protection of wild birds date back to the beginning of the 20th century, with the multilateral 1902 Convention for the Protection of Birds Useful to Agriculture (see under Treaty No. 13 in the present work), and the earliest bilateral Convention for the Protection of Migratory Birds which was concluded between Canada and the USA in August 1916, followed by a similar agreement between Mexico and the United States in February 1936. More recently, and supplementary to global and regional wildlife agreements protecting bird species and habitats (e.g., Nos. 15-18, 20-23, and 27 in the present survey), migratory bird agreements have also been concluded by Japan with the United States (March 1972), the USSR (October 1973) and Australia (February 1974); and between the former USSR and the United States (November 1976).

The Agreement between the Government of Japan and the Government of the People's Republic of China concerning the Protection of Migratory Birds and their Habitats was signed in Beijing on 3 March 1981 and entered into force, after ratification by both Parties, on 8 June 1981 for a period of 15 years (Article 6). Its primary objective is the conservation and management of certain migratory bird species and their habitats. 227 species of migratory birds are protected by the Agreement:

"In order to protect and manage migratory birds and their habitats, the Governments of the two countries shall, in accordance with their respective laws and regulations, establish sanctuaries and shall take other appropriate measures, in particular they shall:

(1)   Explore methods of protecting migratory birds and their habitats from harm;

(2)   Strictly limit the import and introduction of animals and plants that are harmful to protected migratory birds (Article 4).

In addition:

(1)   The Governments of the two countries shall encourage the exchange of data and publications relating to research on migratory birds.

(2)... Encourage the development of cooperative research projects relating to migratory birds (and)

(3)... Encourage the protection of migratory birds, particularly in the case of migratory birds threatened with extinction."

The Parties recognize that "birds constitute an important element of the natural ecosystem and a natural resource having significant value for art, science, culture, recreation, economics and other fields."

Participation is also encouraged by incentives outlined in Article 2, which allows exceptions to the general prohibition against the hunting of migratory birds and the collection of their eggs, under the following circumstances:

"(1)   For scientific and educational purposes, for purposes of domestication and breeding and for other specific purposes that are not inconsistent with the spirit of this Agreement;

(2)   To protect human life and property;

(3)   During hunting seasons ...."

These exceptions allow for the limited developmental use of migratory bird resources, by balancing the Parties' interest in preserving migratory populations against the needs of scientific, social, and public entities.

Current information on the operation and implementation of the Accord is made available to outside Parties through the encouragement of data and publications exchange relating to research and the development of cooperative research projects on migratory birds (Article 3). Five intergovernmental meetings have so far been held under the Agreement, alternatively in Beijing (December 1984, November 1988) and Tokyo (February 1983, November 1986 and December 1991). The operation of the Agreement is illustrated by co-operation for protection of the Japanese ibis; originally considered as extinct in China and therefore not even listed in the appendix of the Agreement, rediscovery of six specimens in China in May 1981 prompted several joint expert meetings and breeding projects, including a comprehensive programme for local habitat protection in China.

Compliance by the Parties with their obligations under the Agreement is monitored by the active participation of the respective Governments in accordance with the laws and regulations of each (Article 1, paragraph 1). There are no specific requirements for data supply or disclosure regarding bird numbers, or otherwise.

The Governments of the two countries may hold consultations on the implementation of the Agreement at the request of the Government of either Party (Article 5). No additional procedures are set out in the event consultations fail.

VI. GENERAL ENVIRONMENTAL CO-OPERATION

The Memorandum of Understanding on Environmental Protection Between the United States Environmental Protection Agency and the Federal Ministry of Housing and Environment of Nigeria was signed in Lagos on 20 September 1980, and entered into force upon signature, for a period of five years which was renewed for another five-year term, but eventually expired in 1991. Its basic aims included the promotion and maintenance of bilateral co-operation in the field of environmental protection on the basis of equality, reciprocity, and mutual benefit. Each Party sought to promote a framework that would enhance co-operation in the field of environmental protection as an appropriate corollary to the two nations' other existing economic and technical programmes of collaboration.

Broadly speaking, the objectives of the programme were contained in Article III which, essentially, stated that the Parties agreed to assist in the development of environmental programmes across broad parameters of their national priorities. The environmental opportunities or programme which both States prioritized were aimed at improving the overall quality of life. In particular, investments in water purification, effluent treatment, and solid and toxic waste management were aims of both States. Improved and effective conservation technology, increased energy efficiency, use of renewable energy, pollution control and clean methodologies, greater recycling and pollution prevention, and wider availability of environmental consulting services were also primary objectives of the Agreement. The Agreement was not intended to function as a one-way technical assistance programme, nor were funds ever allocated by either government for specific programmes.

The actual bearing of co-operation on environmental protection and sustainable development between the two States was marginal[16]. Co-operation under Article V of the Agreement included exchanging scientists, chemical spill response teams, technicians and scholars; organizing bilateral conferences; conducting joint educational programmes; and exchanging information and data in the field of environmental planning and protection. The sharing of these resources-although aimed at encouraging co-operation between Governments, universities, research centers, and other bodies having similar environmental concerns as exist between these two States-was hampered throughout by a lack of sponsorship and funding from both Governments.

Despite this overall lack of support, however, the basic objectives designed to encourage co-operation between the two Parties were successfully met in the area of information exchange and educational opportunity. In addition, scientists, technicians and other experts of third countries or international organizations were invited, with the agreement of both Parties, to

---

[16] Telephone communication, official of the Office of International Activities, United States Environmental Protection Agency (10 February 1992).

participate in the activities carried out under the Agreement, including a conference sponsored by the World Bank[17].

Although membership of the Agreement was limited to Nigeria and the United States, comparable bilateral arrangements on a regional level between the United States and other developing nations have since emerged. According to the US Environmental Protection Agency, the potential success of these new agreements depends on acceptance of the fact that environmental problems relating to large and expanding urban populations, substantial industrial activity, and conservation of the environment take into account the following: (1) States must develop national environmental action plans; (2) they must define and prioritize specific environmental problems and goals; and (3) they must devise development plans which put these goals within reach.

Along these lines, the United States Government on 7 January 1992 launched an environmental co-operation initiative for Asia, the objectives and purposes of which will attempt to match American expertise with the needs of nations where anti-pollution and conservation measures are not keeping pace with industrial development. Unlike the United States-Nigeria Memorandum of Understanding, the United States-Asia Environmental Partnership (USA-AEP) programme will include much larger private sector involvement. American and Asian consultants and companies will be assisted in marketing their skills and technologies to Asian and Pacific nations by 18 United States Government agencies[18]. Several provisions of the Lagos Memorandum and the USA-AEP Agreements are similar and warrant comparison.

The range of co-operation outlined in the Lagos Memorandum (Article IV) was very general. In comparison, the USA-AEP programme specifically identifies the following four component areas in which collaboration shall be directly encouraged: environmental fellowship and training programme, technology co-operation, environmental infrastructure, and regional co-operation[19].

Under the Lagos Memorandum, as stated in Article II, each Party agreed to promote and maintain bilateral co-operation in the field of environmental protection on the basis of equality, reciprocity, and mutual benefit. This clause served to provide for the reservation of certain rights and obligations in accordance with the sovereign freedom of States to utilize their natural resources. More importantly, it served to guarantee that neither State should exercise against the other State political weight in ways inconsistent with the spirit of the Agreement. This is of particular importance still to developing nations seeking to implement global environmental regulatory norms, while also allowing for rational development strategies and economic growth.

The importance of respecting local concerns is borne out in the USA-AEP Agreement. There, the Parties have openly acknowledged the need for public and private co-operation and the necessity of advancing mutual understanding of one another's "unique and valuable"

---

[17] See id.

[18] New York Times, 8 January 1992.

[19] Briefing document, United States-Asia Environmental Partnership, Secretariat Bureau, Washington, D.C. (3 February 1992).

resources[20].

Other measures contained in the Lagos Memorandum, designed to take into account the special circumstances of developing countries, related to sharing patents, designs, and other proprietary property derived from co-operative activities under the agreement (Article VIII). Of additional relevance were provisions stipulating that the internal laws of each Party were to apply regarding activities conducted under the Agreement.

Information on the operation and implementation of this Agreement was made available to interested third persons through the provisions contained in Articles VIII and VI. Article VIII provided that scientific and technical information derived from co-operation activities under the Agreement would be made available, unless otherwise agreed, to the world scientific community through customary channels and in accordance with the normal procedures of the participating parties. In the United States, the Agency for International Development (AID) and the Environmental Protection Agency were the channels through which information was communicated.

Regarding training programmes, EPA and FMHE had joint responsibility for encouraging and facilitating, as appropriate, the dissemination of information to concerned parties, and issuing invitations to experts wishing to participate in activities carried out under the Accord. The termination of the Lagos Memorandum will not mean that these activities will cease[21]. According to the EPA, projects affected by termination of the Memorandum in 1991 will be covered by other programmes.

Compliance by the Parties with the terms of the Agreement was monitored intra-governmentally by each State's respective environmental protection agency. During the period under which the Agreement ran, all activities mutually agreed upon for implementation by the "Cooperating Agencies" (EPA, FMHE) were documented and appended as specific Project Implementation Plans. By this method specific details were available and cooperative dissemination could occur in accordance with Article VIII. However, sponsors and funding did not come forth to implement all specific proposals put forth by the EPA and FMHE, and project plans would go unrealized.

Resolution of conflicts and disputes arising between the Parties regarding implementation of the Agreement or otherwise were handled through negotiations in accordance with Article IX. The Parties fixed the procedures by which cooperative activities could be undertaken pursuant to Article IX (Article X). Each Party agreed also to use its best efforts to facilitate resolution of disputes, and the prompt disposition of materials and resources necessary to that end. During the tenure of the terms of the Agreement however, no appreciable dispute arose.

---

[20] Briefing document, see supra note 19.

[21] Telephone communication, official of the Office of International Activities, United States Environmental Protection Agency (10 February 1992).

CHAPTER XIII

RELATIONSHIP BETWEEN ENVIRONMENTAL AGREEMENTS AND INSTRUMENTS RELATED TO TRADE AND DEVELOPMENT

James O. Cameron, Thobeka Mjolo-Thamage and Jonathan C. Robinson

The relationship between existing international environmental agreements and relevant international trade agreements is an uneasy one. Often the three policy objectives - environment, trade and development - conflict without the benefit of any rational legal structure capable of providing a satisfactory resolution. This paper focuses on those aspects of the international regulation of the environment which most clearly conflict with international trade law and the opportunity for synthesis through development imperatives. The international legal materials we have researched revealed an ad hoc, even opportunistic, approach to global regulation on trade, environment and development. To date there has been little integration. Trade regulation, through the GATT process, benefits from the most stable and consistent forum for the generation of law and policy, but what some perceive as its failure to deal adequately with environmental issues and, some would argue, development issues, raises questions about using international trade law as a base from which to evaluate international environmental agreements or instruments relating to development imperatives.

The European Community, itself a regional international legal system, has through its amendments to the Treaty of Rome, done at Maastricht in December 1991, demonstrated, through the balancing of fundamental principles, how the law can provide a structure for the successful resolution of trade, environment and development conflicts. Of fundamental importance is the equality given to environmental protection alongside trade policy in an economic system created to ensure free movement of goods and services. The synthesis of the dialectic between free movement of goods and services and environmental protection is expressed in the concept of sustainable development or more accurately sustainable growth respecting the environment. Furthermore, the amended Article 130(r) contains express provisions enabling a "fast track - slow track" approach to be pursued, allowing countries of the relatively less economically developed south to continue to develop with less environmental regulatory constraint until such time as they can compete more favourably with their northern European counterparts, who may, in the meantime, be subjected to stricter environmental regulation. Alternatively, an "Environment Fund" or "Cohesion Fund" will provide for the costs of compliance by less developed regions to be met in part by the more developed.

For the most part this paper simply sets out the agreements and the latest initiatives on development. We are not instructed to make any recommendations for change nor any proposals for amendments to any existing international legal regime. Nonetheless, there is one clear message from this work - that, despite the conflict identified, synthesis is necessary and possible. Indeed sustainable development, properly conceived, is that synthesis.

REASONS FOR USING TRADE INSTRUMENTS IN INTERNATIONAL ENVIRONMENTAL AGREEMENTS

The reasons for the use of trade instruments in international environmental agreements differ according to the subject matter of the agreement. The agreements in which trade instruments are used fall into three categories; agreements for the protection of wildlife, agreements to protect the environment of the importing state from harmful products, and agreements to protect the global commons.

AGREEMENTS TO PROTECT WILDLIFE

That trade instruments are fundamental for the effectiveness of agreements for the protection of wildlife is demonstrated by the success of the Convention on the International Trade in Endangered Species (CITES[1], No. 18 in the present survey). Although other agreements to protect wildlife contain incidental trade provisions, CITES is the only convention which seeks to protect wildlife solely by the regulation of international trade. The leading commentator on international wildlife law states that:

"CITES is perhaps the most successful of all international treaties concerned with the conservation of wildlife. Its success is explained primarily by its basic principles... The basic principles of CITES are quite straightforward. It regulates international trade in wild animals and plants which are listed in three Appendices to the Convention"[2].

The success of CITES is demonstrated not only by its success in preventing the decline in populations and in some cases the recovery of endangered species, but also by the number of States which are parties:

"The fact that 87 States are now parties to CITES demonstrates the widespread appeal of a treaty which strictly limits international trade in species in genuine need of protection, allows a controlled trade in those able to sustain some exploitation and sets up a system of international cooperation to help achieve its objectives."

This scheme is attractive both to states with and without populations of endangered species within their jurisdiction:

"The Convention is attractive to the "producer" nations who see controls at the place of import as well as the place of export as essential weapons in their fight to protect their valuable wildlife resources from poachers and illegal traders. The "consumer" nations support it because without controls their legitimate dealers might have no raw material in which to trade in the generations to come."[3]

It is important to note two points. First, the existence of import restrictions in nations which do not have populations of the endangered species in question is considered "essential" for the protection of that species in the exporting state. Secondly, because of the interest which

---

[1] Simon Lyster International Wildlife Law p.241. (Membership as of 1 January 1992: 112).

[2] Simon Lyster International Wildlife Law p.240.

[3] Simon Lyster International Wildlife Law p.241.

dealers in their states have in the survival of species abroad, importing states have an interest in helping to preserve that species by import restrictions. In its refusal to allow states to restrict trade in order to protect the extra-territorial environment, the GATT as currently drafted and interpreted does not take account of either of these points.

Another reason given for the success of CITES is that it contains restrictions on trade with non-parties. This is not only because these restrictions help reinforce the existing system of reciprocal import and export restrictions:

> "The tough line taken in this respect may have contributed to the steadily increasing membership of the Convention since non-Parties may feel that the advantages of being a Party, and therefore in a position to influence the development of the Convention outweigh those of remaining outside where there are even fewer States with which they can freely trade."[4]

It is arguable whether such restrictions on trade with non-parties would be considered "discrimination" contrary to the GATT.

Although CITES is the most important international agreement to use trade instruments to protect wildlife, trade restrictions exist also in numerous other agreements. Their use can be examined by similar reasoning[5].

AGREEMENTS TO PROTECT THE ENVIRONMENT OF THE IMPORTING STATE FROM HARMFUL ORGANISMS AND PRODUCTS

Typical of agreements intended to protect the environment of the importing state from harmful products are agreements on the movement of hazardous waste. Restrictions on import are clearly an important tool for importing states to use in protecting their domestic environment. However, the international agreements regulating trade in hazardous waste demonstrate agreement between both importing and exporting states that such restrictions are not sufficient. International cooperation, and in particular reciprocal restrictions on export, are essential. Article 39 of the Fourth ACP-EEC Lome Convention (see No. 9 in the present survey) provides:

> "The Contracting Parties undertake, for their part, to make every effort to ensure that international movements of hazardous waste and radioactive waste are generally controlled, and they emphasise the importance of efficient international cooperation in this area."

Similarly the preamble to the Resolution on an African Common Position on the Basel Convention (No. 103 in the present survey) of the OAU Pan-African Conference on Environment and Sustainable Development meeting in Mali states that:

> "Regional and International Cooperation is necessary for an effective control of the transboundary movements of hazardous wastes and their elimination."

---

[4] Simon Lyster <u>International Wildlife Law</u> p.256.

[5] See, for example, in relation to wild plants, Cyrille de Klemm <u>Wild Plant Conservation and the Law</u> chapter 4.3.

Restrictions on the export of hazardous waste have been advocated on other grounds. It is in the long term cheaper to dispose of waste safely when and where it arises than to dispose of it unsafely, and then have later to remedy the damage caused. In an increasingly global economy it is in the interest of all states to avoid the waste of resources involved in the unsafe disposal of hazardous waste anywhere.

AGREEMENTS TO PROTECT THE GLOBAL COMMONS

Different considerations apply to agreements intended to protect the global commons. These agreements in particular depend on trade restrictions with non-parties. The benefits of an agreement to protect the global commons accrue to all states. However, in the absence of sanctions on non-parties, it is only the parties to an agreement who bear the cost of any measures. Trade restrictions on non-parties fulfil a double function. First, they seek to prevent free-riders enjoying the benefits of an agreement without contributing to the cost. This argument of equity is a justification in itself. But the prevention of free-riding by sanctions against non-participation also encourages participation in a global agreement. Without such sanctions there will often be greater benefit in remaining a non-party. Where this is the case, international agreement to protect the global commons will be difficult, if not impossible[6].

REFLECTION OF THESE CONSIDERATIONS IN THE GATT

The following section describes trade provisions used in existing international environmental agreements, and discusses their compatibility with the GATT. Some introductory background on GATT law will be useful.

The first point to be made is that GATT only regulates the measures of its contracting parties, not other treaties or agreements as such. The GATT is therefore not in the position of judging environmental agreements for the consistency with GATT of these agreements as such. Furthermore, if a treaty permits its parties to implement it in a GATT-consistent manner -- for instance, through a complete ban on domestic sale or importation of products of endangered species, or hazardous chemicals -- there is no necessary conflict between the provisions of the treaty and the provisions of GATT.

The GATT leaves its contracting parties free to tax or regulate imported products and like domestic products as long as its taxes or regulations do not discriminate against imported products or afford protection to domestic producers: this is the national treatment principle of Article III. A contracting party is also free to tax or regulate domestic production for environmental purposes. Internal taxes or regulations are also subject to the most-favoured-nation clause of the GATT, which requires that such taxes or regulations accord the products of GATT contracting parties treatment no less favourable than that accorded to like products of any other country. In practice, the "likeness" of a product is often a key issue. In the recent

---

[6] As regards participation of developing countries it is imperative that the making of the agreement is legitimised by their participation. That participation needs to be entirely encouraged through funding mechanisms. Thereafter, developing countries invariably need to be assisted to comply with obligations, through direct funding or through transfer of technology or both.

U.S.-Mexico Tuna-Dolphin dispute, for example, the Panel decided that two samples of tuna would be "like" irrespective of the different levels of harm done to dolphins in their capture. Similarly a product manufactured in a way which released ozone depleting CFC's would, under the GATT, be "like" one produced in a way which did not release CFC's.

Article XI of GATT prohibits quantitative restrictions on imports and exports. Article XIII provides that no prohibition or restriction shall be applied by any contracting party on the importation of any product of the territory of any other contracting party or on the exportation of any product destined for the territory of any other contracting party, unless the importation of the like product of all third countries or the exportation of the like product to all third countries is similarly prohibited or restricted: thus, import or export restrictions must be non-discriminatory. However, import and export duties are subject to essentially no regulation other than the concessions in each contracting party's GATT tariff schedule, and the most-favoured-nation clause. Thus, while an export ban may be illegal, an export tax of any amount is in principle completely unregulated. While most developed country import tariffs are bound, and an increasing number of developing countries have bound import tariff concessions, export tariff concessions by developed or developing countries are extremely rare.

GATT also provides general exceptions in Article XX, for certain measures that would <u>otherwise</u> be inconsistent with the GATT. These exceptions are, of course, legally irrelevant for any measure, such as a non-discriminatory ban on imports of a product, coupled with an absolute ban on domestic sale, which is consistent with the positive rules of GATT. Article XX provides:

> "Subject to the requirement that such measures are not applied in a manner which would constitute a means of arbitrary or unjustifiable discrimination between countries where the same conditions prevail, or a disguised restriction on international trade, nothing in this Agreement shall be construed to prevent the adoption or enforcement by any contracting party of measures:
>
> ...
>
> (b)   necessary to protect human, animal or plant life or health;...
>
> (d)   necessary to secure compliance with laws or regulations which are not inconsistent with the provisions of this Agreement, including those relating to customs enforcement... and the prevention of deceptive practices;...
>
> (g)   relating to the conservation of exhaustible natural resources if such measures are made effective in conjunction with restrictions on domestic production or consumption;"

The exception in Article XX(d) could be used, for example, to justify the extension to imported goods of domestic requirements relating to eco-labelling.

Finally, the waiver provisions of GATT Article XXV permit GATT's contracting parties acting together to waive any and all obligations under GATT, for any specified measure of a contracting party, by a 2/3 majority of those voting including a majority of contracting parties (55). It must be noted however that tentative agreement has been reached in the Uruguay Round on a decision which would place a time-limit and annual renewal requirement on waivers.

QUANTITATIVE RESTRICTIONS IN EXISTING INTERNATIONAL ENVIRONMENTAL AGREEMENTS; A SUMMARY OF THEIR USE AND COMPATIBILITY WITH THE GATT

The use of quantitative restrictions in international environmental agreements is not a new phenomenon. There are numerous examples in agreements dating from 1936[7]. But despite this continuous practice, and the convincing policy arguments for it, only a small proportion of these existing restrictions are clearly compatible with the GATT. It can be argued that a large proportion are contrary to the GATT's basic prohibition on quantitative restrictions[8], and that the GATT's general exceptions[9] are too narrowly drawn to allow the use of quantitative restrictions for many generally accepted and legitimate environmental objectives. This section discusses the types of quantitative restrictions that are typically found in different types of agreement, and their compatibility with the GATT.

The way in which trade instruments are used in international environmental agreements, like the reasons for their use, depend on the subject matter of the agreement. The same three categories are discernible; agreements to protect wildlife, agreements to protect the environment of the importing state from harmful organisms and products, and agreements to protect the global commons.

AGREEMENTS FOR THE PROTECTION OF WILDLIFE

Agreements for the protection of wildlife typically use restrictions on export or import between parties, usually based on a permit system. Some also make use of restrictions on transit through party states, and restrictions on trade with non-parties.

Restrictions on Export by Parties

Few agreements intended to protect wildlife expressly impose an absolute ban on exports of specimens of endangered species or derived products. There are no absolute bans on export in the most important agreement in this category, the Convention on the International Trade in Endangered Species of Wild Fauna and Flora ("CITES"). However, the effect of the requirements for the grant of an export permit in CITES is to impose a ban on the export of

---

[7] e.g. Convention on Nature Protection and Wildlife Preservation in the Western Hemisphere (1940, No. 12 in the present survey) Article IX; African Convention on the Conservation of Nature and Natural Resources (1968, No. 15 in the present survey) Article IX; Convention Between the USA and Mexico for the Protection of Migratory Birds and Game Mammals (1936) Article III; Convention Between the Government of the USA and the Government of Japan for the Protection of Migratory Birds in Danger of Extinction, and their Environment (1972) Article 4; Convention on the International Trade in Endangered Species of Wild Fauna and Flora (1973, No. 18 in the present survey) passim; Convention Between the US and the USSR Concerning the Conservation of Migratory Birds and their Environment (1976) Article II; International Convention for the Protection of Birds (1950) Article 3, 4, 9.

[8] GATT Article XI.

[9] GATT Article XX, especially Articles XX(b) and (g).

Appendix I and II species where the export would be detrimental to the survival of the species.

More typical than an express and absolute ban on exports is the requirement for an export permit. Agreements usually specify conditions for the grant of a permit. For example, under CITES a permit for the export of a specimen of an Appendix II species can only be granted when:

"(a) a Scientific Authority of the State of export has advised that such an export will not be detrimental to the survival of that species;

(b) a Management Authority of the State of export is satisfied that the specimen was not obtained in contravention of the laws of that State for the protection of fauna and flora; and

(c) a Management Authority of the State of export is satisfied that any living specimen will be so prepared and shipped as to minimize the risk of injury, damage to health or cruel treatment."

Prohibitions and restrictions on exports such as these are prima facie contrary to GATT Article XI.1 which provides:

"No prohibitions or restrictions other than duties, [taxes] or other charges whether made effective through quotas, import or export licences or other measures, shall be instituted or maintained by any contracting party on the ... exportation ... of any product destined for the territory of any other contracting party."

It could be argued that restrictions on the export of endangered species fall outside the prohibition in Article XI.1 because of the exception in Article XI.2 for "export prohibitions or restrictions temporarily applied to prevent or relieve critical shortages of foodstuffs or other products essential to the exporting contracting party." It is, however, doubtful whether a GATT panel would consider endangered species "essential" to the exporting state, and long term restrictions necessary for the recovery of species are probably not "temporarily applied".

Even if these prohibitions and restrictions were contrary to Article XI.1 and not saved by Article XI.2, they are clearly potentially capable of falling within the general exceptions in Article XX for measures:

"(a) necessary to protect human, animal or plant life or health; ... [or]

(g) relating to the conservation of exhaustible natural resources if such measures are made effective in conjunction with restrictions on domestic production or consumption."

Restrictions on exports of endangered species of plants or animals will fall within Article XX(b) if they can be shown to be "necessary". A measure is not "necessary" if the same level of protection could be achieved by a measure less disruptive of international trade[10]. As the animals or plants being protected are within the jurisdiction of the state prohibiting export the question of whether Article XX(b) can be used to protect species outside the jurisdiction does not arise.

---

[10] See <u>Report of the Panel, Thailand-Restrictions on Importation of, and Internal Taxes on, Cigarettes,</u> 7 November 1990.

It has been assumed by GATT panels that animals are capable of falling within the category of "exhaustible natural resources" under Article XX(g)[11]. In the recent US-Mexico Tuna-Dolphin dispute[12], Mexico argued that the drafting history of the Article showed that it was not intended to apply to "any living being". Because of its decision on the extra-territorial application of environmental standards, the panel did not address Mexico's argument.

Measures do not have to be shown to be "necessary", but do have to be "primarily aimed at the conservation of an exhaustible natural resource" to be considered as "relating to" conservation within the meaning of Article XX(g)[13]. It does not matter that the main motive for the conservation is not economic but ecological; a Panel has "acknowledged that the conservation of natural resources encompasses broader environmental concerns reflecting both economic and non-economic interests"[14].

The chapeau of Article XX requires that measures for which an exception is sought:
"are not applied in a manner which would constitute a means of arbitrary or unjustifiable discrimination between countries where the same conditions prevail, or a disguised restriction on international trade"[15].

Provided that export restrictions are justified on ecological grounds, they should not be considered "disguised restrictions on trade". And provided the restrictions apply equally to exports to all states the issue of "arbitrary or unjustifiable discrimination" should not arise.

A concern does arise, however, where a state of import bans or restricts imports of a product while permitting its domestic sale or consumption, and the issue of an export permit is made conditional on the prior issue of an import permit by the state of import. This is the case under CITES for the export of specimens of Appendix I species[16]. The grant of an import licence is in turn conditional on the relevant authority in the state of import being satisfied, among other things, that the specimen is not to be used for primarily commercial purposes[17]. In making the grant of an export licence conditional on the prior grant of an import licence, which is in turn conditional on the determination of a non-commercial use in the importing state, the state of export may be discriminating between states inconsistently with both Article XIII and the Article XX chapeau reference to "states where the same conditions prevail". Is the fact that

---

[11] See, for example, Final Report of the Panel in the Matter of Canada's Landing Requirement for Pacific Coast Salmon and Herring, October 16th 1989, paragraph 7.02.

[12] Report of the Panel, United States - Restrictions on Imports of Tuna, September 3rd 1991, paragraph 3.43.

[13] Report of the Panel, Canada - Measures Affecting Exports of Unprocessed Herring and Salmon, 20th November 1987, paragraph 4.6.

[14] In the Matter of Canada's Landing Requirement for Pacific Coast Salmon and Herring, U.S.-Canada FTA Panel Report, applying GATT provisions incorporated into the FTA, October 16th 1989.

[15] GATT Article XX. Article XIII also contains a general requirement that quantitative restrictions be applied in a non-discriminatory way.

[16] CITES Article III.2 (d).

[17] CITES Article III.3 (c).

an individual specimen will be used for commercial purposes in one state and not in another sufficient to make the two states ones where "the same conditions [do not] prevail"? If it is not, then the state of export will need to show that discriminating on this basis is not "arbitrary" or "unjustifiable".

This question of compatibility of export restrictions with the GATT arises under CITES only in relation to exports of specimens of Appendix I species. Appendix I species are those most in need of protection, and it is for this reason that export is made conditional on the prior grant of an import licence. The export of the less endangered species listed under Appendix II is not conditional on the prior grant of an import permit. It is ironic that restrictions on the export of Appendix I species are less clearly compatible with the GATT than are the restrictions on the export of Appendix II species.

Restrictions on Imports by Parties

Few agreements for the protection of wildlife contain express and absolute import bans. More common is a requirement that imports be conditional on the grant of an import permit. The requirements which must be met before an import permit is granted vary. Common is a requirement that the specimen has been caught legally in the state of export, or that the exporting state has determined that the export will not be detrimental to the survival of the species.

The compatibility of any of these provisions with the GATT is doubtful, however they do not conflict necessarily. Environment-related import restrictions were interpreted recently in connection with a dispute between Mexico and the United States concerning U.S. imposition of trade sanctions on Mexican tuna exports, under a U.S. law concerning prevention of incidental taking of dolphins during tuna fishing[18]. The dispute settlement panel in that case found that non-discriminatory regulation of imported and like domestic products as such was fully consistent with Article III, even if enforced at the border; but that Article III would not permit enforcement at the border of regulations which related not to the characteristics of a product as such, but to the circumstances of its production. Hence, the trade sanctions were found to be quantitative restrictions contrary to Article XI.1.

It can be argued that restrictions on import imposed in accordance with CITES are incapable of falling within the exceptions in Article XX(b) or (g) as their purpose is to protect endangered species in the exporting state, by reinforcing the system of export restrictions. The Panel in the US-Mexico Tuna-Dolphin dispute[19] interpreted the Article XX exceptions as only allowing measures taken for the protection of plants or animals, or the conservation of exhaustible resources, within the jurisdiction of the state taking the measures.

The principle objective of the U.S. Regulation which was the subject of the Mexico - U.S. tuna dispute was the protection of cetaceans, in particular dolphins, from a form of fishing which was, it was argued, indiscriminate, wasteful and led to large loss of mammal life. In that sense it was irrelevant where, i.e. in what territory, the dolphins were threatened. However, it must be noted that the sanctions which were imposed by the U.S. were not trade regulations

---

[18] Report of the Panel, United States - Restrictions on Imports of Tuna, September 3rd 1991.

[19] Report of the Panel, United States - Restrictions on Imports of Tuna, September 3rd 1991, paragraph 5.27.

agreed under a multilateral treaty, but unilateral sanctions by one country asserting jurisdiction over the environmental priority of another country. It must also be noted that a unilateral sanctions regime inherently favours larger countries over small. The concluding remarks of the Tuna panel decision point to the desirability of expanded international cooperation based on mutual agreement, and of active consideration in GATT of trade and environment issues, as an alternative to an unilateral sanctions regime.

Restrictions on import are an integral part of many international agreements for the protection of wildlife. Without them the effectiveness of agreements would be greatly reduced.

Restrictions on Transit through Parties

There are international agreements for the protection of wildlife, not including CITES, which impose restrictions on the transit of species protected by the agreement through the territory of parties[20].

Since measures restricting transit apply even to goods not imported into the customs territory of a contracting party, they are a different issue from quantitative restrictions on importation as such and different rules apply. These measures may conflict with GATT Article V:1 on freedom of transit, which provides that "There shall be freedom of transit through the territory of each contracting party, via the routes most convenient for international transit, for traffic in transit to or from the territory of other contracting parties. No distinction shall be made which is based on the flag of vessels, the place of origin, departure, entry, exit or destination, or on any circumstances relating to the ownership of goods, of vessels or of other means of transport." This paragraph was taken from the Barcelona Convention and Statute on Freedom of Transit[21]. GATT Article V:5 also provides that "With respect to all charges, regulations and formalities in connection with transit, each contracting party shall accord to traffic in transit to or from the territory of any other contracting party treatment no less favourable than the treatment accorded to traffic in transit to or from any third country." To the extent that measures implementing transit provisions in treaties conflict with Article V, the application of the exceptions in Article XX becomes relevant, and the analysis above would apply.

Restrictions on Trade with Non-Parties

CITES restricts trade not only between parties, but between parties and non-parties. For example, the export of a specimen of an Appendix I species to a non-party is conditional upon the prior grant of an import permit by the importing non-party[22], and the import permit must

---

[20] e.g. Western Hemisphere Convention (No. 12 in the present survey), Article IX.

[21] Concluded 20 April 1921 in Barcelona, entered into force 21 October 1922; 7 LNTS 11; still in force.

[22] CITES Article III.

"substantially conform with the requirements of" CITES[23]. The import of a specimen of an Appendix I species from a non-party is also dependent on the grant of an import permit, which will only be granted if the relevant authority in the importing state advises that the import will not be detrimental to the survival of the species.

As the effect of CITES is to impose the same restrictions on trade with non-parties as on trade with parties, arguments of "discrimination" under Article XX are unlikely to arise, and the same considerations apply as apply to the restrictions on trade with parties. Restrictions on exports are likely to be justifiable under Articles XX(b) or (g), whereas restrictions on imports are likely be prohibited under Article XI.1 and fall outside the Article XX exceptions.

A counter argument might be that if such a permit is seen as relating to the characteristics of the product as such, then under the Tuna panel decision a non-discriminatory system of permits applied to both import and domestic sale of the like product could be consistent with GATT under Article III. If the permit requirement is seen as relating purely to the conditions of production of the product, it falls not under Article III but under the ban on quantitative restrictions on trade in Article XI:1.

Discrimination by a contracting party between the products of other contracting parties gives rise to issues under the GATT's most-favoured-nation clause, Article I, and the non-discrimination requirement in Article XIII. CITES may avoid these problems to the extent that parties' measures do not discriminate between trade with non-parties and trade with parties, and if the permit requirement is itself GATT-consistent and the differences in treatment are necessary for enforcement reasons, these differences may be sheltered by the enforcement exception in Article XX(d).

AGREEMENTS TO PROTECT THE ENVIRONMENT OF THE IMPORTING STATE FROM HARMFUL ORGANISMS OR PRODUCTS

Agreements to protect the environment of the importing state from harmful organisms or products, whether plant pests, hazardous waste, or pesticides, rely primarily upon import restrictions[24]. These are often supported, however, by corresponding export restrictions. Some agreements contain restrictions on exports to non-parties. The restrictions used and the factors affecting their compatibility with the GATT are common to agreements of this type, irrespective of the subject matter.

---

[23] CITES Article X.

[24] International Plant Protection Convention (1951); Plant Protection Agreement for the South East Asia and Pacific Region (1956); North American Plant Protection Agreement (1976); Phyto-Sanitary Convention for Africa South of the Sahara (1954).

Restrictions on Import

Agreements either impose a total restriction on the import of items which may be harmful[25], or make the import conditional on the grant of an import permit[26]. In the case of plant pests this itself may be conditional on the consignment meeting certain phyto-sanitary criteria.

These restrictions, if applied in a non-discriminatory way, are likely to fall within the Article XX exceptions and be compatible with the GATT, as their purpose is to protect plants, animals, humans and resources within the jurisdiction of the state. It could be argued, however, that some regional plant protection agreements require measures to be taken by one state not to protect plants within its own jurisdiction, but within the jurisdiction of other states within the region[27]. Measures such as these may not fall within the Article XX exceptions.

Under some of these agreements discriminatory application of the restrictions may prevent the Article XX exceptions from applying, and the restrictions will therefore remain contrary to the Article XI.1 prohibition[28].

The Basel Convention (No. 103 in the present survey) requires parties to prohibit imports of hazardous waste from non-parties[29]. As hazardous waste produced by non-parties is intrinsically no more hazardous than that produced by parties, it could be argued that this discrimination is "arbitrary", unless the discriminatory import ban could be justified under Article XX (d) as a necessary enforcement measure for measures that are otherwise GATT-consistent. Similar arguments can be made about the requirement in the Bamako Convention (No. 104 in the present survey) that the African parties prohibit the import of hazardous waste originating outside Africa, but not that originating inside Africa[30]. A counter-argument would be that the same conditions do not prevail in countries which are not signatories to the relevant convention, and so the conditions in the chapeau of Article XX are met.

---

[25] Fourth ACP-EEC Lome Convention (under No. 9 in the present survey), Article 39 (waste); Plant Protection Agreement for the South East Asia and Pacific Region, Article IV and Appendix B (plant pests).

[26] Basel Convention (No. 79 in the present survey), Article 4.2 (g) (waste); International Plant Protection Convention Article VI.1 (plant pests).

[27] e.g. under the Phyto-Sanitary Convention for Africa South of the Sahara.

[28] For example, Basel Convention, Bamako Convention, ACP-EEC Fourth Lome Convention.

[29] Basel Convention Article 4.5.

[30] Bamako Convention Article 4.1.

Restrictions on Export

Agreements dealing with hazardous waste typically use export restrictions to support the restrictions on import[31]. Under GATT a country can essentially do anything to imports or exports that it does to its own products, and it can do anything it considers necessary to its own production processes.

A particular form of restriction on export is the system of prior informed consent established by the non-binding London Guidelines for the Exchange of Information on Chemicals in International Trade (No. 103 in the present survey). If a country prohibits export of a product while permitting its domestic sale or consumption, this discrimination may violate the prohibition on export restrictions in Article XI. The procedure of making export dependent on the prior informed consent of the state of import may be inconsistent with Article XIII. It might not be sheltered by Article XX(b), if its purpose is to assist in the protection of extrajurisdictional human, animal, or plant life or health.

Restrictions on Trade with Non-Parties

As explained above many of the agreements in this category impose different restrictions on trade with non-parties from those applied to trade with parties. This may be inconsistent with Article I or XIII, and constitute "arbitrary or unjustifiable" discrimination preventing resort to Article XX.

AGREEMENTS TO PROTECT THE GLOBAL COMMONS

The only existing agreement using trade instruments to protect the global commons is the Montreal Protocol on Substances that Deplete the Ozone Layer (No. 33 in the present survey). It contains no restrictions on trade between parties. There are, however, restrictions on trade with non-parties which are powerful and controversial. The Vienna Convention and Montreal Protocol regime has been effective in large part because of the trade restrictions contained in it. It must be taken as a missed opportunity that no clear statement was made by the signatories that these provisions were to take priority over the GATT.

Restrictions on Import

Parties are progressively to ban the import of ozone depleting substances, products containing these substances, and possibly products produced with, but not containing, these substances[32].

If one simply places these restrictive provisions alongside the GATT, an international trade lawyer would likely argue that they are incompatible with the GATT because they are inconsistent with the ban on quantitative trade restrictions under Article XI, and, being intended

---

[31] Basel Convention Article 4; Bamako Convention Article 4; Fourth ACP-EEC Lome Convention Article 39.

[32] Montreal Protocol, Article 4.1, 3 and 4.

to protect the extraterritorial environment, they fall outside Article XX. A counter argument, would be that the measures may be capable of falling within Article XX, even interpreted narrowly, as depletion of the extra-territorial ozone layer is harmful to the territorial environment. However, to justify the Montreal Protocol in this way demonstrates the artificiality of argument which must be used to justify existing agreements under the GATT; we know that the Montreal Protocol is designed to deal with the environment some way beyond territorial jurisdiction - in the atmosphere above. Yet the disparity between the policy arguments which justify the use of trade provisions in international environmental agreements, and the way those policy arguments are reflected in GATT Articles XX(b) and (g) prevents reliance on that primary objective as a justification.

Furthermore, it should be possible to show that the discrimination between imports from parties and non-parties is not contrary to the Preamble to Article XX, as the differences between production costs in countries accepting and not accepting reductions in production and use of CFCs make them countries where the same conditions do not prevail. The argument that differences in production costs resulting from compliance with environmental protection should be treated as an aspect of countries' competitiveness,[33] even if it is valid in relation to the prevention of purely domestic environmental degradation, should not apply here; in this context it would be based on the assumption of a sovereign right to inflict environmental degradation on other states.

However it has been strongly argued within GATT that it is impossible to distinguish between the sort of cost difference referred to above and that caused, for instance, by differences in the minimum wage. An example is cited in the argument that the cost difference attributable to non-use of CFCs is minimal. This is clearly a very controversial argument.

It should also be possible to show that the measures are "necessary" within the meaning of Article XX(b). We now know that the ozone depletion problem is orders of magnitude more serious than it was in 1985 or 1987. When there is likely to be a threat to the world's ecosystems, not to say a widespread increase in skin cancers and a universal threat to human immune systems (in a world confronted by AIDS), drastic action is necessary and justified.

A further objection to the regime of the Montreal Protocol is that it provides in Article 4(4) for restrictions on imports to be based not only on the characteristics of products (that they contain ozone-depleting substances), but also on the methods used in the production or processing of products. It is argued that Article XX can be used to justify only the first and not the second type of restriction. Support for this view is found in the Report of the Panel in the US-Mexico Tuna-Dolphin dispute. It is based on the argument that the willingness to inflict and suffer environmental degradation is part of a country's competitiveness and should not be restricted under GATT. But so-called domestic environmental degradation is seen increasingly to affect other countries and to be their legitimate concern. Further, the urgency of many environmental problems makes this aspect of competitiveness increasingly unacceptable. A second argument in favour of the narrow interpretation of Article XX is that to allow countries to discriminate on the basis of process and production methods in order to protect the environment would invite discrimination with regard to other factors that contribute towards

---

[33] e.g. <u>Industrial Pollution Control and International Trade</u>, Note by the GATT Secretariat, 9th June 1971, L/3538.

countries' competitiveness, such as low labour costs.   But environmental protection can legitimately be given separate treatment because environmental degradation in one state has a physical impact on others, unlike low labour costs.   An interpretation that accepted the legality of environmental protection would therefore be limited in its effect.

Restrictions on Export

Parties are required to ban the export to non-parties of controlled substances[34], and to discourage the export of technology for producing controlled substances[35].

As with the restrictions on import, the restrictions may be capable of falling within Article XX, but one would be required to demonstrate that the restrictions are "necessary", in the international trade context, and do not involve "arbitrary or unjustifiable discrimination between countries where the same conditions prevail".   For such arguments see above.

The previous two sections of this report have set out the policy reasons which justify the use of quantitative restrictions in international environmental agreements, described typical uses of quantitative restrictions in existing agreements, and demonstrated the conflict which may exist between many of these and the GATT. The following section discusses the way these conflicts are resolved under international treaty law.

THE RELATIONSHIP BETWEEN GATT AND INTERNATIONAL ENVIRONMENTAL AGREEMENTS UNDER INTERNATIONAL TREATY LAW

As is evident from the analysis above, the relationship between the GATT and international environmental agreements is an uneasy one, but is there in any sense a hierarchy of norms which would determine any supremacy of the rules generated by the one over the other? The GATT provides broad flexibility to its contracting parties to tax or regulate for environmental or any other purposes, as long as such taxes do not discriminate. Leaving aside the issue of whether use of the waiver clause is at all a practical policy to pursue in the face of conflicts between international environmental agreements and the GATT. The existence of the waiver clause in the GATT means that the contracting parties can waive GATT obligations, and so there is no <u>necessary</u> conflict between obligations of states under other treaties and their obligations as contracting parties to the GATT.

We have, so far, simply identified conflict which was our principal objective, and hence avoided an answer.   There are good arguments on either side of the compatibility divide, just as there are in terms of hierarchy.   Trade lawyers see clear breaches of GATT in the light of a vision of a world of free(er) trade. Environmental lawyers argue for priority for the newer or more specific or more universal environmental agreements.   Our simple message is that there is no clear answer.   The only matter about which we are sure is the need for change.

The international law of treaties provides some general rules which are of some value in assessing the worth of the competing arguments. The general rules are as follows:

---

[34] Montreal Protocol Article 4.2.

[35] Montreal Protocol Article 4.5.

-later treaties take priority over earlier;

-more specific treaties take priority over the general - generalia specialibus non derogant;

-where a treaty says that it is subject to or is not considered incompatible with another treaty that other treaty will prevail;

-as between parties to a treaty who later become parties to a later, inconsistent, treaty, the earlier will apply only where its provisions are not incompatible with the later treaty;

-as between a party to both treaties and a party to only one of them, the treaty to which both are parties will govern the mutual rights and obligations of the states concerned;

-in determining which treaty is the earlier and which the later, the relevant date is the date of adoption not that of its entry into force;

-the general rules (set out in Article 30 <u>Vienna Convention on the Law of Treaties</u>) are to be considered as residuary rules - that is to say rules which will operate in the absence of express treaty provisions regulating priority[36]; and

-pacta sunt servanda: every treaty in force is binding on the parties to it and must be performed in good faith.

A number of difficulties, which we are unable to address in any detail in this report, arise in determining any priority between the GATT and the various international environmental agreements. The first and most obvious is that we are dealing with different subject matter. The rules are primarily focused on conflict and priority between treaties covering the same subject matter. Here we have treaties dealing with environmental or conservation issues which contain implementation provisions in the form of trade instruments. Against that body of conservation and environmental protection law, containing those trade instruments, we have international trade law which, for these purposes, is contained in the rules of the GATT, designed to regulate different subject matter, namely, the liberalisation of world trade.

Further problems are associated with the idiosyncratic nature of the GATT[37]. The agreement is constantly evolving through practice and further agreement, in that sense it is not a treaty which can be said to have been "adopted" at any one time. One can identify significant moments - say, in 1948, or immediately following a GATT round - but it would be perhaps misleading to pick a point in time where the obligations on the Contracting Parties were characterised in a single text. 1948 is the only candidate. At that time there were far fewer parties and the whole regime of preferences for developing countries absent.

Fixing that early date clearly puts GATT at a disadvantage as against the newer environmental Treaties. But there may be a better, additional and complementary framework for analysis in comparing the differing nature of the trade and environment agreements. Because the GATT was conceived as a kind of contractual agreement, with no supporting, permanent organisation, it has lacked the status of an international legislative body. It cannot compete with the UN, or the UN agencies, as the legitimate creator of what is described as international public law. International organisations, or indeed groups of states dealing with a particular subject matter, can make agreements erga omnes. Indeed environmental agreements, most particularly those dealing with the global commons, or matters of concern to the whole of international

---

[36] Sinclair, The Law of Treaties, p.97-98.

[37] This is a situation which will change significantly on the ratification, if it is forthcoming, of the MTO.

society, are the paradigm examples of agreements made in the global public interest. These features - groups of states acting in a semi-legislative capacity and inherent purpose of regulating the particular subject matter - present in constitutive treaties, were identified generally by Lord McNair in his famous treatise on the Law of Treaties and in particular by reference to international agreements relating to waterways:

"Article 380 of the Treaty of Versailles of 1919 provided that

The Kiel canal and its approaches shall be maintained free and open to the vessels of commerce and war of all nations at peace with Germany on terms of entire equality.

What was in question in this case was not whether the operation of the Treaty of Versailles conferred a right, or imposed a duty, upon a State not party to the Treaty; ...The question was whether or not Article 380... created objective law, produced effects erga omnes."[38]

The Permanent Court of Justice in the Wimbledon case, to which these facts relate, affirmed this rule, stating that the Treaty had created an international regime for the "benefit of all the nations of the world". McNair[39] distinguishes agreements which are intended to operate erga omnes and predominantly contractual treaties which create rights in personam. He argues that these erga omnes agreements are characterised by the leadership of a group of States determined to address a problem of universal concern and that in some sense these agreements are a substitute for the lack of a global legislature.

The agreements relating to the global commons, such as the Vienna Convention and Montreal Protocol and perhaps especially the forthcoming Climate Change Convention, would seem to fall within this category. This raises important issues. If they are considered to be erga omnes agreements does that, of itself, establish them as a higher law, above and superior to the GATT? Specifically, does the existence of an article banning imports of ozone-depleting substances from non-signatories support the erga omnes idea or run counter to it, in that in the context of the desperate attempt to recruit signatories, such as India and China, a special article had to be created to extend the reach of the agreement to third parties. These issues need fuller analysis than we can provide in the context of this report, so that any conclusions we may reach must be considered to be tentative.

That being said it is possible to argue that the Montreal Protocol regime takes priority over the GATT in relation to trade in ozone-depleting substances, because of its subject matter, the urgency in resolving the problem for the benefit of the whole of international society and because trade provisions were agreed upon in order better to carry out the objectives of the agreement.

It is possible to argue, under the general rules cited above, that an agreement such as CITES is an example of the specific having priority over the general. Notwithstanding the reservations we have expressed over the "same subject matter" base for determining priority,

[38] McNair, Law of Treaties, 267.

[39] Ibid. p.256. It is worth recalling that Lord McNair was President of the International Court of Justice and Whewell Professor of International Law at Cambridge. Whilst his book was published in 1961, it is still a most authoritative text.

it is certainly arguable that CITES expressly sets aside existing, prior, GATT rules in order to address the particular problem of endangered species. That there are very many parties to CITES who are also Contracting Parties to GATT supports that view. The same argument could be made in respect of the Montreal Protocol. There is no provision in either agreement constraining the Parties by virtue of their prior GATT obligations.

The potential conflicts between trade instruments in international environmental agreements, and the uncertain resolution of those conflicts by international treaty law demonstrates the need for both debate and the formulation of new rules[40]. If these rules are to fully address environmental issues, and to lead to lasting global security, full account must be taken of issues of development and the role in international society of transnational corporations.

DEVELOPMENT

THE USE OF DEVELOPMENT-RELATED INSTRUMENTS

Development-related agreements or instruments aim at integrating environmental considerations with trade and economic issues in order to advance the more equitable distribution of the welfare of the worlds resources. Amongst other important concerns, these instruments address problems associated with inconsistent existing development, trade and environmental policies and practises. This approach offers new integrated policy formations which if used to amend existing instruments or adopted or implemented in their own right could, it is argued, help to reverse what many have observed as the disastrous economic, social and environmental experiences of the 1980's in developing countries. The problems of the world economy are conceived as systemic and as an economy depends on law, international agreements have assumed a vital importance in confronting what is understood to be the failure of the international economy to serve the whole of international society, the society of all human beings, as Philip Allott has stated:

"The international economy has been unable to ensure the sustained and accelerating development of all its subordinate societies, the ever increasing well-being of the whole

---

[40] In October, 1991, it was agreed to activate the GATT Working Group on Environmental Measures and International Trade. This group held its first substantive meeting in January 1992 and will meet next in March. Its terms of reference focus on examining "any specific matters relevant to the trade policy aspects of measures to control pollution and protect the human environment especially with regard to the application of the provisions of the General Agreement taking into account the particular problems of developing countries." Within this framework, the current agenda of the Group includes examination of (a) trade provisions in existing multilateral environmental agreements (such as CITES, the Montreal Protocol and the Basel Convention), (b) multilateral transparency of national environmental regulations, and (c) trade effects of new packaging and labelling requirements aimed at protecting the environment. The Group thus offers a forum in which contracting parties may discuss such issues in the combined context of trade, environment and developing country concerns. One of the important tasks of the Group will be to examine the current multilateral trade rules to be certain that they do not hinder multilateral efforts to deal with environmental problems.

human race"[41]

We are unable to provide any analysis nor to make any theoretical contribution to the resolution of these fundamental and complex matters in this report, we simply recognise the need to do this work, and in this section will deal briefly with provisions of two United Nations development agreements, one of which suggests strategies, and the other is the Declaration resulting from those strategies. Additionally, we review the current progress towards a United Nations Code of Conduct on Transnational Corporations. These strategies and proposed agreements are then briefly evaluated in terms of their recognition of environmental considerations.

NOTES ON THE INTERNATIONAL DEVELOPMENT STRATEGY FOR THE FOURTH UN DEVELOPMENT DECADE

The UN has noted that developing countries have been subject to shrinking resource flows, declining commodity prices, rising interest rates and increasing barriers to market access during the latter half of the 1980's. Figures for overall growth indicate a growth rate of only 3% annually. For this decline to be halted and reversed a stronger awareness of the interdependence of nations is recommended, but this must look beyond the notion of commercial links in trade and finance alone. In particular, it is noted, environmental threats and epidemics are often global in their scope, and economic stress can only exacerbate the problems they give rise to.

The document preamble stresses that a strong stimulus to global co-operation is provided by the consciousness of the global consequences of environmental problems, and how these problems interact with levels of achieved development in developing countries. Closer integration within developing countries themselves can also assist their progress, and the advancement in the fields of science and communication offer opportunities for accelerated, sustainable, development.

The UN General Assembly Declaration adopted at the 18th Special Session contained a pledge that UN member states will seek to reverse the adverse trends of the 1980's, and followed this with an outline of the goals and objectives for accelerated development in the 1990's; policies and measures to support the objectives are outlined within a reactivating framework. These measures encompass recommendations within the fields of:
-economic policy
-external debt
-development finance
-international trade
-commodities
-science and technology, industrial policies and measures, and
-agriculture

In evaluating these development strategies in relation to trade and the environment, of particular relevance here are the recommendations for international trade and commodities, and for agriculture.

---

[41] Philip Allott, Eunomia, p.355, OUP 1990.

1) International Trade

The outlined goal is to "reactivate trade". The document recommends that protectionism should be halted and reversed. Developing countries, it is argued, should concentrate on rapid Structural Adjustment Programmes (SAP's), and their comparative advantages; suggested trading conditions
include:

a) textile trading to be brought under GATT

b) trade blocks and regional integration not to impede world trade and to conform with the rules of GATT

c) strict adherence to GATT by all contracting parties

The report emphasises that the success of the current round of GATT talks is essential for progress in international trade and for the building up of the capabilities of developing countries.

2) Commodities

The factors contributing to the slow growth caused by the depressed levels of commodity prices will prove difficult to stabilise. Recommended improvements include:

a) International Commodity Agreements need negotiating to improve agreements between producers and consumers - many existing agreements broke down in the 1980's.

b) developing countries should diversify into the processing, marketing and distribution of their commodities.

c) Investment in Science and technology, the creation of industrial policies and measures, and modernisation of agriculture.

That final point, (c) above, can be presented in an integrated manner, namely, that Development requires the modernisation and transformation of industrial and agricultural sectors, through appropriate use of science and technology: e.g.

-narrowing the "knowledge gap" with the industrialized world;

-upgrading of work skills and increasing the use of scientific research;

-using technologies from both abroad and those appropriate to local conditions.

3) Industrial Policies and Measures

Industrialisation is indispensable for economic growth. Policies need to focus on:

-development of appropriate roles for the public and private sectors

-the balance between import substitution and export led industrial production

4) Agriculture

Measures needed to strengthen domestic food security and to promote modernisation, in order to enhance export and agro-business opportunities. Policy suggestions include:

-price incentives to facilitate transition from subsistence to modernised agriculture

-land, credit and infrastructural development

-policies to promote role of women farmers

-investment and training

The "Priority aspects of development" (para 78) emphasises that economic growth alone cannot protect the physical environment. If environmental damage and degradation increase, the natural resource base of the developing countries and the welfare of populations will be harmed, making progress in development unsustainable. The Strategy for the 1990's must, then, give special attention to human resource development, the alleviation of poverty and the environment.

The resolution on the environment (para 95) urges developed countries to take urgent and appropriate measures to halt the flow of pollution, and urges all countries to take effective action for its protection; there can be no sustainable development if environmental degradation persists.

The UN Declaration adopted the Resolutions presented at the eighteenth Special Session. In basing its adoption on a declared global commitment to equitable development and the eradication of poverty, the strategies as outlined above were approved. The assessment of the 1980's as a decade of uneven or lost development by many developing countries, was attributed mainly to such factors as external indebtedness, the one way flow of resources from developing to developed countries, and the long-term downward trend in commodity prices.

In detailing the resolutions the session focused more strongly on the impending environmental and economic disasters that may occur if pollution, desertification, deforestation and climate change are not halted and reversed. Thus future economic development must be 'sound and sustainable', or, it is argued, the world economy is under serious threat.

CODE OF CONDUCT ON TRANSNATIONAL CORPORATIONS

The transnational corporations play a major role in the economy of both developed and developing countries. Although rules exists for international trade, principally at the inter-state level, under the General Agreement on Trade and Tariffs (GATT) there is no corresponding international framework dealing with the conduct and treatment of transnational corporations at the bilateral, regional and multilateral levels. For this reason the UN has proposed this Code.

For the developing countries the main objective in relation to transnational corporations is to achieve such goals as consistency with national laws, regulations and policies, adequate disclosure of information, environmental and consumer protection.

The Code calls for the respect of the permanent sovereignty of countries over their natural resources.

The transnational corporations are urged to carry out their activities in accordance:
- with the relevant national laws, regulations, administrative practices and with:
- policies relating to the preservation of the environment of the countries in which they operate
- and with due regard to relevant international standards.

In performing their activities they should take steps to protect the environment and where damaged to rehabilitate it and should make efforts to develop and apply adequate technologies for this purpose.

They should supply all relevant information concerning characteristics of their products processes and other activities including experimental uses and related aspects which may harm the environment.

The code calls for safe packaging, proper labelling and informative and accurate advertising.

Transnational corporations should be prepared to cooperate with International Organisations in their efforts to develop and promote national and international standards for the protection of the environment.

Efforts should be made to develop and apply adequate, environmentally sound and appropriate technologies.

EVALUATING THE RELATIONSHIP BETWEEN EXISTING AGREEMENTS ON THE
ENVIRONMENT, INTERNATIONAL TRADE AGREEMENTS AND
DEVELOPMENT RELATED AGREEMENTS

In some senses a circle has been created , which in order to avoid becoming vicious, needs to be carefully monitored. The Development-related instruments refer to international trade agreements and the importance of environmental policy in a declared commitment to sustainable development. Indeed, it is a fundamental component of the development strategy that the GATT be strengthened and made more effective. However, as we have already noted, the GATT does not contain provisions which adequately reflect the commitment to sustainable development.

It is axiomatic that an integrated approach is optimal in dealing with trade, environment and development imperatives. It is equally clear that failure to deal with, for example the causes of poverty, will make environmental problems associated with land degradation and water pollution next to impossible to solve. Furthermore, no-one seriously contends that global environmental problems can be solved without cooperation not only between states but also transnational corporations, international organisations, non-governmental organisations and individuals.

Thus, within these Development initiatives certain important environmental issues remain unresolved, for example:

1) The General Assembly Resolution (S-18/3) states that economic policies should have as their ultimate objective the betterment of the human condition. However with the emphasis still on export-led growth, and third world primary resources still entering world markets at unstable price levels, it remains an issue firstly, whether resolutions condemning global economic instability are sufficient to reverse the trend of decline and secondly whether export led primary resource exploitation can be managed in an environmentally wise way. Raw commodity production often requires intensive mining and quarrying for its extraction, and these processes in themselves need monitoring for adverse effects on land degradation, industrial pollution, threats to biodiversity and on human health and safety.

2) The proposed intensification of industrial manufacturing and the modernisation of agriculture are another two sectors which are vulnerable to techniques which degrade the environment. The commitment to developing an appropriate application of technology and science needs to be related to solutions which safeguard the environment from the potential damage to sometimes fragile eco-systems that modernisation may endanger. The crucial word is, of course, "appropriate".

3) The Code of Conduct on Transnational Corporations strongly recommends that governments should adopt policies which are consistent with their priorities for sustainable economic growth. In circumstances where there may be differing standards set to preserve and promote sustainable economic growth, and where regulatory intervention in the market place to achieve environmental objectives is promoted, the Code will need careful coordination with the Uruguay Round Final Act or more generally

with provisions regulating international trade as outlined in the General Agreement on Tariffs and Trade (GATT). In this regard it is clear that multilateral decision-making is preferred to unilateral.

In the light of the above policy recommendations, and the potential problems which could arise for an integrated development programme if environmentally sensitive strategies are not incorporated, it becomes apparent that the ultimate goals for growth and equity in developing countries are dependent upon a more holistic view of economic growth, one that appreciates the life sustaining character of a healthy biosphere.

The development of rules adequately balancing interests of trade, environment and development will require substantial debate. That progress towards such rules is possible, however, is demonstrated by the evolution of the EEC Treaty of Rome through the Single European Act and Maastricht Treaty on Political Union.

RECENT DEVELOPMENTS

AMENDMENTS TO THE EC TREATY - THE MAASTRICHT SUMMIT

Prior to the Maastricht summit the primary aim of the European Community, as stated in Article 2 of the Treaty of Rome was to promote economic growth. Since the Single European Act (SEA) in 1987 introduced environmental policy within the scope of the Treaty of Rome (see No. 9 in the present survey) there has been clear legal authority for environmental policy which may in some circumstances conflict with free movement of goods and services - the principal freedoms used to promote economic growth. Amendments to the Treaty of Rome agreed at the Maastricht summit now place environmental protection concerns alongside economic growth in an amended Article 2. Article 2 now provides for "sustainable ..... growth respecting the environment". The methods for achieving sustainable growth are set out in Article 3 which places environmental policy with free movement of goods and services and competition policy and makes no hierarchical distinction between them.

It is worth looking at the amendments to Article 130(r) in more detail. In Article 130(r)(1) Community policy is given an additional objective (to those present in the SEA), namely that of promoting measures at an international level to deal with regional or worldwide environmental problems. Article 130(r)(2) establishes that "The Community policy on the environment shall aim at a high level of protection taking into account the diversity of situations in the various regions of the Community". Furthermore, and fundamentally, Community policy "shall be based on the precautionary principle and on the principles that preventive action should be taken, that environmental damage as a priority should be rectified at source and that the polluter should pay". This significant step by the Member States of the European Community necessarily involves regulatory action, even in the face of scientific uncertainty, which in some cases will raise a prima facie barrier to the free movement of any goods and services which are produced or carried out in a non-precautionary manner.

The Amended Article 130(r)(2) goes on to say that "Environmental protection requirements must be integrated into the definition and implementation of other Community policies". This is a much stronger commitment to the integrated approach implicit in the Single European Act amendments in 1987. This approach is fundamental to the Community's commitment to sustainable development. Its first fruits are already controversial; the EC Commission is to propose a Directive requiring Member States to assess the environmental implications of all government policies, especially in key areas of transport, agriculture and energy.

Article 130(r)(2) goes on to say "In this context, harmonisation measures ensuring these requirements shall include, where appropriate, a safeguard clause allowing Member States to take provisional measures for non-economic environmental reasons, subject to a Community inspection procedure". Again, reference to safeguard clauses and non-economic justifications for high environmental standards subject to an international inspection procedure offers an indication of what might be in a re-modelled GATT system. The Community recognises, very pragmatically, that there are differences in the capabilities of Member States in the north and south of the Community in adopting and implementing high environmental standards. The new Community regime[42] enables countries such as the Netherlands, Germany and Denmark to adopt more stringent measures than the agreed Community position, and allows for temporary derogations[43], coupled with financial assistance, where the costs are deemed "disproportionate" for the public authorities of any particular Member State. An "Environment Fund" or "Cohesion Fund" is to be set up to provide such financial assistance, predominantly to the southern EC states. It is not difficult to see parallels in international society. The full text of what is now Article 130(s)(5) is as follows:-

> "5.   If a measure adopted pursuant to paragraph 1 involves disproportionate cost for the public authorities of a Member State the Council may, when adopting the said measure, provide for:
>   -   temporary derogations and/or
>   -   financial support from an Environmental Fund."

THE FINAL ACT OF THE URUGUAY ROUND AND THE DRAFT AGREEMENT ESTABLISHING THE MULTILATERAL TRADE ORGANISATION

By contrast the draft Agreement Establishing the Multilateral Trade Organisation (MTO) introduces no specific commitment to environmental protection within a sustainable development framework. The preamble does recognise that relations in the field of trade and economic endeavour should be conducted with a view to, inter alia, "developing the optimal use of the resources of the world at sustainable levels". However there is no mention of the environment under Article 2 ("Scope of the MTO") or Article 3 ("Functions of the MTO"). In Article 2 the MTO does provide for all the agreements and legal instruments set out in Annexes 1, 2 and 3 to the draft Agreement including the Final Act of Uruguay Round. The Uruguay Round includes an agreement on technical barriers to trade which includes in its preamble:

> "Recognising that no country should be prevented from taking measures necessary to ensure the quality of its exports, or for the protection of human, animal or health, or the environment, ... subject to the requirement that they are not applied in a manner which

---

[42] Treaty of Rome,. Article 130(t)

[43] Article 130(s)(5), Treaty of Rome.

would constitute a means of arbitrary or unjustifiable discrimination between countries where the same conditions prevail or a disguised restriction on international trade;"

The Agreement on Subsidies and Countervailing Measures includes a section (Part IV) on non-actionable subsidies where Article 8 identifies what is a non-actionable subsidy. No mention is made of, for example, research and development for environmental purposes. The Uruguay Round Agreement on Agriculture does make reference to the environment in the preamble:

"Noting that commitments under the reform programme should be made in an equitable way among all participants, having regard to non-trade concerns, including food security and the need to protect the environment;"

Annex 2 to the Agricultural Agreement sets out a basis for exemption from the reduction commitments in respect of domestic support policies. Policies in this category involve expenditures (or revenue foregone) in relation to programmes which provide services or benefits to agriculture or the rural community. They will not involve direct payments to producers or processors. One of the programmes listed is

"(i)   Research including general research, research in connection with environmental programmes, and research programmes related to particular products ...

(v)   Inspection services, including general inspection services and inspection of particular products for health, safety, grading and standardisation purposes ...

(vii)   Infrastructural services, including: ...... infrastructural works associated with environmental programmes."

Part C includes a decision by contracting parties on the application of sanitary and phyto-sanitary measures that where an international standard exists (e.g. Codex Alimentarius), and a government wants to apply a higher level of protection, it can only do so if the higher level is scientifically justified. In the first recital of the preamble the following words are included:

"While affirming that no contracting party should be prevented from adopting or enforcing measures necessary to protect human, animal or plant life or health, subject to the requirement that they are not applied in a manner which would constitute a means of arbitrary or unjustifiable discrimination between countries where the same condition prevail or a disguised restriction on international trade;"

The decision goes on to state the basic rights and obligations, which are, inter alia:

"5.   Contracting parties have the right to take sanitary and phyto-sanitary measures necessary for the protection of human, animal or plant life or health, provided that such measures are not inconsistent with the provisions of this decision.

6.   Contracting parties shall ensure that sanitary and phyto-sanitary measures are applied only to the extent necessary to protect human, animal or plant life or health, are based on scientific principles and are not maintained against available scientific evidence. [....]

8.   Sanitary or phyto-sanitary measures which conform to the relevant provisions of this decision shall be presumed to be in accordance with the obligations of the contracting parties under the provisions of the General Agreement which relate to the use of sanitary or phyto-sanitary measures, in particular the provisions of Article XX(b)."

There is no mention of environmental protection in the Agreement on Safeguards. In clear distinction to the EC Treaty amendments at Maastricht, the GATT Agreement states only under

Article 2 "a contracting party may apply a safeguard measure to a product only if the importing contracting party has determined, pursuant to the provision set out below, that such a product is being imported into its territory in such increased quantities, absolute or relative to domestic production, and under such conditions as to cause or threaten to cause serious injury to the domestic industry that produces like or directly competitive products". There is a note attached to the phrase "contracting party" making clear that a customs union may apply a safeguard measure as a single unit or on behalf of a Member State and that when a customs union applies for safeguard measures as a single unit all the requirements for the determination of serious injury or threat under this agreement shall be based on the conditions existing in the customs union as a whole.

CONCLUSION

The environmental, trade and development nexus is now high on the political agenda. Law-makers worldwide are responding. We know that rhetoric is relatively easy, solutions relatively difficult. Nonetheless, apparent complexity need not deter decision-making and the important process of gathering information and formulating ideas has begun. The recent resumption of vigorous debate of environmental issues within the GATT sends encouraging signals. It demonstrates the single most important factor in the resolution of the conflicts so readily identified between international trade, environmental and development policy - that a consciousness is forming in international political (and legal) society that the problems identified can be solved. Solutions, even proposals for solutions, will not satisfy all commentators; it would be unreasonable to expect such a conformity of view, and a little unhealthy when positive criticism and wide public debate are so necessary for the development and success of any proposed solutions.

The opportunity exists through the UNCED process to collect, order and apply these proposed solutions within that special atmosphere which is formed by self interested and public interested co-operation.

ANNEX

Annotated List of International Agreements and Instruments[*]

CONTENTS

---

* Based on the list of agreements and instruments contained in UNCED document A/CONF.151/PC/77, as revised by the Preparatory Committee at its third session (decision 3/25, annex III, A/46/48, volume II). Following the fourth session of the Committee, agreements and instruments on transboundary freshwaters (previously listed in document A/CONF.151/PC/79) were incorporated in the list. In accordance with decisions 3/25/III and 3/28, the relationship with trade and development instruments, sample bilateral agreements, and the prevention and settlement of environmental disputes were included in the present survey; references to the relevant agreements and instruments are contained in chapters XI to XIII.

A.   GENERAL ENVIRONMENTAL CONCERNS

(1) Declaration of the United Nations Conference on the Human Environment (Stockholm, 16 June 1972)

- Objectives: To lay down common principles to inspire and guide the people of the world in the preservation and enhancement of the human environment.
- Non-mandatory; global. After adoption by the Conference, recorded in UNGA Resolution 2994 (XXVII) of 15 December 1972.
- Related instrument: (a) World Charter for Nature (UNGA Resolution 37/7 of 28 October 1982).
- Texts in ELGP 1, ILM 11:1416, IPE 1:1118; (a) ELGP 5, ILM 22:455, IPE I/C/28-10-82.
- Secretariat: United Nations Environment Programme (UNEP), Environmental Law & Institutions Programme Activity Centre (PAC), P.O. Box 30552, Nairobi, Kenya (fax 254-2-226895, phone 254-2-230800).

(2) Nordic Convention on the Protection of the Environment (Stockholm, 19 February 1974) and related agreement
- Objectives: To protect and improve the environment through co-operation to ensure that activities under the jurisdiction of one Party do not cause damage to the environment of other Parties.
- In force 5 October 1976; regional. Membership restricted to signatory Nordic countries; 4 Parties, no developing countries.
- Related instrument: (a) Nordic Agreement on Co-operation Over National Territorial Boundaries with the Aim of Preventing or Limiting Damage to Man or Property or the Environment in the Event of Accidents (Stockholm, 20 January 1989).
- Texts in UNTS 1092:279, SMT 1:403, ILM 13:591, IEL 974:14, IPE 1:70; (a) IPE I/A/20-01-89.
- Secretariat: Nordic Council of Ministers, Store Strandstraede 18, DK-1255 Copenhagen K, Denmark (fax 45-33-114711, phone 45-33-1924000).

(3) OECD Principles Concerning Transfrontier Pollution (Paris, 14 November 1974) and related instruments

- Objectives: To lay down principles designed to facilitate the development of harmonized environmental policies in OECD member countries with a view to solving transfrontier pollution problems.
- Non-mandatory; regional. Recommendation adopted by the Council of the Organisation for Economic Co-operation and Development (OECD), C(74)224.
- Related instruments: Recommendations on (a) Equal Rights of Access in Relation to Transfrontier Pollution (Paris, 11 May 1976); (b) Implementation of a Regime of Equal Right of Access and Non-Discrimination in Relation to Transfrontier Pollution (Paris, 17 May 1977); (c) Strengthening International Co-operation on Environmental Protection in Transfrontier Regions (Paris, 21 September 1978); (d) Decision on the Exchange of Information Concerning Accidents Capable of Causing Transfrontier Damage (Paris, 8 July 1988).

- Texts in ILM 14:242, IPE 1:316; (a) ILM 15:1218, IPE 18:9235; (b) ILM 16:977, IPE 18:9344; (c) IPE 18:9406; (d) ILM 28:247.
- Secretariat: Organisation for Economic Cooperation and Development (OECD), Environment Directorate, 2 rue André-Pascal, F-75775 Paris, France (fax 33-1-45248500, phone 33-1-45248200).

(4) Convention on the Prohibition of Military or Any Other Hostile Use of Environmental Modification Techniques (Geneva, 18 May 1977)

- Objectives: To prohibit military or other hostile use of such techniques in order to consolidate world peace and trust among nations.
- In force 5 October 1978, global. Membership open; 55 Parties, including 29 developing countries.
- Annex on Consultative Committee of Experts.
- Text in UNTS 1108:151, SMT 1:479, ILM 16:88, IEL 977:37, IPE 15:7905.
- Secretariat: United Nations, Department for Disarmament Affairs, New York, N.Y. 10017, USA (fax 1-212-963 1121, phone 1-212-963 5938).

(5) Protocol I (Relating to the Protection of Victims of International Armed Conflicts) Additional to the 1949 Geneva Conventions (Geneva, 8 June 1977)

- Objectives: To reaffirm and develop the provisions protecting the victims of armed conflicts, including protection of the environment against widespread, long-term and severe damage.
- In force 7 December 1978; global. Membership restricted to member States of the 1949 Red Cross Conventions; 107 Parties, including 81 developing countries.
- Related instruments: (a) Protocol II (Relating to the Protection of Victims of Non-International Armed Conflicts) (Geneva, 8 June 1977, in force 7 December 1978).
- Texts in ILM 16:1391, IPE 15:7909; (a) ILM 16:1442.
- Secretariat: International Committee of the Red Cross (CICR), 19 avenue de la Paix, CH-1202 Geneva, Switzerland (fax 41-22-733 2057, phone 41-22-734 6001).

(6) UNEP Principles of Conduct in the Field of the Environment for the Guidance of States in the Conservation and Harmonious Utilization of Natural Resources Shared by Two or More States (Nairobi, 19 May 1978)

- Objectives: To provide guidance for the conduct of States with respect to the conservation and harmonious utilization of shared natural resources.
- Non-mandatory; global. After adoption by UNEP Governing Council Decision 6/14, recorded in UNGA Resolution 34/168 of 18 December 1979.
- Text in ELGP 2, ILM 17:1097, IPE 18:9351.
- Secretariat: UNEP (see No. 1 above).

(7) European Outline Convention on Transfrontier Co-operation Between Territorial Communities or Authorities (Madrid, 21 May 1980)

- Objectives: To facilitate and foster transfrontier co-operation between territorial communities or authorities of each Contracting Party.

- In force 22 December 1981; regional. Membership restricted to member States of the Council of Europe; 16 Parties, no developing countries.
- Text in SMT 2:93, ILM 20:315, IEL 980:40.
- Secretariat: Council of Europe, Directorate of Environment and Local Authorities, B.P. 431 R6, F-67006 Strasbourg, France, (fax 33-88-412781, phone 33-88-412000).

(8) <u>Convention on Prohibition or Restriction on the Use of Certain Conventional Weapons which may be deemed to be excessively injurious or to have indiscriminate effects</u> (Geneva, 10 October 1980)

- Objectives: To codify and develop the rules of international law applicable in armed conflict, including protection against environmental damage by mines and incendiary weapons.
- In force 2 December 1983; global. Membership open; 31 Parties, including 13 developing countries.
- Related instruments: Annexed Protocols I (Non-detectable Fragments), II (Mines, Booby Traps and Other Devices), III (Incendiary Weapons).
- Texts in ILM 19:1529, IPE 28:520.
- Secretariat: UN Department for Disarmament Affairs (see No. 4 above).

(9) <u>Single European Act</u> (Luxembourg, 17 February 1986, and The Hague, 28 February 1986) amending the 1957 Rome Treaties (establishing the European Coal and Steel Community, the European Economic Community and the European Atomic Energy Community) and related instruments

- Objectives: To revise and consolidate the legal and institutional basis of the European Communities, including their mandate in the field of environmental protection.
- In force 1 July 1987; regional. Membership restricted to EC member States; 12 Parties, no developing countries.
- Related instruments: (a) <u>Fourth ACP-EEC Convention</u> (Lomé IV, 15 December 1989); (b) over 200 environment-related EEC decisions, directives and regulations.
- Texts in ILM 25:506; (a) ILM 29:809, IEL 989:93.
- Secretariat: Commission of the European Communities (EC), 200 rue de la Loi, B-1049 Bruxelles, Belgium (fax 32-2-2350144, phone 32-2-2355990).

(10) <u>UNEP Goals and Principles of Environmental Impact Assessment</u> (Nairobi, 17 June 1987)

- Objectives: To promote procedures for taking into account environmental effects, including transboundary effects, prior to undertaking or authorizing activities.
- Non-mandatory; global. After adoption by UNEP Governing Council Decision 14/25, recorded in UNGA Resolution 42/184 of 11 December 1987.
- Text in ELGP 9, IPE I/D/19-06-87.
- Secretariat: UNEP (see No. 1 above).

(11) <u>Convention on Environmental Impact Assessment in a Transboundary Context</u> (Espoo, 25 February 1991)

- Objectives: To prevent, reduce and control significant adverse transboundary environmental impact from proposed activities, by the establishment of an environmental impact assessment procedure that permits public participation.
- Not yet in force; regional. Membership restricted to ECE member States, the EC, and States having consultative status with ECE.
- Appendices: I. List of activities; II. Content of the environmental impact assessment documentation; III. General criteria to assist in the determination of the environmental significance of activities not listed in appendix I; IV. Inquiry procedure; V. Post-project analysis; VI. Elements for bilateral and multilateral co-operation; VII. Arbitration.
- Text in ILM 30:802.
- Secretariat: United Nations Economic Commission for Europe (UN/ECE), Environment and Human Settlements Division, Palais des Nations, CH-1211 Geneva 10 (fax 41-22-749825, phone 41-22-7310211).

B.   NATURE CONSERVATION AND TERRESTRIAL LIVING RESOURCES

(12) <u>Convention on Nature Protection and Wildlife Preservation in the Western Hemisphere</u> (Washington, 12 October 1940)

- Objectives: To preserve all species and genera of native American fauna and flora from extinction, and to preserve areas of extraordinary beauty, striking geological formations or aesthetic, historic or scientific value.
- In force 1 May 1942; regional. Membership restricted to members of the Organization of American States; 17 Parties, including 16 developing countries.
- Annex: List of protected species.
- Text in UNTS 161:193, SMT 1:64, IEL 940:76, IPE 4:1729.
- Secretariat: Organization of American States (OAS), 17th Street and Constitution Avenue NW., Washington DC 20006, USA (fax 1-202-458 3967, phone 1-202-458 3399).

(13) <u>International Convention for the Protection of Birds</u> (Paris, 18 October 1950)

- Objectives: To protect birds in the wild state, considering that in the interests of science, the protection of nature and the economy of each nation, all birds should as a matter of principle be protected.
- In force 17 January 1963; global. Membership open; 10 Parties, including 2 European developing countries.
- Related instruments: (a) <u>Convention for the Protection of Birds Useful to Agriculture</u> (Paris 19 March 1902, in force 6 December 1905, 15 Parties, no developing countries). (b) <u>Benelux Convention Concerning Hunting and the Protection of Birds</u> (Brussels, 10 June 1970, in force 1 July 1972, as amended on 20 June 1977 3 Parties)
- Text in UNTS 638:185, SMT 1:84, IPE 4:1791, IEL 950:77; (a) IEL 902:22, IPE 4:1615; (b) SMT 1:239.

- Depositary: Ministry of Foreign Affairs, 37 Quai d'Orsay, F-76007 Paris (fax 33-1-47539495, phone 33-1-47535353).

(14) <u>Antarctic Treaty</u> (Washington, 1 December 1959) and related instruments

- Objectives: To ensure that Antarctica is used for peaceful purposes, for international co-operation in scientific research, and does not become the scene or object of international discord.
- In force 23 June 1961; regional, but open to States from outside the region. 40 Parties, including 15 developing countries.
- Related instruments: (a) <u>Convention for the Protection of Antarctic Seals</u> (London, 1 June 1972, in force 11 March 1978); (b) <u>Convention on the Conservation of Antarctic Marine Living Resources</u> (Canberra, 20 May 1980, in force 7 April 1982); (c) <u>Convention on the Regulation of Antarctic Mineral Resource Activities</u> (Wellington, 2 June 1988, not yet in force; (d) <u>Protocol on Environment Protection</u> (Madrid, 4 October 1991, not yet in force).
- Texts in UNTS 402:71, SMT 1:150, IEL 959:91, IPE 1:18; (a) SMT 1:272, ILM 11:251, IEL 972:41, IPE 8:3753; (b) SMT 2:86, ILM 19:841, IEL 980:39, IPE III/A/20-05-80; (c) SMT 2:415, ILM 27:868, IEL 988:42; (d) ILM 30:1461.
- Depositary: United States Department of State, Bureau of Oceans and International Environmental and Scientific Affairs, Washington, D.C. 20520, USA, (fax 202-647-1770); (a) Depositary: Foreign and Commonwealth Office, Polar Regions Section, White Hall, London SW1, United Kingdom (fax 44-71-2702086, phone 44-71-2702716); (b) Secretariat: Commission for the Conservation of Antarctic Marine Living Resources (CCAMLR), 25 Old Wharf, Hobart, Tasmania 7000, Australia (fax 2-232714, phone 2-310366).

(15) <u>African Convention on the Conservation of Nature and Natural Resources</u> (Algiers, 15 September 1968)

- Objectives: To encourage individual and joint action by African States for the conservation, utilization and development of soil, water, flora and fauna for the present and future welfare of mankind.
- In force 16 June 1969; regional. Membership restricted to African States; 30 Parties, all developing countries.
- Annex: List of protected species.
- Text in UNTS 1001:3, SMT 1:207, IEL 968:68, IPE 5:2037.
- Secretariat: Organization of African Unity (OAU), ESCAS Department, P.O. Box 3243, Addis Ababa, Ethiopia (fax 251-1-512622, phone 251-1-517700).

(16) <u>Convention on Wetlands of International Importance especially as Waterfowl Habitat</u> (Ramsar, 2 February 1971) as amended

- Objectives: To stem the progressive encroachment on and loss of wetlands now and in the future, recognizing the fundamental ecological functions of wetlands and their economic, cultural, scientific and recreational value.
- In force 21 December 1975; global. Membership open; 64 Parties, including 35 developing countries.

- Related instruments: Amendment Protocols (Paris, 3 December 1982, in force 1 October 1986; and 28 May 1987, not yet in force); List of Wetlands of International Importance.
- Texts in UNTS 996:245, SMT 1:246, ILM 11:969, IEL 971:09, IPE 5:2161, 1983 amendment ILM 22:698, 1987 amendment IEL 971:09/13.
- Secretariat: World Conservation Union, (IUCN) Ramsar Bureau, avenue du Mont-Blanc, CH-1196 Gland, Switzerland (fax 41-22-648375, phone 41-22-649114).

(17) <u>Convention Concerning the Protection of the World Cultural and Natural Heritage</u> (Paris, 23 November 1972)

- Objectives: To establish an effective system of collective protection of the cultural and natural heritage of outstanding universal value, organized on a permanent basis and in accordance with modern scientific methods.
- In force 17 December 1975; global. Membership open; 123 Parties, including 95 developing countries.
- Related instrument: World Heritage List.
- Text in UNTS 1037:151, SMT 1:276, ILM 11:1358, IEL 972:86, IPE 14:7238.
- Secretariat: United Nations Educational, Scientific and Cultural Organization (UNESCO), World Heritage Centre, 7 place de Fontenoy, F-75700 Paris, France (fax 33-1-45671690, phone 33-1-45681000).

(18) <u>Convention on International Trade in Endangered Species of Wild Fauna and Flora</u> (Washington, 3 March 1973) as amended

- Objectives: To protect certain endangered species from over-exploitation by means of a system of import/export permits.
- In force 1 July 1975; global. Membership open; 113 Parties, including 85 developing countries.
- Related instruments: Amendment Protocols (a) Bonn, 27 June 1979, in force 13 April 1987; (b) Gaborone, 30 April 1983, not yet in force.
- Texts in UNTS 983:243, SMT 1:289, ILM 12:1085, IEL 973:18; (a) IPE 22:389.
- Secretariat: UNEP/CITES, 6 rue de Maupas, CH-1000 Lausanne 9, Switzerland (fax 41-21-200084, phone 41-21-200081).

(19) <u>Agreement on Conservation of Polar Bears</u> (Oslo, 15 November 1973)

- Objectives: To achieve protection of the polar bear as a significant resource of the Arctic region through further conservation and management measures.
- In force 26 May 1976; regional. Membership restricted to the original Contracting Parties (States of the Arctic region); 6 Parties, no developing countries.
- Text in SMT 1:401, ILM 13:13, IEL 973:85, IPE 5:2276.
- Secretariat: Ministry for the Environment, P.O. Box 8013 DEP, N-0030 Oslo 1, Norway (fax 47-2-349561, phone 47-2-345968).

(20) <u>Convention on Conservation of Nature in the South Pacific</u> (Apia, 12 June 1976)

- Objectives: To take action for the conservation, utilization and development of the natural resources of the South Pacific region through careful planning and management for the benefit of present and future generations.
- In force 28 June 1990; regional. Membership restricted to member States of the South Pacific Commission; 5 Parties, including 3 developing countries.
- Texts in SMT 1:463, IEL 976:45, IPE 20:10.359.
- Secretariat: South Pacific Regional Environment Programme (SPREP), P.O. Box D5, Noumea Cedex, New Caledonia (fax 687-263818, phone 687-262000).

(21) <u>Treaty for Amazonian Co-operation</u> (Brasilia, 3 July 1978)

- Objectives: To promote the harmonious development of the Amazon region and permit equitable distribution of the benefits of such development among the contracting Parties.
- In force 2 February 1980; regional. Membership restricted to the original Contracting Parties (States of the Amazon region); 8 Parties, all developing countries.
- Text in SMT 1:496, ILM 17:1045, IEL 978:49, IPE 18:9017.
- Depositary: Ministry of External Relations, Department of the Americas, Palacio Itamaraty, 70170 Brasilia, DF (fax 55-61-2237362, phone 55-61-2116864).

(22) <u>Convention on the Conservation of Migratory Species of Wild Animals</u> (Bonn, 23 June 1979)
- Objectives: To protect those species of wild animals that migrate across or outside national boundaries.
- In force 1 November 1983; global. Membership open; 39 Parties, including 20 developing countries.
- Related instrument: (a) <u>Agreement on the Conservation of Seals in the Wadden Sea</u> (Bonn, 17 November 1988, in force 10 October 1991). (b) Agreement on Bats in Europe (Geneva, 25 November 1991).
- Text in SMT 1:500, ILM 19:15, IEL 979:55, IPE 23:1; (a) IEL 990:77, IPE III/A/17-11-88.
- Secretariat: UNEP/CMS, P.O. Box 201448, D-5300 Bonn 2, Germany, (fax 49-228-373237, phone 49-228-302152).

(23) <u>Convention on the Conservation of European Wildlife and Natural Habitats</u> (Berne, 19 September 1979)

- Objectives: To conserve wild fauna and flora and their natural habitats, especially those species and habitats whose conservation requires the co-operation of several States, and to promote such co-operation.
- In force 1 June 1982; regional. Membership restricted to member States of the Council of Europe and the EEC, others upon invitation; 25 Parties, including 4 developing countries.
Related instruments: (a) <u>Benelux Convention on Nature Conservation and Landscape Protection</u> (Brussels, 8 June 1982, in force 10 October 1963, 3 Parties).
- Text in SMT 1:509, IEL 979:70, IPE 23:40; (a) SMT 2:163.

- Secretariat: Council of Europe, Environment Conservation and Management Division, B.P. 431 R6, F-67006 Strasbourg, France (fax 33-88-412784, phone 33-88-412259).

(24) <u>Convention for the Conservation and Management of the Vicuña</u> (Lima, 20 December 1979)

- Objectives: To continue to promote the conservation and management of the Vicuña.
- In force 19 March 1982; regional. Membership restricted to (Andean) range States of the Vicuña; 4 Parties, all developing countries.
- Text in SMT 2:74, IEL 979:94.
- Depositary: Ministry for Foreign Affairs, Calle Azangaro 350, Lima 1, Peru (fax 51-14-323318, phone 51-14-270995).

(25) <u>International Tropical Timber Agreement</u> (Geneva, 18 November 1983)

- Objectives: To provide an effective framework for co-operation and consultation between countries producing and consuming tropical timber, to promote the expansion and diversification of international trade in tropical timber and the improvement of structural conditions in the tropical timber market, to promote and support research and development with a view to improving forest management and wood utilization, and to encourage the development of national policies aimed at sustainable utilization and conservation of tropical forests and their genetic resources, and at maintaining the ecological balance in the regions concerned.
- In force 1 April 1985; global. Membership open to any State which produces or consumes tropical timber; 48 Parties, including 25 developing countries.
- Text in SMT 2:271, IEL 983:85.
- Secretariat: International Tropical Timber Organization (ITTO), Sangyo Boeki Centre, Bldg. 2, Yamashita-cho Naka-ku, Yokohama 231, Japan (fax 81-45-223 1111, phone 81-45-223 1110).

(26) <u>FAO International Undertaking on Plant Genetic Resources</u> (Rome, 23 November 1983) as supplemented

- Objectives: To ensure that plant genetic resorces are preserved and are made as widely available as possible for the purposes of plant breeding, for the benefit of present and future generations.
- Non-mandatory; global. Adopted by Resolution 8/83 of the 22nd FAO Conference.
- Secretariat: Food and Agriculture Organization of the United Nations (FAO), Via delle Terme di Caracalla, 00100 Rome, Italy (fax 39-6-5797 4408, phone 39-6-57971).

(27) <u>ASEAN Agreement on the Conservation of Nature and Natural Resources</u> (Kuala Lumpur, 9 July 1985)

- Objectives: To promote joint and individual State action for the conservation and management of the natural resources of the ASEAN Region.

- Not yet in force; regional. Membership restricted to the 6 member States of the Association of South-East Asian States (ASEAN).
- Text in SMT 2:343, IEL 985:51, IPE I/A/09-07-85.
- Depositary: Ministry of Foreign Affairs, Jallan Wesma Putra 50602, Kuala Lumpur, Malaysia (fax 603-242551, phone 603-2488088).

C. ATMOSPHERE AND OUTER SPACE

(28) Regulations concerning gaseous pollutant emissions from motor vehicles, pursuant to the Agreement Concerning the Adoption of Uniform Conditions of Approval and Reciprocal Recognition of Approval for Motor Vehicle Equipment and Parts (Geneva, 20 March 1958) as amended and supplemented

- Objectives: To define uniform conditions for licensing of motor vehicles and parts in the European region, including the standardization of environmental specifications for vehicle construction.
- In force 20 June 1959; regional. Membership restricted to ECE member States and States having consultative status with ECE; 21 member States, including 2 developing countries.
- Related instruments: Regulations concerning emissions (a) from gasoline engines (Nos. 15/1970 and 833/1989); (b) from motorcycles and mopeds (Nos. 40/1979 and 47/1981); (c) from diesel engines (No. 49/1982 - 1990).
- Texts in UNTS 335:211, 609:290, IEL 958:22, IPE 15:7401; (a) UNTS 740:364, 1078:351; (b) UNTS 1144:308, 1255:158; (c) E/ECE/324/Rev.1/Add.48/Rev.1.
- Secretariat: UN Economic Commission for Europe (UN/ECE), Transport Division, Palais des Nations, CH-1211 Geneva 10 (fax 41-22-733 5435, phone 41-22-731 0211).

(29) Treaty on Principles Governing the Activities of States in the Exploration and Use of Outer Space Including the Moon and Other Celestial Bodies (27 January 1967) and related instruments

- Objectives: To establish an international legal regime for the exploration and use of outer space.
- In force 10 October 1967; global. Membership open; 91 Parties, including 61 developing countries.
- Related instruments: (a) Agreement on the Rescue of Astronauts, the Return of Astronauts and the Return of Objects Launched into Outer Space (22 April 1968, in force 3 December 1968); (b) Convention on International Liability for Damage Caused by Space Objects (29 March 1972, in force 1 September 1972); (c) Agreement Governing the Activities of States on the Moon and Other Celestial Bodies (18 December 1979, in force 11 July 1984); (d) Principles Relating to Remote Sensing of the Earth from Space (after adoption by the Committee, endorsed by U.N. General Assembly Resolution 41/65 of 3 December 1986).
- Texts in UNTS 610:205, ILM 6:386, IEL 967:07, IPE 1:30; (a) UNTS 672:119, ILM 7:151, IEL 968:31, IPE 17:8577; (b) IEL 972:24, IPE 17:8629; (c) ILM 18:1434, IEL 979:92, IPE 29:267.

- Secretariat: United Nations, Outer Space Affairs Division, New York, N.Y. 10017, USA (fax 1-212-963-7998, phone 1-212-963-6051).

(30) <u>Annex 16, vol. II (Environmental Protection: Aircraft Engine Emissions) to the 1944 Chicago Convention on International Civil Aviation</u> (Montreal, 30 June 1981) as amended

- Objectives: To standardize the required emissions limits for aircraft engine emissions, by way of uniform certification procedures.
- In force 18 February 1982 (amendment applicable 17 November 1988); global. Membership restricted to ICAO member States; 164 Parties, including 132 developing countries.
- Related instruments: Annex 16, vol. I (Environmental Protection: Aircraft Noise), 2nd ed. 1988.
- Texts in ICAO International Standards and Recommended Practices; 1944 Convention in UNTS 15:295.
- Secretariat: International Civil Aviation Organization (ICAO), 1000 Sherbrooke Street West, Montreal, Quebec H3A 2R2, Canada (fax 1-514-288-4772, phone 1-514-286-6270).

(31) <u>Convention on Long-range Transboundary Air Pollution</u> (Geneva, 13 November 1979) and related protocols

- Objectives: To protect man and his environment against air pollution and to endeavour to limit and, as far as possible, gradually reduce and prevent air pollution, including long-range transboundary air pollution.
- In force 16 March 1983; regional. Membership restricted to ECE member States, the EC and States having consultative status with ECE; 33 Parties, including 4 developing countries.
- Related instruments: (a) <u>Protocol on Long-term Financing of the Co-operative Programme for Monitoring and Evaluation of the Long-range Transmission of Air Pollutants in Europe</u>, (Geneva, 28 September 1984, in force 28 January 1988); (b) <u>Protocol on the Reduction of Sulphur Emissions or Their Transboundary Fluxes by at least 30 Per Cent</u> (Helsinki, 8 July 1985, in force 2 September 1987); (c) <u>Protocol Concerning the Control of Emissions of Nitrogen Oxides or Their Transboundary Fluxes</u> (Sofia, 1 November 1988, in force 14 February 1991); (d) <u>Protocol Concerning the Control of Emissions of Volatile Organic Compounds or Their Transboundary Fluxes</u> (Geneva, 18 November 1991, not yet in force).
- Texts in SMT 1:519, ILM 18:1442, IEL 979:84, IPE 28:341; (a) SMT 2:285, IEL 979:84; (b) SMT 2:288, ILM 27:707, IEL 979:84; (c) SMT 2:290, ILM 28:214, IEL 979:84.
- Secretariat: UN/ECE (see No. 11 above).

(32) <u>UNEP Provisions for Co-operation Between States on Weather Modification</u> (Nairobi, 29 April 1980)

- Objectives: To ensure mutual notification and consultation in the conduct of weather modification activities likely to have transboundary effects.

- Non-mandatory; global. Recommended by UNEP Governing Council Decision 8/7/A, and circulated to governments in June 1980.
- Related instruments: (a) Draft WMO/UNEP Guidelines for National Legislation concerning Weather Modification (1979).
- Text in ELGP 3; (a) WMO/UNEP/WG.26/6.
- Secretariat: UNEP (see No. 1 above).

(33) <u>Vienna Convention for the Protection of the Ozone Layer</u> (Vienna, 22 March 1985) and Montreal Protocol, 1987 as amended

- Objectives: To protect human health and the environment against adverse effects resulting from modifications of the ozone layer.
- In force 22 September 1988; global. Membership open; 81 Parties, including 49 developing countries.
- Related instruments: (a) <u>Montreal Protocol on Substances That Deplete the Ozone Layer</u> and amendments (Montreal, 16 September 1987, in force 1 January 1989); (b) <u>Amendment to the Montreal Protocol on Substances That Deplete the Ozone Layer</u> (London, 29 June 1990, in force 10 August 1992).
- Texts in SMT 2:301, ILM 26:1529, IEL 985:22; (a) SMT 2:309, ILM 26:1541, IEL 985:22/A; (b) SMT 2:316.
- Secretariat: UNEP Ozone Secretariat, P.O. Box 330552, Nairobi, Kenya (fax 254-2-521930, phone 254-2-521928); Secretariat of Interim Multilateral Ozone Fund, Montreal Trust Bldg., 1800 McGill College Ave., Montreal H3A 3J6, Canada (fax 1-514-2820068, phone 1-514-2821122).

D.   GLOBAL MARINE ENVIRONMENT

(34) <u>International Convention Relating to Intervention on the High Seas in Case of Oil Pollution Casualties</u> (Brussels, 29 November 1969) and related protocol

- Objectives: To enable countries to take action on the high seas in case of a maritime casualty resulting in danger of oil pollution of sea and coastlines.
- In force 6 May 1975; global. Membership open; 57 Parties, including 33 developing countries.
- Related instrument: (a) <u>Protocol Relating to Intervention on the High Seas in Cases of Marine Pollution by Substances Other Than Oil</u> (London, 2 November 1973, in force 30 March 1983) as amended.
- Texts in UNTS 970:211, SMT 1:230, ILM 9:25, IEL 969:89, IPE 1:460; (a) SMT 1:400, ILM 13:605, IEL 973:83, IPE 1:470.
- Secretariat: International Maritime Organization (IMO), 4, Albert-Embankment, London SE1 7SR (fax 44-71-587 3210, phone 44-71-7357611).

(35) <u>Convention on the Prevention of Marine Pollution by Dumping of Wastes and Other Matter</u> (London, 29 December 1972) as amended

- Objectives: To control pollution of the sea by dumping, and to encourage regional agreements supplementary to the Convention.

- In force 30 September 1975; global. Membership open; 67 Parties, including 38 developing countries.
- Text in UNTS 1046:120, SMT 1:283, ILM 11:1294, IEL 972:96, IPE 2:537, 1978 amendment IPE II/A/12-10-78, 1980 amendment IPE II/A/24-09-80, 1989 amendment IEL 972:12/C.
- Secretariat: IMO (see No. 34 above).

(36) <u>International Convention for the Prevention of Pollution from Ships</u> (London, 2 November 1973) as amended

- Objectives: To preserve the marine environment by achieving the complete elimination of international pollution by oil and other harmful substances and the minimization of accidental discharge of such substance.
- In force 2 October 1983; global. Membership open; 70 Parties, including 41 developing countries.
- Related instruments (a) <u>Protocol of 1978 Relating to the International Convention for the Prevention of Pollution From Ships</u> (London, 17 February 1978, in force 2 October 1983).
- Texts in SMT 1:320, ILM 12:1319, IEL 973:84, IPE 2:552; (a) ILM 17:546, IEL 973:84/A, IPE 19:9451.
- Secretariat: IMO (see No. 34 above).

(37) <u>UNEP Guidelines Concerning the Environment Related to Offshore Mining and Drilling within the Limits of National Jurisdiction</u> (Nairobi, 31 May 1982)

- Objectives: To lay down basic standards for incorporation in national and regional rules, regulations, practices and procedures which will ensure that environmental considerations are effectively protected in national and international systems of authorization, environmental assessment, environmental monitoring, consideration of transfrontier impacts, safety measures, contingency planning, liability and compensation.
- Non-mandatory; global. After endorsement by UNEP Governing Council Decision 10/14 (VI), recorded by UN General Assembly Resolution 37/217 of 20 December 1982.
- Text in IPE II/D/31-05-82.
- Secretariat: UNEP (see No. 1 above).

(38) <u>United Nations Convention on the Law of the Sea</u> (Montego Bay, 10 December 1982)
- Objectives: To set up a comprehensive new legal regime for the sea and oceans, including protection and preservation of the marine environment.
- Not yet in force; global. Membership open.
- Text in SMT 2:165, ILM 21:1261, IEL 982:92, IPE II/A/10-12-82.
- Secretariat: United Nations Office of Legal Affairs, Division for Ocean Affairs and the Law of the Sea, New York, NY 10017, USA (fax 1-212-963 5847, phone 1-212-963 3990).

(39) <u>UNEP Montreal Guidelines for the Protection of the Marine Environment against Pollution from Land-based Sources</u> (Montreal, 19 April 1985)

- Objectives: To assist governments in the process of developing appropriate bilateral, regional and multilateral agreements and national legislation for the protection of the marine environment against pollution from land-based sources.
- Non-mandatory; global. After adoption by a UNEP Working Group of Experts, endorsed by UNEP Governing Council Decision 13/18 (II) of 24 May 1985.
- Text in ELGP 7, IPE II/D/ 24-05-85.
- Secretariat: UNEP Oceans and Coastal Areas/Programme Activity Centre (OCA-PAC), P.O.Box 30552, Nairobi, Kenya (fax 254-2-230127, phone 254-2-230800).

(40) <u>International Convention on Salvage</u> (London, 28 April 1989)

- Objectives: To provide for uniform international rules regarding salvage operation in the light of the need for timely operations and to protect the environment.
- Not yet in force; global. Membership open.
- Text in IEL 989:32.
- Secretariat: IMO (see No. 34 above).

(41) <u>International Convention on Oil Pollution Preparedness, Response and Co-operation</u> (London, 29 November 1990)

- Objectives: To prevent marine pollution by oil, to advance the adoption of adequate response measures in the event that oil pollution does occur, and to provide for mutual assistance and co-operation between States for these aims.
- Not yet in force; global. Membership open.
- Text in ILM 30:735.
- Secretariat: IMO (see No. 34 above).

E.   REGIONAL MARINE ENVIRONMENT

(42) <u>Nordic Agreement concerning Co-operation in Measures to Deal with Pollution of the Sea by Oil</u> (Copenhagen, 16 September 1971)

- Objectives: To ensure co-operation in dealing with any significant pollution of the sea by oil which threatens the coasts and related interests of one of the Contracting States.
- In force 16 October 1971; regional. Membership restricted to signatories; 4 Parties, no developing countries.
- Text in IEL 971:69, IPE 2:502.
- Secretariat: Ministry of the Environment, Agency for Environmental Protection, 29 Strandgade, DK-1401 Copenhagen, Denmark (fax 45-31-572449, phone 45-31-578310).

(43) <u>Convention for the Prevention of Marine Pollution by Dumping from Ships and Aircraft</u> (Oslo, 15 February 1972) as amended

- Objectives: To control the dumping of harmful substances from ships and aircraft in the sea.

- In force 7 April 1974; regional. Membership restricted to signatories (European States as specified and EC), others upon invitation; 13 Parties, no developing countries.
- Text in UNTS 932:3, SMT 1:266, ILM 11:262, IEL 972:12, IPE 2:530, 1983 amendment IPE II/A/02-0-83.
- Secretariat: Oslo/Paris Commission, New Court, 48 Carey Street, London WC28 2JE (fax 44-71-817427, phone 44-71-2429927).

(44) Convention on the Protection of the Marine Environment of the Baltic Sea Area (Helsinki, 22 March 1974) as amended

- Objectives: To protect and enhance the marine environment of the Baltic Sea area by means of regional co-operation.
- In force 3 May 1980; regional. Membership restricted to the Baltic Sea states, others upon invitation; 6 Parties, no developing countries.
- Text in SMT 1:405, ILM 13:546, IEL 974:23, IPE 2:733, 1987 amendment IPE II/A/27-02-87, 1989 amendment IPE II/A/17-02-89.
- Secretariat: Helsinki Commission (HELCOM), Mannerheimintie 12A, SF-00100 Helsinki, Finland (fax 35-80-644577, phone 35-80-602366).

(45) Convention on the Prevention of Marine Pollution from Land-based Sources (Paris, 4 June 1974) as amended

- Objectives: The Convention forms part of a comprehensive set of progressive and coherent measures to protect the marine environment from pollution.
- In force 6 May 1978; regional. Membership restricted to signatories (European States as specified and EC), others upon invitation; 13 Parties, no developing countries.
- Related instruments: (a) Amending Protocol 1986.
- Texts in SMT 1:430, ILM 13:352, IEL 974:43, IPE 2:748; (a) IEL 974:43/A, IPE II/A/26-03-86.
- Secretariat: Oslo/Paris Commission (see No. 43 above).

(46) Convention for the Protection of the Mediterranean Sea against Pollution (Barcelona, 16 February 1976) and related protocols

- Objectives: In the light of the special characteristics and vulnerability of the Mediterranean, to achieve international co-operation for a co-ordinated and comprehensive approach to the protection and enhancement of the marine environment in the Mediterranean area.
- In force 12 February 1978; regional. Membership restricted to States invited to the 1976 Barcelona Conference, any State entitled to sign any of the protocols, the EC and other regional economic organizations at least one member of which is a coastal State of the Mediterranean Sea Area. 19 Parties, including 12 developing countries.
- Related instruments (a) Protocol for the Prevention of Pollution of the Mediterranean Sea by Dumping from Ships and Aircraft (Barcelona, 16 February 1976, in force 12 February 1978); (b) Protocol Concerning Co-operation in Combating Pollution of the Mediterranean Sea by Oil and Other Harmful Substances

in Cases of Emergency (Barcelona, 16 February 1976, in force 12 February 1978);
(c) Protocol for the Protection of the Mediterranean Sea Against Pollution from Land-
based Sources (Athens, 17 May 1980, in force 17 June 1983); (d) Protocol
Concerning Mediterranean Specially Protected Areas (Geneva, 3 April 1982, in force
23 March 1986).
- Texts in SMT 1:448, ILM 15:290, IEL 976:13, IPE 19:9497; (a) SMT 1:454, ILM
15:300, IEL 976:14, IPE 19:9515; (b) SMT 1:457, ILM 16:306, IEL 976:15, IPE
19:9506; (c) SMT 2:81, ILM 19:869, IEL 980:37, IPE II/A/17-05-80; (d) SMT
2:154, IEL 982:26.
- Secretariat: UNEP, Co-ordinating Unit for the Mediterranean Action Plan, P.O.
Box 18019, GR-116 10 Athens, Greece, (fax 30-1-7291160, phone 30-1-72445369).

(47) Kuwait Regional Convention for Co-operation on the Protection of the Marine
Environment from Pollution (Kuwait, 24 April 1978) and related protocols

- Objectives: To prevent, abate and combat pollution of the marine environment in
the region.
- In force 30 June 1979; regional. Membership restricted to States invited to the 1978
Kuwait Conference (Gulf coastal States); 8 Parties, all developing countries.
- Related instruments (a) Protocol Concerning Regional Co-operation in Combating
Pollution by Oil and Other Harmful Substances in Cases of Emergency (Kuwait, 24
April 1978, in force 17 June 1979); (b) Protocol Concerning Marine Pollution
Resulting from Exploration and Exploitation of the Continental Shelf (29 March 1989,
in force 17 February 1990); (c) Protocol for the Protection of the Marine
Environment against Pollution from Land-Based Sources (21 February 1990).
- Texts in UNTS 1140:133, SMT 1:486, ILM 17:511, IEL 978:31, IPE 19:9551; (a)
SMT 1:492, ILM 17:526, IEL 978:32, IPE 19:9551.
- Secretariat: Regional Organization for the Protection of the Marine Environment
(ROPME), P.O. Box 26388, 13124 Safat, Kuwait (fax 965-5324172, phone 965-
5312140/3).

(48) Convention for Co-operation in the Protection and Development of the Marine and
Coastal Environment of the West and Central African Region (Abidjan, 23 March 1981) and
related protocol

- Objectives: To protect the marine environment, coastal zones and related internal
waters falling within the jurisdiction of the States of the West and Central African
region.
- In force 5 August 1984; regional. Membership restricted to African States, others
after approval of three quarters of the initial Parties (coastal and island States from
Mauritania to Namibia inclusive); 10 Parties, all developing countries.
- Related instrument: (a) Protocol Concerning Co-operation in Combating Pollution
in Cases of Emergency (Abidjan, 23 March 1981, in force 5 August 1984).
- Texts in SMT 2:118, ILM 20:756, IEL 981:23, IPE II/A/23-03-81; (a) SMT 2:123,
IEL 981:24, IPE II/A/23-03-81.a.
- Secretariat: UNEP (see No. 39 above).

(49) <u>Convention for the Protection of the Marine Environment and Coastal Area of the South-East Pacific</u> (Lima, 12 November 1981) and related protocols

> - Objectives: To protect the marine environment and coastal zones of the south-east Pacific within the 200-mile area of maritime sovereignty and jurisdiction of the parties, and beyond that area, the high seas up to a distance within which pollution of the high seas may affect that area.
> - In force 19 May 1986; regional. Membership restricted to States bordering the South-East Pacific; 5 Parties, all developing countries.
> - Related instruments (a) <u>Agreement on Regional Co-operation in Combating Pollution of the South-East Pacific by Hydrocarbons and Other Harmful Substances in Cases of Emergency</u> (Lima, 12 November 1981, in force 14 July 1986); (b) <u>Supplementary Protocol to the Agreement on Regional Co-operation in Combating Pollution of the South-East Pacific by Oil and Other Harmful Substances in Cases of Emergency</u> (Quito, 22 July 1983, in force 20 May 1987); (c) <u>Protocol for the Protection of the South-East Pacific Against Pollution from Land-Based Sources</u> (Quito, 23 July 1983, in force 23 September 1986); (d) <u>Protocol for the Conservation and Management of Protected Marine and Coastal Areas of the South-East Pacific</u> (Paipa, 21 September 1989, not yet in force); (e) <u>Protocol for the Protection of the South-East Pacific Against Radioactive Contamination</u> (Paipa, 21 September 1989, not yet in force)
> - Texts in SMT 2:130, IEL 981:84, IPE II/A/12-11-81; (a) SMT 2:134, IEL 981:85, IPE II/A/12-11-81.a; (b) SMT 2:137, IEL 983:55; (c) SMT 2:139, IEL 983:54, IPE II/A/22-07-83.a,b; (d) IEL 989:71; (e) IEL 989:70.
> - Secretariat: Permanent Commission of the South Pacific (CPPS), Casilla 16638, Agencia 6400-9, Santiago 9, Chile (fax 562-6951100, phone 562-726652).

(50) <u>Memorandum of Understanding on Port State Control in Implementing Agreements on Maritime Safety and Protection of the Marine Environment</u> (Paris, 26 January 1982) as amended

> - Objectives: To improve and harmonize the system of port State control and strengthen co-operation and the exchange of information for the purpose of ensuring that effective action is taken by port States to prevent the operation of substandard ships and to avoid distorting competition between ports.
> - In force 1 July 1982; regional. Membership restricted to the (European) signatories, others upon their consent; 15 Parties, no developing countries.
> - Text in ILM 21:1, IPE II/A/26-01-82, 1988 amendment IPE II/A/10-02-88.
> - Secretariat: Ministry of Transport, Public Works and Water Management, Plesmanweg 1-6, P.O. Box 20901, 2597JG The Hague, Netherlands (fax 31-70-3517895, phone 31-70-3955555).

(51) <u>Regional Convention for the Conservation of the Red Sea and Gulf of Aden Environment</u> (Jeddah, 14 February 1982) and related protocol

> - Objectives: To ensure rational human use of living and non-living marine and coastal resources in a manner ensuring optimum benefit for the present generation, at the same time maintaining the potential of that environment to satisfy the needs and aspiration of future generations.

- In force 20 August 1985; regional. Membership restricted to members of the Arab League; 7 Parties, all developing countries.
- Related instruments (a) <u>Protocol Concerning Regional Co-operation in Combating Pollution by Oil and Other Harmful Substances In Cases of Emergency</u> (Jeddah, 14 February 1982, in force 20 August 1985)
- Texts in SMT 2:144, ILM 22:219, IEL 982:13, IPE II/A/14-02-82; (a) SMT 2:150, IEL 982:14, IPE II/A/14-02-82.a.
- Secretariat: Red Sea and Gulf of Aden Environment Programme (PERSGA), P.O.Box 1358, Jeddah 21431, Saudi Arabia (fax 966-2-6511424, phone 966-2-6514472).

(52) <u>Convention for the Protection and Development of the Marine Environment of the Wider Caribbean Region</u> (Cartagena, 24 March 1983) and related protocols

- Objectives: To protect and manage the marine environment and coastal areas of the Wider Caribbean region.
- In force 11 October 1986; regional. Membership restricted to States and regional economic integration organizations invited to the 1983 Cartagena Conference, others upon approval of three-fourths of the Parties; 19 Parties, including 15 developing countries.
- Related instruments (a) <u>Protocol Concerning Co-operation in Combating Oil Spills in the Wider Caribbean Region</u> (Cartagena, 24 March 1983, in force 11 October 1986); (b) <u>Protocol Concerning Specially Protected Areas and Wildlife to the Convention for the Protection and Development of the Marine Environment of the Wider Caribbean Region</u> (Kingston, 18 January 1990, not yet in force).
- Texts in SMT 2:258, IEL 983:23, ILM 22:221, IPE II/A/24-03-83.a; (a) SMT 2:265, IEL 983:24, IPE II/A/24-03-83.b; (b) IEL 990:85.
- Secretariat: UNEP, Regional Coordinating Unit for the Caribbean Environment Programme (CAR/RCU), 14-20 Port Royal Street, Kingston, Jamaica (fax 1-809-9229292, phone 1-809-9229267).

(53) <u>Agreement for Co-operation in Dealing with Pollution of the North Sea by Oil and Other Harmful Substances</u> (Bonn, 13 September 1983)

- Objectives: To ensure co-operation between the coastal States in providing manpower supplies, equipment and scientific advice at short notice to deal with discharges of oil or other harmful substances in the North Sea.
- In force 1 September 1989; regional. Membership restricted to States invited to the 1983 Bonn Conference of Plenipotentiaries and the EC, others upon unanimous invitation; 9 Parties, no developing countries.
- Text in SMT 2:268, IEL 983:68, IPE II/A/13-09-83.
- Secretariat: Oslo/Paris Commission (see No. 43 above).

(54) <u>Convention for the Protection, Management and Development of the Marine and Coastal Environment of the Eastern African Region</u> (Nairobi, 21 June 1985) and related protocols

- Objectives: To protect and manage the marine environment and coastal areas of the Eastern Africa region.

- Not yet in force; regional. Membership restricted to States and regional economic integration organisations invited to the 1982 Nairobi Conference, others upon prior approval of three-fourths of the Parties.
- Related instruments (a) <u>Protocol Concerning Protected Areas and Wild Fauna and Flora in the Eastern African Region</u> (Nairobi, 21 June 1985, not yet in force); (b) <u>Protocol Concerning Co-operation in Combating Marine Pollution in Cases of Emergency in the Eastern African Region</u> (Nairobi, 21 June 1985, not yet in force).
- Texts in SMT 2:324, IEL 985:46, IPE II/A/21-06-85.a; (a) SMT 2:331, IEL 985:47, IPE II/A/21-06-85.b; (b) SMT 2:337, IEL 985:48, IPE II/A/21-06-85.c.
- Secretariat: UNEP (see No. 39 above).

(55) <u>Convention for the Protection of the Natural Resources and Environment of the South Pacific Region</u> (Noumea, 24 November 1986) and related protocols

- Objectives: To protect and manage the natural resources and environment of the South Pacific region.
- In force 18 August 1990; regional. Membership restricted to States invited to participate in the 1986 Noumea Conference, other States after prior approval by three-quarters of the Parties; 10 Parties, all developing countries.
- Related instruments (a) <u>Protocol for the Prevention of Pollution of the South Pacific Region by Dumping</u> (Noumea, 25 November 1986, in force 18 August 1990); (b) <u>Protocol Concerning Co-operation in Combating Pollution Emergencies in the South Pacific Region</u> (Noumea, 25 November 1986, in force 18 August 1990).
- Texts in SMT 2:372, ILM 26:38, IEL 986:87, IPE II/A/24-11-86; (a) SMT 2:381, IEL 986:87/A, IPE II/A/24-11-86.b; (b) SMT 2:386, IEL 986:87/B, IPE II/A/24-11-86.a.
- Secretariat: SPREP (see No. 20 above).

(56) <u>Agreement on Co-operation for Combating Pollution in the Northeast Atlantic</u> (Lisbon, 17 October 1990)

- Objectives: To protect the coastal regions of the Northeast Atlantic against pollution by hydrocarbons and other noxious substances; in particular, the agreement aims at the provision of rapid response measures in case of accidents to ships and platforms resulting in such pollution.
- Not yet in force; regional. Membership restricted to the 5 signatories and other States unanimously invited by the Parties.
- Text in ILM 30:1231.
- Depositary: Ministry of Foreign Affairs, Largo do Rilvas, Lisbon, Portugal (fax 35-11-671518, phone 35-11-3965041).

F.   MARINE LIVING RESOURCES

(57) <u>International Convention for the Regulation of Whaling</u> (Washington, 2 December 1946) as amended

- Objectives: To protect all species of whales from overfishing and safeguard for future generations the great natural resources represented by whale stocks; to establish

a system of international regulation for the whale fisheries to ensure proper conservation and development of whale stocks.
- In force 10 November 1948; global. Membership open; 37 Parties, including 18 developing countries.
- Text in UNTS 161:72, SMT 1:67, IEL 946:89, IPE 7:3539, 1956 amendment UNTS 338:366, IPE 7:3539.
- Secretariat: International Whaling Commission, Station Road, Histon, Cambridge CB4 4NP, United Kingdom (fax 44-223-232876, phone 44-223-233971).

(58) Agreement for the Establishment of the Indo-Pacific Fisheries Commission (Baguio, 26 February 1948) as amended

- Objectives: To promote the full and proper utilization of living aquatic resources by the development and management of fishing and culture operations and by the development of related processing and marketing activities.
- In force 9 November 1948; regional. Membership restricted to FAO member States, other States upon admission by a two-thirds majority of the member States; 19 Parties, including 13 developing countries.
- Text in UNTS 120:59, IEL 948:15.
- Secretariat: Indo-Pacific Fisheries Commission (IPFC), c/o FAO (see No. 26 above), Room F-217 (fax 39-6-57976500, phone 39-6-57976422).

(59) Convention for the Establishment of an Inter-American Tropical Tuna Commission (Washington, 31 May 1949) and related agreements

- Objectives: To maintain populations of yellow fin and skipjack tuna in the eastern Pacific Ocean to permit maximum sustained catches year after year.
- In force 3 March 1950; regional. Membership restricted to States whose nationals participate in the fisheries covered by the Convention; 7 Parties, including 4 developing countries.
- Related instruments: (a) Convention Establishing the Eastern Pacific Tuna Organization (Lima, 21 July 1989, not yet in force).
- Text in UNTS 80:3, SMT 1:76, IEL 949:41, IPE 6:2848.
- Secretariat: Inter-American Tropical Tuna Commission (IATTC), 5604 La Jolla Shores Drive, La Jolla, CA 92037, USA (fax 1-619-546 7133, phone 1-619-546 7100).

(60) Agreement for the Establishment of the General Fisheries Council for the Mediterranean (Rome, 24 September 1949) as amended

- Objectives: To promote the development and proper utilization of the resources of the Mediterranean and contiguous waters through international co-operation.
- In force 20 February 1952; regional, but membership open to States from outside the region. 20 Parties, including 13 developing countries.
- Related instruments: Amendments (a) 1963 (in force 3 December 1963); (b) 1976 (in force 9 December 1976).
- Texts in UNTS 126:237, SMT 1:80, IEL 949:72, IPE 6:2857; (a) UNTS 490:444, IPE 6:2862.

- Secretariat: General Fisheries Council for the Mediterranean (GFCM), c/o FAO (see No. 58 above).

(61) <u>International Convention for the High Seas Fisheries of the North Pacific Ocean</u> (Tokyo, 9 May 1952) as amended

- Objectives: To ensure maximum sustained productivity of the fishery resources of the north Pacific Ocean. To co-ordinate research and conservation measures to this end.
- In force 12 June 1953; regional. Membership restricted to signatory States; 3 Parties, no developing countries.
- Related instruments: Amending Protocols: (a) 1962, (b) 1978, (c) 1986.
- Texts in UNTS 205:65, SMT 1:96, IEL 952:35, IPE 6:2876, (a) IPE 6:2894; (b) IPE III/A/25-04-78; (c) IPE III/A/09-04-86.
- Secretariat: International North Pacific Fisheries Commission (INPFC), 6640 Northwest Marine Drive, Vancouver, B.C. V6T 1X2, Canada (fax 1-604-228 1135, phone 1-604-228 1128).

(62) <u>Convention on the Organization of the Permanent Commission on the Exploitation and Conservation of the Marine Resources of the South Pacific</u> (Santiago, 18 August 1952) and related agreements

- Objectives: To obtain the greatest benefits from the conservation, protection and regulation of the utilization of the natural resources off the coasts of the party states up to the 200-mile-limit.
- In force 18 August 1952; regional. Membership restricted to member States of the Permanent Commission of the South Pacific; 4 Parties, all developing countries.
- Related instruments: (a) <u>Convention on Licensing for Exploitation of the Natural Resources of the South Pacific</u> (4 December 1954); (b) <u>1981 Lima Convention</u> (see No. 49 above).
- Text in UNTS 1006:324, IEL 952:62, IPE 6:2897.
- Secretariat: Permanent Commission of the South Pacific (see No. 49 above).

(63) <u>Convention for the International Council for the Exploration of the Sea</u> (Copenhagen, 12 September 1964) as amended

- Objectives: To provide a new constitution for the International Council for the Exploration of the Sea established in Copenhagen in 1902.
- In force 22 July 1968; regional (Atlantic Ocean). Membership restricted to the original participating States, others upon prior approval by three quarters of the Parties; 17 Parties, no developing countries.
- Text in UNTS 652:237, SMT 1:195, ILM 7:302, IEL 964:68, IPE 1:425.
- Secretariat: International Council for the Exploration of the Sea (ICES), Palaegade 2-4, DK-1261 Copenhagen, Denmark (fax 45-33-934215, phone 45-33-154225).

(64) <u>International Convention for the Conservation of Atlantic Tunas</u> (Rio de Janeiro, 14 May 1966) as amended

- Objectives: To maintain populations of tuna and tunal-like fish in the Atlantic Ocean at levels permitting the maximum sustainable catch for food and other purposes.
- In force 21 March 1969; regional, but open to States from outside the region. 22 Parties, including 14 developing countries.
- Text in UNTS 673:63, SMT 1:202, ILM 6:293, IEL 966:38, IPE 6:3018, 1984 amendment IPE III/A/10-07-84.
- Secretariat: International Commission for the Conservation of Atlantic Tunas (ICCAT), Principe de Vergara, 17-7, 28001 Madrid, Spain (fax 34-1-5761968, phone 34-1-4310329).

(65) <u>Convention on Fishing and Conservation of the Living Resources in the Baltic Sea and Belts</u> (Gdansk, 13 September 1973) as amended

- Objectives: To achieve greater and closer co-operation between the parties in order to maintain maximum stable productivity of the living resources of the region.
- In force 28 July 1974; regional. Membership restricted to the original signatories and others interested in the preservation and rational exploitation of living resources in the Baltic Sea and Belts upon invitation from the Parties; 5 Parties, no developing countries.
- Related instruments: (a) Amendment Protocol (Warsaw, 11 November 1982, in force 10 February 1984).
- Texts in SMT 1:317, ILM 12:1291, IEL 973:68, IPE 7:3367; (a) ILM 22:704, IPE III/A/11-11-82.
- Secretariat: International Baltic Sea Fisheries Commission (IBSFC), 20 Hoza Ul., PL-00528 Warsaw, Poland (phone 48-2-6288647).

(66) <u>Convention on Future Multilateral Co-operation in the Northwest Atlantic Fisheries</u> (Ottawa, 24 October 1978)

- Objectives: To promote the conservation and optimum utilization of the fishery resources of the North West Atlantic area within a framework appropriate to the regime of extended coastal State jurisdiction over fisheries, and accordingly to encourage international co-operation and consultation with respect to these resources.
- In force 1 January 1979; regional. Membership restricted to States represented at the 1978 Ottawa Conference, to others upon prior approval by the Parties; 11 Parties, including 2 developing countries.
- Text in SMT 2:60, IEL 978:79, IPE 22:107.
- Secretariat: Northwest Atlantic Fisheries Organization (NAFO), P.O. Box 638, Dartmouth, Nova Scotia B2Y 3Y9, Canada (fax 1-902-4695729, phone 1-902-4699105).

(67)   South Pacific Forum Fisheries Convention (Honiara, 10 July 1978) and related agreements

    - Objectives: To increase the benefits from management and conservation of marine living resorces in the South Pacific region.
    - In force 9 August 1979; regional. Membership restricted to the independent and self-governing territories of the South Pacific; 16 Parties, including 14 developing countries.
    - Related instruments: (a) Agreement Concerning Co-operation in the Management of Fisheries of Common Interest (Nauru, 11 February 1982, in force 23 April 1983); (b) Treaty on Fisheries Between the Governments of Certain Pacific Island States and the Government of the United States of America (Port Moresby, 2 April 1987, in force 15 June 1988); (c) Convention for the Prohibition of Fishing with Long Driftnets in the South Pacific (Wellington 23 November 1989, in force 17 May 1991) and two protocols (Noumea, 20 October 1990).
    - Texts in IEL 979:57; (b) IEL 987:26; (c) ILM 29:1454, IEL 989:87.
    - Secretariat: South Pacific Forum Fisheries Agency (FFA), P.O. Box 629, Honiara, Solomon Islands (fax 677-23995, phone 677-21124).

(68)   Convention on Future Multilateral Co-operation in the North-East Atlantic Fisheries (London, 18 November 1980)

    - Objectives: To promote the conservation and optimum utilization of the fishery resources of the north-east Atlantic area within a framework appropriate to the regime of extended coastal State jurisdiction over fisheries, and accordingly to encourage international co-operation and consultation with respect to these resources.
    - In force 17 March 1982; regional. Membership restricted to the original Contracting Parties and the EC, other States upon approval of three-quarters of the contracting parties; 9 Parties, no developing countries.
    - Text in SMT 2:107, IPE III/A/18-11-80.
    - Secretariat: Northeast Atlantic Fisheries Commission (NEAFC), Nobel House, 17 Smith Square, London SWIP 3JR, United Kingdom (fax 44-71-238 5721, phone 44-71-238 5919).

(69)   Convention for the Conservation of Salmon in the North Atlantic Ocean (Reykjavik, 2 March 1982)

    - Objectives: To promote the conservation, restoration, enhancement and rational management of salmon stock in the North Atlantic Ocean through international co-operation, as well as the acquisition, analysis and dissemination of appropriate scientific information.
    - In force 1 October 1983; regional. Membership restricted to the original signatories, other States exercising fisheries jurisdiction in the North Atlantic Ocean or States of origin for salmon stocks subject to this Convention upon approval of the Council; 9 Parties, no developing countries.
    - Text in SMT 2:157, IEL 982:17, IPE III/A/22-01-82.

- Secretariat: North Atlantic Salmon Conservation Organization (NASCO), 11 Rutland Square, Edinburgh EH1 2AS, United Kingdom (fax 44-31-228 4384, phone 44-31-228 2551).

(70) Agreement on the Network of Aquaculture Centres in Asia and the Pacific (Bangkok, 8 January 1988)

- Objectives: To assist the Member States in their efforts to expand aquaculture development.
- In force 11 November 1990; regional. Membership restricted to States invited to participate in the 1988 Bangkok Conference, other States subject to prior approval by two-thirds of the members; 9 Parties, all developing countries.
- Text in SMT 2:408.
- Secretariat: Network of Aquaculture Centres in Asia (NACA), c/o UNDP, G.P.O. Box 618, Bangkok 10200, Thailand (fax 662-5611727, phone 662-5611728).

G.   TRANSBOUNDARY FRESHWATERS

(71) Convention Relating to the Development of Hydraulic Power Affecting More Than One State (Geneva, 9 December 1923)

- Objectives: To promote international agreement for the purpose of facilitating the exploitation and increasing the yield of hydraulic power.
- In force 30 June 1925; global. Membership open, 11 Parties, including 4 developing countries.
- Related instrument: (a) Convention and Statute on the Regime of Navigable Waterways of International Concern (Barcelona, 20 April 1921) and additional protocol.
- Texts in League of Nations Treaty Series 36:75, IPE 11:5506, (a) League of Nations Treaty Series 7:35, 65 IEL 921:30.
- Secretariat: United Nations Department of Technical Co-operation for Development, Water Resources Branch, New York, NY 10017, USA (phone 1-212-963 8593).

(72) Declaration Concerning the Industrial and Agricultural Use of International Rivers (Montevideo, 24 December 1933)

- Objectives: To lay down principles of co-operation between American States regarding the industrial and agricultural use of watercourses of an international character.
- Non-mandatory: regional. Adopted by the Seventh International Conference of American States.
- Related instrument: Declaration (reservation) by the US delegation (reproduced in: Carnegie Foundation for International Peace, The International Conferences of American States, First Supplement 1933-1940, Washington, D.C., pp. 105-106).
- Text in: Pan American Union, Minutes of the antecedents of the Seventh International Conference of American States (1933), p. 114.
- Secretariat: OAS (see No. 12 above)

(73)   <u>Protocol to Establish a Tripartite Standing Committee on Polluted Waters</u> (Brussels, 8 April 1950)

   - Objectives: To deal with problems raised by the pollution of waters in the boundary area between Belgium, France and Luxembourg.
   - In force 8 April 1950; regional. Membership restricted to signatories; 3 Parties, no developing countries.
   - Text in UNTS 66: 285, IEL 950:38.
   - Secretariat: Standing Commission and Sub-committee, alternating/shared between Parties.

(74)   <u>Convention on the Protection of Lake Constance Against Pollution</u> (Steckborn, 27 October 1960).

   - Objectives: To co-operate in the protection of Lake Constance against pollution and in the improvement of its water quality.
   - In force 10 November 1961, regional. Membership restricted to riparian States; 3 Parties, no developing countries.
   - Related instruments: (a) <u>Agreement Concerning the Withdrawal of Water from Lake Constance</u> (Berne, 30 April 1966, in force 25 November 1967); (b) <u>Convention on Navigation on Lake Constance</u> (1 June 1973, in force 1 January 1976).
   - Texts in IEL 960:80 IPE 10:4814; (a) UNTS 620:191, IEL 966:32, IPE 10:4825; (b) IEL 973:42.
   - Secretariat: International Commission for Protecting the Waters of Lake Constance, c/o Federal Office for Environment Protection (BUWAL), CH- 3003 Berne, Switzerland (fax 41-31-619981, phone 41-31-619311).

(75)   <u>Protocol Concerning the Constitution of an International Commission for the Protection of the Mosel Against Pollution</u> (Paris, 20 December 1961)

   - Objectives: To establish cooperation between the Contracting Parties for the protection of the Mosel river against pollution.
   - In force 1 July 1962, regional. Membership restricted to riparian States; 3 Parties, no developing countries.
   - Related instrument: (a) <u>Agreement on the Canalization of the Mosel</u> (Luxembourg, 27 October 1956, in force 31 December 1956).
   - Texts in UNTS 940:211, SMT 1:165, IEL: 961:94 IPE: 11:5618; (a) IEL 956:80.
   - Secretariat: International Commission for the Protection of the Mosel and the Saar against Pollution, 29a Güterstr., D-5500 Trier, Germany (fax 49-651-76606, phone 49-651-73147).

(76)   <u>Agreement on the International Commission for the Protection of the Rhine Against Pollution</u> (Berne, 29 April 1963) as amended

   - Objectives: To improve cooperation between the riparian States of the Rhine river, prevent pollution and improve water quality.
   - In force 1 May 1965, regional. Membership restricted to signatories; 6 Parties, no developing countries.

-Related instruments: (a) Amendment, (Bonn 3 December 1976); (b) <u>Revised Convention Relating to the Navigation of the Rhine</u> (Mannheim, 17 October 1868, as amended to 17 October 1979).
- Texts in UNTS 994:3, SMT 1: 176, IEL 963:31 IPE 10:4820; (a) IEL 976:91; (b) IEL 868:77.
- Secretariat: International Commission for the Protection of the Rhine against Pollution (ICPRP), P.O. Box 309, D-5400 Koblenz, Germany (fax 49-261-36572, phone 49-261-12495).

(77)   <u>Act regarding Navigation and Economic Co-operation between the States of the Niger Basin</u> (Niamey, 26 October 1963) and related agreements

- Objectives: To develop close co-operation for the judicious exploitation of the resources of the Niger River basin as well as to guarantee freedom of navigation on the River and its tributaries, and to ensure equality of treatment to users.
- In force 1 February 1966; regional. Membership restricted to signatories; 8 Parties, all developing countries.
- Related instruments: (a) <u>Agreement Concerning the River Niger Commission and the Navigation and Transport on the River Niger</u> (Niamey, 25 November 1964 as revised), (b) <u>Convention Creating the Niger Basin Authority</u> (Faranah, 21 November 1980) with a <u>Protocol Relating to the Development Fund of the Niger Basin</u>.
- Texts in UNTS 587:9, SMT 1:186, IPE 11:5648, IEL 963:80. (a) SMT 1:188, IEL 964:87; (b) SMT 2: 112, IEL 980:86.
- Secretariat: Niger Basin Authority, B.P. 729, Niamey, Niger.

(78)   <u>Convention and Statute relating to the Development of the Lake Chad Basin</u> (N'Djamena, 22 May 1964) as amended and supplemented

- Objectives: To establish principles for the utilization of the resources of the Lake Chad Basin for economic goals, including water management.
- In force 1964, amended at Yaoundé, 22 October 1972, and at Enugu, 3 December 1977; regional. Membership restricted to signatories; 4 Parties, all developing countries.
- Texts in IEL 964:38; 1973 amendment in IEL 973:80.
- Secretariat: Lake Chad Basin Commission, B.P. 727, N'Djamena, Chad.

(79)   <u>European Water Charter</u> (Strasbourg, 6 May 1968)

- Objectives: To promote collective action on a European scale on water problems, for the qualitative and quantitative conservation of water resources.
- Non-mandatory; regional.   Adopted by the Consultative Assembly and the Committee of Ministers of the Council of Europe in 1967, and proclaimed in 1968.
- Text in Yearbook of the International Law Commission 1974, vol. II., pp. 342-343.
- Secretariat: Council of Europe (see No. 7 above).

(80)   <u>Treaty on the River Plate Basin</u> (Brasilia, 23 April 1969)
- Objectives: To promote the harmonious development and physical integration of the River Plate Basin and its zones of direct and measurable influence.

- In force 14 August 1970; regional. Membership restricted to basin States; 5 Parties, all developing countries.
- Texts in UNTS 875:3, ILM 8:905, IEL 969:31, IPE 11:5768.
- Secretariat: La Plata River Basin Authority, c/o UNDP, P.O. Box 2257, Buenos Aires, Argentina.

(81)   Conventions concerning the Status of the Senegal River, and Establishing the Senegal River Development Organization (Nouakchott, 11 March 1972) as amended and supplemented

- Objective: To promote and intensify cooperation and economic exchanges and to pursue joint efforts of economic development through utilization of the resources of the Senegal river.
- In force 1974, amended 17 December 1975; regional. Membership restricted to riparian States; Parties, all developing countries.
- Texts in IEL 972:19, 1975 amendment IEL 972:20.
- Secretariat: Organisation pour la Mise en Valeur du Fleuve Sénégal, (OMVS), B.P. 3152, Dakar, Senegal.

(82)   Convention for the Protection of the Rhine River Against Chemical Pollution (Bonn, 3 December 1976).

- Objective of: To protect the Rhine against chemical pollution with the purpose of ameliorating the standards of water for specified uses.
- In force 1 February 1979, regional. Membership restricted to signatories: 6 Parties, no developing countries.
- Related instrument: (a) Convention for the Protection of the Rhine River Against Pollution by Chlorides (Bonn, 3 December 1976 as amended, in force 5 July 1985).
- Texts in UNTS 1124:375, SMT 1:468, ILM 16:242, IPE 25:440, IEL 976:89, (a) SMT 2:55, ILM 16:265, IEL 976:90, IPE 26:1.
- Secretariat: ICPRP (see No. 76 above).

(83)   Action Plan of the United Nations Water Conference (Mar del Plata, 25 March 1977),

- Objectives: To promote the accelerated development and orderly administration of water resources as a key factor in efforts to improve the economic and social conditions of mankind, especially in the developing countries.
- Non-mandatory; global. Approved by General Assembly resolution 32/158 of 19 December 1977.
- Text in IPE 26:166.
- Secretariat: UN Department of Technical Co-operation for Development (see No. 71 above).

(84)   Agreement for the Establishment of an Organization to Manage and Develop the Kagera River Basin (Rusumo, 24 August 1977) and related agreement

- Objectives: To establish the Kagera River Basin Authority as a basis for cooperation between the riparian States.

- In force 5 February 1978, amended 19 May 1978; regional. Membership restricted to riparian States; 4 Parties, all developing countries.
- Texts in UN Natural Resources/Water Series No. 13 (ST/ESA/141, 1984), p. 32, 1978 amendment p. 70.
- Secretariat: Kagera River Basin Authority, B.P. 1357, Kigali, Rwanda.

(85)   <u>OECD Recommendations on Water Management Policies and Instruments</u>, (Paris, 5 April 1978)

- Objectives: To protect water resources against pollution and excessive use; to preserve the water environment and ecology; to safeguard and improve the hydrological cycle in general; and to provide adequate water supply, in quality and quantity, for domestic, industrial and agricultural purposes, account being taken of long-term demands.
- Non-mandatory; regional. Adopted by OECD Council Recommendation OECD C978)4 (Final).
- Text in IPE 26:239.
- Secretariat: OEDC (see No. 3 above).

(86)   <u>Convention relating to the Status of the River Gambia, and the Creation of the Gambia River Basin Development Organization</u> (Kaolack, 30 June 1978) as amended

- Objectives: To ensure co-ordinated development of the Gambia River for the rational exploitation of its natural resources.
- In force 1979, amended on 6 June 1981; regional. Membership restricted to riparian States; 3 Parties, all developing countries.
- Texts in UN Natural Resources/Water Series No. 13 (ST/ESA/141, 1984), p. 39.
- Secretariat: Organization pour la Mise en Valeur du Fleuve Gambia (OMVG), B.P. 74, Kaolack, Senegal.

(87)   <u>Declaration on Co-operation by the Danube States in Matters of Water Management of the Danube, in particular for Protection of the Waters of the Danube Against Pollution</u> (Bucharest, 13 December 1985)

- Objectives: To cooperate towards the conservation and rational use of water resources and towards the prevention, abatement and monitoring of water pollution in the Danube River.
- Non-mandatory; regional. Restricted to the 8 riparian States of the Danube, including 2 European developing countries.
- Related instruments: (a) <u>Convention Concerning the Regime of Navigation in the Danube</u> (Belgrade, 18 August 1948, as amended on 7 January 1960); (b) <u>Convention Concerning Fishing in the Waters of the Danube</u> (Bucharest, 29 January 1958).
- Texts in Österreichische Zeitschrift für öffentliches Recht und Völkerrecht, vol. 37 (1987) pp. 430-435; (a) UNTS 33:181, IEL 948:61; (b) UNTS 339:23, SMT 1:123, IEL 958:8.
- Secretariat: Danube Commission, Benczur Utca 25, H-1068 Budapest, Hungary (phone 36-1-122 8085).

(88)   UN/ECE Principles Regarding Co-operation in the Field of Transboundary Waters, (Geneva, 10 April 1987)

> - Objectives: To provide direction for fostering and strengthening co-operation to overcome problems associated with the harmonious development, use and conservation of transboundary waters.
> - Non-mandatory; regional. Adopted by Decision I (42) at the 42nd session of the United Nations Economic Commission for Europe.
> - Text in ECE/ENVWA/2, p. 25.
> - Secretariat: UN/ECE (see No. 11 above).

(89) Agreement on Co-operation on Management of Water Resources in the Danube Basin (Regensburg, 1 December 1987)

> - Objectives: To improve as far as possible the quality of the waters in the Danube Basin forming a common frontier between Austria and Germany.
> - Membership restricted to riparians; though bilateral in scope, concluded with the participation of the European Community (EC).
> - Text in Official Journal of the European Communities No. L 90/20 (1990).
> - Secretariat: Standing Committee on Management of Water Resources, alternating/shared between Austria and Germany.

(90)   Agreement on the Action Plan for the Environmentally Sound Management of the Common Zambezi River System (Harare, 28 May 1987)

> - Objectives: To develop regional cooperation on environmentally sound water resources management of the common Zambezi River system for sustainable development.
> - In force 28 May 1987, regional. Membership restricted to signatories and Angola, Malawi and Namibia. 5 Parties, all developing countries.
> - Texts in ILM 27:1109, IEL 987:40.
> - Secretariat: Southern African Development Coordination Conference (SADCC), P.O. Box 4595, Maputo, Mozambique.

(91)   UN/ECE Charter on Ground-Water Management (Geneva, 21 April 1989)

> - Objectives: To promote the sustainable use of ground-water and to preserve its quality.
> - Non-mandatory; regional. Adopted by Decision E(44) at the 44th session of the United Nations Economic Commission for Europe.
> - Text in E/ECE/1197, ECE/ENVWA/12.
> - Secretariat: UN/ECE (see No. 11 above).

(92)   UN/ECE Code of Conduct on Accidental Pollution of Transboundary Inland Waters (Geneva, 27 April 1990)

> - Objectives: To guide governments in the protection of transboundary inland waters against pollution resulting from hazardous activities in case of accidents or natural

disasters and in mitigating their impacts on the aquatic environment.
- Non-mandatory; regional. Adopted by Decision C(45) at the 45th session of the
United Nations Economic Commission for Europe.
- Texts in E/ECE/1225, ECE/ENVWA/16.
- Secretariat: UN/ECE (see No. 11 above).

(93) Convention on the International Commission for the Protection of the Elbe
(Magdeburg, 8 October 1990)

- Objectives: To prevent further pollution of the Elbe River and to improve its current
state.
- Not yet in force; regional. Membership restricted to riparians; though bilateral in
scope, concluded with the participation of the European Community (EC).
- Text in IEL 990:75
- Secretariat: International Commission for the Protection of the Elbe, Am Domplatz,
P.O. Box 1647/1648, 0-3010 Magdeburg, Germany (fax 49-91-343162, phone 49-91-
343155).

(94) ILC Draft Articles on the Law of the Non-Navigational Uses of International
Watercourses (Geneva, 19 July 1991)

- Objectives: To codify the rules applicable to uses of international watercourses and
of their waters for purposes other than navigation and to measures of conservation
related to the uses of those watercourses and their waters.
- Non-mandatory; global. Adopted in first reading by the International Law
Commission of the United Nations at its 43rd session.
- Text in A/CONF.151/PC/79, appendix 3; ILM 30:1575.
- Secretariat: United Nations Office of Legal Affairs, New York, N.Y. 10017, USA
(phone 1-212-963 5323).

H.   HAZARDOUS SUBSTANCES

(95) ECOSOC Recommendations on the Transport of Dangerous Goods (Geneva, 26 April
1957) as revised

- Objectives: To present a basic scheme of provisions that will allow national and
international regulations governing the various modes of transport to develop within
it in a uniform fashion, thus contributing to worldwide harmonization in this field.
- Non-mandatory; global. Recommendations adopted and periodically revised by the
United Nations Committee of Experts on the Transport of Dangerous Goods, and
published in accordance with ECOSOC Resolution 645/G/XXIII and subsequent
resolutions.
-Related instruments: (a) Recommendations on Tests and Criteria for the
Classification of Dangerous Goods.
- Text in ST/SG/AC.10/1/Rev.7 (1991); (a) ST/SG/AC.10/11/Rev.1 (1991).
- Secretariat: UN/ECE (see No. 28 above).

(96) <u>European Agreement Concerning the International Carriage of Dangerous Goods by Road</u> (Geneva, 30 September 1957) as amended

- Objectives: To increase the safety of international transport by road by regulating the carriage of specified dangerous goods, including wastes.
- In force 29 January 1968; regional. Membership restricted to ECE member States and States having consultative status with ECE; 20 Parties, including 1 developing country.
- Text in UNTS 619:77, 1297:406, IEL 957:72.
- Secretariat: UN/ECE (see No. 28 above).

(97) <u>European Agreement on the Restriction of the Use of Certain Detergents in Washing and Cleaning Products</u> (Strasbourg, 16 September 1968)

- Objectives: To protect the supply of water against pollution by detergents and cleaning products.
- In force 16 February 1971; regional. Membership restricted to member States of the Council of Europe; 10 Parties, no developing countries.
- Related instruments: (a) 1983 Amendment Protocol.
- Text in UNTS 788:181, SMT 1:214, IEL 968:69; (a) IEL 968:69/A.
- Secretariat: Council of Europe (see No. 7 above).

(98) <u>Convention for the Mutual Recognition of Inspections in Respect of the Manufacture of Pharmaceutical Products</u> (Geneva, 8 October 1970)

- Objectives: To contribute towards the removal of obstacles in international trade while ensuring strict quality control of the manufacture of pharmaceutical products.
- In force 26 May 1971; global. Membership open; 16 Parties, including 1 developing country.
- Text in UNTS 956:3.
- Secretariat: European Free Trade Association (EFTA), Rue de Varembé 9-11, 1211 Geneva 20 (fax 41-22-733 9291, phone 41-22-749 1325).

(99) <u>Convention on the Prohibition of the Development, Production and Stockpiling of Bacteriological (Biological) and Toxic Weapons, and on their Destruction</u> (London, Moscow, Washington, 10 April 1972)

- Objectives: To prohibit the development of biological weapons and eliminate them, as a step towards general disarmament for the sake of all mankind.
- In force 26 March 1975; global. Membership open; 117 Parties, including 84 developing countries.
- Text in UNTS 1015:163, SMT 1:269, ILM 11:309, IEL 972:28, IPE 15:7858.
- Secretariat: UN Department for Disarmament Affairs (see No. 4 above).

(100)   OECD Recommendations on Mutual Acceptance of Data in the Assessment of Chemicals and Good Laboratory Practices (Paris, 1981-1983) and related instruments

- Objectives: To minimize the cost burden associated with testing chemicals and to utilize more effectively scarce test facilities and specialist manpower as well as the number of animals used in testing through concerted action amongst OECD member States in protecting man and his environment from exposure to hazardous chemicals.
- Non-mandatory; regional. Adopted by the Council of the Organisation for Economic Cooperation and Development on 12 May 1981 and on 26 July 1983, respectively.
- Related instruments: (a) Decision C(87)90 (Final) of 26 June 1987 on the Systematic Investigation of Existing Chemicals; (b) Decision C(89)23 (Final) of 30 March 1989 supplementing the Decision of the Council concerning the Mutual Acceptance of Data in the Assessment of Chemicals; (c) Decision C(90)163 (Final) of 31 January 1991 on the Co-operative Investigation and Risk Reduction of Existing Chemicals.
- Texts in OECD C(81)30 Final and C(83)95 Final.
- Secretariat: OECD (see No. 3 above).

(101)   FAO International Code of Conduct on the Distribution and Use of Pesticides (Rome, 28 November 1985) as amended

- Objectives: To provide a practical framework for the control of pesticides, especially in countries that do not have adequate pesticide registration and control schemes.
- Non-mandatory; global. Adopted by Resolution 10/85 of the 23rd FAO Conference, amended by Resolution 6/89 of the 25th FAO Conference.
- Secretariat: FAO (see No. 26 above).

(102)   UNEP London Guidelines for the Exchange of Information on Chemicals in International Trade (Nairobi, 17 June 1987) as amended

- Objectives: To assist Governments in the process of increasing chemical safety in all countries through the exchange of information on chemicals in international trade.
- Non-mandatory; global. Amended text adopted by UNEP Governing Council Decision 15/30 of 25 May 1989.
- Text in UNEP/GC.15/9/Add.2/Supplement 3, appendix.
- Secretariat: UNEP International Register of Potentially Toxic Chemicals (IRPTC), Palais des Nations, 1211 Geneva 10 (fax 41-22-7332673, phone 41-22-7985850).

(103)   Basel Convention on the Control of Transboundary Movements of Hazardous Wastes and their Disposal (Basel, 22 March 1989)

- Objectives: To ensure that the measures taken by States in the management of hazardous wastes and other wastes including their transboundary movement and disposal are consistent with the protection of human health and the environment whatever the place of their disposal.
- In force 5 May 1992; global. Membership open; 23 Parties.
- Text in SMT 2:449, 28 ILM 657, IEL 989:22.

- Secretariat: UNEP Secretariat for the Basel Convention, 266 Route de Lausanne, 1292 Geneva-Chambésy (fax 41-22-7581189, phone 41-22-7582510).

(104) <u>Convention on the Ban of the Import into Africa and the Control of Transboundary Movements and Management of Hazardous Wastes within Africa</u> (Bamako, 30 January 1991)

- Objectives: To protect human health and the environment from the dangers posed by hazardous wastes by reducing their generation to a minimum in terms of quantity and/or hazard potential.
- Not yet in force; regional. Membership restricted to member States of the Organization of African Unity.
- Text in ILM 30:775 (Annexes in ILM 31:163), IEL 991:08.
- Secretariat: OAU (see No. 15 above).

I.   NUCLEAR SAFETY

(105) <u>UNGA Resolution 913 (X) Establishing the Scientific Committee on the Effects of Atomic Radiation</u> (New York, 3 December 1955)

- Objectives: To distribute as wide as possible all available scientific data on the short-term and long-term effects upon man and his environment of ionizing radiation, including radiation levels and radio-active "fall-out".
- Non-mandatory; global. Membership restricted to 21 States by UNGA Resolution A/RES/41/62B, including 9 developing countries.
- Text in IPE 13:6517.
- Secretariat: United Nations Scientific Committee on the Effects of Atomic Radiation (UNSCEAR), Vienna International Centre, P.O. Box 500, A-1400 Vienna, Austria (fax 43-1-232156, phone 43-1-211310).

(106) <u>Treaty Banning Nuclear Weapon Tests in the Atmosphere, in Outer Space and Under Water</u> (Moscow, 5 August 1963)

- Objectives: To obtain an agreement on general and complete disarmament under strict international control in accordance with the objectives of the United Nations; to put an end to the armaments race and eliminate incentives to the production and testing of all kinds of weapons, including nuclear weapons.
- In force 10 October 1963; global. Membership open; 117 Parties, including 85 developing countries.
- Text in UNTS 480:43, SMT 1:185, IEL 963:59, IPE 1:422.
- Depositary: Ministry for Foreign Affairs of the Russian Federtion, Smolenskaea-Somnaea Square 32/34, 121200 Moscow, USSR (fax 7-095-2442203, phone 7-095-2442469).

(107)   <u>Treaty for the Prohibition of Nuclear Weapons in Latin America</u> (Tlatelolco, 14 February 1967)
- Objectives: To strengthen peace and security in the region, to prevent the possibility of nuclear-weapons race in the region and to protect the parties against possible nuclear attacks on one hand and to contribute to the prevention of the proliferation

of nuclear weapons and to general disarmament on the other hand.
- In force 29 January 1968; regional. Membership restricted to the Latin American Republics and other sovereign States situated in their entirety south of latitude 35 North in the Western hemisphere; 23 Parties, all developing countries.
- Text in UNTS 634:281, 362, 364, ILM 6:521, IEL 967:13, IPE 15:7827.
- Depositary: Ministry of Foreign Affairs, Ricardo Flores Magon 1, Colonia Noalco, 06995 Tlatelolco, Mexico D.F. (fax 525-7823582, phone 525-7823932).

(108) South Pacific Nuclear-Free Zone Treaty (Raratonga, 8 August 1985)

- Objectives: To establish a nuclear free zone in the region and to keep the region free of environmental pollution by radioactive wastes.
- In force 11 December 1986; regional. Membership restricted to member States of the South Pacific Forum; 10 Parties, including 8 developing countries.
- Text in SMT 2:352, ILM 24:1440, IEL 985:58.
- Secretariat: South Pacific Forum (see No. 67 above).

(109) IAEA Convention on Early Notification of a Nuclear Accident (Vienna, 26 September 1986) and related convention on assistance

- Objectives: To provide relevant information about nuclear accidents as early as possible in order that transboundary radiological consequences can be minimized.
- In force 27 October 1986; global. Membership open; 58 Parties, including 28 developing countries.
- Related instruments (a) Convention on Assistance in the Case of a Nuclear Accident or Radiological Emergency (Vienna, 26 September 1986, in force 27 February 1987).
- Texts in SMT 2:363, ILM 25:1370, IEL 986:71; (a) SMT 2:367, ILM 25:1377, IEL 986:72.
- Secretariat: International Atomic Energy Agency (IAEA), Vienna International Centre, P.O. Box 100, A-1400 Vienna, Austria (fax 43-1-234564, phone 43-1-23600).

J.   WORKING ENVIRONMENT

(110) ILO Convention Concerning the Protection of Workers Against Ionizing Radiations (Geneva, 22 June 1960)

- Objectives: To protect workers, as regards their health and safety, against ionizing radiations.
- In force 17 June 1962; global. Membership restricted to member States of the International Labour Organisation; 39 Parties, including 19 developing countries.
- Text in UNTS 431:41, SMT 1:156, IEL 960:48, IPE 12:5966.
- Secretariat: International Labour Organization (ILO), 4 route des Morillons, 1211 Geneva (fax 41-22-7988685, phone 41-22-7996111).

(111) <u>ILO Convention Concerning Protection Against Hazards of Poisoning from Benzene</u> (Geneva, 23 June 1971)

- Objectives: To protect workers from hazards arising from the production, handling or use of benzene.
- In force 24 July 1973; global. Membership restricted to member States of the International Labour Organisation; 28 Parties, including 18 developing countries.
- Text in UNTS 885:45, SMT 1:251, IEL 971:47, IPE 15:7503.
- Secretariat: ILO (see No. 110 above).

(112) <u>ILO Convention Concerning Prevention and Control of Occupational Hazards Caused by Carcinogenic Substances and Agents</u> (Geneva, 26 June 1974)

- Objectives: To protect workers from hazards arising from occupational exposure to carcinogenic substances and agents.
- In force 10 June 1976; global. Membership restricted to member States of the International Labour Organisation; 25 Parties, including 14 developing countries.
- Text in UNTS 1010:5, IEL 974:48, IPE 17:8682.
- Secretariat: ILO (see No. 110 above).

(113) <u>ILO Convention Concerning Protection of Workers Against Occupational Hazards in the Working Environment Due to Air Pollution, Noise and Vibration</u> (Geneva, 20 June 1977)

- Objectives: To protect workers against occupational hazards in the working environment.
- In force 11 July 1979; global. Membership restricted to member States of the International Labour Organisation; 25 Parties, including 13 developing countries.
- Text in SMT 1:482, IEL 977:46, IPE 28:335.
- Secretariat: ILO (see No. 110 above).

(114) <u>ILO Convention Concerning Occupational Safety and Health and the Working Environment</u> (Geneva, 22 June 1981)

- Objectives: To prevent accidents and injury to health by minimizing the causes of hazards inherent in the working environment.
- In force 11 August 1983; global. Membership restricted to member States of the International Labour Organisation; 15 Parties, including 7 developing countries.
- Text in SMT 2:126.
- Secretariat: ILO (see No. 110 above).

(115) <u>ILO Convention Concerning Safety in the Use of Asbestos</u> (Geneva, 24 June 1986)

- Objectives: To prevent and control the exposure of workers to asbestos and to protect them against health hazards due to occupational exposure to asbestos.
- In force 16 June 1989; global. Membership restricted to member States of the International Labour Organisation; 10 Parties, including 6 developing countries.
- Text in SMT 2:359.
- Secretariat: ILO (see No. 110 above).

(116) <u>ILO Convention on Safety in the Use of Chemicals at Work</u> (Geneva, 24 June 1990)

- Objectives: To classify chemicals according to their health hazards and set up safety provisions for their use at the workplace.
- Not yet in force; global. Membership restricted to member States of the International Labour Organisation.
- Text in International Labour Organization: Convention No. 170.
- Secretariat: ILO (see No. 110 above).

K.   LIABILITY FOR ENVIRONMENTAL DAMAGE

(117) <u>Convention on Third Party Liability in the Field of Nuclear Energy</u> (Paris, 29 July 1960) as amended and supplemented

- Objectives: To ensure adequate and equitable compensation for persons who suffer damage caused by nuclear incidents, whilst ensuring that the development of nuclear energy for peaceful purposes is not thereby hindered. To unify the basic rules in various countries relating to liability incurred for such damage.
- In force 1 April 1968; regional. Membership restricted to member States of OECD and associated states, others upon unanimous assent of the Contracting Parties; 14 Parties, 1 developing country.
- Related instruments (a) <u>Additional Protocol to the Convention on Third Party Liability in the Field of Nuclear Energy</u> (Paris, 28 January 1964); (b) <u>Protocol to Amend the Convention on Third Party Liability in the Field of Nuclear Energy</u> (Paris, 16 November 1982); (c) <u>Convention Supplementary to the Paris Convention on Third Party Liability in the Field of Nuclear Energy</u> (Brussels, 31 January 1963); (d) <u>Additional Protocol to the Convention of 31 January 1963 Supplementary to the Paris Convention</u> (Paris, 28 January 1964); (e) <u>Protocol to Amend the Convention of 31 January 1963 Supplementary to the Paris Convention</u> (Paris, 16 November 1982);
- Texts in UNTS 956:251, SMT 1:159, IEL 960:57, IPE 12:5972; (a) SMT 1:161, ILM 2:685, IEL 964:10, IPE 12:5990; (b) IEL 960:57/B; (c) SMT 1:171, IEL 963:10; (d) IEL 963:10/A; (e) IEL 963:10/B.
- Secretariat: OECD (see No. 3 above).

(118) <u>Convention on Civil Liability for Nuclear Damage</u> (Vienna, 21 May 1963) and related protocols

- Objectives: To establish minimum standards to provide financial protection against damage resulting from peaceful uses of nuclear energy.
- In force 12 November 1977; global. Membership open; 14 Parties, including 12 developing countries.
- Related instruments: (a) <u>Optional Protocol Concerning the Compulsory Settlement of Disputes</u> (Vienna, 21 May 1963, not yet in force); (b) <u>Joint Protocol Relating to the Application of the Vienna Convention and the Paris Convention</u> (Vienna, 21 September 1988, not yet in force)
- Texts in UNTS 1063:265, SMT 1:179, ILM 2:727, IEL 963:40, IPE 12:6082; (a) SMT 1:184, IEL 963:41, (b) SMT 2:447, IEL 988:78.
- Secretariat: IAEA (see No. 109 above).

(119) <u>Convention Relating to Civil Liability in the Field of Maritime Carriage of Nuclear Material</u> (Brussels, 17 December 1971)

- Objectives: To ensure that the operator of a nuclear installation will be exclusively liable for damage caused by a nuclear incident occurring in the course of maritime carriage of nuclear material.
- In force 15 July 1975; global. Membership open; 14 Parties, including 4 developing countries.
- Text in UNTS 974:255, SMT 1:253, ILM 11:277, IEL 971:93, IPE 2:504.
- Secretariat: IMO (see No. 34) above.

(120) <u>Convention on the Liability of Operators of Nuclear Ships</u> (Brussels, 25 May 1962)

- Objectives: To determine uniform rules concerning liability of operators of nuclear ships.
- Not yet in force; global. Membership open.
- Text in IEL 962:40, IPE 1:405.
- Depositary: Ministry of Foreign Affairs, 162 Boulevard Emille Jacquemain, 1021 Brussels, Belgium (phone 32-2-5168785).

(121) <u>International Convention on Civil Liability for Oil Pollution Damage</u> (Brussels, 29 November 1969) as amended

- Objectives: To ensure that adequate compensation is available to persons who suffer damage caused by pollution resulting from the escape or discharge of oil from ships. To standardize internation rules and procedures for determining questions of liability and adequate compensation in such areas.
- In force 19 June 1975; global. Membership open; 71 Parties, including 47 developing countries.
- Related instruments: (a) 1976 Protocol; (b) 1984 Protocol.
- Texts in UNTS 973:3, SMT 1:235, ILM 9:45, IEL 969:88, IPE 1:470; (a) IEL 976:86, IPE 19:9443; (b) IEL 969:88/A.
- Secretariat: IMO (see No. 34 above).

(122) <u>International Convention on the Establishment of an International Fund for Compensation for Oil Pollution Damage</u> (Brussels, 18 December 1971) and related protocols
- Objectives: To supplement the International Convention on Civil Liability for Oil Pollutions Damage, 1969; to ensure that adequate compensation is available to persons who suffer damage caused by pollution resulting from the escape or by discharge of oil from ships; and to ensure that the oil cargo interests bear a part of the economic consequences of such oil pollution damage, to the relief of the shipping industry.
- In force 16 October 1978; global. Membership open; 47 Parties, including 29 developing countries.
- Related instruments: (a) 1976 Protocol; (b) 1984 Protocol.
- Texts in UNTS 1110:57, SMT 1:255, ILM 11:284, IEL 971:94; (a) ILM 16:621, IEL 976:87, IPE 19:9447; (b) IEL 971:94/A, IPE II/A/25-05-84.b.
- Secretariat: IMO (see No. 34 above).

(123) <u>Convention on Civil Liability for Oil Pollution Damage Resulting from Exploration for and Exploitation of Sea-Bed Mineral Resources</u> (London, 1 May 1977)

- Objectives: To ensure that adequate compensation is available to victims of pollution damage from offshore activities, by means of the adoption of uniform rules and procedures for determining questions of liability and for providing such compensation.
- Not yet in force; regional. Membership restricted to signatories, others upon unanimous invitation.
- Text in SMT 1:474, ILM 16:1450, IEL 977:33.
- Depositary: Foreign and Commonwealth Office, King Charles Street, London SW1A 2AH, United Kingdom (fax 44-71-2702767, phone 44-71-2703000).

(124) <u>Convention on Civil Liability for Damage Caused During Carriage of Dangerous Goods by Road, Rail and Inland Navigation Vessels</u> (Geneva, 10 October 1989)

- Objectives: To establish uniform rules ensuring adequate and speedy compensation for damage during inland carriage of dangerous goods.
- Not yet in force; global. Membership open.
- Text in ECE/TRANS/79.
- Secretariat: UN/ECE (see No. 28 above).

ABBREVIATIONS

UNTS United Nations Treaty Series (United Nations: New York), English/French

SMT Selected Multilateral Treaties in the Field of the Environment, vol. 1, 1983 (United Nations Environment Programme: Nairobi), English/French; vol. 2, 1991 (Grotius Publications: Cambridge/England), English only

ELGP Environmental Law Guidelines and Principles (United Nations Environment Programme: Nairobi), Arabic/Chinese/English/French/Russian/Spanish

ILM International Legal Materials (American Society of International Law: Washington, DC), English only

IEL International Environmental Law: Multilateral Treaties, V vols. loose-leaf 1974 - (Erich Schmidt Verlag: Berlin), English/French/German

IPE International Protection of the Environment, 30 vols. 1975-1983, III vols. loose-leaf 1990- (Oceana Publishers: Dobbs Ferry, NY), English only